Global Environmental Politics

Praise for *Global Environmental Politics*

'In **Global Environmental Politics**, three top scholars have written a superb textbook introducing students to both the facts and the theories and concepts they need to analyze and understand how global environmental politics work. The authors clarify complex theoretical issues, provide detailed and sophisticated summaries of interesting cases, and illustrate key points with well-designed figures and tables, while introducing students to the most important and current scholarship. Students will find this book a pleasure to read and faculty will find that it covers all topics central to an introductory course on global environmental politics.'

Ronald B. Mitchell, Professor of Political Science and Environmental Politics, University of Oregon, USA.

'Finally, a well-organized empirically rich and theoretically driven textbook on global environmental politics. This state of the art volume presents some of the major forces involved in GEP, presented clearly and critically. It combines insights from IR, comparative politics, environmental psychology, political economy and policy analysis, along with extremely effective graphics.'

Peter M. Haas, Professor, Department of Political Science, University of Massachusetts Amherst, USA.

'**Global Environmental Politics** provides broad and engaging perspectives on core topics such as environmental science and policy, ideas, actors, institutions, and their roles in steering, contesting and shaping the governance of global environmental challenges. It prompts critical thinking and inquiry, and as such is a must have resource in the classroom and larger debates.'

Liliana B. Andonova, Professor, Department of IR/Political Science, Graduate Institute of International and Development Studies, Geneva, Switzerland.

'**Global Environmental Politics** is a remarkably sophisticated as well as comprehensive analysis of environmental practices, institutions, and policies. Morin, Orsini, and Jinnah examine how varying state preferences, the variety of transnational activity, and international bargaining generate the complex patterns of behaviour that we see today.'

Robert O. Keohane, Professor (Emeritus) of Public and International Affairs, Princeton University, USA.

Global Environmental Politics

Jean-Frédéric Morin

Amandine Orsini

Sikina Jinnah

OXFORD
UNIVERSITY PRESS

OXFORD
UNIVERSITY PRESS

Great Clarendon Street, Oxford, OX2 6DP,
United Kingdom

Oxford University Press is a department of the University of Oxford.
It furthers the University's objective of excellence in research, scholarship,
and education by publishing worldwide. Oxford is a registered trade mark of
Oxford University Press in the UK and in certain other countries

Impression: 1

Illustrator: L'Atelier de cartographie de Sciences.

Published in the United States of America by Oxford University Press
198 Madison Avenue, New York, NY 10016, United States of America

British Library Cataloguing in Publication Data
Data available

Library of Congress Control Number: 2019952166
ISBN 978–0–19–882608–8

Printed in Great Britain by
Bell & Bain Ltd., Glasgow

Acknowledgements

We are grateful for the many forms of support we have received in preparing this book. In particular, an amazing cadre of current and former graduate students has made important contributions to this project. We offer deep thanks to: Corentin Bialais, Dominique De Wit, Zach Dove, Jane Flegal, Mette Frederiksen, Véronique Fournier, Mathilde Gauquelin, Rosalie Gauthier-Nadeau, Noémie Laurens, Megan Martenyi, Diana Moanga, Laura Mortelet, and Helena Veum. We are also grateful to the editorial and support staff at Oxford University Press, especially Sarah Iles, Emily Spicer, and Francesca Walker. We would like to thank our colleague Maya Jegen for her contribution to a previous book published at Presses de Sciences Po. The manuscript also benefited greatly from the insightful comments from at least six anonymous reviewers.

How to use the online resources

GUIDED TOUR OF THE ONLINE RESOURCES

 www.oup.com/he/morin1e

The Online Resources that accompany this book provide students and instructors with a range of ready to use teaching and learning resources.

ADDITIONAL RESOURCES

Interactive figures

A range of interactive figures to further engage your comprehension of key ideas and concepts.

Multiple-choice questions

Self-marking multiple-choice questions for each chapter of the text, to enable you to test your understanding of key themes, and to act as an aid to revision.

Web Links

Relevant web links to reliable online content and databases related to topics covered in the book are provided in the Online Resources for easy access.

Contents

List of figures   x
List of tables   xi
List of boxes   xii
List of acronyms and abbreviations   xiv

Introduction   **1**

0.1   Key issues in global environmental politics   2
0.2   The emergence of global environmental action   4
0.3   Global environmental politics as a field of study   9
0.4   How to use this book   14
       Annex 0.1: Key multilateral environmental agreements   18

PART 1 **Defining global environmental issues**   **25**

1   **Interconnections between science and politics**   **27**
1.1   Cooperation under scientific uncertainty   28
1.2   Experts as political actors   34
1.3   The co-production of science and politics   37
1.4   The interface of science and politics   43
1.5   Conclusion   48

2   **Ideas about environmental protection**   **54**
2.1   Are there universal environmental values?   56
2.2   Does the environment have an intrinsic value?   61
2.3   Does human intervention cause more harm than good?   66
2.4   Does economic growth help or harm environmental protection?   71
2.5   Intragenerational versus intergenerational equity   80
2.6   Conclusion   85

PART 2 **Actors and interests**   **93**

3   **States**   **95**
3.1   Domestic sources of state preferences   96
3.2   International sources of state preferences   107
3.3   Conclusion   120

4   Non-state actors   **126**

4.1   NGOs in global environmental governance   129

4.2   Business engagement in global environmental governance   132

4.3   Non-state actor influence   137

4.4   Transnational governance   145

4.5   Conclusion   153

PART 3   Bargaining over the environment   **161**

5   The tragedy of the commons and sovereign rights   **163**

5.1   The tragedy of the commons   164

5.2   The common heritage of humankind   170

5.3   Sovereignty over natural resources   176

5.4   Conclusion   187

**6   Development and the environment: From the Stockholm
     Summit to the Sustainable Development Goals**   **192**

6.1   Three views on environment and development   193

6.2   Stockholm, 1972: an initial compromise between systemic and structural views   199

6.3   The Brundtland Report, 1987: the birth of sustainable development   204

6.4   Rio, 1992: the rise of the liberal view   207

6.5   Johannesburg, 2002: dilution of the systemic view   211

6.6   Rio+20, 2012: towards a new equilibrium?   215

6.7   Conclusion   220

PART 4   Institutions and policies   **227**

7   International institutions   **229**

7.1   The birth of environmental concerns in international institutions   231

7.2   The autonomy of international institutions   235

7.3   Interactions between international institutions   241

7.4   Designing global environmental governance   248

7.5   Conclusion   252

8   Policy instruments and effectiveness   **259**

8.1   The effectiveness of global environmental politics   260

8.2   Types of policy instruments   265

8.3   The diffusion of instruments   274

8.4   What are the political effects of instruments?   279

8.5   Conclusion   284

PART 5 **Cross-cutting issues**   **291**

  9 **Natural resources, security, and conflicts**   **293**
     9.1   The ambiguous concept of environmental security   294
     9.2   Environmental degradation as a trigger for armed conflict   297
     9.3   Human and environmental security   305
     9.4   Environmental impact of security policies   307
     9.5   Conclusion   311

 10 **Trade and the environment**   **318**
     10.1 Is trade good or bad for the environment?   319
     10.2 Trade dimensions of environmental regimes   328
     10.3 Environmental dimensions of the global trade regime   335
     10.4 Conclusion   348

Appendix: Databases and useful websites   357
Glossary   359
Index   365

List of figures

Figure 0.1   Global trends in environmental degradation   10

Figure 0.2   Timeline of the main treaties and declarations   12

Figure 1.1   Annual number of scientific publications (1970–2012)   31

Figure 1.2   The inequalities in scientific production   41

Figure 2.1   The environment in the opinion polls   57

Figure 2.2   Ecological footprint and per capita GDP   74

Figure 2.3   Oil production, oil price, and forecasts 1910–2016   75

Figure 2.4   The environmental Kuznets Curve   78

Figure 2.5   Renewable energy as a function of GDP per capita   78

Figure 2.6   Comparison of greenhouse gas emissions   83

Figure 3.1   Number of environmental agreements ratified 1945–2018   97

Figure 3.2   Wealth and the ratification of environmental agreements as of 1 January 2019   99

Figure 3.3   Democracy and the ratification of environmental agreements as of 1 January 2019   101

Figure 3.4   Indicators of national groups' environmental activism   103

Figure 3.5   Number of national delegates per country–negotiations on climate and biodiversity 2018   111

Figure 3.6   Overlap between the main coalitions in climate negotiations   115

Figure 4.1   Number of non-state actors registered as observers—international negotiations on climate, and biodiversity (1994–2018)   127

Figure 4.2   Cumulative number of transnational climate initiatives (1990–2018)   146

Figure 4.3   Selected transnational city networks involved in global environmental governance   148

Figure 5.1   Territorial claims in Antarctica   172

Figure 5.2   Coastal state zones   175

Figure 5.3   Distribution of biotechnology capacities (2010–2015)   181

Figure 5.4   Distribution of biological diversity (2018)   181

Figure 6.1   Three ideal-type views on environment and development   194

Figure 6.2   World map of ecological footprint of consumption per country (2017)   195

Figure 6.3   World map of adjusted net savings per country (2015)   196

Figure 6.4   World map of ecosystem vitality per country (2018)   197

Figure 6.5   Distribution of cross-national environmental agreements by level of development (1918–2018)   199

Figure 6.6   Four summits, three views   215

Figure 6.7   Public development aid for environmental protection (1995–2015)   216

Figure 7.1   Relationship between the number of parties to an environmental treaty and the creation of a secretariat   237

Figure 7.2   Environmental regime complexes centred on biodiversity and climate change   244

Figure 8.1   Number of treaties ratified and environmental performance   262

Figure 8.2   Environmentally related tax revenue (2018)   267

Figure 9.1   The Homer-Dixon model   299

Figure 9.2   Cooperation and conflicts over water   302

Figure 9.3   The resource curse?   304

Figure 9.4   Number of natural disaster events (1970–2017)   306

Figure 10.1 CO_2 emissions in traded goods as a share of domestic emissions   324

Figure 10.2 Solar prices vs cumulative capacity worldwide 2006–2016   326

Figure 10.3 Fossil fuel consumption subsidies in selected countries, 2017   340

Figure 10.4 Environmental provisions in preferential trade agreements 1947–2016   341

List of tables

Table 0.1   Selected international environmental issues   5

Table 3.1   Expected behaviour of states according to their interests   98

Table 4.1   Typology of modes of interaction between non-state actors and decision makers   141

Table 5.1   Typology of goods   165

Table 5.2   Four solutions to the tragedy of the commons   169

Table 5.3   The sovereignty trade-off   186

Table 7.1   A few intergovernmental organizations and the treaties associated with them   231

Table 7.2   The emergence of environmental issues in the organizational landscape   232

Table 7.3   Modes of interaction between regimes   246

Table 8.1   Implementation instruments   268

Table 8.2   Verification instruments   271

Table 8.3   Examples of instrument diffusion   275

Table 10.1   Disputes involving Article XX(b) and (g) of the General Agreement
on Tariffs and Trade (1980–2018)   337

Table 10.2   Canada's environmental disputes under the NAFTA Investment Chapter (1993–2018)   344

List of boxes

Box 0.1	Welcome to the Anthropocene	2
Box 0.2	Space exploration and planetary consciousness	8
Box 1.1	Nanotechnology—opportunities and uncertainties	29
Box 1.2	The multiple interpretations of the precautionary principle	31
Box 1.3	The cultural cognition hypothesis	33
Box 1.4	The epistemic community on ozone depletion	36
Box 1.5	The science and politics of transboundary air pollution	42
Box 1.6	What is geoengineering? Risks and potentials	44
Box 1.7	Climate science, negotiated	46
Box 2.1	Conspicuous conservation	58
Box 2.2	The Vatican and the environment: an activist pope?	60
Box 2.3	Ecofeminism: connections between women, nature, and oppression	64
Box 2.4	The global politics of whaling	67
Box 2.5	Scarcity or abundance? A wager between Julian Simon and Paul Ehrlich	76
Box 3.1	The coherency of national delegations	105
Box 3.2	A bottom-up approach to addressing climate change: nationally determined contributions	108
Box 3.3	The Group of 77 in climate negotiations: an unstable balance	116
Box 3.4	Negotiations over desertification: developing countries taking the lead	117
Box 4.1	The representation of indigenous people	130
Box 4.2	Corporate involvement in climate change negotiations	135
Box 4.3	Plastic pollution—an emerging environmental problem	140
Box 4.4	Monsanto and the international negotiations on genetically modified organisms	144
Box 4.5	Corporate social responsibility	147
Box 4.6	Transnational climate change initiatives	149
Box 4.7	The Forest Stewardship Council: a model for legitimacy?	151
Box 5.1	Overfishing in international waters	166
Box 5.2	Orbital space debris—a common pool resource problem	173
Box 5.3	The Trail Smelter dispute: establishing principles of prevention and compensation for pollution	177
Box 5.4	Governing marine pollution: a classic collective action problem	178
Box 5.5	Traditional knowledge and genetic resources	183
Box 6.1	Vandana Shiva: representing the structural view and beyond	197
Box 6.2	Summit diplomacy: multilateralism to galvanize efforts for sustainable development	200
Box 6.3	Maurice Strong: a bridge-maker between businesses, civil society groups, and governments	202
Box 6.4	Gro Harlem Brundtland: the lead architect of sustainable development	205
Box 6.5	Debt-for-nature swaps—a win-win solution for conservation and development?	208
Box 6.6	The politics of environmental aid	212
Box 6.7	Sustainable Development Goals: defining the global development agenda	219

Box 7.1   The politics of funding environmental projects: the World Bank   234

Box 7.2   The Global Environment Facility: a key financial mechanism   238

Box 7.3   Convention secretariats as political players   240

Box 7.4   A foundational thinker on global environmental institutions: the work of Oran Young   242

Box 7.5   The European Union as a green international actor?   251

Box 7.6   Regulating greenhouse gas emissions in international aviation and maritime transport   253

Box 8.1   Market-based instruments for addressing climate change   266

Box 8.2   The commodification of nature: payments for ecosystem services   276

Box 8.3   The international politics of green technology innovation and transfer   280

Box 8.4   Unintended consequences in policymaking   283

Box 9.1   The difficulty in classifying environmental migrants   296

Box 9.2   Avoiding ecological collapse: what can we learn from Easter Island?   298

Box 9.3   The myth of water wars   302

Box 9.4   The threat of environmental terrorism   309

Box 10.1   Recycling waste trade between China and the US   320

Box 10.2   The Bamako Convention: addressing hazardous waste dumping in
                 developing countries through a regional agreement   330

Box 10.3   The World Trade Organization Shrimp/Turtle dispute   339

Box 10.4   Vattenfall vs Germany dispute   345

Box 10.5   Climate clubs: using trade barriers to support climate mitigation   346

Box 10.6   Addressing climate change through trade agreements   347

List of acronyms and abbreviations

ALBA	Bolivarian Alliance for the Peoples of Our America
AOSIS	Alliance of Small Island States
BINGO	business and industry NGO
CAFE	Corporate Average Fuel Economy regulation
CBD	Convention on Biological Diversity
CDP	Carbon Disclosure Project
CFC	chlorofluorocarbon
CGIAR	Consultative Group on International Agricultural Research
CITES	Convention on International Trade in Endangered Species of Wild Fauna and Flora
Codex	Codex Alimentarius Commission
EU	European Union
FAO	Food and Agriculture Organization
FAOSTAT	FAO website providing data on food and agriculture
FSC	Forest Stewardship Council
G7	Group of Seven (an informal organization of seven rich countries)
G20	Group of Twenty (an international forum for the governments and central bank governors from 19 countries and the European Union)
G77	Group of 77 (a coalition of 135 developing countries)
GDP	Gross domestic product
GEF	Global Environment Facility
GEP	global environmental politics
GMO	genetically modified organism
ICTSD	International Centre for Trade and Sustainable Development
IGC	International Growth Centre
INDCs	Intended Nationally Determined Contributions
IPBES	Intergovernmental Science-Policy Platform on Biodiversity and Ecosystem Services
IPCC	Intergovernmental Panel on Climate Change
IR	international relations
ITPGRFA	International Treaty on Plant Genetic Resources for Food and Agriculture
ITTO	International Tropical Timber Organization
IUCN	International Union for Conservation of Nature
ISO	International Organization for Standardization
JUSCANZ	coalition including Japan, the United States, Canada, Australia, and New Zealand
MARPOL	International Convention for the Prevention of Pollution from Ships
NASA	National Aeronautics and Space Administration

NATO	North Atlantic Treaty Organization
NGO	non-governmental organization
ODA	overseas development assistance
OECD	Organisation for Economic Co-operation and Development
OILPOL	International Convention for the Prevention of Pollution of the Sea by Oil
OPEC	Organization of the Petroleum Exporting Countries
OSPAR	Convention for the Protection of the Marine Environment of the North-East Atlantic
PEFC	Programme for the Endorsement of Forest Certification
RINGO	research and independent NGO
SDGs	Sustainable Development Goals
TUNGO	trade union NGO
UN	United Nations
UNCCD	United Nations Convention to Combat Desertification
UNEP	United Nations Environment Programme
UNFCCC	United Nations Framework Convention on Climate Change
UNESCO	United Nations Educational, Scientific and Cultural Organization
UN-REDD	United Nations collaborative Programme on Reducing Emissions from Deforestation and Forest Degradation in developing countries
UPOV	Union for the Protection of New Varieties of Plants
WIPO	World Intellectual Property Organization
WIPO GREEN	WIPO's online platform for green technology
WTO	World Trade Organization
WWF	World Wide Fund for Nature/World Wildlife Fund
YMCA	Young Men's Christian Association

Introduction

This introductory chapter presents global environmental politics as an important area of international and transnational cooperation and as a distinct field of study. First, as an area of cooperation, global environmental politics emerged out of the need to work together internationally and transnationally to address some pressing environmental problems, such as biodiversity loss, climate change, the depletion of the ozone layer, and the rapid reduction of global fish stocks. Independent state action at the local and national levels is not sufficient to address global environmental issues: these issues require cooperation through global governance. Second, as a field of study, global environmental politics investigates the various dimensions of emerging actions on global environmental issues. It is a diverse field of study from both theoretical and disciplinary perspectives. This book reflects this diversity and introduces readers to a wide range of environmental problems and academic approaches to studying them.

 Learning objectives

After reading this introduction, readers will be able to:

- Understand why international cooperation is required to address some important environmental challenges;

- Discuss how international environmental cooperation emerged in the 1970s and has evolved in the last 50 years;

- Explain how various different international declarations and treaties govern environmental issues; and

- Recognize global environmental politics as a distinct interdisciplinary field of study, influenced by international relations theories and earth sciences, among others.

Introduction

Interest in global environmental politics is a relatively recent phenomenon. In the 1960s, only a few researchers in the social sciences were actively working on environmental issues, such as depletion of fisheries in international waters, global **biodiversity** loss, and transboundary air pollution. Examination of these issues was largely dominated by natural and physical sciences. Since then, however, the scope and scale of human impacts on natural systems have become increasingly clear. This has led some to refer to the current geological epoch as the 'Anthropocene' (see Box 0.1), reflecting the deep and wide imprint of human systems on the earth, including on isolated ecosystems such as Antarctica, the Amazon rainforest, the Sahara Desert, and the deep seabed. The severe degradation of our planet, driven by humans, raises a fundamental question for social scientists: how can human societies organize themselves and cooperate to reverse, slow, or mediate this self-destructive behaviour?

Underlying this fundamental question are numerous more specific questions, such as: Why are certain environmental problems addressed by the international community and not others? How can global solutions to environmental degradation accommodate the diversity of cultures and levels of economic development across the world? Is a **governance** system based on state **sovereignty** optimal for environmental protection? How can **non-state actors**, such as **non-governmental organizations**, business groups, scientists, and other **stakeholders**, organize themselves transnationally to contribute to environmental protection? What is the most effective design for international **institutions** and **policy instruments** to encourage environmental protection? How does global environmental governance interact with non-environmental issues, such as trade and security? This book details the answers to these questions.

First, however, this introductory chapter defines and presents the core issues and institutions involved in global environmental politics. It is organized into four sections. Section 0.1 presents the diversity of environmental issues that form the empirical focus of global environmental politics. Section 0.2 outlines the key international declarations and treaties that work to address these issues. Section 0.3 details global environmental politics as a field of study, presenting the theoretical approaches that have inspired scholars to think about these issues. Section 0.4 concludes with an outline of this textbook and a discussion of how to use it.

0.1 Key issues in global environmental politics

Climate change is one of the greatest challenges facing humanity. Climate change attracts considerable attention in public debates as well as in research communities (Dauvergne and Clapp 2016; Green and Hale 2017). However, in the current epoch of the Anthropocene (see Box 0.1), climate change is just one among many environmental issues that have a clear international dimension.

Box 0.1 Welcome to the Anthropocene

Since the mid-twentieth century, the earth has seen a rapid increase in carbon dioxide emissions, rising sea levels, rapid deforestation, and mass extinction of species. Human activity has led to such profound change to the earth's systems that some scientists argue that we have ushered in a new geological epoch, the Anthropocene—i.e. the Age of Humans. This rapid evolution of the earth marks a departure from the previous geological epoch, the Holocene, in which human civilization developed over 10,000 years in a relatively stable environment following the last ice age and the last mass extinction of megafauna in Europe, Oceania, and the Americas.

It was not until around 2011 that the term 'Anthropocene' emerged in public debates. With the mainstreaming of this term came a far-reaching and new realization of the extent, scale, and permanence of the effects of human activity on the earth's environment. It has become part of an expanding academic and political debate across the natural sciences, and social sciences, on its definition and its policy implications.

Regarding its definition, a central focus of the Anthropocene debate has concerned when this new geological era actually began. The first scientists to propose the term in its current form—Dutch chemist and Nobel Prize winner Paul Crutzen and American biologist Eugene F. Stoermer—argued that the Anthropocene began in 1784, the year Watt invented the steam engine and ushered in the Industrial Revolution in Europe. Others argue that it began in 1945 with the explosion of the first atomic bomb. Still others suggest that the Anthropocene began in 1492 with the arrival of Europeans in the Americas, followed soon after by the formation of the modern capitalist world system, founded on imperial conquest, slavery, and a desire for unlimited economic growth and expansion.

Although the use of the term Anthropocene to define a distinct geological epoch is based on scientific evidence, support for officially accepting the Anthropocene is not unanimous in the International Union of Geological Sciences. Opposition is pronounced among some stratigraphers (scientists who study rock layers), for example, who have argued that evidence of human impacts has not yet systematically or significantly made its way into the lithosphere (the layer beneath the outer layer of the earth's crust).

Critical social scientists also question the political implications of the term. Most common are critiques of its broad conception of 'human'. For example, some warn that the term 'Anthropocene' implies a uniform human responsibility for environmental degradation, whereas in reality certain populations—the rich elite—or similarly, a set of specific social relations—capitalism—are primarily responsible. These scholars argue that fossil-fuelled capitalism accrued benefits to the few at the expense of the many. In other words, it would be unfair to blame all of humanity for global environmental change, while in fact more specific social groups should be blamed. Some in this camp have suggested alternative terms such as the 'Capitalocene' to stress the relationship between power, profit, and environmental change.

Other debates centre around setting goals and devising strategies for governance in the Anthropocene, calling for a new way of thinking about **sustainable development**. Some argue that the Anthropocene creates a new need to develop effective institutions for global cooperation and coordination, due to increases in the interdependence and integration of societies on multiple scales. More critical scholars have argued that the Anthropocene requires us to radically rethink how our society is structured and how development is achieved. They have discussed ways of 'remaking' the world around us in a way that responds more effectively to the environmental harms and societal inequalities that characterize the Anthropocene. This includes responding to the earth's system change by exploring ways in which political economic systems need to be transformed.

Together, these debates seek to identify the scope of the problem, its root causes, and equitable and effective solutions to changing human livelihoods. They also point to the complicated relationship not only between humans and nature, but also between natural and social sciences. Further conversation between these elements will be helpful for considering accurate and innovative ways to conceive of the complex planetary changes that define the conditions of the Anthropocene. To understand the emergence of the Anthropocene and governance solutions within it, requires drawing from a wide and often ontologically diverging set of conversations.

Sources: Autin and Holbrook 2012; Biermann 2014; Biermann and Lövbrand 2019; Crutzen and Stoermer 2000; Demos 2017; Hickmann et al. 2018; Lövbrand et al. 2015; Moore 2017; Nicholson and Jinnah 2016; Waters et al. 2016; Young 2017.

There are three types of environmental issues that have international dimensions, and so are addressed by global environmental politics. First, some territories and associated natural resources, such as outer space and the high seas, are shared by the whole international community and should be protected in the name of humankind's common heritage. These environments are beyond the territories of sovereign states and must be managed collectively.

The second type of international environmental issues are those related to transnational ecosystems and migratory species. Rivers and migratory birds, for example, often cross national borders. This means that protection of these environments requires states to work together, bilaterally or regionally, knowing that pollution or degradation that occurs in one state will affect the environment in other states as well.

Third, several local sources of pollution have global effects. Local chlorofluorocarbon emissions contribute to the thinning of the stratospheric **ozone layer**, leading to increased skin cancer rates globally. Likewise, local carbon dioxide emissions contribute to global climate change, affecting the health, development, and security of communities, regardless of their own contribution to climate change. This type of problem requires state intervention to control local pollution, as well as multilateral intervention to coordinate state actions.

Although this typology of international environmental issues is helpful in understanding what makes an environmental issue the subject of global governance, these delineations are not always clear-cut. Some environmental problems can be simultaneously global, transnational, and local. Table 0.1 presents a selection of environmental issues with international dimensions and shows that the three types of environmental issues are not mutually exclusive. Overfishing, for example, can be seen either as a global, transnational, or local problem. Moreover, environmental issues are linked to one another. For instance, climate change catalyses biodiversity loss, and biodiversity loss reinforces the impacts of climate change.

Despite the importance of these international issues, their international dimension is sometimes contested. Some states consider that the governance of their forests is strictly a domestic issue. They assert sovereign rights over their forests and deny the legitimacy of the claims made by **intergovernmental organizations**, non-governmental organizations, and other states regarding the international community's duty to engage in protection of their territorial forests. Likewise, some states consider that desertification is mainly a local issue, caused by poor agricultural practices and inappropriate land use planning. They see little point in international cooperation to address desertification.

While Table 0.1 presents a selection of environmental issues that have already been on states' agenda for several decades, new issues can also emerge that were previously unknown and overlooked. For example, plastic pollution in the oceans and space debris are two new environmental issues—states were unaware of their full scope and impacts until very recently. The next section briefly presents how the field of global environmental politics has evolved, with the creation of several international institutions and initiatives to address environmental issues, in parallel with the continued improvement of our scientific understanding of such issues.

0.2 The emergence of global environmental action

States have long cooperated with one another to manage and protect natural resources. European countries adopted regulations on the transport of dangerous goods on the Rhine in 1868. The United States, Russia, Japan, and the United Kingdom signed the North Pacific Fur Seal Convention in 1911. These early actions were relatively rare, but reveal that international initiatives for the protection of natural resources are not new.

From the 1940s onwards, various events began to attract media attention, and increased public awareness of environmental problems and the limits of the planet. Examples include the United States' controversial nuclear testing in the Marshall Islands between 1946 and 1962,

Table 0.1 Selected international environmental issues

	Why should we care about this resource or ecosystem?	Why action is needed to protect it	Why action is needed at the international level
Freshwater pollution	Freshwater is a vital resource for numerous ecosystems and species. Human societies use it for drinking water, agriculture, fisheries, transportation, and electricity production. It is also precious, as only 3% of the earth's water is freshwater and most of it is frozen in the polar ice caps.	Rivers and lakes around the world are polluted by fertilizers and pesticides used in agriculture. In some regions, untreated human sewage and industrial wastes are still dumped into waterways.	Freshwater pollution is often a transnational issue, as drainage basins are often shared by several countries. Activities conducted by countries upstream necessarily affect the quality and quantity of freshwater downstream. Hundreds of regional treaties have been concluded to regulate the use of freshwater.
Climate change	Climate stability is essential to all ecosystems and species. Moreover, all sectors of our society, including agriculture, tourism, energy, transportation, security, and human health, benefit from a relatively stable climate.	Global average surface temperatures have already risen by almost 1°C and could still rise by up to 3.4°C this century. We are already observing significant impacts of warming, including ocean acidification and increased frequency and intensity of extreme weather events such as droughts, floods, and hurricanes. These impacts have negative consequences on ecosystems and human systems, especially on those who have the least capacity to adapt to these changes.	Climate change is mostly the result of greenhouse gases (such as carbon dioxide) that are emitted locally and then spread in the atmosphere. As the earth's atmosphere is shared globally, emissions in one area or country affect climate change in other areas or countries. One state alone, even a major emitter such as China or the United States, cannot unilaterally reduce emissions enough to stabilize the earth's average temperature at a level that avoids dangerous climate change impacts. There is also little incentive to act unilaterally as reducing emissions can negatively affect an economy's competitiveness.
Ozone layer depletion	The ozone layer prevents UV-B radiation from reaching the earth's surface, reducing UV-B radiation exposure that causes skin cancer, suppresses the human immune system, and inhibits plant growth, including that of key crops such as cotton and beans, and phytoplankton, the organism at the base of the marine food chain.	A hole in the ozone layer was caused in the southern polar region by the widespread use of ozone-depleting substances such as chlorofluorocarbons. Until the 1990s, chlorofluorocarbons were used in various products, including refrigerants, propellants, and fertilizers. Atmospheric levels of nearly all ozone-depleting substances have declined substantially in the past two decades, and the ozone layer is on track to recover.	Ozone-depleting substances are emitted locally but travel in the atmosphere and deplete the ozone layer in areas that are not necessarily above the country of emission. It is thus necessary to make concerted efforts to reduce local emissions of ozone-depleting substances.

(Continued)

	Why should we care about this resource or ecosystem?	Why action is needed to protect it	Why action is needed at the international level
Biological diversity loss	Biodiversity is defined as the diversity of the living, split into diversity within species (genetic diversity), between species (species diversity), and between ecosystems (ecosystem diversity). Biodiversity is important for ecosystem functions and for agriculture, medicinal, spiritual, and recreational/aesthetic values.	The current rate of diversity loss is so exceptionally high that biologists refer to the current period as the sixth great extinction. At least 26,000 known species of amphibians, reptiles, freshwater fish, plants, and invertebrates are under threat of extinction. The previous episode of massive extinction occurred more than 60 million years ago when dinosaurs disappeared from the earth.	The causes of biodiversity loss include habitat destruction, resource overexploitation, climate change, transboundary pollution, industrial agriculture, and invasive species. In many cases these causes have international origins, such as habitat destruction to make way for agricultural production for export markets, or invasive species crossing national borders through trade. Although biodiverse countries can and do act to address biodiversity conservation unilaterally, international cooperation is necessary to address these international drivers.
Wildlife trade and trafficking	Wildlife trade and trafficking is a major threat to the survival of numerous endangered species, such as elephants and rhinos. It also poses threats to human security, where profits from such traffic have been used to finance civil conflicts and terrorist activities. Governments have also recognized the threat these markets pose to hinder social and economic development and contribute to the spread of disease, for example through the trade in illegal bush meat.	Illegal trade in wildlife is estimated to be worth billions of dollars annually, making it one of the most lucrative criminal activities in the world.	Trade in wildlife happens worldwide, across all borders. It is driven by consumer demand for plant and animal species (and their derivatives), coupled with widespread weak management, law, and policies to control the trade. This is why cooperation between exporting and importing countries is required.

	Why should we care about this resource or ecosystem?	Why action is needed to protect it	Why action is needed at the international level
Overfishing	Fisheries provide a growing source of food for direct human consumption and for livestock. They also provide income and livelihoods to millions of households. In 2016, 60 million people were engaged in fisheries and aquaculture.	The share of stocks fished at unsustainable levels is increasing and is currently above 30%. The Mediterranean seas, the Black Sea, the Southeast Pacific, and Southwest Atlantic are maritime areas with the highest proportion of fish stocks at biologically unsustainable levels.	In 2016, about 35% of global fish production entered international trade in various forms. Protection for fish stocks requires international cooperation because many fisheries are beyond the jurisdiction of any one state.
Forest degradation and deforestation	Forests are home to most species found on land and produce a large share of the world's oxygen. Moreover, hundreds of millions of people, particularly in developing countries, live in forests or directly depend on the forest for their livelihood. Deforestation is also an important driver of climate change, contributing directly and indirectly to global greenhouse gas emissions.	Millions of hectares of forest are destroyed every year. Expanding agriculture is responsible for most of the world's deforestation. Illegal logging is another driver of the degradation of the world's forests.	Deforestation is associated with local and global consumer demand for meat, crops, wood, and paper. Protecting forests requires the development of robust institutions to incentivize the protection of these common heritage resources, which have commercial value and are within the sovereign control of one or more states.
Desertification	Desertification is not just a natural process of existing deserts expanding. It is a type of land degradation that is caused by various climatic and human factors, such as overcultivation, overgrazing, deforestation, poor irrigation practices, and prolonged droughts and floods. Desertification damages ecosystems and disrupts human activities.	Africa is the continent most severely affected by desertification, with two-thirds of the continent covered by deserts or drylands. Other regions that are greatly impacted by desertification include Asia and South America, and increasingly parts of North America and Europe. Desertification is estimated to directly affect 250 million people and a third of the planet's land surface.	Desertification is partly caused by socio-economic factors, and has negative consequences for the livelihoods of the people who live in affected areas, particularly in developing countries. These socio-economic causes and consequences can be reduced with the assistance of developed countries.

Source: Authors, with data from the United Nations Environment Programme, the Food and Agriculture Organization, and the International Union for Conservation of Nature

the United States Army's use of defoliant agents as a weapon during the Vietnam War, the wreck of the Torrey Canyon oil tanker in 1967 off the coast of England, the underwater films of Jacques-Yves Cousteau, and the first photos of earth taken from space by the United States National Aeronautics and Space Administration (see Box 0.2).

Box 0.2 Space exploration and planetary consciousness

The pictures of the earth taken from space by the American National Aeronautics and Space Administration (known as NASA) resonated with political imagination, and were powerful catalysts for environmental governance. These pictures contributed to creating a planetary consciousness by revealing the earth as a finite territory, with clear limits. The corresponding 'spaceship Earth', an expression used by the American engineer Buckminster Fuller in 1969, was going to become a central image in the formation of global environmental consciousness.

In particular, two American missions to the moon contributed to this planetary consciousness: Apollo 8 in 1968 and Apollo 17 in 1972. These missions produced the first high-quality colour pictures of the earth seen from space. The Apollo 8 picture, named *Earthrise*, is a photograph of the earth taken from lunar orbit. It presents our planet half-cloaked in shadow, with only part of it visible. It is floating in a black, sepulchral universe. The Apollo 17 picture, named *The Whole Earth*, represents the full planet in all its unity and isolation, suspended in space.

The Apollo pictures of the earth rapidly became important symbols of environmentalism. They have been featured on the covers of numerous books, reports, and journals over the last several decades. This view of earth as seen from space has also been widely shared and adapted for different purposes: for postcards, lapel buttons, flags, calendars, political manifestos, commercial advertisements, and T-shirts. In various stylized forms, it has become the logo of many organizations, including firms and non-governmental organizations wishing to emphasize their transnational scope or their planetary consciousness.

These images of the earth have helped to raise people's awareness about environmental issues—first, because they show the planet as a closed system, fragile in the middle of a dark, hostile universe. They have therefore paved the way for the emergence and diffusion of several new environmental movements concerned about the viability of such a closed system. For instance, in the 1970s the Gaia hypothesis, developed by the NASA scientist James Lovelock, presented the planet as a living, self-regulating organism that needs to be protected. The idea of the planet as a closed system is also a fundamental premise of the complex models that were developed from the 1960s onwards, such as the models embedded in the **Club of Rome's** *Limits to Growth* (1972).

Second, the unity of earth seen from space makes clear the superficiality of man-made political borders. It calls for global cooperation, instead of national conflicts over sovereignty claims, and has been a trigger for multilateral initiatives. In this sense, the image of earth seen from space planted the seeds for the creation of multilateral initiatives such as the Man and the Biosphere Programme initiated in 1971.

However, while these images of earth from space have promoted international cooperation, some commentators consider that the Apollo photographs carry with them neocolonial connotations. These commentators recall the imperialist and racist orientations of some Western environmentalists who asked for **preservation** initiatives in foreign countries, especially in Africa. The totalizing socio-environmental discourses of 'One-World' or 'Whole-Earth', both terms associated with the images, can be used as an excuse by Western countries to promote preservation areas in the global South (the African continent is particularly visible on the *Whole Earth* photograph) while practising business as usual at home.

Another criticism comes from a postmodernist perspective. Postmodern scholars argue that representing the earth as a single entity communicates the need for a unitary and global vision, while in fact the earth is far from being socially and culturally homogeneous. Instead of celebrating the planet's unity, postmodernists propose to embrace its diversity, including its inherent divisions, layering, and recurrent patterns that form a mixed and complex picture to which all could contribute.

Sources: Cosgrove 1994; Jasanoff 2001, 2004; Lekan 2014; Petsko 2011.

Some bestselling books published in the 1960s also contributed to raising public awareness, including Rachel Carson's landmark book *Silent Spring*, which exposed the deleterious effects of pesticides on biodiversity, and Paul Ehrlich's book *The Population Bomb*, which made alarming predictions on the environmental impact of population growth. Depletion of natural resources, industrial pollution, overconsumption, and overpopulation gradually became major concerns in developed countries. In response, new environmental advocacy groups were created to address these concerns, such as Friends of the Earth in 1969 and Greenpeace in 1970.

Environmental concerns, initially expressed locally and nationally, spread to many parts of the world. It became clear that solutions to many environmental problems, such as biodiversity loss, could only be reached through international cooperation. In 1968, the United Nations Educational, Scientific and Cultural Organization (known as UNESCO), organized the first intergovernmental conference on global biosphere protection, and in 1971 it launched the 'Man and the Biosphere Programme' to protect key ecosystems. In 1972, the United Nations organized the Stockholm Conference on the Human Environment, after which the United Nations Environment Program was created. The number of environmental treaties increased rapidly after this (Mitchell 2002–2019).

In the 1980s, the most pressing environmental issues included ozone depletion, acid rain, whaling, oil spills, and open-air nuclear tests. Over time, international cooperation has contributed to mitigating some of these issues, most famously ozone depletion. However, as Figure 0.1 (page 10) shows, other environmental problems appear even more pressing today than they were in the 1980s. Climate change, which was not well documented in the 1980s, became a ubiquitous problem in the 1990s.

International cooperation further increased in intensity in the early 1990s at the United Nations Conference on the Environment and Development, which was held in Rio de Janeiro, Brazil. The Rio conference is hailed as a high point of environmental cooperation because it defined several key principles, such as **common but differentiated responsibilities**, and laid the groundwork for a series of **international environmental agreements** on issues such as climate change and biodiversity (Meyer et al. 1997; see Chapter 6).

Figure 0.2, a timeline of the main multilateral treaties and declarations in global environmental governance, illustrates how they proliferated after the 1972 Stockholm Conference on the Human Environment, and their intense development around the 1992 Rio Conference on the Environment and Development. It also reveals the diversity of the environmental issues that these treaties and declarations address.

Annex 0.1 at the end of this introduction presents a selection of the most important multilateral environmental agreements from Figure 0.2, giving background information on their main obligations and political context—specific aspects of these agreements are discussed in detail in later chapters.

0.3 Global environmental politics as a field of study

The emergence of global environmental politics as an academic field of study followed a historical trajectory similar to the development of environmental governance in practice (Boardman 1997; Davidson and Frickel 2004). Before the 1972 Stockholm Conference, very few researchers in politics, economics, sociology, or law were studying the international

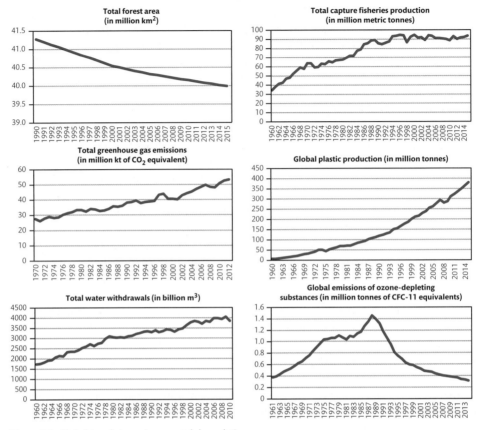

Figure 0.1 Global trends in environmental degradation

Source data from: Food and Agriculture Organization; World Bank; www.ourworldindata.org; Geyer et al. 2017.

dimensions of environmental issues. Some social scientists, such as Harold and Margaret Sprout (1957), had been working on the relationship between environmental damage and armed conflict since the 1950s. However, the first publications related to environmental politics that had a strong impact on public debates were authored by biologists, such as Rachel Carson, Paul Ehrlich, and Garrett Hardin.

Only after the 1972 Stockholm Conference did global environmental politics take shape as a field of study in its own right. For the first time in 1972, a key journal in international politics, *International Organization*, devoted a special issue to environmental challenges. After the 1992 Rio Conference the field grew even further. This growth was reflected in the increasing number of research centres, academic programmes, scientific associations, specialized journals, annual conferences, scientific prizes, research grants, and special collections from university presses devoted to global environmental politics. Journals particularly active in the field include *Global Environmental Politics*, *Journal of Environment & Development*, *Environmental Politics*, *Global Environmental Change*, *International Environmental Agreements: Politics, Law and Economics*, and *Earth System Governance*.

Global environmental politics is a multidisciplinary field, with contributions from various disciplines (sociology, political science, geography, law, economics etc.), that addresses these analytical questions and many others. It explores everything from the definition of environmental issues to the evaluation of policy solutions (Mitchell 2002). Studying global environmental politics is not about blindly condemning polluters or uncritically supporting environmental activists' claims. It is first necessary to understand and explain political dynamics before one can adopt an informed and critical position on environmental problems and how to address them.

The field of global environmental politics is not unified by a grand theory, a unique scale of analysis, a precise epistemological perspective, or a single methodology. Just as genetic diversity contributes to the health and resilience of an ecosystem, intellectual diversity makes the field of global environmental politics vibrant and innovative. Although global environmental politics is multidisciplinary, international relations scholarship has been particularly influential in this field. All the traditional theoretical approaches to the study of international relations are reflected in global environmental politics (Barkdull and Harris 2002; Boardman 1997). These include *realism*, *liberal institutionalism*, *constructivism*, and *critical theories*.

Realists study how states compete for power and security in an anarchical system. In global environmental politics, realist-inspired studies look particularly at the relationship between scarcity of natural resources and the emergence of armed conflicts. Realist theories can also explain non-cooperative behaviours in global environmental politics, such as when states do not join international treaties or institutions, or when they fail to respect their commitments under these institutions (Grundig 2006; Purdon 2014).

Liberal institutionalist accounts are rooted in the assumption that states aim to maximize their absolute gains, meaning their own gains, irrespective of the gains of other players. Liberal institutionalists insist on the fact that states can reach optimal solutions by establishing international institutions. The multiplicity and diversity of international institutions devoted to environmental protection provide liberal institutionalists with rich empirical material to test their hypotheses (Bernauer 1995; Haas et al. 1993; Mitchell 2003).

Constructivists pay attention to the ideas that structure the behaviour of international actors, including states and non-state actors. In the field of global environmental politics, scholars inspired by constructivism look at a wide range of social constructs, such as the meaning we assign to nature, or the **social norms** defining how the environment should be protected (Haas 2015).

Finally, *critical theories* uncover the biases underlying the foundation of global politics. Those working on global environmental politics using insights from critical theories trace the political origins of environmental problems, uncovering how the unequal distribution of power is reflected in international environmental governance (Dalby 2007; Newell 2008).

But studies of global environmental politics do not merely replicate the traditional theoretical debates of international relations. They have also generated specific contributions to the study of international relations. The environment is a particularly useful field for analysing a variety of phenomena, including the influence of non-state actors, the role of science, summit diplomacy, the ethical aspects of international relations, the problems of collective action, interactions between international institutions, or the effectiveness of transnational initiatives.

Global environmental politics scholars have also developed conceptual tools that have subsequently been adopted by other fields of international relations. For example, the concepts of '**epistemic community**' (a network of experts) and '**regime** complex' (a cluster of overlapping international institutions) were first introduced in global environmental politics, by Peter Haas (1989) and by Kal Raustiala and David Victor (2004) respectively. The concepts

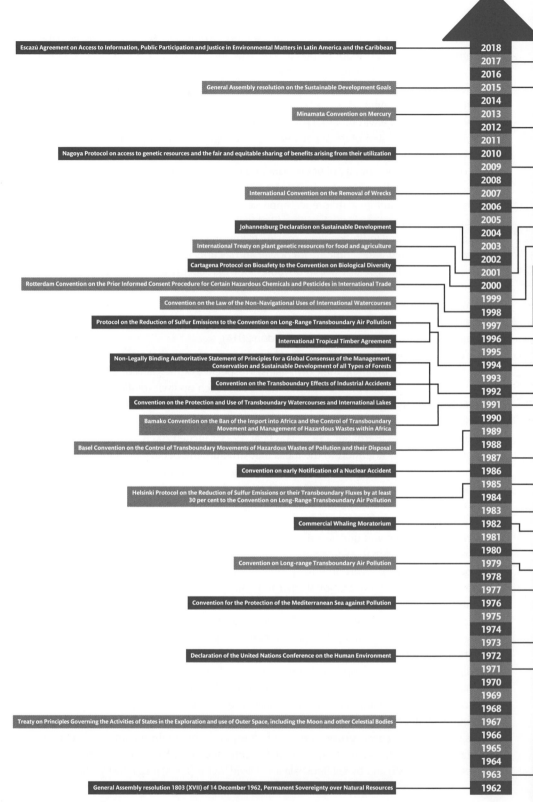

Figure 0.2 Timeline of the main treaties and declarations

Treaty on the Prohibition of Nuclear Weapons

Paris Agreement under the United Nations Framework Convention on Climate Change

The Future We Want, final document of the United Nations Conference on Sustainable Development Rio + 20

Agreement on Port State Measures to Prevent, Deter and Eliminate Illegal, Unreported and Unregulated Fishing

International Tropical Timber Agreement

Stockholm Convention on Persistent Organic Pollutants

Aarhus Convention on Access to Information, Public Participation in Decision-Making and Access to Justice in Environmental Matters

Kyoto Protocol to the United Nations Framework Convention on Climate Change

Comprehensive Nuclear Test Ban Treaty

Convention to Combat Desertification in those Countries Experiencing Serious Drought and Desertification, particularly in Africa

Convention on Nuclear Safety

Convention on Biological Diversity

United Nations Framework Convention on Climate Change

Agenda 21

Rio Declaration on Environment and Development

Madrid Protocol on Environmental Protection to the Antarctic Treaty

Espoo Convention on Environmental Impact Assessment in a Transboundary Context

Montreal Protocol on Substances that Deplete the Ozone Layer

Vienna Convention for the Protection of the Ozone Layer

International Tropical Timber Agreement

United Nations Convention on the Law of the Sea

Convention on the Conservation of Antarctic Marine Living Resources

Convention on the Conservation of Migratory Species of Wild Animals

Convention on the Prohibition of Military or any other Hostile use of Environmental Modification Techniques

Convention on International Trade in Endangered Species of Wild Fauna and Flora

Ramsar Convention on Wetlands of International Importance especially as Waterfowl Habitat

Treaty Banning Nuclear Weapon Tests in the Atmosphere, in Outer Space and under Water

are now frequently used by the broader community of researchers in international relations (Morin et al. 2013). Similarly, polycentric and network governance approaches, which emphasize relationships between actors instead of their individual interests, had already been adopted in the environmental field, when other fields were still confined to interstate paradigms (Young 1997).

Yet global environmental politics remains under-represented in international relations, compared to more traditional fields such as military conflict and trade (Green and Hale 2017; Morin et al. 2013). Only a small fraction of international relations scholars identify the environment as their primary field of investigation, and only a modest share of articles in generalist journals of international relations are devoted to environmental governance. With this book, we hope to contribute to training a new generation of global environmental politics analysts, who might make this field more prominent in scholarly and public debates.

0.4   How to use this book

The diversity of empirical issues and theoretical perspectives that are reflected in global environmental politics scholarship inform the approach we adopt in this book. Although climate change is of fundamental importance and frequently makes the headlines, other issues are equally instructive in understanding international environmental politics—for example, desertification, hazardous waste, biodiversity protection, acid rain, ozone-depleting substances, freshwater, overfishing, and air quality. Moreover, this book pays special attention to the interactions between environmental politics and other governance fields, such as trade, development, and security.

The book goes beyond empirical description of environmental issues by introducing the reader to concepts, theories, methods, and debates from the academic literature. In doing so, it favours an analytical approach that exposes the reader to a wide variety of political perspectives and discusses the strengths and weaknesses of the literature. By providing these analytical insights, it equips the reader with the necessary analytical tools to develop their own conceptual mindsets, normative frameworks, and research endeavours.

Newcomers to global environmental politics might enter this field with existing strong convictions. They might assume, for example: that there is a scientific consensus on the best way to measure a country's contribution to environmental degradation; that the United States is always falling behind the European Union on environmental protection; that multilateral cooperation has so far never succeeded in protecting the environment; that political declarations are futile if they are not accompanied by strong **enforcement** mechanisms; that all multinational corporations are opposed to environmental regulation; that trade agreements weaken environmental regulations; or that a number of military conflicts are being fought for access to freshwater. However, these assumptions are not always borne out by empirical evidence. The analytical approach favoured in this book might call into question the reader's certainties and preconceptions by testing them against empirical evidence. This might be intellectually destabilizing, but also stimulating and engaging.

To further promote an analytical approach, the book is organized along analytical lines. Rather than offering a chronological narrative or studying each issue area independently, it is structured in ten conceptually-based chapters, grouped in pairs, each looking at cross-cutting issues.

The first pair of chapters explores why environmental cooperation is necessary. Chapter 1 looks at how scientific evidence informs policy debates and motivates political actions. Chapter 2 discusses the role of non-scientific ideas, such as social norms and ethical values, as they also structure the way actors engage with environmental cooperation. These first two chapters openly question some common unexamined assumptions related to the necessity of international environmental cooperation.

The following two chapters look at the actors who engage in global environmental governance. Chapter 3 focuses on states, to expose the diversity and (dis)similarity of their interests and preferences. It explains how national interests are constructed, how they inform state preferences in international negotiations, and how states adjust these preferences collectively, through interactions with one another. Chapter 4 points to the contribution of a broad range of non-state actors, including non-governmental organizations, business associations, and cities, to global environmental governance. It explains how these non-state actors complement public policies by establishing their own governance schemes.

The next pair of chapters looks at the interactions among these actors. Chapter 5 studies collective action problems in different types of geographical spaces. Some natural resources fall under state sovereignty while some ecosystems belong to the common **heritage of humankind**, creating different challenges for international cooperation. Chapter 6 takes a historical perspective on how developed and **developing countries** have come to consensual decisions since 1972. It shows how the articulation between environmental protection and economic development has gradually evolved over time.

The two next chapters present the institutional results of these interactions. Chapter 7 discusses the development of international environmental institutions, including treaties and intergovernmental organizations, to tackle environmental challenges. It also questions the interactions between these international institutions, as an increasing number of them have an impact on global environmental governance. Chapter 8 reviews the variety of policy instruments adopted to ensure that international commitments are implemented. It explains how the effectiveness of global environmental politics could be measured, and discusses **implementation** as well as verification instruments.

The last two chapters broaden the discussion by studying the relationship between environmental governance and non-environmental issues. Chapter 9 examines how security and environmental protection are closely intertwined. While environmental degradation can increase tension within and among societies, armed conflicts can also contribute to environmental degradation. Chapter 10 analyses the complex interactions between environmental and trade governance. It explains the theoretical underpinnings of this relationship in the literature and discusses how environmental agreements use trade provisions and trade agreements use environmental ones.

Overall, each chapter combines empirical descriptions and analytical insights from a range of theoretical approaches, allowing for in-depth analytical discussions. Each chapter concludes with a series of 'Critical thinking questions' that can guide the reader in analytical discussions of the concepts and ideas presented in the chapter. Additional review questions are also available in the online resources that accompany the book.

This book can be read in two ways. Readers who are new to the field can read it straight through, chapter by chapter. The book is written on the assumption that readers have no prior knowledge in global environmental politics or international relations. Each chapter takes great care to include essential contextual information and make explicit underlying assumptions. Readers who are more familiar with the terrain of global environmental politics can navigate non-consecutively between chapters using the table of contents and index, which together list the main themes discussed in the book. While the structure follows a logical order, each chapter can be read independently. This enables the reader to jump straight to their specific interests.

Either way, the book provides readers with tools to enhance their understanding and their critical thinking surrounding environmental politics. It includes numerous text boxes, maps, plots, and tables. It also offers carefully selected references at the end of each chapter, a glossary, and a list of resources available online. Glossary terms in the text are indicated by blue bold font. Interactive figures, which illustrate for example the geographical distribution of environmental technologies and historical trends in the adoption of environmental treaties, are also available in the online resources.

The aim of this book is to make readers aware of and familiar with global environmental politics, as a phenomenon and as a field of study, with the hope of inspiring them to take up the challenge by undertaking further action and research in this field.

 For additional material and resources, please visit the online resources at: www.oup.com/he/morin1e

Chapter references

Autin, Whitney J., and John M. Holbrook. 2012. 'Is the Anthropocene an Issue of Stratigraphy or Pop Culture'. *GSA Today* 22 (7): 60–61.

Barkdull, John, and Paul G. Harris. 2002. 'Environmental Change and Foreign Policy: A Survey of Theory'. *Global Environmental Politics* 2 (2): 63–91.

Bernauer, Thomas. 1995. 'The Effect of International Environmental Institutions: How we Might Learn More'. *International Organization* 49 (2): 351–377.

Biermann, Frank. 2014. 'The Anthropocene: A Governance Perspective'. *The Anthropocene Review* 1 (1): 57–61.

Biermann, Frank, and Eva Lövbrand. 2019. *Anthropocene Encounters: New Directions in Green Political Thinking*. Cambridge: Cambridge University Press.

Boardman, Robert. 1997. 'Environmental Discourse and International Relations Theory: Towards a Proto-Theory of Ecosation'. *Global Society: Journal of Interdisciplinary International Relations* 11 (1): 31–44.

Cosgrove, Denis. 1994. 'Contested Global Visions: One-World, Whole-Earth, and the Apollo Space Photographs'. *Annals of the Association of American Geographers* 84 (2): 270–294.

Crutzen, Paul, and Eugene Stoermer. 2000. 'The "Anthropocene"'. *Global Change Newsletter* 41 (May): 17–18.

Dalby, Simon. 2007. 'Anthropocene Geopolitics: Globalisation, Empire, Environment and Critique'. *Geography Compass* 1 (1): 103–118.

Dauvergne, Peter, and Jennifer Clapp. 2016. 'Researching Global Environmental Politics in the 21st Century'. *Global Environmental Politics* 16 (1): 1–12.

Davidson, Debra J., and Scott Frickel. 2004. 'Understanding Environmental Governance: A Critical Review'. *Organization & Environment* 17 (4): 471–492.

Demos, T. J. 2017. *Against the Anthropocene: Visual Culture and Environment Today*. New York: Sternberg Press.

Geyer, Roland, Jenna R. Jambeck, and Kara Lavender Law. 2017. 'Production, Use, and Fate of all Plastics Ever Made'. *Science Advances* 3 (7): e1700782.

Green, Jessica F., and Thomas N. Hale. 2017. 'Reversing the Marginalization of Global Environmental Politics in International Relations: An Opportunity for the Discipline'. *PS: Political Science & Politics* 50 (2): 473–479.

Grundig, Frank. 2006. 'Patterns of International Cooperation and the Explanatory Power of Relative Gains: An Analysis of Cooperation on Global Climate Change, Ozone Depletion, and International Trade'. *International Studies Quarterly* 50 (4): 781–801.

Haas, Peter M. 1989. 'Do Regimes Matter? Epistemic Communities and Mediterranean Pollution Control'. *International Organization* 43 (3): 377–403.

Haas, Peter M. 2015. *Epistemic Communities, Constructivism, and International Environmental Politics.* Abingdon and New York: Routledge.

Haas, Peter M., Robert O. Keohane, and Marc A. Levy (eds). 1993. *Institutions for the Earth: Sources of Effective International Environmental Protection.* Cambridge, MA: MIT Press.

Hickmann, Thomas, Lena Partzsch, Philipp Pattberg, and Sabine Weiland. 2018. *The Anthropocene Debate and Political Science.* Abingdon and New York: Routledge.

Jasanoff, Sheila. 2001. 'Image and Imagination: The Formation of Global Environmental Consciousness'. In *Changing the Atmosphere: Expert Knowledge and Environmental Governance*, edited by Clarck Miller and Paul Edwards, 309–337. Cambridge, MA: MIT Press.

Jasanoff, Sheila. 2004. 'Heaven and Earth: The Politics of Environmental Images'. In *Earthly Politics: Local and Global in Environmental Governance*, edited by Sheila Jasanoff and Marybeth Long Martello, 31–54. Cambridge, MA: MIT Press: 31–54.

Lekan, Thomas M. 2014. 'Fractal Eaarth: Visualizing the Global Environment in the Anthropocene'. *Environmental Humanities* 5 (1): 171–201.

Lövbrand, Eva, Silke Beck, Jason Chilvers, Tim Forsyth, Johan Hedrén, Mike Hulme, Rolf Lidskog, and Eleftheria Vasileiadou. 2015. 'Who Speaks for the Future of Earth? How Critical Social Science Can Extend the Conversation on the Anthropocene'. *Global Environmental Change* 32 (May): 211–218.

Meyer, John, David J. Frank, Ann Hironaka, Evan Schofer, and Nancy Brandon Tuma. 1997. 'The Structuring of a World Environmental Regime, 1870–1990'. *International Organization* 51 (4): 623–651.

Mitchell, Ronald. 2002. 'International Environment'. In *Handbook of International Relations*, edited by Walter Carlsnaes, Thomas Risse, and Beth Simmons, 500–516. London: Sage.

Mitchell, Ronald B. 2002–2019. *International Environmental Agreements Database Project* (Version 2018.1). Available at: http://iea.uoregon.edu/, accessed October 2019.

Mitchell, Ronald B. 2003. 'International Environmental Agreements: A Survey of their Features, Formation, and Effects'. *Annual Review of Environment and Resources* 28 (1): 429–461.

Moore, Jason. 2017. 'The Capitalocene, Part I: On the Nature and Origins of our Ecological Crisis'. *Journal of Peasant Studies* 44 (3): 594–630.

Morin, Jean-Frédéric et al. 2013. 'Insights from Global Environmental Governance'. *International Studies Review* 15 (4): 562–589.

Newell, Peter. 2008. 'The Political Economy of Global Environmental Governance'. *Review of International Studies* 34 (3): 507–529.

Nicholson, Simon, and Sikina Jinnah. 2016. *New Earth Politics: Essays from the Anthropocene.* Cambridge, MA: MIT Press.

Petsko, Gregory A. 2011. 'The Blue Marble'. *Genome Biology* 12 (4): article 112.

Purdon, Mark. 2014. 'Neoclassical Realism and International Climate Change Politics: Moral Imperative and Political Constraint in International Climate Finance'. *Journal of International Relations and Development* 17 (3): 301–338.

Raustiala, Kal, and David G. Victor. 2004. 'The Regime Complex for Plant Genetic Resources'. *International Organization* 58 (2): 277–309.

Sprout, Harold, and Margaret Sprout. 1957. 'Environmental Factors in the Study of International Politics'. *Conflict Resolution* 1 (4): 309–328.

Waters, Colin N., Jan Zalasiewicz, Colin Summerhayes, Anthony D. Barnosky, Clément Poirier, Agnieszka Galuszka, Alejandro Cearreta, Matt Edgeworth, Erle C. Ellis, and Michael Ellis. 2016. 'The Anthropocene is Functionally and Stratigraphically Distinct from the Holocene'. *Science* 351 (6269): aad2622-1–aad2622-10.

Young, Oran R. (ed.) 1997. *Global Governance: Drawing Insights from the Environmental Experience.* Cambridge, MA: MIT Press.

Young, Oran R. 2017. *Governing Complex Systems: Social Capital for the Anthropocene.* Cambridge, MA: MIT Press.

Annex 0.1: Key multilateral environmental agreements: Obligations and political context

---

International Convention for the Regulation of Whaling

Place of signature: Washington, DC, United States

Adoption year: 1946   **Entry into force**: 1948   **Number of parties (as of Jan. 2019)**: 87

Main obligations: Establish an International Whaling Commission to adopt regulations for the conservation of whale stocks, including the identification of protected species, whaling seasons, and permitted waters for whaling, as well as collect information on whale stocks and the impact of whaling activities.

Political context: The Convention was originally designed as an agreement between whaling nations, aiming to regulate this activity for sustained harvesting. Non-whaling states later joined, shifting the balance away from strictly commercial concerns and adopting an environmental, preservation-oriented agenda as well.

Convention on International Trade in Endangered Species of Wild Fauna and Flora

Place of signature: Washington, DC, United States

Adoption year: 1973   **Entry into force**: 1975   **Number of parties (as of Jan. 2019)**: 183

Main obligations: Regulate trade in species listed in Appendices: I (species threatened with extinction due to international trade), II (species that may become threatened if trade remains unregulated), and III (species that are subject to national regulation and require other parties' cooperation). It also established a permit scheme for the import and export of regulated species, based on a scientific evaluation of potential impacts.

Political context: The negotiations originated in the International Union for Conservation of Nature and reflected concerns about the overexploitation of biological resources. The treaty's original adoption raised little controversy. Over the years, however, protection of some species, particularly those that are considered commercially viable, such as bluefin tuna, has been extremely contentious.

International Convention for the Prevention of Pollution from Ships (MARPOL)

Place of signature: London, United Kingdom

Adoption year: 1973   **Entry into force**: 1983   **Number of parties (as of Jan. 2019)**: 156

Main obligations: Prevent pollution of the marine environment by banning the discharge of harmful substances from ships; make pollution subject to sanctions by the government under whose authority the ship operates; cooperate in the enforcement of the Convention, including through inspections.

Political context: Oil spills increased public pressure on governments to adopt stricter regulations. The MARPOL initiative was led by the United States, but met opposition from several major maritime shipping nations, which tended to favour less strict regulation to minimize the impact on ship owners. In the end, environmental concerns prevailed, though ratification of the Convention was very slow.

Convention on Long-range Transboundary Air Pollution

Place of signature: Geneva, Switzerland

Adoption year: 1979 **Entry into force**: 1983 **Number of parties (as of Jan. 2019)**: 51

Main obligations: Develop policies and strategies to combat the discharge of air pollutants; encourage research and development of technologies to reduce and monitor emissions; exchange information on and review policies concerning air pollution; implement an existing European cooperative programme on air pollution monitoring; negotiate protocols on specific targets.

Political context: The negotiation of the Convention came as a response to concerns about acid rain. Norway and Sweden unsuccessfully pushed for more stringent provisions, but pollutant states in Eastern Europe opposed sulphur dioxide reduction targets, resulting in a 'loose' framework convention that sets out general objectives but does not set numerical targets. Later on, several protocols were negotiated to reinforce the obligations of states with regard to air pollution.

Convention on the Conservation of Antarctic Marine Living Resources (CCAMLR)

Place of signature: Canberra, Australia

Adoption year: 1980 **Entry into force**: 1982 **Number of parties (as of Jan. 2019)**: 37

Main obligations: Prevent decrease in size of populations of living resources in Antarctica, maintain ecological relationships between populations, and restore depleted populations; establish a Commission for the Conservation of Antarctic Marine Living Resources to formulate conservation measures and to facilitate research and data collection on populations; establish a Scientific Committee to serve as a consultative body to the Commission.

Political context: Fishing states such as Japan and the Soviet Union, which had a commercial interest in exploiting marine living resources, were opposed to conservationists who pushed for quotas to protect Antarctic species. Countries that could claim a right to Antarctic territory were interested in leveraging the Convention to further their claims, while non-claiming countries opposed this strategy.

Vienna Convention for the Protection of the Ozone Layer

Place of signature: Vienna, Austria

Adoption year: 1985 **Entry into force**: 1988 **Number of parties (as of Jan. 2019)**: 197

Main obligations: Protect humans and the environment from the adverse effects of human-induced ozone layer depletion; cooperate in research, monitoring, and policymaking; negotiate protocols on emission targets.

Political context: The process started with bilateral negotiations between the European Community and the United States, with the United States advocating for stricter regulations on chlorofluorocarbons and the European Community opposed to specific targets. It then expanded into multilateral negotiations in 1981.

Montreal Protocol on Substances that Deplete the Ozone Layer

Place of signature: Montreal, Canada

Adoption year: 1987	**Entry into force**: 1989	**Number of parties (as of Jan. 2019)**: 197

Main obligations: Restrict production and use of ozone-depleting substances; ban the import of controlled substances from and their export to non-parties to the Protocol; establish a system for licensing the import and export of new, used, recycled, and reclaimed controlled substances; add or remove substances from the list covered by the Protocol and re-evaluate their potential impact on the ozone layer.

Political context: The European Community and Japan supported lower reduction targets, while the United States, Canada, Norway, and Sweden supported strong cuts. The United States' proactive stance can be in part explained by the fact that Dupont, an American corporation, had developed a substitute for some ozone-depleting substances.

Basel Convention on the Control of Transboundary Movements of Hazardous Wastes and their Disposal

Place of signature: Basel, Switzerland

Adoption year: 1989	**Entry into force**: 1992	**Number of parties (as of Jan. 2019)**: 186

Main obligations: Maintain and update a national list of hazardous wastes; establish the right to prohibit the import of hazardous wastes into national territory; prohibit the export of hazardous wastes to countries where import is domestically prohibited; if applicable, obtain the prior informed consent of the state of import and ensure safe transportation; reduce production of hazardous wastes and ensure their safe disposal.

Political context: Developed and developing countries' interests were in opposition to one another during the negotiations, due to the flow of hazardous wastes primarily from the former to the latter. The United States is the only developed country that has not ratified the Convention.

Bamako Convention on the Ban of the Import into Africa and the Control of Transboundary Movement and Management of Hazardous Wastes within Africa

Place of signature: Bamako, Mali

Adoption year: 1991	**Entry into force**: 1998	**Number of parties (as of Jan. 2019)**: 27

Main obligations: Maintain and update a national list of hazardous wastes; take measures to prohibit the import of hazardous wastes into Africa from non-contracting parties; prevent export of hazardous wastes to states that have prohibited such imports; prohibit the dumping of hazardous wastes at sea, or in internal waters and waterways; impose liability on waste generators and reduce waste generation under state jurisdiction; adopt a precautionary approach.

Political context: Because they felt that the 1989 Basel Convention (see above) did not adequately account for their specific interests, several African countries decided to negotiate their own regional convention to account for their specific circumstances and protect the interests of developing countries.

Convention on Environmental Impact Assessment in a Transboundary Context		
Place of signature: Espoo, Finland		
Adoption year: 1991	**Entry into force**: 1997	**Number of parties (as of Jan. 2019)**: 45

Main obligations: For the party of origin, prepare an assessment before authorizing activities listed in the appendix that may have transboundary effects; during the assessment process, respect procedural obligations regarding the other party's notification and public participation requirements; enter consultations once the assessment is completed and take the assessment into account for the final decision.

Political context: European countries advocated for a specific list of activities triggering an environmental impact assessment obligation, while the United States and Canada preferred broader but more vague obligations, without listing specific activities.

United Nations Framework Convention on Climate Change		
Place of signature: New York, United States		
Adoption year: 1992	**Entry into force**: 1994	**Number of parties (as of Jan. 2019)**: 197

Main obligations: Stabilize greenhouse gas concentrations in the atmosphere at a level that avoids dangerous anthropogenic interference with the climate system and considering common but differentiated responsibility; develop national inventories of emissions.

Political context: The negotiations were characterized by a difference in perception between many developed and developing countries, especially related to the historical contribution of the former and the right to development of the latter. Developing countries also requested that developed countries bear the costs of abatement measures. The United States, a major greenhouse gas emitter, favoured less specific provisions than most other developed countries.

Convention on Biological Diversity		
Place of signature: Rio de Janeiro, Brazil		
Adoption year: 1992	**Entry into force**: 1993	**Number of parties (as of Jan. 2019)**: 196

Main obligations: Require environmental impact assessment of projects likely to have an impact on biodiversity; develop national strategies, establish protected areas, and cooperate for the conservation of biodiversity; monitor national components of biodiversity and exchange information; ensure the equitable sharing of benefits arising from the use of genetic resources and traditional knowledge; recognize state sovereignty over genetic resources; facilitate other parties' access to genetic resources, subject to prior informed consent.

Political context: Developing countries, as providers of biodiversity, argued for national sovereignty provisions on their natural and genetic resources. The United States was opposed to the Convention's benefit sharing provisions, which they saw as a risk to intellectual property protection.

United Nations Convention to Combat Desertification in those Countries Experiencing Serious Drought and/or Desertification, Particularly in Africa

Place of signature: Paris, France

Adoption year: 1994   **Entry into force**: 1996   **Number of parties (as of Jan. 2019)**: 197

Main obligations: Adopt an integrated approach to combat desertification; develop national action programmes; for affected countries, establish strategies and raise awareness; for developed countries, provide financial or other assistance to affected countries; promote the availability of financial mechanisms and establish new ones.

Political context: African countries, as the countries most affected by desertification, were in favour of the Convention. In contrast, developed countries were unconvinced of the need for a convention, and some opposed the conclusion of an international convention on what they defined as a cluster of local issues.

Kyoto Protocol to the United Nations Framework Convention on Climate Change

Place of signature: Kyoto, Japan

Adoption year: 1997   **Entry into force**: 2005   **Number of parties (as of Jan. 2019)**: 192

Main obligations: Developed countries were required to reduce greenhouse gas emissions to approximately 5% below 1990 levels by 2012, implement measures to minimize the adverse effects of climate change, and establish a national system to estimate anthropogenic greenhouse gas emissions by sources and removals by sinks; developing countries could participate in the Clean Development Mechanism to reduce emissions on a voluntary basis; for all parties, cooperate in research, training and policy development.

Political context: The negotiations were characterized by many opposing interests, largely divided according to the following groups: the Umbrella group (United States, Canada, Japan, and others); the European Union and the Group of 77 (a coalition of developing states) including China; the Association of Small Island States; the Group of 11 (a coalition bringing together transitioning European economies); and the Environmental Integrity Group, led by Switzerland. Each of these groups had different views on how to calculate reduction targets for each country.

Convention on Access to Information, Public Participation in Decision-Making and Access to Justice in Environmental Matters

Place of signature: Aarhus, Denmark

Adoption year: 1998   **Entry into force**: 2001   **Number of parties (as of Jan. 2019)**: 47

Main obligations: Make environmental information available to the public on request; allow the public to participate during the elaboration of specific plans, programmes, regulations, and activities; ensure public access to justice in cases where participation rights or environmental law may have been breached.

Political context: States' preferences were generally aligned during the negotiations. Public involvement fit into the democratization process that took place in Central and Eastern Europe in the 1990s, and which was supported by Western European countries.

Rotterdam Convention on the Prior Informed Consent Procedure for Certain Hazardous Chemicals and Pesticides in International Trade

Place of signature: Rotterdam, Netherlands

Adoption year: 1998 **Entry into force**: 2004 **Number of parties (as of Jan. 2019)**: 160

Main obligations: Notify the Convention Secretariat of national bans and restrictions on covered products; ensure that once a threshold is reached, the Chemical Review Committee evaluates the measures and agrees to make the product subject to the prior informed consent procedure; notify the importing party when a substance is exported from a party that has banned or restricted it.

Political context: The negotiations reflected the diverging interests of two main groups of developed countries, led by the United States and the European Union. These groups respectively favoured a narrow versus a wide application of the prior informed consent procedure, and the prevalence of World Trade Organization rules versus the Convention's rules in cases of inconsistency.

Cartagena Protocol on Biosafety to the Convention on Biological Diversity

Place of signature: Montreal, Canada

Adoption year: 2000 **Entry into force**: 2003 **Number of parties (as of Jan. 2019)**: 171

Main obligations: Ensure that the development, handling, transport, use, transfer, and release of any living genetically modified organisms are undertaken in a manner that prevents or reduces the risks to biological diversity; follow an advanced informed agreement procedure for transboundary movement of living modified organisms.

Political context: Negotiating interests were divided among numerous groups. Developing countries, as both exporters and importers of living modified organisms, were in favour of the advance informed agreement procedure applying to all products. The Miami Group, consisting of the main exporters of agricultural commodities containing living modified organisms, was against it. Other groups included the European Union, the Compromise Group, and the Central and East European Countries.

Stockholm Convention on Persistent Organic Pollutants

Place of signature: Stockholm, Sweden

Adoption year: 2001 **Entry into force**: 2004 **Number of parties (as of Jan. 2019)**: 182

Main obligations: Prohibit or take legal and administrative measures necessary to eliminate production, use, import, and export of certain listed chemicals; prevent the production of new pesticides; take measures to reduce anthropogenic releases of certain listed chemicals; appropriately identify and manage existing stockpiles of chemicals; allow for amendments to the lists to add chemicals with significant adverse effects on human health or the environment.

Political context: The main cleavage was between the European Union, which had already adopted regulations on many organic pollutants and encouraged more restrictive provisions, on one side, and Japan, Canada, the United States, Australia, and New Zealand, which preferred softer provisions, on the other. Both sides nevertheless agreed to use existing financial mechanisms, whereas the Group of 77 (a coalition of developing countries) and China preferred the establishment of a new one.

Nagoya Protocol on Access to Genetic Resources and the Fair and Equitable Sharing of Benefits Arising from their Utilization to the Convention on Biological Diversity

Place of signature: Nagoya, Japan

Adoption year: 2010   **Entry into force**: 2014   **Number of parties (as of Jan. 2019)**: 105

Main obligations: Ensure the fair and equitable sharing of benefits arising from the use of genetic resources and traditional knowledge; ensure that the prior informed consent of the country of origin is obtained according to a set procedure; exchange information through a clearing house; ensure that genetic resources used under a party's jurisdiction were obtained in accordance with the principles of the Convention on Biological Diversity.

Political context: The negotiating positions of several developed and developing countries were in opposition. Debates focused on the economic scope of domestic benefit sharing provisions, the Protocol's relationship with other international instruments, and the level of precision of the obligations on domestic compliance monitoring.

Minamata Convention on Mercury

Place of signature: Kumamoto, Japan

Adoption year: 2013   **Entry into force**: 2017   **Number of parties (as of Jan. 2019)**: 92

Main obligations: Prohibit new initiatives of primary mercury mining and end existing ones within 15 years; prohibit manufacture, export, or import of mercury-added products; dispose of existing stocks of mercury in an environmentally sound manner; prohibit the export of mercury unless the importing party has given its consent and the planned use is allowed under the Convention; control and reduce mercury emissions at the source and releases to land and water.

Political context: While there was general agreement on the need to regulate mercury emissions for both environmental and health reasons, the United States originally favoured voluntary measures rather than a binding convention. Once it changed its position negotiations went forward, and the main division occurred between developed and developing nations on mercury emissions from polluting power plants, which several developing countries relied on to supply electricity to their citizens.

Paris Agreement on Climate Change

Place of signature: Paris, France

Adoption year: 2015   **Entry into force**: 2016   **Number of parties (as of Jan. 2019)**: 184

Main obligations: Limit global average temperature to 2°C increase over pre-industrial levels (and pursue efforts to limit temperature increase even further to 1.5°C), by committing to nationally determined contributions of emission reductions, to be ratcheted up every five years; conduct national evaluations of emissions in a transparent manner; cooperate to increase the ability to adapt to and mitigate climate change, with a country-driven and participatory approach; for developed parties, provide financial resources to developing parties for mitigation and adaptation; conserve and enhance carbon sinks.

Political context: Among the complex manoeuvrings that led to the Paris Agreement, a 'high ambition coalition' bridged the historic political gap between developed and developing countries, including the European Union, small island states, and later the United States, Canada, Australia, Brazil, and South Africa.

Part 1

Defining global environmental issues

Interconnections between science and politics

This chapter discusses the complex and multifaceted relationship between science and politics. Although science and politics each follow a distinct logic and pursue distinct objectives, they are inextricably connected to one another. On the one hand, science influences political debates, by drawing attention to certain problems and providing necessary justifications for political action. On the other hand, political dynamics, including political values and power relations, structure the conduct of science. This chapter highlights the different aspects of the co-production of science and politics, in the framework of international environmental debates.

◉ Learning objectives

After reading this chapter, readers will be able to:

- Articulate why political action on environmental issues is needed in the face of scientific uncertainty;

- Explain the role of scientists and scientific knowledge in the development of international environmental policymaking across several issue areas, including climate change, ozone depletion, and food security;

- Understand how the production of environmental science is influenced by diverse political values and different national capacities; and

- Explain how organizations that straddle the interface between science and politics operate and engage in environmental policymaking.

Introduction

One of the prominent characteristics of modernity is its faith in science, and particularly natural sciences. There is a widespread belief that science can objectively define environmental problems and identify the most appropriate policy solutions (Pammett 2015). This faith in science is a frequent assumption when discussing global environmental **governance**. It is also an assumption that is often left unquestioned.

Another commonly held belief is that political leaders fail to implement policy prescriptions provided by scientists. Science and politics are often seen as two antithetical approaches. Science is perceived as rational, objective, consensual, neutral, and universal, whereas politics is seen as emotive, subjective, conflicting, partial, and contextual. Scientists are often thought to contribute to the common good of humanity, while politicians are frequently seen as protecting vested interests, which may be the interests of their class, their constituency, or their country. Under this logic, it is tempting to explain the failures of global environmental governance as the result of political leaders' tendency to pursue vested interests, rather than adopting the solutions that science proposes.

Although these assumptions are frequently expressed in public debates, they are simplistic and misleading (Gulbrandsen 2008; Koetz et al. 2012). They suggest a rather limited view of what global environmental governance really is and how it operates. In reality, science rarely offers politically neutral solutions, and politics is often responsive to scientific arguments. Rather than being antagonistic, science and politics are interconnected in complex ways.

This chapter deconstructs some prevailing assumptions about science and politics to broaden the scope of how and why international cooperation unfolds in response to environmental problems. It explores four different dimensions of the complex and multifaceted relations between science and politics: the necessity to take political action under scientific uncertainty (Section 1.1), scientists' involvement in the political arena (Section 1.2), the political context of scientific inquiries (Section 1.3), and organizations that straddle the worlds of science and politics (Section 1.4).

1.1 Cooperation under scientific uncertainty

The ubiquity of scientific uncertainty

Science offers very few certitudes. Most of the time, science reasons in terms of probabilities, and avoids making strong deterministic predictions. In fact, science makes progress precisely thanks to a healthy dose of scientific doubt and self-criticism.

Computer modelling is a good example (Lewis 2014; Pulver and VanDeveer 2009). Models used in environmental sciences often include a vast quantity of diverse input variables, including climatic, economic, agricultural, technological, demographic, biological, etc. On the basis of historical trends and observations of the interaction between the variables, these models can be used to make probabilistic predictions, for example on the price of natural resources, the magnitude of climate change, or the rate of extinction of biological species. These predictions constitute a valuable source of information to guide public policies.

However, predictions derived from models are imprecise. Several predictions made in the 1970s about the 2000s proved to be inaccurate. The most famous example is undoubtedly the report *The Limits to Growth*. Published in 1972, the report was based on one of the very first complex computer simulations. The simulation was conducted by a team from the Massachusetts Institute of Technology, directed by Donella and Dennis Meadows, and commissioned by a think tank called the **Club of Rome**. The report made references—albeit cautiously—to catastrophic predictions for the end of the twentieth century, such as an increasing inability to meet the population's food requirements. These predictions were very topical in the 1970s, but they did not all materialize, thanks to an unexpected improvement in agricultural yields.

One can adopt two positions when predictions have proven to be inaccurate. The first and most optimistic position claims that past failures do not mean that current models are incorrect. Models are becoming increasingly complex and accurate—current climate change models are far more nuanced than Donella and Dennis Meadows' first modelling attempts. Despite their inevitable imperfections, it seems more rational to base environmental policies on these models, rather than on anecdotal evidence.

However, some scholars consider that social and environmental systems are too complex, unstable, and chaotic to be modelled accurately (Mayer 2012). We will never be able to collect all the relevant data, and a plethora of feedback loops prevent us from isolating causal relationships. The emergence of new technologies further increases this complexity and uncertainty (see Box 1.1). In this context of uncertainty, some analysts are campaigning against state interventions in social, economic, and environmental systems. Even if these interventions are benevolent in intention, they could have unintended adverse effects and cause more harm than good. When considering complex systems, it would be preferable to show some humility, refrain from direct intervention, and resist being lured by the illusion of control that modelling may give us. The economist Friedrich von Hayek defended this view in his speech on receiving the Nobel Prize in 1974 for his work on economic fluctuations:

> *What looks superficially like the most scientific procedure is often the most unscientific [. . .]. There are definite limits to what we can expect science to achieve. This means that to entrust to science—or to deliberate control according to scientific principles—more than scientific method can achieve may have deplorable effects. [. . .] It is often difficult enough for the expert, and certainly in many instances impossible for the layman, to distinguish between legitimate and illegitimate claims advanced in the name of science. The enormous publicity recently given by the media to a report pronouncing in the name of science on The Limits to Growth, and the silence of the same media about the devastating criticism this report has received from the competent experts, must make one feel somewhat apprehensive about the use to which the prestige of science can be put. (Hayek 1974)*

Hayek's view is only shared by a minority of people in either the political or scientific worlds. Increasingly, quantitative models prevail in the natural, physical, and social sciences, and shape environmental policies (Pulver and VanDeveer 2009). Few decision makers fully consider the methodological problems that occur in science, or the difficulties involved in predicting the evolution of the biosphere.

Box 1.1 Nanotechnology—opportunities and uncertainties

Nanotechnology is an emerging branch of technology that manipulates materials at the atomic level—equal to and smaller than one billionth of a metre. It allows scientists to construct specific molecular structures and new materials with new characteristics, and to improve the internal properties or surface qualities of conventional materials. For example, silver nanoparticles can be added to plastics to make them antibacterial. This fast-moving area of science has opened up a new spectrum of opportunities and technological advances in a large number of fields, including military, transportation, construction, food production, manufacturing, and optics. It has significant applications in the medical field, where it can be used to improve detection, diagnosis, and treatment of various cancers. Through nanotechnology, engineering systems can create more efficient energy sources, and offer new solutions to current environmental and waste management issues. The United States, the European Union, and China, among others, have developed programmes to support research and development of nanotechnologies.

But even though nanotechnology can deliver significant social benefits, its use also creates ethical, societal, and legal concerns. When starting to manipulate the order and composition of atoms, scientists can create elements that could behave in unexpected ways. Some believe that these novel properties

(continued...)

unleash a wide spectrum of uncertainties, raising concerns, for example, regarding the toxicity and environmental impact of nanomaterials, risks to workers and consumers, and potential effects on global economics.

The rapid evolution and broad applications of nanotechnologies make it difficult to fit them into any existing regulatory model or system. In most countries, nanotechnology is not regulated as a particular technology by any single regulatory agency. Rather, it is regulated by a number of different agencies, depending on the particular products and uses involved. As the number of nanoproducts entering the market increases, new challenges emerge for regulatory agencies, creating a myriad of complex policy considerations. For instance, the European Union requires the term 'nano' to be included on the list of ingredients for foods that contain engineered nanomaterials. The United States instead focuses on developing regulations that are product-focused, encouraging manufacturers to consult with the Food and Drug Administration before taking their products to market. This discrepancy can potentially create international legal issues for transatlantic trade, with identical products being labelled differently for different markets.

Given differing national and regional regulatory approaches, some have advocated that nanotechnology requires the development of novel soft law mechanisms. These soft law approaches would ensure broad industry participation, and voluntary data disclosure, risk management, and safety testing, and would thus provide public reassurance that new technologies are being evaluated and regulated appropriately. Others advocate for the need to develop a coordinated international effort, such as a new treaty containing substantive regulatory commitments. Ultimately, the next decades will be critical for the development of international standards in nanotechnology regulation, and provide an opportunity to strengthen current regulatory frameworks.

Sources: Bowman and Hodge 2007; Grieger et al. 2016; Mandel 2008; Marchant and Abbott 2013.

Political action under uncertainty

A high degree of scientific certainty is not a guarantee of political action. For example, the immediate causes of deforestation and desertification are well known, and several forestry and agricultural techniques are available to alleviate the problems, yet states have adopted very few multilateral norms in response to these two environmental issues. Multilateral initiatives specifically geared to the problem of deforestation are still modest, and the 1994 UN Convention to Combat Desertification primarily calls on regions, countries, and local authorities to develop their own programmes of action. Thus, identifying a problem and the available solutions does not necessarily mean that those solutions will be effectively implemented and coordinated on a multilateral level (Dimitrov 2006).

Even more surprising, scientific certitude is not a prerequisite for international cooperation. As Figure 1.1 suggests, some international treaties have been adopted prior to the proliferation of scientific studies on the environmental issue they address. The 2000 Cartagena Protocol on Biosafety is a case in point. During negotiations, the scientific community disagreed about the risks posed by **genetically modified organisms** (GMOs) for human health and biological diversity. In this context, the Cartagena Protocol is based on the **precautionary principle** and obliges exporters of modified living organisms to inform the importing countries (see Box 1.2). The latter can then refuse to allow the importation if they consider that harm is possible, even if the risk itself remains highly uncertain (Gupta 2010).

States have adopted several other international treaties, despite the high degree of uncertainty about the scale and immediate causes of the environmental problems targeted: the 1963 *Partial Nuclear Test Ban Treaty* was signed when the effects of low-level radioactive

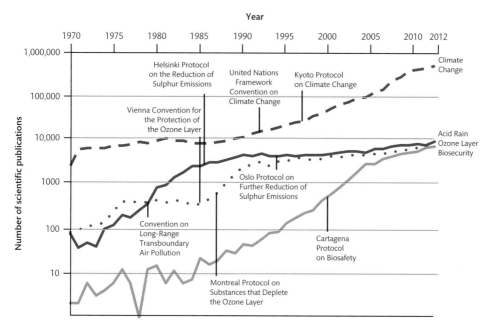

Figure 1.1 Annual number of scientific publications (1970–2012)

Box 1.2 The multiple interpretations of the precautionary principle

Applied to global environmental politics, the **precautionary principle** states that a lack of absolute scientific certainty about environmental risks is not a legitimate reason for postponing the adoption of measures that would help to reduce these potential risks. Unlike the **prevention principle**, which is applicable once science has confirmed the risk of harmful effects and which requires that all necessary measures must be taken to limit associated damage, the precautionary principle is invoked when science is unable to determine with absolute certainty whether there is indeed a risk. In short, environmental damage is considered possible but its likelihood is not confirmed scientifically.

Several international **institutions** rely on this principle, but they invoke it in different ways. According to the Rio Declaration on Environment and Development, precautionary measures can be taken only in cases of 'serious or irreversible' potential damage (Principle 15). The United Nations Framework Convention on Climate Change adds that precautionary measures 'should be cost-effective so as to ensure global benefits at the lowest possible cost' (Article 3). The Cartagena Protocol on Biosafety specifies that precautionary measures may only be taken following risk assessment carried out 'in a scientifically sound manner' and 'taking into account recognized risk assessment techniques' (Article 15). The World Trade Organization's Agreement on the Application of Sanitary and Phytosanitary Measures does not explicitly use the term 'precautionary principle', but nonetheless authorizes precautionary measures as long as they are provisional and the authorities that adopt them seek to quickly obtain 'the additional information necessary for a more objective assessment of risk' (Article 5.7). Overall, more than a hundred different **international environmental agreements** refer to one version or another of the precautionary principle.

The diversity of the definitions is greater still if we consider national laws. Numerous countries have also integrated the precautionary principle into their respective legal systems, and each has interpreted

(continued...)

it in a specific way that aligns with its own political culture regarding risk management and uncertainty. For example, while American political authorities tend to view the precautionary principle as an optional approach rather than a legal principle, European authorities are generally more inclined to see it as a legal principle and to act even in the absence of scientific evidence.

This regulatory variation favours strategic behaviours on the part of governments, as they can invoke one principle or another to either justify or contest an environmental measure. The European Union's 1999 moratorium on genetically modified organisms (GMOs), for example, preventing imports of GMOs into European countries, was adopted to forcefully implement a narrow understanding of the precautionary principle, as articulated in the 2000 Cartagena Protocol on Biosafety. This narrow understanding contradicted the restrictive version of the precautionary principle set out in the 1995 Agreement on the Application of Sanitary and Phytosanitary Measures.

In addition, there is a debate with regard to the types of uncertainties that can be invoked under the precautionary principle. The **policy instruments** that rely on the precautionary principle generally focus on uncertainty with regard to environmental damage. However, the same principle may potentially lose relevance when confronted with other types of uncertainty. For example, several environmental measures can have negative effects on the economic system, and economics as a scientific field is characterized by a degree of uncertainty that is at least as high as that seen in environmental sciences. Yet, if the precautionary principle accounts for uncertainty relating to environmental damage and uncertainty relating to economic damage to an equal extent, the principle risks losing its relevance since action for environmental protection can lead to economic damage, or the other way around.

There is therefore no single precautionary principle, but several different interpretations, which vary in scope and from one international **regime** to another. Although policymakers and academics refer to 'the' precautionary principle, it would be more accurate to talk about multiple precautionary approaches.

Sources: Andrée 2005; Falkner and Jaspers 2012; Foster et al. 2000; Lieberman and Gray 2008; Mitchell 2019; Pellizzoni and Ylönen 2008; Sachs 2011; Stephan 2012; Sunstein 2005.

contamination were uncertain (Andresen et al. 2000; Harrison and Bryner 2004); the 1992 *Convention on Biological Diversity* was concluded even though the actual economic value of **genetic resources** was poorly estimated; the 1997 *Kyoto Protocol on Climate Change* was signed when climate models were unable to establish stable predictions; the 1985 *Vienna Convention for the Protection of the Ozone Layer* was signed despite inconclusive research on the causes, scale, and effects of the depletion of the **ozone layer** (see Box 1.4).

Therefore, the lack of scientific certainty is not necessarily a constraint on international co-operation. In some cases, uncertainty actually encourages cooperation because it masks the scale of the challenges, and thus conceals the interests of the different parties. It is conceivable that the high degree of uncertainty about the quantity, value, and location of minerals in the Antarctic encouraged the adoption of a ban on mining activities on the continent. Similarly, the high degree of uncertainty about the spread of pollution in the Mediterranean Sea encouraged Mediterranean states, which overestimated that spread, to cooperate to reduce land-based pollution (Haas 1989).

In some cases, the increase in scientific data could even be an obstacle to international cooperation because it fuels controversial debate. A profusion of data can strengthen the positions of all the **stakeholders** and exacerbate conflict (see Box 1.3). For example, the proliferation of indicators and assessments slowed the negotiations between Sweden and Finland about pollution in the Baltic Sea. The Swedish and Finnish governments were equally determined that negotiations would be based on data and solutions proposed by their own

Box 1.3 The cultural cognition hypothesis

Conventional wisdom suggests that the more people know about scientific results, the more they will make decisions in line with those results. However, several empirical studies reveal that this is not necessarily the case. Instead of adapting their opinions and behaviours according to evolving scientific evidence, most people filter scientific evidence to support their initial opinion. As a result, the way people interpret scientific findings can be vastly different. This phenomenon is known as the 'cultural cognition' hypothesis and means that the subjective interpretation of science, more than science itself, drives environmental choices.

One of the first studies to reveal the cultural cognition phenomenon, although without clearly labelling it as such, was a study by Stephen Zehr in the 1990s. Analysing debates on acid rain in the United States Congress, Zehr remarked that the contributions of the various scientists consulted by members of Congress did nothing to help clarify the problem of acid rain and its possible solutions. Rather, Congress members interpreted the various scientific opinions through the lens of their own pre-existing preferences. The slightest nuance expressed by a scientist was amplified by the members of Congress to support their own points of view. As a result, the process of consulting scientists left political decision makers with the false impression that scientists were profoundly divided on the question of acid rain, and that there was significant scientific uncertainty. In this case, the use of scientific expertise served to polarize and prolong political debates rather than to help bring them to a conclusion.

Following on from this work, a team from Yale University examined the relationship between individuals' levels of scientific awareness and their political opinions. In one of their studies, the researchers conducted a survey on a representative sample of 1,500 Americans. A first series of questions tested the respondents' aptitude for understanding basic scientific concepts and for interpreting statistical data. A second series of questions focused on their political opinions, including their opinions on climate policies. Contrary to what one might expect, the results of this study indicate that respondents who were against their government acting to reduce **greenhouse gas** emissions did not necessarily have a poorer understanding of the scientific arguments linking emissions to climate change. Furthermore, the respondents with the most scientific knowledge did not always prove to be more concerned about climate change. Instead, the survey results indicate that scientific awareness is in fact associated with political polarization. The more respondents were capable of understanding scientific discourse and statistical data, the more likely they were to hold extreme views either for or against greenhouse gas-reduction policies. The Yale researchers therefore concluded that scientific knowledge and abilities allow individuals to better select scientific evidence that supports their pre-existing values and ideas. In other words, a person's perception of science depends less on their level of knowledge than on their political inclinations, in line with the 'cultural cognition' hypothesis.

Other researchers have come up with a major reformulation of the hypothesis, indicating that a certain level of scientific consensus is needed for cultural cognition to happen, and that scientific consensus can also play against cultural cognition by orientating people's opinion on environmental problems. Indeed, these studies find that science is likely to influence public opinion when the public perceives that there is clear scientific consensus surrounding a particular issue. They argue that an important way of allowing science to change public opinion would be to communicate more on scientific consensus and scientific agreement, rather than insisting on remaining uncertainties, when consensus and agreement do exist.

However, the degree of trust that people have in scientific consensus can vary from one issue to another. In Europe, many informed citizens trust the consensus on the findings of climate science, while being very sceptical of the scientific consensus that genetically modified foods are safe to consume. This suggests that people's cultural and cognitive biases filter their understanding of scientific evidence to support their initial opinion. This also shows that people are particularly sensitive to the way scientific consensus is communicated in the media.

Sources: Hulme 2009; Kahan 2015; Kahan et al. 2012, 2011, 2009; Pechar et al. 2018; Sarewitz 2004; van der Linden et al. 2017; Zehr 1994.

national scientific institutions, which were all valid and legitimate, but their technical measures were not exactly compatible (Auer 2010). The development of scientific knowledge does not necessarily lead to the emergence of political consensus.

The types of scientific knowledge that matter

Environmental cooperation depends less on the degree of scientific certainty than on the type of scientific knowledge available (Dimitrov 2003, 2006; Kailis 2017). The type of scientific knowledge that is most conducive to international cooperation focuses on interdependence between different countries. For example, scientific evidence revealing that a single state cannot effectively tackle **biosecurity** in isolation boosted international negotiations related to genetically modified organisms. This context of interdependence prompted some states to join forces, despite the high degree of uncertainty on the effects of genetically modified organisms for human health or ecosystems.

However, knowledge that focuses on the magnitude of environmental damage or socio-economic consequences is often insufficient to encourage international cooperation. International cooperation seems more likely for environmental issues with well-documented global interdependence but uncertain socio-economic impacts, than for issues with uncertain global interdependence but well-documented socio-economic impacts. Examples of the latter type of environmental issues are desertification and deforestation. Scientific research tends to highlight the local causes of these problems, such as agricultural or forestry practices, rather than their transnational causes, like those linked to the structure of international trade. We also know more about the local effects of deforestation and desertification, particularly on temperature, soil stability, and air quality, than we know about their global effects. Consequently, even though science can provide solid evidence of the scale of desertification and deforestation, what we know about the context of interdependence is not enough to boost international cooperation.

1.2 Experts as political actors

The concept of epistemic community

The transmission of expert and specialized knowledge to political decision makers is not automatic. Stakeholders must actively promote specific empirical evidence to ensure that it is actually taken into account, and even then there are no guarantees. Since the 1970s, scientists in particular have played a central role in structuring the international governance of environmental issues by promoting the transmission of knowledge through various associations and networks (Meyer et al. 1997).

The concept of '**epistemic community**' is key to understanding how scientists influence political decision makers. Peter Haas defines an epistemic community as 'a network of professionals with recognized expertise and competence in a particular domain and an authoritative claim to policy relevant knowledge within that domain' (Haas 1992b: 3). An epistemic community is a more limited network than an entire discipline or profession. Its members must share *causal beliefs* (for example, the belief that CO_2 emissions significantly contribute to climate change) and *validity criteria for knowledge* (for example, the capacity to reproduce research results to ensure they are considered scientific). Not only that: they must also share *normative principles* (for example, the idea that future generations should be able to benefit from a healthy environment) and a *common political project* (for example, catalysing action from decision makers on the risks of climate change).

However, members of an epistemic community may have different functions and be involved in diverse organizations. They may be members of the academic community, employees of private companies, or civil servants. They may also be located in several countries and exert an influence on several governments at the same time. They often constitute a transnational network.

Scientists and experts do not usually have the required political and economic leverage to influence public opinion or the electoral calculations of elected representatives. However, they are socially recognized as being privileged bearers of knowledge, which gives them some intellectual authority to persuade political leaders to adopt their ideas. This position allows them not only to provide governments with information, but also to help build a cognitive frame, which subsequently filters and interprets the information received. For example, by framing **biodiversity** as an essential input for biotechnology research, an epistemic community can strategically put this environmental issue on the political agenda of governments concerned about the biotech industry's durability. In this way, the epistemic community's action is more a matter of persuasion than pressure.

The actual influence of epistemic communities

Epistemic communities can have a major influence on international environmental negotiations. This was particularly the case for certain aspects of the negotiations on the ozone layer, acid rain, genetic resources, land-based pollution in the Mediterranean Basin, and climate change (see Box 1.4). In each case, they managed to attract the attention of political decision makers, impose their particular framing of the problem, and encourage the conclusion of an international agreement corresponding to that frame—albeit to varying degrees. For example, to encourage international cooperation to clean up the Mediterranean Basin, an epistemic community presented the problem in terms of interdependence. Scientists aggregated national data on land-based pollution to deflect blame from specific polluting countries, suggesting instead that currents could easily transport pollutants from one Mediterranean shore to another. When the problem was presented in this way, the Mediterranean countries genuinely engaged in a joint effort to reduce land-based pollution (Haas 1989).

However, epistemic communities do not always have a significant influence. One example of an epistemic community failing to exert influence is that of cetologists (biologists who study whales and other cetaceans) surrounding an international moratorium on whaling. The whaling industry (favouring large-scale commercial whaling) and environmental non-governmental organizations (NGOs) (looking for a complete ban on whaling) have had a greater influence on governments than have cetology experts (who favoured limited quotas for commercial whaling) (see Box 2.4). Countries that advocate an international whaling ban, as well as those opposing it, have paid relatively little attention to the nuanced arguments raised by cetologists (Peterson 1992).

How can we explain this variation in influence? The size of the epistemic community does not appear to be a determining factor. However, professional and ideological proximity to

Box 1.4 The epistemic community on ozone depletion

When the Vienna Convention for the Protection of the Ozone Layer was signed in 1985, the significance and causes of ozone layer depletion were still highly uncertain. As a result, the Vienna Convention was merely a call for increased international cooperation on the issue, and did not set out any specific obligations on how to stop ozone layer depletion.

Yet only two years later, in September 1987, a highly precise international **protocol** to the Vienna Convention, called the Montreal Protocol on Substances that Deplete the Ozone Layer, was agreed. The Montreal Protocol requires drastic reductions in the production and use of eight specific substances that were found to deplete the ozone layer, such as chlorofluorocarbons (CFCs). This marked acceleration in the precision of the objectives contrasts with the usual slow tempo of international negotiations. The strength of the obligations contained in the Montreal Protocol is all the more surprising given that CFCs had an important economic and technological value, being widely used in several industries, including as coolant gases in refrigerators, as propellants in aerosols, and as solvents in the electronics industry. How can such rapid progress be explained?

This remarkable advancement was brought about by the actions of an 'epistemic community'. As evidenced by Peter Haas, the epistemic community on ozone depletion was initially primarily made up of American atmospheric scientists working for various agencies in the United States government. Experts from the United Nations Environment Programme joined this community, as well as experts in Germany, the United Kingdom, and even the then Soviet Union, confirming the community's transnational reach.

The epistemic community on ozone depletion was catalysed just a few weeks after the Vienna Convention was signed, when the British geophysicist Joseph Farman brought to light a significantly thinned area of the ozone layer above the Antarctic. The 'ozone hole' became a symbolic image, exposing the environmental damage in graphic and simple terms. It played an important role in raising awareness among both the broader public and political decision makers.

Although the scientists involved in the epistemic community did not yet know what scale of CFC reductions would be needed to rebuild the ozone layer, they nonetheless started to lobby together for the adoption of an additional international agreement to limit CFC emissions. They published numerous reports and high-profile journal articles, and they organized major conferences on the issue, strategically avoiding exposure of their uncertainties.

The epistemic community also had a number of channels for policy influence. Drawing on its membership connections, it had access to the resources and network of the United Nations Environment Programme for widely circulating reports, data, and documents. The community also had access to key players in the United States government. Richard Benedict, an active expert in the epistemic community, eventually became head of the United States delegation for the Montreal Protocol negotiations. The community progressively succeeded in persuading the highest authorities in the American government to take on a leading role. The Reagan administration, though hostile to regulatory approaches and distrustful of the United Nations, even came to argue for strict CFC restriction.

Therefore, the epistemic community's political actions played a key role in the adoption of the Montreal Protocol in 1987. However, the role of science per se in this outcome is unclear. As Peter Haas has recognized: 'the epistemic community's influence was thus exercised in part through usurpation of decision-making channels and in part through persuasion'.

Sources: Benedick 1991; Haas 2015, 1992a; Litfin 1995; Parson 2003; Zehr 1994.

decision makers are important variables explaining an epistemic community's capacity to put a new issue on the global agenda and impose its cognitive frame (Haas 1992a). Other factors that can enhance an epistemic community's influence are a strong alliance with NGOs, a transnational presence in a diverse range of countries, a high degree of uncertainty, a context of crisis, and weak political opposition (Andresen et al. 2018; Biermann 2002; Gough and Shackley 2001; Kailis 2017; Meijerink 2005; Zito 2001).

However, studies that assess the influence of epistemic communities are not without their critics. The criticisms are often of a methodological order and claim that the epistemic communities' influence is overestimated. The first methodological challenge is to map the epistemic community. While network analysis may suit the experts' modus operandi, the analyst may struggle to demarcate the limits of an epistemic community and identify its members. The next methodological challenge is in attributing influence to specific actors: what the analyst interprets as the influence of an epistemic community can actually be the result of parallel action led by NGOs. It is difficult to assess the influence of a group of stakeholders in isolation from the influence exerted by their allies. Third, a feedback loop between the presumed cause (the epistemic community's actions) and the presumed effect (political leaders' reactions) can interfere with the measure of epistemic communities' influence. Sometimes, some political leaders may even encourage the scientific community to conduct research and pressure their peers. Although the concept of epistemic community may make it easier to conceptualize the integration of science into politics, it overlooks the politicization of science (Lidskog and Sundqvist 2002; Litfin 1995; Toke 1999). Section 1.3 discusses this point.

1.3 The co-production of science and politics

An increasing number of studies on global environmental governance suggest that science and politics are co-produced. As they shape each other, it is impossible to understand one without considering the other. Political interactions are partly based on available knowledge, and scientific production is a social practice that is conditioned by its political context (Lidskog and Sundqvist 2015).

Knowledge-based politics

References to science are omnipresent in political debates on environmental protection. Rationalist and scientific arguments provide the justification for a variety of different standpoints and political positions (Grundmann 2007). Supporters and opponents of controversial environmental policies alike use social and natural scientific evidence to substantiate their opinions—for example, in the case of shale gas extraction or resorting to geoengineering to address climate change. They point to scientific studies, raise empirical facts, show charts, and try to make arguments that appear as logical as possible. The growing number of **environmental impact assessments** conducted by governments support this constant need to ground policy actions in scientific and rational terms. Other types of arguments—spiritual or aesthetic, for example—are rarely mentioned in political debates.

Consequently, science largely defines what constitutes credible, legitimate, and authoritative knowledge (see Box 1.4). It dictates who is an 'expert' and who is merely a 'layperson', which determines their respective claims to political influence. With regard to climate change, the majority of scientists who acknowledge the anthropogenic causes of global warming, as much as the isolated individuals who deny it, tend to use technical language to appear as authoritative experts and to discredit their opponents. They depict their adversaries as partisan ideologues corrupted by oil companies or the vanity of winning a Nobel Prize (Goeminne 2012; Jacques 2012).

Expert discourse does not merely discredit opponents; it can also help establish new political actors. For example, in the 1990s, scientists working on climate change drew the political world's attention to 'Arctic citizens' (Martello 2004b). Scientists recognized that Arctic communities have a legitimate voice in interpreting climate change and its implications for the region. By echoing the voice of Arctic communities, scientists helped establish them as international actors. They portrayed Arctic communities as legitimate transnational stakeholders, who are particularly vulnerable to climate change and whose point of view should be considered. In 1996, the Arctic Council became the first **intergovernmental organization** to acknowledge the legitimacy of Arctic communities as political stakeholders. It recognizes six Arctic communities as 'Permanent Participants'. As such, these communities may address the Arctic Council meetings, they must be consulted by member states, and they can formally propose cooperative activities.

Similarly, biologists and anthropologists have helped indigenous communities become recognized stakeholders in international debates over biological diversity. Scientific studies have revealed the extent of the interdependence between indigenous communities' traditional practices and the protection of biological diversity. This view was later institutionalized in the 1992 Convention on Biological Diversity, in particular its Article 8(j), which underlines the importance of protecting indigenous communities' traditional practices. Since then, indigenous communities have become widely recognized as legitimate holders of traditional ecological knowledge and active participants in the biodiversity regime (Esguerra et al. 2017; Löfmarck and Lidskog 2017; Montana 2017; Morin et al. 2017). While Western science remains the dominant paradigm, some international bodies now attribute greater importance to the non-scientific knowledge that Arctic citizens and indigenous communities possess.

The political foundations of knowledge

Whether scientific or traditional, knowledge is not inherently neutral. All forms of knowledge, including scientific knowledge, are based on value judgements and normative assumptions. The political scientist Ernst Haas makes this point clearly:

> Knowledge incorporates scientific notions relating to the social goal. Such notions are rarely free from ideological elements. Nor are they necessarily free from the self-interest of their proponents. Questionable metaphors, imperfect analogies, exaggeration, and other epistemological sins abound in science for policy as well as in policy for science. Economists adjust their models to the kind of society they prefer, and advocate the results of their simulations as the findings of science. So do ecologists, energy specialists, and lawyers drawing up regulations for technology transfers. None of this matters for our purposes. As long as these activities are accepted as a basis for public policy by groups and individuals professing varying political ideologies, we consider such notions as consensual. Knowledge is the professionally mediated body of theory and information that transcends prevailing lines of ideological cleavage. (Haas 1980: 368)

For example, qualifying a species as 'invasive' is not politically neutral and it carries various implicit assumptions (Warren 2007). The notion of invasion is a metaphor that ecology borrows from military terminology. It is a way of reporting the rapid spread of certain species that have come from elsewhere, which calls for a specific policy response (i.e. to stop their entry). Yet the distinction between 'native species' and 'alien species' is arbitrary. They are socially constructed categories, based on a segmented vision of space and time. They reflect a static vision of the environment, since species have always migrated and ecosystems have always evolved. In addition, the notion of 'alien' and 'invasive' species relies on anthropocentric assumptions, since the scientific literature does not use these adjectives to describe humans, their livestock, and their domestic animals, although these species have spread rapidly and exert great pressure on ecosystems. The scientific discourse on invasive species may appear purely technical, but it is implicitly political.

Moreover, the validity of scientific arguments and findings is deeply embedded in power structures and political preferences. An extreme example is that of the controversies raised by the publication of the book *The Skeptical Environmentalist* in 2001. In the book, the Danish political scientist Bjørn Lomborg argues that several international development issues should be given priority over environmental protection, on the grounds of economic efficiency. More human lives could be saved, he claims, if investments to reduce greenhouse gases were allocated to eradicating HIV/AIDS in **developing countries**. This seemingly rational preference for one **public good** over another provoked uncompromising reactions from many scientists, particularly from the natural sciences, who accused Lomborg of tampering with his data. A Danish government committee even led an enquiry, concluding that Lomborg's work was indeed biased and partial. However, following the election of a centre-right government, the Danish Ministry of Science overruled the decision due to lack of evidence. A few years later, when the social democrats regained power, the funds allocated to Lomborg's research projects were severely cut. Irrespective of the scientific value of Lomborg's research, the controversies surrounding his work clearly illustrate the fact that the conduct of science, as a social process, is not free from politics (Pielke 2004; Sarewitz 2004).

More fundamentally, governments can influence an entire scientific discipline through resource allocation. For example, investment from the United States government in the early days of the Cold War shaped our understanding of the earth's climate system (Allan 2017). The US military, in particular, poured money into aeronautics, oceanography, meteorology, and atmospheric physics. The immediate objective of the United States military was to sustain technological development in strategic fields like submarine navigation, nuclear test detection, and weather modification. This military patronage accelerated the progress of geophysical sciences, and shaped our knowledge of the earth's climate by contributing to a particular geophysical representation of the earth system. For several decades, the climate was perceived as a vast machine that engineers could model with the hope of gaining operational control over it. Alternative framing of earth science, informed by biology, ecology, or complexity science, could have pointed instead to non-linearity and volatility of the climate. However, these perspectives remained marginal in our understanding of the earth's climate until the 1990s, as they did not benefit from the same financial support as geophysical sciences.

The asymmetry between developed and developing countries also structures scientific research. The overwhelming majority of scientific research is conducted in developed countries (see Figure 1.2). Yet scientists' geographic and cultural origin has an important impact on their point of view. A survey involving 1,030 scientists from 72 different countries reveals that

(a) **Number of publications in the area 'Environmental Science' (1996–2017)**

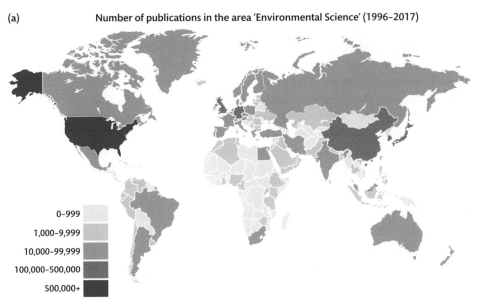

This map shows that the larger a country's population, the more likely it is to have published several scientific studies. This figure also reveals that high-income countries, such as the United States, the United Kingdom, and Germany, conduct the overwhelming majority of research in environmental science. Some middle-income countries, like China and India, are also important players. However, most African countries publish very few studies in environmental sciences. This distribution matters because scientists' origin has an important impact on their perception of environmental problems.

(b) **Number of authors or contributors to the sixth assessment report of the Intergovernmental Panel on Climate Change**

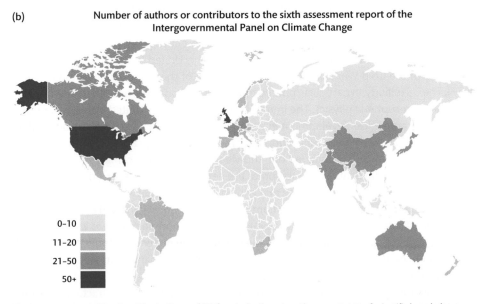

The Intergovernmental Panel on Climate Change (IPCC) periodically reviews the current state of scientific knowledge on climate change. This map shows that most authors and contributors to the sixth IPCC report come from high-income countries in North America and Europe, and some middle-income countries like China, India, and Brazil. Few researchers from Africa, South-East Asia, Central America, and the Middle East are contributing to the IPCC, although climate change severely affects these regions.

(c) **Number of patents granted to residents for environmental technology (2011–2016)**

	0
	1–99
	100–999
	1,000–9,999
	10,000+

Patents confer to inventors exclusive rights on the commercialization of their invention for a period of 20 years. This map shows the country of residence of the inventors of patented environmental technologies. A significant number of these inventors are located in North America, Europe, China, and Japan. Few of them live in Africa, South-East Asia, the Middle East, or Latin America. This indicates that some countries have greater capacity than others to develop new environmental technologies. It also suggests that high-income countries are likely to benefit disproportionately from the commercialization of environmental technologies.

Figure 1.2 The inequalities in scientific production

Source data from: www.scimagojr.com; www.ipcc.ch; www.wipo.org

 Take your learning further by viewing the interactive version of this figure
www.oup.com/he/morin1e

the way they define and rank environmental problems depends as much on their origin as on their discipline (Pavé et al. 1998). In this context, it is not surprising that the scientific community prioritizes research themes and analytical perspectives that reflect the ideas that prevail in developed countries. Initially, research on climate change focused on reducing greenhouse gas emissions in developed countries, before considering the question of **adaptation** in developing countries (Biermann 2002; Borland et al. 2018; Parikh 1992). Similarly, more studies focus on problems of access to water, which strike the Western imagination, rather than sanitation issues, which are equally important for the health of populations in developing countries (Gupta and van der Zaag 2009). The prevailing scientific practices and discourses are no more universal than they are politically neutral. Certain views, generally those of the weaker stakeholders, are systematically sidelined.

Due to this structural asymmetry, governments in developing countries are sometimes sceptical about scientific claims made by developed countries' representatives (Biermann 2002). They want their own scientists to have a voice, rather than rely solely on findings produced by scientists from developed countries. For example, scientists can use different methods to calculate carbon dioxide emissions caused by logging in tropical forests and methane emissions generated by rice paddies. The method chosen and the type of data used can significantly modify the perceived contribution of different countries to climate change (Agarwal and Narain 1991; Hulme 2009; Kanie et al. 2010). Thus, for developing countries, it is important to increase the representation of their scientists in international bodies, such as the **Intergovernmental Panel on Climate Change**. They also argue that developed countries should provide technical and financial assistance to help them develop their own research capabilities.

Science rests on politics and vice versa. Each approach structures and determines the other's options for action. Scientific research and international negotiations have a mutual influence on one another. For example, the Paris Agreement's goal of limiting temperature rise to 2°C above pre-industrial levels is just as much the result of scientific research as it is of political negotiation (Cointe et al. 2011; Lahn and Sundqvist 2017; Mayer 2012). In the late 1990s, this 2°C threshold was merely the outcome of a few climate models that were designed to assess the likely impact of a twofold increase in the concentration of CO_2 in the atmosphere. It was subsequently endorsed by some NGOs and the European Union, before being politically established at the Copenhagen climate conference in 2009. Accepted as a long-term political goal, the 2°C threshold was reintroduced into scientific studies to serve as a guide for modelling, rather than as the model's outcome. Although the 2°C threshold is somewhat arbitrary, both scientifically and politically, it helps to structure debates and provides a reference point for scientific inquiries and political processes. Science is not prior to politics: both are co-produced as part of a continuous dynamic movement (see Box 1.5).

Box 1.5 The science and politics of transboundary air pollution

The negotiations concerning transboundary air pollution provide an illustrative example of the co-production between science and politics. Co-production is a term used to describe the iterative process through which science informs policy and policy informs science. In the 1960s, several scientific studies suggested that industrial atmospheric pollution from Central Europe may contribute to the acidification of lakes and rivers in Scandinavian countries through acid rain. This acidification had serious environmental consequences, damaging trees and water resources and leading, among others, to fish extinction and bird population decline. In 1972, at the United Nations Conference on the Human Environment in Stockholm, the Swedish government raised the issue of acid rain among European countries. In response, the member states of the Organisation for Economic Co-operation and Development (OECD) set up a technical cooperation institution, called the Long Range Transport Project, for the exchange of transboundary air pollution data over the period 1972 to 1977. Scientists working in this field in several countries developed information sharing networks, and a transnational epistemic community was formed.

In 1975, Leonid Brezhnev, the Secretary General of the Communist Party of the Soviet Union, saw in these emerging environmental problems an opportunity for cooperation between Eastern and Western Europe. He proposed negotiating a new international convention on transboundary air pollution, and the idea was favourably received by the governments of the West. Their objective was not only to reduce air pollution emissions but also to consolidate the climate of 'détente' between the two rival blocs of the Cold War. Both the Eastern and Western blocs worked to emphasize the technical aspects of transboundary air pollution in order to encourage ideological neutrality and foster political cooperation.

These technical discussions ultimately resulted in the adoption of the Convention on Long-Distance Transboundary Air Pollution in 1979, under the auspices of the United Nations Economic Commission for Europe. While this **framework convention** is rather general, it did act as a catalyst for the collection of new data, which allowed for development of maps pinpointing emissions sources for affected areas. Modelling has also been key in moving political negotiations forward on this topic, through initiatives such as the Regional Acidification Information System, a computer model for assessing the impact of air pollution. In this context, a series of eight protocols have been adopted, each establishing targets for reducing emissions of a specific damaging chemical substance (sulphur, nitrogen oxide, volatile organic compounds, heavy metals, **persistent organic pollutants**, and ammonia), based on scientific studies. Today, the Convention is a major regional environmental agreement. Its dynamism towards the reduction of transboundary air pollution was the result of a constant relationship between pollution science and political cooperation, with each fuelling the other.

Sources: Byrne 2015; Lidskog and Sundqvist 2011, 2002; Tuinstra et al. 2006, 1999.

1.4 The interface of science and politics

The need for a communication channel

Smooth communication between science and politics is essential. As explained earlier, scientific findings do not automatically get taken up in political forums. Moreover, scientific research often needs political input to build on value judgements. Climate change research provides a good example of this need for political input. The UN Framework Convention on Climate Change from 1992 defines goals that concern science and politics simultaneously:

> *The ultimate objective of this Convention [is to achieve] stabilization of greenhouse gas concentrations in the atmosphere at a level that would prevent dangerous anthropogenic interference with the climate system. Such a level should be achieved within a time-frame sufficient to allow ecosystems to adapt naturally to climate change, to ensure that food production is not threatened and to enable economic development to proceed in a sustainable manner. (Article 2)*

Science alone cannot determine when anthropogenic interference becomes 'dangerous', when food production is 'threatened', and when economic development ceases to be 'sustainable'. From the outset, these notions necessarily involve value judgements. Science can provide useful information to assess the danger, the threat, and the sustainability, but that is not enough. These assessments depend equally on the values that a given society attributes to ecological and economic systems, the level of risk that it considers tolerable, and the scope of the time horizon.

Science cannot rank environmental goals either. Yet, several measures that alleviate one environmental problem may cause another. Nuclear energy produces less greenhouse gas emissions than fossil fuels but raises the question of radioactive waste storage. Genetically modified organisms may lead to a reduction in the use of pesticides but are also a threat to agricultural diversity. There is no simple solution to environmental problems, and science alone cannot solve these political dilemmas.

Environmental politics also raises ethical questions, which science cannot answer by itself. Should governments take into account historical emissions of greenhouse gases when setting national targets for **climate mitigation**? Should developing countries have the right to develop their economies following the Western model, despite the environmental consequences this development would cause? Should governments control birth rate to reduce the anthropogenic pressure on the environment? Should solar geoengineering be used to buy more time to address climate change, even if it may commit future generations to use of these technologies (see Box 1.6)? Science cannot answer these ethical questions; only

Box 1.6 What is geoengineering? Risks and potentials

Geoengineering, also called climate engineering, involves the large-scale use of technology to alter the global climate. These technologies are typically discussed in the context of the potential role they could play in response to global climate change alongside greenhouse gas mitigation. It is important to note from the outset that geoengineering technologies are still in their earliest stages of development. Scientists still know very little about whether large-scale deployment is even possible, and if so what unintended impacts it might have on social and natural systems. Nevertheless, they are already highly controversial, in large part because many people worry that turning to a so-called 'technological fix' for climate change would divert attention away from ambitious greenhouse gas mitigation. This view, typically referred to as the 'moral hazard' argument, has gained much traction in both academic and policy-oriented circles.

Geoengineering technologies are typically grouped into two baskets, known as *carbon dioxide removal* and *solar geoengineering*. *Carbon dioxide removal* involves extracting carbon dioxide from the atmosphere and storing it in oceans, soils, biomass, or geological formations. Technologies currently being explored include ocean fertilization, which increases the oceans' absorptive capacity for carbon. Another carbon dioxide removal technology is bioenergy with carbon capture and storage, which involves growing biomass, such as trees, burning that biomass as fuel to generate power, then capturing the resulting emissions and storing them underground.

Although carbon dioxide removal technologies could reduce the concentration of carbon dioxide in the atmosphere, this does nothing to actually reduce emissions. This is a problem because it could lock societies into a remedial technology rather than actually solving the underlying problem of unsustainable greenhouse gas emissions.

The second basket, *solar geoengineering*, or solar radiation management technologies, reduce the amount of solar radiation that is trapped in the earth's atmosphere. This is done either by increasing the earth's reflectivity, or by making it easier for solar radiation to escape the earth's atmosphere. For example, marine cloud brightening increases the reflectivity of clouds over the ocean, and so reduces the amount of solar radiation that reaches the earth's surface. The current leading proposal in solar geoengineering involves the deposition of reflective aerosol particles into the stratosphere. This is expected to generate a global dimming, or cooling response similar to what we observe with large-scale volcanic eruptions.

Because solar geoengineering strategies reduce global temperatures by simply reflecting solar radiation back into space, they do nothing to reduce either emissions or carbon dioxide concentrations in the atmosphere. As such, they do not resolve non-temperature-related effects of climate change, such as ocean acidification. Importantly, solar geoengineering technologies merely mask the temperature impacts of carbon in the atmosphere by reflecting sunlight and thereby cooling the earth. Therefore, if societies suddenly stopped using solar geoengineering for some reason the scale of impacts could be devastating, as the cooling effect would be removed without addressing the underlying problem of greenhouse gas concentrations in the atmosphere. This is called the 'termination shock' problem.

For many years, geoengineering was considered a taboo topic in climate science and policy circles. Recently, however, these technologies have been gaining more attention. This is in no small part because predictions from scientists about the expected impacts from climate change are increasingly dire, and the pledges from countries for addressing these challenges remain inadequate. In this context, some scientists have suggested that the only high-confidence way to keep temperatures below the 1.5°C threshold is to couple deep global emissions cuts with climate engineering.

One open question relates to how power dynamics would play out in decisions about the deployment of geoengineering technologies. Who would control the global thermostat? It is conceivable, for example, that one state that wishes to avoid costly emission reductions might develop and deploy a solar engineering technology, which then impacts rainfall patterns in other countries. Even faced with the same objective risks, two populations might have a different degree of risk tolerance. This situation raises concerns about democracy and justice: how can civil society be involved in decision-making? If solar geoengineering has transboundary impacts, how can those who will potentially be impacted have recourse to remedy in the face of any future injury? There are also critical ethical and moral concerns: how might technological 'lock-in' impact our responsibility to future generations? Should humans be tinkering with the climate in this way at all?

All of these concerns point to a need for governance of these technologies to steer the development and possible future deployment in societally beneficial directions. This could involve a moratorium, prohibiting any future research or deployment. It could also involve softer governance mechanisms, such as criteria for allocation of public funding for research, transparency mechanisms, standards of best practice, and public oversight of evaluation processes for outdoor experiments. Some scholars have proposed using parametric insurance schemes to pay states that might face detrimental impacts from deployment of geoengineering techniques, as a way to lessen their opposition to such deployment by other states. Centrally, geoengineering governance will need to evolve over time as we learn more about these technologies and the potential risks and benefits they present to society.

Sources: Burns and Nicholson 2017; Fuentes-George 2017; Horton et al. 2016; Horton 2018; Jinnah 2018; Jinnah et al. 2019; Jinnah and Nicholson 2019; Keith 2013; Nicholson et al. 2018; Rabitz 2019; Rayner et al. 2013; Victor 2008.

political means can arbitrate them. In particular, political processes that allow open delibera-tions and the articulation of political values should guide environmental policies.

Each society has its own way of defining the balance between efficiency, fairness, and rationality. As far as genetically modified organisms are concerned, different countries have reached radically different conclusions on the basis of the same scientific information. In ac-cordance with their prevailing social values and their national agricultural production system, the French government considers that it is still preferable to avoid the use of these organisms, whereas the United States government believes that their benefits outweigh the risks they may represent (Pechar et al. 2018). Whereas the French have taken a precautionary approach, the American approach is based on scientific risk management (Vogel 2012). This reflects a cultural, economic, and political divergence, rather than a scientific disagreement.

Political representatives often ask scientists for their views on issues that go beyond their area of expertise. Also, since decision makers are often uncomfortable with ambivalence, sci-entists may feel pressure to accentuate their research findings and hide their own doubts and differences, if they want positive political feedback. Yet science is never complete, certain, and unanimous. These limitations call for certain political measures, such as continuous reas-sessment mechanisms and public debates (Andresen et al. 2000; Cash et al. 2003; Dilling and Lemos 2011; Farrell et al. 2001; Höllermann and Evers 2017; Martello 2004a; Vogel et al. 2007).

Boundary organizations

Science and politics are distinct endeavours, but the boundary between them is fuzzy. What is considered to be 'political' or 'scientific' is not always obvious and depends on the social con-text. Organizations known as '**boundary organizations**' are located at the unstable interface between the 'scientific' and 'political' worlds (Litfin 1995). They have the mandate to facilitate the bidirectional flow of communication between science and politics. The Intergovernmen-tal Panel on Climate Change (see Box 1.7), the Science–Policy Interface on Desertification

Box 1.7 Climate science, negotiated

The Intergovernmental Panel on Climate Change (IPCC) was created in 1988 by the United Nations Environment Programme and the World Meteorological Organization. Its mission is to review the current state of scientific knowledge on climate change, its socio-economic impacts, and to provide options for adaptation and mitigation. For example, in October 2018 the IPCC released a special report to support the work of the next **Conference of the Parties** to the Paris Agreement. This special report illuminated the differences in expected impacts of the Paris Agreement's two stated targets of limiting global warming to 1.5°C versus 2°C. The report clearly shows, for example, that a 1.5°C increase presents much less extreme weather event threats than does a 2°C increase.

The IPCC does not conduct original scientific research itself. It primarily reviews available scientific publications. About 2,500 experts are consulted in order to conduct this literature review process. They receive no salary from the IPCC but travel expenses are reimbursed to enable the participation of a broad range of experts. High prestige is the main reward scientists receive for acting as IPCC reviewers. Indeed, in 2007 the IPCC shared the Nobel Peace Prize with former American vice president and climate activist, Al Gore.

Based on an extensive literature review, the IPCC produces assessment reports, which synthesize research and produce a corresponding summary for policymakers. Although the IPCC does not provide explicit political recommendations, political input is actually sought in the context of the IPCC. Indeed, the member states of the IPCC engage in several steps of political negotiations in order to produce these scientific reports: governments approve the main points to be covered, they appoint experts to serve on the IPCC, and they examine the reports before final versions are released. Importantly, the summary for policymakers is negotiated, line by line, by government representatives. Certain governments have not hesitated to take advantage of such opportunities to frame elements of the report that reflect their own interests. For example, as Joanna Depledge has documented, certain member states of the IPCC, such as Saudi Arabia, are openly hostile to efforts to reduce greenhouse gas emissions, and work to emphasize any uncertainty and minimize any potential risks.

As a result of diverse political interests, there have been instances where the same IPCC report has used different adjectives to describe the level of certainty regarding the human causes of climate change or its consequences. For instance, the fifth assessment report of the IPCC, published in 2014, is not clear about the causal relationship between climate change and human security. The report's human security chapter is dismissive of the relationship between climate change and conflicts on one page, but recognizes that climate change increases the risk of civil war on the next. To reach scientific consensus, therefore, the IPCC must operate politically to smooth out any disagreements and represent all viewpoints, even if they conflict.

Some analysts have argued that although it has become more inclusive over time, the IPCC is not inclusive enough. In particular, it has been accused of neglecting expertise from developing countries. In 1990, only 21 out of 265 IPCC experts were from developing countries. In 2014, 101 out of 279 were from developing countries. Despite this improvement, an imbalance persists in the geographical distribution of experts. The discrepancy is even stronger when one looks at the research cited in the reports, which mostly comes from developed countries.

The IPCC has also been criticized for marginalizing social scientific research. In the social sciences, several disciplines, such as anthropology and sociology, have been neglected to the benefit of economics. From this perspective, scientific uncertainty does not stem only from a lack of knowledge but also from a lack of integration among the various disciplines, each of which holds a legitimate normative point of view. Another criticism concerns the lack of integration, in IPCC reports, of knowledge that falls outside scientific publication standards, such as local and **traditional knowledge**.

Finally, the IPCC has recently been criticized for being inappropriately driven by certain networks of scientists, who control the review process by only selecting what they consider relevant sources (notably their own research or research from close colleagues) to the detriment of others, therefore 'narrowing' the climate field. Some scientists are also suspected of reorienting their own research agenda in certain directions so that they can quote their own work in later IPCC reports.

That being said, the IPCC has greatly helped to publicly disseminate scientific research, increase the legitimacy, credibility, and relevance of climate science, and put pressure on international negotiations. This boundary organization has also improved in terms of its procedural transparency, now being more transparent on the selection process for its experts. Despite its imperfections, the IPPC has made an important contribution to climate change science and politics, and is trying to adapt to contemporary challenges.

Sources: Biermann 2002; Depledge 2008; Gleditsch and Nordås 2014; Hughes 2015; Hughes and Paterson 2017; Lahn and Sundqvist 2017; Lidskog and Sundqvist 2015; Malnes 2006; Silke et al. 2014.

(Akhtar-Schuster et al. 2016), and the **Intergovernmental Science-Policy Platform on Biodiversity and Ecosystem Services** (Dunkley et al. 2018; Löfmarck and Lidskog 2017; Morin et al. 2017) are examples of international boundary organizations.

In boundary organizations, scientists and decision makers can collaborate in numerous types of activities. These activities include: identifying common environmental indicators for a set of stakeholders (Auer 2010; Miller 2001); making explicit the assumptions underlying models and scenarios (Pulver and VanDeveer 2009; Tuinstra et al. 1999); and conducting environmental impact assessments in an inclusive and participatory manner (Koetz et al. 2012; Lemos and Morehouse 2005; Mitchell et al. 2006; Weichselgartner and Kasperson 2010). These activities provide the opportunity to establish fruitful dialogue between science and politics. This dialogue may encourage scientists and decision makers to learn from each other, develop a common understanding of the world, and to cooperate to solve environmental problems.

Boundary organizations can play an important role in assigning political meaning to scientific evidence. One example is the Technical Working Group of the 1989 Basel Convention on the Control of Transboundary Movements of Hazardous Wastes, which was charged with developing a definition of 'hazardous' (Lucier and Gareau 2016). This Convention regulates trade of hazardous waste (see Box 10.2), and in the 1990s its Technical Working Group had the mandate to identify which waste was to be deemed 'hazardous', and hence subject to the Convention's provisions. Participants in the Technical Working Group included delegates from signatory countries, industry representatives, and experts employed by NGOs. Two different views emerged in this boundary organization. Some participants, mainly from developed countries and industry, focused on the hazards associated with waste when handled under ideal conditions. Other participants considered the conditions under which wastes are *actually* handled, as different countries have different levels of capacity for handling wastes safely. Clearly, science alone cannot establish what is and is not hazardous, and a decision involving political considerations had to be made. In the end, the first perspective prevailed and products like lead scrap were considered as non-hazardous, even though they can be hazardous when handled improperly.

One major concern is that particular groups can have excessive influence over the internal processes in boundary organizations—it might be some private interest or powerful governments. Conversely, some scientists might use boundary organizations to their own advantage to distort discussions, by exaggerating doubts and uncertainties. In these circumstances, boundary organizations may become echo chambers amplifying scientific doubt for political purposes. During the international negotiations on acid rain, ozone layer protection, and climate change, for example, some complacent scientists minimized the environmental problems and received a political echo that was out of proportion with the minority view they expressed (Oreskes and Conway 2010).

Despite these legitimate concerns, it is widely accepted that the majority of international boundary organizations make a positive contribution to environmental cooperation (Andresen et al. 2018). They ensure that scientists are well informed about political objectives and that decision makers are aware of scientific data. For example, as far as endangered species are concerned, scientific committees associated with the Convention on International Trade in Endangered Species of Wild Fauna and Flora have helped scientists produce pertinent, legitimate, and credible findings and have helped states adopt rational decisions (Gehring and Ruffing 2008). Boundary organizations help science by ensuring that it is guided by values defined by legitimate political processes, and also raise awareness about the limitations of science in defining policy. They encourage the exchange of information and build trust between the worlds of science and politics, while keeping them clearly distinct.

1.5 Conclusion

Acknowledging that scientific production is a social dynamic, influenced by politics and values, does not mean that science is futile or that it should not inform international environmental governance. Instead, it is a reminder that science cannot resolve environmental problems on its own. As Chapter 2 explains, the human environment is not made up of material structures alone, but also of ideational structures such as social values and norms. Yet science cannot be mobilized objectively to arbitrate conflicting norms or prioritize certain values. Political processes, not scientific processes, should establish the political priorities. From this perspective, politics does not simply appear as an obstacle to environmental protection, but also as an essential component of solutions to environmental problems. It is with this perspective in mind that this book offers analytical tools to understand global environmental governance.

Critical thinking questions

1. Why is it simplistic to present scientists as knowledge producers and political leaders as knowledge consumers?
2. What can increase the influence of epistemic communities in political debates?
3. What was the context of scientific uncertainty during the negotiations on the Vienna Convention for the Protection of the Ozone Layer and the Montreal Protocol?
4. How is the Intergovernmental Panel on Climate Change influenced by political dynamics?

 Test your knowledge and understanding further by trying this chapter's Multiple Choice Questions www.oup.com/he/morin1e

Key references

Dimitrov, Radoslav. 2006. *Science and International Environmental Policy: Regimes and Nonregimes in Global Governance*. Lanham, MD: Rowman & Littlefield.

This book explains clearly under what conditions scientific knowledge is a prerequisite for international action on environmental issues. It sets out why certain environmental problems—including some characterized by great scientific uncertainty—are governed by strong international institutions, while other environmental problems—even some that are well documented scientifically—are left poorly governed.

Haas, Peter M. 1992. 'Epistemic Communities and International Policy Coordination'. *International Organization* 46 (1): 1–35.

Peter Haas introduced the concept of 'epistemic communities' at the end of the 1980s. This introduction to a special issue in the journal International Organization *explains the meaning and the implications of this important conceptual innovation.*

Jasanoff, Sheila. 2004. 'Heaven and Earth: The Politics of Environmental Images'. In *Earthly Politics: Local and Global in Environmental Governance*, edited by Sheila Jasanoff and Marybeth Long Martello, 31–54. Cambridge, MA: MIT Press.

Sheila Jasanoff is a leading scholar in Science and Technologies Studies. In this chapter, published in a book she co-edited with Marybeth Long Martello, Jasanoff looks at the role of visual representations, including images produced by scientists, in the construction of global environmentalism.

Lidskog, Rolf, and Göran Sundqvist. 2015. 'When Does Science Matter? International Relations Meets Science and Technology Studies'. *Global Environmental Politics* 15 (1): 1–20.

This article is one of the first—but certainly not the last—to bring together International Relations (IR) and Science and Technology Studies (S&TS). These two different fields have grown in isolation from each other for several decades, but their combination opens new avenues of research for global environmental politics.

 For additional material and resources, please visit the online resources at: www.oup.com/he/morin1e

Chapter references

Agarwal, Anil, and Sunita Narain. 1991. 'Global Warming in an Unequal World: A Case of Environmental Colonialism'. *Earth Island Journal* 6 (2): 39–40.

Akhtar-Schuster, Mariam, F. Amiraslani, C. F. Diaz Morejon, R. Escadafal, E. Fulajtar, A. Grainger, et al. 2016. 'Designing a New Science-Policy Communication Mechanism for the UN Convention to Combat Desertification'. *Environmental Science & Policy* 63 (September): 122–131.

Allan, Bentley B. 2017. 'Producing the Climate: States, Scientists, and the Constitution of Global Governance Objects'. *International Organization* 71 (1): 131–162.

Andrée, Peter. 2005. 'The Cartagena Protocol on Biosafety and Shifts in the Discourse of Precaution'. *Global Environmental Politics* 5 (4): 25–46.

Andresen, Steinar, Prativa Baral, Steven J. Hoffman, and Patrick Fafard. 2018. 'What can be Learned from Experience with Scientific Advisory Committees in the Field of International Environmental Politics?' *Global Challenges* 2 (9): article 1800055.

Andresen, Steinar, Tora Skodvin, Arild Underdal, and Jørgen Wettestad. 2000. *Science and Politics in International Environmental Regimes: Between Integrity and Involvement*. New York: Manchester University Press.

Auer, Matthew. 2010. 'Better Science and Worse Diplomacy: Negotiating the Cleanup of the Swedish and Finnish Pulp and Paper Industry'. *International Environmental Agreements* 10 (1): 65–84.

Benedick, Richard. 1991. *Ozone Diplomacy: New Directions in Safeguarding the Planet*. Cambridge, MA: Harvard University Press.

Biermann, Frank. 2002. 'Institutions for Scientific Advice: Global Environmental Assessments and their Influence in Developing Countries'. *Global Governance* 8 (2): 195–219.

Borland, R., Morrell, R., and Watson, V. 2018. 'Southern Agency: Navigating Local and Global Imperatives in Climate Research'. *Global Environmental Politics* 18 (3): 47–65.

Bowman, D. M., and G. A. Hodge. 2007. 'A Small Matter of Regulation: An International Review of Nanotechnology Regulation'. *The Columbia Science and Technology Law Review* 8 (1): 1–36.

Burns, Wil, and Simon Nicholson. 2017. 'Bioenergy and Carbon Capture with Storage (BECCS): The Prospects and Challenges of an Emerging Climate Policy Response'. *Journal of Environmental Studies and Sciences* 7 (4): 527–534.

Byrne, Adam. 2015. 'The 1979 Convention on Long-Range Transboundary Air Pollution: Assessing its Effectiveness as a Multilateral Environmental Regime after 35 Years'. *Transnational Environmental Law* 4 (1): 37–67.

Cash, David W., William C. Clark, Frank Alcock, Nancy M. Dickson, Noelle Eckley, David H. Guston, Jill Jäger, and Ronald B. Mitchell. 2003. 'Knowledge Systems for Sustainable Development'. *Proceedings of the National Academy of Sciences* 100 (14): 8086–8091.

Cointe, Béatrice, Paul-Alain Ravon, and Emmanuel Guérin. 2011. '2°C: The History of a Policy–Science Nexus'. Working Paper No. 19/11. Paris: Institute for Sustainable Development and International Relations.

Depledge, Joanna. 2008. 'Striving for No: Saudi Arabia in the Climate Change Regime'. *Global Environmental Politics* 8 (4): 9–35.

Dilling, Lisa, and Maria Carmen Lemos. 2011. 'Creating Usable Science: Opportunities and Constraints for Climate Knowledge Use and their Implications for Science Policy'. *Global Environmental Change* 21 (2): 680–689.

Dimitrov, Radoslav. 2003. 'Knowledge, Power, and Interests in Environmental Regime Formation'. *International Studies Quarterly* 47 (1): 123–150.

Dimitrov, Radoslav. 2006. *Science and International Environmental Policy: Regimes and Nonregimes in Global Governance*. Lanham, MD: Rowman & Littlefield.

Dunkley, R., S. Baker, N. Constant, and A. Sanderson-Bellamy. 2018. 'Enabling the IPBES Conceptual Framework to Work across Knowledge Boundaries'. *International Environmental Agreements: Politics, Law and Economics* 18 (6): 779–799.

Esguerra, A., S. Beck, and R. Lidskog. 2017. 'Stakeholder Engagement in the Making: IPBES Legitimization Politics'. *Global Environmental Politics* 17 (1): 59–76.

Falkner, Robert, and Nico Jaspers. 2012. 'Regulating Nanotechnologies: Risk, Uncertainty and the Global Governance Gap'. *Global Environmental Politics* 12 (1): 30–55.

Farrell, Alex, Stacy D. VanDeveer, and Jill Jäger. 2001. 'Environmental Assessments: Four Underappreciated Elements of Design'. *Global Environmental Change* 11 (4): 311–333.

Foster, Kenneth R., Paolo Vecchia, and Michael H. Repacholi. 2000. 'Science and the Precautionary Principle'. *Science* 288 (5468): 979–981.

Fuentes-George, Kemi. 2017. 'Consensus, Certainty, and Catastrophe: Discourse, Governance, and Ocean Iron Fertilization'. *Global Environmental Politics* 17 (2): 125–143.

Gehring, Thomas, and Eva Ruffing. 2008. 'When Arguments Prevail over Power: The CITES Procedure for the Listing of Endangered Species'. *Global Environmental Politics* 8 (2): 123–148.

Gleditsch, Nils Petter, and Ragnhild Nordås. 2014. 'Conflicting Messages? The IPCC on Conflict and Human Security', *Political Geography* 43: 82–90.

Goeminne, Gert. 2012. 'Lost in Translation: Climate Denial and the Return of the Political'. *Global Environmental Politics* 12 (2): 1–8.

Gough, Clair, and Simon Shackley. 2001. 'The Respectable Politics of Climate Change: The Epistemic Communities and NGOs'. *International Affairs* 77 (2): 329–346.

Grieger, K. D., S. F. Hansen, N. P. Mortensen, S. Cates, and B. Kowalcyk. 2016. 'International Implications of Labeling Foods Containing Engineered Nanomaterials'. *Journal of Food Protection* 79 (5): 830–842.

Grundmann, Reiner. 2007. 'Climate Change and Knowledge Politics'. *Environmental Politics* 16 (3): 414–432.

Gulbrandsen, Lars H. 2008. 'The Role of Science in Environmental Governance: Competing Knowledge Producers in Swedish and Norwegian Forestry'. *Global Environmental Politics* 8 (2): 99–122.

Gupta, Aarti. 2010. 'Transparency as Contested Political Terrain: Who Knows What about the Global GMO Trade and Why does it Matter?' *Global Environmental Politics* 10 (3): 32–52.

Gupta, Joyeeta, and Pieter Van Der Zaag. 2009. 'The Politics of Water Science: On Unresolved Water Problems and Biased Research Agendas'. *Global Environmental Politics* 9 (2): 14–23.

Haas, Ernst B. 1980. 'Why Collaborate?: Issue-Linkage and International Regimes'. *World Politics* 32 (3): 357–405.

Haas, Peter M. 1989. 'Do Regimes Matter? Epistemic Communities and Mediterranean Pollution'. *International Organization* 43 (3): 377–403.

Haas, Peter M. 1992a. 'Banning Chlorofluorocarbons: Epistemic Community Efforts to Protect Stratospheric Ozone'. *International Organization* 46 (1): 187–224.

Haas, Peter M. 1992b. 'Epistemic Communities and International Policy Coordination'. *International Organization* 46 (1): 1–35.

Haas, Peter M. 2015. *Epistemic Communities, Constructivism, and International Environmental Politics*. Abingdon and New York: Routledge.

Harrison, Neil E., and Gary C. Bryner. 2004. *Science and Politics in the International Environment*. Lanham, MD: Rowman & Littlefield.

Hayek, Friedrich August von. 1974. 'The Pretence of Knowledge'. Lecture to the memory of Alfred Nobel (11 December 1974). Available at: http://www.nobelprize.org/nobel_prizes/economic-sciences/laureates/1974/hayek-lecture.html, accessed October 2019.

Höllermann, B., and M. Evers. 2017. 'Perception and Handling of Uncertainties in Water Management— A Study of Practitioners' and Scientists' Perspectives on Uncertainty in their Daily Decision-making'. *Environmental Science & Policy* 71: 9–18.

Horton, Joshua B. 2018. 'Parametric Insurance as an Alternative to Liability for Compensating Climate Harms'. *Carbon and Climate Law Review* 12 (4): 285–296.

Horton, Joshua B., David W. Keith, and Matthias Honegger. 2016. *Implications of the Paris Agreement for Carbon Dioxide Removal and Solar Geoengineering*. Cambridge, MA: Harvard Project on Climate Agreements.

Hughes, Hannah Rachel. 2015. 'Bourdieu and the IPCC's Symbolic Power'. *Global Environmental Politics* 15 (4): 85–104.

Hughes, Hannah Rachel, and Matthew Paterson. 2017. 'Narrowing the Climate Field: The Symbolic Power of Authors in the IPCC's Assessment of Mitigation'. *Review of Policy Research* 34 (6): 744–766.

Hulme, Michael. 2009. *Why we Disagree about Climate Change: Understanding Controversy, Inaction and Opportunity*. Cambridge: Cambridge University Press.

Jacques, Peter J. 2012. 'A General Theory of Climate Denial'. *Global Environmental Politics* 12 (2): 9–17.

Jinnah, Sikina. 2018. 'Why Govern Climate Engineering? A Preliminary Framework for Demand-Based Governance'. *International Studies Review* 20 (2): 272–282.

Jinnah, Sikina, and Simon Nicholson. 2019. 'Governing Solar Radiation Management: How, Why, and for Whom?' *Environmental Politics* 28 (3): 385–396.

Jinnah, Sikina, and Simon Nicholson, and Jane Flegal. 2019. 'Toward Legitimate Governance of Solar Geoengineering Research: A Role for Sub-State Actors'. *Ethics, Policy and Environment* 21 (3): 362–381.

Kahan, Dan M. 2015. 'What is the "Science of Science Communication"?' *Journal of Science Communication* 14 (3): 1–10.

Kahan, Dan M., Donald Braman, Paul Slovic, John Gastil, and Geoffrey Cohen. 2009. 'Cultural Cognition of the Risks and Benefits of Nanotechnology'. *Nature Nanotechnology* 4 (2): 87–90.

Kahan, Dan M., Hank Jenkins-Smith, and Donald Braman. 2011. 'Cultural Cognition of Scientific Consensus'. *Journal of Risk Research* 14 (2): 147–174.

Kahan, Dan M., Ellen Peters, Maggie Wittlin, Paul Slovic, Lisa L. Ouellette, Donald Braman, and Gregory Mandel. 2012. 'The Polarizing Impact of Science Literacy and Numeracy on Perceived Climate Change Risks'. *Nature Climate Change* 2 (10): 732–735.

Kailis, A. 2017. 'The Influential Role of Consensual Knowledge in International Environmental Agreements: Negotiating the Implementing Measures of the Mediterranean Land-Based Sources Protocol (1980)'. *International Environmental Agreements: Politics, Law and Economics* 17 (2): 295–311.

Kanie, Norichika, Hiromi Nishimoto, Yasuaki Hijioka, and Yasuko Kameyama. 2010. 'Allocation and Architecture in Climate Governance Beyond Kyoto: Lessons From Interdisciplinary Research on Target Setting'. *International Environmental Agreements* 10 (4): 299–315.

Keith, David. 2013. *A Case for Climate Engineering*. Cambridge, MA: MIT Press.

Koetz, Thomas, Katharine N. Farrell, and Peter Bridgewater. 2012. 'Building Better Science-Policy Interfaces for International Environmental Governance: Assessing Potential Within The Intergovernmental Platform for Biodiversity and Ecosystem Services'. *International Environmental Agreements* 12 (1): 1–21.

Lahn, B., and G. Sundqvist. 2017. 'Science as a "Fixed Point"? Quantification and Boundary Objects in International Climate Politics'. *Environmental Science & Policy* 67: 8–15.

Lemos, Maria Carmen, and Barbara J. Morehouse. 2005. 'The Co-Production of Science and Policy in Integrated Climate Assessments'. *Global Environmental Change* 15 (1): 57–68.

Lewis, Kirsty. 2014. 'Climate Science in Climate Security Scenarios'. *Climatic Change* 123 (1): 11–22.

Lidskog, Rolf, and Göran Sundqvist. 2002. 'The Role of Science in Environmental Regimes: The Case of LRTAP'. *European Journal of International Relations* 8 (1): 77–101.

Lidskog, Rolf, and Göran Sundqvist. 2011. *Governing the Air*. Cambridge, MA: MIT Press.

Lidskog, Rolf, and Göran Sundqvist. 2015. 'When Does Science Matter? International Relations Meets Science and Technology Studies'. *Global Environmental Politics* 15 (1): 1–20.

Lieberman, Sarah, and Tim Gray. 2008. 'The World Trade Organization's Report on the EU's Moratorium on Biotech Products: The Wisdom of the US Challenge to the EU in the WTO'. *Global Environmental Politics* 8 (1): 33–52.

Litfin, Karen T. 1995. 'Framing Science: Precautionary Discourse and the Ozone Treaties'. *Millennium* 24 (2): 251–277.

Löfmarck, E., and R. Lidskog. 2017. 'Bumping Against the Boundary: IPBES and the Knowledge Divide'. *Environmental Science & Policy* 69: 22–28.

Lucier, C. A., and B. J. Gareau. 2016. 'Obstacles to Preserving Precaution and Equity in Global Hazardous Waste Regulation: An Analysis of Contested Knowledge in the Basel Convention'. *International Environmental Agreements: Politics, Law and Economics* 16 (4): 493–508.

Malnes, Raino. 2006. 'Imperfect Science'. *Global Environmental Politics* 6 (3): 58–71.

Mandel, G. 2008. 'Nanotechnology Governance'. *Alabama Law Review* 59 (5): 1324–1362.

Marchant, Gary E., and Kenneth. W. Abbott. 2013. 'International Harmonization of Nanotechnology Governance through "Soft Law" Approaches'. *Nanotechnology Law & Business* 9 (4): 393–410.

Martello, Marybeth Long. 2004a. 'Expert Advice and Desertification Policy: Past Experience and Current Challenges'. *Global Environmental Politics* 4 (3): 85–106.

Martello, Marybeth Long. 2004b. 'Global Change Science and the Arctic Citizen'. *Science and Public Policy* 31(2): 107–115.

Mayer, Maximilian. 2012. 'Chaotic Climate Change and Security'. *International Political Sociology* 6 (2): 165–185.

Meijerink, Sander. 2005. 'Understanding Policy Stability and Change. The Interplay of Advocacy Coalitions and Epistemic Communities, Windows of Opportunity, and Dutch Coastal Flooding Policy 1945–2003'. *Journal of European Public Policy* 12 (6): 1060–1077.

Meyer, John W., David John Frank, Ann Hironaka, Evan Schofer, and Nancy Brandon Tuma. 1997. 'The Structuring of a World Environmental Regime, 1870–1990'. *International Organization* 51 (4): 623–651.

Miller, Clark. 2001. 'Hybrid Management: Boundary Organizations, Science Policy, and Environmental Governance in the Climate Regime'. *Science, Technology & Human Values* 26 (4): 478–500.

Mitchell, Ronald B. 2019. *International Environmental Agreements Database Project*. Available at: https://iea.uoregon.edu/, accessed October 2019.

Mitchell, Ronald B., William C. Clark, and David W. Cash. 2006. 'Information and Influence'. In *Global Environmental Assessments: Information and Influence*, edited by Ronald B. Mitchell, William C. Clark, David W. Cash, and Nancy M. Dickson, 307–338. Cambridge: MIT Press.

Montana, J. 2017. 'Accommodating Consensus and Diversity in Environmental Knowledge Production: Achieving Closure through Typologies in IPBES'. *Environmental Science & Policy* 68: 20–27.

Morin, J.-F., S. Louafi, A. Orsini, and M. Oubenal. 2017. 'Boundary Organizations in Regime Complexes: A Social Network Profil of IPBES'. *Journal of International Relations and Development* 20 (3): 543–577.

Nicholson, Simon, Sikina Jinnah, and Alexander Gillespie. 2018. 'Solar Radiation Management: A legal Justification and Policy Framework for Immediate Governance'. *Climate Politics* 18 (3): 322–334.

Oreskes, Naomi, and Erik Conway. 2010. *Merchants of Doubt: How a Handful of Scientists Obscured the Truth on Issues from Tobacco Smoke to Global Warming*. New York: Bloomsbury Paperbacks.

Pammett, Jon H. 2015. 'Faith that Science will Solve Environmental Problems: Does it Hurt or Help?' *Environmental Politics* 24 (4): 553–574.

Parikh, Jyoti K. 1992. 'IPCC Strategies Unfair to the South'. *Nature* 360 (6404): 507–508.

Parson, Edward A. 2003. *Protecting the Ozone Layer: Science and Strategy*. New York: Oxford University Press.

Pavé, Alain, Catherine Courtet, and Jean-Luc Volatier. 1998. 'Environnement: Comment la communauté scientifique voit les problèmes'. *Courrier de l'environnement de l'INRA* 34 (July): 109–114.

Pechar, Emily, Thomas Bernauer, and Frederick Mayer. 2018. 'Beyond Political Ideology: The Impact of Attitudes towards Government and Corporations on Trust in Science'. *Science Communication* 40 (3): 291–313.

Pellizzoni, Luigi, and Marja Ylönen. 2008. 'Responsibility in Uncertain Times: An Institutional Perspective on Precaution'. *Global Environmental Politics* 8 (3): 51–73.

Peterson, M. J. 1992. 'Whalers, Cetologists, Environmentalists, and the International Management of Whaling'. *International Organization* 46 (1): 147–186.

Pielke, Roger A. 2004. 'When Scientists Politicize Science: Making Sense of Controversy Over the Skeptical Environmentalist'. *Environmental Science & Policy* 7 (5): 405–417.

Pulver, Simone, and Stacy D. Vandeveer. 2009. 'Thinking About Tomorrows: Scenarios, Global Environmental Politics, and Social Science Scholarship'. *Global Environmental Politics* 9 (2): 1–13.

Rabitz, Florian. 2019. 'Governing the Termination Problem in Solar Radiation Management'. *Environmental Politics* 28 (3): 502–522.

Rayner, Steve, Clare Heyward, Tim Kruger, Nick Pidgeon, Catherine Redgwell, and Julian Savulescu. 2013. 'The Oxford Principles'. *Climatic Change* 121 (3): 499–512.

Sachs, Noah M. 2011. 'Rescuing the Strong Precautionary Principle from its Critics'. *University of Illinois Law Review* (4): 1285–1338.

Sarewitz, Daniel. 2004. 'How Science Makes Environmental Controversies Worse'. *Environmental Science & Policy* 7 (5): 385–403.

Silke Beck, Maud Borie, Jason Chilvers, Alejandro Esguerra, Katja Heubach, Mike Hulme, Rolf Lidskog, Eva Lövbrand, Elisabeth Marquard, Clark Miller, Tahani Nadim, Carsten Nesshoever, Josef Settele, Esther Turnhout, Eleftheria Vasileiadou, and Christoph Goerg. 2014. 'Towards a Reflexive Turn in the Governance of Global Environmental Expertise. The Cases of the IPCC and the IPBES'. *GAIA* 23 (2): 80–87.

Stephan, Hannes R. 2012. 'Revisiting the Transatlantic Divergence over GMOs: Toward a Cultural-Political Analysis'. *Global Environmental Politics* 12 (4): 104–124.

Sunstein, Cass R. 2005. *Laws of Fear: Beyond the Precautionary Principle*, The Seeley Lectures (Book 6). New York: Cambridge University Press.

Toke, Dave. 1999. 'Epistemic Communities and Environmental Groups'. *Politics* 19 (2): 97–102.

Tuinstra, Willemijn, Leen Hordijk, and Markus Amann. 1999. 'Using Computer Models in International Negotiations: The Case of Acidification in Europe'. *Environment: Science and Policy for Sustainable Development* 41 (9): 32–42.

Tuinstra, Willemijn, Leen Hordijk, and Carolien Kroeze. 2006. 'Moving Boundaries in Transboundary Air Pollution: Co-Production of Science and Policy Under the Convention of Long-Range Transboundary Air Pollution'. *Global Environmental Change* 16 (4): 349–363.

Van der Linden, Sander L., Anthony A. Leiserowitz, and Edward W. Maibach. 2017. 'Gateway Illusion or Cultural Cognition Confusion?' *JCOM: Journal of Science Communication* 16 (5): 1–17.

Victor, David. 2008. 'On the Regulation of Geoengineering'. *Oxford Review of Economic Policy* 24 (2): 322–336.

Vogel, Coleen, Susanne C. Moser, Roger E. Kasperson, and Geoffrey D. Dabelko. 2007. 'Linking Vulnerability, Adaptation, and Resilience Science to Practice: Pathways, Players, and Partnerships'. *Global Environmental Change* 17 (3–4): 349–364.

Vogel, David. 2012. *The Politics of Precaution: Regulating Health, Safety, and Environmental Risks in Europe and the United States*. Princeton, NJ: Princeton University Press.

Warren, Charles R. 2007. 'Perspectives on the "Alien" Versus "Native" Species Debate: A Critique of Concepts, Language and Practice'. *Progress in Human Geography* 31 (4): 427–446.

Weichselgartner, Juergen, and Roger Kasperson. 2010. 'Barriers in the Science-Policy-Practice Interface: Toward a Knowledge-Action-System in Global Environmental Change Research'. *Global Environmental Change* 20 (2): 266–277.

Zehr, Stephen. 1994. 'Accounting for the Ozone Hole'. *The Sociological Quarterly* 35 (4): 603–619.

Zito, Anthony. 2001. 'Epistemic Communities, Collective Entrepreneurship and European Integration'. *Journal of European Public Policy* 8 (4): 585–603.

Ideas about environmental protection

Ideas play a central role in shaping the preferences and behaviours of governments, non-governmental organizations, businesses, and other stakeholders. However, ideas are not universally shared, which means that ideological clashes are a feature of global environmental governance. Some people think that communities should each be free to establish their own environmental regulations, while others believe that universal principles should be applied across the board. Some argue that the environment should be protected for the services it provides to humanity, while others recognize its intrinsic value, irrespective of the services it provides. Some people recommend actively managing nature, while others think we should avoid interfering with nature in order to better preserve it. Some people are worried about the fact that natural resources are limited, while others are confident that technological innovation can overcome these limitations. Some people suggest that we should take into account the rights of future generations, while others think that the needs of the current generation are a priority. This chapter explores these debates, which shape global environmental politics.

 Learning objectives

After reading this chapter, readers will be able to:

- Understand the arguments in favour of and against a communitarian view of environmental regulations;

- Explain the assumptions underlying both biocentric and anthropocentric motivations for environmental protection;

- Identify international institutions building on preservationist and conservationist logics to environmental protection;

- Analyse critically both neo-malthusian and cornucopian theories related to economic development and the environment; and

- Distinguish the policy implications of calls for greater intergenerational and intra-generational equity in global environmental politics.

Introduction

The environment is not simply a material structure made up of living organisms and their habitats. The environment also consists of the ideas people attach to these living and non-living ecosystem components. Depending on the social context, one can perceive a forest as a resource pool to be exploited, a paradise bequeathed by God, a source of artistic inspiration, a fragile and complex ecosystem, a sacred territory where spirits live, or a threat that must be tamed (Fuentes-George 2013). From this perspective, preferences regarding environmental protection do not depend on material conditions alone. Preferences are also social constructs, meaning that they depend on ideas that are produced and reproduced through social interactions. As John Dryzek (2005: 10) put it, 'While real problems exist, our interaction with them can only ever be through a culturally constructed lens—meaning that we can never know nature except through the interpretive mechanism of culture, which means that all perspectives are partial and contestable.'

At least three types of socially constructed ideas play a key role in international environmental **governance**: *world views*, *causal beliefs*, and **social norms** (Goldstein and Keohane 1993). *World views* are very broad value systems that define how the world is and how it should be. Classic economic liberalism, for example, is a world view that considers that individuals are the basic units of society and that their rational maximization of gains contribute to the common good. Therefore, liberalism leads to policy proposals that are quite different from more holistic visions, which consider the whole to be greater than the sum of its parts (Clapp and Dauvergne 2011).

Causal beliefs focus on relationships of cause and effect. Some causal beliefs are informed by modern science, such as the fact that emissions of **greenhouse gases** cause climate change. Causal beliefs can also rely on traditional belief systems (Eisenstadt and Jones West 2017a), such as the belief that a shaman can cure someone who is ill by invoking the gods. Finally, *social norms* are guidelines that define the behaviour deemed socially appropriate for a given identity. Contributing to the funding of environmental protection in **developing countries**, for example, is a behaviour expected from countries considered as 'high-income' (Eckersley 2016).

World views, causal beliefs, and social norms vary from one community to another. While some communities are transnational (such as a profession or a religion), most communities are geographically bounded. A town, a nation, and a civilization refer to communities at three different geographical scales. In many cases, members of a community share a number of ideas, providing them with a shared identity and allowing them to build **institutions** to govern their interactions.

Considering the global heterogeneity of ideas, **stakeholders** involved in international environmental politics have to be persuasive when communicating their ideas. Ideas provide legitimacy for the most powerful actors, who strive to make their institutions universal and durable, as well as for marginal stakeholders, who question the established order. Over time, prevailing ideas at the top of the international agenda evolve through ideational debates. These interactive and changing dynamics help explain why the definition of environmental problems and the preferred solutions to alleviate them vary from one region to another and from one period to another.

This chapter presents five of the major ideological debates that have marked the evolution of global environmental governance. The first two debates present conflicting world views. The first concerns the scope of environmental values (Section 2.1); the second examines the intrinsic values of non-human organisms (Section 2.2). The following two debates concern causal beliefs. One is about the relationship between human intervention and environmental protection (Section 2.3), while the other concerns the relationship between economic growth and environmental degradation (Section 2.4). The last debate looks at different social norms related to **environmental justice** and the appropriate behaviours expected towards historically marginalized populations (Section 2.5).

These five debates are presented in the form of dichotomies, and we pay special atten-tion to extreme positions. In reality, most actors navigate in the grey areas between these extremes, with varying degrees of (in)coherence. Nonetheless, for the purpose of this chapter, presenting ideological debates as dichotomies makes it easier to understand the ideational structures that explicitly or implicitly provide the basis for international debates on environ-mental protection.

2.1 Are there universal environmental values?

National variations in environmental ideas

The importance of environmental protection is recognized throughout the world (Leiserowitz et al. 2006). According to the opinion polls conducted by the World Values Survey between 2010 and 2014 in 60 countries, 75 per cent of surveyed individuals believe that looking after the environment is important. Respondents from developed and developing countries equally share this positive attitude towards the environment. Even more striking, in most countries, most respondents believe that environmental protection should be a political pri-ority, even if it probably means slower economic growth and higher unemployment. The World Values Survey observes this prioritization of the environment over the economy in countries as diverse as Brazil (60.3 per cent of respondents), China (56.6 per cent), India (58.4 per cent), Libya (54.4 per cent), and Sweden (62.9 per cent).

Yet that does not mean that humanity shares identical ideas about how environmental protection should be pursued. A close examination of the findings of the World Values Survey reveals important variations from one country to another (see Figure 2.1). There are also significant variations of opinion within each country.

This variation in opinion is partly a function of material interests (Eisenstadt and Jones West 2017b). On average, the more someone is negatively affected by environmental degradation, the more likely they are to express support for environmental protection. However, economic conditions and the distribution of costs associated with environmental protection are not al-ways strong predictors of opinion about environmental policy (McGrath and Bernauer 2017). Citizens from countries that are particularly vulnerable to drought, flooding, and soil erosion do not consistently express stronger concern for climate change than citizens from other countries. Citizens from countries with greater material and technological capacity to address climate change are not systematically more supportive of climate policies than those from developing countries (Kim and Wolinsky-Nahmias 2014). Economic downturns do not reduce the prior-ity given to climate policy action (Mildenberger and Leiserowitz 2017). Perhaps more surpris-ingly from an international politics perspective, public support for unilateral climate policy does not drop substantially when respondents are confronted with the free-riding problem of other countries that remain inactive (Anderson et al. 2017; McGrath and Bernauer 2017).

Cultural background is often a better predictor of opinion on environmental policies than material interests. How we should protect the environment and, more fundamen-tally, how we define the environment to be protected, varies from one community to another. These cultural divergences are apparent when we examine certain emblematic animal species and food taboos. While Americans may attribute special intelligence to marine mammals, which justifies exceptional protection measures under American law,

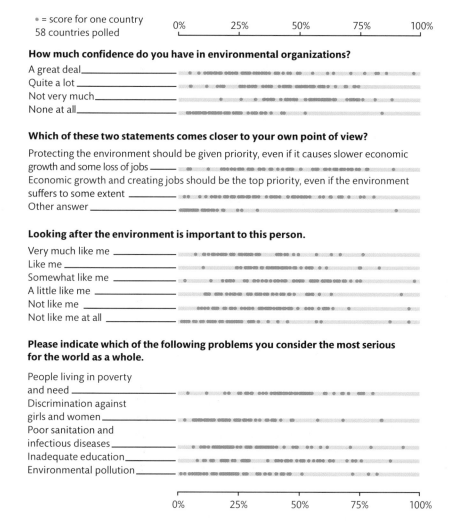

Figure 2.1 The environment in the opinion polls

Source data from: World Values Survey (2010–2014)

Take your learning further by viewing the interactive version of this figure
www.oup.com/he/morin1e

they would be highly unlikely to protect cows in the same way. In contrast, several states in India strictly prohibit the slaughter of cows, which for their population symbolize generosity and nurturing.

There are also significant cultural differences between Western countries, in terms of what is considered appropriate behaviour towards a particular species. For example, the Canadian practice of killing seals with clubs is shocking to most Europeans, as demonstrated by the European import ban on seal hunting products. In turn, the French practice of force-feeding ducks and geese for foie gras shocks many Americans. Foie gras is a treat for French guests at end-of-year feasts, but its sale has been prohibited in California since 2012. California also banned the sale of horsemeat in 1998 because the horse has a special place in the imagery and history of the western frontier. Yet horse butchers are not uncommon in several countries in continental Europe.

Local cultures also frame our perceptions of vegetation and natural spaces (Stephan 2012). In Europe, farming is often treated as a cultural heritage. This is reflected in the policies geared to protecting landscape and traditional agricultural practices. In North America, the natural heritage is associated with areas of wilderness, like Grand Canyon National Park in the United States or Banff National Park in Canada. These parks are symbols of the countries' national identity and history. In fact, in some countries, national parks are the responsibility of the ministry of culture rather than the ministry of the environment.

Discussions held at the **Conference of the Parties** to the Convention on International Trade in Endangered Species of Wild Fauna and Flora crystallize these cultural differences. During the 2013 conference, for example, several countries proposed adding the polar bear to appendix 1 of the convention, which prohibits international trade in species whose survival would be threatened by that trade. In the collective imagination, the polar bear is a charismatic animal that has become a totemic symbol of the victims of climate change. Canada, however, strongly opposed this proposal, arguing that polar bear trading does not threaten the species' survival. In addition, as far as the Canadian authorities are concerned, polar bear hunting is essential to protect the traditional practices of Inuit communities, for whom the bearskin trade represents a source of additional income. Canada's arguments managed to convince a majority of countries at the 2013 conference that the polar bear should not be included in appendix 1.

There is reason to believe that Canada might change its mind at a future Conference of the Parties if other countries mount a public campaign to add the polar bear to appendix 1. In fact, countries that are economically penalized by a trade ban on a species often support the measure when they realize there is an emerging international consensus on the issue (Gehring and Ruffing 2008). International norms do not always have to be internalized to produce an effect. The fear of public reprobation or the desire to enhance reputation may be sufficient to modify an actor's preferences (see Box 2.1).

Box 2.1 Conspicuous conservation

The behaviour of individuals is influenced not only by their own beliefs about the environment, but also by the social norms that are shared in their communities. These social norms can act as powerful incentives for individuals to willingly invest in the protection of the environment when environmental action has a 'signalling' effect. Several studies have shown that people are more inclined to choose organic food products when shopping in public, and when these products cost more. Luxury clientele will also more easily turn to sustainable luxury if those products are conspicuous and expensive. These studies confirm reputation, but also social status, as new environmental motivations.

Steven Sexton and Alison Sexton (2014) have illustrated this argument by analysing hybrid car purchases in the United States. Several models of hybrid car are available on the American market, among them the Toyota Prius, which is noted for its relatively high price compared with competing hybrid models and for its unique and easily recognizable design. The design of other models, such as the Honda Civic hybrid and the Ford Escape hybrid, does not differ significantly from that of their regular versions powered by fossil fuels. The Prius therefore has a strong 'conspicuous' capacity, meaning that, thanks to its unique design, it clearly communicates its owner's environmental concerns. Yet sales of the Prius compared to those of its hybrid competitors vary significantly from region to region in the United States. In regions where citizens are more concerned about the environment, as indicated by their voting choices, proportionally more hybrid car buyers choose the Prius rather than competing hybrid models. This is the case even when a series of control variables that affect car choices are introduced into the statistical model, such as owner age, family size, access to public transport, median income, population density, and average journey distance. In other words, individuals who live in communities that are sensitive to environmental issues are not only more likely to buy a hybrid car; they are also more likely to be willing to pay for a more expensive model in order to clearly communicate their environmental concerns to their neighbours, and therefore to publicly display that they belong in that community. This behaviour is a form of 'conspicuous conservation'.

This gives interesting new insights for global environmental governance. International regulations are needed to harmonize environmental measures and ensure that everyone, not only the wealthy, engage in environmental behaviour. However, the environmental behaviours with the greatest 'conspicuous' capacity are not always the most rational from an environmental point of view. Installing solar panels on the front-facing side of a roof gives a strong signal, but thermally insulating a house, which is more discreet, often proves to be more energy efficient. At the national level, the creation of national parks clearly communicates a government's environmental concerns, but can prove to be less effective in protecting **biodiversity** than, for instance, technical regulations on the use of chemical products. International cooperation for the protection of charismatic animals, such as elephants and whales, also has a stronger conspicuous capacity than efforts to protect amphibians and insects, but the latter play a no less important role in ecosystem maintenance. This suggests that we should aim to ensure that the most effective environmental protection measures also have a conspicuous signalling capacity.

Sources: Cervellon 2013; Griskevicius et al. 2010; Sexton and Sexton 2014.

Communitarianism and universalism

The global diversity of ideas raises the question of whether certain minimal common rules should regulate the whole of humanity and its relationships with the environment. Do some environmental norms have universal scope, as human rights do, which might justify proselytizing even in communities that do not recognize them a priori or are even hostile towards them? For example, should the taboo on whale hunting be imposed on Inuit communities, for whom the activity is an opportunity to connect with an ancestral practice? The International Whaling Commission, which adopted a moratorium on whaling in 1982, authorizes indigenous communities to hunt for subsistence as an exception. However, on an ethical level, if an exception is granted for Inuits, how can we justify not extending it to the Japanese as well? After all, whale meat has had a special place on their national menu for centuries.

On this issue, a *universal world view* contrasts with a *communitarian world view* (Elliott 2006). *Universalism* suggests that humanity constitutes a single moral community, within which individuals share rights and moral obligations (see Box 2.2). Some criteria of justice, fairness, and righteousness are universal and timeless. In contrast, *communitarianism* suggests that an individual is shaped culturally by a specific community. Communities are not free associations of individuals; rather, individuals are the products of communities. This explains why individuals tend to be far more concerned about the environmental quality of their own community than about the state of the world as a whole. Moreover, communities have different cultural representations, risk tolerance, and political priorities. Therefore, the scope of social and legal norms is, and should be, limited to each community.

International environmental governance oscillates between these universalist and communitarian poles. For example, the preamble to the 1972 Stockholm Declaration of the United Nations Conference on the Human Environment underlined 'the need for a common outlook and for common principles to inspire and guide the peoples of the world in the preservation and enhancement of the human environment'. Yet the declaration also recognized that 'it will be essential in all cases to consider the systems of values prevailing in each country' (Principle 23). The 2015 Paris Agreement on climate change aimed to strike a balance between the universalist and communitarian poles by combining nationally determined contributions, in which parties define their own objectives for greenhouse gas reductions domestically, with an international review mechanism which holds them accountable to those national targets in the international system (Pickering et al. 2015).

The universalist idea of adopting a founding legal document, specifying universal environmental principles and values (like the two International Covenants on Human Rights), has been raised several times. For example, it was one of the recommendations of the 1987 Brundtland Report of the World Commission on Environment and Development: 'There is now a need to consolidate and extend relevant legal principles in a new charter to guide state behaviour in the transition to sustainable development' (paragraph 85). However, the project failed during the preparations leading up to the 1992 United Nations Conference on the Environment and Development, held in Rio, and again during the preparations for the World Summit on Sustainable Development, held in Johannesburg in 2002. Disagreements over the normative principles and the thematic priorities have impeded a global consensus. More recently, in May 2018, the UN General Assembly adopted a resolution calling for the negotiation of a 'Global Pact for the Environment' to address gaps in international environmental law. However, so far, states have failed to agree on an international treaty that specifies universal environmental values in detail.

Box 2.2 The Vatican and the environment: an activist pope?

The relationship between religion and environmental issues has received attention from scholars, policymakers, and activists in recent years. Researchers have examined how religious attitudes and beliefs shape public perceptions about various environmental problems, including climate change, finding that the influence of religion on environmental perceptions and actions is often ambiguous. For their part, religious leaders themselves have intervened in ongoing environmental discussions. Pope Francis' June 2015 encyclical—the most authoritative decree a pope can issue—on climate change is an example of this kind of intervention.

In this encyclical, entitled *Laudato Si: On Care for Our Common Home*, he declared that care for the environment is central to moral and spiritual life. He argued that our common environment is in crisis—not just driven by climate change, but a wide-ranging ecological crisis that is comprised of several environmental issues, including climate change, pollution and waste, diminishing water quality, and biodiversity loss. In the document he emphasizes that, despite the shared nature of 'our common home', widespread inequality means that the poor are most vulnerable to environment-related risks. His insistence that environmental, social, moral, spiritual, and political life are interrelated is notable, as is his argument that rather than taking 'dominion' over the earth, humans should be responsible caretakers of nature. The encyclical also included discussion on the importance of engaging local community networks and institutions in climate governance, the need for governance of various 'global commons' through strengthened international institutions, and a critique of carbon trading and reliance on market forces.

Pope Francis has made climate change one of the central issues of his papacy. The Vatican is a permanent **observer** at the United Nations, and has strongly supported the 2015 Paris Agreement. He has called on the United States to revisit its position on climate change, and his chief environmental advisor, Cardinal Peter Turkson, has publicly criticized United States President Donald Trump's position on climate change. In a first of its kind collaboration with two California-based venture capital firms, the Vatican also hosted a contest for start-up technology companies that aim to address climate change. Through this initiative it funded nine companies at $100,000 each—and provided them with offices at the Vatican—to pursue environmental projects.

Additionally, climate change was a key issue at the 2018 Third Vatican Conference on Impact Investing, which had the objective of moving capital into investments that target the poorest and most vulnerable. The Vatican is also actively participating in the negotiations on a new treaty on marine biological diversity, despite the fact that it does not have fishing vessels or even a coastline. Through initiatives such as this, Pope Francis is pushing the boundaries of what the Vatican can do to engage in environmental politics.

Sources: Albanese and Follain 2017; Albanese and Rotondi 2017; Clingerman and O'Brien 2014; Funk and Alper 2015; O'Neill 2016.

2.2 Does the environment have an intrinsic value?

Anthropocentrism versus biocentrism

Anthropocentrism and **biocentrism** are two world views that disagree about the intrinsic value of the environment (Eckerlsey 1992; Hayward 1998; Naess 1973). *Anthropocentrism* places humans at the centre of the moral universe and considers the environment around them as a pool of resources. This world view does not mean that humans can freely mistreat animals or exploit natural resources until they are exhausted. It simply assumes that ethical criteria governing the treatment of animals and the exploitation of resources must relate to the interests of humans. If the environment must be protected, it is because it has an instrumental value for humanity. It might even be argued from an anthropocentric perspective that the long-term interests of humanity demand a radical shift in current modes of production and consumption (Hawken et al. 2013).

In contrast, *biocentrism* considers living organisms to have an intrinsic value, independent of the services they may provide for humanity. According to biocentrism, no ethical argument can justify humans ignoring the interests of non-human organisms. Living organisms have their own specific interests, which should be defended. This does not mean that we should treat all creatures equally and provide them with the same rights. While some biocentric thinkers argue that all kinds of organisms have moral standing, including plants, bacteria, and holistic entities such as ecosystems, others limit their argument to sentient beings, such as mammals. Also, biocentrism does not mean that harm to non-human organisms is never justified. However, all biocentric thinkers agree that humans should take into account the specific interests of non-human organisms and should aim to satisfy the maximum number of interests when making decisions that affect non-human organisms.

Anthropocentric institutions

The first environmental agreements were clearly based on anthropocentric justifications. They defended the immediate interests of hunters, fishermen, and farmers. One of the very first international environmental treaties was adopted in 1881 to protect European vine-yards, which were seriously threatened by phylloxera, an insect that originated from the US. The treaty created a notification system to prevent the introduction and propagation of the insect. Then, in 1900, the European colonial powers signed the Convention for the Preserva-tion of Wild Animals, Birds and Fish in Africa. This Convention explicitly distinguished two categories of animals. The first included those that were useful or harmless to humans, like giraffes and zebras. The second included animals that were a threat to humans, like crocodiles and pythons. The Convention protected the former but encouraged hunting and the destruc-tion of eggs for the latter. A third example is the Convention for the Protection of Birds Useful to Agriculture, signed by several European countries in 1902. This Convention prohibits the hunting of insectivorous birds and the destruction of their nests because they are the farm-ers' natural allies. A last example of this first generation of anthropocentric instruments is the North Pacific Fur Seal Convention, ratified in 1911 by the US, Russia, Japan, and the UK. The Convention did not aim to protect seals, but to ensure the durability of the sealskin trade and industry through rational hunting management.

Several more recent treaties have similar anthropocentric goals, aiming to protect the interests of hunters, fishermen, and farmers. For example, this is the case with numerous conventions on deep-sea fish stocks, which aim to guarantee the viability of the fishing in-dustry (see Box 5.1). It also applies to the International Treaty on Plant Genetic Resources for Food and Agriculture, signed in 2001. This treaty aims to conserve genetic material that has a potential value for food, particularly **genetic resources** that could improve cultivated varie-ties through crossing, to enhance their resistance, attractiveness, and productivity. Here, the value of genetic material is appreciated in terms of its usefulness to farmers and consumers and not for its intrinsic value.

Anthropocentric considerations are not limited to economic activities. Several treaties also aim to protect the environment's scientific, historic, or aesthetic value. In 1933, the London Convention Relative to the Preservation of Fauna and Flora in their Natural State targeted the creation of national parks to guarantee 'the preservation of objects of aesthetic, geo-logical, prehistoric, historical, archaeological, or other scientific interest' (Article 2.1). Then, in 1940, the Convention on Nature Protection and Wild Life Preservation in the Western Hemisphere encouraged the creation of parks to conserve 'areas of extraordinary beauty, striking geological formations or regions of aesthetic, historic or scientific value' (preamble). The 1971 Ramsar Convention on Wetlands of International Importance justifies the protec-tion of these zones because they 'constitute a resource of great economic, cultural, scientific and recreational value' (preamble). Lastly, the Convention Concerning the Protection of the World Cultural and Natural Heritage was concluded at UNESCO in 1972 to protect natural sites or other natural areas 'of outstanding universal value from the point of view of science, **conservation** or natural beauty' (Article 2). In all these cases, the justifications that form the basis of international cooperation refer to the appreciation of the environment by humans, and not the intrinsic environmental value.

Biocentric perspectives

Biocentrism can also be broken down into a range of different positions. For some, bio-centrism encompasses anthropocentric values because humans are also living beings and should be valued and protected like other living organisms. They consider that biocentrism and anthropocentrism could be reconciled if people agree to focus on the interests of future generations (Barkin 2006; Kauffman and Martin 2014). *Bioregionalism* is one way of achieving this reconciliation. It defines the appropriate boundaries of political, economic, and social systems at the level of ecosystems in order to bring nature and culture closer together and to find greater harmony between humans and their environment (Carr 2005).

Without looking for any reconciliation, '**deep ecology**' calls for immediate fundamental changes in our social, cultural, and economic systems to protect non-human life, even if it implies a smaller human population with reduced standards of living (Naess 1973). Some deep ecologists assert that the interests of ecological systems should take precedence over the interests of individuals, living or unborn. The eras that people view as the 'Dark Ages', those periods characterized by famine, conflicts, and the collapse of economic and social systems, are not necessarily disasters from a biocentric point of view. They are seen as a fair return to equilibrium after centuries of human overexploitation of nature (Chew 2002). These views are widely shared in the deep ecology advocacy group Earth First! (Foreman 2004). They are also echoed by the Voluntary Human Extinction Movement, which claims not to be misanthropic but still advocates reducing the human population through birth control (Ormrod 2011).

Some proponents of biocentrism lay claim to *ecofeminism* (Bretherton 2003). Although ecofeminism is itself a very diverse movement, a number of its supporters consider that the same patriarchal system keeps women and nature under the domination of men and culture (see Box 2.3). In both cases, individualism and rationalism are used as instruments of control and exploitation. Random hierarchical demarcations that distinguish gender and species are artificial, but so deeply rooted in Western culture that androcentrism (centred on men) and anthropocentrism (centred on humans) are taken for granted. A fairer and more sustain-able world would be based on a more communitarian and holistic vision of the relationships between genders and living organisms. Therefore, under this view, the struggle for wom-en's emancipation and the struggle for the environment's emancipation are closely linked (Fox 1989).

The *Gaia hypothesis* proposes a different biocentric perspective (Litfin 2005). This hypothesis, which takes its name from the Greek goddess personifying the earth, was developed by James Lovelock in the 1970s. It is a holistic hypothesis, according to which the different elements can only be understood through their complex relationships. The whole is greater than the sum of its parts, and the parts can only be understood in relation to the whole. The earth itself is seen as a living, evolving, and adaptive organism. It forms a system composed of several sub-systems, such as the biosphere, the atmosphere, the hydrosphere, and the geosphere, which are in turn composed of sub-subsystems. The different elements are linked to each other by feedback loops and their constant dynamics maintain the earth's system in a certain balance.

Box 2.3 Ecofeminism: connections between women, nature, and oppression

Ecofeminism is a theory and practice that examines how the widespread subordination of women is inseparably linked to the devastating exploitation of the natural environment. The term ecofeminism was first used by French feminist author and activist Francoise d'Eaubonne in her book *Le Féminisme ou la mort (Feminism or Death)* in 1974. D'Eaubonne contended that the liberation of women is interdependent with the liberation of the environment, and that the environment could only be saved with the total abolishment of women's oppression.

Since the 1980s ecofeminist analysis has centred around the connections between the subordination of women and of nature. Prominent ecofeminist scholar Carolyn Merchant has organized these developments into four distinct categories, each with a different perspective on the sources of domination. The first, *liberal ecofeminism*, focuses on reformist environmentalism that aims to amend society's harmful relationship with nature through new ecologically sustainable and gender-focused policies, regulations, and laws. Liberal ecofeminists are likely to emphasize the need for greater representation of women in sites of environmental decision-making: in extractive industries, political institutions, environmental organizations, and international institutions.

The second strand, *cultural ecofeminism* (also referred to as radical ecofeminism) argues that patriarchy has devalued women's psychology, physiology, and social roles by associating them with an understanding of nature that has been deemed inferior to man and culture. One example of an endeavour that radical ecofeminists support is the creation of new forms of social organization, such as women-led cooperatives, which are designed to increase the autonomy and power of women in a community.

The third, *social ecofeminism*, identifies hierarchical human relations that result in centralized societies (such as the state) as the cause of domination between people, and also the source of the double subordination of women and nature. According to this viewpoint, non-hierarchical human organization is required to ameliorate the domination of both women and nature.

The fourth is *socialist ecofeminism*, which identifies capitalism specifically as the source of women's and nature's subordination, arguing that capitalism is the modern manifestation of the patriarchal system. For these ecofeminists, the links between the subordination of women and the environment are rooted in the 'capitalist patriarchy'—a global economic system embedded within the long history of women's oppression and exploitation. Thus, for socialist ecofeminists, capitalism must be replaced with a socialist system to address the domination of women and nature.

Importantly, there are tensions and conflict between these four strands, particularly between the liberal and other categories of ecofeminism: liberal ecofeminists generally do not believe that significant transformations in social, economic, and political institutions are necessary.

Ecofeminism is also an ecological movement, which emerged in women-led environmental and climate justice activism, and other initiatives that look to remedy the impact that environmental destruction has on women's political power, bodies, and labour. For example, in 1977 in Kenya, women in the Green Belt Movement, founded by Professor Wangari Maathai, organized themselves to collect water and firewood, gather seeds, and plant trees to strengthen the soil in response to drought and food scarcity that were hindering women's work in the area. Similarly, Indian women of the Chipko movement held on to trees in order to peacefully resist deforestation as early as 1730, then again in 1973. Across the globe, women have been at the forefront of protesting against nuclear plants, pollution, and toxic waste, emphasizing the consequences these have on women's reproductive systems and the rearing of children. For example in 1978, in the American neighbourhood of Love Canal in New York state, Lois Gibbs mobilized local women to investigate and reveal that miscarriages, birth defects, and serious illness among adults and children were being caused by toxic waste and pollution from a nearby landfill site.

Ecofeminism also sees women's traditional work and their historical understanding of plant life, herbal medicines, and midwifery as knowledge that is both closely linked to the earth and as inherently ecologically sustainable. Some ecofeminists claim that women have a closer connection to nature because of their capacity to give birth to children and because they are biologically more caring, emotional, and nurturing than men. This line of thought has resulted in strong critiques of ecofeminism for essentializing women, mothers, and genders into the same fixed biological categories that have so heavily contributed to women's oppression to begin with. These debates have also brought attention to tendencies to universalize the experiences of all women. Indigenous women and women in developing countries, for example, are impacted by capitalism and patriarchy in drastically different ways than women in many developed countries. In some cases, this has created a geographical divide within the ecofeminist literature and movement, and these tendencies have also spurred accusations that ecofeminism is an endeavour dominated by white, middle-class academics.

Sources: Dankelman 2010; d'Eaubonne 1974; Hessing 1993; Merchant 1980, 2005; Mies 1998; Nagel 2016; Plumwood 1993; Salleh 1997; Sargisson 2001; Warren 1997.

From this point of view, it is necessary to protect the different individual animal and plant species, as well as the ecosystems and even the planet, understood as a living organism in its own right.

The limited influence of biocentrism

Biocentric outlooks remain marginal when it comes to international negotiations (Kauffman and Martin 2014). It is interesting to note that the very first principle of the 1972 Stockholm Declaration of the United Nations Conference on the Human Environment is that 'Man has a fundamental right to freedom, equality and adequate conditions of life, in an environment of a quality that permits a life of dignity and well-being' (Principle 1). And 20 years later, the first principle of the 1992 Rio Declaration on Environment and Development reflects the same unequivocal anthropocentrism: 'Human beings are at the centre of concerns for sustainable development' (Principle 1).

Some international instruments clearly recognize the environment's intrinsic value, but they systematically add anthropocentric justifications to the biocentric perspective. Thus, the World Charter for Nature, a political declaration adopted by the United Nations General Assembly in 1982, recognizes that 'every form of life is unique, warranting respect regardless of its worth to man', but also that humanity 'depends on the uninterrupted functioning of natural systems which ensure the supply of energy and nutrients' (preamble). Similarly, the Convention on Biological Diversity states that 'the contracting parties [are] conscious of the intrinsic value of biological diversity', but also of 'the value of biodiversity and its ecological, genetic, social, economic, scientific, educational, cultural, recreational and aesthetic components' (preamble).

States have incorporated very few concrete ideas inspired by biocentrism into international instruments. They have considered from time to time the proposal for the international recognition of '**ecocide**' as a crime alongside genocide. The notion of ecocide would place a crime against nature on a par with a crime against humanity. This proposal emerged in the 1970s, when the United States sprayed defoliant on the Vietnamese jungle. It was also considered in the 1990s during the negotiations on the Rome Statute of the International Criminal Court. Each time, however, an anthropocentric and state-centric world view prevailed over the recognition of the ecocide idea. The 1976 Convention on the Prohibition of Military or Any Other Hostile Use of Environmental Modification Techniques does not prohibit all environmental modification techniques that have widespread, long-lasting, or severe effects. It only prohibits those used by a state, and only those that aim to 'cause destruction, damage or injury to any other State **Party**' (Article 1). Similarly, the war crimes recognized in the Rome Statute are conditioned by the anthropocentric context of military conflicts. They include, for example, 'intentionally launching an attack in the knowledge that such an attack will cause [. . .] widespread, long-term or severe damage to the natural environment which would be clearly excessive in relation to the concrete and direct overall military advantage anticipated' (Article 8).

Over and above the notion of ecocide, the very idea of any international recognition of animal rights remains fiercely contested. The animal liberation movement has made some significant advances since its emergence in the 1970s (Singer 1975). National legislation and the codes of conduct of several transnational corporations now limit the cruelty and suffering that can be imposed on animals. Some species and even some ecosystems with particular symbolic value, such as the Whanganui River in New Zealand, enjoy exceptional legal rights (O'Donnell and Talbot-Jones 2018). However, national and international law is still deeply marked by what some proponents of biocentrism call 'speciesism'. This term refers to the discriminatory treatment of living beings based on their species. Debates on the 2010 Nagoya Protocol clearly illustrate that the norms relative to genetic resources, including their patentability, are not the same for human genes and non-human genes. At the Rio+20 Earth Summit in 2012, when Ecuador proposed that nature's rights, as well as our responsibilities towards nature, should be recognized, the proposal was quickly removed from the negotiation table (Kauffman and Martin 2014).

Despite some biocentric advances, mainly at the local level, shifting from a rather anthropocentric vision of the world to a more biocentric vision would mark a fundamental change in international environmental law. Several key elements of Western culture are fundamentally anthropocentric, including: 'the emblematic faith in the modernity of technology, the doctrine of progress, the centrality of the utilitarian rationale, the inviolability of individual liberty and the denial of the sacred' (Litfin 2003: 30). In Judeo-Christian traditions, the human is a creature made in God's image, placed at the centre of creation. God's injunction, recorded in Genesis, is anthropocentric in the extreme: 'be fruitful and multiply, and fill the earth and subdue it; and have dominion over the fish of the sea and the birds of the air and over every living thing that moves upon the earth' (The Book of Genesis, chapter 1, verses 28–29). Given these deep cultural roots, it is highly unlikely that the biocentric perspective will become the dominant representation of the world in the near future.

2.3 Does human intervention cause more harm than good?

Conserving versus preserving

Beyond the question of what motivates environmental protection is the question of how to protect the environment. More specifically, should humans intervene directly in ecosystems to ensure that resources last, or step back and let nature take its course? This debate on the causal effect of human intervention has been going on for several generations.

More than a century ago, the conservationist views of Gifford Pinchot (1865–1946), the first chief of the United States Forest Service, clashed with the preservationist views of John Muir (1838–1914), co-founder of the Sierra Club. Pinchot actually coined the term 'conservation ethics', while Muir used the term **preservation** to distance himself from the environmental approach favoured by Pinchot.

The proponents of *conservationism*, like Pinchot, consider that humans should actively intervene to manage the environment in a sustainable manner. For example, some forestry techniques can maintain a certain degree of biological diversity while helping to ensure the regular renewal of forestry resources. On a larger scale, geoengineering techniques (see Box 1.6), such as catalysing intensive plankton production at the ocean surface, can serve to capture greenhouse gases and lessen the impacts of climate change.

In contrast, the supporters of *preservationism*, such as John Muir, consider that humans are more likely to exacerbate environmental problems by interfering. Preservationists perceive humans as the main threat to the environment, even if they are well intentioned and care for the environment. Preservationists consider natural destructive processes like epidemics and forest fires, that humans try to prevent, as regenerative episodes that should not necessarily be prevented. According to preservationists, the best way to achieve environmental goals is to minimize any human interference with natural processes.

This ongoing debate between conservationists and preservationists has lasted over a century (see Box 2.4; Epstein 2006; Robinson 2004; Steel et al. 1990). Groups of hunters, fishermen, and farmers were the first to defend the conservationist view to maintain stocks of natural resources. In contrast, hikers' associations were among the first to campaign for a preservationist approach that would allow them to appreciate natural beauty in its wild state. The Sierra Club in the United States and the Royal Society for the Protection of Birds in the United Kingdom are both preservationist **non-governmental organizations** (NGOs), founded at the end of the nineteenth century, that each have over a million members today.

Box 2.4 The global politics of whaling

The whaling debate is one of the most well-known environmental conflicts of the past century. By the mid-twentieth century, hundreds of thousands of whales were being captured each decade by industrial whaling operations, as a result of high demand for whale oil and baleen (used heavily in industrial processes as an energy source and raw material). In an effort to ensure the continuity of the whaling industry in the face of declining populations, 15 nations signed the International Convention for the Regulation of Whaling in 1946, and under this Convention created the International Whaling Commission. The Commission was designed to set limits on the number of whales that could be captured.

Although the International Whaling Commission emerged in its early years as a conservationist **regime**, over time it became more preservationist in its approach. Between 1946 and the early 1960s the Commission was characterized as a 'whalers' club', whose policies served the short-term economic interests of industrial whaling companies and their respective countries. By the 1970s, the anti-whaling movement had begun to emerge amid growing concern about the plight of whale populations. In many countries, whales came to be seen as exceptional animals, possessing an intrinsic value, that must be

(continued...)

protected independently of whether or not the species was threatened with extinction. Many began to see whaling as a cruel and morally reprehensible practice.

Reflecting these concerns, the 1972 Stockholm Conference on the Human Environment adopted a resolution that recommended a ten-year moratorium on commercial whaling. Non-whaling and anti-whaling states began to join the International Whaling Commission after it repeatedly failed to pass a moratorium, more than doubling it in size from its 15 original signatories to 33 members. Environmental NGOs, in particular Greenpeace, paid the membership fees for a number of anti-whaling developing countries to join the International Whaling Commission. The United States also used economic incentives to encourage like-minded states to join the International Whaling Commission. With this growth, the International Whaling Commission could now secure a three-quarters majority in support of a ten-year moratorium on commercial whaling, which passed in 1982.

Despite the moratorium on commercial whaling, three general exemptions allow International Whaling Commission members to engage in whaling: *indigenous whaling*, *scientific purposes*, and '*under objection*'. *Indigenous subsistence whaling* is permitted under the moratorium, meaning that indigenous communities can continue to hunt if whales provide for their basic needs and have been central to their livelihoods. Countries can also issue *scientific whaling permits*, which allow whales to be harvested for the purposes of scientific research. Finally, whaling can be undertaken '*under objection*', meaning that International Whaling Commission members that have filed objections to the moratorium can continue to engage in whaling. Currently, only Norway and Iceland catch whales under this exemption.

Japan's position on whaling highlights the tension between protection of endangered species and preservation of cultural practices. Japan has long argued that whaling is an important aspect of traditional Japanese culture, and therefore Japan should be allowed to conduct its traditional cultural practices. In parallel to these cultural claims, Japan has been whaling under the scientific research exemption since 1986. Further, Miller and Dolsak (2007) have shown that Japan uses its bilateral aid programme to encourage developing countries that receive this aid to vote in favour of pro-whaling interests. Arguing that far more whales are taken annually than are needed for scientific purposes, environmental groups and some governments dispute Japan's scientific exemption, and assert that this is simply a disguise for commercial whaling. These tensions have been the cause of battles between whalers and activists, with activists sinking whaling ships in ports and deliberately running into whalers' boats at sea. Two of the most well-known anti-whaling activist organizations are Greenpeace and Sea Shepherd Conservation Society.

Some, including the pro-whaling countries and members of the Scientific Committee of the International Whaling Commission, argue that the moratorium should be lifted and replaced with scientifically derived quotas for sustainable use, including for commercial whaling. Importantly, because some species of whales, such as the grey whale, are not in danger of extinction, some pro-whaling countries argue that catch limits should be provided for them, although certain populations of non-threatened species may still be endangered. Nevertheless, in 2018 the International Whaling Commission passed the Florianópolis Declaration, which affirmed the moratorium on commercial use, despite strong objections from pro-whaling nations. In reaction, Japan announced that it is withdrawing from the International Whaling Commission and it is expected to resume commercial whaling.

Sources: Andresen 2008; Blok 2008; Epstein 2008; Hirata 2005; Hurd 2012; Miller and Dolsak 2007; Singleton 2016.

Three waves of preservationists

Conservationist and preservationist ideas have evolved considerably over the years. The preservationist movement in particular can be divided into three major currents, which tend to overlap rather than succeed each other (Epstein 2006). The first, which emerged in the late nineteenth century and is still at the heart of contemporary environmental politics, involves preserving *natural spaces* in their wild state and strictly regulating human activities in these places. Emblematic of this first preservationist current, is the United States government's creation of a series of national parks at the end of the nineteenth and in the early twentieth century, driven partly by a romantic and nostalgic representation of nature. International instruments later helped diffuse this American **policy instrument** in other countries. For example, the 1940 Convention on Nature Protection and Wild Life Preservation in the Western Hemisphere urged its signatories to create reserves of pristine wilderness in their respective territories. The Convention defines these reserves as 'regions under public control characterized by primitive conditions of flora, fauna, transportation and habitation wherein there is no provision for the passage of motorized transportation and all commercial developments are excluded' (Article 1(4)).

The second preservationist current, which swept across the world in the 1970s, is also of American origin (Epstein 2006). However, instead of focusing on specific areas, it targeted the preservation of certain *species*. This approach underpins the 1973 Convention on International Trade in Endangered Species of Wild Fauna and Flora and the 1979 Bonn Convention on the Conservation of Migratory Species of Wild Animals. Both conventions list, in their annexes, specific species that must be preserved. The Convention on International Trade in Endangered Species regulates the trade in animals and plants, including products derived from them, such as crocodile-skin boots or shark fins. The Bonn Convention regulates migratory species, with measures that range from a strict hunting ban for the most endangered species to the recovery of populations of less endangered species.

Without a global approach to preservation, measures that target particular species may actually be futile and even disrupt the ecological balance between different populations. This situation, combined with insight from scientific advances on species interactions, led to the third current of preservationism, which focuses on entire *ecosystems* (Meyer et al. 1997). The Ramsar Convention on Wetlands of International Importance, concluded in 1971, was the first multilateral treaty that targeted a specific type of ecosystem. Its parties have to register at least one wetland area located within their territory on a common list—for example, a marsh or peat bog that is of 'international significance in terms of ecology, botany, zoology, limnology or hydrology' (Article 2). They are then required to implement development plans to preserve the site's ecological characteristics.

These three preservationist currents imprinted the International Antarctic Regime. Reflecting the first current, the 1959 Antarctic Treaty limited human activities on the continent, although security concerns in the context of the Cold War largely motivated this preservationist approach. The 1972 Convention for the Conservation of Antarctic Seals, which echoes the second preservationist current, focuses on a vulnerable and emblematic species. Lastly, the 1982 Convention on the Conservation of Antarctic Marine Living Resources favours an ecosystem approach to preservation, by protecting all marine resources living within natural thermal boundaries.

Different considerations motivate preservationist instruments, ranging from a romantic representation of wildlife that underlies the creation of the first parks, to a scientific representation that underpins the ecosystem approach. However, the desire to conserve a stock of natural resources for future exploitation is not one of these motivations. Preservationists from all three currents tend to ignore social and economic activities, which is the primary reason why conservationists criticize them.

The new generation of conservationists

Over the past century, the conservationist movement has also changed considerably. It is no longer run exclusively, or even mainly, by hunters, fishermen, and farmers worried about the continuing viability of their activities. The new standard-bearers of the conservationist movement are now developing countries and NGOs that are sensitive to their concerns. In their view, environmental protection should promote the sustainable use of natural resources and go hand in hand with development strategies.

This new generation of conservationists sometimes criticizes preservationists as being a by-product of colonialism. All too often, environmental policies devised in high-income countries for developing countries involve measures to protect animal and plant species to the detriment of local populations, who live by the use of these resources, and in some cases have done so for centuries. Local communities have been displaced from their ancestral land to create natural parks, from which human populations are excluded. Although this practice is highly controversial, it has not ended with decolonization. In the 2000s, hundreds of people were displaced from the Nechisar National Park in Ethiopia (Adams and Hutton 2007; Cernea and Schmidt-Soltau 2006). This type of preservationist policy fails to alleviate the precarious living conditions that local populations have to cope with (Duffy et al. 2019; Holmes 2012; Luke 1997).

The International Union for Conservation of Nature is actively striving to establish and diffuse a revised conservationist approach. Even before the publication of the Brundtland Report in 1987, the International Union for Conservation of Nature was already using the concept of **sustainable development** to defend the idea that economic development can be compatible with environmental protection (International Union for Conservation of Nature 1980). The organization is working closely with several governments and businesses to improve the sustainability of their policies and practices. It presents ecotourism and environmental certification, for example, as instruments that combine economic development and environmental protection.

The 1992 Convention on Biological Diversity endorses the revised conservationism promoted by the International Union for Conservation of Nature. Far from excluding local populations, the Convention explicitly recognizes that the 'knowledge, innovations and practices of indigenous and local communities [are] relevant for the conservation and sustainable use of biological diversity' (Article 8j). It urges signatory countries to preserve and maintain the knowledge, innovations, and practices of these communities. In addition, the Convention uses **market mechanisms** to create incentives for conservation. Its signatories must take measures to ensure that users of genetic resources, such as biotech companies, share their research findings and the benefits derived from the commercial use of the genetic resources with the country that provided the resources (Article 15). Thus, the Convention on Biological Diversity does not set human activities against environmental protection. Instead, it reconciles the two, by creating a synergy between the social, economic, and environmental objectives of sustainable development.

Since the adoption of the Convention on Biological Diversity, conservationist ideas have gained influence to the point of overturning some of the earlier preservationist instruments (Holmes 2011). The case of African elephants clearly illustrates this shift (Stiles 2004). In 1989, with the rapid decline in African elephant populations, the parties to the Convention on

International Trade in Endangered Species decided to add the species to appendix 1, which lists the species that are subject to a trade ban. However, several southern African countries oppose this preservationist decision. In their view, the elephant populations in southern Africa are less threatened than those in central Africa. Sustainable management simultaneously guarantees species conservation and the maintenance of hunting practices. Southern African countries claim that controlled hunting is actually necessary to ensure that an increase in elephant numbers does not put too much pressure on their ecosystem. Otherwise, local farmers might cull elephants to protect their harvests. In addition, the regulated trade in ivory would guarantee incomes that could then be reinvested in conservation efforts. The parties to the Convention on International Trade in Endangered Species are sensitive to these arguments. They have occasionally authorized southern African countries to sell a set quantity of stockpiled ivory from legal government-owned stocks, to a pre-identified international buyer. For example, in 1997 Namibia, Botswana, and Zimbabwe were authorized to sell 50 tonnes of stockpiled ivory to Japan, raising US$5 million for elephant conservation. A similar one-off sale in 2008 to China and Japan raised more than US$15 million for elephant conservation. Although the impacts of these sales on elephant poaching are unclear (Bulte et al. 2007), southern African countries are now making the case for minimizing international restrictions on the ivory trade. The debate between preservationists and conservationists is by no means over.

2.4 Does economic growth help or harm environmental protection?

Neo-Malthusian theories

Two opposing causal beliefs, *neo-Malthusian* and *cornucopian* theories, suggest different relationships between economic growth and environmental degradation. It is important to note that most authors described here as neo-Malthusian do not actually acknowledge that they are the intellectual successors of Thomas Malthus. Similarly, those described as cornucopians do not actually perceive nature as a horn of plenty (known as a *cornucopia* in classical mythology). In fact, 'neo-Malthusians' and 'cornucopians' are simplistic labels, often used by their opponents with a pejorative connotation to discredit them as oversimplistic. However, understanding these caricatures is useful for grappling with the conflicts that shape public debates over natural resources (Bernstein 2001; Clapp and Dauvergne 2011; Dryzek 2005).

In his book *An Essay on the Principle of Population*, the British economist Thomas Malthus (1766–1834) examined the relationship between the availability of agricultural resources and demographic growth. He observed that agricultural production increases at an arithmetic rate (1, 2, 3, 4, etc.), whereas demographic growth increases at a geometric rate (2, 4, 8, 16, etc.). Malthus believed that if this demographic growth is not deliberately slowed down, it will trigger self-regulating mechanisms, such as wars, famines, and epidemics, which will restore a certain equilibrium between resource availability and population size. To avoid these catastrophic scenarios, Malthus proposed different measures to reduce population growth, such as delaying marriage. This perspective resurfaced in the 1960s, with the spread of environmental concerns and the rapid population growth in developing countries.

However, this neo-**Malthusianism** was methodologically more sophisticated than the origi-nal work of Malthus, thanks to the advent of the first computers, which made it possible to develop more complex models.

The common trend between Malthus and neo-Malthusians is the shared assumption that planet earth is a finite system with limited natural resources. The earth's system relies en-tirely on its internal dynamics. It is on its own, like a lone vessel on the high seas or a shuttle launched into space. There are no external inputs, apart from solar radiation. To guarantee the system's durability, the earth's internal dynamics must maintain certain equilibria, includ-ing a balance between resource consumption and regeneration, and a balance between the emission and absorption of pollution. According to neo-Malthusians, these balances deter-mine the earth's **carrying capacity**: in other words, the maximum pressures that the planet can bear while safeguarding its durability.

Most neo-Malthusians believe that humanity has already upset the earth's natural equilib-ria and exceeded its carrying capacity. With its dual demographic and economic growth, hu-manity has now ceased to live on the regenerative fruits that nature provides and has begun to drain its natural capital (Hawken et al. 2013). The quantity of resources consumed exceeds the quantity of resources regenerated. Likewise, the quantity of pollution emitted exceeds the quantity of pollution absorbed. As a result, humanity is drawing perilously close to a point of no return. If we fail to adopt sweeping changes soon, there will be no turning back. The economic, health, social, and environmental subsystems are in danger of collapse. Lengthy recessions, epidemics, conflicts, and natural disasters could potentially restore a new equi-librium to the planetary system after several millennia, but at the expense of life expectancy and quality of life, which are likely to be substantially reduced. The new equilibrium may even threaten humanity's very survival.

The biologist Paul Ehrlich, from Stanford University, is one of the leading authors in this Malthusian resurgence. In 1968, when the world was in the grip of the Cold War, living in constant fear of the atomic bomb (the A-bomb) and the hydrogen bomb (H-bomb), Ehrlich published *The Population Bomb*, in which he presented demographic growth as the primary threat to humanity. According to Ehrlich, resources would soon be insufficient to satisfy the requirements of all human beings. In addition, he claimed that the environmental degrada-tion associated with every additional individual would increase along with population size. Based on this premise, Ehrlich envisioned future scenarios suggesting a rapid depletion of resources in the 1980s and a sharp decline in life expectancy before the end of the twentieth century. To mitigate these disasters, Ehrlich was in favour of vigorous birth control policies, particularly in developing countries.

The biologist Garrett Hardin (1974) also blamed developing countries and their lack of demographic control for environmental problems. He was opposed to international food aid donations, even during famines or natural disasters, because he thought prohibiting aid would encourage governments in developing countries to implement restrictive birth control policies. According to Hardin, aid makes governments in overpopulated coun-tries believe that food resources are unlimited, which leads to dangerously high fertility rates.

These extreme views have obviously been harshly criticized for being neocolonial and rac-ist (Connelly 2009; Sasser 2014). Ehrlich and Hardin blamed the world's poorest populations, those who actually pollute the least per capita and do not have easy access to voluntary birth control. As biologists, they perceived poor women in developing countries as distant popula-tions that should be controlled from the United States, rather than individual human beings who should be free to control their own bodies.

However, demographic growth is not the neo-Malthusians' only concern. They are also worried about economic growth. In 1972, the **Club of Rome**, a group of business executives, policy leaders, and scientists concerned by the effects of economic growth, published *The Limits to Growth* report. The Club of Rome did not actually write the report; it commissioned a team from the Massachusetts Institute of Technology, which had access to the computer tools required for complex modelling (Meadows et al. 1972). The report focused on the inter-actions between certain variables, including agricultural production, technological advances, life expectancy, industrial production, and the emission of pollutants. Past trends for each of these variables and their interactions informed several scenarios. Some of the scenarios deemed likely predicted major shortages of raw materials, a sharp population decline, and a marked deterioration in living conditions in the coming decades.

Much like *The Population Bomb* before it, *The Limits to Growth* had a resounding impact in the 1970s and sparked numerous debates around the world on the desirability of growth. Some analysts argued in favour of a stationary state economy that distributes its wealth more fairly but does not grow any more (Daly and Cobb 1994). Others evoked the downsizing of production and consumption as a means of avoiding disasters. Such de-growth might create greater unemployment and poverty, but it would offer more leisure time and family time, and, more fundamentally, align our activities with the earth's carrying capacity.

In the US, Jimmy Carter's administration commissioned a similar study and published the report *Global 2000* in 1980. The report's conclusions were just as pessimistic as *The Limits to Growth*: 'If present trends continue, the world in 2000 will be more crowded, more polluted, less stable ecologically, and more vulnerable to disruption than the world we live in now. [. . .] Despite greater material output, the world's people will be poorer in many ways than they are today' (Barney 1980: 1). However, a few months after the report was published, the Reagan administration moved into the White House and ignored it completely.

Neo-Malthusian assumptions are still present in international debates on environ-mental protection (Bührs 2009). They form, among other things, the basis of the notion of **ecological footprint** that was developed in the 1990s (Rees and Wackernagel 1994). The ecological footprint is a quantitative measure of environmental impact, generally ex-pressed as a number of hectares per year. The ecological footprint of an individual, a good, or a nation can be measured. The ecological footprint of an individual, for example, refers to the amount of land required to support that individual's lifestyle through the goods consumed and the pollution generated (see Figure 2.2). Since the ecological footprint is measured in land units, it conveys more clearly the idea that available resources are limited than if it was expressed in terms of money or tonnes of pollution. For example, the ecological footprint of the entire human population exceeds the amount of land avail-able on earth. In other words, the global population would need more than one earth to sustain its current level of consumption and pollution in the long term. NGOs frequently use this concept to condemn unsustainable lifestyles, especially in developed economies (Wackernagel et al. 2002). Although measures of the ecological footprint lack methodo-logical precision, they are frequently used in public debates for education and awareness purposes (Turner 2014).

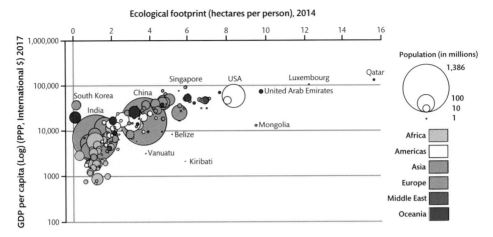

Figure 2.2 Ecological footprint and per capita GDP

Source data from: World Bank; Global Footprint Network

Critics of neo-Malthusianism

Neo-Malthusian theories are criticized on several grounds. At the empirical level, several of the catastrophic scenarios and predictions have proven to be mistaken. Famine has become rarer over time, even though the world's population has more than doubled since the publication of *The Population Bomb* in 1968. The population in developed countries has stabilized and developing countries appear to be experiencing an accelerated demographic transition. In parallel, new agricultural techniques, the increase in the area of arable land, and new food conservation methods have made a global food shortage very unlikely. Catastrophic neo-Malthusian predictions that have not materialized are sometimes used a posteriori to discredit neo-Malthusian theories overall (Simon and Kahn 1984).

Even the frequent predictions—which appear both logical and cautious—about the depletion of oil reserves have proven to be mistaken. Following the work conducted by Marion King Hubbert in the 1950s, a number of scholars think that oil production will follow a bell curve (Figure 2.3). Once the peak is reached, production will start to fall and the price will rise constantly as the reserves are depleted. However, the discovery of new oil fields, lower extraction costs, and the development of new techniques and technologies to enable access to new territories have belied the predictions of an imminent peak in production, which have been repeated for decades.

To counter these empirical criticisms, certain neo-Malthusians maintain that the failure of some past predictions does not necessarily mean that their concerns for the future are misplaced. Models are now more sophisticated and more accurate. The technological advances may simply have delayed the moment when we go beyond the point of equilibrium, and the expected disasters may occur sooner or later (Turner 2008).

Nevertheless, over and above the question of empirical accuracy, criticisms remain at the theoretical level. In particular, criticism has been levelled at the idea that feedback loops could generate vicious cycles and draw the planet into a spiral of systemic collapse.

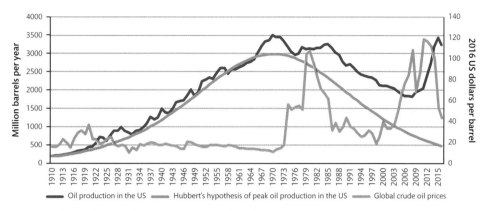

Figure 2.3 Oil production, oil price, and forecasts 1910–2016

Source data from: US Energy Information Administration; BP. Reproduced with permission from Cavallo, A.J. Hubbert's petroleum production model: an evaluation and implications for World Oil Production Forecasts. *Nat Resour Res*, 13: 211. Copyright © 2004, International Association for Mathematical Geology. https://doi.org/10.1007/s11053-004-0129-2

On the contrary, several self-regulating mechanisms, embedded in social and economic institutions, could keep the system in place. For example, neo-Malthusians sometimes imagine that economic growth drives demographic growth and vice versa, in a vicious cycle that contributes to environmental destruction. However, several studies have observed the opposite relationship: over time, economic growth encourages a drop rather than a rise in fertility rates, and therefore eases the demographic pressure on the environment.

The most damaging criticisms of neo-Malthusian theories are perhaps of an ethical and political order. Voluntary measures to limit birth rate and consumption are insufficient, on their own, to reverse the trends condemned by neo-Malthusians. To bring about a demographic downturn and production decline, political authorities would have to intervene with strong coercive measures. This would be to the detriment of the people's will and democratic processes. It is difficult to imagine a government being elected democratically on an electoral platform advocating mandatory birth control and a programmed recession. Such policies would almost certainly face strong resistance, bringing together a heterogeneous alliance of NGOs defending the right to development, pro-life religious movements, businesses defending the right to trade, unions defending workers' incomes, and feminist organizations defending the right of women to control their own fertility. Therefore, neo-Malthusianism is often criticized for potentially being an elitist anti-democratic movement (Dryzek 2005). Most neo-Malthusian policy prescriptions have gradually receded in the face of these criticisms. Coercive birth control methods, especially, are no longer promoted with the same urgency as in the 1970s.

Cornucopian theories

In contrast to neo-Malthusian theory, *cornucopian theories* maintain that humanity is not a destabilizing population that must be managed, but an exceptional species with an extraordinary capacity to innovate. This ability to innovate is capable of constantly pushing back the earth's 'carrying capacity'. It weakens the neo-Malthusian idea that all resources are limited. To quote Julian

Simon, a prominent cornucopian economist, the capacity to innovate is the 'ultimate resource', which makes every other resource virtually unlimited as well (Simon 1981).

Innovation is particularly useful for developing substitute products when natural resources are depleted or when a specific form of pollution becomes intolerable. For example, in order to move around, humans went from the horse to the steam engine, then on to the combustion engine and electric batteries. Each of these sources of energy uses different natural resources and generates different forms of pollution. The shift from animal traction to the engine reduced the amount of droppings in the street, but increased CO_2 emissions. The move to renewable energies will reduce atmospheric emissions, but increase the pressure on the mineral resources required to make batteries. Given that types of pollution evolve, worrying about the intensive extraction of a specific natural resource or the emission of a specific type of pollution is misplaced—they are both transient. The only stable indicator of the future prospects for humanity is life expectancy, which is increasing constantly thanks in large part to innovation in various fields of technology (Barnett and Morse 1967; Simon 1984; Simon and Kahn 1984).

Humans' ability to innovate also means that they can develop less polluting and more sustainable methods of production and consumption (see Box 2.5). They can even innovate on an institutional and political level to improve the relationships between humanity and its environment. This is the project of **ecological modernization** (Hajer 1995; Mol 2001). As a policy approach as well as a discourse, ecological modernization emerged in the 1980s in Germany. It argues that economic development and environmental protection can potentially go hand in hand. Societies can achieve these two objectives simultaneously by radically changing their old industrial structures for structures that better favour innovation in all aspects of life, including technologies, management, political organizations, and lifestyle.

From this perspective, deliberately slowing down demographic growth makes no sense. Humans are not just mouths to feed and emitters of pollution. They are also beings with the capacity to innovate. Each additional human being on the planet increases humanity's capacity to innovate. Similarly, it would be foolish to slow down growth in production. A constant rise in income leads to greater investment in research and development, which means that technical solutions can be found and diffused on a planetary scale to solve humanity's problems (Simon and Kahn 1984).

Box 2.5 Scarcity or abundance? A wager between Julian Simon and Paul Ehrlich

In 1980, two academics placed a bet over the projected price of five commodities over a ten-year period: chromium, copper, nickel, tin, and tungsten. Biologist Paul Ehrlich believed that resource pressures resulting from a growing population would drive up the prices of these metals over the decade, while economist Julian Simon held that economic forces—including technological innovation—would result in lower prices. Ultimately, Ehrlich would lose the bet (and $576.07); the prices of all five commodities fell between 1980 and 1990. This wager was a microcosm of a much larger debate over whether, as human population and resource consumption increased alongside technological advancement, humans would be faced with conditions of resource scarcity, on one hand, or material abundance, on the other.

Paul Ehrlich's famous book *The Population Bomb*, published in 1968, predicts that hundreds of millions of people will starve to death because, according to Ehrlich, the earth's growing population will outstrip the available food supply. Ehrlich's views on this topic also led him to found the organization Zero Population Growth, which advocated population control. Ehrlich was thrust into the public spotlight in 1970 when, on *The Tonight Show* with Johnny Carson, Ehrlich confidently proclaimed that it was 'already too late to avoid famines that would kill millions' (Sabin 2013: 2). By contrast, Julian Simon, who was then a little known economist, believed that we should be 'thrilled' about population growth: '[h]uman beings are not just more mouths to feed, but are productive and inventive minds that help find creative solutions to man's problems, thus leaving us better off over the long run' (Simon 1981: 415). Inspired by proponents of laissez faire capitalism at the University of Chicago, Simon moreover believed that markets would react to the depletion of natural resources by spurring the innovation and production of substitutes and by moderating demand.

Although Simon ultimately won the bet, the implications of this wager remain opaque. The price of the five metal commodities is merely a small piece of a larger puzzle involving population, economic growth, consumption, environmental degradation, technology, and natural resources. Yet these debates over scarcity and abundance continue to shape ongoing discussion over environmental problems, including climate change and access to energy. Ehrlich's proposal for state-mandated population control and Simon's preference for a reliance on market forces are not the only options available for environmental governance. We might ask, therefore, whether there are more nuanced positions, between the optimistic faith of cornucopians in technology and markets, on the one hand, and the Malthusians' apocalyptic premonitions of ecological catastrophe, on the other.

Sources: Aligica 2009; Ehrlich 1968; Sabin 2013; Simon 1981; Simon and Kahn 1984.

The environmental Kuznets curve

Proponents of the cornucopian theory often express the relationship between increases in revenue and improved environmental conditions using the **environmental Kuznets curve**. Simon Kuznets, an economist, was not actually interested in the question of environmental degradation. However, Gene Grossman and Alan Krueger (1995) argue that the inverted U-shaped curve that Kuznets drew in the 1950s to illustrate the relationship between per capita income and the equality of income distribution can also be applied to environmental degradation (see Figure 2.4). An increase in per capita income might cause greater environmental degradation initially, but after per capita income reaches a certain level, environmental degradation begins to decrease. This is because when income reaches a certain threshold, the population has satisfied its immediate needs, such as sanitation and food provision, and can focus on environmental protection. People can invest financial and technological means to reduce pollution and gear their economy towards less polluting activities, such as services and advanced technology rather than industry and the extraction of raw materials. From this point of view, allowing developing countries to focus on economic development, rather than environmental protection, will nonetheless yield environmental benefits in the longer term. Ultimately, according to the environmental Kuznets curve, an increase in per capita income will yield environmental protection.

For example, as Figure 2.5 suggests, there is an environmental Kuznets curve for renewable energy consumption: poor populations in Nepal and Nigeria use traditional biomass for most of their energy, while rich populations in Norway, Iceland, and Sweden also rely on renewable energy sources, including sunlight, wind, rivers, and geothermal heat. Populations with an average income level, such as Turkey, Russia, and Mexico, are more likely to use non-renewable sources for 80 per cent of their energy.

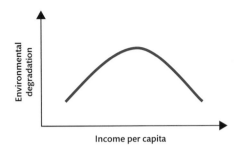

Figure 2.4 The environmental Kuznets curve

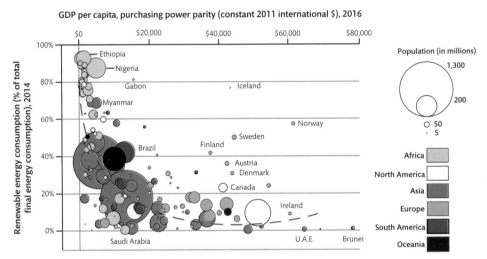

Figure 2.5 Renewable energy as a function of GDP per capita

Source data from: World Bank—World Development Indicators

The environmental Kuznets curve is fiercely debated and critiqued in the literature (Arrow et al. 1995; Dinda 2004; Stern 2004). For example, some developing countries do not wait to reach a high per capita income before investing in environmental protection and adopting environmental norms, which are sometimes as strict (or more so) as those in force in developed countries. Moreover, part of the reason that richer countries appear to emit less pollution is because their polluting activities have simply been moved to other regions. High-income populations do not stop consuming products that are polluting to manufacture; they import them from abroad, instead of actually producing them domestically (Suri and Chapman 1998). Overall, the environmental Kuznets curve is mainly valid for certain forms of pollution, which have an immediate and local impact, like air quality in urban areas and domestic waste treatment. In most other cases, notably the emission of greenhouse gases, environmental degradation increases with economic development (de Bruyn and Opschoor 1997). An environmental Kuznets curve does appear for renewable energy as Figure 2.5 suggests, but this is because renewable energy includes traditional biomass, such as the direct combustion of wood and charcoal, which is not a healthy or environmentally friendly energy source.

Critics of cornucopianism

Several authors, including neo-Malthusians, do not consider economic growth or techno-logical development to be viable solutions for environmental problems. Both contribute to environmental degradation, by encouraging the extraction of natural resources and the emis-sion of pollutants. The market equilibrium between supply and demand, as understood by classical economics, bears no relation to the planet's natural balances. Industrial capitalism recognizes the value of private property as capital, but it neglects the value of natural capital in its accounting principles (Hawken et al. 2013; Porritt 2012). More fundamentally, produc-tion costs cannot fully internalize the damage caused by producing a good or providing a service—also known as environmental externalities—because some of this damage is irrevers-ible. Economic growth and technological development are not substitutes for natural capital (Barkin 2006; Wackernagel et al. 2002).

The field of ecological economics builds on this assumption that the natural capital should be maintained. Unlike environmental economics, which aims at a weak form of sustainabil-ity and the preservation of the current economic system, ecological economics strives for a strong form of sustainability and the preservation of the natural capital (Neumayer 2003). Ecological economics does not consider nature as a simple input for the economic system. It also studies the economic system's effects on nature. One of the founders of this field, Nicholas Georgescu-Roegen, criticizes classical economic theories for being based on sim-plistic mechanical principles that are comparable to classical Newtonian physics. By draw-ing from the laws of thermodynamic physics, Georgescu-Roegen claims that resources are not created, but simply transformed, and that the process of transformation reduces the resources' usefulness: 'Economists are fond of saying that we cannot get something for noth-ing. The **Entropy** Law teaches us that the rule of biological life and, in man's case, of its eco-nomic continuation is far harsher. In entropy terms, the cost of any biological or economic enterprise is always greater than the product. In entropy terms, any such activity necessarily results in a deficit' (1993: 80).

However, this systemic representation, which underlines the earth's limits and predicts the system's imminent collapse, has few supporters in international institutions. On the contrary, the prevailing assumptions in policy circles reflect the most optimistic vision, which is based on economic growth and technological development. For example, the countries that signed the 2012 declaration of the UN Conference on Sustainable Development agreed to 'promote investment in science, innovation and technology for sustainable development' and men-tioned 'the role of foreign direct investment, international trade and international coopera-tion in the transfer of environmentally sound technologies' (paragraph 271). The causal belief that progress is propelled by technological advancement and economic growth is deeply rooted in the modern world view (Pammett 2015).

2.5 Intragenerational versus intergenerational equity

The impacts and responsibilities associated with environmental protection are unevenly distributed. In this respect, climate change is one of the most striking examples (Moellendorf 2009; Nicholson and Chong 2011; Vanderheiden 2008). The impacts of climate change are greater on poorer populations, which produce the least greenhouse gas emissions; they are also the most vulnerable to climate change impacts because they have the least capacity to adapt to them.

To some extent, international instruments can help to rebalance these inequities. They can impose higher costs on the most advantaged populations and transfer resources to the most disadvantaged. Thus, international negotiations raise fundamental normative questions that must be resolved in the name of environmental justice. However, enforcing equitable and just solutions is not that simple. Ethical principles are sometimes controversial and cause genuine moral dilemmas.

Intergenerational equity

Several important debates have emerged surrounding the equity between generations (*intergenerational equity*). According to some political actors, fairness requires that international instruments for climate change take account of the historic emissions produced by previous generations (Shue 1999). Societies that were built, historically, by polluting should pay a greater share of the costs of alleviating and adapting to climate change, for the benefit of the most vulnerable societies (Moore 2012). For example, the UK should pay the costs associated with the pollution emitted since the Industrial Revolution. This is the position held by the Bolivarian Alliance for the Peoples of Our America (ALBA), which includes Venezuela, Cuba, Bolivia, and Ecuador (Audet 2013). It is also the view frequently reported in news media outlets from developing countries (Pandey and Kurian 2017).

However, the impact of greenhouse gas emissions on the climate was unknown in the nineteenth century. In fact, it remained unclear until the 1990s. The industrialists who emitted greenhouse gases during the Industrial Revolution had no way of knowing that they were already contributing to climate change. Ignorance is not necessarily a valid excuse for failing to redress an unfair situation, however. It helps explain certain behaviour, but does not remove the moral responsibility for the harm caused, even if involuntarily. Supporters of historical cost accounting for greenhouse gases maintain that the aim is not to punish polluters, who were unaware of the consequences of their actions, but to ensure that they assume their liability for a problem they helped to create (Page 2011).

Some philosophers are opposed to using historical cost accounting to calculate the rights and obligations of each country. In their view, it is a violation of the **'polluter pays' principle** (Caney 2005). According to this principle, polluters should be held responsible for their own emissions, but not necessarily for those of their ancestors. Environmental liability is not inherited from one generation to the next. To reconcile historical cost accounting with the polluter pays principle, the entities considered as the polluters should not be mortal individuals, but relatively permanent entities, such as states or businesses. A state could be held responsible for actions that occurred over a century ago. However, considering states as units with environmental rights and obligations is a tenuous idea (Grubb et al. 1992; Harris et al. 2013; Rao 2014).

The demographic and economic characteristics of states are so heterogeneous that recognizing their rights over the atmosphere is likely to cause unfair situations, both between states and between individuals within the same state. Is it fair that multimillionaires living in poor countries do not contribute financially to the reduction of greenhouse gases, whereas all taxpayers in rich countries, including the poorest, contribute?

Some proponents of historical cost accounting, such as Henry Shue (1999), reject the polluter pays principle in preference for the 'beneficiary pays' principle. According to Shue, the populations that have inherited economic development from past generations (development that caused greenhouse gas emissions) should pay the price because they are the main beneficiaries. But this argument is also tenuous. The benefits of economic development associated with greenhouse gas emissions are not limited geographically. Some of the twentieth century's scientific and technological developments, such as medical advances, benefit the whole of humanity and contribute to improving living conditions in all countries, even in countries that did not produce large quantities of greenhouse gases. Therefore, it is difficult to calculate the share of benefits induced by historic greenhouse gas emissions on a per country basis.

It is equally difficult to take into account the interests of future generations, particularly in the long term (Gardiner 2006). Humans are worried about the fate of their children and grandchildren, and it is possible to identify broad trends that are likely to mark their lives. However, it is difficult to empathize with people that will be on earth in over a century. Not only are they distant from us, but their identity is completely unknown. It is hard to predict the world that they will be living in, and it is equally hard to guess at their preferences and their risk tolerance. They would most likely prefer a stable climate, but how far would they be willing to sacrifice their level of economic development to achieve this objective? And would they be comfortable with us experimenting with climate engineering techniques that can reduce global warming but have other unintended consequences for the earth's systems (McKinnon 2018)?

Nonetheless, in the interest of future generations, the Stern Review on the economics of climate change suggests investing rapidly and massively to reduce greenhouse gas emissions (Stern 2007). This lengthy report was commissioned by the British government and written by the economist Nicholas Stern. It concludes that it will be more profitable to invest to reduce greenhouse gas emissions, even if this leads to a slight drop in world production in the short term (estimated at 1 per cent), than to pay the high costs brought about by climate change, which is likely to cause a sharp and lasting decline in the value of world production (up to 20 per cent).

To reach this conclusion, Stern estimates the discount rate to be 1.4 per cent. The discount rate is the ratio between the value attributed to the current consumption of a resource and the value attributed to its future consumption. If a resource remains constant, its current consumption always seems more attractive than its future consumption. People are willing to make sacrifices and invest for the future only when the value of a resource increases with time. Some critics claim that Stern underestimates the discount rate and artificially increases the profitability of environmental investments. If a higher discount rate is applied, similar to interest rates used in financial markets, the profitability of investing in the reduction of greenhouse gas emissions would be unclear. With a high discount rate, it might be more attractive to enjoy the benefits of emitting greenhouse gases now, even if the long-term costs of these emissions are high. In Stern's (2010) view, applying a high discount rate would be unfair because it would deny the interests of future generations with regard to a relatively stable climate. Some analysts go even further and suggest that the discount rate should be zero because future generations, however distant they may be, have the same right to a stable climate as today's generations (Barkin 2006).

Intragenerational equity

Some critics contrast the principle of intergenerational equity with the principle of *intra-generational equity*. Is it fair to invest large sums of money to protect the interests of future generations, when a share of the present population is suffering from a lack of investment in their livelihoods now? Arguably, we have a greater responsibility towards people alive today than we have towards future generations, because they can act reciprocally and are part of our moral community. Bjørn Lomborg makes a similar argument in his controversial book *The Skeptical Environmentalist* (2001). In his view, it would be wiser for public authorities to invest their limited resources to address current problems, such as eradicating poverty, funding health research, or providing universal access to drinking water, rather than to reduce greenhouse gas emissions, because their impact on living conditions is difficult to predict.

To some extent, the existential crisis faced by members of the **Alliance of Small Island States (AOSIS)**, such as Vanuatu, the Seychelles, or Surinam, whose territories will literally disappear as sea levels rise, also highlights the importance of intragenerational equity. For small island states, the central issue in climate change negotiations is not the long-term reduction of greenhouse gas emissions or the development capacity of future generations. Rather, it is financing measures to adapt to immediate climate change. Their main concern is the **vulnerability** of today's populations. Yet international institutions governing climate change, including the 2015 Paris Agreement, are more focused on the problem of mitigation for future generations than on the problem of **adaptation** for current generations (Audet 2013; Ciplet et al. 2013; Grasso 2010; Hall and Persson 2017; Moore 2012). Developing countries see the 2013 Warsaw International Mechanism for Loss and Damage as a rare step in the right direction to address intragenerational equity. This mechanism supports research, dialogue, and actions tackling loss and damage associated with the impact of climate change in vulnerable developing countries. However, it remains modest in comparison with the resources and attention devoted to climate change mitigation.

Other developing countries underline another form of intragenerational inequity when it comes to efforts to reduce greenhouse gas emissions. Arguably, it is unfair to criticize densely populated countries, like India and China, for their combined emissions without taking their population size into account (Agarwal and Narain 1991). Although these developing countries have become major greenhouse gas emitters, their emissions on a per capita basis are still significantly lower than those of developed countries (see Figure 2.6). Therefore, instead of setting targets for reduction on a country basis, international agreements could set a per capita emission threshold. This would benefit highly populated countries, whereas Australia, Canada, and the US, where per capita emissions are particularly high, would have to radically change their economic structures.

In addition, some scholars argue that it is important to differentiate between the sources of the greenhouse gases emitted (Agarwal and Narain 1991). The carbon dioxide emissions

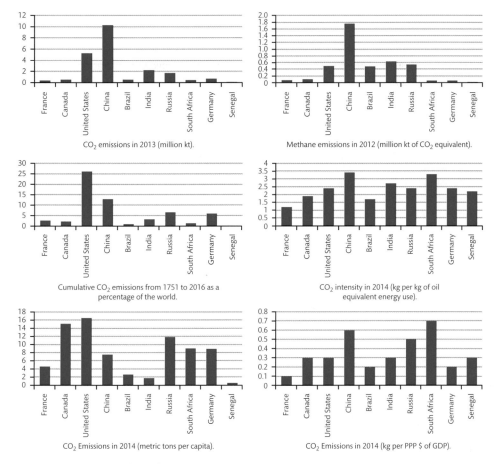

Figure 2.6 Comparison of greenhouse gas emissions

Source data from: World Bank – World Development Indicators

produced by industry or transport, primarily in developed countries, cannot be put on an equal footing with the methane emitted by livestock and rice paddies, which supply basic food for populations in developing countries. From this perspective, it would be unfair to impose the same reduction on 'survival' emissions and 'luxury' emissions.

According to Agarwal and Narain (1991), if Western NGOs and international institutions continue to confuse 'survival' emissions with 'luxury' emissions, it is because the views of vulnerable populations in developing countries are poorly represented in public debates and political decision-making bodies. These populations do not just suffer from environmental and economic injustice because they emit fewer greenhouse gases per capita and are less well equipped to cope with climate change. They are also exposed to a third form of climate injustice, namely political injustice. Some African countries, in particular, are seriously under-represented in international bodies because of financial, technical, and administrative constraints. Women and indigenous peoples from developing countries are even more under-represented. As such, their interests and concerns are not sufficiently reflected in international negotiations.

Nonetheless, some scholars have expressed reservations about prioritizing intragenerational equity at the expense of problem-solving efficiency (Kanie et al. 2010; Stadelmann et al. 2014; Victor and Coben 2005). Developing countries are among those that produce the most greenhouse gases in relation to the value of their economic production. In addition, it costs less to reduce emissions in developing countries (see Figure 2.6). A million dollars or euros invested in Africa enables the reduction of a larger quantity of greenhouse gases than the same amount invested in Europe, where the most affordable energy gains have already been achieved. From the perspective of these scholars, efficiency gains justify focusing global efforts to reduce emissions of greenhouse gases on developing countries' emissions, especially if these reductions are financed by developed countries.

There is also great resistance in Western countries to the idea of reducing per capita emissions to a level similar to that in developing countries, because doing so would shake their economic and social foundations. Bringing the emissions produced by the average American down to the level of the average Indian would require massive changes in lifestyle choices in the United States. Some scholars have argued that for certain segments of the American population, the disruption created by mitigation policies could possibly be as devastating in socio-economic terms as climate change itself (Baer et al. 2010; Singer 2002). From this perspective, restoring intragenerational equity could only be achieved at the expense of other principles, such as democratic decision-making and self-determination.

The 1992 United Nations Framework Convention on Climate Change and its 1998 Kyoto Protocol attempt to reconcile intergenerational equity with intragenerational equity (Paavola and Adger 2006). The Convention actually states that it 'is the Parties' responsibility to preserve the climate system in the interests of present and future generations, on the basis of equality and according to their common but differentiated responsibilities and their respective capacities' (Article 3.1). Although the **Framework Convention** mentions present and future generations, it omits the historic emissions of past generations. Instead, it aims to reduce carbon dioxide emissions compared to 1990 levels, which implies that historic emissions are not taken into account. However, the Framework Convention defines different country categories in its annexes, and under the Kyoto Protocol concrete emission reductions are required from developed countries but those from developing countries are made voluntary, in line with the principle of common but differentiated responsibilities. In short, the obligations imposed on different countries are defined in relation to their level of economic development.

The precise meaning of '**common but differentiated responsibility**' remains an important topic of negotiation in international climate negotiations (Bushey and Jinnah 2010; Jinnah 2016, 2017; Okereke 2008). The 2015 Paris Agreement provides that the Agreement should be 'implemented to reflect equity and the principle of common but differentiated responsibility and respective capabilities, in the light of different national circumstances' (Article 2.2). However, it does not provide specific guidance on the actual operationalization of this principle. It merely notes 'the importance for some of the concept of "climate justice" when taking action to address climate change' (preamble).

Some scholars consider that we are now in a 'post-equity era' of country-based and voluntary measures (Klinsky et al. 2017). This is based on the idea that emphasizing equity concerns could be detrimental to the effectiveness of the international climate regime. Some governments from developed countries might be willing to reduce their emissions of greenhouse gases, but only if emerging economies are also taking significant steps in this direction. Thus, the idea that developed and developing countries should be subject to different standards is doomed to be rejected by some developed country governments, and might block collective action. From this perspective, international institutions that contribute to climate change mitigation should be considered a step in the right direction, even if they are not perfectly equitable.

However, others believe that equity concerns should be at the core of global environmental governance. Otherwise, international institutions risk being perceived as illegitimate, which could negatively affect participation and **compliance**. More fundamentally, ignoring equity when addressing climate change is antithetical to the aims of climate policy, since equity towards present and future generations is a main reason for climate change mitigation in the first place. Only a shared understanding of climate justice can temper the political resistance to the economic transformations required to limit global temperature increase to 1.5°C as dictated by the Paris Agreement. From this second perspective, it is important to publicly debate equity issues with a view to building a common understanding of effort sharing (Patterson et al. 2018; Pickering et al. 2015).

Debates on equity do not only relate to negotiations on climate change. They underpin all international environmental negotiations. Should the principle of intragenerational equity guide access to genetic resources? How can radioactive waste management address the principle of intergenerational equity? Do developed countries have a 'common but differentiated responsibility' when it comes to addressing the desertification that prevails in several developing countries? These types of ethical debates on intragenerational and intergenerational equity are a central feature of international environmental policymaking and will undoubtedly remain so for years to come.

2.6 Conclusion

This chapter has presented five major debates on environmental protection: (1) universalism versus communitarianism; (2) anthropocentrism versus biocentrism; (3) conservationism versus preservationism; (4) neo-Malthusianism versus cornucopian theory; (5) and intragenerational equity versus intergenerational equity. These major debates, which are sometimes explicit, but often implicit, structure global environmental politics.

Most political actors fall in the spectrum between the extreme positions on each of these debates. As the following chapters make clear, the process of international negotiation encourages parties to amalgamate or combine ideas, rather than oppose them. In some cases, the negotiation process marginalizes extremes and encourages intermediary positions or formulas for compromise. In cases where negotiators fail to reach a clear position, they can rely on conceptual ambiguity to allow each party to interpret the outcome as they see fit.

The report by the World Commission on Environment and Development, *Our Common Future* (1987), sometimes referred to as the Brundtland Report, is a great example of compromise between different normative poles. The introduction underlines the need for common norms, but the conclusion recognizes that a 'wide variation in national legal systems and practices makes it impossible to propose an approach that would be valid everywhere' (paragraph 84). The report also recalls the numerous possible justifications for environmental protection by stating that 'utility aside, there are also moral, ethical, cultural, aesthetic, and purely scientific reasons for conserving wild beings' (paragraph 53). The chapter of the Brundtland Report devoted to biological diversity focuses as much attention on conservation approaches that are 'opportunities for development', as on approaches focusing on 'wildlife preservation' (paragraph 47). And the report explicitly recognizes the notion of ecological limits, which is core to neo-Malthusian perspectives, but also the capacity of technologies to push those limits, as proposed by cornucopians (paragraph 27). Finally, the report integrates intra- and intergenerational equity in the concept of sustainable development, defined as development 'that meets the needs of the present without compromising the ability of future generations to meet their own needs' (paragraph 27).

Making comprises between extreme positions, as the report *Our Common Future* does, can federate different parties and help to bring about a global consensus. The concept of sustainable development, in particular, unites and mobilizes different normative points of view in a common project. Its normative ambiguity constitutes its main political value (Bernstein 2001; Dryzek 2005). As shown in the following chapters, it federates divergent ideas and interests across states (Chapter 3) and **non-state actors** (Chapter 4).

Critical thinking questions

1. Provide examples of some anthropocentric and biocentric arguments for a preservationist approach to managing biodiversity loss.
2. Explain two different approaches to allocating targets for greenhouse gas emission reduction among countries. How are least-developed countries, emerging economies, and developed countries each impacted by these different approaches?
3. Is neo-Malthusianism biocentric or anthropocentric? Explain your answer.
4. In what way do some neo-Malthusian ideas conflict with the principle of intragenerational equity?
5. Does the integration of intragenerational equity into environmental policy require universal norms that are binding for all, to the detriment of cultural specificities?

 Test your knowledge and understanding further by trying this chapter's Multiple Choice Questions www.oup.com/he/morin1e

Key references

Agarwal, Anil, and Sunita Narain. 1991. 'Global Warming in an Unequal World: A Case of Environmental Colonialism'. *Earth Island Journal* 6 (2): 39–40.
This article expresses a 'non-Western view' of global climate governance and criticizes the unfair bias of some Western environmental organizations. Despite the fact that it was published even before the adoption of the United Nations Framework Convention on Climate Change in 1992, it is still relevant today and remains widely cited, as such inequalities are still sensitive.

Clapp, Jennifer, and Peter Dauvergne. 2011. *Paths to a Green World: The Political Economy of the Global Environment.* Cambridge, MA: MIT Press.
This book presents four world views of environmental changes: those of market liberals, institutionalists, bioenvironmentalists, and social greens. This typology is used to examine the complex relations between political economy and ecological change.

Dryzek, John. 2005. *The Politics of the Earth: Environmental Discourses*. Oxford: Oxford University Press.

This book analyses very clearly different discourses on environmental protection, including survivalism, prometheanism (called cornucopianism in this chapter), administrative rationalism, democratic pragmatism, economic rationalism, and ecological modernization.

Neumayer, Eric. 2003. *Weak versus Strong Sustainability: Exploring the Limits of Two Opposing Paradigms*. Cheltenham: Edward Elgar Publishing.

The distinction between weak and strong sustainability helps to uncover important tensions within the sustainable development umbrella. The central question examined by Neumayer is whether natural capital can be substituted by other forms of capital.

For additional material and resources, please visit the online resources at:
www.oup.com/he/morin1e

Chapter references

Adams, William M., and Jon Hutton. 2007. 'People, Parks and Poverty: Political Ecology and Biodiversity Conservation'. *Conservation and Society* 5 (2): 147–183.

Agarwal, Anil, and Sunita Narain. 1991. 'Global Warming in an Unequal World: A Case of Environmental Colonialism'. *Earth Island Journal* 6 (2): 39–40.

Albanese, Chiara, and John Follain. 2017. 'The Pope Wants Vatican Startups to Fix Climate Change'. *Bloomberg* website. Available at: https://www.bloomberg.com/news/articles/2017-12-19/silicon-valley-is-bringing-the-startup-hub-to-the-vatican, accessed 10 April 2018.

Albanese, Chiara, and Flavia Rotondi. 2017. 'Vatican Sees a Way Around Trump on Climate Change, Official Says'. *Bloomberg* website. Available at: https://www.bloomberg.com/news/articles/2017-12-05/vatican-sees-way-around-trump-on-climate-change-official-says, accessed 10 April 2018.

Aligica, Paul Dragos. 2009. 'Julian Simon and the "Limits to Growth" Neo-Malthusianism'. *The Electronic Journal of Sustainable Development* 1 (3): 49–60.

Anderson, Brilé, Thomas Bernauer, and Stefano Balietti. 2017. 'Effects of Fairness Principles on Willingness to Pay for Climate Change Mitigation'. *Climatic Change* 142 (3–4): 447–461.

Andresen, Steinar. 2008. 'The Volatile Nature of the International Whaling Commission: Power, Institutions and Norms'. In *International Governance of Fisheries Ecosystems: Learning from the Past, Finding Solutions for the Future*, edited by Michael G. Schechter, Nancy J. Leonard, and William W. Taylor, 173–189. Bethesda, MD: American Fisheries Society.

Arrow, Kenneth, Bert Bolin, Robert Costanza, Partha Dasgupta, Carl Folke, Crawford S. Holling, Bengt-Owe Jansson, Simon Levin, Karl-Goran Mäler, Charles Perrings, and David Pimentel. 1995. 'Economic Growth, Carrying Capacity, and the Environment'. *Science* 268 (5210): 520–521.

Audet, René. 2013. 'Climate Justice and Bargaining Coalitions: A Discourse Analysis'. *International Environmental Agreements: Politics, Law and Economics* 13 (3): 369–386.

Baer, Paul, Tom Athanasiou, Sivan Kartha, and Eric Kemp-Benedict. 2010. 'Greenhouse Development Rights. A Framework for Climate Protection That is "More Fair" Than Equal Per Capita Emission Rights'. In *Climate Ethics: Essential Readings*, edited by Stephen M. Gardiner, Simon Caney, Dale Jamieson, and Henry Shue, 215–230. Oxford: Oxford University Press.

Barkin, J. Samuel. 2006. 'Discounting the Discount Rate: Ecocentrism and Environmental Economics'. *Global Environmental Politics* 6 (4): 56–72.

Barnett, Howard, and Chandler Morse. 1967. *Scarcity and Growth: The Economics of Natural Resources Availability*. Baltimore: Johns Hopkins University Press.

Barney, Gerald. O. 1980. *The Global 2000 Report to the President: Entering the 21st Century*, Volume 1. Washington, DC: United States Government Printing Office.

Bernstein, Steven F. 2001. *The Compromise of Liberal Environmentalism*. New York: Columbia University Press.

Blok, Anders. 2008. 'Contesting Global Norms: Politics of Identity in Japanese Pro-Whaling Countermobilization'. *Global Environmental Politics* 8 (2): 39–66.

Bretherton, Charlotte. 2003. 'Movements, Networks, Hierarchies: A Gender Perspective on Global Environmental Governance'. *Global Environmental Politics* 3 (2): 103–119.

Bührs, Ton. 2009. 'Environmental Space as a Basis for Legitimating Global Governance of Environmental Limits'. *Global Environmental Politics* 9 (4): 111–135.

Bulte, Erwin H., Richard Damania, and G. Cornelis Van Kooten. 2007. 'The Effects of One-Off Ivory Sales on Elephant Mortality'. *The Journal of Wildlife Management* 71 (2): 613–618.

Bushey, Douglas, and Sikina Jinnah. 2010. 'Evolving Responsibility? The Principle of Common but Differentiated Responsibility in the UNFCCC'. *Berkeley Journal of International Law, Publicist* 28 (6): 1–10.

Caney, Simon. 2005. 'Cosmopolitan Justice, Responsibility, and Global Climate Change'. *Leiden Journal of International Law* 18 (4): 747–775.

Carr, Mike. 2005. *Bioregionalism and Civil Society: Democratic Challenges to Corporate Globalism.* Vancouver: UBC Press.

Cernea, Michael M., and Kai Schmidt-Soltau. 2006. 'Poverty Risks and National Parks: Policy Issues in Conservation and Resettlement'. *World Development* 34 (10): 1808–1830.

Cervellon, Marie-Cécile. 2013. 'Conspicuous Conservation: Using Semiotics to Understand Sustainable Luxury'. *International Journal of Market Research* 55 (5): 695–717.

Chew, Sing C. 2002. 'Globalisation, Ecological Crisis, and Dark Ages'. *Global Society* 16 (4): 333–356.

Ciplet, David, J. Timmons Roberts, and Mizan Khan. 2013. 'The Politics of International Climate Adaptation Funding: Justice and Divisions in the Greenhouse'. *Global Environmental Politics* 13 (1): 49–68.

Clapp, Jennifer, and Peter Dauvergne. 2011. *Paths to a Green World: The Political Economy of the Global Environment.* Cambridge, MA: MIT Press.

Clingerman, Forrest, and Kevin O'Brien. 2014. 'Playing God: Why Religion Belongs in the Climate Engineering Debate'. *Bulletin of the Atomic Scientists* 70 (3): 27–37.

Connelly, Matthew James. 2009. *Fatal Misconception: The Struggle to Control World Population.* Cambridge, MA: Harvard University Press.

D'Eaubonne, Françoise. 1974. *Le féminisme ou la mort.* Paris: Femmes en Mouvement, P. Horay.

Daly, Herman E., and John B. Cobb. 1994. *For the Common Good: Redirecting the Economy toward Community, the Environment, and a Sustainable Future.* Boston, MA: Beacon Press.

Dankelman, Irene. 2010. *Gender and Climate Change: An Introduction.* London, Sterling: Earthscan.

De Bruyn, Sander M., and John B. Opschoor. 1997. 'Developments in the Throughput–Income Relationship: Theoretical and Empirical Observations'. *Ecological Economics* 20 (3): 255–268.

Dinda, Soumyananda. 2004. 'Environmental Kuznets Curve Hypothesis: A Survey'. *Ecological Economics* 49 (4): 431–455.

Dryzek, John. 2005. *The Politics of the Earth: Environmental Discourses.* Oxford: Oxford University Press.

Duffy, Rosaleen, Francis Massé, Emile Smidt, Esther Marijnen, Bram Büscher, Judith Verweijen et al. 2019. 'Why we must Question the Militarisation of Conservation'. *Biological Conservation* 232: 66–73.

Eckersley, Robyn. 1992. *Environmentalism and Political Theory: Toward an Ecocentric Approach.* New York: SUNY Press.

Eckersley, Robyn. 2016. 'National Identities, International Roles, and the Legitimation of Climate Leadership: Germany and Norway Compared'. *Environmental Politics* 25(1): 180–201.

Ehrlich, Paul.1968. *The Population Bomb.* New York: Sierra Club/Ballantine Books.

Eisenstadt, Todd A., and Karleen Jones West. 2017a. 'Indigenous Belief Systems, Science, and Resource Extraction: Climate Change Attitudes in Ecuador'. *Global Environmental Politics* 17 (1): 40–58.

Eisenstadt, Todd A., and Karleen Jones West. 2017b. 'Public Opinion, Vulnerability, and Living with Extraction on Ecuador's Oil Frontier: Where the Debate between Development and Environmentalism Gets Personal'. *Comparative Politics* 49 (2): 231–251.

Elliott, Lorraine. 2006. 'Cosmopolitan Environmental Harm Conventions'. *Global Society* 20 (3): 345–363.

Epstein, Charlotte. 2006. 'The Making of Global Environmental Norms: Endangered Species Protection'. *Global Environmental Politics* 6 (2): 32–54.

Epstein, Charlotte. 2008. *The Power of Words in International Relations: Birth of an Anti-Whaling Discourse.* Cambridge, MA: MIT Press.

Foreman, Dave. 2004. *Rewilding North America: A Vision for Conservation in the 21st Century.* Washington, DC: Island Press.

Fox, Warwick. 1989. 'The Deep Ecology–Ecofeminism Debate and its Parallels'. *Environmental Ethics* 11 (1): 5–25.

Fuentes-George, Kemi. 2013. 'Neoliberalism, Environmental Justice, and the Convention on Biological Diversity: How Problematizing the Commodification of Nature Affects Regime Effectiveness'. *Global Environmental Politics* 13 (4): 144–163.

Funk, Cary, and Becka A. Alper. 2015. 'Religion and Views on Climate and Energy Issues'. In *Religion and Science*, Pew Research Center Report, 32–42. Washington, DC: Pew Research Center.

Gardiner, Stephen M. 2006. 'A Perfect Moral Storm: Climate Change, Intergenerational Ethics and The Problem of Moral Corruption'. *Environmental Values* 15 (3): 397–413.

Gehring, Thomas, and Eva Ruffing. 2008. 'When Arguments Prevail over Power: the CITES Procedure for the Listing of Endangered Species'. *Global Environmental Politics* 8 (2): 123–148.

Georgescu-Roegen, Nicholas. 1993. 'The Entropy Law and the Economic Problem'. In *Valuing the Earth: Economics, Ecology, Ethics*, edited by Herman E. Daly and Kenneth N. Townsend, 75–88. Cambridge: MIT Press.

Goldstein, Judith, and Robert Owen Keohane. 1993. *Ideas and Foreign Policy: Beliefs, Institutions, and Political Change*. Ithaca, NY: Cornell University Press.

Grasso, Marco. 2010. 'An Ethical Approach to Climate Adaptation Finance'. *Global Environmental Change* 20 (1): 74–81.

Griskevicius, Vladas, Joshua M. Tybur, and Bram Van den Bergh. 2010. 'Going Green to be Seen: Status, Reputation, and Conspicuous Conservation'. *Journal of Personality and Social Psychology* 98 (3): 392–404.

Grossman, Gene M., and Alan B. Krueger. 1995. 'Economic Growth and the Environment'. *The Quarterly Journal of Economics* 110 (2): 353–377.

Grubb, Michael, James Sebenius, Antonio Magalhaes, and Susan Subak. 1992. 'Sharing the Burden'. In *Confronting Climate Change: Risks, Implications and Responses*, edited by Irving M. Mintzer, 305–322. Cambridge: Cambridge University Press.

Hajer, Marteen A. 1995. *The Politics of Environmental Discourse: Ecological Modernization and the Policy Process*. Oxford: Oxford University Press.

Hall, Nina, and Åsa Persson. 2017. 'Global Climate Adaptation Governance: Why is it not Legally Binding?' *European Journal of International Relations* 24 (3): 540–566.

Hardin, Garrett. 1974. 'Living on a Lifeboat'. *BioScience* 24 (10): 561–568.

Harris, Paul G., Alice S. Y. Chow, and Rasmus Karlsson. 2013. 'China and Climate Justice: Moving Beyond Statism'. *International Environmental Agreements* 13 (3): 291–305.

Hawken, Paul, Amory B. Lovins, and L. Hunter Lovins. 2013. *Natural Capitalism: The Next Industrial Revolution*. Abingdon and New York: Routledge.

Hayward, Tim. 1998. *Political Theory and Ecological Values*. Cambridge: Polity Press.

Hessing, Melody. 1993. 'Women and Sustainability: Ecofeminist Perspectives'. *Alternatives* 19 (4): 14–21.

Hirata, Keiko. 2005. 'Why Japan Supports Whaling'. *Journal of International Wildlife and Policy* 8 (2–3): 129–149.

Holmes, George. 2011. 'Conservation's Friends in High Places: Neoliberalism, Networks, and the Transnational Conservation Elite'. *Global Environmental Politics* 11 (4): 1–21.

Holmes, George. 2012. 'Biodiversity for Billionaires: Capitalism, Conservation and the Role of Philanthropy in Saving/Selling Nature'. *Development and Change* 43 (1): 185–203.

Hurd, Ian. 2012. 'Almost Saving Whales: The Ambiguity of Success at the International Whaling Commission'. *Ethics & International Affairs* 26 (1): 103–112.

International Union for Conservation of Nature. 1980. *World Conservation Strategy: Living Resource Conservation for Sustainable Development*. Gland: International Union for Conservation of Nature (IUCN) in collaboration with the United Nations Environment Programme (UNEP) and the World Wide Fund for Nature (WWF).

Jinnah, Sikina. 2016. 'Climate'. In *Why Govern?: Rethinking Demand and Progress in Global Governance*, edited by Amitav Acharya, 192–210. Cambridge: Cambridge University Press.

Jinnah, Sikina. 2017. 'Makers, Takers, Shakers, Shapers: Emerging Economies and Normative Engagement in Climate Governance'. *Global Governance* 23 (2): 285–306.

Kanie, Norichika, Hiromi Nishimoto, Yasuaki Hijioka, and Yasuko Kameyama. 2010. 'Allocation and Architecture in Climate Governance Beyond Kyoto: Lessons From Interdisciplinary Research on Target Setting'. *International Environmental Agreements* 10 (4): 299–315.

Kauffman, Craig M., and Pamela L. Martin. 2014. 'Scaling up Buen Vivir: Globalizing Local Environmental Governance from Ecuador'. *Global Environmental Politics* 14 (1): 40–58.

Kim, So Young, and Yael Wolinsky-Nahmias. 2014. 'Cross-National Public Opinion on Climate Change: The Effects of Affluence and Vulnerability'. *Global Environmental Politics* 14 (1): 79–106.

Klinsky, Sonja, J. Timmons Roberts, Saleemul Huq, Chukwumerije Okereke, Peter Newell, Peter Dauvergne et al. 2017. 'Why Equity is Fundamental in Climate Change Policy Research'. *Global Environmental Change* 44: 170–173.

Leiserowitz, Anthony A., Robert W. Kates, and Thomas M. Parris. 2006. 'Sustainability Values, Attitudes, and Behaviors: A Review of Multinational and Global Trends'. *Annual Review of Environment and Resources* 31: 413–44.

Litfin, Karen T. 2003. 'Towards an Integral Perspective on World Politics: Secularism, Sovereignty and the Challenge of Global Ecology'. *Millennium* 32 (1): 29–56.

Litfin, Karen T. 2005. 'Gaia Theory: Intimations for Global Environmental Politics'. In *Handbook of Global*

Environmental Politics, edited by Peter Dauvergne, 502–517. Cheltenham: Edward Elgar Publishing.

Lomborg, Bjørn. 2001. *The Skeptical Environmentalist: Measuring the Real State of the World*. Cambridge: Cambridge University Press.

Luke, Timothy W. 1997. 'The World Wildlife Fund: Ecocolonialism as Funding the Worldwide "Wise Use" of Nature'. *Capitalism Nature Socialism* 8 (2): 31–61.

McGrath, Liam F., and Thomas Bernauer. 2017. 'How Strong is Public Support for Unilateral Climate Policy and What Drives it?' *Climate Change* 8(6): 484.

McKinnon, Catriona. 2018. 'Sleepwalking into Lock-In? Avoiding Wrongs to Future People in the Governance of Solar Radiation Management Research'. *Environmental Politics* 28 (3): 441–459.

Meadows, Donella H., Dennis L. Meadows, Jørgen Randers, and William W. Behrens III. 1972. *The Limits to Growth: A Report for the Club of Rome's Project on the Predicament of Mankind*. New York: Universe Books.

Merchant, Carolyn. 1980. *The Death of Nature: Women, Ecology and the Scientific Revolution*. San Francisco, CA: Harper & Row Publishers.

Merchant, Carolyn. 2005. *Radical Ecology: The Search for a Livable World*. 2nd ed. New York and London: Routledge, Taylor & Francis Group.

Meyer, John W., David John Frank, Ann Hironaka, Evan Schofer, and Nancy Brandon Tuma. 1997. 'The Structuring of a World Environmental Regime, 1870–1990'. *International Organization* 51 (4): 623–651.

Mies, Maria. 1998. *Patriarchy and Accumulation on a World Scale: Women in the International Division of Labour*. London and New York: Zed Books Ltd.

Mildenberger, Matto, and Anthony Leiserowitz. 2017. 'Public Opinion on Climate Change: Is there an Economy–Environment Tradeoff?' *Environmental Politics* 26 (5): 801–824.

Miller, Andrew R., and Nives Dolšak. 2007. 'Issue Linkages in International Environmental Policy: The International Whaling Commission and Japanese Development Aid'. *Global Environmental Politics* 7 (1): 69–96.

Moellendorf, Darrel. 2009. 'Treaty Norms and Climate Change Mitigation'. *Ethics & International Affairs* 23 (3): 247–265.

Mol, Arthur P. J. 2001. *Globalization and Environmental Reform: The Ecological Modernization of the Global Economy*. Cambridge, MA: MIT Press.

Moore, Frances C. 2012. 'Negotiating Adaptation: Norm Selection and Hybridization in International Climate Negotiations'. *Global Environmental Politics* 12 (4): 30–48.

Naess, Arne. 1973. 'The Shallow and the Deep, Long-Range Ecology Movement: A Summary'. *Inquiry* 16 (1): 95–100.

Nagel, Joane. 2016. *Gender and Climate Change: Impacts, Science, Policy*. New York: Routledge.

Neumayer, Eric. 2003. *Weak versus Strong Sustainability: Exploring the Limits of Two Opposing Paradigms*. Cheltenham: Edward Elgar.

Nicholson, Simon, and Daniel Chong. 2011. 'Jumping on the Human Rights Bandwagon: How Rights-Based Linkages Can Refocus Climate Politics'. *Global Environmental Politics* 11 (3): 121–136.

O'Donnell, Erin, and Julia Talbot-Jones. 2018. 'Creating Legal Rights for Rivers: Lessons from Australia, New Zealand, and India'. *Ecology and Society* 23.1: article 7.

Okereke, Chukwumerije. 2008. 'Equity Norms in Global Environmental Governance'. *Global Environmental Politics* 8 (3): 25–50.

O'Neill, Eoin. 2016. 'The Pope and the Environment: Towards an Integral Ecology?' *Environmental Politics* 25 (4): 749–54.

Ormrod, James S. 2011. '"Making Room for the Tigers and the Polar Bears": Biography, Phantasy and Ideology in the Voluntary Human Extinction Movement'. *Psychoanalysis, Culture and Society* 16 (2): 142–161.

Paavola, Jouni, and W. Neil Adger. 2006. 'Fair Adaptation to Climate Change'. *Ecological Economics* 56 (4): 594–609.

Page, Edward A. 2011. 'Climate Justice and the Fair Distribution of Atmospheric Burdens. A Conjunctive Account'. *The Monist* 94 (3): 412–432.

Pammett, Jon H. 2015. 'Faith that Science will Solve Environmental Problems: Does it Hurt or Help?' *Environmental Politics* 24 (4): 553–574.

Pandey, Chandra Lal, and Priya A. Kurian. 2017. 'The Media and the Major Emitters: Media Coverage of International Climate Change Policy'. *Global Environmental Politics* 17 (4): 67–87.

Patterson, James J., Thomas Thaler, Matthew Hoffmann, Sara Hughes, Angela Oels, Eric K. Chu et al. 2018. 'Political Feasibility of 1.5°C Societal Transformations: The Role of Social Justice'. *Current Opinion in Environmental Sustainability* 31: 1–9.

Pickering, Jonathan, Frank Jotzo, and Peter J. Wood. 2015. 'Sharing the Global Climate Finance Effort Fairly with Limited Coordination'. *Global Environmental Politics* 15 (4): 39–62.

Plumwood, Val. 1993. *Feminism and the Mastery of Nature*. London and New York: Routledge.

Porritt, Jonathon. 2012. *Capitalism as if the World Matters*. London: Routledge.

Rao, Narasimha D. 2014. 'International and Intranational Equity in Sharing Climate Change Mitigation Burdens'. *International Environmental Agreements* 14 (2): 129–146.

Rees, William E., and M. Wackernagel. 1994. 'Ecological Footprints and Appropriated Carrying Capacity: Measuring the Natural Capital Requirements of the Human Economy'. In *Investing in Natural Capital: The Ecological Economics Approach to Sustainability*, edited by AnnMari Jansson, Monica Hammer, Carl Folke, and Robert Costanza, 362–390. Washington, DC: Island Press.

Robinson, John. 2004. 'Squaring the Circle? Some Thoughts on the Idea of Sustainable Development'. *Ecological Economics* 48 (4): 369–384.

Sabin, Paul. 2013. *The Bet: Paul Ehrlich, Julian Simon, and Our Gamble over Earth's Future*. New Haven, CT: Yale University Press.

Salleh, Ariel. 1997. *Ecofeminism as Politics: Nature, Marx and the Postmodern*. New York: Zed Books.

Sargisson, Lucy. 2001. 'What's Wrong with Ecofeminism'. *Environmental Politics* 10 (1): 52–64.

Sasser, Jade. 2014. 'From Darkness into Light: Race, Population, and Environmental Advocacy'. *Antipode* 46 (5): 1240–1257.

Sexton, Steven E., and Alison Sexton. 2014. 'Conspicuous Conservation: The Prius Halo and Willingness to Pay for Environmental Bona Fides'. *Journal of Environmental Economics and Management* 67 (3): 303–317.

Shue, Henry. 1999. 'Global Environment and International Inequality'. *International Affairs* 75 (3): 531–545.

Simon, Julian L. 1981. *The Ultimate Resource*. Princeton, NJ: Princeton University Press.

Simon, Julian L. 1984. 'Bright Global Future'. *Bulletin of the Atomic Scientists* 40 (9): 14–17.

Simon, Julian L., and Herman Kahn. 1984. *The Resourceful Earth: A Response to Global 2000*. New York and Oxford: Basil Blackwell.

Singer, Peter. 1975. *Animal Liberation*. New York: New York Review of Books.

Singer, Peter. 2002. *One World: The Ethics of Globalization*. New Haven, CT: Yale University Press.

Singleton, Benedict E. 2016. 'Clumsiness and Elegance in Environmental Management: Applying Cultural Theory to the History of Whaling'. *Environmental Politics* 25 (3): 414–433.

Stadelmann, Martin, Åsa Persson, Izabela Ratajczak-Juszko, and Axel Michaelowa. 2014. 'Equity and Cost-Effectiveness of Multilateral Adaptation Finance: Are They Friends or Foes?' *International Environmental Agreements* 14 (2): 101–120.

Steel, Brent S., Mary Ann E. Steger, Nicholas P. Lovrich, and John C. Pierce. 1990. 'Consensus and Dissension among Contemporary Environmental Activists: Preservationists and Conservationists in the US and Canadian Context'. *Environment and Planning C: Government and Policy* 8 (4): 379–393.

Stephan, Hannes R. 2012. 'Revisiting the Transatlantic Divergence over GMOs: Toward a Cultural-Political Analysis'. *Global Environmental Politics* 12 (4): 104–124.

Stern, David I. 2004. 'The Rise and Fall of the Environmental Kuznets Curve'. *World Development* 32 (8): 1419–1439.

Stern, Nicholas. 2007. *The Economics of Climate Change: The Stern Review*. Cambridge: Cambridge University Press.

Stern, Nicholas. 2010. 'The Economics of Climate Change'. In *Climate Ethics: Essential Readings*, edited by Simon Caney, Dale Jamieson, and Henry Shue, 39–75. Oxford: Oxford University Press.

Stiles, Daniel. 2004. 'The Ivory Trade and Elephant Conservation'. *Environmental Conservation* 31 (4): 309–321.

Suri, Vivek, and Duane Chapman. 1998. 'Economic Growth, Trade and Energy: Implications for the Environmental Kuznets Curve'. *Ecological Economics* 25 (2): 195–208.

Turner, Graham M. 2008. 'A Comparison of *The Limits to Growth* With 30 Years of Reality'. *Global Environmental Change* 18 (3): 397–411.

Turner, James Morton. 2014. 'Counting Carbon: The Politics of Carbon Footprints and Climate Governance from the Individual to the Global'. *Global Environmental Politics* 14 (1): 59–78.

Vanderheiden, Steve. 2008. *Atmospheric Justice*. Oxford: Oxford University Press.

Victor, David G., and Lesley A. Coben. 2005. 'A Herd Mentality in the Design of International Environmental Agreements?' *Global Environmental Politics* 5 (1): 24–57.

Wackernagel, Mathis, Niels B. Schulz, Diana Deumling, Alejandro Callejas Linares, Martin Jenkins, Valerie Kapos, Chad Monfreda, Jonathan Loh, Norman Myers, Richard Norgaard, and Jorgen Randers. 2002. 'Tracking the Ecological Overshoot of the Human Economy'. *Proceedings of the National Academy of Sciences* 99 (14): 9266–9271.

Warren, Karen J. 1997. *Ecofeminism: Women, Culture, Nature*. Bloomington: Indiana University Press.

Part 2

Actors and interests

3 | States

States are central actors in international relations, and global environmental politics is no exception. State preferences are very diverse because they are rooted in often divergent national interests. Their preferences also fluctuate over time as they are partly shaped by interactions with other states. This chapter helps us to understand how state preferences are formed and reformed at the domestic and international levels. It first investigates the way national interests are defined and then translated into state preferences. It then shows how state preferences evolve during international negotiations through interactions with other states.

 Learning objectives

After reading this chapter, readers will be able to:

- Identify international and domestic factors that shape the formation of state interests in global environmental politics;

- Understand the rational choice model of state interest formation in global environmental politics;

- Describe how domestic administrative units represent national interests;

- Explain the models of interstate interaction in international negotiations and how these interactions shape state preferences; and

- Discuss how working and contact groups, interstate coalitions, and leadership can shape state preferences during international negotiations.

Introduction

All of the main international relations theories—including realism, liberal institutionalism, constructivism, and critical theories—consider states as important actors in understanding international politics. Compared to other international actors, states are in a unique position to create international law, establish **intergovernmental organizations**, control the flow of trade, compel private actors to comply with regulations, and provide fiscal incentives. Therefore, regardless of the theoretical lens used to study global environmental politics, it is essential to consider how and why states behave in particular ways.

This chapter focuses on state preferences (i.e. their positions on international issues under negotiation), which are largely defined by national interests (i.e. the domestic factors related to these international issues) and interstate interactions (i.e. the process of engaging with other states during international negotiations). Although ideas and values are also key in shaping state interests and behaviour (Chapter 2), as are institutional dynamics (Chapter 7), this chapter looks primarily at how domestic interests and interstate dynamics shape state preferences in global environmental politics. Centrally, it provides tools to understand how state preferences form, and how they either combine to lead to multilateral action or alternatively fail to reach consensus. Therefore, this chapter views the dynamics of preference formation as occurring simultaneously at two distinct levels: the domestic and the international (Putnam 1988).

Section 3.1 investigates the domestic sources of state preference formation. It first draws on rational choice theory to discuss the domestic factors that come into play for states as they identify their national interests related to global environmental issues. In particular, two important domestic factors are the degree of environmental **vulnerability** and the abatement costs of environmental measures. The section also discusses the limits of presenting state preference formation as determined through a straightforward calculation of national interests. Other factors, including domestic ones, also shape the formulation of state preferences. Among these other factors, the nature of the political **regime** works as a filter through which states arbitrate conflicting interests. The domestic administrative structure, made up of various agencies, ministries, and departments working on environmental protections within a single state, can also affect how a state articulates and represents its preferences.

In international negotiations, states must defend their positions in relation to the positions of other states. Therefore, Section 3.2 moves the discussion of state preference from the domestic to the international level. In international negotiations, states must defend their positions in relation to the positions of other states. Section 3.2 investigates this interactive context and identifies some of the many international factors that further (re)shape state preferences, such as the emergence of interstate coalitions. It details the practices deployed by states internationally to define, defend, and negotiate for their individual preferences. Importantly, state preferences are not necessarily settled before, or even during, international negotiations; a state might construct or change its preferences in the course of its interactions with other states. As such, the logic between the internal (i.e. domestic) and the external (i.e. international) definition of state preferences is not necessarily sequential— it is a co-evolving process.

3.1 Domestic sources of state preferences

Ecological vulnerability and abatement costs

Why do states display very different levels of involvement in global environmental politics despite sharing the same planet? For instance Figure 3.1, which represents the number of environmental agreements ratified by different states over the period 1945–2018, shows that Kuwait has ratified just a few agreements, while Germany has ratified more than 120. This significant variation between states calls for an explanation. This first section looks at different domestic factors that explain this variation, which is rooted in how states define their interests with respect to environmental issues.

Rational choice theory provides a useful starting point for understanding variation in state preferences. In its simplest form, rational choice theory argues that states make decisions, such as whether or not to ratify a treaty, based on their national interests. Like any model, it does not provide a perfect description of reality, but can be used to understand the broad contours of state behaviour in global environmental politics (Barkdull and Harris 2002; Roberts et al. 2004; Thompson 2010).

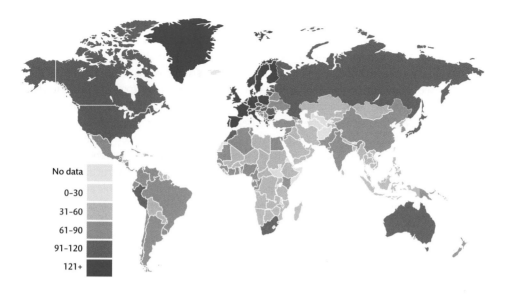

Figure 3.1 Number of environmental agreements ratified 1945–2018

Source data from: Mitchell. R.B., et al (2019).

  Take your learning further by viewing the interactive version of this figure
www.oup.com/he/morin1e

In particular, rational choice theory assumes that national interests are a reflection of a comparative analysis of the costs and benefits associated with each policy option. It assumes that states choose the option that presents the greatest benefits at the least cost. In other words, states use a utility function in order to define their preferences. Under rational choice theory, states are rational on the basis of three distinct premises. First, they have the full capacity to make choices that deviate from past practice: they are free from routine that would blindly make them follow the same path. Second, they are able to systematically analyse and organize their different possible policy options in order of preference. This order is complete, meaning that it includes all options and that the preferences are consistent with one another. Third, states act in accordance with the option that is most beneficial to them—the one that will maximize their level of satisfaction, taking the associated costs and benefits into consideration. States do not brush aside their preferences simply for the sake of conforming to moral imperatives or traditions. They also maintain the possibility of not acting if no option appears satisfactory (Morin and Paquin 2018).

Global environmental politics scholars have found at least two specific variables useful in the calculation of a country's national interest. These are environmental vulnerability, which is an estimate of the benefits of action to avoid environmental harm, and the costs of abatement, which are the monetary costs of taking such actions (Sprinz and Vaahtoranta 1994). Environmental vulnerability is measured by the extent of the damage that would be suffered or potentially suffered by a state, its territory, or its population if no environmental action was taken. Some states are particularly vulnerable to extreme environmental events, such as hurricanes or floods (Eisenstadt et al. 2019). The costs of abatement include the costs of substitution (i.e. of replacing polluting equipment or developing a new technology), the costs of abandonment (i.e. of stopping the use of a technology for which no substitute is available), and the costs of handling (i.e. the cost of providing financial support to the affected industrial sectors) (Davenport 2005).

By overlaying these two variables with rational choice theory, Detlef Sprinz and Tapani Vaahtoranta (1994) expect four types of state behaviour: *dragger, bystander, intermediate, and pusher* (see Table 3.1). States that enthusiastically push for the adoption of environmental regulations—the *pushers*—are those that are both the most vulnerable to environmental degradation and the least affected by abatement costs. Inversely, states that are most obstructive to adopting environmental standards are those that are the least environmentally vulnerable and would bear the highest abatement costs—these are the *draggers*. When states are vulnerable to environmental problems but also face high abatement costs, their behaviour is *intermediate*. When they are not vulnerable to environmental problems and do not face high abatements costs they can be expected to observe environmental debates from the outside, embracing a *bystander* behaviour.

Sprinz and Vaahtoranta (1994) use examples, including the negotiations on the Montreal Protocol on the protection of the **ozone layer** (see Annex 0.1 at p. 19) to illustrate the relevance of their theoretical model. As they explain, Scandinavian countries have a particularly high rate of skin cancer, a risk that has increased with the depletion of the ozone layer. In addition, Scandinavian countries have always produced low amounts of chlorofluorocarbons, one of the main gases that deplete the ozone layer. These two variables explain why Scandinavian countries have been among the most ardent pushers of the Montreal Protocol. In contrast, France was a significant producer and exporter of chlorofluorocarbons in the 1980s. This meant that France would face high abatement costs, which according to Sprinz and Vaahtoranta explains why France initially played the role of dragger, stalling negotiations on the protection of the ozone layer, and raising doubts about the validity of the scientific knowledge on the subject. According to this model, both the enthusiasm of the Scandinavian countries and France's initial reluctance with regard to protecting the ozone layer were guided by rational choice-based decision making.

Environmental vulnerability and the costs of abatement can change depending on the issue at hand, and this in turn modifies state interests across issues and over time. A small Pacific island such as Tuvalu is highly vulnerable to climate change, but is not particularly affected by ozone layer depletion. Consequently, since interests vary in line with the particular environmental problem, the same country may be a promoter of environmental action on one issue, but prove to be an obstructionist on another. The United States, having suffered from

Table 3.1 Expected behaviour of states according to their interests

		Degree of vulnerability	
		Low	High
Abatement costs	Low	Bystanders	Pushers
	High	Draggers	Intermediates

Source: Reproduced with permission from D.F. Sprinz and T. Vaahtoranta. National Self-interest: a Major Factor in International Environmental Policy Formulation. Volume 4, Responding to global environmental change, pp. 323–328. In *Encyclopedia of Global Environmental Change*. Copyright © 2002, John Wiley & Sons, Ltd, Chichester.

several severe oil spills in the 1970s, has been a promoter in the fight against marine pollution and ratified the International Convention for the Prevention of Pollution from Ships (known as the MARPOL Convention) and its annexes. But in relation to climate change it has been obstructive, partly due to the high costs of abatement that its reduced fossil fuel consumption would provoke. Environmental vulnerability can also change over time. For instance, China was a dragger during the Kyoto Protocol climate negotiations in the mid- to late 1990s, but is now becoming more proactive in the Paris Agreement due in part to the emerging relevance of domestic air pollution, which is linked to **greenhouse gas** emissions (Tambo et al. 2016).

For poorer countries, the costs of abatement may seem insurmountable for a large number of environmental issues (Nakada 2006). Figure 3.2 presents the number of environmental treaties ratified by states according to wealth, calculated by per capita gross domestic product. The graph suggests that it is necessary, but not sufficient, for a state to have a certain level of wealth for it to make a substantial commitment to ratifying environmental treaties. Once the wealth threshold is reached, the condition of wealth is no longer sufficient (see also Tobin 2017). The number of agreements signed by countries with similar per capita gross domestic products, such as France and Singapore, varies greatly. This suggests that other variables besides the gross domestic product come into play in defining states' preferences as they become wealthier.

Abatement costs also depend on a country's degree of trade openness, coupled with the nature of its exports (Cao and Prakash 2010). The degree of trade openness is generally measured by the proportion of imports and exports accounted for in the gross domestic product. Countries with relatively closed markets (i.e. they do not trade much with other countries) are often less sensitive to multilateral cooperation efforts because their economic well-being is less dependent on other countries, whereas states with open markets will be sensitive to their

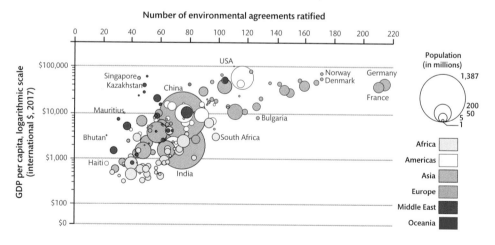

Figure 3.2 Wealth and the ratification of environmental agreements as of 1 January 2019

Source data from: World Bank; https://iea.uoregon.edu/

 Take your learning further by viewing the interactive version of this figure
www.oup.com/he/morin1e

trading partners' preferences. For example, although Japan has long practised whale hunting for cultural reasons, it accepted a ban on whaling within the International Whaling Commission in 1986 due to the threat of trade sanctions from the United States, one of its key trading partners (Andresen 1989).

There is variation among countries who have similar levels of trade openness, depending on the nature of their exports. For example, India and China are both countries with high levels of trade openness, but they have different preferences with regard to the liberalization of environmental goods at the World Trade Organization. China exports a growing quantity of environmental technologies and is more likely to see commercial opportunities in an accelerated liberalization of environmental goods. In contrast, India expressed opposition to an increased liberalization of environmental goods, fearing that it would not be able to protect some of its domestic producers from foreign competition (Harashima 2008).

In summary, the rational choice model can be helpful in understanding how national interests form and in turn shape states' preferences and behaviour at the international level. However, it also has limitations. In its simplest form, the model rests on the assumption that national interests can be easily calculated and that the state is a unitary and monolithic actor. In practice, however, interest formation can be quite complex. Ideas can intervene and modify the way interests are calculated (see Chapter 2), international interactions can change the way states define their preferences (see Section 3.2), and the domestic political regime acts as an intermediary variable between material interests and state preferences. We now turn to the latter.

A state's political regime as an intermediate variable

The structure of the state's political regime is also an important factor to consider for explaining variation in state preferences. A state's political regime can be conceptualized as an **intermediate variable** between environmental vulnerability and abatement costs, on the one hand, and state preferences on the other. In other words, a state's political regime can alter the way state leaders comparatively weigh their vulnerability and abatement costs. For example, autocracies are more likely to support environmental regulation if a powerful minority, such as the ruling class or a politically connected corporation, is highly vulnerable to environmental degradation, and abatement costs are low. On the other hand, democracies are more likely to promote environmental standards if the majority of the population is vulnerable to environmental degradation, even if the abatement costs are high, as long as they are highly concentrated on a minority, such as a single industrial sector or a small region.

The construction of state preferences surrounding climate politics in the Maldives highlights these differences well because the country has had both autocratic and democratic regimes. When under autocratic regimes the Maldives has been absent from climate negotiations, partly because the wealthy class would need to shoulder a large share of the abatement costs of **adaptation** and mitigation. In contrast, when the Maldives has been governed by a democratic regime, it has been a key player in global climate negotiations, because the entire country is highly vulnerable to the impacts of climate change (Hirsch 2015). Although abatement costs remain important under a democratic regime, the Maldives has advocated strongly in global climate negotiations for a large portion of these costs to be shouldered by developed countries.

Since the costs of abatement are often concentrated on one group within a country, whereas vulnerability is often spread across the country's population, democracies are, on average, more committed to protecting the environment than autocracies. Figure 3.3 presents the relationship between a country's democracy index (a measure of how democratic its regime is), and the number of environmental treaties ratified by that country. It shows that only democracies have adopted a substantial number of environmental agreements. Once again, democracy is a necessary but insufficient condition to predict environmental treaty **ratification**, as demonstrated by democracies such as India and the United States, which have ratified a relatively small number of environmental agreements (see Figure 3.3).

In addition to the way vulnerability and abatement costs are distributed, several other factors also help to explain the correlation between democracy and higher levels of environmental treaty ratification (Bättig and Bernauer 2009). First, democracies respect individual rights and allow environmental activists to express themselves openly, including by pressuring their governments to address environmental issues through treaties and other means. Also, because political elites in democracies rely on elections to maintain their power, they are more attentive to public opinion, which is often favourable to environmental agreements, especially when vulnerability is high. Democracies more often allow public access to information; this allows environmental data to be exchanged, advertised, and compared, which can point to the need to take action for environmental protection. Democratic states are also more likely to cooperate with one another on environmental issues because they produce and exchange information on environmental problems. And as democracies are generally more open to trade liberalization, some of their businesses may benefit from the

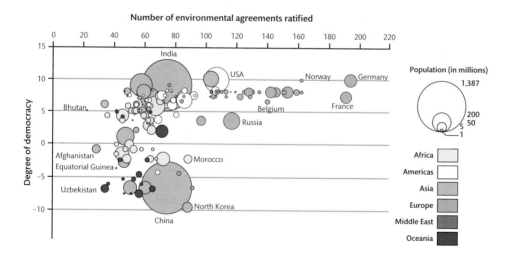

Figure 3.3 Democracy and the ratification of environmental agreements as of 1 January 2019

Source data from: www.Systemicpeace.org; World Bank; https://iea.uoregon.edu/

 Take your learning further by viewing the interactive version of this figure
www.oup.com/he/morin1e

harmonization of environmental standards, and so may favour environmental treaties as a mechanism to help create harmonization (Carbonell and Allison 2015).

However, the involvement of democracies in global environmental **governance** is uneven. Even when they are elected as part of a democratic regime, political leaders remain preoccupied by short-term objectives, which can be more easily and visibly addressed within their terms in office, thus helping them win the next election. Elections and short electoral cycles decrease the incentives for politicians to address environmental problems that require long-term action to see results, such as some elements of climate change and **biodiversity** loss. Elected representatives try above all to respond to the preferences of their voters and political supporters, which can create a counter-incentive to long-term environmental action (Hovi et al. 2009).

Even in a democracy, a limited group of influential individuals may manage to block environmental policy development. For example, in Indonesia elected politicians have forged clientelist relations (consisting of distributing goods or services in exchange for political support) with palm oil producers (Dauvergne 2018). These producers use slash-and-burn farming, which generates polluting smoke, to increase the surface area for production, and are therefore firmly opposed to the adoption of any environmental agreement on sustainable palm oil production or on air pollution, which would limit their commercial activity. So, although Indonesia is one of the most democratized countries in South East Asia, it is among the most obstructionist in discussions surrounding a regional agreement on air pollution (Varkkey 2014).

Democracies are also more sensitive to pressure from interest groups (see Chapter 4). The United States' preferences in global environmental politics, for example, are strongly influenced by powerful industry groups, which benefit from major political leverage offered by the American democratic system due to their influence over political campaign donations. For example, the fact that the United States is one of the only countries that has not ratified the Convention on Biological Diversity can be explained by the opposition of several American biotechnology companies, who opposed the provisions in the agreement related to **benefit sharing** and biosafety (Chasek 2007). In other cases, however, American industrial groups have supported the creation of multilateral environmental agreements. American businesses in the fur sector, for example, pushed the United States to adopt the Convention on International Trade in Endangered Species of Wild Fauna and Flora. They did so because the United States government was planning to adopt domestic fauna protection measures anyway, and the industry wanted the costs of this to be borne across the fur industry in other countries as well, rather than solely by US businesses (DeSombre 2000).

As discussed in further detail in Chapter 4, other types of **non-state actors** can also influence national preferences (Bernauer et al. 2013). Although there is much variation across different countries, non-state environmental activism, combined with the political regime type, can be useful in understanding the dynamics of environmental interest groups and their likelihood of influencing policy decisions. This can be seen partly in Figure 3.4, which presents two different measures of state environmental activism. As shown in Figure 3.4, interest group politics are particularly helpful in understanding European countries' high rate of environmental treaty ratification. Proportionally speaking, several European countries have a high number of organizations affiliated with the International Union for Conservation of Nature, and a high number of businesses that have voluntarily adopted the international

(a)

Number of domestic organizations affiliated with the IUCN (2018)

No Data 0   1   2   5   15   70

(b)

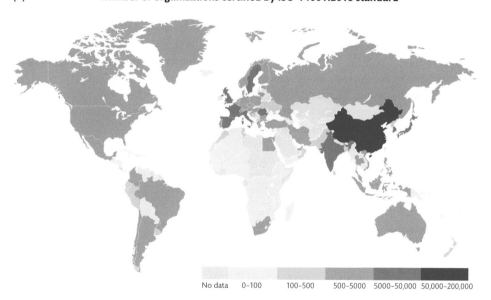

Number of organizations certified by ISO-14001:2015 standard

No data   0–100   100–500   500–5000   5000–50,000   50,000–200,000

Figure 3.4 Indicators of national groups' environmental activism
Sources data from: (a) www.IUCN.org and (b) iso.org

'ISO 14001' standard on environmental performance. Nonetheless, these indicators are less helpful in understanding the United States case, which has a low rate of ratifying **international environmental agreements** despite American interest groups being very active on environmental issues. Indeed, the number of environmentally active non-state actors is similar to that for Europe. This difference between the United States and Europe suggests that their respective political **institutions** and leaders consider interest group concerns differently.

The nature of the political regime varies in important ways, even among democracies. For example, that Canada, a democracy, signed the Kyoto Protocol while the United States, another democracy, did not was due in part to the differences between their democratic systems. Both are producers and major consumers of fossil fuels, but Canada functions under a parliamentary regime while the American political system is a presidential regime. The Canadian prime minister has the political authority to ratify an international agreement without consulting the Parliament (as Prime Minister Jean Chrétien did in 2002 with the Kyoto Protocol), or to withdraw from an agreement (as Prime Minister Stephen Harper did in 2011, also with the Kyoto Protocol). In contrast, although the American president has the power to negotiate treaties, only the Senate can ratify an international treaty, which is needed for a treaty to become legally binding on the United States. This separation of powers became clear in the case of the Kyoto Protocol, which was negotiated and signed by President Bill Clinton in 1998 but was never ratified by the United States Senate, and thus never became binding on the United States (Harrison 2007; Hovi et al. 2010; Tamura 2006).

The Canadian and American electoral systems are both based on first-past-the-post voting. Several other democracies' electoral systems are based on proportional representation, which promotes the emergence of a wide diversity of political parties, including green parties. The presence of a large green **party** in a country can substantially favour the adoption of environmental policies. Germany, Finland, and Sweden are countries where green parties have been quite successful at influencing their national governments. Their mobilization partly explains these states' proactive stance on certain environmental issues, such as sustainable energy and climate change (van Haute 2016). This is just another example showing that national interests are mediated through a particular political regime to give rise to particular state preferences.

Representing state preferences

The state is not a unitary and monolithic actor—it is made of a multiplicity of different administrative units. Together, these units are responsible for articulating and defending state preferences. In this section, we detail the state administrative apparatus, which represents state preferences on environmental issues.

When a country engages in environmental issues at the international level, it assigns responsibilities for representing its national interests on these issues to a domestic administrative unit (a department or ministry). Sometimes a new unit is created specifically for environmental issues, but they may be assigned to an existing unit. The latter is the case in the United States with respect to climate change, which is negotiated by the Department of State, not a specialized environmental department. Creating a new domestic ministry or a department of the environment is often a sign that environmental protection has become a central and permanent concern for the state, requiring public policies to be created and implemented, and national positions to be communicated at the international level.

States have been relatively slow to develop ministries of the environment. The vast majority of these ministries were only set up in the early 1970s, following the creation of the United Nations Environment Programme in 1972. Japan even waited until 2001 to convert its environmental agency into a proper ministry of the environment. This slow pace is a sign that environmental issues still remain in the realm of 'low politics' in comparison to issues such as trade and security, which are housed in widespread ministries of trade and foreign affairs.

In several countries, the creation of ministries of the environment was catalysed by action at the international level (Busch and Jörgens 2005: 874; Meyer et al. 1997: 638). The 1972 Stockholm Summit on Human Environment and the 1992 **Rio Summit** on Environment and Development were major driving forces behind this dynamic (see Chapter 6). During these conferences, states were called on to participate in preparatory meetings, write reports, and implement new policies. Often, new administrative units had to be created to execute these tasks. For example, the first global environmental summit in 1972 in Stockholm called on states to create 'appropriate national institutions [. . .] entrusted with the task of planning, managing or controlling the 9 environmental resources of States with a view to enhancing environmental quality' (Stockholm declaration, Principle 17). These international actions led to the creation of environmental ministries in several countries.

The waves of democratization in the 1970s and 1990s also led to the creation of ministries of the environment. This can be explained by several factors, including that: democracies learn from and replicate one another; public pressure is more important in democracies, meaning that environmental groups and citizens in favour of creating a ministry of the environment were more easily heard; and international aid is more easily available for democratic regimes, suggesting that they may have received more funding to support the creation of a ministry of the environment in their government (Aklin and Urpelainen 2014).

Although ministries of the environment can be important in translating national interests to the international level, they do not have a monopoly on negotiating environmental issues for the state. Several other ministries whose primary occupation is not the environment can also play an important role. France, for example, first set up a ministry dedicated to the environment in 1972, followed by an Environment and Energy Management Agency in 1991, and an environment and climate subdivision within the Ministry of Foreign Affairs in 2012. Although there are benefits to multiple ministries with different types of expertise working together to represent the state at the international level, this does not always result in smooth cooperation (see Box 3.1).

Box 3.1 The coherency of national delegations

When attending international negotiations, each state is represented by a national delegation. These delegations are typically made up of one or more administrative units, including but not limited to ministries of the environment. For example, during the negotiations of the 2000 Cartagena Protocol on Biosafety, the members of the ten most active delegations could, on average, be broken down as follows: 35 per cent were officers from a ministry of the environment or equivalent, 11 per cent were from a

(continued...)

ministry of agriculture, 11 per cent were from a ministry of foreign affairs, 8 per cent were from a ministry of science and technology, and 6 per cent were from a ministry of trade.

Each administrative unit defends its interests according to its own bureaucratic culture. This results in differing views on the challenges of environmental negotiations and the priorities that should be attributed to them. For example, Brazil is divided when it comes to the need to place the Amazon rainforest under an international protection regime. On the one hand, its Ministries of Foreign Affairs, Science and Technology, and Agriculture are all supported by the oil company Petrobas, military organizations, and major producers of soy, timber, and livestock. It is not surprising, therefore, that they oppose any international agreement that would restrict logging operations. On the other hand, Brazil's Ministry of the Environment—supported by the scientific community, several governors of federated states, the ethanol industry, renewable energy producers, national and local businesses, and NGOs—argues that the Amazon should be the subject of an international agreement on the protection of forests.

In these bureaucratic conflicts, administrative units do not compete on an equal footing. Often, ministries of the environment have fewer financial and human resources than other ministries, and in inter-ministry dynamics, they are often marginalized compared with more powerful ministries, such as ministries of trade, finance, or industry.

The composition of delegations can influence the way in which negotiating positions evolve. For instance, the idea of implementing a CO_2 emissions trading system in Europe was partly the result of a change in staff at the European Commission, just after the Kyoto Protocol was adopted. Officers in the European Commission's climate unit were initially in favour of a carbon tax rather than an emissions trading system. However, the arrival of the economist Jos Delbeke in a key position in the Commission, and the subsequent recruitment of economists in Delbeke's new team, marked a change in preferences. This new team took initiatives, drew from external expertise, and mobilized to obtain the political support necessary for a European CO_2 emissions trading system.

To alleviate the risk of incoherency, certain governments have set up internal coordination procedures. For example, at the end of the 1990s, Switzerland established inter-agency coordination procedures for the negotiations on access to **genetic resources**. However, several delegations still lack the material or political means to implement this type of coordination. This difference accentuates inequalities between developed countries, which are more capable of coordinating their positions, and **developing countries**, for which such inter-ministerial coordination is more difficult.

Sources: Morin and Orsini 2014; Nakanabo Diallo 2015; Orsini 2010; Skjærseth and Wettestad 2009; Skovgaard 2017; van Asselt et al. 2009; Vieira 2013.

Finally, how issues are assigned to one ministry rather than another is an important indication of how a state perceives particular environmental issues. For example, in the United States, the State Department leads the negotiations on climate change, but the much smaller Fish and Wildlife Service within the Department of Interior leads the negotiations and **implementation** of the Convention on International Trade in Endangered Species of Wild Fauna and Flora. Similarly, the administrative unit appointed as the national focal point for the United Nations Framework Convention on Climate Change reflects and influences state preferences—in some cases it is the ministry of energy (for instance, in Saudi Arabia), or the ministry of foreign affairs and trade (as in Australia), instead of the ministry of the environment. Thus, it is not just the existence of a ministry of the environment, but also the nature of the tasks that are assigned to it (or not) that are important in understanding preference formation.

Regardless of whether a specific environment ministry is created, how it shares its responsibilities with other ministries, or which ministry is assigned primary responsibility, a central task of any administrative body is to represent the state in international negotiations. Indeed, the state preference formation discussed in this section can be modified during international negotiations, the topic which we now discuss in Section 3.2.

3.2 International sources of state preferences

Interstate negotiations: a long and complicated process

International negotiations are primarily about meeting one imperative: reconciling numerous and often diverging state preferences within a single written agreement. As discussed in Section 3.1, national interests are often quite diverse, and initial state preferences are often divergent. In this context, negotiated agreements are forged gradually, through the juxtaposition of different proposals, from different countries. The negotiating process creates ample opportunities for states to recalculate their preferences as they interact with one another and new proposals emerge. States use various mechanisms, such as creating working and **contact groups**, appointing negotiating chairs, forming interstate coalitions, and following leaders, to increase the possibility that international interactions will yield consensus among their preferences. Before examining these mechanisms in turn, this section first stresses the challenge of reconciling different states' preferences.

One good indicator of the difficulty in aligning state preferences is the length of the negotiation process. Negotiating a new multilateral environmental agreement often takes several years. The United Nations Convention on the Law of the Sea, for example, took ten years to negotiate. Most of the time, the procedure for the adoption of the text follows the consensus principle, whereby no votes are explicitly called for, but all states must agree—in practice, this means that no state expresses disagreement with the proposed text. To reach this high bar of international consensus, states must work together over a long period of time and revise their preferences until they find common ground (Brunnée 2002; Campbell et al. 2014; Chasek 2001; Chasek and Wagner 2012).

The negotiation of a multilateral environmental agreement is not only lengthy, but also intense. It typically involves several fast-paced negotiation sessions, each lasting a couple of weeks. These negotiation sessions are conducted under high pressure due to the significant funding and staff they require, the political capital they entail, and the media attention they generate (Muñoz et al. 2009). During the sessions, a delegate's typical day is incredibly busy, rushing between back-to-back meetings. Discussions begin early in the morning with coordination efforts at the national or regional level or in ad hoc interstate coalitions, and end late at night in extended sessions (Campbell et al. 2014). Images of negotiators sleeping at their desks can be found online accompanying the reports published by the *Earth Negotiations Bulletin*, a publication of the International Institute for Sustainable Development that provides daily summaries and concluding analyses of many international environmental negotiations. These images illustrate that aligning various state preferences is not an easy task.

Game theory is useful to conceptualize the challenges of reconciling numerous and diverging state preferences into a consensual agreement. Game theory is a mode of deductive reasoning based on formal modelling. It typically rests on the assumption that actors are interdependent, meaning that what they get out of an interaction depends not only on their own actions, but also on the actions of other participating actors. This means that all actors must behave strategically—they must take into account the behaviour of other states to define their best course of action. State preferences are thus partly determined by the anticipated actions and reactions of other states.

One of the most widely known games analysed in game theory is the '**prisoner's dilemma**'. In this game, actors share an optimal cooperative solution, but they all have an incentive to defect from this collective interest in order to maximize their individual gain. Their challenge is to design an agreement that provides an additional incentive for cooperation or sanctions for defection (Pittel and Rübbelke 2012).

Negotiations on climate change correspond well to the logic of the prisoner's dilemma game: all states share a collective interest in mitigating global emissions of greenhouse gases, but they would prefer other states to take most of this responsibility, and they are not willing to act alone. For example, during the Kyoto Protocol and early Paris Agreement negotiations, the United States declared that it opposed making any commitments unless similar commitments were also made by emerging countries, particularly China and India. Similarly, China initially insisted that developed countries should bear the primary costs of mitigation, partly because of their historical contribution to emissions. Eventually, the United States and China both shifted their preferences and adopted the Paris Agreement (although the United States later withdrew from the Agreement when the Trump administration took office). This can be explained to some extent by the interactions among states that led to the Paris Agreement's voluntary and bottom-up approach, which created a satisfactory compromise for these two countries (Hilton and Kerr 2017) (see Box 3.2).

Box 3.2 A bottom-up approach to addressing climate change: nationally determined contributions

Unlike the top-down emission-reduction targets under the Kyoto Protocol, which were politically negotiated and set as a percentage of each country's actual emissions in 1990, emission-reduction targets under the Paris Agreement were defined from the bottom up. In other words, each party defines for itself what it is willing to do to reduce emissions. Specifically, in the lead-up to the 21st **Conference of the Parties** to the United Nations Framework Convention on Climate Change in 2015, where the Paris Agreement was adopted, countries were invited to submit plans that outlined their intentions to take action on climate change after the Kyoto Protocol's second commitment period ends in 2020. These plans, initially called *Intended* Nationally Determined Contributions (INDCs), addressed national ambition by setting targets for reducing greenhouse gas emissions, among other things. As countries ratified the Paris Agreement their INDCs were converted into Nationally Determined Contributions, or if they had not yet submitted INDCs they were required to submit a Nationally Determined Contribution along with their instrument of ratification. These Nationally Determined Contributions are the primary way in which parties aim to achieve the Paris Agreement goal of 'holding the increase in the global average temperature to well below 2°C' (Article 2(1)a). Parties are expected to ratchet up their Nationally Determined Contributions approximately every five years, beginning in 2023.

This approach marks a significant shift from the Kyoto Protocol's top-down targets and legally binding commitments. Under the Paris Agreement, Nationally Determined Contributions are voluntary, meaning that countries that fail to uphold their pledges will not be breaking international law. States are nevertheless subject to legally binding procedural requirements, such as reporting, and to normative expectations that they make their pledges as ambitious as possible.

This voluntary approach was the result of significant divisions among parties with varying levels of ambition to reduce emissions. During the negotiations for the agreement, the United States and other countries opposed internationally determined, legally binding commitments. Other states agreed to a voluntary system to keep all parties at the negotiating table.

This voluntary approach has nonetheless been heavily criticized. Some argue that voluntary contributions have negative implications for efficiency, because the objectives are not necessarily optimal. Although there is an expectation that Nationally Determined Contributions will be ratcheted up over time, recent analyses highlight that they are currently insufficient to achieve the goals of the Paris Agreement. Assuming these voluntary plans are fully implemented, the average global temperature will still increase by about 3°C above pre-industrial levels by 2100 according to estimates by the United Nations Environment Programme. Others argue that voluntary contributions pose equity issues, because countries do not share the same responsibility for climate change or capabilities for addressing it.

Sources: Bretschger 2017; Dimitrov 2016; Falkner 2016; Höhne et al. 2017; Jernnäs and Linnér 2019; Rajamani and Brunnée 2017; Spencer et al. 2015; UNEP 2018.

Another game that is useful in understanding how negotiation dynamics structure state interactions, and in turn shape their preferences, is the 'chicken' game (Pittel and Rübbelke 2012). It is a game that recalls a famous scene from American cinema: two reckless teenagers measure up their courage by driving their cars into each other to see who makes the other turn away first. The negotiators of environmental agreements often follow a similar pattern: they stick to their initial positions as long as they can, hoping others will be the first to make concessions. However, they are also interested in reaching an agreement, even if only a weak one, rather than failing to reach agreement at all. This logic pushes delegates to negotiate for as long as possible, up to the last minute or even a little beyond. These protracted sessions test the mettle of state preferences, as the collective outcome is very much dependent on how strongly states defend those preferences and risk collapse of the negotiations, or allow their preferences to be shaped by the positions of others in an effort to reach consensus.

This chicken game helps to explain why the negotiation of multilateral environmental agreements often requires numerous negotiation sessions. The final text of an agreement is typically presented for adoption on the last of several scheduled negotiation days, often in a closing plenary session in the early hours of the morning, far later than the negotiation session was scheduled to conclude. This was the case for the Convention to Combat Desertification negotiations, for which the plenary session to adopt the treaty started much later than scheduled, a full day after the negotiations were supposed to conclude, at 4 a.m. on 18 June 1994. At this plenary session, the majority of delegates were too exhausted to celebrate the text's adoption (Najam 2004).

The dynamics of international negotiations shape how states interact with one another, and in turn create pathways for them to influence one another's preferences. Thus, interstate negotiations are not a smooth or linear process, from an opening plenary session to a closing one, during which states naturally converge on a median position. Instead, the adoption of multilateral environmental agreements is often the result of unpredictable dynamics of interactions (Brunnée 2002). The following sub-sections discuss four pathways through which state preferences are further shaped at the international level: establishing working and contact groups, appointing negotiation chairs, creating interstate coalitions, and following a leader.

Creating working and contact groups

States have adopted various diplomatic practices for maximizing the likelihood that their interactions in international negotiations will reach consensus. These include conducting negotiations in restricted but often representative subgroups (Campbell et al. 2014), which allow for coordination of positions among a limited number of delegations, before presenting a potential consensus to other states. Indeed, the negotiation of multilateral environmental agreements does not only take place in the emblematic United Nations large plenary sessions where each member state is represented, but also in smaller more intimate forums for negotiations.

These subgroups are known as contact groups or working groups. The idea behind their creation is to facilitate consensus. For example, the negotiation of the Kyoto Protocol's Clean Development Mechanism took place mainly between American and Brazilian negotiators, who had opposing views on this issue, before opening up the discussion to other delegations (Boyd et al. 2008). The progress made in groups like this is sometimes kept secret until the final hours of negotiation. Partly for this reason, the Paris Agreement was largely negotiated behind closed doors (Dimitrov 2016).

The system of working and contact groups has both advantages and drawbacks. On one hand, secrecy allows the delegates in these restricted groups to express their views freely without fear of information leaking to the media. On the other hand, delegations that are left out only hear partial, vague echoes of the progress of the texts. This runs counter to the general norm of transparency and participation in global environmental politics. Exclusion can lead (and has led) to the collapse of some agreements, as was the case with the predecessor to the Paris Agreement, the 2009 Copenhagen Accord.

The division of negotiations into subgroups also exacerbates existing inequalities in levels of state representation at international treaty negotiations (see Figure 3.5). For example, at the 24th Conference of the Parties to the United Nations Framework Convention on Climate Change, which took place in Poland in 2018, the island nation of Dominica sent three delegates while the United States sent 51. This is a problem for small states such as Dominica, which are particularly vulnerable to climate change and need international assistance in bearing abatement costs, but cannot participate fully because there are often many more than three working groups held simultaneously. These smaller states are therefore at a disadvantage in comparison to the United States and other well-resourced states when it comes to participating in all of these sessions.

Appointing chairs as entrepreneurs

States often designate negotiation chairs to facilitate the negotiation process (Chasek and Wagner 2012, Tallberg 2010). Negotiation chairs can be selected to be representative of diverse interests. For instance, there can be two negotiation chairs, one from a developed country and one from a developing country. The negotiations surrounding several environmental agreements, including the Convention on the Law of the Sea (1973-1982), the Vienna Convention for the Protection of the Ozone Layer and its Montreal Protocol (1982-1987), the Framework Convention on Climate Change and its Protocol (1991-1997), and the Nagoya Protocol on Access and Benefit Sharing (2006-2010), were overseen by negotiation chairs. For example, for the Nagoya Protocol, Fernando Casa (Colombia) and Timothy

Number of national delegates per country–negotiations on biodiversity

14th Conference of the Parties to the Convention on Biological Diversity, Sharm El Sheikh, Egypt, 2018.

No data   1   10   20   40   80   >80

Number of national delegates per country–negotiations on climate change

24th Conference of the Parties to the United Nations Framework Convention on Climate Change, Katowice, Poland, 2018.

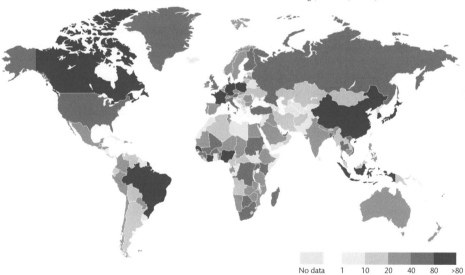

No data   1   10   20   40   80   >80

Figure 3.5 Number of national delegates per country–negotiations on climate and biodiversity 2018

Source data from: CBD secretariat; UNFCCC secretariat

Hodges (Canada) acted as co-chairs, Colombia being a provider, and Canada a user, of genetic resources.

Chairs can also be appointed to facilitate negotiation through smaller groups, such as working groups or contact groups. These working group chairs are charged with guiding and monitoring the progress made during these smaller groups' negotiations. Negotiation chairs and working group chairs usually work cooperatively, with negotiation chairs appointing working group chairs using similar criteria to those used for their own appointment.

Chairs facilitate the negotiations and often encourage the adoption of agreements or the taking of important decisions under existing agreements (Tallberg 2010). On one hand, chairs are asked to respect the mandate given to them by states; on the other hand, states sometimes delegate authority to them. For example, during the negotiations on climate change, chairs frequently reminded states of their responsibilities by affirming that they were 'in the hands' of state negotiators and could do nothing without their active involvement. Sometimes, however, the delegates declared themselves 'in the hands' of the chairs, signalling that it was time for the chairs to exert their authority in guiding states towards consensus. This requires a delicate diplomatic balance for chairs, who must accommodate very different state preferences (Depledge 2007).

Certain conditions favour the emergence of more entrepreneurial chairs. When negotiation mandates are not clearly defined and states have widely diverging preferences, negotiations become difficult to manage. The large number of participants, their varied preferences, and the need to reach a consensus push delegates to look for chairs with entrepreneurial qualities. In these circumstances, chairs perform the role of agreement drafters, negotiation mediators, or negotiation catalysers.

Chairs sometimes draft their own versions of the texts to be negotiated, which they then present to the states. For example, although the United Nations Seabed Committee, under the Convention on the Law of the Sea, failed to propose a preparatory negotiation text, state delegates were confronted with approximately 100 competing proposals from individual states. This led to a deadlock in the negotiations. States therefore tasked the chairs with developing a single text proposal that reflected points of agreement from the proposals, and gave them a large amount of leeway to do this. Similar situations arose during the negotiations on the Montreal Protocol on Substances that Deplete the Ozone Layer and the Kyoto Protocol on Climate Change (Depledge 2007).

Chairs also play an important role as mediators to facilitate the adoption of texts. In the delicate negotiations over financial arrangements in the Convention on the Law of the Sea, the negotiation chair, Tommy Koh (from Singapore), played a decisive role: he established an informal secretariat to gather the available information and write informed proposals; he progressively synthesized the discussions by gradually limiting the size of negotiation groups; he used a financial model developed by American researchers as a basis for negotiation; and he created bridges between the most important points of negotiation to open up possibilities for compromise (Tallberg 2010: 256).

Chairs have specific strategies for moving discussions forward. One of these strategies is to initially limit the number of states allowed in the negotiating room, selecting the ones who hold the most radical positions. Once an agreement has been reached among this restricted group, chairs push for its adoption by all the other delegations. In the negotiations on the ozone layer, the negotiation chair, Winfried Lang (from Austria), and the then executive director of the United Nations Environment Programme, Mustafa Tolba, used this strategy. They organized informal, closed group discussions in a 'friends of the chairs' group. This group produced a single negotiation text, called 'Tolba's personal text'. The chairs then presented the text to the plenary session, where other delegations received it with enthusiasm (Tallberg 2010: 257).

Chairs are sometimes highly inventive in the ways they catalyse negotiations. When the negotiations surrounding the Cartagena Protocol on **genetically modified organisms** had reached a standstill, the negotiation chair Veit Koester (from Denmark) used teddy bears to mediate the debates. Only the delegates holding a teddy bear were allowed to speak (Orsini 2010). The chair used humour to disarm negotiators, enabling him to reorganize the debates, which had been chaotic up to that point, and to help an agreement to be reached. In recent international negotiation processes such as those surrounding the adoption of the 2015 **Sustainable Development Goals**, states have even been calling for a 'new type' of environmental diplomacy, one that is more heavily based on informal exchanges under the leadership of chairs (Chasek and Wagner 2016).

Forming interstate coalitions

Interstate coalitions are another mechanism through which state preferences can be (re) shaped at the international level. States in a coalition typically have similar interests and preferences on important issues. Coalitions thus operate to amplify state preferences in international negotiations by creating a mechanism for states to put forward a collective voice, which carries more weight than individual states acting alone, and can push other states to alter their preferences towards a consensus outcome.

Coalitions are generally created around common or overlapping interests, which often apply both to and beyond environmental negotiations. For example, there are several coalitions that are formed on a regional basis, such as the African Group, the Group of Arab Countries, and the Latin American and Caribbean Group. These groups work together both on environmental negotiations and in other issue areas, such as international trade and development.

Other coalitions are specific to environmental negotiations, and can even develop around a very specific environmental issue at a particular point in time. For example, the Latin American Initiatives Group (known as GRILA), a coalition between Bolivia, Chile, Costa Rica, and Colombia among others, was created in 1999 and was active for only a few years to promote the successful inclusion of **carbon sinks** in the Kyoto Protocol's Clean Development Mechanism. Another example is the Coalition of Rainforest Nations, which was created in 2005 to group together forested tropical countries to support the creation of the United Nations Reducing Emissions from Deforestation and Forest Degradation Mechanism, designed for forest **conservation** and as a mechanism to fight climate change.

In their composition, coalitions do not necessarily follow the classical split between regions, or between developed and developing countries. For example, during the negotiations on the Cartagena Protocol on Biosafety, the Miami Group united Argentina, Australia, Canada, Chile, the United States, and Uruguay. While Argentina, Chile, and Uruguay are members of another intergovernmental coalition, the Group of 77 (G77), they disengaged from the G77 during these negotiations to align themselves with other states that were also major exporters of genetically modified products.

In climate change negotiations, developed countries have also formed coalitions that go beyond regional groupings (Gupta 2014). The Umbrella Group brings together several non-European developed countries, including Australia, Japan, and Norway. This group is generally opposed to climate change measures that affect economic interests, and insists on developing countries also being on board to implement climate measures. The Environmental Integrity Group unites six countries—Switzerland, South Korea, Mexico, Liechtenstein, Monaco, and Georgia—who wish to reconcile developed and developing country preferences in order to work for a fair climate regime. The same state can be a member of several coalitions in global environmental politics. This results in a great deal of overlap within and between coalitions. Figure 3.6 illustrates these overlaps using climate change as an example.

Intergovernmental coalitions are rarely institutionalized, and are therefore relatively unstable. It is uncommon for such coalitions to be institutionalized in the form of permanent organizations. For example, JUSCANZ is a coalition that includes Japan, the United States, Canada, Australia, and New Zealand, sometimes joined by Norway and Switzerland in global environmental politics. Between 1993 and 2007, at the Commission on Sustainable Development, the JUSCANZ members generally discussed their positions together before each negotiation session. In the process, JUSCANZ members probably influenced one another's preferences behind closed doors, even if only at the margins. However, JUSCANZ never voiced a common position at those sessions, and its members sometimes expressed diverging views. In other words, JUSCANZ acted only as an informal discussion forum, and did not lead to the unification of its members' positions in that forum.

One coalition that is highly institutionalized and cohesive is the Bolivarian Alliance for the Peoples of Our America (known as ALBA). This coalition groups together ten countries in South and Central America, and works primarily on regional economic cooperation, but is nonetheless attentive to environmental negotiations. In climate negotiations, its members stand together to oppose the use of **market mechanisms** to reduce carbon emissions, arguing instead for alternatives to mainstream international economic governance.

Coalitions like ALBA are important and effective tools for states to both express their preferences and convince others to bring their own preferences into alignment. They enable states to pool their resources, expertise, and skills to push for their shared ideas and preferences within broader international negotiations. Importantly, they reduce the need for participating states to attend all meetings, as a coalition leader can represent them. For example, negotiations on forests may be held in several separate locations, such as the United Nations Food and Agriculture Organization's Committee on Forestry, the United Nations Forum on Forests, and the International Tropical Timber Organization, requiring negotiators to move frequently between locations. This situation exerts increasing pressure on national administrations, and especially on small and poor countries with limited resources, as their negotiators must shuttle between multiple forums (Andresen 2001). Coordinating with like-minded countries through coalitions can help these countries to cover all of these parallel sessions and take unified positions on issues to amplify their voice in international negotiations.

Although coalitions can provide a forum for countries to interact and adjust their preferences towards consensus outcomes, their unity is not a given. Conflicting subgroups and new coalitions often emerge. For example, Brazil disengaged from the Latin American Initiatives Group at the sixth **Conference of the Parties** on climate change in 2000 in The Hague because it was not willing to change its position relating to the inclusion of carbon sink projects in the Clean Development Mechanism (Boyd et al. 2008). This is not uncommon, with many coalitions shifting and evolving as discussions progress between their members (Tobin et al. 2018; see also Box 3.3). In the next sub-section, we turn to another mechanism through which state preferences are shaped at the international level: leadership.

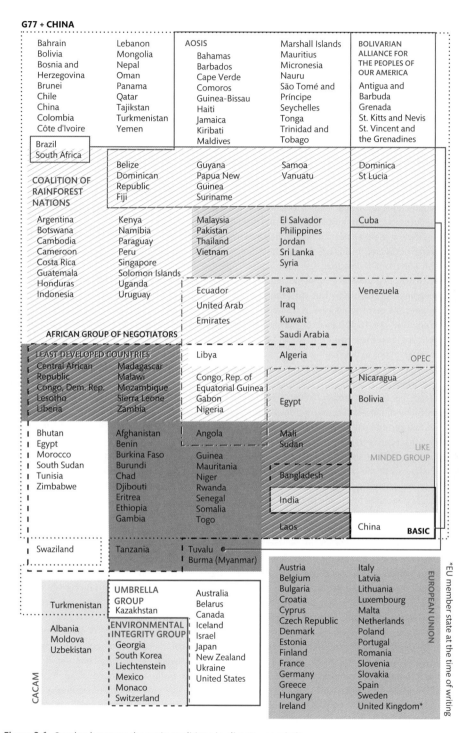

Figure 3.6 Overlap between the main coalitions in climate negotiations

Source: UNFCCC secretariat

Box 3.3 The Group of 77 in climate negotiations: an unstable balance

Originally created by 77 developing countries, the Group of 77 (known as G77) now brings together 134 developing states. It is a coalition that is not specific to global environmental politics: the group was created at the first United Nations Conference on Trade and Development in Geneva in 1964. Its initial objective was to defend the economic interests of developing countries through the creation of a new international economic order. Ever since, the G77 has remained one of the main coalitions of developing countries in the United Nations, including as related to global environmental politics. It enables its members to articulate and collectively promote their interests, and to improve their negotiation capabilities.

The G77 is not based on a clear political programme, but brings together its members' different points of view and political agendas. The G77 rarely conducts coordination meetings prior to international negotiations. Instead, it endeavours to elaborate its common position during international meetings, which reduces its ability to quickly prepare and react to the points being negotiated.

Nonetheless, the G77 has put up a united and influential front in global environmental negotiations on several occasions, including during the climate change negotiations. G77 members share four common important claims that they have consistently expressed. First, they promote an approach to climate change that takes economic development issues into consideration. Second, they advocate for the recognition of '**common but differentiated responsibilities and respective capabilities**' as a guiding principle that should govern relationships between developed and developing countries. Third, they emphasize the importance of transferring technologies and related expertise from developed to developing countries. Fourth, they call for additional financial resources to be provided for climate change programmes in developing countries. Finance was a red line issue for the G77 in the adoption of the Paris Agreement. These general claims have all been reflected in the adopted international agreement in various ways.

The fact that the G77 remains a central coalition for so many developing countries is quite surprising. CO_2 emissions and levels of economic development vary greatly between its members. This variation has resulted in a recent split between emerging countries, such as China, India, and Brazil, and other G77 members that have seen less intense economic development.

Moreover, several subcoalitions within the G77 have diametrically opposed interests. One need only briefly look at the preferences of the **Alliance of Small Island States** and the Organization of the Petroleum Exporting Countries (OPEC) to verify this. Members of the Alliance of Small Island States are particularly vulnerable to climate change, especially to a future rise in sea levels, and they contribute very little to CO_2 emissions. They therefore defend a position that strongly favours the adoption of ambitious commitments to reduce greenhouse gases. In particular, they advocate for limiting global warming to 1.5°C above pre-industrial levels. In contrast, OPEC's members are opposed to any measure to reduce CO_2 emissions and to any tax on carbon emissions. They insist on the economic consequences of climate change mitigation, and demand compensation for reduction in petroleum consumption. One of OPEC's objectives is to make it the responsibility of the G77 as a whole to block negotiations on climate change. The chair of the G77 rotates, but OPEC members have several times acted as G77 chairs, including Saudi Arabia, which has also come to act as an 'anti-developed countries' advocate.

Despite diverging views in the G77, there are two factors that explain the group's continued presence in climate negotiations. Firstly, unity has always been one of its central values, particularly to ensure the visibility of developing countries' shared concerns. Secondly, several developing countries share the sentiment that they are politically and economically vulnerable on the international stage. As a result, the G77 appears to them as a mode of cohesion by default. Even if this sometimes means making concessions, several G77 members believe they will benefit more from following the group's leaders than they would by defecting from the group.

When disagreements become too lively, bargaining is often what restores unity in the G77. The day before the 1992 Rio Summit, while African countries were advocating for the adoption of a treaty on desertification, the other members of the G77 remained indifferent to this demand. They preferred to concentrate their efforts on blocking a potential agreement on forests that threatened the interests of Brazil and Indonesia. But the G77 decided to support the position of the African countries on desertification and became very active in these negotiations, in exchange for African countries' commitment to abandon their support for the creation of a treaty on forests. Although it experiences significant internal tensions, the G77 often appears as a united coalition.

Sources: Barnett 2008; Bhandary 2017; Corneloup and Mol 2014; Depledge 2008; Dimitrov 2016; Kasa et al. 2008; Najam 2004; Nelson 2016.

Following a leader

Leadership is a notion used to measure the level of state engagement in international negotiations. Although sometimes correlated with power, both developed and developing countries can exert leadership. For example, Box 3.4 explains how several African countries led the desertification negotiations, and in doing so shaped the preferences of stronger players such as the United States and the European Union. Leadership can thus be important in understanding how state preferences are shaped at the international level.

Box 3.4 Negotiations over desertification: developing countries taking the lead

Desertification and land degradation have been on the international agenda since 1977 through the United Nations Conference on Desertification. This conference was motivated by the severe droughts in the African Sahel region in the 1960s and 1970s and it led to the adoption of a plan of action to combat desertification. Even so, in 1991 the United Nations Environment Programme stressed that the problem had become worse and that current efforts to address desertification were ineffective. The United Nations Environment Programme therefore, with strong support from African countries, called for additional action at the international level on this issue. Initially the United States and the European Community opposed a new international treaty, largely due to financial concerns and because they considered desertification to be a local problem rather than an international one. However, in 1992, during the initial negotiation phase of the United Nations Conference on Environment and Development (the Rio Summit), the European Community offered to support a new convention on desertification in exchange for support from developing countries on a forest convention.

At first, this strategic move from the European Community created tensions and disagreements among developing countries, including among the African countries, as some developing countries were critical of the proposed forest convention's narrow focus on tropical forests. However, after intense internal negotiations, the developing countries came together in support of the African countries' call for a convention on desertification, but rejected the European Community's demand for a forest convention. The European Community eventually caved in to pressure when the United States decided to change its own position during the negotiations and support the new desertification treaty. In his careful documentation of these negotiations, Adil Najam argues that it is unclear exactly why the United States changed its position and the European Community let go of their forest convention condition during the Rio process. One possible explanation is that the United States and European Community feared that a rejection of developing countries' demands for a desertification treaty could endanger agreement on

(continued...)

other Rio issues that they were pushing forward. Another possible explanation is that the United States, in particular, faced pressure from bad publicity at home over its stance on other issues discussed in the Rio process. However, irrespective of the true explanation, the decision to establish a convention on desertification has been celebrated as an effort led by developing countries.

After agreement was finally reached during the Rio Summit to pursue a treaty on desertification, countries then called on the United Nations General Assembly to establish a negotiating committee to develop the text of the convention, which was adopted in 1994. The 1994 United Nations Convention to Combat Desertification entered into force in 1996 and currently has 197 parties.

The Convention combats desertification and land degradation through local participation and a bottom-up approach. More specifically, it provides that each party must develop a national action programme that involves local communities and civil society in both the design and implementation of projects targeting desertification. This includes engaging local communities in the process of identifying problems, collecting information, and solving local challenges. The Convention also emphasizes the importance of cooperation among countries and the development of partnerships, for example in relation to scientific data and technological knowledge.

One critical controversy during the negotiations on the Convention concerned financing. Central to the debate was the scope of the financial mechanism and through which channels funding should be provided. Developing countries feared that developed countries would prioritize issues such as biodiversity and climate change unless a central fund for desertification was established. The United States and the European Community showed no willingness to compromise on this issue, which has challenged effective implementation of the Convention. However, at the Conference of the Parties in 2017, a new global private sector fund, the Land Degradation Neutrality Fund, was established which brings together public and private investors in an effort to secure more funding for restoration of degraded land.

Sources: Akhtar-Schuster et al. 2016; Johnson et al. 2006; Najam 2004.

We can better understand how states shape one another's preferences through leadership by dividing leadership into three types: structural, intellectual, and entrepreneurial (Papa and Gleason 2012: 917; Young 1991). We explain each leadership type below.

Structural leadership relies on states' material resources, which can be either general or specific to the negotiations in question. *General* resources, such as economic or military resources, allow a state to lead by increasing its bargaining power and thus its capacity to influence the preferences of other states. For example, the European Union successfully convinced Russia to sign the Kyoto Protocol in 2004 by making this a condition of European Union support for Russia's membership in the World Trade Organization. The European Union was able to bargain in this way as it is a significant actor in the World Trade Organization and has a powerful voice in opposing the entry of new members (Afionis and Chatzopoulos 2010; Henry and Sundstrom 2007). This example highlights how political linkages across international treaties can play a role in shaping state preferences.

Structural leadership can also depend on states' *specific* resources, with respect to the particular issue under negotiation. This would apply, for example, in negotiations surrounding the management of a specific resource that is primarily located in one or a small number of states. In that scenario, the state or states that hold the majority of that specific resource are generally more involved and potentially even disproportionately more powerful than others in international negotiations surrounding that resource. This is the case for the 'megadiverse countries', a coalition of 15 states that together are home to 70 per cent of the world's biodiversity. This coalition, though made up of several countries that are not generally considered powerful, has been a structural leader in the international negotiations on biodiversity. This is reflected in their success in placing on the agenda of the Convention on Biological Diversity the principle of sharing the benefits that arise out of the use of genetic resources, despite strong resistance from developed countries. This disproportionate influence by countries that are typically considered less powerful is called the 'power to destroy' because if the countries with specific resources within their sovereign territory reject an agreement, the entire agreement could collapse (Downie 1999). As such, the 'power to destroy' can shape state preferences at the international level.

Intellectual leadership involves a state shaping the way other states understand environmental problems, and convincing them to alter their preferences. Intellectual leadership can rest on scientific knowledge (see Chapter 1); but it can also rest on more constructivist understandings related to discourses and issue framing. The **Alliance of Small Island States**, for example, displayed great intellectual leadership in climate negotiations by shifting the discourse from the economic costs of mitigation and adaptation to the existential dimensions of failing to mitigate and adapt. At the 2009 Copenhagen climate change conference, numerous small island states portrayed climate change as a threat to their survival, destroying their houses, their crops, and even the burial grounds of their loved ones. Their shift in discourse aimed to affect how other countries understood climate change, as an emotional issue, not just an economic one. This intellectual leadership is often used by delegations of modest stature, and sometimes proves to be a formidable rhetorical weapon in shaping how other states redefine their preferences in international negotiations (Rosendal 2007).

Entrepreneurial leadership refers to states' negotiating skills. These skills are measured by the ability to collectively organize and guide negotiations between states with diverse preferences towards consensus outcomes (Kaasa 2007). Entrepreneurial leaders might be adept at proposing compromises or fostering strategic alliances.

For example, the European Union has been considered a leader in global environmental politics, because it successfully convinced many states to adopt the Kyoto Protocol, despite the United States' reticence, at the Bonn climate conference in 2001. However, at the 2009 Copenhagen conference, the European Union failed in its efforts to build consensus around a new climate agreement, signalling a decline in its entrepreneurial leadership (Afionis 2011; Vogler and Stephan 2007). This decline is also a reflection of the European Union's internal political dynamics. The lack of coordination between the European member states and the European Commission, along with the change in European Union presidency every six months, made Europe slower to react to the pace of international negotiations. In 2007, the European Union had anticipated this problem and created the troika system, in which three chairs (the former presidency, the current presidency, and the future presidency) come together to establish the forthcoming 18-month negotiation agenda. However, in the midst of the Copenhagen climate negotiations, the European Union struggled to speak with one voice, even with the troika system (Skjærseth 2017). Some believe that the idea that Europe is a strong leader in global environmental governance is a myth invented by Eurocrats to legitimize their actions (Lenshow and Sprungk 2010). Yet, the project of a European Green Deal, presented by the European Commission in December 2019 and aiming to make Europe a climate-neutral continent by 2050, might create a new momentum in Europe in favour of environmental protection.

Entrepreneurial leaders must be able to guide both the content and process of negotiations. Typically, such leaders are intimately familiar with a particular negotiation setting and have followed the process for many years. Yet, because negotiating multilateral agreements can take several years to complete, few delegates are involved consistently throughout the entire process. As a result, negotiators who keep up with meetings over time are often more able to influence the preferences of others through entrepreneurial leadership. For example, during the Cartagena Protocol on Biosafety negotiations, more than 75 per cent of delegates only attended 2 out of 30 meetings. The negotiators from Ethiopia and Malaysia participated in all 30 meetings, and were therefore able to consistently and credibly stress the importance of adopting a binding agreement, and eventually convinced other states in the African Group and the G77 to adopt it, despite their initial lack of mobilization on the issue (Orsini 2010).

All three of the leadership types discussed above can either proactively facilitate the adoption of agreements by shaping state preferences towards consensus, as in the European and Ethiopian/Malaysian cases discussed above, or adopt an obstructive strategy (Barnett 2008; Depledge 2006). A proactive leader will use its resources to convince reluctant countries to build consensus and often increase their level of commitment. In contrast, an obstructionist leader will become the most reluctant country itself, guiding negotiations towards a lower common denominator, and attempting to create or entrench divisions between states with diverging preferences.

For example, the United States, which has strong potential for structural leadership due to its general resources, has played both proactive and obstructionist leadership roles. It promoted the creation of international standards for the protection of mammals as early as 1972, under the Marine Mammal Protection Act. However, it has also actively obstructed the negotiations on climate change by insisting that states shift their positions to be more in line with its preferences on responsibility for mitigation (Chasek 2007; DeSombre 2000).

The United States is not, however, the only dragger on climate change. Saudi Arabia—like most other member states of the Organization of the Petroleum Exporting Countries—strategically ratified the United Nations Framework Convention on Climate Change and the Kyoto Protocol in order to influence negotiations from within (Depledge 2008). Saudi Arabia also used the expertise of an experienced negotiator, Mohamed Al Sabban. According to Joanna Depledge (2008), who studied his behaviour in multilateral negotiations, Al Sabban is a 'brilliant and stubborn' negotiator (Kjellén (2008: 77), quoted in Depledge 2008: 19) with all of the qualities needed to influence negotiations: self-confidence, tenacity, eloquence, and profound knowledge of the problem being negotiated. The fact that Mohamed Al Sabban was a consistent participant in all of the Conferences of the Parties in the climate negotiations, from 1991 to 2008, enabled him to acquire a certain intellectual leadership and to play a key obstructionist role in the negotiations. Saudi Arabia significantly slowed down the Kyoto Protocol negotiation process by opposing the adoption of a negotiation mandate, blocking the appointment of facilitators to the negotiation process, and preventing the recognition of important milestones during the negotiations (Depledge 2008). In playing the dragger role in climate politics, the United States and Saudi Arabia didn't shape state preferences directly, but rather hindered other states' ability to secure their own preferences in a consensus-based international negotiation.

3.3 Conclusion

States have very different preferences in global environmental politics. These state preferences are formed and shaped in a co-evolving process at both the domestic and international levels. Domestically, a rational choice analysis shows how environmental vulnerability and the costs of abatement contribute to defining a state's national interests in environmental politics. But the rational choice model, though useful, has its limits. It often presents the state as a unitary and monolithic actor, whereas in fact states come in multiple institutional forms and are made up of numerous actors with varying and sometimes conflicting interests.

Several international factors also play an important role in shaping state preferences. Some of those international factors revolve around how states interact with one another in international negotiations. Models of negotiation dynamics—such as the prisoner's dilemma and chicken games—help us to better understand how state interactions through international negotiations can play a role in structuring state preferences. In addition, state preferences can be revised during international negotiations via states' interactions in working and contact groups, with negotiating chairs, in coalitions, and through leadership efforts.

State preference formation is the joint result of these dynamics at the domestic and the international level (Putnam 1988). In global environmental politics, state negotiators must often go back and forth between domestic pressures and foreign demands in solidifying their preferences (Kroll and Shogren 2008). Domestic constraints such as pressure from interest groups, ratification procedures, or national elections are important in determining what states ultimately agree to include in international agreements. Equally important is the way in which states are able to defend their positions to others, while successfully concluding international environmental negotiations. International interactions, alongside domestic factors, shape the evolution of state preferences that are ultimately captured in international environmental agreements.

Although these domestic and international factors are central in helping us understand how states' preferences might converge towards consensus in global environmental negotiations, the process is extremely complex and other factors are also important. Centrally, in these efforts for collective action, states will also interact with many transnational non-state actors. We turn to these important players in global environmental governance in Chapter 4.

Critical thinking questions

1. Why might states' national interests vary from one environmental issue to another? Use examples to illustrate your answer.
2. Explain the rational choice model and its limitations in explaining states' preferences in global environmental politics.
3. How might usually less powerful states operate to shape the preferences of more powerful states in international environmental negotiations?
4. Explain how leadership works to help states secure their interests in international environmental negotiations.

 Test your knowledge and understanding further by trying this chapter's Multiple Choice Questions
www.oup.com/he/morin1e

Key references

Aklin, Michaël, and Johannes Urpelainen. 2014. 'The Global Spread of Environmental Ministries: Domestic–International Interactions'. *International Studies Quarterly* 58 (4): 764–780.
This article discusses domestic and international factors that explain the creation of environmental ministries by states. It shows how the democratization of states makes them more sensitive to the salience of environmental issues at the international level.

Chaek, Pamela, and Lynn Wagner (eds). 2012. *The Roads from Rio: Lessons Learned from Twenty Years of Multilateral Environmental Negotiations.* London: Routledge.

This book analyses multilateral environmental negotiations over the period 1992 to 2012 on ten issue areas. It identifies the different steps by which international agreements are negotiated. Pamela Chasek is one of the founders of the Earth Negotiation Bulletin, a reporting service on environmental negotiations, of which Lynn Wagner is also a very active member. Their expert knowledge of the details of international negotiations is clear.

Desombre, Elizabeth R. 2000. *Domestic Sources of International Environmental Policy: Industry, Environmentalists, and US Power.* Cambridge, MA: MIT Press.

This book illustrates the interactions between domestic and international interests in global environmental politics. It shows how national interest groups can create alliances to push for the adoption of environmental regulations at home and abroad. The book uses the United States context as a case study, covering three environmental issues: endangered species, air pollution, and fisheries conservation.

Sprinz, Detlef F., and Tapani Vaahtoranta. 1994. 'The Interest-Based Explanation of International Environmental Policy'. *International Organization* 48 (1): 77–105.

This article applies the rational choice model to explain the behaviour of states in two international negotiations: the Montreal Protocol on Substances that Deplete the Ozone Layer and the Helsinki Protocol on acid rain. On the basis of environmental vulnerability and abatement costs, the authors identify 'pushers', 'draggers', 'intermediates', and 'bystanders' in international environmental negotiations.

 For additional material and resources, please visit the online resources at: **www.oup.com/he/morin1e**

Chapter references

Afionis, Stavros. 2011. 'The European Union as a Negotiator in the International Climate Change Regime'. *International Environmental Agreements* 11 (4): 297–319.

Afionis, Stavros, and Ioannis Chatzopoulos. 2010. 'Russia's Role in UNFCCC Negotiations Since the Exit of The United States in 2001'. *International Environmental Agreements* 10 (1): 45–63.

Akhtar-Schuster, M., F. Amiraslani, C. F. Diaz Morejon, R. Escadafal, E. Fulajtar, A. Grainger, K. Kellner, S. I. Khan, O. Perez Pardo, U. Sauchanka, L. C. Stringer, Fasil Reda, and R. J. Thomas. 2016. 'Designing a New Science-Policy Communication Mechanism for the UN Convention to Combat Desertification'. *Environmental Science & Policy* 63: 122–131.

Aklin, Michaël, and Johannes Urpelainen. 2014. 'The Global Spread of Environmental Ministries: Domestic-International Interactions'. *International Studies Quarterly* 58 (4): 764–780.

Andresen, Steinar. 1989. 'Science and Politics in the International Management of Whales'. *Marine Policy* 13 (2): 99–117.

Andresen, Steinar. 2001. 'Global Environmental Governance: UN Fragmentation and Co-ordination'. In *Yearbook of International Cooperation on Environment and Development 2001–2002*, edited by Olav Schram Stokke and Øystein B. Thommessen, 19–25. London: Earthscan.

Barkdull, John, and Paul G. Harris. 2002. 'Environmental Change and Foreign Policy: A Survey of Theory'. *Global Environmental Politics* 2 (2): 63–91.

Barnett, Jon. 2008. 'The Worst of Friends: OPEC and G-77 in the Climate Regime'. *Global Environmental Politics* 8 (4): 1–8.

Bättig, Michèle B., and Thomas Bernauer. 2009. 'National Institutions and Global Public Goods: Are Democracies More Cooperative in Climate Change Policy?' *International Organization* 63 (2): 281–308.

Bernauer, Thomas, Tobias Böhmelt, and Vally Koubi. 2013. 'Is there a Democracy–Civil Society Paradox in Global Environmental Governance?' *Global Environmental Politics* 13 (1): 88–107.

Bhandary, Rishikesh Ram. 2017. 'Coalition Strategies in the Climate Negotiations: An Analysis of

Mountain-Related Coalitions'. *International Environmental Agreements* 17 (2): 173–190.

Boyd, Emily, Esteve Corbera, and Manuel Estrada. 2008. 'UNFCCC Negotiations (pre-Kyoto to COP-9): What the Process Says About the Politics of CDM-sinks'. *International Environmental Agreements* 8 (2): 95–112.

Bretschger, Lucas. 2017. 'Equity and the Convergence of Nationally Determined Climate Policies'. *Environmental Economics and Policy Studies* 19 (1): 1–14.

Brunnée, Jutta. 2002. 'COPing with Consent: Law-Making Under Multilateral Environmental Agreements'. *Leiden Journal of International Law* 15 (1): 1–52.

Busch, Per-Olof, and Helge Jörgens. 2005. 'The International Sources of Policy Convergence: Explaining the Spread of Environmental Policy Innovations'. *Journal of European Public Policy* 12 (5): 860–884.

Campbell, Lisa M., Catherine Corson, Noella J. Gray, Kenneth I. Macdonald, and Peter Brosius. 2014. 'Studying Global Environmental Meetings to Understand Global Environmental Governance: Collaborative Event Ethnography at the Tenth Conference of the Parties to the Convention on Biological Diversity'. *Global Environmental Politics* 14 (3): 1–20.

Cao, Xun and Aseem Prakash. 2010. 'Trade Competition and Domestic Pollution: A Panel Study, 1980-2003.' *International Organization* 64 (3): 481–503.

Carbonell, Joel R., and Juliann E. Allison. 2015. 'Democracy and State Environmental Commitment to International Environmental Treaties'. *International Environmental Agreements* 15 (2): 79–104.

Chasek, Pamela S. 2001. *Earth Negotiations:Analyzing Thirty Years of Environmental Diplomacy*. Tokyo: UNU Press.

Chasek, Pamela S. 2007. 'US Policy in the UN Environmental Arena: Powerful Laggard or Constructive Leader?' *International Environmental Agreements* 7 (4): 363–387.

Chasek, Pamela, and Lynn Wagner (eds). 2012. *The Roads from Rio: Lessons Learned from Twenty Years of Multilateral Environmental Negotiations*. London: Routledge.

Chasek, Pamela S., and Lynn M. Wagner. 2016. 'Breaking the Mold: A New Type of Multilateral Sustainable Development Negotiation'. *International Environmental Agreements* 16 (3): 397–413.

Corneloup, Inés de Águeda, and Arthur P. J. Mol. 2014. 'Small Island Developing States and International Climate Change Negotiations: the Power of Moral "Leadership"'. *International Environmental Agreements* 14 (3): 281–297.

Dauvergne, Peter. 2018. 'The Global Politics of the Business of "Sustainable" Palm Oil'. *Global Environmental Politics* 18 (2): 34–52.

Davenport, Deborah S. 2005. 'An Alternative Explanation for the Failure of the UNCED Forest Negotiations'. *Global Environmental Politics* 5 (1): 105–130.

Depledge, Joanna. 2006. 'The Opposite of Learning: Ossification in the Climate Change Regime'. *Global Environmental Politics* 6 (1): 1–22.

Depledge, Joanna. 2007. 'A Special Relationship: Chairpersons and the Secretariat in the Climate Change Negotiations'. *Global Environmental Politics* 7 (1): 45–68.

Depledge, Joanna. 2008. 'Striving for No: Saudi Arabia in the Climate Change Regime'. *Global Environmental Politics* 8 (4): 9–35.

Desombre, Elizabeth R. 2000. *Domestic Sources of International Environmental Policy: Industry, Environmentalists, and US Power*. Cambridge, MA: MIT Press.

Dimitrov Radovslav S. 2016. 'The Paris Agreement on Climate Change: Behind Closed Doors'. *Global Environmental Politics* 16 (3): 1–11.

Downie, David L. 1999. 'The Power to Destroy: Understanding Stratospheric Ozone Politics as a Common Pool Resource Problem'. In *Anarchy and the Environment: The International Relations of Common Pool Resources*, edited by Samuel J. Barkin and George Shambaugh, 97–121. Albany, NY: State University of New York.

Eisenstadt, Todd A., Daniel J. Fiorino, and Daniela Stevens. 2019. 'National Environmental Policies as Shelter from the Storm: Specifying the Relationship between Extreme Weather Vulnerability and National Environmental Performance'. *Journal of Environmental Studies and Sciences* 9 (1): 96–107.

Falkner, Robert. 2016. 'The Paris Agreement and the New Logic of International Climate Politics'. *International Affairs* 92 (5): 1107–1125.

Gupta, Joyeeta. 2014. *The History of Global Climate Governance*. Cambridge: Cambridge University Press.

Harashima, Yohei. 2008. 'Trade and Environment Negotiations in the WTO: Asian Perspectives'. *International Environmental Agreements* 8 (1): 17–34.

Harrison, Kathryn. 2007. 'The Road not Taken: Climate Change Policy in Canada and the United States'. *Global Environmental Politics* 7 (4): 92–117.

Henry, Laura A., and Lisa McIntosh Sundstrom. 2007. 'Russia and the Kyoto Protocol: Seeking an Alignment of Interests and Image'. *Global Environmental Politics* 7 (4): 47–69.

Hilton, Isabel, and Oliver Kerr. 2017. 'The Paris Agreement: China's "New Normal" Role in International Climate Negotiations'. *Climate Policy* 17 (1): 48–58.

Hirsch, Eric. 2015. ' "It Won't be any Good to have Democracy if we don't have a Country": Climate Change and the Politics of Synecdoche in the Maldives'. *Global Environmental Change* 35: 190–198.

Höhne, Niklas, Takeshi Kuramochi, Carsten Warnecke, Frauke Röser, Hanna Fekete, Markus Hagemann, Thomas Day et al. 2017. 'The Paris Agreement: Resolving the Inconsistency between Global Goals and National Contributions'. *Climate Policy* 17 (1): 16–32.

Hovi, Jon, Detlef F. Sprinz, and Guri Bang. 2010. 'Why the United States did not Become a Party to The Kyoto Protocol: German, Norwegian, and US Perspectives'. *European Journal of International Relations* 18 (1): 129–150.

Hovi, Jon, Detlef F. Sprinz, and Arild Underdal. 2009. 'Implementing Long-Term Climate Policy: Time Inconsistency, Domestic Politics, International Anarchy'. *Global Environmental Politics* 9 (3): 20–39.

Jernnäs, Maria, and Björn-Ola Linnér. 2019. 'A Discursive Cartography of Nationally Determined Contributions to the Paris Climate Agreement'. *Global Environmental Change* 55 (March): 73–83.

Johnson, Pierre Marc, Mayrand Karel, and Marc Paquin. 2006. *Governing Global Desertification: Linking Environmental Degradation, Poverty and Participation*. Aldershot: Ashgate.

Kaasa, Stine Madland. 2007. 'The UN Commission on Sustainable Development: Which Mechanisms Explain its Accomplishments?' *Global Environmental Politics* 7 (3): 107–129.

Kasa, Sjur, Anne T. Gullberg, and Gørild Heggelund. 2008. 'The Group of 77 in the International Climate Negotiations: Recent Developments and Future Directions'. *International Environmental Agreements* 8 (2): 113–127.

Kroll, Stephan, and Jason F. Shogren. 2008. 'Domestic Politics and Climate Change: International Public Goods in Two-Level Games'. *Cambridge Review of International Affairs* 21 (4): 563–583.

Lenshow, Andrea, and Carina Sprungk. 2010. 'The Myth of a Green Europe'. *Journal of Common Market Studies* 48 (1): 133–154.

Meyer, John W., David John Frank, Ann Hironaka, Evan Schofer, and Nancy Brandon Tuma. 1997. 'The Structuring of a World Environmental Regime, 1870–1990'. *International Organization* 51 (4): 623–651.

Mitchell, Ronald B., Liliana B. Andonova, Mark Axelrod, Jörg Balsiger, Thomas Bernauer, Jessica F. Green, James Hollway, Rakhyun E. Kim, and Jean-Frédéric Morin. 2010. 'What We Know (and Could Know) About International Environmental Agreements'. *Global Environmental Politics* 20 (1): 103–121.

Morin, Jean-Frédéric, and Amandine Orsini. 2014. 'Policy Coherence and Regime Complexes: The Case of Genetic Resources'. *Review of International Studies* 40 (2): 303–324.

Morin, Jean-Frédéric, and Jonathan Paquin. 2018. *Foreign Policy Analysis: A Toolbox*. Cham, Switzerland: Palgrave Macmillan.

Muñoz, Miguel, Rachel Thrasher, and Adil Najam. 2009. 'Measuring the Negotiation Burden of Multilateral Environmental Agreements'. *Global Environmental Politics* 9 (4): 1–13.

Najam, Adil. 2004. 'Dynamics of the Southern Collective: Developing Countries in Desertification Negotiations'. *Global Environmental Politics* 4 (3): 128–154.

Nakada, Minoru. 2006. 'Distributional Conflicts and the Timing of Environmental Policy'. *International Environmental Agreements* 6 (1): 29–38.

Nakanabo Diallo, Rozenn N. 2015. 'Conservation Philanthropy and the Shadow of State Power in Gorongosa National Park, Mozambique'. *Conservation Society* 13 (2):119–128.

Nelson, Michael Byron. 2016. 'Africa's Regional Powers and Climate Change Negotiations'. *Global Environmental Politics* 16 (2): 110–129.

Orsini, Amandine. 2010. *La biodiversité sous influence? Les lobbies industriels face aux politiques internationales d'environnement*. Brussels: Éditions de l'Université de Bruxelles.

Papa, Mihaela, and Nancy W. Gleason. 2012. 'Major Emerging Powers in Sustainable Development Diplomacy: Assessing Their Leadership Potential'. *Global Environmental Change* 22 (4): 915–924.

Pittel, Karen, and Dirk T. G. Rübbelke. 2012. 'Transitions in the Negotiations on Climate Change: From Prisoner's Dilemma to Chicken and Beyond'. *International Environmental Agreements* 12 (1): 23–39.

Putnam, Robert D. 1988. 'Diplomacy and Domestic Politics: The Logic of Two-Level Games'. *International Organization* 42 (3): 427–460.

Rajamani, Lavanya, and Jutta Brunnée. 2017. 'The Legality of Downgrading Nationally Determined Contributions under the Paris Agreement: Lessons from the US Disengagement'. *Journal of Environmental Law* 29 (3): 537–551.

Roberts, J. Timmons, Bradley C. Parks, and Alexis A. Vásquez. 2004. 'Who Ratifies Environmental Treaties and Why? Institutionalism, Structuralism and

Participation by 192 Nations in 22 Treaties'. *Global Environmental Politics* 4 (3): 22–64.

Rosendal, G. Kristin. 2007. 'Norway in UN Environmental Policies: Ambitions and Influence'. *International Environmental Agreements* 7 (4): 439–455.

Skjærseth, Jon Birger. 2017. 'The European Commission's Shifting Climate Leadership'. *Global Environmental Politics* 17 (2): 84–104.

Skjærseth, Jon Birger, and Jørgen Wettestad. 2009. 'The Origin, Evolution and Consequences of the EU Emissions Trading System'. *Global Environmental Politics* 9 (2): 101–122.

Skovgaard, Jakob. 2017. 'Limiting Costs or Correcting Market Failures? Finance Ministries and Frame Alignment in UN Climate Finance Negotiations'. *International Environment Agreements* 17 (1): 89–106.

Spencer, Thomas, Roberta Pierfederici, Henri Waisman, Michel Colombier, Christoph Bertram, Elmar Kriegler, Gunnar Luderer, Florian Humpenoeder, Alexander Popp, and Ottmar Edenhofer et al. 2015. 'Beyond the Numbers: Understanding the Transformation Induced by INDCs'. IAEA INIS (INIS-FR-17-0724). Paris: IDDRI.

Sprinz, Detlef F., and Tapani Vaahtoranta. 1994. 'The Interest-Based Explanation of International Environmental Policy'. *International Organization* 48 (1): 77–105.

Tallberg, Jonas. 2010. 'The Power of the Chair: Formal Leadership in International Cooperation'. *International Studies Quarterly* 54 (1): 241–265.

Tambo, Ernest, Duo-quan Wang, and Xiao-Nong Zhou. 2016. 'Tackling Air Pollution and Extreme Climate Changes in China: Implementing the Paris Climate Change Agreement'. *Environment International* 95: 152–156.

Tamura, Kentaro. 2006. 'Climate Change and the Credibility of International Commitments:

What is Necessary for the US to Deliver on Such Commitments?' *International Environmental Agreements* 6 (3): 289–304.

Thompson, Alexander. 2010. 'Rational Design in Motion: Uncertainty and Flexibility in the Global Climate Regime'. *European Journal of International Relations* 16 (2): 269–296.

Tobin, Paul. 2017. 'Leaders and Laggards: Climate Policy Ambition in Developed States'. *Global Environmental Politics* 17 (4): 28–47.

Tobin, Paul, Nicole M. Schmidt, Jale Tosun, and Charlotte Burns. 2018. 'Mapping States' Paris Climate Pledges: Analysing Targets and Groups at COP21'. *Global Environmental Change* 48: 11–21.

United Nations Environment Programme. 2018. *Emissions Gap Report*. Nairobi: UNEP.

Van Asselt, Harro, Norichika Kaine, and Masahiko Iguchi. 2009. 'Japan's Position in International Climate Policy: Navigating Between Kyoto and the APP'. *International Environmental Agreements* 9 (3): 319–336.

Van Haute, Emilie (ed.) 2016. *Green Parties in Europe*. London: Routledge.

Varkkey, Helena. 2014. 'Regional Cooperation, Patronage and the ASEAN Agreement on Transboundary Haze Pollution'. *International Environmental Agreements* 14 (1): 65–81.

Vieira, Marco A. 2013. 'Brazilian Foreign Policy in the Context of Global Climate Norms'. *Foreign Policy Analysis* 9 (4): 369–386.

Vogler, John, and Hannes R. Stephan. 2007. 'The European Union in Global Environmental Governance: Leadership In The Making?' *International Environmental Agreements* 7 (4): 389–413.

Young, Oran R. 1991. 'Political Leadership and Regime Formation: On the Development of Institutions in International Society'. *International Organization* 45 (3): 281–308.

4 Non-state actors

Non-state actors, such as NGOs, corporations, and transnational networks, play an increasingly significant role in global environmental politics. Some of them, such as Greenpeace and Shell, became well known by communicating directly with the public or consumers. Others, such as the Indigenous Peoples' International Centre for Policy Research and Education or the International Council for Local Environmental Initiatives, are less visible to the wider public but no less influential. The scope, diversity, preferences, methods of engagement, and contributions of non-state actors to global environmental governance are often overshadowed by a focus on state actors. This chapter sheds light on how non-state actors engage in global environmental governance and highlights how they shape the political landscape in this field.

 Learning objectives

After reading this chapter, readers will be able to:

● Identify different types of non-governmental organizations in global environmental governance;

● Explain the different strategies and modes of engagement that non-state actors deploy in environmental politics;

● Assess how and how much non-state actors influence global environmental politics; and

● Discuss the nature and consequences of governance instruments developed by non-state actors.

Introduction

Non-state actors engage in a host of important political activities in global environmental **governance**. These range from direct action campaigns, to provision of expertise, to facilitating negotiations between states, to highlighting violations of international environmental law. For example, on 1 June 2018, Greenpeace organized a direct action event at the shareholders' meeting of the oil and gas firm Total. Greenpeace's objective was to raise public and government awareness concerning Total's decision to drill for oil in the Amazon rainforest, where extensive exploration activities threaten **biodiversity**. In a very different example of non-governmental organizations' (NGO) activities in global environmental politics, later that year the World Wildlife Fund (known as WWF) released its *Living Planet Report*, which periodically presents current trends with regard to global biodiversity and the health of the planet. The 2018 report finds evidence that global biodiversity has declined by over 50 per cent in less than 50 years. This report has been used to catalyse action and scholarship on biodiversity **conservation**, with the earlier reports, for example, being cited over 200 times on these issues. These are just two examples of how even the same types of non-state actors, in this case environmental NGOs, deploy very different strategies in their approach to engagement with global environmental politics.

The number of non-state actors active in global environmental politics is impressive. In 2018, 4,000 of the accredited non-state organizations at the United Nations had environmental protection listed as one of their aims, and as of 2018 there were 482 non-state organizations accredited to the United Nations Environment Assembly of the United Nations Environment Programme.

The number of international non-state actors is still growing, as illustrated by their increasing participation in international environmental conferences (see Figure 4.1). In most environmental **institutions**, non-state actors can become accredited and subsequently register and attend intergovernmental meetings as **observers**. In some cases, there are so many non-state observers that their presence raises significant logistical challenges for conference organizers. At the 2009 United Nations climate change conference held in Copenhagen, for example, more than two-thirds of registered participants were NGO representatives, causing overcrowding, and the Danish, as the host government, made a controversial decision to limit NGOs' access to the negotiation process (Fisher 2010: 12; Orr 2016).

Several factors explain this growing involvement of non-state actors, including a widespread goal to increase transparency at international institutions, the development of

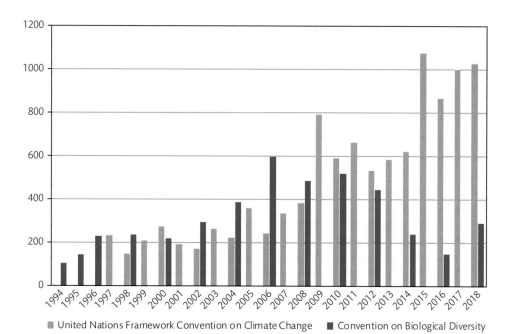

Figure 4.1 Number of non-state actors registered as observers—international negotiations on climate, and biodiversity (1994–2018)

Source data from: https://unfccc.int; cbd.int

communication technologies, and governments' renewed trust in and reliance on non-state actors to implement their policies (Green and Colgan 2013; Reimann 2006). Transparency and public participation have become established norms in international environmental politics. This is exemplified by the adoption of the 1998 Aarhus Convention on Access to Information, Public Participation in Decision-Making and Access to Justice in Environmental Matters and the 2018 Escazú Agreement on Access to Information, Public Participation and Justice in Environmental Matters. Alongside this ubiquity of non-state actors, there are a host of ways they engage and matter in global politics, which this chapter illuminates.

At the United Nations Conference on Environment and Development held in Rio in 1992, states identified nine categories of non-state actors whose participation is deemed essential if we are to reach **sustainable development**. Called '**major groups**', these nine categories are: women, children and youth, indigenous people and their communities, NGOs, local authorities, workers and trade unions, business and industry, the scientific and technological community, and farmers. The relevance of this categorization was restated in *The Future We Want*, the outcome document of the RIO+20 Summit in 2012.

The major group categorization highlights the diversity of non-state actors in global environmental politics. In particular, it makes clear that non-state actors include for-profit (such as businesses and farmers) as well as not-for-profit organizations (such as NGOs or local authorities). Although several actors in civil society are organized into NGOs, reducing non-state actors to the simple category of NGOs would be an oversimplification. For example, cities and other substate actors are not NGOs, but they have been increasingly involved as participants in global environmental governance.

While the United Nations list of nine 'major groups' captures a wide range of non-state actors, it is not exhaustive. It neglects non-state actors that are less institutionalized. For example, it does not include informal movements of individuals defending specific environmental claims. There are some movements in global environmental politics that intentionally distance themselves from more institutionalized NGOs because they believe the NGOs do not challenge the status quo aggressively enough, and because they often work closely with governments and/or corporations. For example, Earth First! is a radical environmental advocacy group that uses direct action strategies such as protests, performances, and sit-ins. Other non-state actors do not necessarily distance themselves from the major groups categories, but they do not have the financial, human, or logistical means to become actively involved in environmental politics. This is particularly the case for marginalized and vulnerable populations such as certain indigenous groups (see Box 4.1).

Normative debates on non-state actors' contribution to international politics are lively. For some, their contribution is positive, representing a clear step towards the advent of an 'international civil society' (Wapner 1996), which would help to bring a more direct involvement of citizens and other affected populations in international environmental politics. Others are concerned about the privatization of global environmental politics (Clapp 1998). They warn of a retreat by state actors as legitimate public authorities in international politics, in favour of non-state actors that are not elected or representative, are less transparent, and whose power is more difficult to monitor and counterbalance. Alongside these normative debates, considerable efforts have been made to better understand non-state actors' contributions to global environmental governance, both as rule influencers and as rule producers (Green 2013). We unpack these various debates in the remainder of this chapter.

The chapter gives particular attention to NGOs, businesses, and transnational networks (on the role of scientific organizations see Chapter 1; on the role of secretariats see Chapter 7). It first introduces how NGOs engage in global environmental governance and how that engagement has evolved over time (Section 4.1). It goes on to discuss the strategies and interests of businesses in global environmental politics (Section 4.2), and then introduces conceptual tools to understand NGO and business influence in this issue area (Section 4.3). The last section of the chapter examines the direct involvement of transnational actors as rule producers, a role that has become more and more visible and that raises concerns over the privatization of global environmental politics (Section 4.4).

4.1 NGOs in global environmental governance

Defining NGOs

NGOs receive a lot of attention in international environmental policy forums and academic studies. The United Nations defines NGOs as 'any such organization that is not established by a governmental entity or intergovernmental agreement' (United Nations Economic and Social Council resolution 1996/31). This indicates that an NGO is defined first and foremost by its non-governmental nature; its members are not states and it is independent from state influence. Though useful, this criterion sometimes proves difficult to operationalize, and there are numerous ambiguous cases.

Although NGOs are non-governmental in nature, in practice they can have relationships with governments that become porous, in terms of objectives, funding, direction, or work agenda. For example, the All-China Environment Federation, an organization accredited to the United Nations Environment Programme as an environmental NGO, is financially supported by the Chinese government. Although most NGOs are financially independent of their governments, several of them maintain strong connections with government agencies, sometimes even influencing their governments' positions. This dynamic is particularly visible in large federations of NGOs, such as Friends of the Earth International. Although united in a global structure, national chapters of these NGO federations can develop different interests in relation to their host governments' objectives, leading to divergence between chapters (Doherty 2006).

NGOs are also defined as not-for-profit actors, even if this criterion is not directly stated as part of the definition in the United Nations resolution. The resolution says that the main resources of the organization should come from national affiliates or other components or individual members. According to this definition, individual corporations are not NGOs, because their resources come from their economic activities, but organizations that bring together a number of individual corporations are considered as NGOs. For example, industrial associations, the members of which are corporations, are considered NGOs in the United Nations major groups designation. The International Chamber of Commerce and the European Roundtable of Industrialists, for example, are industrial associations that are NGOs. Businesses are also eager to create or fund NGOs in order to promote ideas that align with their interests in international forums (see Box 4.4).

The range of interests represented by NGOs is vast and not always coherent. Although examples such as WWF's campaigns to protect large mammals, or Greenpeace's anti-nuclear actions come to mind when we think of NGOs operating in this issue area, the field of sustainable development actually inspires a great diversity of actors and interests. Even NGOs that are not strictly focused on environmental protection are also part of the sustainable development NGO landscape. For example, development NGOs, such as Oxfam International and Third World Network, and NGOs specializing in human rights, such as Global Witness and Human Rights Watch, have programmes related to environmental protection (see Box 4.1). NGOs following climate change negotiations include organizations specializing in agriculture, development, energy, religion, transport, engineering, and indigenous issues, among others (Muñoz Cabré 2011; see also Kuchler 2017).

Box 4.1 The representation of indigenous people

Indigenous peoples increasingly leverage the international stage to pursue their interests and raise awareness on their issues of concern, including those related to territorial claims and their limited political autonomy.

Indigenous representation in international politics started in the 1980s in the International Labour Organization, which in 1989 hosted the Indigenous and Tribal Peoples Convention, the first international treaty to give rights to indigenous people. Some indigenous organizations, empowered by the Convention, then started to draw the attention of the international community to environmental issues that were directly impacting their daily lives, such as deforestation and biodiversity erosion.

Certain governments and renowned activists have also been successful in bringing indigenous and local communities' interests to the international stage. For example, in 1977 in Kenya, Wangari Maathai created the Green Belt Movement. This movement aims to empower local communities, and women in particular, by teaching them to restore the forest cover on their degraded lands. In 2004, the benefit of such an initiative was recognized, when Wangari Maathai was awarded the Nobel Peace Prize. Another early example is the creation of the Communal Areas Management Programme for Indigenous Resources initiative in Zimbabwe in 1989, which combines biodiversity conservation with protection of indigenous communities' territorial rights.

In the 1990s, indigenous people and local communities began to organize their actions within umbrella organizations. The Indigenous Peoples' International Centre for Policy Research and Education was created in 1996, and the International Indigenous Peoples Forum on Climate Change formed in 2001. These organizations aim to create what Margaret Keck and Kathryn Sikkink have called a 'boomerang effect', in which local organizations use international actors and networks to 'send out' their demands at the international level, in the hope that these networks can leverage political action to 'come back' at the national and local levels in support of their interests. More recently, during the negotiations of the 2010 Nagoya Protocol on **genetic resources**, indigenous organizations' demands regarding the protection of their **traditional knowledge** were supported by NGOs such as the Third World Network and the European Network for Ecological Reflection and Action. This contributed to the adoption of Nagoya Protocol Article 7, recognizing the rights of indigenous and local communities to grant access to the genetic resources and associated traditional knowledge present on their territories.

Most international institutions do not formally recognize any special status for indigenous organizations. However, there are a few exceptions to the under-representation of indigenous organizations in global environmental politics. Since 2000, six indigenous peoples' organizations have gained permanent status in the Arctic Council. In forest governance, the mechanism 'Reduction Emissions from Deforestation and forest Degradation, plus the sustainable management of forests, and the conservation and enhancement of forest carbon stocks', initiated in 2010 to fight deforestation and forest degradation, has been an opportunity for indigenous peoples in Indonesia and Tanzania to have their rights recognized.

Overall, even without formal recognition, the importance of indigenous and local community rights and knowledge is increasingly referred to on the international scene. Since its fourth assessment in 2007, the **Intergovernmental Panel on Climate Change** has mentioned in its reports indigenous knowledge on the impacts of climate change or on **adaptation** strategies as a key resource for climate change mitigation and adaptation. Indigenous and local communities often have unique approaches to environmental management and protection that could be highly valuable in tackling global environmental challenges.

Sources: Jodoin 2017; Keck and Sikkink 1998; Lindroth and Sinevaara-Niskanen 2013; Marion Suiseeya 2014.

Evolution of environmental NGO engagement over time

Some **intergovernmental organizations** have developed ad hoc systems to classify the NGOs they interact with regularly. For instance, the United Nations Framework Convention on Climate Change secretariat adopted a system mirroring the nine United Nations major groups. This system distinguishes six different types of NGOs: environmental NGOs, business and industry NGOs (known as BINGOs), farmers and agricultural NGOs, research and independent NGOs (known as RINGOs), trade union NGOs (known as TUNGOs), and youth NGOs.

Despite their shared interest in climate change issues, important divisions still exist within and between these types of NGOs. In this sub-section we explain the diversity among environmental NGOs. Although there are various ways to slice this up, we identify three generations of environmental NGOs, which differ in terms of the types of environmental issues they address, the ideas they espouse (see Chapter 2), and their modes of engagement in environmental politics.

The first generation of environmental NGOs, from the end of the nineteenth century until the end of the 1950s, were created by those who were exclusively interested in protecting natural spaces and species, such as ornithologists, hunters, and hikers. These NGOs used an anthropocentric vision of environmental protection to advocate nature conservation and **preservation** policies, such as the creation of national parks, through direct contact with policymakers. The Sierra Club, the Wildlife Conservation Society, and Birdlife International, created in 1892, 1895, and 1922 respectively, belong to this category and are still active today.

The second-generation environmental NGOs are those created in the 1960s and 1970s by activists aspiring to tackle environmental issues beyond mere conservation, embrace a more biocentric view, and use more radical modes of engagement in politics. For example, the founders of Friends of the Earth, created in 1969, and Greenpeace, created in 1971, were originally members of the Sierra Club, a first-generation environmental NGO. However, they came to see the Sierra Club as limited in scope, and therefore felt that new NGOs were needed. In both cases, they first campaigned on nuclear energy, but quickly embraced broader environmental issues such as industrial pollution. Still active today, they joined forces with other similar organizations such as Earthlife Africa, which favours a more radical tone and uses more visible strategies such as protests, boycotts, and demonstrations to attract attention from the public, decision makers, and the media.

Emerging in the 1980s, the third-generation environmental NGOs invested their efforts in production and dissemination of expertise. They worked alongside decision makers in their search for policy solutions to environmental problems. In the United States, for example, third-generation NGOs such as the International Institute for Sustainable Development, the Worldwatch Institute, the World Resources Institute, and the Advocates Coalition for Development and Environment maintain close relationships with political leaders. They operate as think tanks, occupying a middle ground between research centres and consultancies, producing data as well as providing advice on how to tackle environmental issues. Third-generation NGOs invest in research, rely on technical expertise, advise decision makers, and cover numerous themes related to the environment and sustainable development.

Many environmental NGOs have evolved from generation to generation in a cumulative way. Without losing their historical or ideological roots, they have gradually diversified their portfolio of activities. For example, WWF, a first-generation environmental NGO, and Greenpeace, a second-generation NGO, have professionalized in recent years and now offer policy expertise in a similar way to third-generation NGOs.

Other environmental NGOs have chosen one particular kind of action to the exclusion of all others. For example, a former Greenpeace member, Paul Watson, did not support Greenpeace's evolution and created a more radical NGO, the Sea Shepherd Conservation Society, in 1977, which used even more direct action methods to protect whales, seals, and other marine species. The Sea Shepherd Conservation Society still follows this line of action several decades after its creation.

NGOs are therefore very diverse and can support opposite positions. For example, the NGO Action Group on Erosion, Technology and Concentration is opposed to commercial use of genetic resources, whereas the World Resources Institute sees such use as a possible funding source for protecting biodiversity (Bled 2010). And the Environmental Defense Fund is more supportive of market-based mechanisms for reducing **greenhouse gas** emissions than the Climate Action Network (Alcock 2008). In this context, NGOs sometimes have to directly compete with one another to gain support for their positions. They also compete to recruit new members, for media attention, and for funding. Inter-NGO competition is particularly intense, for instance, in the domain of sea turtle conservation (Botetzagias et al. 2010: 118) or climate change activism (Hadden 2015). As Section 4.2 discusses, diversity and competition are also characteristic of business groups in environmental politics.

4.2 Business engagement in global environmental governance

How and why businesses engage in global environmental politics

Businesses initially became significant actors in global environmental governance at the 1992 **Rio Summit** on Environment and Development. Businesses were slower to engage in international forums, not because their role is less important, but because they initially favoured work at the national level, where they already hold influence in political decision-making.

Maurice Strong, the Secretary General of the 1992 Rio Summit (see Box 6.3), supported the creation of the first international industry organization with environmental concerns, the Business Council for Sustainable Development. Strong sought to increase private sector awareness of the challenges of sustainable development. At the Rio Summit, he asked the entrepreneur Stephen Schmidheiny to provide a list of important business executives,

48 of whom were invited to become the initial members of the Business Council for Sustainable Development—with that decision, industry participation was formalized at the 1992 Rio Summit. In January 1995, the Business Council for Sustainable Development merged with the World Industry Council for the Environment, to create the World Business Council for Sustainable Development, which is now the largest international industrial coalition on environmental issues. It brings together 200 businesses and 70 national business councils around six programmes, including climate and energy, circular economy, cities and mobility, and food and nature. It primarily engages with global environmental politics by attending international meetings and lobbying governments to follow its positions on relevant issues.

The relationship between corporations and environmental policies is complicated. On one hand, businesses have a major impact on the environment. They consume natural resources in large quantities and generate significant negative externalities such as waste and pollution. According to the Climate Accountability Institute, 90 entities are responsible for 63 per cent of greenhouse gas emissions over the period 1854 to 2010, and 56 of these 90 entities are oil and gas corporations (Heede 2014). So it is not surprising that few businesses are strong supporters of environmental regulation, which often interferes with their economic activities.

On the other hand, corporations often have the expertise needed to develop effective environmental technologies, and can gain a competitive advantage if they can shape environmental policies to suit their specific interests. For example, the American corporation DuPont played a key role in the international negotiations on the protection of the **ozone layer** (Falkner 2008). After the adoption of the Vienna Convention, DuPont, the world's largest commercial producer of chlorofluorocarbons, made an important declaration recognizing that a connection between its products and the depletion of the ozone layer was highly likely and that regulation of these products was inevitable. Instead of denying the harmful environmental impacts of chlorofluorocarbons, DuPont embraced a long-term perspective and a proactive stance, investing in the search for substitutes from 1988 onwards. The company declared that it was in favour of limiting emissions internationally and was soon successful in identifying a substitute for chlorofluorocarbons—called hydrochlorofluorocarbons. In this context, the United States government came fully on board with the aggressive chlorofluorocarbons phaseouts proposed under the Montreal Protocol, and it became difficult for European countries that were initially sceptical to remain opposed to the move. Of course, DuPont developed these substitutes not just for environmental reasons, but also to maximize its own profits by becoming a leader in a new market. Even so, thanks to this technological innovation, DuPont's support of an international agreement to protect the ozone layer significantly helped to alleviate the initial misgivings of American negotiators (Haas 1992).

Two perspectives on the role of business in global environmental governance

There are many competing views regarding the role played by the business sector in global environmental governance. We distinguish here between two main views: a *neo-Gramscian perspective* and a *pluralist perspective*.

The former puts forward a vision that is explicitly critical of corporations (Levy and Newell 2005). *Neo-Gramscian* analysts consider global environmental politics to be dominated by a hegemonic combination of forces, institutions, and ideas that help maintain the economic and financial order, even though it is detrimental to the environment. In their view, corporations are among the main beneficiaries and the main architects of the hegemonic order: they are closely associated with government elites and take advantage of existing institutions and ideas to establish their own legitimacy. According to this perspective, businesses will always pursue business-as-usual practices when asked to handle global environmental problems, changing their behaviour only at the margins and in line with their market interests (Newell 2018).

For instance, faced with the threat of climate change, biotechnology corporations work hard to market 'climate-smart agriculture', which they see as including the development of seeds that are resistant to climate impacts, such as temperature extremes and inconsistent rainfall. According to these biotechnology corporations, developing these adapted seeds necessitates even stronger intellectual property protection, since it involves a large capital expenditure in research and development costs. Stronger intellectual property rights over 'climate-smart agriculture' would result in even more business control over the agri-food system (Newell and Taylor 2018). Alternative understandings of what 'climate-smart agriculture' might consist of are possible, such as agricultural methods that would use fewer climate-constrained inputs such as water, or improvements to food distribution that would reduce food waste. However, these alternative understandings are marginalized by powerful actors who seek to create a 'climate-smart' agricultural system that also serves their own economic interests.

Neo-Gramscian scholars concentrate on the power discrepancies that exist in global environmental politics. They denounce the slow violence of domination, which gives powerful economic actors control over less powerful actors through the domination of key systems. They are particularly concerned about business influence in **developing countries**, who have limited power to resist market forces. Such violence is visible, for example, in the mining industry, which not only displaces local populations from their land, but also deprives them of natural resources, and subjects them to increased local pollution (Gamu and Dauvergne 2018).

In this context, neo-Gramscian voices, including those of environmental activists and marginalized populations, resist the capitalist hegemonic bloc. However, such counter-hegemonic forces often struggle to get their voices heard. This has been the case for several decades in Nigeria, for instance, where farmers and fishermen have been trying to have a voice with regard to pollution caused by oil spills by Shell. After several national and regional court cases in which they were unsuccessful—due to, among other things, the tight links between Shell and the Nigerian government—farmers and a Dutch NGO have tried to bring cases to the American and Dutch courts, hoping for recognition and compensation (Enneking 2014). In 2013 the American Supreme Court declared that it could not judge cases outside United States territory. As of 2019 there is no resolution yet of the case brought in front of the Dutch court.

A second lens through which to view the corporate relationship to the environment is the *pluralist perspective*. This perspective questions the main premises of the neo-Gramscian view by focusing on the heterogeneity of corporations' interests and preferences (Falkner 2008). Although corporations are motivated by profit above all, this is not their only motivation, and in some circumstances they actively support binding environmental measures. As explained in Box 4.2, some corporations have made a positive contribution to climate change politics.

Box 4.2 Corporate involvement in climate change negotiations

Business positions regarding multilateral negotiations on climate change differ in terms of both preferences and intensity. However, they can be grouped into four categories, ranging from opposition to climate change science to more proactive stances for addressing climate change through policy action.

The first category of corporations strongly *oppose* action to address global warming, denying the importance of climate change as a policy issue. For instance, the Global Climate Coalition, an industry association created in 1989 by corporations from the oil, gas, and automobile industries, held this position before it was dissolved in 2002. From 1992 to 1997, during the Kyoto Protocol negotiations, the Global Climate Coalition contested the validity of the conclusion of the Intergovernmental Panel on Climate Change, the international scientific authority on this issue, and questioned the science behind global warming. Then, to discourage the United States from signing the Protocol, members of the Global Climate Coalition invested a vast amount of money in an advertising campaign in the United States that denounced the Protocol's economic costs and the damage it would pose to the competitiveness of American corporations if ratified. To substantiate its arguments, the Global Climate Coalition collaborated with conservative think tanks such as the Heritage Foundation, the Heartland Institute, the George C. Marshall Institute, the Hoover Institution, and the Cato Institute. Some of these think tanks received substantial financial support from Global Climate Coalition member corporations and expressed scepticism that climate change is linked to CO_2 emissions.

The second category of businesses hold a more *moderate and passive* position. This is the case for the corporate energy users represented by, among others, the International Climate Change Partnership. As consumers of energy, including fossil fuels, these corporations do not necessarily have the same interests as energy producers. During the Kyoto Protocol negotiations, for example, they acted as observers of the debates, neither advocating for binding policies nor forcefully opposing them. This passive position was also adopted by businesses in the energy sectors that produce relatively low quantities of greenhouse gases, such as nuclear energy producers. Industrial associations that represent corporations with diverging interests, such as the International Chamber of Commerce, also tend to adopt this position of passive bystander in climate change negotiations.

The third category of businesses embrace a *moderate but active* position. This includes a few corporations in the energy and automobile sectors, such as energy corporation BP ('Beyond Petroleum') and car maker Toyota, who have been taking an increasingly proactive approach towards reducing greenhouse gas emissions since 2002, in order to set themselves apart from their competitors. These corporations favour long-term growth, and take an active part in the negotiations in hopes of shaping the negotiations in their interests.

Finally, the fourth category of businesses are strongly *in favour of* binding and ambitious commitments to reduce greenhouse gases. This position is endorsed by insurers, who are concerned by the enormous costs that natural disasters caused by climate change could provoke. The renewable energy industry also takes this proactive position in favour of a rapid reduction in greenhouse gases in the hope of increasing market share for their sector. Corporations specializing in the greenhouse gas emissions markets, represented by the International Emissions Trading Association, have also favoured this active position.

Sources: Carpenter 2001; Meckling 2015; Nasiritousi 2017; Orsini and Compagnon 2011; Sæverud and Skjærseth 2007; Vormedal 2008.

Several factors may explain why certain corporations are favourable to environmental regulations (Falkner 2008). In many cases, business actors seek a certain predictability level in order to maintain the stability of their markets and guarantee their investments in the long term. They may therefore prefer binding environmental regulations, as long as these are clear and stable, in order to avoid an uncertain and unpredictable regulatory framework.

For example, many European biotechnology corporations supported labelling **genetically modified organisms** in the late 1990s. They could see that labelling would bring more predictability to an agricultural commodities market which was blocked by the ban on genetically modified organisms in place in Europe between 1998 and 2004 (Orsini 2010: 113).

Corporations' preferences also depend on their place in the production chain and their relationship to the final consumers. The more a corporation is subjected to consumer pressure, the more its environmental behaviour will align with that of its consumers. Corporations that sell their products in highly competitive markets and that must deal with the ever-changing nature of demand will be more inclined to support environmental regulations. This is both because they are more vulnerable to 'name and shame' campaigns by NGOs like Greenpeace, and because they can increase their market share by making their environmental concerns known. Thus, in the early 1990s, several furniture corporations declared themselves in favour of forest certification, as discussed in Box 4.7.

Corporations' preferences regarding international regulations can be shaped by domestic law. If corporations are bound by strict regulations at home, they will tend to seek to spread them to other countries so that their competitors are bound by the same regulations. For example, the Swedish firm Electrolux lobbied at the European level in favour of adopting regulations for recycling certain electronic components, in order to force its competitors to follow its Swedish practices (Dauvergne 2008: 123). In California, strong environmental regulations supported by citizens and civic movements were accepted by local corporations, who then pushed for similar strong regulations at the federal level. This process is now known as the 'California effect' (Vogel 2018).

International regulations can potentially simplify product development and marketing procedures. This explains why, for example, the transnational cosmetics firm Natura supported the adoption of the Nagoya Protocol on genetic resources, which calls for traceability of genetic resources and clarifies providers' and users' expectations (Orsini 2010: 149). Similarly, corporations in the nuclear industry support international liability agreements on state responsibility in case of a nuclear accident in order to reduce any potential for corporate responsibility. Moreover, international environmental regulations can create new markets. Indeed, environmental certification, in the tourism sector or for carbon accounting for example, has led to the creation of a flourishing new certification business (Cashore 2002).

Finally, the way in which broader business interests are represented when environmental regulations are elaborated also influences individual business positions. Industrial associations often hold more aggressive positions than individual firms. For example, in 1992 the Industrial Biotechnology Association opposed America's signing of the Convention on Biological Diversity, whereas Merck and Genentech, two major corporations in the fields of pharmaceuticals and biotechnology, worked with environmental NGOs to demand that it be signed (Raustiala 1997: 52).

It is important to give nuance to the initial intuition that businesses routinely oppose environmental standards while many NGOs support them. This antagonism is not a universal rule. Although this opposition is true in certain circumstances, businesses and environmental NGOs are heterogeneous groups and can defend many varied positions. Moreover, as Section 4.3 shows, NGOs and corporations also use similar resources to influence public decision makers.

4.3 Non-state actor influence

How non-state actors influence environmental politics

The various types of non-state actors discussed earlier not only participate in environmental politics, but also mobilize different resources to influence environmental politics (Betsill and Corell 2008; Jinnah 2014; Tamiotti and Finger 2001). Although there are several ways to think about how non-state actors influence politics, one useful way to understand this dynamic is by splitting such resources into three types: *material, organizational, or discursive* (Bernhagen 2008; Botetzagias et al. 2010). Each of these types of influence reflects a mechanism through which non-state actors' power is deployed to influence political processes.

Non-state actors' *material resources* essentially consist of their budget and their employees. In general, corporations possess more material resources than do NGOs, as NGOs are not-for-profit organizations. Not only are corporations able to invest large amounts of money in influencing policymaking by paying lobbyists to support their interests, but they can also remind political leaders that corporations contribute to economic growth and employment—two key public policy goals. Corporations deploy these material resources to influence policymakers. Some NGOs also possess significant resources. In 2017, for example, according to its annual report, Greenpeace International received no less than 1.4 million dollars in donations from individuals and more than 92 million dollars from its national organizations. Greenpeace uses these material resources to influence politics by for instance funding the attendance of its staff at international negotiations or financing its communication campaigns.

Material resource gaps are particularly important between non-state actors in developed countries and those in developing countries. For example, the vast majority of NGOs and corporations that attend international negotiations come from developed countries. The costs required to participate in multiple meetings all over the world are prohibitive enough to discourage organizations with few material resources—that is, the majority of non-state actors in developing countries (Orsini 2011). The meetings prior to the adoption of the United Nations Convention to Combat Desertification were a rare exception to this. At some of these meetings, half of the non-state actor participants were from Africa. These large numbers of developing country participants were made possible by funding provided by the Convention secretariat and individual member states, who recognized the importance of having on board actors directly concerned by the desertification issue (Corell and Betsill 2001).

The second type of resources that non-state actors can use to influence politics are *organizational* in nature, which are particularly important for non-state actors with few material resources. For example, a non-state actor's ability to network is a particularly important organizational resource. Networking resources are measured by the contact and relationships that non-state actors have with other state and non-state actors. These relationships help them to access and quickly share information, pool resources for a common purpose, and increase their visibility, credibility, and legitimacy. During the United Nations Convention to Combat Desertification negotiations, the NGOs that were present created a coalition, the Réseau d'ONG sur la désertification et la sécheresse, to give more weight to their common declarations (Corell and Betsill 2001). On climate change, the Climate Action Network International, created in 1989, now brings together more than 1,300 NGOs from over 120 countries to promote action to limit climate change. On biodiversity, conservation NGOs including WWF, The Nature Conservancy, African Wildlife Foundation, Wildlife Conservation Society,

Conservation International, and Birdlife International network closely, and collaborated with the World Conservation Union and public decision makers to develop conservation strategies, such as ecotourism, which have been supported by several donors and adopted by a number of developing states such as Gabon (Holmes 2011).

Although networks allow for horizontal coordination across non-state actors with similar interests, networks are not entirely horizontal structures, in that they are subject to subtle control processes, patronage, and elitism (Orsini 2011). This can make it difficult to maintain cohesion within networks, even when their members' interests converge. During the negotiations on climate change, for example, NGOs that were initially close-knit became divided over the use of forests as **carbon sinks** (Carpenter 2001). Other networks, such as those working on turtle conservation in the Mediterranean, never saw the light of day due to the misgivings that NGOs working in this field have towards one another (Botetzagias et al. 2010).

The third type of resources available to non-state actors are *discursive* resources. These consist of the knowledge and credibility that an actor possesses to articulate a convincing and unifying message. Corporations' discursive resources are generally derived from their access to technical and market data, which are often protected by intellectual property rights. Governments must often rely on corporations' expertise in evaluating the costs and feasibility of environmental measures. For example, with the chemical industry introducing over a thousand new products to the market each year, governments struggle to keep up. It is difficult to gather data regarding the added value and the environmental risks of each new chemical product (Arnold and Whitford 2006). Some corporations therefore possess key discursive resources that enable them to strongly influence politics. One concrete example of how corporations have deployed discursive resources to influence politics is the debate about how to classify chemical products as 'wastes' on the one hand, or 'recyclable' or 'reusable' materials on the other. By providing data on the possible future uses of their products, corporations can avoid their products being categorized as 'waste' by the international institutions that deal with these issues, such as the Basel Convention on the Control of Transboundary Movements of Hazardous Wastes. This is important because in avoiding a 'wastes' classification, they also avoid the much stricter controls on movement under the Basel Convention (Clapp 1994).

NGOs also deploy discursive resources to influence environmental politics (Boström and Tamm Hallström 2010; Botetzagias et al. 2010). First and foremost, several NGOs also produce scientific expertise, technical information, and knowledge, and have access to privileged information that is of use to policymakers. For example, NGO expertise on traditional knowledge practices to limit soil degradation, and on carbon sinks, proved vital during the negotiations surrounding the Convention to Combat Desertification and the Kyoto Protocol, respectively (Corell and Betsill 2001). Also, information about environmental issues that comes from NGOs is often seen as more credible than similar data produced by corporations. When Greenpeace and the oil industry present contradicting data regarding environmental degradation, for example, many people may trust Greenpeace's data more. However, NGO data is not necessarily any less biased or more accurate. For example, following the Shell Brent Spar offshore oil rig scuttling, Greenpeace, mobilizing lots of public support, had announced that the rig still contained 5,500 tons of oil, which was factually inaccurate (Mitchener 1995).

NGOs are also well equipped to produce powerful new framings of environmental issues, which can shape political decision making. For instance, NGOs used the powerful frame of climate justice throughout the United Nations Framework Convention on Climate Change negotiations to successfully push for a new article of the Paris Agreement on loss and damage (Allan and Hadden 2017). Some NGOs have even specialized in the diffusion of environmental information. For instance, Climate Tracker, created in 2015, is an NGO that trains young journalists to diffuse information on climate change to increase governmental and public awareness.

While presented separately here, the different types of resources most operate in tandem, and can reinforce one another. For instance, the fact that Greenpeace International is a federation of 27 national and regional organizations gives it important material, organizational, and discursive resources; the organization uses its international networks and material resources to fund large information campaigns that deploy technical expertise across the globe.

Influence during different policy phases

Resources alone, whether material, organizational, or discursive, are not sufficient to explain the extent of non-state influence. Indeed, there is quite a bit of variation in the extent to which non-state actors influence environmental politics. There are several strategic decisions that these actors can make to increase their influence. One of these is to select the phase of policymaking in which a specific non-state actor can most efficiently deploy its resources to maximize its impact. In the context of international institutions, there are three policymaking phases for non-state influence: *pre-negotiation*, during which non-state actors practise issue-framing and agenda-setting; *negotiations*, during which they try to influence governmental positions; and **implementation**, during which they attempt to influence the way governments convert their international commitments into domestic law and policy (Betsill and Corell 2008).

During the *pre-negotiation* phase, non-state actors can work to frame the problems being addressed by an emerging **regime**. For example, in 1993 the Rural Advancement Foundation developed and deployed the term 'biopiracy', as opposed to the corporately preferred term 'bioprospecting', to shape the emerging discussions under the Convention on Biological Diversity on access and **benefit sharing**. This framing tactic played a key role in denouncing the misappropriation of genetic resources, framing the issue as one of genetic piracy, which was reflected in the Nagoya Protocol on Access and Benefit Sharing which resulted from these early discussions (Bled 2010: 582; Morin 2008). Non-state actors can also shape the agenda during this phase, by emphasizing the urgency or importance of certain problems that need to be put on the agenda of intergovernmental discussions. For example, the International Union for Conservation of Nature, a hybrid organization whose members include several NGOs as well as governmental organizations, largely contributed to putting biological diversity on the Rio Summit agenda in 1992 by documenting and disseminating information about the accelerated extinction rate of many species (Orsini 2010). More recently, a number of NGOs orchestrated campaigns around the world on plastic pollution and contributed to putting this issue on the global agenda of the Group of Seven (see Box 4.3).

Non-state actors can also act during the *negotiation* phase, in particular by sending proposals to decision makers or providing them with relevant information, such as scientific evidence, to shape their positions on proposals. For example, the International Tropical Timber Organization's provisions on local communities' rights in 2000 were initially proposed by NGOs before being relayed by negotiators (Humphreys 2004). Another way non-state actors can influence decision-making during the negotiation phase is by funding the participation of like-minded state actors. Although non-state actors usually do not have voting rights in intergovernmental organizations, they can still influence which states are present to cast their votes. For example, as a majority rule vote on a whaling moratorium approached at the International Whaling Commission, Greenpeace funded the membership of eight additional governments that favoured the moratorium in the 1970s and 1980s, to increase the likelihood that its position would be reflected in the vote (Skodvin and Andresen 2003: 81).

Finally, during the *implementation* phase, once a treaty has been adopted, non-state actors can attempt to influence **ratification** and/or how international commitments are translated into domestic **policy instruments** (see also Chapter 8). For example, the Global Climate Coalition significantly helped to stoke the American government's scepticism of the anthropogenic origin of climate change, which greatly contributed to the United States' refusal to ratify the Kyoto Protocol (see Box 4.2).

Box 4.3 Plastic pollution—an emerging environmental problem

Since the 1960s there has been a sharp increase in plastic production and consumption around the globe. Consequently, plastic pollution has become a significant problem, affecting terrestrial and marine ecosystems, wildlife, and human health. Plastics are not biodegradable, some are toxic, and all are characterized by a complex life cycle. Waste plastics are often transported by wind and ocean currents and therefore pollute areas thousands of miles away from their place of origin.

One particularly important emerging issue with plastic pollution is related to microplastics. Microplastics are pieces of plastic that are less than 5 mm in size. They are widely used in cosmetics and clothing, and are particularly problematic for marine ecosystems because they can be ingested by marine organisms, become embedded in their tissues, and enter the entire food chain.

Plastic pollution is a transboundary problem, with no clear-cut solution. Some argue that there is a need to work downstream and design better recycling and waste management facilities. Others advocate the importance of working upstream, improving plastics' **ecological footprint**, and helping to reduce consumption of plastic.

Transnational initiatives include governments, industries, and businesses joining together to fight plastic pollution. In 2018 five members of the Group of Seven (G7), Canada, France, Germany, Italy, and the UK, adopted the Ocean Plastics Charter. This non-binding voluntary agreement recognizes that the current approach to producing, using, managing, and disposing of plastics poses a significant threat to the environment, and focuses on designing new ways to recycle and repurpose plastics. The agreement is innovative in that it allowed for private actors, such as Coca-Cola and other companies and industry leaders, to join governments in signing the agreement. However, the agreement also has several weaknesses. For example, it does not include reduction strategies and targets, nor does it ban single-use plastics. Ultimately, a paradigm shift in the current patterns of consumption is needed in order to be able to effectively tackle the problem of plastic pollution.

A large number of NGOs around the world have started to fight plastic pollution, adopting a bottom-up approach which attempts to reduce plastic use through international campaigns. Some companies, such as Starbucks and Nestlé, have reacted by announcing initiatives to phase out plastic straws and other single-use plastics. A growing number of cities have started to ban containers made of polystyrene. In the United States, some states such as California have banned single-use plastic bags in large retail stores, and others such as Hawaii aim to replace plastic straws with paper straws. With the growing use of plastics, their limited disposal options, and their extremely long decomposition time in the environment, these types of initiatives are starting to proliferate around the globe.

Sources: Dauvergne 2018; O'Neill 2017, 2018.

Different strategies of influence

Once non-state actors decide at which policy phase(s) they want to intervene, they must also choose their strategy of influence. This depends on the degree of proximity and of formality that they adopt with policymakers (Arts and Mack 2003). Their strategies can be categorized into four types (see Table 4.1): advice, informal pressure, public pressure, and promotion.

Advice consists of maintaining direct, formal interactions with public decision makers by providing them with information and relevant knowledge, often at a policymaker's request. Sometimes non-state actors even draft working documents and text proposals for state actors. For example, NGOs were instrumental in drafting the text for the Forest Annex to the United States–Peru trade agreement, which laid out a host of forest management requirements that Peru had to undertake as a condition of that agreement entering into force (Jinnah 2011). Non-state actors can also influence states' political decisions through lobbying activities. Most lobbying activities are legal, and from a pluralist viewpoint it could even be considered a civic duty to make one's specific interests known to political leaders in defining the public interest.

Non-state actors can also join national delegations to give advice. In this way, they benefit from special access to information and to decision-making forums. For example, the NGOs Friends of the Earth International, the Centre for International Environmental Law, Greenpeace, and WWF provided small island state delegations with scientific support and political guidance during the United Nations Framework Convention on Climate Change negotiations (Gulbrandsen and Andresen 2004: 60). Being included in national delegations might seem like the ideal strategy for non-state actors to express their views. However, in practice it also comes with constraints: they must follow the rules set by the delegation they are part of, such as attending coordination meetings, and they will have reduced opportunities for direct contact with non-state actors from other countries. As a result, just as non-state actors can influence government interests, so too governments can influence non-state interests (Orsini 2010).

In international forums, non-state actors can often have a direct relationship with governments and practise advice by participating as observers. If time permits, observers are allowed to express their views directly to state delegates by addressing the assembly of states after all states involved have expressed their own views. Observer status nonetheless provides limited opportunities to influence negotiations. Indeed, negotiations do not always take place in open meetings to which observers have access, but often in more closed and smaller informal sessions. This can marginalize observers from key negotiation processes, driving them to creative—and some might say extreme—measures to access information.

Table 4.1 Typology of modes of interaction between non-state actors and decision makers

		Degree of proximity	
		Direct	Diffuse
Degree of formality	Formal	Advice	Promotion
	Informal	Informal pressure	Public pressure

Source: inspired by Arts and Mack 2003

For example, during the Kyoto Protocol climate change negotiations in the late 1990s, observers rifled through rubbish bins in an attempt to obtain information from these smaller sessions to which their access was limited (Corell and Betsill 2001). Even with access to the decision-making processes, several negotiation sessions are often scheduled at the same time, which makes participation difficult for many non-state actors which, generally speaking, do not have sufficient resources to dispatch enough people to attend every session.

This problem, known as the 'negotiation burden' problem, is exacerbated when several international institutions hold conferences on the same subject (Orsini 2013). This is the case for negotiations on genetic resources, which take place in the World Intellectual Property Organization's Intergovernmental Committee on Intellectual Property and Genetic Resources, in the World Trade Organization's Council for Trade-Related Aspects of Intellectual Property Rights, at the **Conference of the Parties** to the Convention on Biological Diversity, and in the Governing Body to the United Nations Food and Agriculture Organization's International Treaty on Plant Genetic Resources. As a result, it is particularly difficult for non-state actors to follow all of the debates, and some non-state actors strategically choose to try to influence negotiations by other means. Networks among various non-state actors, as described above, can also be helpful in coordinating participation and sharing information to alleviate the 'negotiation burden'.

Informal pressure can complement the formal advice provision just described. Informal pressure operates through close proximity and informal interactions between non-state actors and governmental officials. Proximity can take very varied forms, from conversations in corridors, or invitations to receptions, to the famous NGO party that is held alongside all United Nations climate conferences. Informal pressure strategies sometimes come close to being unethical, if not unlawful. For example, during the Cartagena Protocol negotiations on biosafety, American biotechnology firms contacted the Malaysian and Ethiopian governments to discredit some of their delegates, who were attending the Protocol negotiations, by complaining about their lack of professionalism and accusing them of misrepresenting their governments' positions. In fact, these delegates were legitimate experts who were arguing for strong environmental provisions, in direct opposition to what these American firms were advocating, and were indeed in line with their governments' positions. Rather, the US firms were hoping to temporarily remove these 'unwanted' delegates from the negotiation process—a goal in which they were unsuccessful (Orsini 2010: 137).

Public pressure attempts to influence negotiators indirectly through public opinion. Sometimes NGOs prefer not to have direct relationships with policymakers, but rather to influence them from the outside. By publicly attacking a government's reputation, they aim to influence its preferences and behaviour via the pressure of public opinion. Public pressure strategies include protests, demonstrations, naming and shaming campaigns, open letters published in newspapers, litigation, and press releases. For example, several activists chained themselves to the buses that were taking national delegates to the first Conference of the Parties to the United Nations Convention on Climate Change negotiations in Berlin in 1995 to attract governmental and public attention (Hadden 2014).

Counter-summitry is an additional mechanism to influence governments through public pressure. Counter-summits are organized by non-state actors and held in parallel (i.e. in the same city and at the same time) to official intergovernmental summits. In 2012, for example, in parallel to the Rio+20 summit, several social movements, NGOs, and indigenous communities held the 'People's Summit in Rio+20 for Social and Environmental Justice in Defense of the Commons, Against the Commodification of Life'. This counter-summit sought to insist on issues of social and **environmental justice** and **common goods**, in opposition to what these organizations perceived as an intergovernmental agenda centred on the marketization and economic privatization of the environment. It was attended by 15,000 participants, a significant number compared to the 45,000 participants attending the official summit (Meek 2015). Climate summit protesters are also very active in parallel to official United Nations climate negotiations (Wahlström et al. 2013).

NGOs have often embraced new technological tools to increase the scope and reach of their public pressure strategies. In particular, they have used web-based tools such as online petitions or social media (Hestres 2015). They have even used social media to condemn environmental wrongdoing by social media itself. For example, Greenpeace has attacked Facebook's own energy policy by using Facebook itself (Katz-Kimchi and Manosevitch 2015).

Public pressure can also mean litigation. An increasing number of NGOs take governments or local authorities to court for non-compliance with their environmental commitments. In some cases, NGOs have used judiciary mechanisms to change regulations or government practices. For instance, in 2018 the NGO ClientEarth won its third case against the United Kingdom for not respecting its air pollution commitments. However, in other cases NGOs aim to use tribunals as a public stage to draw public attention to their issues, and create political pressure. It might be more important for their long-term objectives to win their case in the tribunal of public opinion than in front of a judge.

Finally, *promotion* consists of communicating ideas to decision makers through formalized means such as books, reports, and conferences. In contrast to public pressure strategies, promotion strategies target decision makers themselves, but in a more diffuse way than when providing advice or exercising informal pressure. For example, in 1988 the International Institute for Environment and Development published a report showing that only a tiny fraction of the world's rainforests was being used in a sustainable manner. This report indirectly influenced the International Tropical Timber Organization's adoption of its Objective 2000 on forest management (Humphreys 2004). Similarly, in 2017 the World Resources Institute published a methodology for estimating private climate finance and, in doing so, helped promote private sector involvement in the implementation of the Paris Agreement (Green and Westphal 2017). These publications were not widely circulated among the public and they did not target specific decision makers, but they were nevertheless influential.

Depending on available resources, each non-state actor can adopt multiple strategies at different phases of the negotiation process. Advice, informal pressure, public pressure, and promotion are not mutually exclusive. In fact, Table 4.1 shows that when ideal-types are put into practice, they create more of a continuum than separate categories. Box 4.4 illustrates this multitude of strategies using the case of Monsanto. It also shows that non-state actors sometimes act under the cover of various coalitions and networks, making it difficult to identify their individual actions. Non-state actors' influence on environmental politics is difficult to establish and varies from one non-state actor to another. Careful and long-term process tracing is needed to understand how and to what extent non-state actors influence global environmental politics (Downie 2014, 2016).

Box 4.4 Monsanto and the international negotiations on genetically modified organisms

In 1996, as negotiations on a biosafety **protocol** to regulate the potential risks of genetically modified organisms were beginning, Monsanto was the world leader in agricultural biotechnology. However, the corporation went on to make several strategic choices that proved to be counterproductive in influencing international biosafety standards, forcing it to continuously redefine its actions. This is one interesting example for understanding the many strategies corporations use to influence international environmental politics, sometimes without success.

In the early 1990s, Monsanto intervened very little in framing the problem to be negotiated—biosafety. At that time, the corporation was more preoccupied with American regulations and had little belief that an international treaty on genetically modified organisms would be adopted. This turned out to be its first strategic error as the 1992 Convention on Biological Diversity, in its Article 19.3, contained a mandate for the negotiation of a protocol on biosafety.

Then Monsanto began to follow international debates more closely and developed a multifaceted advice strategy. First, the corporation registered as an observer to the negotiations of the protocol and maintained close relationships with the American delegation. Given the vehemence of several other delegations in advocating for a binding protocol, Monsanto gradually created connections with other corporations in order to undertake actions that would complement its individual participation as an obstructive observer. From 1996, the corporation actively participated in the actions of the Biotechnology Industry Organization, an American coalition which lobbied for soft guidelines on genetically modified organisms to facilitate international trade in these products. Individually and within the Biotechnology Industry Organization, Monsanto continued to support the American delegation and the interstate coalition known as the 'Miami Group', uniting the largest exporters of genetically modified organisms in favour of a flexible genetically modified organisms-friendly protocol. But Monsanto's advice proved to be insufficient and the negotiations moved towards the adoption of a binding agreement.

In 1998, as debates came closer to reaching a binding agreement, Monsanto participated in setting up a new industrial coalition, the Global Industry Coalition, to strengthen its influence in the negotiations and, in particular, its promotion activities. Calling it the 'Global Industry Coalition' suggested that it included several industrial sectors and not just biotechnology firms, in the hope that this would increase the coalition's legitimacy. Again, the adoption of the Cartagena Protocol in 2000, which recognized genetically modified organisms' potential environmental risks, was a crushing defeat for Monsanto.

In reaction to the adoption of the Cartagena Protocol, Monsanto reformed the way the Global Industry Coalition functioned by setting up a management committee that would guide its actions in a more decisive manner. In addition, in order to restore the image of agricultural biotechnologies, the corporation was involved in the creation in 2001 of a new NGO, CropLife International. This NGO's main objective was to promote genetically modified organisms, insisting on their virtues, particularly for developing countries' agricultural systems. The idea was to reorient the debate surrounding genetically modified organisms, demonstrating that they are not only safe, but also strategic tools for sustainable development to replace traditional agricultural crops. By announcing projects such as 'golden rice', a genetically modified rice variety rich in vitamin A, which is needed to fight malnutrition, the corporation's objective was to convince governments in developing countries of the value of genetically modified organisms. Since 2004, biotechnology firms have also joined the Public Research and Regulation Initiative, a scientific coalition offering advice and promotion, to show that the Protocol is an obstacle not only to trade, but also to scientific progress. The Public Research and Regulation Initiative attends international negotiations dealing with genetically modified organisms and organizes side events, publishes reports, and hosts conferences to convince governments of their benefits.

As this example illustrates, corporations can intervene in international negotiations by relying on various strategies during different phases of the negotiation cycle. It also shows that businesses can act according to different formats: as individual corporations, by actively participating in business associations, by creating NGOs, and by acting as scientific experts. The effects of such diverse strategies are difficult to assess, but their multiplication through time is a clear sign of attempts by business to have its voice heard by all means.

Sources: Orsini 2010; Tienhaara et al. 2012.

4.4 Transnational governance

The rise of transnational governance

Scholars have traditionally considered intergovernmental institutions as the centrepiece of global environmental governance. Since the early 2000s, however, this has begun to change. Transnational forms of governance, which involve non-state actors operating across borders, are becoming increasingly relevant to global politics, including in global environmental politics.

Non-state actors can cooperate transnationally to adopt standards, rules, and instruments. In doing so, they create what are called 'transnational governance schemes'. These schemes move away from traditional forms of 'public governance' because they involve both public and private actors, and because they are not hierarchical like their public counterparts. Why and how do these transnational governance schemes emerge, and what effect do they have on global environmental politics?

Transnational networks are sometimes formalized through partnerships, such as cooperative arrangements with a low level of institutionalization, non-hierarchical decision-making structures, and public problem-solving objectives (Andonova et al. 2009). There are three categories of such partnerships: *public partnerships*, which only include governments; *public–private partnerships*, which include state and non-state actors; and *private partnerships*, which include exclusively non-state actors. The last two partnership types are transnational in that they involve non-state actors. For example, the Prototype Carbon Fund, created in 2000, is a public–private partnership, which brings together six governments and 17 corporations under the management of the World Bank to implement greenhouse gas reduction projects. The Greenhouse Gas Protocol, created in 1997, is an entirely private partnership between the World Resources Institute and the World Business Council for Sustainable Development, which aims to develop standardized greenhouse gas accounting measures.

In the 1990s, transnational initiatives were primarily mandated by governments, but they gradually made their way towards ad hoc partnerships between state and non-state actors (Bäckstrand 2008; Chan and Pattberg 2008: 107). At the 2002 Johannesburg Summit, more than 400 public–private partnerships—called 'Type II' partnerships—were announced on sustainable development issues. Figure 4.2 presents the growth in transnational climate partnerships over time, demonstrating that their growth rate has increased, especially from 2007 onwards.

There are at least three explanations for this growth in transnational governance (Falkner 2003). A first explanation emphasizes the economic elite's proactive transnationalization strategy to exert hegemony over global environmental politics. According to this explanation, certain corporations will create partnerships to promote flexible regulatory mechanisms

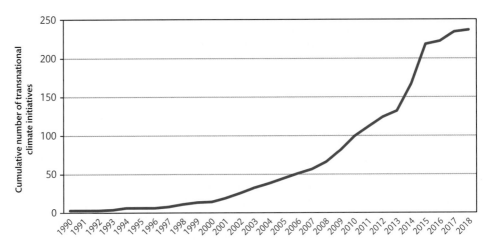

Figure 4.2 Cumulative number of transnational climate initiatives (1990–2018)

Source: networks' website, compiled by Marielle Papin

 Take your learning further by viewing the interactive version of this figure
www.oup.com/he/morin1e

and voluntary initiatives, and therefore marginalize or bypass binding mechanisms. These partnerships aim at keeping **corporate social responsibility** as a voluntary business initiative (see Box 4.5).

A second explanation for the flourishing of partnerships is based on an acknowledgement of the growing number of non-state actors, and of their expanding range of interventions and dynamism in all environmental domains. Since non-state actors often have restricted access to international negotiations, they can find opportunities in transnational governance to be directly involved and to conduct direct actions, bypassing classical intergovernmental politics.

A third explanation points to the decline of states' capacities in a context of economic liberalization and globalization. This state decline translates into political and financial disengagement, in turn leading to interstate regime fragmentation and weakening. Public decision makers face budget reductions, whereas civil society demands appear to be growing when it comes to environmental protection. According to this perspective, partnerships are an alternative, which can enable the implementation of projects that governments are no longer able or willing to complete alone.

Transnational city networks

Cities are also emerging as increasingly important actors in global environmental governance. While cities are public actors, they are not sovereign states and they have transnational activities beyond states. The rise of cities as transnational actors is in part due to difficulties in getting states to agree to take meaningful action on global issues, such as climate change (Gordon and Johnson 2017). As cities around the world pledge to reduce emissions,

Box 4.5 Corporate social responsibility

Corporate social responsibility has long been a hotly debated topic in global environmental politics. It has been defined as corporate 'practices that improve the workplace and benefit society in ways that go above and beyond what companies are legally required to do' (Vogel 2005: 2). These practices include efforts to promote environmental protection, the respect of indigenous and local communities' rights, and participatory approaches.

In 1991, the *Organisation for Economic Co-operation and Development Guidelines for Multinational Enterprises* were revised to include corporate social responsibility. In the same year, the International Chamber of Commerce adopted the Business Charter for Sustainable Development, which lists 16 principles that corporations are invited to voluntarily embrace, such as a 'precautionary approach', 'openness to concerns', or 'corporate priority'. This last principle calls on corporations 'to recognise environmental management as among the highest corporate priorities and as a key determinant to sustainable development [and] to establish policies, programmes and practices for conducting operations in an environmentally sound manner'.

Corporate social responsibility also appeared at the 1992 Rio Summit. Certain activists, delegates, and even a few entrepreneurs hoped that governments would use the summit as an opportunity to ask corporations to internalize the environmental externalities of their production processes. These hopes were not realized, however. The adopted action plan, **Agenda 21**, primarily highlights the positive contribution economic actors make in the search for environmental solutions, and demands the adoption of flexible environmental regulations, compatible with market dynamics. The only effort required for corporations is that they recognize 'environmental management as among the highest corporate priorities and as a key determinant to sustainable development'.

Agenda 21 was followed by a series of international initiatives that also favour a voluntary, rather than binding, approach to corporate social responsibility. In 1997, the Global Reporting Initiative was set up, and successfully fostered the adoption of voluntary reporting standards by corporations, now adopted by more than 90 per cent of the 250 major transnational corporations. In 2000, also, the United Nations Secretary-General launched the **Global Compact**. The Compact is essentially a voluntary agreement between private corporations and several organizations of the United Nations system on a series of principles, including environmental responsibility promotion. For businesses, it is evident that a commitment to *promote* environmental and social responsibility is much less binding than a commitment to *assume* that responsibility.

At the 2002 Johannesburg Summit on Sustainable Development, the International Chamber of Commerce and the World Business Council for Sustainable Development again advocated voluntary measures. Their requests were heard, and were confirmed in paragraph 140(f) of the Johannesburg Implementation Plan, which encourages states to promote corporate responsibility and the exchange of good practices. In 2003, a new initiative was launched in the financial sector known as the 'Equator Principles' that again set voluntary standards in international finance projects.

Several NGOs advocate that these voluntary commitments should be transformed into more binding obligations. In 2002, following the Bhopal disaster in India, in which an explosion at an American pesticides firm claimed thousands of victims, Friends of the Earth International and Greenpeace International wrote a proposal for binding liability standards for the chemical industry. The industry responded in 2006 by adopting a voluntary code of conduct, Responsible Care, based on information exchange.

Thus, gradually, by its persistence, the voluntary approach seems to have become the norm for addressing corporate social responsibility in international debates, a norm that remains challenged by environmental activists.

Sources: Auld et al. 2008; Boiral 2013; Clapp 2005, 2017; Givel 2007; Vogel 2005.

a catchphrase has emerged that exemplifies the progressive action that cities are adopting in the face of stagnant parallel state activities: 'Cities act, while nations talk' (Teffler 2015: 1). For instance, in response to President Donald Trump's May 2017 announcement that the United States would withdraw from the Paris Agreement on climate change, several American cities, such as New York and Chicago, pledged concrete emission-reduction targets. Other cities across the world, such as Beijing, Tokyo, Berlin, and Mexico City, have made similar commitments. Such city-level activities are important in an increasingly urbanized world.

The growing scope of private city governance can perhaps best be seen when looking at how cities are positioning themselves in international arenas that have historically been reserved primarily for state actors. For example, delegates from more than 400 cities, representing over 650 million citizens, attended the 2015 Paris climate conference to display collective leadership on fighting climate change. At that conference, these cities highlighted a wide swathe of urban actions undertaken to fight climate change, ranging from creating greener and more sustainable cities, to local policies and initiatives, to saving energy and drawing from more renewable sources (Teffler 2015; Box 4.6).

The number of transnational municipal and regional networks created to connect cities and regions transnationally is proliferating, with the C40 Cities Climate Leadership Group, the Covenant of Mayors, and the Cities for Climate Protection programme, among others (Bansard et al. 2017; see Figure 4.3). These networks of cities play an essential role in global climate governance based on their coordinated efforts across the world (Gordon and Johnson 2017).

One of the earliest instances of transnational urban climate governance emerged in the early 1990s, with the creation of the International Council for Local Environmental Initiatives, representing more than 200 local governments from 43 countries. This transnational city-network was created to coordinate local governments in designing and implementing climate change policies and sustainable development initiatives.

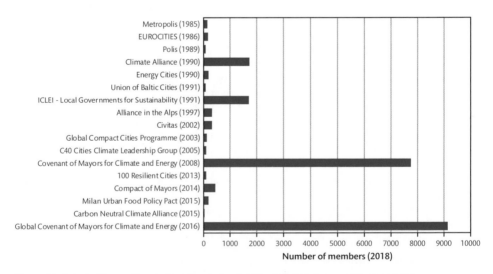

Figure 4.3 Selected transnational city networks involved in global environmental governance

Source data from: UNEP, and UNEP-DTU partnership, Climate Initiatives Platform

The International Council for Local Environmental Initiatives facilitates regular independent interactions between cities and local actors across national boundaries, not operating on behalf of any national government or intergovernmental organization (Betsill and Bulkeley 2004). The Council played an important role in supporting local officials that championed climate action, offering technical, normative, and material support (Gordon and Johnson 2017).

City-networks' contributions to climate governance have historically been criticized for being largely symbolic, observing that cities' greenhouse gas-reduction commitments were often not backed with governance activities in practice (Bulkeley and Kern 2009; Hakelberg 2014). Recently, however, cities have become more actively engaged in climate governance— setting more ambitious reduction targets, providing assistance to other cities, holding other cities accountable to their pledges, and concluding partnerships with transnational NGOs and business actors (Gordon and Johnson 2017). Cities are also becoming engaged in adaptation and mitigation planning, building climate change into other planning processes, and conducting inventories of local emissions (Aylett 2014). Part of their more active engagement could be attributed to cities converging around a more common understanding of their role in the global domain, and particular norms and practices enabling cooperation and action (Gordon 2016).

Despite the rapid growth and proliferation of transnational city networks, there are additional reasons to be sceptical of their potential to provide a solution to otherwise stalled climate governance. For example, membership in city networks remains skewed towards Europe and North America, with cities from the global South under-represented. This suggests that city networks replicate existing governance networks, rather than form alternative means of governance. Further, only a minority of these networks commit to quantified emission reductions, and the requirements for monitoring and reporting emissions are less rigorous than within the United Nations Framework Convention on Climate Change (Bansard et al. 2017). But despite critiques of the effectiveness and governance potential of city networks, because much of the world's population lives in cities, and some cities have larger economies than many states, cities will continue to matter in global environmental governance for years to come.

Box 4.6 Transnational climate change initiatives

Transnational networks have been particularly prolific in addressing climate change. Climate change is ripe for this style of networked governance for many reasons: the arena of climate governance is heavily populated by advocacy and business interests that span borders; the problem of climate change is complex and requires coordination across scales and sectors; and climate governance's embrace of **market mechanisms** requires a new range of governance structures to implement new markets.

Transnational climate change initiatives include networks of cities pledging targets to lower their carbon emissions, corporations setting their own targets to reduce emissions, and institutionalized rules that govern carbon markets. These initiatives engage in governance through a wide range of activities, including information sharing and networking, pressing for standards and commitments to limit emissions and energy use, and setting rules for creating and linking markets for carbon trading.

Non-state actors often participate in transnational initiatives for market-based or normative incentives, or to circumvent domestic and local problems. Multinational corporations and investors are

(continued...)

generally supportive of such initiatives as a way to level the playing field (ensuring that their competitors are held to the same regulations) and as a way to preempt more costly forms of governance. For example, the main function of the International Climate Change Partnership, composed of 22 industries primarily in the fossil fuel and chemical sectors, is to advocate flexible market-based climate policies that do not put certain industries at a disadvantage, thereby intending to preempt costly policies. Yet, transnational initiatives led by private corporations have fewer concrete mitigation targets than other initiatives, and it is still unclear whether these initiatives are effective in reducing emissions.

Some argue that the competitive and institutionally dense nature of climate governance encourages the rapid development of private transnational initiatives. This is because such initiatives can be set up quickly among a few actors and they are able to find a 'niche' to operate within. Another major impetus for the turn towards transnational governance in this area has to do with the failure of important states to engage in climate action. With the US withdrawal from the Paris Agreement, there have been efforts to integrate subnational actors from the United States into the broader climate regime. For example, a coalition called America's Pledge (formed in 2017 by former California governor Jerry Brown and former New York mayor Michael Bloomberg), consisting of 227 cities and counties, nine states, and approximately 1,650 businesses and investors, announced it would uphold the US' commitments under the Paris Agreement.

However, while these efforts are welcomed by supporters of climate action, there are doubts about whether these subnational actors can actually uphold the mitigation targets of the US' commitment in the presence of active opposition on both federal and state levels. This is especially the case considering the counterproductive efforts at the federal level to lower efficiency standards and increase coal, oil, and gas production. There has thus been considerable debate on the merits of a decentralized form of governance involving numerous cooperative, market-oriented voluntary initiatives, as an alternative to state-led multilateralism. However, some argue that transnational initiatives are supposed to supplement, rather than replace, national policy.

Because non-state actors are not democratically elected representatives and may have conflicting interests, there are concerns about the democratic legitimacy of transnational governance. Transnational initiatives broaden the range of actors involved in governance, but they also complicate questions of participation, deliberation, accountability, and legitimacy, as well as the role non-state actors should play in governance. It is important to consider how the average citizen might participate in decision making within a transnational initiative, especially when elected representatives are not involved, citizens are not major shareholders of a corporation that is involved, nor are they collectively organized in any other way.

Sources: Abbott 2012; Andonova et al. 2009; Bäckstrand et al. 2017; Cao and Ward 2017; Chan et al. 2016; Dryzek 2017; Hale and Roger 2014; Michaelowa and Michaelowa 2017; Roger et al. 2017.

Does transnational governance reinforce or counter interstate governance?

The contribution of transnational partnerships to global environmental politics is mixed (Andonova 2010; Arnold and Whitford 2006; Bäckstrand 2008; Bruno and Karliner 2000; Cashore 2002; Falkner 2003). On one hand, transnational partnerships can present a threat of privatizing global environmental governance, whereby it would be largely or entirely in the hands of non-state actors. Such a move from interstate authority to transnational actor authority would raise several risks. First, non-state actors, and corporations in particular, defend specific interests more often than the public interest, and could tend to favour minimal environmental standards. Second, most transnational schemes address environmental issues in a fragmented manner, by focusing on selected issues or specific geographical areas to the exclusion of others. Third, transnational governance reiterates and sometimes exacerbates the inequalities and structural imbalances between actors by involving only actors with sufficient resources. Fourth, the voluntary standards adopted by non-state actor networks are often weak, and failure to comply is rarely met with sanctions. Fifth, transnational initiatives can give a false impression of action, that disguises the fact that in reality the status quo has been maintained.

On the other hand, transnational initiatives can be seen as a positive functional response to the multilateralism crisis. They compensate for international governance shortfalls by injecting more legitimacy from citizen participation, greater material means, high-level technical expertise, operational flexibility, and resilience in the face of fluctuating governmental preferences. This perspective is well illustrated by the case of global forest governance. Due to opposition from developing countries, the idea of adopting a convention on forests at the 1992 Rio Summit was abandoned. Instead, states adopted a voluntary set of standards on forest governance. Since then, no other significant intergovernmental agreement has been finalized to curb forest degradation (Dimitrov et al. 2007). Faced with governmental inaction, several non-state actors have considered acting, and have established standards, certifications, and forums, such as the Forest Stewardship Council, that fill part of the intergovernmental governance gap on forest governance (see Box 4.7).

Box 4.7 The Forest Stewardship Council: a model for legitimacy?

The Forest Stewardship Council is a certification label created in 1993 on the initiative of WWF in partnership with other NGOs and corporations in the forestry industry. This certification label intends to promote responsible forest management according to social, environmental, and economic criteria. The Forest Stewardship Council is often presented as a model for external legitimacy, due to the wide endorsement of its label, and for internal legitimacy, due to its organizational structure which reflects and gives equal weight to a diversity of interests.

The Forest Stewardship Council's success is due in part to its structure, which is highly inclusive, giving it a high level of internal legitimacy. It is directed by a general assembly made up of three separate chambers. The first, known as the economic chamber, brings together producers, certification institutes, industrial associations, traders, and retailers. The second, known as the social chamber, primarily brings together indigenous peoples, development NGOs, and social movements. The third, known as the environmental chamber, brings together various different NGOs. Each chamber reflects equal representation from developed and developing countries. When reaching decisions, the three chambers have equal voting rights and decisions are passed by a two-thirds majority. This complex structure favours fair representation, transparency, and participation—three important criteria for internal legitimacy.

The Forest Stewardship Council also stands out due to its external legitimacy, which can be understood as its ability to produce results. Thanks to the Council, several actors in the timber sector have contributed to improving forest management in numerous countries across the globe. Legislative advancements have also been made with respect to raising awareness among local populations about their rights and the importance of such rights for sustainable forest management techniques, and with regard to limiting intensive farming practices that have strong deforestation consequences. The Forest Stewardship Council has also garnered results by supporting constructive exchanges and learning between actors. Through its reports, it has been active in sharing information on sustainable forest management and on the causes inherent in forest degradation. Because they are grouped in different but equally important chambers within the Forest Stewardship Council, different actors learn from one another: wood retailers have become aware of the number of intermediaries that destabilize their sector,

(continued...)

while NGOs are better equipped to propose solutions that are compatible with business practices. The Forest Stewardship Council has thus become an informal conflict resolution mechanism between actors who exploit forests and those who would like to protect them.

However, the Forest Stewardship Council also has several limitations that challenge its legitimacy. Internally, the participants in the economic chamber have more resources to promote their interests than those in the social and environmental chambers, creating a risk that commercial interests could be over-represented. Moreover, the Forest Stewardship Council's funding structure, which primarily relies on philanthropic donations, is not sustainable. To avoid damaging its credibility, the organization does not wish to increase its membership and certification prices, but must nonetheless address structural financial difficulties.

Externally, there are major geographical disparities when it comes to Forest Stewardship Council forest certification. Almost 75 per cent of European and North American forests are certified, compared with only 25 per cent in Africa, Asia, Oceania, and Latin America. Developing countries are disadvantaged by the certification cost, by the complexity of tropical forest management, and by the small size of plots, which reduces the cost-effectiveness of the certification label. For the moment, the Forest Stewardship Council has not been able to modify the forest product trade structure. The demand for certified wood remains marginal: 5 per cent in Europe, and only 0.02 per cent in Japan, the world's largest importer of tropical wood. Furthermore, the increased price of wood brought about by this certification label has often been blocked upstream without benefiting local producers.

Although the Forest Stewardship Council's success is mixed, that it serves as an example to other partnerships is an illustration of its perceived success. In 2000, for example, the Marine Stewardship Council was created to label fishing products, and adopted a functioning method similar to that of the Forest Stewardship Council. Concurrent partnerships have even been created by the forestry industry, such as the Sustainable Forestry Initiative set up in 1994 as a North American certification scheme and the 1999 Pan European Forest Certification Council as its European equivalent. Analysts have pointed to the limits of such new certification labels compared to the Forest Stewardship Council, particularly with regard to the type of forests to be covered (mostly in developed states) or the environmental standards they promote (found to be rather weak). It is unclear, therefore, if they have an overall positive effect on global forest governance. However, the fact that they were created in response to the Forest Stewardship Council's established practice is a sign of the importance of the Forest Stewardship Council itself.

Sources: Auld 2014; Auld and Gulbrandsen 2010; Chan and Pattberg 2008; Pattberg 2007; Pattberg et al. 2012.

In practice, the majority of transnational partnerships are developed in cooperation with public authorities. In certain cases, transnational partnerships were initiated by governments themselves. The Extractive Industries Transparency Initiative, for example, was launched in 2002 by the British Prime Minister Tony Blair (Haufler 2010). Other partnerships are actively supported by international institutions, such as those funded by the United Nations Fund for International Partnerships and by the Global Environment Facility (see Box 7.2). In fact, all intergovernmental organizations working on environmental issues act as entrepreneurs and have their own partnership programmes (Andonova 2010).

A trend towards a polycentric vision of global environmental politics has gained favour, in which a wide swathe of actors engages directly with policymaking. Elinor Ostrom was one of the first scholars to talk about polycentric governance. Essentially, polycentric governance reflects new forms of governance emerging 'spontaneously from the bottom-up, producing a more dispersed and multilevel pattern of governing' (Jordan et al. 2018: 9; see also Ostrom 2010). These new forms of governance are taking place at all levels of policymaking (local, regional, national, global), in different policy sectors (transport, agriculture, building, energy etc.), and performed by a great diversity of actors and combinations of actors. Polycentricity differs from multilevel governance in that it attributes a stronger degree of autonomy to substate and non-state actors, whereas multilevel governance usually assumes a stronger involvement of governmental actors in both the setting and implementation of policies (Wurzel et al. 2017). It also differs from other related concepts such as regime complexity, institutional fragmentation, or political federalism in the way that 'it is more directly concerned with the role of non-governmental units and/or situations in which jurisdictions overlap' (Jordan et al. 2018).

Polycentricity has de facto been adopted as a model for the implementation of the Paris Agreement and more generally for climate governance. The Paris Agreement indeed fostered the creation, among others, of a non-state action platform, the 2018 Talaona Dialogue, where all actors are invited to communicate on their climate actions. This platform comes in combination with more traditional top-down intergovernmental actions (Bäckstrand et al. 2017). Non-state actor autonomy in relation to governmental and intergovernmental authorities on climate change is therefore limited. It is indeed closely connected with public actor politics, which tries to orchestrate non-state actions (Abbott 2018; Compagnon et al. 2012). Several concerns arise, though, with the concept of polycentricity, and in particular the issue of reactivity (will decision-making be fast enough in a polycentric system?) and power distribution.

Does the emergence of transnational initiatives lead to governance dominated by market forces, or to more open and democratic governance? Opinions remain divided, but a consensus is emerging regarding a move away from the dichotomous vision of environmental governance, which would position private initiatives in opposition to public initiatives. Rather than reinvent the intergovernmental system and initiate a changeover of authority, transnational initiatives seem to supplement the governance already in place by creating niches complementary to those of public authorities.

4.5 Conclusion

This chapter has described the primary categories of non-state actors, explained their interests with respect to environmental regulations, summarized their participation in global environmental politics, and presented their efforts to set up private or public–private partnerships. Importantly, the chapter has illustrated the diversity of non-state actors' interests and strategies, and explained an approach to evaluating their influence on environmental politics.

This chapter has also problematized non-state actor participation in global environmental politics. Although their participation can be a potential solution, compensating for governmental shortfalls, non-state actors' responsibility and legitimacy is questionable as they are ad hoc, unelected, self-interested actors in international politics (Dombrowski 2010).

Whereas in the 1990s NGOs in developed countries were seen as agents of change, working to mobilize local demands (Keck and Sikkink 1998; Princen and Finger 1994), their role as a communication channel for such interests now seems more uncertain. Sometimes, NGOs mobilize for their own causes and neglect certain categories of actors. For example, few NGOs represent small farmers in major events surrounding the negotiations on climate change (Dombrowski 2010).

Although their legitimacy is sometimes called into question, it is undeniable that non-state actors galvanize global environmental politics by stimulating governments and catalysing innovative mechanisms such as public–private partnerships. In this way, non-state actors make a significant contribution, particularly to the collective action problems addressed in global environmental politics, which is the subject of Chapter 5.

Critical thinking questions

1. How do international environmental negotiations enable and constrain the participation of non-state actors?
2. To what extent does private governance compensate for shortcomings in public global environmental governance?
3. How might non-state actors' involvement lead to the commodification of global environmental politics?
4. Explain the phases of the policy cycle in which non-state actors are more likely to intervene. Give some examples of how non-state actors might engage at each phase.
5. Why do corporations sometimes support environmental regulations?
6. What strategies do non-state actors use to participate in environmental governance, and how has this changed over time?

 Test your knowledge and understanding further by trying this chapter's Multiple Choice Questions www.oup.com/he/morin1e

Key references

Betsill, Michele M., and Elisabeth Corell (eds). 2008. *NGO Diplomacy: The Influence of Nongovernmental Organizations in International Environmental Negotiations.* Cambridge, MA: MIT Press.

This edited volume analyses the influence of several categories of non-state actors, including NGOs, during the negotiations of multilateral environmental agreements. It proposes a definition of influence as information transmission that affects behaviour and measures it through analysis of the activity, access, and resources of non-state actors. The book covers a wide range of issue areas such as desertification, biosafety, climate change, forests, and whaling.

Falkner, Robert. 2008. *Business Power and Conflict in International Environmental Politics.* Basingstoke: Palgrave Macmillan.

This book introduces the neo-pluralist framework to study businesses in global environmental politics. It develops three case studies—ozone depletion, climate change, and agrobiotechnology—demonstrating the diversity of business positioning on these environmental problems.

Green, Jessica F. 2013. *Rethinking Private Authority Agents and Entrepreneurs in Global Environmental Governance.* Princeton, NJ: Princeton University Press.

This book discusses the contribution of private actors to global environmental governance, investigating cases in which states delegate actions to private actors and cases in which private actors develop their own

rules. After presenting a framework explaining both situations, the book applies this framework to global governance on climate change.

Hadden, Jennifer. 2015. *Networks in Contention: The Divisive Politics of Climate Change.* New York: Cambridge University Press.

This book analyses divisions within civil society movements engaged in climate activism worldwide. It traces back the emergence of competing frames and strategies for climate activism, from conventional climate advocacy to climate justice activism, and discusses the effects of such divergences on climate politics.

Levy, Marc, and Peter Newell (eds). 2005. *The Business of Global Environmental Governance.* Cambridge, MA: MIT Press.

This edited volume introduces the neo-Gramscian framework to study businesses in global environmental politics. It discusses the role of businesses, markets, and private actors at the international and regional levels of governance.

 For additional material and resources, please visit the online resources at:
www.oup.com/he/morin1e

Chapter references

Abbott, Kenneth. 2012. 'The Transnational Regime Complex for Climate Change.' *Environment and Planning C: Politics and Space* 30 (4): 571–590.

Abbott, Kenneth W. 2018. 'Orchestration: Strategic Ordering in Polycentric Climate Governance'. In *Governing Climate Change: Polycentricity in Action?*, edited by Andrew Jordan, Dave Huitema, Harro van Asselt, and Johanna Forster, 188–209. Cambridge: Cambridge University Press.

Alcock, Franck. 2008. 'Conflicts and Coalitions Within and Across the ENGO Community'. *Global Environmental Politics* 8 (4): 66–91.

Allan, Jen Iris, and Jennifer Hadden. 2017. 'Exploring the Framing Power of NGOs in Global Climate Politics'. *Environmental Politics* 26 (4): 600–620.

Andonova, Liliana B. 2010. 'Public–Private Partnerships for the Earth: Politics and Patterns of Hybrid Authority in the Multilateral System'. *Global Environmental Politics* 10 (2): 25–53.

Andonova, Liliana B., Michele M. Betsill, and Harriet Bulkeley. 2009. 'Transnational Climate Governance'. *Global Environmental Politics* 9 (2): 52–73.

Arnold, Richard, and Andrew B. Whitford. 2006. 'Making Environmental Self-Regulation Mandatory'. *Global Environmental Politics* 6 (4): 1–12.

Arts, Bas, and Sandra Mack. 2003. 'Environmental NGOs and the Biosafety Protocol: A Case Study on Political Influence'. *European Environment* 13 (1): 19–33.

Auld, Graeme. 2014. *Constructing Private Governance: The Rise and Evolution of Forest, Coffee, and Fisheries Certification.* New Haven, CT: Yale University Press.

Auld, Graeme, Steven Bernstein, and Benjamin Cashore. 2008. 'The New Corporate Social Responsibility'. *Annual Review of Environment and Resources* 33: 413–435.

Auld, Graeme, and Lars H. Gulbrandsen. 2010. 'Transparency in Nonstate Certification: Consequences for Accountability and Legitimacy'. *Global Environmental Politics* 10 (3): 97–119.

Aylett, Alexander. 2014. *Progress and Challenges in the Urban Governance of Climate Change: Results of a Global Survey.* Cambridge, MA: MIT Press.

Bäckstrand, Karin. 2008. 'Accountability of Networked Climate Governance: The Rise of Transnational Climate Partnerships'. *Global Environmental Politics* 8 (3): 74–102.

Bäckstrand, Karin, Jonathan W. Kuyper, Björn-Ola Linnér, and Eva Lövbrand. 2017. 'Non-State Actors in Global Climate Governance: From Copenhagen to Paris and Beyond'. *Environmental Politics* 26 (4): 561–579.

Bansard, Jennifer S., Phillipp H. Pattberg, and Oscar Widerberg. 2017. 'Cities to the Rescue? Assessing the Performance of Transnational Municipal Networks in Global Climate Governance'. *International Environmental Agreements: Politics, Law and Economics* 17 (2): 229–246.

Bernhagen, Patrick. 2008. 'Business and International Environmental Agreements: Domestic Sources of Participation and Compliance by Advanced Industrialized Democracies'. *Global Environmental Politics* 8 (1): 78–110.

Betsill, Michele M., and Elisabeth Corell. 2008. *NGO Diplomacy: The Influence of Nongovernmental Organizations in International Environmental Negotiations*. Cambridge, MA: MIT Press.

Betsill, Michele M., and Harriet Bulkeley. 2004. 'Transnational Networks and Global Environmental Governance: The Cities for Climate Protection Program'. *International Studies Quarterly* 48 (2): 471–493.

Bled, Amandine. 2010. 'Technological Choices in International Environmental Negotiations: An Actor-Network Analysis'. *Business & Society* 49 (4): 570–590.

Boiral, Olivier. 2013. 'Sustainability Reports as Simulacra? A Counter-Account of A and A+ GRI Reports'. *Accounting, Auditing & Accountability Journal* 26 (7): 1036–1071.

Boström, Magnus, and Kristina Tamm Hallström. 2010. 'NGO Power in Global Social and Environmental Standard-Setting'. *Global Environmental Politics* 10 (4): 36–59.

Botetzagias, Iosif, Prue Robinson, and Lily Venizelos. 2010. 'Accounting for Difficulties faced in Materializing a Transnational ENGO Conservation Network: A Case-Study from the Mediterranean'. *Global Environmental Politics* 10 (1): 115–151.

Bruno, Kenny, and Joshua Karliner. 2000. *Tangled up in Blue: Corporate Partnerships at the United Nations*. San Francisco, CA: Transnational Resource and Action Centre.

Bulkeley, Harriet, and Kristine Kern. 2009. 'Cities, Europeanization and Multi-Level Governance: Governing Climate Change through Transnational Municipal Networks'. *Journal of Common Market Studies* 47 (2): 309–322.

Cao, Xun, and Hugh Ward. 2017. 'Transnational Climate Governance Networks and Domestic Regulatory Action'. *International Interactions* 43 (1): 76–102.

Carpenter, Chad. 2001. 'Businesses, Green Groups and the Media: The Role of Non-Governmental Organizations in the Climate Change Debate'. *International Affairs* 77 (2): 313–328.

Cashore, Benjamin. 2002. 'Legitimacy and the Privatization of Environmental Governance: How Non-State Market-Driven (NSMD) Governance Systems Gain Rule-Making Authority'. *Governance. An International Journal of Policy, Administration, and Institutions* 15 (4): 503–529.

Chan, Sander, Clara Brandi, and Steffen Bauer. 2016. 'Aligning Transnational Climate Action with International Climate Governance: The Road from Paris'. *Review of European Community and International Environmental Law* 25 (2): 238–247.

Chan, Sander, and Philipp Pattberg. 2008. 'Private Rule-Making and the Politics of Accountability: Analyzing Global Forest Governance'. *Global Environmental Politics* 8 (3): 103–121.

Clapp, Jennifer. 1994. 'The Toxic Waste Trade with Less-Industrialised Countries: Economic Linkages and Political Alliances'. *Third World Quarterly* 15 (3): 505–518.

Clapp, Jennifer. 1998. 'The Privatization of Global Environmental Governance: ISO 14000 and the Developing World'. *Global Governance* 4 (3): 295–316.

Clapp, Jennifer. 2005. 'Global Environmental Governance for Corporate Responsibility and Accountability'. *Global Environmental Politics* 5 (3): 23–34.

Clapp, Jennifer. 2017. 'Responsibility to the Rescue? Governing Private Financial Investment in Global Agriculture'. *Agriculture and Human Values* 34 (1): 223–235.

Compagnon, Daniel, Sander Chan, and Ayşem Mert. 2012. 'The Changing Role of the State'. In *Global Environmental Governance Reconsidered*, edited by Frank Biermann and Philipp Pattberg, 237–263. Cambridge, MA: MIT Press.

Corell, Elisabeth, and Michele M. Betsill. 2001. 'A Comparative Look at NGO Influence in International Environmental Negotiations: Desertification and Climate Change'. *Global Environmental Politics* 1 (4): 86–107.

Dauvergne, Peter. 2008. *The Shadows of Consumption: Consequences for the Global Environment*. Cambridge, MA: MIT Press.

Dauvergne, Peter. 2018. 'Why is the Global Governance of Plastic Failing the Oceans?' *Global Environmental Change* 51 (July): 22–31.

Dimitrov, Radoslav S., Detlef F. Sprinz, Gerald M. DiGiusto, and Alexander Kelle. 2007. 'International Nonregimes: A Research Agenda'. *International Studies Review* 9 (2): 230–258.

Doherty, Brian. 2006. 'Friends of the Earth International: Negotiating a Transnational Identity'. *Environmental Politics* 15 (5): 860–880.

Dombrowski, Kathrin. 2010. 'Filling the Gap? An Analysis of Non-Governmental Organizations Responses to Participation and Representation Deficits in Global Climate Governance'. *International Environmental Agreements. Politics, Law and Economics* 10 (4): 397–416.

Downie, Christian. 2014. 'Transnational Actors in Environmental Politics: Strategies and Influence in Long Negotiations'. *Environmental Politics* 23 (3): 376–394.

Downie, Christian. 2016. 'Prolonged International Environmental Negotiations: The Roles and Strategies of Non-State Actors in the EU'. *International Environmental Agreements, Politics, Law, Economics* 16 (5): 739–755.

Dryzek, John S. 2017. 'The Meanings of Life for Non-State Actors in Climate Politics'. *Environmental Politics* 26 (4): 789–799.

Enneking, Liesbeth. 2014. 'The Future of Foreign Direct Liability: Exploring the International Relevance of the Dutch Shell Nigeria Case'. *Utrecht Law Review* 10 (1): 44–54.

Falkner, Robert. 2003. 'Private Environmental Governance and International Relations: Exploring the Links'. *Global Environmental Politics* 3 (2): 72–87.

Falkner, Robert. 2008. *Business Power and Conflict in International Environmental Politics*. Basingstoke: Palgrave Macmillan.

Fisher, Dana R. 2010. 'COP-15 in Copenhagen: How the Merging of Movements Left Civil Society Out in the Cold'. *Global Environmental Politics* 10 (2): 11–17.

Gamu, Jonathan Kishen, and Peter Dauvergne. 2018. 'The Slow Violence of Corporate Social Responsibility: The Case of Mining in Peru'. *Third World Quarterly* 39 (5): 959–975.

Givel, Michael. 2007. 'Motivation of Chemical Industry Social Responsibility through Responsible Care'. *Health Policy* 81 (1): 85–92.

Gordon, David. 2016. 'From Global Cities to Global Governors: Power, Politics, and the Convergence of Urban Climate Governance'. Thesis, Department of Political Science, University of Toronto.

Gordon, David J., and Craig A. Johnson. 2017. 'The Orchestration of Global Urban Climate Governance: Conducting Power in the post-Paris Climate Regime'. *Environmental Politics* 26 (4): 694–714.

Green, Ashley, and Michael I. Westphal. 2017. 'Designing and Testing a Methodology to Estimate Private Climate Finance Mobilization from Policy and other Causal Factors'. Working Paper. Washington, DC: World Resources Institute.

Green, Jessica F. 2013. *Rethinking Private Authority Agents and Entrepreneurs in Global Environmental Governance*. Princeton, NJ: Princeton University Press.

Green, Jessica F., and Jeff Colgan. 2013. 'Protecting Sovereignty, Protecting the Planet: State Delegation to International Organizations and Private Actors in Environmental Politics'. *Governance: An International Journal of Policy, Administration, and Institutions* 26 (3): 473–497.

Gulbrandsen, Lars H., and Steinar Andresen. 2004. 'NGO Influence in the Implementation of the Kyoto Protocol: Compliance, Flexibility Mechanisms, and Sinks'. *Global Environmental Politics* 4 (4): 54–75.

Haas, Peter M. 1992. 'Banning Chlorofluorocarbons: Epistemic Community Efforts to Protect Stratospheric Ozone'. *International Organization* 46 (1): 187–224.

Hadden, Jennifer. 2014. 'Explaining Variation in Transnational Climate Change Activism: The Role of Inter Movement Spillover'. *Global Environmental Politics* 14 (2): 7–25.

Hadden, Jennifer. 2015. *Networks in Contention: The Divisive Politics of Climate Change*. New York: Cambridge University Press.

Hakelberg, Lukas. 2014. 'Governance by Diffusion: Transnational Municipal Networks and the Spread of Local Climate Strategies in Europe'. *Global Environmental Politics* 14 (1): 107–129.

Hale, Thomas, and Charles Roger. 2014. 'Orchestration and Transnational Climate Governance'. *Review of International Organizations* 9 (1): 59–82.

Haufler, Virginia. 2010. 'Disclosure as Governance: The Extractive Industries Transparency Initiative and Resource Management in the Developing World'. *Global Environmental Politics* 10 (3): 53–73.

Heede, Richard. 2014. *Carbon Majors: Accounting for Carbon and Methane Emissions 1854–2010: Methods & Results Report*. Snowmass, CO: Climate Mitigation Services.

Hestres, Luis E. 2015. 'Climate Change Advocacy Online: Theories of Change, Target Audiences, and Online Strategy'. *Environmental Politics* 24 (2): 193–211.

Holmes, George. 2011. 'Conservation's Friends in High Places: Neoliberalism, Networks, and the Transnational Conservation Elite'. *Global Environmental Politics* 11 (4): 1–21.

Humphreys, David. 2004. 'Redefining the Issues: NGO Influence on International Forest Negotiations'. *Global Environmental Politics* 4 (2): 51–74.

Jinnah, Sikina. 2011. 'Strategic Linkages: The Evolving Role of Trade Agreements in Global Environmental Governance'. *Journal of Environment and Development* 20 (2): 191–215.

Jinnah, Sikina. 2014. *Post-Treaty Politics: Secretariat Influence in Global Environmental Governance*. Cambridge, MA: MIT Press.

Jodoin, Sebastien. 2017. *Forest Preservation in a Changing Climate: REDD+ and Indigenous and Community Rights in Indonesia and Tanzania*. Cambridge: Cambridge University Press.

Jordan, A., D. Huitema, H. Van Asselt, and J. Forster (eds). 2018. *Governing Climate Change: Polycentricity in Action?* Cambridge: Cambridge University Press.

Katz-Kimchi, Merav, and Idit Manosevitch. 2015. 'Mobilizing Facebook Users against Facebook's Energy Policy: The Case of Greenpeace Unfriend Coal Campaign'. *Environmental Communication* 9 (2): 248-267.

Keck, Margaret E., and Kathryn Sikkink. 1998. *Activists Beyond Borders: Advocacy Networks in International Politics*. Ithaca, NY: Cornell University Press.

Kuchler, Magdalena. 2017. 'The Human Rights Turn: ENGOs' Changing Tactics in the Quest for a more Transparent, Participatory and Accountable CDM'. *Environmental Politics* 26 (4): 648-668.

Levy, Marc, and Peter Newell (eds). 2005. *The Business of Global Environmental Governance*. Cambridge, MA: MIT Press.

Lindroth, Marjo, and Heidi Sinevaara-Niskanen. 2013. 'At the Crossroads of Autonomy and Essentialism: Indigenous Peoples in International Environmental Politics'. *International Political Sociology* 7 (3): 275-293.

Marion Suiseeya, Kimberly R. 2014. 'Negotiating the Nagoya Protocol: Indigenous Demands for Justice'. *Global Environmental Politics* 14 (3): 102-124.

Meckling, Jonas. 2015. 'Oppose, Support, or Hedge? Distributional Effects, Regulatory Pressure, and Business Strategy in Environmental Politics'. *Global Environmental Politics* 15 (2): 19-37.

Meek, David. 2015. 'Counter-Summitry: La Via Campesina, the People's Summit, and Rio+20'. *Global Environmental Politics* 15 (2): 11-18.

Michaelowa, Katharina, and Axel Michaelowa. 2017. 'Transnational Climate Governance Initiatives: Designed for Effective Climate Change Mitigation?' *International Interactions*. 43 (1): 129-155.

Mitchener, Brandon. 1995. 'Environmentalists Apologize to Shell for Using Faulty Data: Greenpeace Admits Slip on Oil Rig Risk'. *New York Times*, 6 September.

Morin, Jean-Frédéric. 2008. 'Rhetorical Discourses in International Patent Lawmaking: Property, Fairness, and Well-Being'. *Asian Journal of WTO and International Health Law and Policy* 3 (2): 505-537.

Muñoz Cabré, Miquel. 2011. 'Issue-Linkages to Climate Change Measured through NGO Participation in the UNFCCC'. *Global Environmental Politics* 11 (3): 10-22.

Nasiritousi, Naghmeh. 2017. 'Fossil Fuel Emitters and Climate Change: Unpacking the Governance Activities of Large Oil and Gas Companies'. *Environmental Politics* 26 (4): 621-647.

Newell, Peter. 2018. 'Trasformismo or Transformation? The Global Political Economy of Energy Transitions'.

Review of International Political Economy 26 (1): 25-48, doi: 10.1080/09692290.2018.1511448.

Newell, Peter, and Olivia Taylor. 2018. 'Contested Landscapes: The Global Political Economy of Climate-Smart Agriculture'. *The Journal of Peasant Studies* 45 (1): 108-129.

O'Neill, Kate. 2017. *The Environment and International Relations*. Cambridge: Cambridge University Press.

O'Neill, Kate. 2018. 'The New Global Political Economy of Waste.' In *A Research Agenda for Global Environmental Politics*, edited by Peter Dauverge and Justin Alger, 87-100. Cheltenham: Edward Elgar.

Orr, Shannon K. 2016. 'Institutional Control and Climate Change Activism at COP 21 in Paris'. *Global Environmental Politics* 16 (3): 23-30.

Orsini, Amandine. 2010. *La Biodiversité sous influence*. Brussels: Presses de l'Université de Bruxelles.

Orsini, Amandine. 2011. 'Thinking Transnationally, Acting Individually: Business Lobby Coalitions in International Environmental Negotiations'. *Global Society* 25 (3): 311-329.

Orsini, Amandine. 2013. 'Navigating the Regime Complexes for Forestry and Genetic Resources'. *Global Environmental Politics* 13 (3): 34-55.

Orsini, Amandine, and Daniel Compagnon. 2011. 'Corporate Lobbying and Multilateral Environmental Agreements. Examples from the Climate Change and Biosecurity Sectors'. *Revue française de science politique* 61 (2): 47-64.

Ostrom, E. 2010. 'Polycentric Systems for Coping with Collective Action and Global Environmental Change'. *Global Environmental Change* 20 (4): 550-557.

Pattberg, Philipp. 2007. *Private Institutions and Global Governance: The New Politics of Environmental Sustainability*. Cheltenham and Northampton, MA: Edward Elgar.

Pattberg, Philipp, Frank Biermann, Sander Chan, and Aysem Mert. 2012. *Public–Private Partnerships for Sustainable Development: Emergence, Influence and Legitimacy*. Cheltenham, Northampton: Edward Elgar.

Princen, Thomas, and Matthias Finger. 1994. *Environmental NGOs in World Politics: Linking the Local and the Global*. London: Routledge.

Raustiala, Kal. 1997. 'Domestic Institutions and International Regulatory Cooperation—Comparative Responses to the Convention on Biological Diversity'. *World Politics* 49 (4): 482-509.

Reimann, Kim D. 2006. 'A View from the Top: International Politics, Norms and the Worldwide Growth of NGOs'. *International Studies Quarterly* 50 (1): 45-67.

Roger, Charles, Thomas Hale, and Liliana Andonova. 2017. 'The Comparative Politics of Transnational Climate Governance'. *International Interactions* 43 (1): 1–25.

Sæverud, Ingvild A., and Jon B. Skjærseth. 2007. 'Oil Companies and Climate Change: Inconsistencies between Strategy Formulation and Implementation?' *Global Environmental Politics* 7 (3): 42–62.

Skodvin, Tora, and Steinar Andresen. 2003. 'Nonstate Influence in the International Whaling Commission, 1970–1990'. *Global Environmental Politics* 3 (4): 61–86.

Tamiotti, Ludivine, and Matthias Finger. 2001. 'Environmental Organizations: Changing Roles and Functions in Global Politics'. *Global Environmental Politics* 1 (1): 56–76.

Teffler, Peter. 2015. 'Climate Change: Nations Talk, but Cities Act'. *EU Observer*, 19 October. Available at: https://euobserver.com/regions/130259, accessed 4 September 2018.

Tienhaara, K., A. Orsini, and R. Falkner. 2012. 'Global Corporations'. In *Global Environmental Governance Reconsidered*, edited by F. Biermann and P. Pattberg, 45–68. Cambridge, MA: MIT Press.

Vogel, David. 2005. *The Market for Virtue: The Potential and Limits of Corporate Social Responsibility*. Washington, DC: Brookings Institution Press.

Vogel, David. 2018. *California Greenin' How the Golden State Became an Environmental Leader*. Princeton, NJ: Princeton University Press.

Vormedal, Irja. 2008. 'The Influence of Business and Industry NGOs in the Negotiation of the Kyoto Mechanisms: The Case of Carbon Capture and Storage in the CDM'. *Global Environmental Politics* 8 (4): 36–65.

Wahlström, Mattias, Magnus Wennerhag, and Christopher Rootes. 2013. 'Framing "The Climate Issue": Patterns of Participation and Prognostic Frames among Climate Summit Protesters'. *Global Environmental Politics* 13 (4): 101–122.

Wapner, Paul. 1996. *Environmental Activism and World Civic Politics*. New York: SUNY Press.

Wurzel, R. K. W., J. Connely, and D. Liefferink. 2017. 'Introduction: European Union Climate Leadership'. In *The European Union in International Climate Change Politics: Still Taking a Lead?*, edited by R. K. W. Wurzel, J. Connely, and D. Liefferink, 3–19. Abingdon and New York: Routledge.

Part 3

Bargaining over the environment

5 The tragedy of the commons and sovereign rights

This chapter focuses on rights governing access to globally shared natural resources, such as fish stocks, deep seabed minerals, and clean air. These access rights determine states' incentives for the use of different resources, and structure their behaviour. Changing the international rules governing who can exploit natural resources, and under what conditions, can potentially improve environmental protection. However, there is no consensus about whether these new rules should be based on the principle of national sovereignty or the principle of common heritage. This chapter presents the debate.

◉ Learning objectives

After reading this chapter, readers will be able to:

- Explain how the 'tragedy of the commons' helps us to understand the overexploitation of natural resources and the policy implications for global environmental governance, as well as its limitations in helping us understand these things;

- Analyse the role that the 'common heritage of humankind' has played in the governance of areas outside sovereign control, such as the international seabed, outer space, and the Antarctic; and

- Discuss the constraints and the opportunities that the principle of state sovereignty presents for effective environmental governance.

Introduction

'The Earth is one but the world is not' (Brundtland Report: World Commission on Environment and Development 1987: 28). The international system is based on the principle of national **sovereignty**, which says that each state has absolute, perpetual, and exclusive rights within its national territory. This construction does not, however, match ecological realities. Rivers and migratory birds, for example, do not stop at border crossings. The CO_2 emissions in London do not have a greater impact on climate change in the United Kingdom than they do in Australia. There is a stark contrast between states' territorial divisions and the biosphere's ecological connectedness.

This chapter explores this tension and its relationship to decision-making in natural resource management. How can sovereign states manage the earth's resources if they are fragmented in separate territories that overlap complex ecosystems? This question is often approached using the '**tragedy of the commons**' metaphor. Although the metaphor's empirical validity is contested, it is a useful starting point for exploring the problems of collective action raised by the rights of access to natural resources (see Section 5.1 of this chapter). When the metaphor is applied to the global commons, two main policy options emerge. The first is a coordinated approach building on the notion of a 'common **heritage of humankind**' (see Section 5.2). This common heritage status could arguably provide the normative foundation for a central- ized response to the tragedy of the commons. The second policy option is a decentralized approach based on states' sovereign rights (see Section 5.3). Parcelling the global commons into distinct domains, each under the authority of a sovereign state, would alter the structure of the problem, changing the covert incentives for overexploitation of natural resources into incentives for long-term **conservation**. This chapter discusses how these two policy options have been applied in different issue areas; neither has proved to be fully effective in reducing overexploitation of natural resources.

5.1 The tragedy of the commons

A powerful metaphor

In 1968, the ecologist Garrett Hardin published an article in the journal *Science*, titled 'The Tragedy of the Commons', which is one of the most widely cited publications in environ- mental studies. In his article, Hardin summarized his ideas about the link between the type of property rights that characterize a particular good and actors' behaviour in relation to utilizing that good. The article describes the problem structure (Mitchell 2006) underlying several environmental issues. Hardin's ideas were not entirely novel; mathematicians and economists working on game theory had already made a similar argument (Hardin himself cited a paper from 1833 by the mathematician William Forster Lloyd). Nonetheless, Hardin presented his ideas in an original and appealing way, using simple terms, and without resort- ing to complex equations or technical jargon.

Hardin asked his readers to picture a pasture that is freely accessible to all the shepherds in the area. Each shepherd can gain from grazing as many sheep as possible, given that each extra animal represents an additional source of profit, while the cost of its feed (the quantity of grass consumed) is shared by all the shepherds. However, there is no incentive for any of the shepherds to invest individually in reseeding the pasture, because all the shepherds would share the benefits of the investment. In these circumstances, each shepherd gains by grazing as many sheep as possible, as quickly as possible, before the grass has been com- pletely grazed. As a result of this logic, the pasture becomes overexploited. The inevitable depletion of the pasture is what Hardin calls the 'tragedy of the commons'. The tragedy, ac- cording to Hardin (1968: 1244), 'resides in the solemnity of the remorseless working of things'.

This 'tragedy' is the result of overexploitation of a particular type of good, known as '**common goods**' (see Table 5.1). Common goods meet two criteria. First, access to the good must be unrestricted, which means it must not be controlled by any public authority or private body. For example, high-seas fishing for certain species is accessible to all, with no

Table 5.1 Typology of goods

	Open access	Limited access
Rivalrous	Common good	Private good
Non-rivalrous	Public good	Club good

territorial rights in the open ocean and no restrictions on the quantity of fish a fisherman can catch (see Box 5.1). Second, the consumption of common goods must be 'rival'—for every unit that is consumed or destroyed, the available stock diminishes by one unit (Barkin and Shambaugh 1996). For example, although some may think air is a non-rival good because it appears to be inexhaustible, clean air is in fact a rival good because the pollution of one unit of air reduces the supply of clean air available for others. High-seas fish stocks and clean air are both common goods.

Common goods are particularly vulnerable to rapid depletion, since no one has a vested interest in bearing the cost individually to protect them, even if everybody stands to gain from that investment. This is because, although the costs are borne by one (or a few), the benefits are shared by all, even those who did not contribute to the costs of protecting the resource. Thus, the tragedy of the commons illustrates the tension between individual and collective interests. On the one hand, communities—or the international community—would gain from investing in environmental protection to ensure their sustainability. On the other hand, individuals—or states as monolithic units—would benefit from contributing as little as possible towards the costs of environmental protection. In other words, a pattern of individual rational behaviour—to consume an available resource before your competitors do—may lead to an irrational collective outcome—the depletion of the resources that everyone depends on. This conclusion runs counter to classic economic liberalism, according to which the pursuit of individual interests contributes to collective well-being. The metaphor of the commons suggests that the rational pursuit of individual interests conflicts with the collective interest.

For example, the geostationary orbit constitutes an international common good (Soroos 1987). It is an orbit situated at an altitude of just over 35,000 km above the equator. A satellite on this orbit follows the earth's rotation exactly, which means it is always located above the same point on earth. This feature is particularly useful for communication satellites and meteorological satellites. However, there is a limit to the number of satellites that can be located on this orbit because they cause mutual radio interference. If the states with the capacity to launch satellites into space all rushed to fill this strategic position, they would pollute space, create congestion, and increase the risk of collision. If there was no supranational authority capable of managing the allocation of satellite positions (in this case the International Telecommunication Union), the rational behaviour of these states would lead to a suboptimal outcome for the international community. The result would also be unfair for states that do not yet have the capacity to send a satellite into space.

Potential solutions to the tragedy of the commons

The tragedy of the commons metaphor does not merely describe a problem of collective action. It provides analysts with a framework for imagining possible solutions (Barkin and Shambaugh 1999). If the problem reflects a discrepancy between individual and collective interests, then for environmental protection the incentives provided to individual actors must be adjusted in ways that make them more compatible with collective interests (see Chapter 8). However, not everyone agrees on the best way to achieve this. *Regulation*, *taxation*, *subsidies*, and *private property rights* are the most common solutions to the tragedy of the commons.

Public regulations, combined with monitoring and sanction mechanisms, can alleviate the tragedy of the commons. Going back to the example of grazing land, we can imagine that a central authority limits the maximum number of sheep per shepherd. Since some shepherds may be tempted to break this rule and exceed their quota, inspections and fines should be imposed for those who violate the rules. Several international agreements governing high-seas fishing are based on this model (see Box 5.1). It is also the model underlying the Convention on Long-Range Transboundary Air Pollution. These international treaties restrict the amount of natural resources that states can extract or pollute, and states are expected to enforce these restrictions on their citizens.

Box 5.1 Overfishing in international waters

International waters are those beyond the jurisdiction of coastal states. Because historically there was no system of rules or rights governing fishing in these global commons, this has resulted in a tragedy of the commons whereby global fish stocks are in rapid decline, largely as a result of unhindered industrial fishing. According to the Food and Agriculture Organization of the United Nations, the percentage of fish stocks that are being harvested at unsustainable levels has grown from 10 per cent in 1974 to 33 per cent in 2015.

The UN Convention on the Law of the Sea in 1982 established 'exclusive economic zones', in which coastal states maintain sovereign rights to the waters within 200 miles of their coastlines. This structure echoed Garrett Hardin's argument that individual property rights could solve the problem of the tragedy of the commons. Under the Convention on the Law of the Sea, coastal states have jurisdiction over their exclusive economic zone, and are therefore responsible for protecting and preserving the marine environment there.

Yet, several coastal governments have increased their fishing efforts within their own exclusive economic zones. Because the convention also requires that coastal states allow others to fish within their exclusive economic zone if they are not fully utilizing the fish stocks, coastal states have an incentive to exploit the fish stocks as much as possible. And because many commercially valuable fish species do not stay within exclusive economic zones, the zones do little to protect migratory fish stocks such as tuna and cod.

Other governments, such as Canada, New Zealand, and Iceland, have created individual transferable quota systems within their exclusive economic zones. Under these systems, a specific total allowable catch is set for a given time period, and the government assigns a quota to each individual fisherman, who may then harvest their assigned amount or transfer their quota to others. When combined with an effective monitoring system, well-designed individual transferable quota systems have allowed some countries to avoid the collapse of certain fisheries through **enforcement** of their total allowable catch.

Regional fisheries management organizations, such as the Northwest Atlantic Fisheries Organization, are also an important part of governing these global commons. These organizations are designed to share responsibility for regulating fishing, setting catch limits, and monitoring fish stocks, and cover the majority of the high seas with major fisheries. Some analysts, however, criticize these organizations on the basis that they aim at optimum exploitation of fishery resources, rather than at conserving them. Critics also point out that the drivers of fish stock depletion come not only from fishing, but also from pollution and climate change, while some argue that limiting regulation to specific species ignores the complexity of marine ecosystems and the interdependence between different animal and plant species.

Despite high levels of cooperation on global fisheries, there have been several disputes between coastal countries and those of the factory ships fishing in international waters. In such cases, coastal states' attempts to enforce regional rules in areas beyond their national jurisdiction have been challenged by other states who claim that states lack the authority to unilaterally enforce these rules. For example, in 1995 a conflict emerged between Canada and the European Union involving fishing violations by Spanish and Portuguese vessels in international waters outside Canada's exclusive economic zone. The Northwest Atlantic Fisheries Organization is the international body responsible for managing fishing in this area.

The members of this organization established a total allowable catch and quotas for the 1995–1996 fishing season, following a warning from scientists that the turbot (also known as halibut) was overfished in that area. Members are required to keep to their limits, although they retain the right to opt out of these proposed limits and assign their own quotas. The European Union, arguing that its quota of 12.6 per cent of the total allowable catch was unfair, objected to the quota and adopted a much higher one. Shortly afterwards, a Canadian gunboat arrested the crew of a Spanish fishing trawler just outside the exclusive economic zone, charging them with overfishing under Canadian domestic law. This led to a series of disputes, known as the 'Turbot War', which dramatically raised tensions between Canada and Spain, along with the rest of the European Union. The 'war' was partially resolved when Canada and the European Union reached an agreement that effectively transferred part of Canada's turbot quota to the European Union and required Canada to release the seized Spanish ship. In return, the European Union agreed to stronger mechanisms that would allow all parties, not just the vessel's own country, to enforce member quotas set by the Northwest Atlantic Fisheries Organization.

Looking forward, there are ongoing intergovernmental negotiations to create a new treaty governing marine **biodiversity** beyond the national jurisdictions created under the 1982 Convention on the Law of the Sea. Although delegations to the negotiations recognize that fishing is the greatest threat to marine biodiversity, a number of fishing states are arguing that fishing should not be included in the treaty because current regional and international arrangements already adequately regulate fishing, Therefore, while it is still too early to say how the new treaty will address fishing, some argue that it could help address the tragedy of the commons with respect to overfishing by establishing marine protected areas and providing a coherent and integrated approach to international fishing regulation, thereby closing gaps in both regional and international **governance** of fishing on the high seas.

Sources: Cullis-Suzuki and Pauly 2010; Dieter 2014; Food and Agriculture Organization 2018; Sovacool 2009; Springer 1997; Teece 1997; Wright et al. 2016.

The advantage of regulations as a solution to the tragedy of the commons is that this appears fair and makes it likely that set targets are achieved. However, because they require monitoring and penalty procedures, regulations can be difficult and complex to enforce. Several states are reluctant to authorize international monitoring schemes on their territory and to open their citizens and corporate actors to international sanctioning mechanisms. Other states do not always have the human, financial, or technical capacity to guarantee effective surveillance and to impose sanctions on those who are in violation of established regulations. Therefore, they may end up with regulations that are strict on paper but seldom enforced in reality.

An alternative solution to the tragedy of the commons is to *subsidize* those who adopt virtuous behaviour. If we go back to the tragedy of the commons metaphor, we could envisage paying compensation to the shepherds who voluntarily limit the number of sheep they graze on the area of common land. In a way, international financial **institutions** and developed countries do just that when they make their assistance to **developing countries** conditional on the adoption of more environmentally friendly practices. On a political level, positive incentives such as this are attractive because they rarely spark opposition. However, this option would require public funding, which comes from all taxpayers, including those who are not major polluters.

Another form of financial incentives involves *taxing* resource use in such a way that the environmental externalities—i.e. the cost of environmental damage associated with an activity—are built into the costs of production. Without imposing a limit on the number of sheep, shepherds could pay a tax per head for all the sheep they graze on the common land. They could then use the revenue collected from this tax to invest in reseeding the pasture. This would be one manifestation of the **'polluter pays' principle**, whereby the financial onus is placed on those responsible rather than on the community as a whole, in contrast to public subsidies.

Environmental taxation is frequently used by governments at the domestic level (see Figure 8.2), but seldom at the international level. The main obstacle to the use of taxation to govern global commons is the absence of a global government with the legitimacy and the necessary authority to impose taxes directly. One rare exception is the Convention on the Law of the Sea, which requires states to pay fees to an international organization for deep-sea mining activities. However, the aim of the fee is to redistribute a share of the income to developing countries, rather than to internalize the environmental costs.

An additional challenge with the use of taxation to solve the tragedy of the commons is that environmental externalities are difficult to quantify in monetary terms. What monetary value should be attributed to the exploitation of a hectare of tropical forest, where the **genetic resources** and their potential biotechnology applications are unknown? What does the pleasure of walking in a forest or the aesthetic value of a natural landscape represent in hard cash? How can we quantify the value of an endangered butterfly species? (Funtowicz and Ravetz 1994). If environmental externalities are overestimated, businesses and taxpayers are likely to oppose a new tax, which they consider unjustified. On the other hand, if they are underestimated, environmental degradation will continue, as environmental taxes then essentially serve as pollution licences that rich people and corporations can afford to pay for the common goods they extract.

Other solutions to the tragedy of the commons avoid centralized state intervention (i.e. regulations and state-sponsored incentives) and instead encourage greater decentralization with self-regulation. In this case, public authorities do not have to quantify the environment's monetary value, but must clearly establish *property rights*, guarantee that these rights are protected, and create a market system with the lowest possible transaction costs to trade those rights. To go back once more to the grazing metaphor, this would involve dividing the pasture into individual plots and allocating each plot to one of the shepherds. The shepherds could then choose to use their plot themselves, rent it to another shepherd, or even sell it. In all cases, **market mechanisms** would create economic incentives to guarantee the pasture's sustainability, either by preserving the land's grazing potential or by maintaining its commercial value.

For example, private property rights are used to protect a common good in the creation of a market for air pollution. Public authority can create such a market by allocating every business a set number of emission credits. This allows them to emit a certain quantity of pollutants per year. The credits are essentially property rights for a virtual quantity of air, which the business can choose to use, rent, or sell. When growth in production generates an increase in demand for credits or when the state withdraws them from the market, their price tends to rise as a result. Businesses are then encouraged to develop new technology to reduce their emissions, so that they no longer have to buy credits. They may even make a profit by selling the credits initially allocated to them. This system can potentially encourage private investment in research and development for greener technology (Anderson and Leal 2001; Pennington 2008).

However, adopting private property rights and market mechanisms might be conducive to opportunistic behaviour. For example, we might presume that the owner of a plot of forested land could guarantee his property's long-term market value by investing in reforestation. But he may be tempted to proceed with clear cutting for short-term gain. Similarly, let us consider the example of a fishing community that has the right to water which is clean enough for consumable fish to live in. The community may strategically delay taking legal action against a business which contaminates the water and undermines their right, in order to increase the damages awarded by the court.

In fact, whatever solution is adopted for the tragedy of the commons (regulations, subsidies, taxes, or private property), there is always the risk that unexpected strategic behaviour and adverse effects will ensue. Instead of reconciling individual and collective interests, users of natural resources may have incentives to cause further environmental damage in order to circumvent the rules, increase the subsidies they receive, or avoid environmental taxes.

However, different types of solutions to the tragedy of the commons may be moderately effective in specific circumstances. There is no silver bullet solution, but none of the solutions are necessarily doomed to failure in all circumstances (see Table 5.2). The fundamental question is not which solution is intrinsically superior, but which of the proposed solutions are most likely to succeed in a given situation (Feeny et al. 1990).

Critics of the tragedy of the commons

In fact, some criticisms of the tragedy of the commons metaphor argue that it is an inaccurate description of the problem at hand and therefore cannot point to any genuine solution (Berkes 1989). This was the argument made by the late Elinor Ostrom, the first woman

Table 5.2 Four solutions to the tragedy of the commons

	Main pros	Main cons
Regulations	• Appear likely to achieve the objectives if implemented well	• Sovereignty costs of international monitoring and enforcement schemes • Administrative costs of domestic monitoring and enforcement schemes
Subsidies	• Politically attractive	• Public funding required
Taxation	• Fair, and complies with the polluter pays principle	• Politically unappealing • Difficult to measure environmental externalities
Market mechanisms	• Create continuous incentive for research and development	• Administratively burdensome to establish • Risks of unanticipated opportunistic behaviours

to receive the Nobel Prize for Economics in 2009 (Dietz et al. 2003; Ostrom 1990, 2001). In Ostrom's view, the commons that Hardin describes are rare if not non-existent, at least at a local level. Even in traditional societies unfamiliar with Western property rights, **social norms** almost always govern access to key resources. These norms are sometimes informal and implicit, but they exist nonetheless.

According to Ostrom, it is the introduction of exogenous rules, not the absence of rules, that destabilizes the relationships between society and nature, accelerating the degradation of resources. Centralized public authorities, be it the state or **intergovernmental organizations**, have a limited capacity for action, and their efforts are often counterproductive when it comes to managing shared resources. When local **stakeholders** consider that distant public authorities lack both credibility and legitimacy, they may be suspicious of any policy solution imposed from above by those authorities, and be tempted to overexploit the resources they share. For example, when several developing countries nationalized pastures, forests, and sources of drinking water in the 1960s, some local populations, which had lived in relative harmony with their environment for centuries, adopted new behavioural patterns that were detrimental to the environment. Paradoxically, central authority intervention and the establishment of formal property rights have exacerbated environmental problems.

In Ostrom's view, the sustainable use of shared resources cannot be guaranteed by regulations, tax incentives, subsidies, or market-based solutions. She suggests instead that it would be advisable to establish locally based norms to govern access to resources. The multiplicity of these local norms would create a polycentric governance system involving a wide range of stakeholders rather than a clear hierarchical structure of authority (see Chapter 4). These ideas are attracting increasing attention and a growing number of scholars now study the actual or potential contribution of a polycentric approach to global environmental governance (Cole 2015; Dorsch and Flachsland 2017; Jordan et al. 2015; Keohane and Victor 2016; Zelli and Van Asselt 2013).

However, most natural resource management problems studied by Ostrom are local issues, like clean water and fisheries management, and not global issues, such as ozone depletion or climate change (Downie 1999). There is no certainty that the polycentric governance approach that Ostrom advocated could reduce pressure on natural resources on a global scale. A polycentric governance system also raises difficult questions in terms of legitimacy and accountability. At best, a multiplicity of local initiatives can trigger a positive dynamic and act 'as a spur to international **regimes** to do their part' (Ostrom 2012: 353).

5.2 The common heritage of humankind

Two opposing approaches to solving the tragedy of the commons are unique to the governance of the global commons. One is the extension of the *common heritage of humankind* principle. This principle provides the normative basis for legitimate collective public management at the international level. The other approach is the *extension of sovereignty rights* to global common goods. Sovereignty rights could then operate on global common goods in a way analogous to how private property rights could work for local commons: they change the problem structure by abandoning the common character of the goods. This section and Section 5.3 look at these two alternatives in turn.

The principle of *common heritage of humankind* is frequently put forward as a solution to the tragedy that afflicts the global commons. By formally recognizing humankind's environmental heritage, the international community is invited to establish mechanisms to guarantee a sustainable use of natural resources, held in trust for future generations (Okereke 2008). The notion of humankind's heritage provides a basis for environmental stewardship as it suggests that humanity shares a custodial responsibility for the planet (Falkner and Buzan 2019). For example, the Declaration on the Responsibilities of the Present Generations Towards Future Generations, adopted by the United Nations Educational, Scientific and Cultural Organization in 1997, stresses that 'the present generations may use the common heritage of humankind, as defined in international law, provided that this does not entail compromising it irreversibly' (Article 8).

However, there is no clear definition of what actually constitutes the common heritage of humankind. The concept's meaning and scope are ambiguous. For example, the Convention for the Protection of the World Cultural and Natural Heritage allows a state to propose an outstanding natural site for registration on the list of world heritage sites, on condition that its heritage value is considered to be universal. Once a natural site has been formally recognized as part of the world natural heritage, the state becomes its trustee in the name of humankind (Sand 2004). Yet, registering a site on the list does not entail surrendering sovereign rights or the transfer of ownership. The state simply makes a commitment to ensure that the site is identified, protected, conserved, and enhanced. If the state lacks the necessary funds to fulfil these duties, it is eligible for aid from the 'World Heritage Fund'.

Antarctica is sometimes referred to as a continent that is the common heritage of humankind, but this is slightly misleading (Vogler 2012). The preamble of the 1959 Antarctic Treaty declares that it 'is in the interest of all mankind that Antarctica shall continue forever to be used exclusively for peaceful purposes and shall not become the scene or object of international discord'. With this in mind, the treaty prohibits any military activity on the continent and promotes international cooperation in scientific research. However, it does not actually state that the Antarctic is the common heritage of humankind. Before the Antarctic Treaty was concluded, several signatory countries had claimed parts of its territory and have not yet relinquished their territorial claims (see Figure 5.1).

Nonetheless, by dedicating the continent to peaceful activities, the 1959 Antarctic Treaty provided the normative basis for strong environmental cooperation. The reference to 'the interest of all mankind' established in 1959 led to what is arguably the strictest environmental regime in the world. In 1964, the signatories to the Antarctic Treaty agreed to ban the hunting of indigenous birds and mammals and to plan further protection measures for certain zones and particular species. In 1972, a convention was signed for the protection of all Antarctic seal species. The Convention on the Conservation of Antarctic Marine Living Resources was adopted in 1980 to protect all marine living resources south of the 60th parallel. And in 1991, the Madrid Protocol on Environmental Protection established particularly stringent new regulations. Antarctica was designated as a natural reserve devoted to peace and science, and all activities harmful to flora and fauna were prohibited from then on. Tourism or scientific projects which could have repercussions for the environment, however minor or transient, had to be preceded by an **environmental impact assessment**. Furthermore, they were made subject to strict preventive measures, particularly for waste disposal. More recently, in 2016, parties to the 1980 convention established the Ross Sea marine park, a 1.5 million km² park

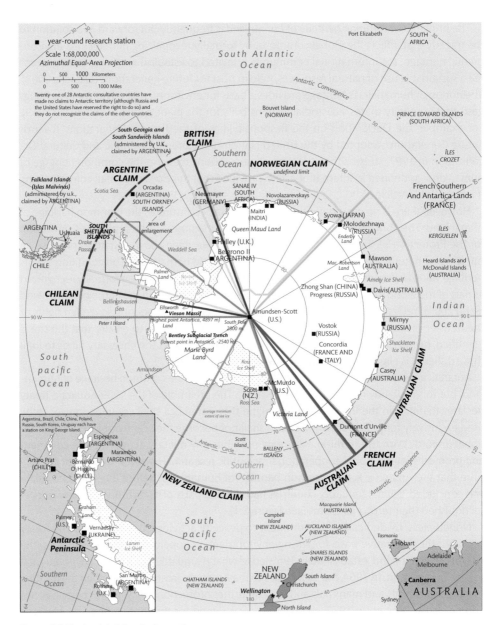

Figure 5.1 Territorial claims in Antarctica

Source: https://commons.wikimedia.org/wiki/File:Antarctic_Region.png

where commercial fishing is completely banned. The tragedy of the commons appears to have been avoided in Antarctica, thanks in part to institutions building on the reference to the 'humankind interest'.

Yet, in other fields, the principle of the common heritage of humankind does not suffice on its own to provide the legal basis for strict environmental protection or to solve the tragedy of the commons. The example of outer space is revealing in this respect.

The 1967 Space Treaty clearly provides that 'outer space, including the Moon and other celestial bodies, is not subject to national appropriation by claim of sovereignty' (Article II) and that the exploration and use of space 'shall be the province of all mankind' (Article I). Despite these principles, though, few environmental measures were envisaged in the 1967 treaty. The key provisions prohibit placing weapons of mass destruction in orbit around the earth, on the moon, or in a space station. The only environmental measure in the 1967 treaty requires signatory countries to conduct 'exploration [. . .] so as to avoid their harmful contamination and also adverse changes in the environment of the Earth resulting from the introduction of extraterrestrial matter' (Article IX). The aim of this provision is to protect the earth's environment rather than outer space. In a similar way, the 1972 Convention on International Liability for Damage Caused by Space Objects provides that a 'launching State shall be absolutely liable to pay compensation for damage caused by its space object on the surface of the Earth or to aircraft flight' (Article II). Here again, the objective was to protect the earth's environment from space activities, rather than protecting space from human activities, including old satellites and spent rocket stages. Although the use of space is formally 'the province of all mankind', the tragedy of the commons is still unfolding in this global common, and the proliferation of space garbage increases the risk of collisions (see Box 5.2).

Box 5.2 Orbital space debris—a common pool resource problem

The term *orbital space debris* refers to any man-made object in the earth's orbit that is no longer in use. The concept encompasses a wide range of objects of various sizes, such as: fragments and component parts of decommissioned satellites, rocket debris, unmanned robotic space probes, even small spacecraft paint particles, and tools dropped by astronauts. Over the past decades, scientific innovations have led to an increased number of artificial objects orbiting the earth. In 2016, the United States recorded a total of 17,852 artificial objects in orbit.

Even small debris can be extremely dangerous because it orbits the earth at very high velocities, posing a serious risk to space travel. As a result, it greatly increases the operational costs of space launches, and can delay the launches if it is projected to be in a shuttle's trajectory. Given the high density of orbital debris, chain reactions can occur when it collides with other debris, or with other objects. These collisional cascades generate even more debris and space fragments, thus increasing the likelihood of future collisions—a phenomenon known as the Kessler syndrome. Past collisions—such as the destruction of a Chinese weather satellite, and the collision of a Russian communication satellite with a privately owned satellite—drastically worsened the amount of space debris, creating the need for an effective global governance system on this issue.

Even though the growing hazardous layer of space debris has hit a critical point, this issue does not have a clear-cut solution. This is a common pool resource problem, as outer space is owned by no entity, nation, or institution, which makes regulation and enforcement difficult.

Some argue that to abate the proliferation of orbital debris there is an imminent need to develop a strong, uniform, and comprehensive binding regulatory regime—in the form of a multilateral treaty. But others believe that spacefaring nations have an incentive to work together, even in the absence of a comprehensive treaty, to mitigate the problem of orbital debris before it transforms into the tragedy of the commons. However, a regime created only by states that already conduct activities in space risks marginalizing the interests of countries that do not yet have space capacities.

(continued...)

A number of technological solutions have been proposed. Innovative approaches such as creating large nets, lasers, and harpoons to gather and destroy debris have been designed, even though their application on a wide scale remains challenging. Transnational collaborations have also been established. For example, in 2018 Japan and Australia joined forces in developing a single, high-power propulsion system using a novel bidirectional plasma beam arrangement that may be able to remove space debris. Laboratory tests have proven successful, offering a promising outlook. This collaboration is an example of the type of innovation, joint research capabilities, and international cooperation that will be necessary to tackle the common pool resource problem of space debris.

Sources: Ferreira-Snyman 2013; Hollingsworth 2013; Kellman 2014; Kurt 2015; Takahashi et al. 2018.

The main multilateral treaty that covers environmental protection in outer space is the 1979 Agreement Governing the Activities of States on the Moon and Other Celestial Bodies. The agreement stipulates that: 'in exploring and using the Moon, States Parties shall take measures to prevent the disruption of the existing balance of its environment by introducing adverse changes in that environment' (Article 7). In particular, the harmful contamination of the moon is prohibited 'through the introduction of extra-environmental matter' (Article 7). However, this measure is modest compared to those prescribed by the Madrid Protocol on the Antarctic. Therefore, the reference to the common heritage of humankind is not a magic formula or a miracle solution for overcoming the tragedy of the commons.

The international seabed beyond the continental shelf (see Figure 5.2) is a further example of the limitations of the common heritage principle in governing global commons (Moore and Squires 2016). It is one of the least explored and least understood parts of the planet. Like the Antarctic regime and the Space Treaty, the international regime for the deep seabed was drafted in the context of the Cold War. At the time, security was a greater concern than the environment, and the notion of a common heritage of humankind was used primarily to promote peaceful relations. In 1970, via resolution 2749, the UN General Assembly declared that 'the seabed and ocean floor, and the subsoil thereof, beyond the limits of national jurisdiction, as well as the resources of the area, are the common heritage of mankind'. This resolution provided the normative basis for the adoption, a year later, of the 1971 Treaty on the Prohibition of the Emplacement of Nuclear Weapons and Other Weapons of Mass Destruction on the Sea-Bed and the Ocean Floor. Like Antarctica and outer space, the deep seabed was first dedicated to peaceful activities before environmental concerns emerged.

While the 1982 United Nations Convention on the Law of the Sea was being negotiated, large quantities of much sought-after minerals were discovered on the international seabed. Developing countries were worried that some countries would act unilaterally, using their technological advantage to monopolize these natural resources. In this context, one of the aims of the Convention on the Law of the Sea was to guarantee the equal distribution of the economic advantages derived from mineral extraction from the seabed. It created the International Seabed Authority, which possesses jurisdiction over the mineral resources of most of the world's deep-sea areas. Revenues generated from mineral exploration contracts are meant to benefit all countries, and especially the **least-developed countries**. The convention also sets measures to limit the adverse impacts of drilling, dredging, excavation, and the construction of pipelines. However, these environmental goals were of secondary

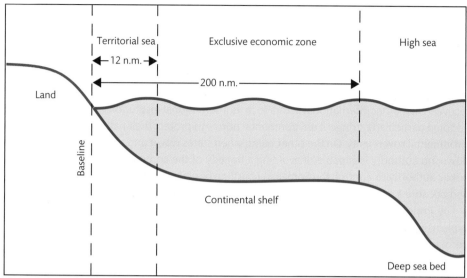

1 nautical mile (n.m.) = 1.15 mile = 1.85 kilometre

Figure 5.2 Coastal state zones

importance to negotiators, compared to the goal of ensuring that the international seabed's natural resources are not captured by a few actors. 'The interest of mankind', as defined in the Convention on the Law of the Sea, refers primarily to the principle of intragenerational equity between countries with and without the capacity to exploit natural resources, as opposed to intergenerational equity concerning future generations (Jacques and Lobo 2018).

The outer space and international seabed cases illustrate that the common heritage of humankind principle does not guarantee the resolution of the tragedy of the commons. The Antarctic case stands out as it led to particularly stringent environmental regulations. So why has the principle been more successful in protecting against the tragedy of the commons in the Antarctic case? This can largely be explained by the fact that, for years, the continent's resources were too difficult or too expensive to extract on a large scale. The number of states with claims over the Antarctic is also particularly small, which might have facilitated the creation of the first protected areas there (Hughes and Grant 2017). As such, the Antarctic regime's relatively strict environmental regulations cannot be attributed exclusively to the principle of the common heritage of humankind, which is not actually recognized by the Antarctic Treaty.

Despite this mixed review, the principle of the common heritage of humankind still appeals to a number of environmentalists because it calls for cooperation and conservation. The principle is sometimes mentioned as a potential solution to the threats facing fresh water reserves, tropical forests, and the global climate. Nonetheless, some developing countries are wary and see it as an indirect means for developed countries to pursue their economic interests. In the Brazilian government's view, for example, the Amazon rainforest is a genuine Brazilian heritage, not the planet's lungs (Conca 1994). An increasing number of natural resources are governed, not by the principle of a common heritage of humankind, but by the principle of state sovereignty.

5.3 Sovereignty over natural resources

Sovereignty as a safeguard for environmental protection

The *extension of sovereignty rights* can appear to be an alternative solution to the extension of the common heritage of humankind to solve the tragedy of the global commons. Sovereign states can set regulations, levy taxes, and impose sanctions on offenders more effectively than other international actors such as international institutions. Several states have adopted particularly stringent environmental norms to protect their natural heritage and environmental sovereignty. On the other hand, when states waver and their sovereignty breaks down, no authority is capable of avoiding a tragedy of the commons. Left with no effective public authority or control, the Somalian coastline has fallen victim to unbridled overfishing and become a dumping ground for foreign vessels' hazardous waste (Lal Panjabi 2010).

The importance of sovereign rights for effective governance of natural resources partly explains why several environmental agreements and declarations refer to the principle of permanent sovereignty over natural resources. One of the early mentions of this principle was in resolution 1803 of 14 December 1962, adopted by the UN General Assembly during the decolonization period:

> The right of peoples and nations to permanent sovereignty over their natural wealth and resources must be exercised in the interest of their national development and of the well-being of the people of the State concerned. The exploration, development and disposition of such resources, as well as the import of the foreign capital required for these purposes, should be in conformity with the rules and conditions which the peoples and nations freely consider to be necessary or desirable with regard to the authorization, restriction or prohibition of such activities. (Resolution 1803)

Moreover, clear sovereignty rights can facilitate international transactions over environmental issues, much as private property rights provide the foundation for market transactions. Legally, when their national territory is affected by foreign sources of pollution, sovereign states have the legal capacity to appeal to international tribunals, as happened in the US when it appealed against Canada in the Trail Smelter dispute (see Box 5.3). Economically, when sovereign states have sovereign rights over certain resources, they do not have an interest in overexploiting them for short-term commercial gains, but rather in maintaining a stock for long-term exploitation. Politically, sovereign states also have the capacity to generate patriotic feelings to exert diplomatic pressure, which was Canada's tactic during the Turbot War against Spain (see Box 5.1). These logics informed the governance of marine resources and genetic resources, as discussed below.

The extension of sovereignty rights over marine resources

Some multilateral environmental agreements have extended the scope of state sovereignty under the assumption that this would favour the protection of the global commons. The most poignant example is the 1982 Convention on the Law of the Sea. The convention extended states' sovereign rights to cover a maritime area called the 'exclusive economic zone', which can stretch up to 200 nautical miles from the coast. This represents a considerable extension of states' sovereign rights. Until World War II, state sovereignty over the sea environment was generally limited to a state's territorial seas, and could cover a distance of up to 12 nautical miles from the coast.

Box 5.3 The Trail Smelter dispute: establishing principles of prevention and compensation for pollution

The 1941 Trail Smelter dispute between Canada and the United States is a landmark international environmental law case regarding the regulation of transboundary pollution. The dispute is also an illustrative example of the tragedy of the commons, because it shows how the 'use' of a common good in one country—in this case air—can cause environmental impacts in other countries that share the resource. The Trail Smelter dispute concerned pollution drifting across the US–Canadian border in 1925 from a privately owned Canadian lead and zinc smelter located in Trail, British Columbia. Landowners in the state of Washington were complaining about the large quantities of sulphur dioxide that the smelter was emitting into the atmosphere, claiming that it was causing significant damage to their property on the US side of the border. However, the landowners faced jurisdictional barriers to claim private remedy since neither the courts in Canada nor the US could hear the case. The courts in British Columbia did not have jurisdiction over injury physically located in the US, and the courts in the state of Washington did not have jurisdiction over businesses located in Canada.

The US government initiated the case as an international nuisance claim, with the two national governments the representing the private parties in the dispute. At first the case was referred to the International Joint Commission, a body set up to deal with transboundary water issues between the US and Canada. The commission presented its findings in 1931. However, because the US disapproved of the outcome, the two governments agreed instead to resolve the dispute through a three-member arbitral tribunal, consisting of one member from each of the two states plus one member from a third state; the US and Canadian governments also agreed to accept the results of the arbitration as binding. The tribunal started its work in 1935. The Trail Smelter dispute was one of the first cases to consider the issue of territorial sovereign rights in relation to transboundary environmental harm, and the first transboundary pollution case that was settled by arbitration through an international tribunal. There was no international treaty on this issue, so the tribunal looked to **customary international law** and court cases on transboundary pollution disputes between US states for precedent.

After the long judicial process, in 1941 the international arbitral tribunal ruled that the Canadian government was responsible for the impacts of the Trail Smelter on US territory. Centrally, the tribunal found that 'no State has the right to use or permit the use of its territory in such a manner as to cause injury by fumes in or to the territory of another or the properties of person therein, when the case is of serious consequence and the injury is established by clear and convincing evidence' (Plater et al. 2010: 937). The Trail Smelter case established a new principle, the 'principle of prevention', stating that governments have an obligation to adopt measures to avoid serious environmental harm in the territory of another country.

One of the critical issues raised by the Trail Smelter dispute is the difficulty of proving injury and assessing damage from industrial pollution—especially in cases where there could be several point sources, and when determining a cause of harm that is not visible. The dispute also highlighted how these issues become increasingly complex when a case concerns transboundary pollution and has to consider the sovereign territorial rights and responsibilities of more than one country and a diverse range of actors and interests. The Trail Smelter case involved not only farmers and landowners, the smelter, and the two governments, but also scientists, federal agencies, and provincial government interests. On the Canadian side, the industry, scientists, and government had the same interests regarding the outcome, whereas the US position faced competing interests from within—for instance, between the US Department of Agriculture and the US Bureau of Mines, who disagreed over what aspects and solutions to focus on. The latter supported the smelting industry and technical solutions, whereas the former supported the farmers and tried to bring attention to the harmful effects of the air pollution on the forests, crops, and soil. Moreover, the case illustrates the importance of the broader political context in environmental disputes: in this case, the anticipation of World War II. Both sides had an interest in not closing down the smelter, as it was the largest of its kind in the British Empire and therefore an important supplier of lead and zinc to the British government's war production.

Sources: Allum 2006; Bratspies and Miller 2006; Plater et al. 2010; Read 2006; Rubin 2006; Wirth 1996.

But with the official establishment of the exclusive economic zone in 1982, some states saw their sovereign rights stretch across immense areas. For example, France's exclusive economic zone covers a territory of over 11 million km^2, which is 17 times greater than the size of France itself. Most global fish catches are made within the exclusive economic zone of one country or another.

Within its exclusive economic zone, a coastal state enjoys 'sovereign rights for the purpose of exploring and exploiting, conserving and managing the natural resources' (Convention on the Law of the Sea, Article 56). However, the exclusive economic zone is not entirely under state sovereignty and cannot be assimilated into the territorial sea. In particular, other states are free to navigate, fly over, and lay submarine cables and pipelines in these zones. It is a matter of jurisdiction, not full sovereignty.

The coastal state plays the role of trustee of the exclusive economic zone. The Convention on the Law of the Sea clearly specifies that the coastal state has jurisdiction over this zone regarding 'the protection and preservation of the marine environment' (Article 56). In particular, it should determine 'the allowable catch of the living resources in its exclusive economic zone' and ensure through 'proper conservation and management measures that the maintenance of the living resources in the exclusive economic zone is not endangered by over-exploitation' (Article 61).

Dividing up the oceans into exclusive economic zones and attributing environmental jurisdiction to coastal states have, nevertheless, failed to prevent the problem of the tragedy of the commons in terms of fishing and land-based pollution (see Box 5.4). The incentives provided by the prospect of long-term exploitation of their exclusive economic zones seem to have failed to induce radical changes in the practices of most states (Miller 2000).

To some extent, the Convention on the Law of the Sea even provides an incentive for the intensive extraction of living resources. If the coastal state does not fully exploit the available resources up to the permitted 'optimum utilization' limit, it is obliged to give other states 'access to the surplus of the allowable catch' (Article 62). This means national authorities may be tempted to allow their own fishermen to exploit a maximum of resources to avoid being forced to allow foreign competitors to fish in their exclusive economic zone. Despite the creation of the exclusive economic zone, the problem of the tragedy of the commons remains (Alcock 2002).

Box 5.4 Governing marine pollution: a classic collective action problem

The pollution of the marine environment is a prominent example of a collective action problem following the tragedy of the commons scenario. The ocean acts as a major sink for all outputs of human activity, such as industrial waste and emissions pollution from transportation, and because much of the ocean is beyond national jurisdiction, individual states have little incentive to rein in their own pollution of this global common. Yet pollution is a major threat to marine biodiversity, and also has large negative impacts on humans: in the degradation of the various services we obtain from the ocean, such as fisheries and recreation, and the effects on human health, for example from increased exposure to pesticides that make their way from agriculture through waterways to the ocean. In efforts to address this collective action problem, scientists and policymakers have sought to understand how humans are polluting the ocean, which nations are polluting the most, what impacts this pollution has on marine ecosystems and organisms, and how we can control marine pollution on the regional and global levels.

Marine pollution refers to the introduction of contaminants by humans into the marine environment. A few major contaminants include chemicals, oils, heavy metals, pathogens, waste, and debris. Some forms of pollution come from shipping, including accidental oil and chemical spills, operational dumping of waste, ballast water used to stabilize ships, waste water, and air emissions from ships' engines. The majority of international law and governance surrounding marine pollution targets pollution from shipping.

The International Maritime Organization, for example, coordinates several instruments that form a framework for international law on pollution from shipping, including the 1973 International Convention for the Prevention of Pollution from Ships and its 1978 Protocol. As a response to a series of tanker accidents, this convention addresses the need to reduce pollution from vessels by requiring that all vessels are fitted with certain equipment intended to minimize the risk of accidental spills, and that vessels follow certain practices intended to restrict intentional dumping. However, resistance from the shipping industry and from maritime nations to increases in the costs of production and/or transport of goods has hampered the effectiveness of the convention. Representatives of the shipping industry and shipping states pushed for less costly, but also less effective, forms of equipment; for changes to ship design only to apply to new vessels, rather than existing vessels; and for an enforcement system based on the authority of the state where the vessel is registered, rather than any other state that may be more interested in enforcing regulations. Further amendments did impose additional requirements for reducing vessel discharges; for example, a number of additional annexes negotiated after 1980 required that tankers are equipped with double hulls, banned discharge of untreated sewage within 12 miles of land, and limited the emissions of ozone-depleting substances from exhausts.

Additional treaties that address pollution from shipping include: the 1990 International Convention on Oil Pollution Preparedness, Response and Co-operation, the 1996 Protocol to the Convention on the Prevention of Marine Pollution by Dumping of Wastes and Other Matter, the 2000 Protocol on the Preparedness, Response and Co-operation to Pollution Incidents by Hazardous and Noxious Substances, and the 2004 International Convention for the Control and Management of Ships' Ballast Water and Sediment. These treaties comprise a variety of requirements designed to reduce the amount of pollution entering the ocean from both normal operations and accidents. In addition to these multilateral treaties, the United Nations Environment Programme has favoured the conclusion of several regional agreements on the control of pollution from ships.

Paradoxically, while most governance activity has concentrated on pollution emitted by ships, the bulk of marine pollution originates from land-based sources such as industry, agriculture, and dumping of municipal waste. Multilateral treaties only superficially or indirectly address this pollution. However, the recently negotiated international Minamata Convention on Mercury requires states to address the pollution of mercury into the marine environment, for example by controlling releases of mercury-contaminated industrial waste water into the ocean and by strengthening requirements for storing and disposing of other forms of mercury waste.

Marine plastic litter is receiving growing attention at all levels of governance. According to one estimate, up to 12.7 million tons of plastic entered the ocean in 2010. The millions of tons of plastic that float in the Northern Pacific like a continent of waste—referred to as the Great Pacific Garbage Patch—represent one of the most striking illustrations of this pollution. Many marine animals are harmed by entanglement in plastic debris, by ingestion of plastic litter, and through the accumulation of microplastics up through the food chain. In light of this, some argue that the ongoing negotiations for a new international treaty on the protection of marine biodiversity in areas beyond national jurisdiction should incorporate discussion of plastic pollution, although they are so far focusing on other issues. Furthermore, the Group of 7, the meeting of the most powerful developed nations, signed an Ocean

(continued...)

Plastics Charter in 2018, committing to work with industry towards 100 per cent reusable, recyclable, or recoverable plastics by 2030, although it is not clear that this will effectively address plastic pollution. According to one estimate, only 9 per cent of all plastic waste had been recycled as of 2015.

While there is an emerging norm against the use of plastic microbeads in personal care products, phasing out the products remains vastly uneven across jurisdictions. The same can be said for plastic bag bans. While bans on the use of plastic bags are becoming more common, Jennifer Clapp has demonstrated that industry has been particularly adept at challenging these regulations, resulting in a 'regulatory chill', whereby public authorities refrain from implementing regulations to avoid costly litigation. Therefore, due to the widespread use of plastics in numerous industries and products and growing revenue in the global plastic industry, some scholars are sceptical of the prospects for limited government bans and corporate voluntary initiatives to control plastic pollution. Instead, many are arguing for global plastic governance, consisting of an international treaty with legally binding targets and timelines, that will effectively reduce the pollution of plastic in the global marine commons.

Sources: Clapp 2012; Dauvergne 2018a, 2018b; Derraik 2002; Griffin 1994; Lister et al. 2015; Tiller and Nyman 2018.

Sovereignty rights over genetic resources

The Convention on Biological Diversity constitutes a further attempt to resolve the tragedy of the commons by extending national sovereignty. Until the Convention on Biological Diversity was concluded in 1992, genetic resources largely eluded national sovereignty. The International Undertaking on Plant Genetic Resources stated that genetic resources 'are a heritage of mankind and consequently should be available without restriction' (Article 1). Western biotech and pharmaceutical companies, among others, were able to take advantage of this regime and collect samples freely in the tropical forests. These samples were subsequently used for research, which sometimes resulted in the commercialization of new biotech or pharmaceutical products. Excluding the state of origin of the genetic resources deprived it of potentially high incomes. Some environmental activists, like the Indian Vandana Shiva (see Box 6.1), qualify this misapplication of genetic resources as 'biopiracy':

> The United States has accused the Third World of piracy. [However], if the contributions of Third World people are taken into account, the roles are dramatically reversed: the United States would owe Third World countries $302 million in agriculture royalties and $5.1 billion for pharmaceuticals. (Shiva 1997: 56)

The parallel extension of intellectual property rights in the field of biotechnology has exacerbated developing countries' demands for the control of their genetic resources. Until the 1980s, most countries did not allow the patenting of biological material. A new plant or microorganism could not be protected by a patent, and remained in the public domain. However, starting in the early 1990s, an increasing number of countries accepted the idea that a biological invention can be private property. The biotech industry defended this extension of intellectual property rights, by underlining that it represented a fair reward for inventive activities and a necessary incentive to stimulate innovation (see Figure 5.3). In response to this discourse, several developing countries argued that paying dividends to the countries that supplied the genetic resources required for the development of biotech products also represented a fair reward and a necessary incentive for conservation activities in developing countries, where the richest biological diversity is found in its natural state (see Figure 5.4).

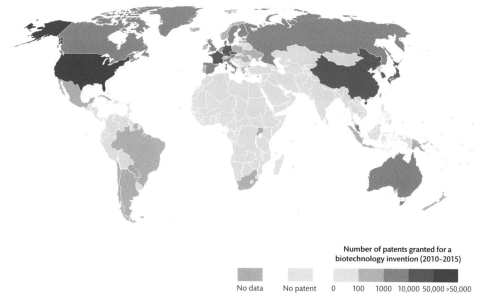

Figure 5.3 Distribution of biotechnology capacities (2010–2015)

Source data from: www.WIPO.org

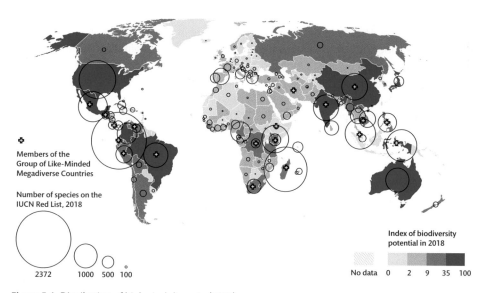

Figure 5.4 Distribution of biological diversity (2018)

Source data from: World Bank; www.IUNC.org; www.cbd.int

Faced with these demands from developing countries, the 1992 Convention on Biological Diversity broke with the regime of a common heritage, affirming that 'states have . . . the sovereign right to exploit their own resources pursuant to their own environmental policies' (Article 3). This sovereignty implies that governments now have the power to determine the conditions of access to genetic resources. In exchange for their consent, the countries that supply genetic resources can ask biotech companies to share 'in a fair and equitable way the results of research and development and the benefits arising from the commercial and other utilization of genetic resources' (Article 15).

Therefore, the Convention on Biological Diversity is based on a contractual approach to resolving the tragedy of the commons. The suppliers and users of genetic resources should negotiate the exact procedures for access to genetic resources and for sharing the benefits derived from their use on 'mutually agreed terms' (Article 15). The monetary and technological advantages that the suppliers obtain from the users of genetic resources can ultimately be reinvested in biodiversity conservation. In addition, the prospect of signing new contracts and continuing to obtain new advantages is a further incentive for developing countries to conserve their genetic resources in their natural state (ten Kate and Laird 2002).

Several contracts for the transfer of genetic material have actually been signed, although their content is rarely disclosed. However, it appears that the number of contracts on offer and the value of the shared advantages have not been sufficient to make a significant contribution to the conservation of biological diversity (Morin 2003). The commercial value of genetic resources is not enough to provide a real incentive for conservation, and the shared monetary and technological advantages are seldom reinvested in the conservation of biodiversity. They tend to be used instead for local economic development, to enhance the reputation of the biotech companies, or to improve the integration of suppliers into the biotech industries.

Opinions are divided about the possibilities for future improvements in genetic resource management (Oberthür and Rosendal 2014). Some experts maintain that the genetic resource market is structurally limited and cannot develop. On the supply side, genetic resources are overabundant. They originate from various different countries, collections, and botanical gardens. On the demand side, the biotech industry's need for natural genetic material is lower than was expected in the early 1990s because of the development of synthetic substitutes. 'Green gold' was just a mirage. Other scholars are more optimistic. In their view, the number of contracts and the value of shared advantages could be increased by clarifying the laws governing access to genetic resources, helping the suppliers of genetic resources to negotiate, proposing model contracts, improving contract monitoring, and imposing sanctions when contracts are breached.

The Nagoya Protocol on Access to Genetic Resources and the Fair and Equitable Sharing of Benefits Arising from their Utilization, concluded in 2010, gambles on this more optimistic vision (Jinnah and Jungcurt 2009). The **protocol's** main objectives are to clarify the laws pertaining to the different parties, to reduce transaction costs to encourage the development of the market in genetic resources, and to protect **traditional knowledge** (see Box 5.5). In particular, a multilateral mechanism has been set up for transboundary genetic resources. It facilitates the negotiation of access rights and the shared benefits of genetic resources when the sovereign rights of different countries overlap.

Box 5.5 Traditional knowledge and genetic resources

Traditional knowledge consists of the knowledge and practices that are passed from generation to generation within a cultural community. Some of that knowledge, including knowledge about the medicinal properties of plants, is of particular interest to the biotechnology and pharmaceutical industries, as they may be able to use it in the development of new products derived from genetic and biological resources. When traditional knowledge is in the public domain, biotechnology and pharmaceutical companies may freely use it to guide their research and develop new products. As such, the protection of both traditional knowledge and genetic resources are tightly intertwined.

Traditional knowledge has long been considered by states and their private sector actors as belonging in the public domain. However, in the late 1990s several activists, including Vandana Shiva, began to contest this assumption. According to these activists, the use of traditional knowledge by a third party, without authorization from the community to which it belongs, is an immoral and reprehensible act. Traditional knowledge should therefore be protected, they argue, just like other types of knowledge, through intellectual property rights. Pushing back on this claim, many in the biotechnology industry have argued that their inventions are novel, and result from an inventive step that sets them apart from the traditional knowledge on which they are based. Only modern inventions, in their view, which often demand significant investment and expertise, should be incentivized and compensated by intellectual property rights.

The debate surrounding the equivalence between traditional knowledge and contemporary scientific knowledge on genetic resources has been fuelled by the granting of a few controversial patents for inventions using genetic resources and traditional knowledge from developing countries. The most widely publicized of these cases are those of turmeric, basmati rice, hoodia, and neem. Neem, for example, is a tree originating in South Asia that has been used for centuries by local farmers for its fungicidal and insecticidal properties. Yet in 1994 the European Patent Office granted a patent to W. R. Grace, a chemical company, for a fungus prevention method using neem oil. A coalition of several hundred **non-governmental organizations** (NGOs) led a public campaign to revoke the patent. The patent was finally revoked in 2000 on the grounds that the invention was not new, novelty being one of the essential criteria in obtaining a patent. Some saw this as the result of intense social mobilization, while others considered it proof that the patent system is flexible enough to correct its own mistakes.

Several solutions have been put forward to prevent the appropriation of traditional knowledge by third parties. Some suggest creating publicly accessible records of traditional knowledge that would help to ensure that such knowledge is known and recognized. Patent office examiners could then consult these records to determine the existing status of knowledge and so establish whether an invention meets the novelty criterion. The World Intellectual Property Organization manages one online listing system, which includes more than 100 databases and registries of traditional knowledge and genetic resources worldwide.

Others suggest going one step further and setting up a system that would enable communities to generate revenue from their traditional knowledge whenever it is used by a third party. This would involve a form of community-based intellectual property right specifically adapted to traditional knowledge. Businesses wishing to use such knowledge for commercial purposes would then have to pay royalties to the community. This debate, which takes place primarily in the World Intellectual Property Organization's Intergovernmental Committee on Intellectual Property and Genetic Resources, Traditional Knowledge and Folklore, has not yet resulted in a new international treaty on intellectual property for traditional knowledge. However, in 2017 the Intergovernmental Committee adopted a negotiation mandate for 2018/2019 on 'reaching an international legal instrument(s), without prejudging the nature of outcome(s), relating to intellectual property which will ensure the balanced and effective protection of genetic resources, traditional knowledge and traditional cultural expressions'.

(continued...)

While no new global intellectual property instrument has yet been created to protect traditional knowledge, progress has been made with the 1992 Convention on Biological Diversity and the 2010 Nagoya Protocol with regard to the access conditions for traditional knowledge and associated **benefit sharing**. Article 8(j) of the Convention on Biological Diversity states that:

> Each contracting party shall [. . .] respect, preserve and maintain knowledge, innovations and practices of indigenous and local communities embodying traditional lifestyles relevant for the conservation and sustainable use of biological diversity and promote their wider application with the approval and involvement of the holders of such knowledge, innovations and practices and encourage the equitable sharing of the benefits arising from the utilization of such knowledge, innovations and practices.

There are two key elements here: the idea of **prior informed consent** from indigenous and local communities, meaning that misappropriation is no longer legitimate; and benefit sharing, meaning that users of traditional knowledge should share part of the benefits they gain from this knowledge with the indigenous and local communities. The Nagoya Protocol has established the Access and Benefit-Sharing Clearing-House as a platform where all legislation and cases of access to genetic resources and associated traditional knowledge are registered, which will facilitate the **implementation** of the protocol.

Sources: Gibson 2005; Jinnah and Jungcurt 2009; Morgera et al. 2014; Shiva 1997.

Sovereignty as a hindrance to environmental cooperation

While there is evidence that the extension of sovereignty rights over marine and genetic resources does not yield the environmental benefits expected, it is also possible that the principle of permanent sovereignty over natural resources could hinder international efforts to protect the environment. If each state can determine its policies and set its own levels of protection, in the name of sovereignty, it is by definition free to ignore the international cooperative efforts. Under this scenario, states would have little incentive to ratify a convention, join an intergovernmental organization, or authorize foreign inspectors to enter their territory. They might be tempted to maintain particularly lax environmental standards to minimize the costs of production for businesses and to attract foreign investors. In this sense, the principle of sovereignty could incentivize a race to the lowest environmental standards and contribute to the tragedy of the commons.

In addition, if a state feels that its sovereignty is under threat, it may take measures that contribute to environmental degradation. For example, in the 1980s Brazil intensified its military presence in the north of the Amazon rainforest, especially near the border with Guyana, Venezuela, and Colombia. The operation aimed at affirming Brazil's effective control over the territory in the face of claims made by indigenous communities, and backed by foreign NGOs. However, in clearing forest and building roads for military use, it paved the way for further degradation of the rainforest. More recently, Canada increased its military presence in the Arctic in order to clearly establish its sovereignty over the Northwest Passage, which is disputed by the US. These Canadian activities also endangered the fragile Arctic ecosystems. These two cases illustrate that the occupation of territory, which the principle of national sovereignty implies and requires, can exacerbate environmental degradation.

The principle of sovereignty over natural resources does not, however, allow states to isolate themselves from the international community and freely damage the environment. Economic, political, and legal forces transcend international relations and break through sovereignty's apparent barriers. For example, international law acknowledges that a state cannot allow its territory to be used in a way that would cause major harm to the environment of another state (see Box 5.3). This is the principle of prevention, which was politically endorsed by the 1972 Stockholm Declaration and the 1992 Rio Declaration. It was also legally recognized by the International Court of Justice in its advisory opinion on the Legality of the Threat or Use of Nuclear Weapons in 1996. The principle of prevention is generally referred to jointly with the principle of sovereignty over natural resources in a single sentence. There is a good reason for this: it is a reminder that sovereign rights come with responsibilities. This is implicit, for example, in the 1992 Rio Declaration:

> States have, in accordance with the Charter of the United Nations and the principles of international law, the sovereign right to exploit their own resources pursuant to their own environmental and developmental policies, and the responsibility to ensure that activities within their jurisdiction or control do not cause damage to the environment of other States or of areas beyond the limits of national jurisdiction. (The 1992 Rio Declaration, Principle 2)

Apart from the legal principles, numerous political and economic forces encourage states to cooperate and overcome the atomism implied by a narrow interpretation of the concept of sovereignty. Even when 'formal sovereignty' remains intact, 'operational sovereignty' is limited by the interdependence between states and the international institutions that unite them (Levy et al. 1993). As discussed in more detail in Chapter 10, several environmental treaties prohibit the trade in certain goods with states that are not party to the relevant agreement, which puts pressure on those states to join. In this way, the Montreal Protocol banned imports of air-conditioning devices, aerosols, and other products which may contain ozone-depleting substances originating from non-signatory countries. The Basel Convention prohibits trade in hazardous waste with countries that have not ratified the convention. Thus, a country where businesses produce aerosols or provide hazardous waste treatment services will have an economic incentive to sign these treaties (DeSombre 2005).

In addition to the increasing interdependence of states, new forms of authority are emerging on the international stage (see Chapter 4 on non-state actors). For example, in the Arctic Council, Inuit communities take part in the environmental governance of the Arctic, alongside states (Shadian 2010). In Europe, the European Union enjoys increasing autonomy in international environmental negotiations, and can no longer be considered simply an instrument of the most influential member states (Delreux 2011).

Environmental cooperation increasingly brings together different kinds of stakeholders through partnerships, networks, and delegation mandates (Green and Colgan 2013). For example, the efforts to clean up the Great Lakes involve Canadian and American federal governments, two Canadian provinces, eight American states, several towns and municipalities, indigenous communities, environmental NGOs, scientific groups, and industrial associations. All these stakeholders cooperate through diverse institutions, including the Great Lakes Commission, the International Joint Commission, and local management and regeneration schemes. Environmental governance appears to be increasingly more horizontal than hierarchical, and more inclusive than exclusive (Karkkainen 2004).

The debate between sovereignty as an instrument for environmental protection and as an obstacle to environmental protection seems somewhat sterile. The principle of sovereignty can be used for environmental purposes, but applying it is no guarantee that the tragedy of the commons will be resolved. Above all, the exercise of sovereignty is not without limitations, so the (positive or negative) effects of sovereignty on environmental protection are themselves limited.

Bargaining over sovereignty

There is also a debate about the effects of environmental cooperation on sovereignty. To consider this question we must acknowledge that sovereignty is not a dichotomous variable, either absolute or non-existent—environmental cooperation is not sufficient in itself either to create new sovereign states or to entirely dissolve a country's sovereignty. Instead, the effect of environmental cooperation on sovereignty is a matter of degree.

One way to clarify this issue is to divide sovereignty into different dimensions; *control*, *autonomy*, and *legitimacy* are three dimensions of sovereignty that might be differentially impacted by environmental cooperation (Litfin 1997; Hochstetler et al. 2000). In some cases, as states cooperate and establish institutions to govern the global commons, there may be a trade-off between these three dimensions. For example, a commitment to reduce greenhouse gas emissions could be linked to the acquisition of foreign technologies. Acquiring the new technologies is a way of increasing state *autonomy*, but it may have a negative impact on state *legitimacy* because the state's contribution to **climate mitigation** is conditional on receiving material gains. Another trade-off between sovereignty dimensions would occur if a state delegates control over defining targets for reducing **greenhouse gas** emissions to an international scientific committee. This would increase the state's *legitimacy*, but decrease its *control* over policymaking. Table 5.3 presents other hypothetical examples.

Table 5.3 The sovereignty trade-off

Exchange Y against X	Gain autonomy	Increase control	Increase legitimacy
Lose autonomy	____	Condition public support offered to developing countries for the implementation of specific environmental policies.	Delegate the determination of greenhouse gas reduction targets to an international scientific committee.
Lose control	Delegate to the importing state the control of the trade of a range of endangered species, as determined by the state of origin.	____	Transfer financial resources to indigenous communities for them to develop conservation policies that are consistent with traditional practices.
Lose legitimacy	Condition the reduction of greenhouse gas emissions to the acquisition of new environmental technologies.	Move local communities out of a certain geographical area to create a protected natural park.	____

Sources: inspired by Litfin (1997) and Hochstetler et al. (1999)

From this perspective, sovereignty is neither a cause of the tragedy of the commons nor a solution to it. It is not restricted or strengthened by international cooperation either. This makes it a multidimensional concept, which has to be redefined constantly through sovereignty trade-offs like the ones illustrated in Table 5.3 (Conca 1994; Miller 2000).

However, states do not negotiate these sovereignty trade-offs on an equal footing. From the outset, some states enjoy greater legitimacy, control, and autonomy than others. They can take advantage of this asymmetry to extract greater concessions from other states when they negotiate sovereignty trade-offs. In the end, states with smaller degrees of control, legitimacy, and autonomy might have to sacrifice greater sovereignty than other states in order to participate in environmental cooperation. This explains, as Chapter 6 discusses, the initial reluctance of some developing countries to participate in international environmental institutions, and their insistence on receiving assistance to increase their autonomy, control, and legitimacy.

5.4 **Conclusion**

The tragedy of the commons can help us to understand the drivers of several environmental problems, including fish stock depletion, genetic resource exploitation, outer space pollution, international seabed mining, pollution of the atmosphere, and exploitation of Antarctic resources. In each of these issue areas, revising the rights of access to natural resources or to certain geographic areas may result in the modification of actors' incentives, a behavioural shift, and ultimately the resolution of the tragedy of the commons.

Although Garrett Hardin recommended private property and individual responsibility as a solution to the tragedy of the commons, the suggestion that any single formula is pertinent for all natural resources and all ecosystems has proven unrealistic. There is no ideal solution to the tragedy of the commons. The various different solutions can all be relevant, but only under certain conditions. For example, the notion of a common heritage of humankind has encouraged the protection of some environmental resources, such as the natural sites registered on the heritage list of the United Nations Educational, Scientific and Culture Organization. However, carbon markets rely on sovereignty and property rights to create incentives to innovate and to achieve the targets for reducing greenhouse gas emissions.

The most effective solution to the tragedy of the commons is highly contextual. It depends on the environmental problem being addressed, including the degree of scientific certainty, the degree of ecological interdependence, the presence of international institutions, and the type of resources at stake. All of these factors influence the relative appeal of the principles of sovereignty versus common heritage of humankind in addressing environmental problems. In particular, resources that are limited to a specific area, such as the Amazon rainforest or Antarctic fauna, benefit from supranational attention, and thus a common heritage of humankind approach. In contrast, some global resources, such as the **ozone layer**, can be managed more effectively by granting exclusive rights to economic agents, and thus a sovereignty-based approach. Across the board, however, despite the utility of the tragedy of the commons metaphor in helping us understand the drivers of environmental degradation, it also has limitations. Importantly, the problems facing shepherds on a local level cannot always be scaled up to an international level.

Chapter 6 reveals that the preferred solution to the tragedy of the commons evolves not only in relation to the environmental problem itself, but also in relation to the prevailing ideologies related to economic growth (Jacques and Lobo 2018). As a result of this evolution, the notion of common heritage appears to have gradually lost its appeal in the last 40 years, and solutions based on private property and free markets are gaining in popularity.

Critical thinking questions

1. Is solar energy a common, a private, a public, or a club good? Why?
2. Some people suggest that fresh water should be considered as part of the common heritage of humankind in order to improve its management. What are the arguments in favour of and against this proposal?
3. Explain how biodiversity loss is a tragedy of the commons issue, and what types of solutions might be used to address this issue through common heritage and sovereignty-based approaches.
4. How did the Convention on the Law of the Sea modify the incentives for coastal states with regard to the utilization and conservation of maritime areas?
5. How did the Cold War affect the development of key principles in the regimes that govern the Antarctic, outer space, and the international seabed?

 Test your knowledge and understanding further by trying this chapter's Multiple Choice Questions www.oup.com/he/morin1e

Key references

Hardin, Garrett. 1968. 'The Tragedy of the Commons'. *Science* 162 (3859): 1243–1248.
This landmark article from 1968 remains one of the most widely cited publications in environmental governance. By building on the metaphor of a freely accessible pasture, Hardin expresses clearly the tension between individual and collective interests. The empirical validity and the normative implications of this article continue to be debated.

Litfin, Karen T. 1997. 'Sovereignty in World Ecopolitics'. *Mershon International Studies Review* 41 (2): 167–204.
In this article, Karen Litfin examines the impact of global environmental governance on state sovereignty. Instead of understanding sovereignty as a dichotomous variable that is either existing or non-existing, she unpacks the principle of sovereignty in three dimensions—autonomy, control, and legitimacy—and finds that they are affected in different ways by environmental cooperation.

Ostrom, Elinor. 2012. 'Nested Externalities and Polycentric Institutions: Must We Wait for Global Solutions to Climate Change before Taking Actions at other Scales?' *Economic Theory* 49 (2): 353–369.
Elinor Ostrom received a Nobel prize in economics for her work on the governance of the commons. Instead of seeing them as unregulated goods that require central management, Ostrom reveals their existing and valuable decentralized governance schemes. In this article, she discusses the value of a polycentric system of governance, involving local governments and non-state stakeholders, to address climate change.

Vogler, John. 2012. 'Global Commons Revisited'. *Global Policy* 3 (1): 61–71.
In this short but very clear article, Vogler discusses the governance of global commons that are located beyond sovereign jurisdiction, such as the international seabed, Antarctica, outer space, and the global atmosphere. He pays particular attention to attempts that have been made to regulate these global commons through common heritage status.

 For additional material and resources, please visit the online resources at:
www.oup.com/he/morin1e

Chapter references

Alcock, Franck. 2002. 'Bargaining, Uncertainty, and Property Rights in Fisheries'. *World Politics* 54 (4): 437–461.

Allum, James R. 2006. '"An Outcrop of Hell": History, Environment, and the Politics of the *Trail Smelter* Dispute'. In *Transboundary Harm in International Law: Lessons from the Trail Smelter Arbitration*, edited by Rebecca M. Bratspies and Russell A. Miller, 13–26. Cambridge: Cambridge University Press.

Anderson, Terry Lee, and Donald Leal. 2001. *Free Market Environmentalism*. New York; Basingstoke: Palgrave.

Barkin, J. Samuel, and George E. Shambaugh. 1996. 'Common-Pool Resources and International Environmental Politics'. *Environmental Politics* 5 (3): 429–447.

Barkin, J. Samuel, and George E. Shambaugh. 1999. *Anarchy and the Environment: The International Relations of Common Pool Resources*. Albany, NY: SUNY Press.

Berkes, Fikret. 1989. *Common Property Resources: Ecology and Community-Based Sustainable Development*. London: Belhaven Press (Pinter Publishers).

Bratspies, Rebecca M., and Russell A. Miller (eds). 2006. *Transboundary Harm in International Law: Lessons from the Trail Smelter Arbitration*. Cambridge: Cambridge University Press.

Clapp, Jennifer. 2012. 'The Rising Tide against Plastic Waste: Unpacking Industry Attempts to Influence the Debate'. In *Histories of the Dustheap: Waste, Material Cultures, Social Justice*, edited by Stephanie Foote and Elizabeth Mazzolini, 199–226. Cambridge, MA: MIT Press.

Cole, Daniel H. 2015. 'Advantages of a Polycentric Approach to Climate Change Policy'. *Nature Climate Change* 5 (2): 114.

Conca, Ken. 1994. 'Rethinking the Ecology–Sovereignty Debate'. *Millennium* 23 (3): 701–711.

Cullis-Suzuki, Sarika, and Daniel Pauly. 2010. 'Failing the High Seas: A Global Evaluation of Regional Fisheries Management Organizations'. *Marine Policy* 34 (5): 1036–1042.

Dauvergne, Peter. 2018a. 'The Power of Environmental Norms: Marine Plastic Pollution and the Politics of Microbeads'. *Environmental Politics* 27 (4): 579–597.

Dauvergne, Peter. 2018b. 'Why is the Global Governance of Plastic Failing the Oceans?' *Global Environmental Change* 51 (July): 22–31.

Delreux, Tom. 2011. *The EU as International Environmental Negotiator*. Surrey: Ashgate.

Derraik, José G. B. 2002. 'The Pollution of the Marine Environment by Plastic Debris: A Review'. *Marine Pollution Bulletin* 44 (9): 842–852.

Desombre, Elizabeth R. 2005. 'Fishing under Flags of Convenience: Using Market Power to Increase Participation in International Regulation'. *Global Environmental Politics* 5 (4): 73–94.

Dieter, Austin. 2014. 'From Harbor to High Seas: An Argument for Rethinking Fishery Management Systems and Multinational Fishing Treaties'. *Wisconsin International Law Journal* 32 (4): 725–751.

Dietz, Thomas, Elinor Ostrom, and Paul Stern. 2003. 'The Struggle to Govern the Commons'. *Science* 302 (5653): 1907–1912.

Dorsch, Marcel J., and Christian Flachsland. 2017. 'A Polycentric Approach to Global Climate Governance'. *Global Environmental Politics* 17(2): 45–64.

Downie, David Leonard. 1999. 'The Power to Destroy: Understanding Stratospheric Ozone Politics as a Common-Pool Resource Problem'. In *Anarchy and the Environment: The International Relations of Common Pool Resources*, edited by J. Samuel Barkin and George E. Shambaugh, 97–120. Albany, NY: SUNY Press.

Falkner, Robert, and Barry Buzan. 2019. 'The Emergence of Environmental Stewardship as a

Primary Institution of Global International Society'. *European Journal of International Relations* 25 (1): 131–155.

Feeny, David, Fikret Berkes, Bonnie J. McCay, and James M. Acheson. 1990. 'The Tragedy of the Commons: Twenty-two Years Later'. *Human Ecology* 18 (1): 1–19.

Ferreira-Snyman. A. 2013. 'The Environmental Responsibility of States for Space Debris and the Implications for Developing Countries in Africa'. *The Comparative and International Law Journal of Southern Africa* 46 (1): 19–51.

Food and Agriculture Organization. 2018. *The State of World Fisheries and Aquaculture 2018: Meeting the Sustainable Development Goals*. Rome: FAO. Available online at: http://www.fao.org/3/I9540EN/i9540en.pdf, accessed 26 November 2018.

Funtowicz, Silvio O., and Jerome R. Ravetz. 1994. 'The Worth of a Songbird: Ecological Economics as a Post-Normal Science'. *Ecological Economics* 10 (3): 197–207.

Gibson, Johanna. 2005. *Community Resources: Intellectual Property, International Trade and Protection of Traditional Knowledge*. London: Routledge.

Green, Jessica F., and Jeff Colgan. 2013. 'Protecting Sovereignty, Protecting the Planet: State Delegation to International Organizations and Private Actors in Environmental Politics'. *Governance* 26 (3): 473–497.

Griffin, Andrew. 1994. 'MARPOL 73/78 and Vessel Pollution: A Glass Half Full or Half Empty Comment'. *Indiana Journal of Global Legal Studies* 1 (2): 489–514.

Hardin, Garrett. 1968. 'The Tragedy of the Commons'. *Science* 162 (3859): 1243–1248.

Hochstetler, Kathryn, Ann Marie Clark, and Elisabeth J. Friedman. 2000. 'Sovereignty in the Balance: Claims and Bargains at the UN Conference on the Environment, Human Rights, and Women'. *International Studies Quarterly* 44 (4): 591–614.

Hollingsworth. Gabrielle. 2013. 'Space Junk: Why the United Nations Must Step in to Save Access to Space'. *Santa Clara Law Review* 53 (1): 239–266.

Hughes, Kevin A., and Susie M. Grant. 2017. 'The Spatial Distribution of Antarctica's Protected Areas: A Product of Pragmatism, Geopolitics or Conservation Need?' *Environmental Science & Policy* 72 (June): 41–51.

Jacques, Peter J., and Rafaella Lobo. 2018. 'The Shifting Context of Sustainability: Growth and the World Ocean Regime'. *Global Environmental Politics* 18 (4): 85–106.

Jinnah, Sikina, and Stefan Jungcurt. 2009. 'Could Access Requirements Stifle Your Research?' *Science* 323 (5913): 644–645.

Jordan, Andrew J., et al. 2015. 'Emergence of Polycentric Climate Governance and its Future Prospects'. *Nature Climate Change* 5 (11): 977.

Karkkainen, Bradley. 2004. 'Post-Sovereign Environmental Governance'. *Global Environmental Politics* 4 (1): 72–96.

Kellman. Barry. 2014. 'Space: The Fouled Frontier: Adjudicating Space Debris as an International Environmental Nuisance'. *Journal of Space Law* 39: 227.

Keohane, Robert O., and David G. Victor. 2016. 'Cooperation and Discord in Global Climate Policy'. *Nature Climate Change* 6 (6): 570–575.

Kurt, J. 2015. 'Triumph of the Space Commons: Addressing the Impending Space Debris Crisis without an International Treaty'. *William & Mary Environmental Law and Policy Review* 40 (1): 305–334.

Lal Panjabi, Ranee Khooshie. 2010. 'The Pirates of Somalia: Opportunistic Predators or Environmental Prey?' *William & Mary Environmental Law and Policy Review* 34 (2): 377–491.

Levy, Marc A., Robert O. Keohane, and Peter Haas. 1993. 'Improving the Effectiveness of International Environmental Institutions'. In *Institutions for the Earth: Sources of Effective International Environmental Protection*, edited by Peter M. Haas, Robert O. Keohane, and Marc A. Levy, 397–426. Cambridge, MA: MIT Press.

Lister, Jane, René Taudal Poulsen, and Stefano Ponte. 2015. 'Orchestrating Transnational Environmental Governance in Maritime Shipping'. *Global Environmental Change* 34 (September): 185–195.

Litfin, Karen T. 1997. 'Sovereignty in World Ecopolitics'. *Mershon International Studies Review* 41 (2): 167–204.

Miller, Marian A. L. 2000. 'Third World States and Fluid Sovereignty: Development Options and the Politics of Sustainable Ocean Management'. *Ocean & Coastal Management* 43 (2): 235–253.

Mitchell, Ronald B. 2006. 'Problem Structure, Institutional Design, and the Relative Effectiveness of International Environmental Agreements'. *Global Environmental Politics* 6 (3): 72–89.

Moore, Scott, and Dale Squires. 2016. 'Governing the Depths: Conceptualizing the Politics of Deep Sea Resources'. *Global Environmental Politics* 16(2): 101–109.

Morgera, Elisa, Elsa Tsioumani, and Matthias Buck. 2014. *Unraveling the Nagoya Protocol: A Commentary on the Nagoya Protocol on Access and Benefit-Sharing to the Convention on Biological Diversity*. Leiden: Koninklijke Brill nv.

Morin, Jean-Frédéric. 2003. 'Les accord de bioprospection favorisent-ils la conservation des ressources génétiques?' *Revue de droit de l'Université de Sherbrooke* 34 (1): 307–343.

Nordhaus, William. 1982. 'How Fast Should we Graze the Global Commons?' *American Economic Review* 72 (2): 242–246.

Oberthür, Sebastian, and G. Kristin Rosendal. 2014. *Global Governance of Genetic Resources: Access and Benefit Sharing after the Nagoya Protocol*. Abingdon; New York: Routledge.

Okereke, Chukwumerije. 2008. 'Equity Norms in Global Environmental Governance'. *Global Environmental Politics* 8 (3): 25–50.

Ostrom, Elinor. 1990. *Governing the Commons: The Evolutions of Institutions for Collective Action*. Cambridge: Cambridge University Press.

Ostrom, Elinor. 2001. 'Reformulating the Commons'. In *Protecting the Commons: A Framework for Resource Management in the Americas*, edited by Joanna Burger, Elinor Ostrom, Richard B. Norgaard, David Policansky, and Bernard D. Goldstein, 17–41. Washington, DC: Island Press.

Ostrom, Elinor. 2012. 'Nested Externalities and Polycentric Institutions: Must we Wait for Global Solutions to Climate Change before Taking Actions at other Scales?' *Economic Theory* 49 (2): 353–369.

Pennington, Mark. 2008. 'Classical Liberalism and Ecological Rationality: The Case for Polycentric Environmental Law'. *Environmental Politics* 17 (3): 431–448.

Plater, Zygmunt J. B., Robert H. Abrams, Robert L. Graham, Lisa Heinzerling, David A. With, and Noah D. Hall, 2010. *Environmental Law and Policy: Nature, Law, and Society*. 4th ed. New York: Aspen Publishers.

Read, John E. 2006. 'The *Trail Smelter* Dispute [Abridged]'. In *Transboundary Harm in International Law: Lessons from the Trail Smelter Arbitration*, edited by Rebecca M. Bratspies and Russell A. Miller, 27–33. Cambridge: Cambridge University Press.

Rubin, Alfred P. 2006. 'Pollution by Analogy: The *Trail Smelter* Arbitration [Abridged]'. In *Transboundary Harm in International Law: Lessons from the Trail Smelter Arbitration*, edited by Rebecca M. Bratspies and Russell A. Miller, 46–55. Cambridge: Cambridge University Press.

Sand, Peter H. 2004. 'Sovereignty Bounded: Public Trusteeship for Common Pool Resources'. *Global Environmental Politics* 4 (1): 47–71.

Schrijver, Nico. 1997. *Sovereignty over Natural Resources: Balancing Rights and Duties*. Cambridge: Cambridge University Press.

Shadian, Jessica. 2010. 'From States to Polities: Reconceptualizing Sovereignty through Inuit Governance'. *European Journal of International Relations* 16 (3): 485–510.

Shiva, Vandana. 1997. *Biopiracy: The Plunder of Nature & Knowledge*. Boston, MA: South End Press.

Soroos, Marvin. 1987. 'Global Commons, Telecommunications, and International Space Policy'. In *International Space Policy: Legal, Economic and Strategic Options for the 21st Century*, edited by John R. Mcintyre and Daniel S. Paap, 139–155. New York: Quorum Books.

Sovacool, Benjamin K. 2009. 'A Game of Cat and Fish: How to Restore the Balance in Sustainable Fisheries Management'. *Development of International Law* 40 (1): 97–125.

Springer, Allen L. 1997. 'The Canadian Turbot War with Spain: Unilateral State Action in Defense of Environmental Interests'. *The Journal of Environment & Development* 6 (1): 26–60.

Takahashi, Kazunori, Christine Charles, Rod W. Boswell, and Akira Ando. 2018. 'Demonstrating a New Technology for Space Debris Removal using a Bi-Directional Plasma Thruster'. *Scientific Reports* 8 (1): article no. 14417.

Teece, David R. 1997. 'Global Overfishing and the Spanish–Canadian Turbot War: Can International Law Protect the High-Seas Environment?' *Colorado Journal of International Environmental Law & Policy* 8 (1): 89–126.

Ten Kate, Kerry, and Sarah A. Laird. 2002. *The Commercial Use of Biodiversity: Access to Genetic Resources and Benefit-Sharing*. London: Earthscan.

Tiller, Rachel, and Elizabeth Nyman. 2018. 'Ocean Plastics and the BBNJ Treaty—Is Plastic Frightening Enough to Insert Itself into the BBNJ Treaty, or Do we Need to Wait for a Treaty of its Own?' *Journal of Environmental Studies and Sciences* 8 (4): 411–415.

Vogler, John. 2012. 'Global Commons Revisited'. *Global Policy* 3 (1): 61–71.

Wirth, John D. 1996. 'The Trail Smelter Dispute: Canadians and Americans Confront Transboundary Pollution, 1927–41'. *Environmental History* 1 (2): 34–51.

World Commission on Environment and Development. 1987. *Our Common Future*. Oxford: Oxford University Press.

Wright, Glen, Julien Rochette, Lucie Blom, Duncan Currie, Carole Durussel, Kristina Gjerde, and Sebastien Unger. 2016. *High Seas Fisheries: What Role for a New International Instrument?*, IDDRI Study No. 3. Paris: IDDRI.

Zelli, Fariborz, and Harro Van Asselt. 2013 'Introduction: The Institutional Fragmentation of Global Environmental Governance: Causes, Consequences, and Responses'. *Global Environmental Politics* 13 (3): 1–13.

6

Development and the environment

From the Stockholm Summit to the Sustainable Development Goals

Environmental protection and economic development are objectives that are at once contradictory and complementary. They cannot be considered separately as one necessarily affects the other. This chapter adopts a historical approach and studies how interactions between these two policy objectives have been understood since the early 1970s. To do so, it first introduces three different views on how environmental protection and economic development interact. It goes on to assess the resonances of each of these views in key global instruments adopted in the last 50 years: the 1972 Stockholm Declaration, the 1987 Brundtland Report, the outcomes of the 1992 Rio Summit, the 2002 Declaration of the Johannesburg Summit and the 2012 Rio Declaration. One of the main conclusions of the chapter is that a liberal understanding of the relationship between environmental protection and economic development has been gaining increased prominence over time.

 Learning objectives

After reading this chapter, readers will be able to:

- Articulate different views surrounding the relationship between economic development and environmental protection;
- Explain the importance of issues related to economic development for the political success of early important global environmental governance efforts;
- Critically examine the assumptions underlying the concept of sustainable development;
- Understand the structural significance of the 1992 Rio Summit in the evolution of debates on environment and development;
- Compare how environment and development were treated at the various world summits between 1972 and 2012; and
- Contextualize the different summits' declarations in light of key economic events and global trends.

Introduction

Are environmental protection and economic development contradictory or complementary? This is a complex question, around which a debate has been raging for 50 years. In this chapter, we study how this debate has developed over time, by examining it through the lenses of three different views on this issue: systemic, liberal, and structural views. As explained in Section 6.1, each of these views understands the relationship between environmental protection and economic development in a different way.

The core of the chapter assesses how these three views are reflected in the outcome documents of five key events in the history of global environmental politics over five decades. The first is the 1972 Stockholm Conference, considered as a founding moment in the history of multilateral cooperation on the environment. The second is the **Brundtland Commission** and the publication of its report in 1987, which popularized the concept of '**sustainable development**' and framed the debate on environment and development for decades to come. The final three are the United Nations summits organized on the decadal anniversaries of the Stockholm Conference: the **Rio Summit** of 1992, the Johannesburg Summit of 2002, and the Rio+20 Summit of 2012. These major global conferences involved thousands of delegates, under the watchful eye of the media and civil society organizations, and were crucial events in the history of multilateral cooperation on the environment.

For each of these five key events, we contrast the relative importance of the systemic, liberal, and structural views in their outcome documents. This analysis enables us to determine whether each of these three views has either gained or lost prominence over the last 50 years. In doing so, we trace how the global debate on the relationship between environmental protection and economic development has evolved. The objective is neither to determine which view is the most accurate nor to explain why a certain view was prevalent at a particular time. Instead, this chapter offers an understanding of how the relative importance of the three views has evolved historically.

Section 6.1 introduces the three views we use to analyse these events: systemic, liberal, and structural views. The following five sections look in turn at the historical context and the outcome documents of the 1972 Stockholm Conference (Section 6.2), the Brundtland Commission (Section 6.3), the 1992 Rio Summit (Section 6.4), the 2002 Johannesburg Summit (Section 6.5), and the Rio+20 Summit held in 2012 (Section 6.6).

6.1 Three views on environment and development

The relationship between environmental protection and economic development can be articulated in different ways (Clapp and Dauvergne 2011; Dryzek 2005). We introduce here a typology of three different views on this issue (see Figure 6.1). They are ideal types, in the sense that, in the real world, they are rarely endorsed in their purest form by political actors. However, as extreme characterizations, these ideal types are useful analytical tools that can serve as reference points to study the evolution of the debate on environmental protection and economic development.

	Systemic view	Liberal view	Structural view
Human beings are . . .	one species among others.	innovative.	equal in rights.
Resources are . . .	limited.	unlimited.	unevenly distributed.
Market forces are . . .	destructive.	productive.	unfair.
Environmental degradation is worsened by . . .	demographic and economic growth.	economic stagnation.	under-development.
Poverty is . . .	a consequence of environmental degradation.	a cause of environmental degradation.	both a consequence and a cause of environmental degradation.
Environmental governance is ineffective when . . .	it is based on voluntary measures.	it disincentivizes innovation.	priorities of the rich are imposed on underprivileged.
We should condemn . . .	leap forwards.	stagnation.	unfairness.

Figure 6.1 Three ideal-type views on environment and development

 Take your learning further by viewing the interactive version of this figure
www.oup.com/he/morin1e

The first ideal type is the *systemic view*. It is based on the idea that the biosphere is a closed system made up of tightly linked economic, biophysical, and social subsystems (Meadows et al. 1972; Rockström et al. 2009; Steffen et al. 2011; Steffen et al. 2015). In this closed system, resources are limited and human beings depend on the biosphere. For these reasons, the systemic view advocates maintaining a balance within the biosphere, including for example between consumption and regeneration of resources, and between pollution and absorption of pollution. If economic development exceeds the earth system's **carrying capacity** or its natural equilibrium is disrupted, the whole earth system risks collapsing in unpredictable and potentially catastrophic ways. Social and economic subsystems could be brought down along with the environmental ones (see neo-**Malthusianism**, as presented in Chapter 2, Section 2.4).

The systemic view also maintains that human societies have already disrupted these balances by generating an **ecological footprint** that outstrips the planet's regenerative capacity. The transgression of the planet's carrying capacity is particularly obvious in the areas of climate change, **biodiversity** loss, and nitrogen production (Steffen et al. 2011). Polluters must therefore urgently reduce their environmental footprint, even if this comes at the expense of short-term sacrifices in economic development. High-income countries might have to undergo a period of voluntary economic recession, and **developing countries** should achieve their development goals in ways that are not defined by reaching the rates of consumption enjoyed in developed countries. In short, the systemic view is rooted in the idea that the earth has a defined carrying capacity to which humans must adapt or risk societal collapse.

Figure 6.2 is an incarnation of this systemic view. It is a map of ecological footprints, indicating for each country the area (in hectares) needed to provide resources and absorb pollutants for its average citizen. This map reveals how unsustainable current levels of economic development are, particularly in high-income countries. The more economically developed a country is, the more it appears to exceed a sustainable ecological footprint. This suggests there is an urgent need to restore balance in the biophysical environment as most countries exceed the earth's carrying capacity.

A second ideal-type view on the relationship between economic development and environmental protection is the *liberal view*. The term 'liberal' here refers to classical economic theories on the importance of free markets, 'liberated' from state control. In contrast to the systemic view, the liberal view argues that economic development can be the cause of environmental improvements. Free markets, in particular, can increase environmental protection by providing resources and incentives for reductions in pollution (Bernstein 2001). According to the liberal view, freeing individuals and businesses from regulatory constraints can promote research, development, and the dissemination of new technologies, including those that can reduce natural resource consumption and pollution. For liberals, technological innovation is unlimited and will surely help to solve environmental problems. Therefore, under this view, there is little need to worry about the limited nature of natural resources. Rather, liberals argue for the creation of conditions that favour economic growth and innovation (see cornucopianism, as presented in Chapter 2, Section 2.4).

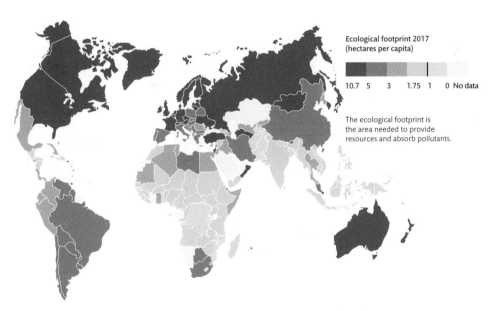

Ecological footprint 2017
(hectares per capita)

10.7   5   3   1.75   1   0   No data

The ecological footprint is
the area needed to provide
resources and absorb pollutants.

Figure 6.2 World map of ecological footprint of consumption per country (2017)

Source data from: Global Footprint Network

Figure 6.3 communicates this liberal view. This world map is based on a measure of adjusted net savings that was developed by the World Bank. This measure expresses the rate of saving in an economy after taking into account investments in human capital, depletion of natural resources, and damage caused by pollution. It relies on the assumption that the consumption of natural resources can be offset by economic investment and expenditure on education. Therefore, it suggests that natural capital can be substituted by economic or human capital. If a specific natural resource is exhausted, economic and human capital can be used to develop new technologies that would serve the same purpose. As a result, the view of the world presented by this map is far more optimistic about our capacity to combine environmental protection and economic growth than the previous map showing ecological footprints.

The third ideal-type view on environment and development is the *structural view*. It emphasizes the structural inequalities that exist between developing and developed countries (Najam 2005; Shiva 2004; Williams 2005). Developing countries have contributed the least to environmental problems, yet they are often the first to suffer. They provide much of the natural resources and cheap labour that generate profit in developed countries, but cause environmental degradation at home. Developing countries are also more likely than developed countries to lack the necessary resources to adapt to changing environmental conditions. Furthermore, this material inequality is accompanied by political inequality, as developing countries do not always have the power and influence to secure their preferred outcomes in international forums. The structural view argues that environmental problem-solving requires the transfer of funding, expertise, and technologies to developing countries. It also requires the guarantee of developing countries' **sovereignty**, to enable these countries to contribute to environmental **preservation**, rather than sacrificing their rights to economic development (see Box 6.1).

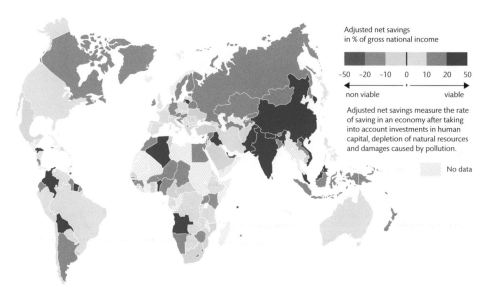

Figure 6.3 World map of adjusted net savings per country (2015)

Source data from: World Bank

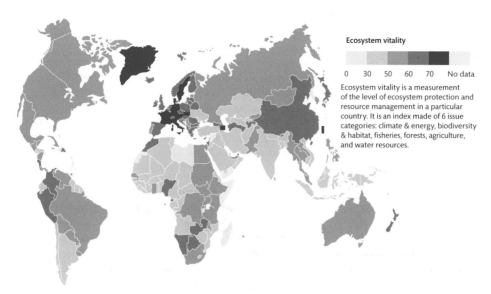

Ecosystem vitality

0   30   50   60   70   No data

Ecosystem vitality is a measurement of the level of ecosystem protection and resource management in a particular country. It is an index made of 6 issue categories: climate & energy, biodiversity & habitat, fisheries, forests, agriculture, and water resources.

Figure 6.4 World map of ecosystem vitality per country (2018)

Source data from: Environmental Performance Index: https://epi.envirocenter.yale.edu, 2018

Take your learning further by viewing the interactive versions of these figures
www.oup.com/he/morin1e

Figure 6.4 is consistent with the structural view. It shows how countries with low levels of development experience real difficulties in maintaining the vitality of their ecosystems. The ecosystem vitality index measures ecosystem protection and resource management in six issue categories: climate and energy, biodiversity and habitat, fisheries, forests, agriculture, and water resources. The resulting map shows that ecosystem vitality is particularly weak in developing countries.

Box 6.1 Vandana Shiva: representing the structural view and beyond

Vandana Shiva is a major environmental activist and ecofeminist figure. Born in India in 1952, she completed a PhD in physics in 1978 at the University of Western Ontario in Canada. During her studies, she returned every summer to the region in the Himalayas where she grew up to participate in the Chipko movement, which was founded by women to campaign for the recognition of the inherent—rather than merely economic—value of healthy soils, clean water, and clean air. As a result of the efforts of the Chipko movement and other civil society actors, private logging was banned in the Himalayas in 1979 and public logging was forbidden at an altitude over 1,000 m.

Studying in Canada brought the inequalities between developed and developing countries into sharp relief for Shiva. After her PhD, she returned to India to help the large community of farmers who, she felt, suffered from the legacy of colonization and its intensive industrial agricultural system based on monocultures. In 1982, she established the Research Foundation for Science, Technology and Ecology,

(continued...)

an institute dedicated to research and advocacy on the synergies between biodiversity **conservation** and human rights.

Over the years, she became increasingly interested in issues surrounding the destruction of agricultural biodiversity. Multinational organizations were selling infertile seeds to farmers, maintaining control over them through intellectual property rights so that the farmers could not breed crops or save seed from year to year. For ten years she supported legal fights at the European Patent Office to revoke patents on traditional Indian plants. One of the most prominent successes was the revocation of a patent on an anti-fungal product derived from neem, a tree species which had long been used in India for this purpose. Similarly, her organization successfully lobbied the Indian government to ban the use of infertile genetically modified seeds in India, under the Protection of Plant Varieties and Farmers' Rights Act passed in 2001.

Through these activities Shiva constantly criticized the mainstream agricultural system, in which countries invest in chemicals and feed for animals instead of preserving biodiversity and soils. This mainstream behaviour, she argued, is dictated by the patriarchal and capitalist logic of developed states towards developing countries. She believes that the growing world population is not to be blamed for poverty and the depletion of natural resources. Rather, in line with the structural view, she argues that it is the unequal distribution of both resources and rights among people, and especially between developed and developing countries, that drives these problems.

While she is a key representative of the structural view, fighting the domination of the developed world over developing countries especially for agriculture and biodiversity conservation, Vandana Shiva is also known for her feminist activism. According to Shiva, environmental protection and women's rights are inherently interconnected. Most farmers in the world are women. While they produce more food than men, they are, at the same time, the first victims of violence and malnutrition. For Shiva, the destruction of nature and the denial of women's freedom is a result of the same patriarchal and capitalist logic that developed countries have imposed on developing countries for agriculture. The solution to the global environmental crisis therefore also involves the emancipation of women, as they have, according to Shiva, a better understanding of environmental issues.

Vandana Shiva is a famous but controversial figure. Some believe that she caricatures the drawbacks of the green revolution, omitting to mention that it has also lifted a large number of people out of poverty and hunger. She has also been blamed for exaggerating the potential health impacts of **genetically modified organisms** and glyphosate-based herbicides, implying that they can lead to autism, Alzheimer's, or diabetes, even though scientific data has not confirmed such a link. Arguably, being provocative has always been part of Shiva's strategy to raise awareness on development, environment, and gender issues.

Sources: Shiva 1989, 1991, 1997, 2005, 2014.

It suggests, as the structural view would have it, that correcting economic, political, and technical inequalities between countries can lead to better environmental protection globally.

The systemic, liberal, and structural views are ideal types that help us to understand political outcomes. In practice, when one or other of these views is expressed, it is generally more nuanced. The three views are not mutually exclusive; they can appear in different proportions and with varying degrees of coherence within a single case. Nevertheless, one of these three views is usually predominant. Analysing which of the three views a particular political event embodies is important because it helps us to understand the visions that influence political choices as well as the lineage of ideas that have come to prevail across global environmental politics.

6.2 Stockholm, 1972: an initial compromise between systemic and structural views

The preparation for the Stockholm Summit

The 1972 United Nations Conference on the Human Environment was a milestone in international environmental politics. Since the 1960s, environmental protection had been a concern for an increasing number of people in developed countries. However, the environment was not yet a central theme of multilateral cooperation. There was no specialized United Nations agency devoted to environmental protection and there were only a handful of multilateral environmental agreements (see Figure 0.2).

At the time of the 1972 Conference, environmental cooperation was mainly governed by bilateral and regional agreements. These agreements regulated a number of key environmental issue areas, such as water resources, fisheries, and nuclear energy. Figure 6.5 shows the distribution of North–North, North–South, and South–South environmental agreements concluded for each year since World War I. It reveals that initially most bilateral and regional environmental agreements were concluded among developed countries. Even at the time of the 1972 Stockholm Summit, while most members of the United Nations were developing countries, there were relatively few environmental agreements concluded among developing countries.

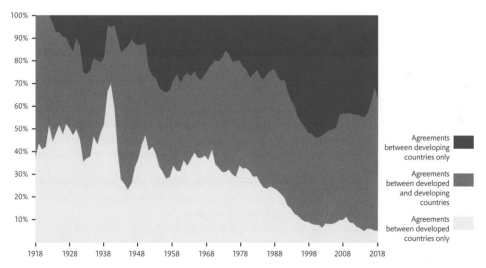

Figure 6.5 Distribution of cross-national environmental agreements by level of development (1918–2018)

Source data from: https://iea.uoregon.edu/

Take your learning further by viewing the interactive version of this figure
www.oup.com/he/morin1e

The Swedish government showed pioneering spirit, therefore, when in 1968 it proposed to host an international United Nations conference on environmental issues. Sweden was keen to promote multilateral environmental cooperation, as it had recently been a victim of extensive transboundary pollution from neighbouring countries. In 1969, the United Nations General Assembly accepted Sweden's proposal, and it was decided that the conference would be held in Stockholm (see Box 6.2).

Box 6.2 Summit diplomacy: multilateralism to galvanize efforts for sustainable development

Summit diplomacy refers to the pursuit of international cooperation through large, high-profile, high-level meetings between governments. These summits offer several advantages. First, the preparatory process encourages governments to *reflect on their domestic conditions*, and so can lead to important national reforms. For example, several governments established environment ministries in the wake of the 1972 Stockholm Summit.

Summits also create *concrete deadlines*, which can catalyse negotiation processes. Without the deadline of the Rio Summit, for example, the Convention on Biological Diversity would probably not have been opened for signature in 1992.

Summits attract *heads of state* and other government leaders, which creates increased diplomatic and media pressure to achieve demonstrable political outcomes. This pressure can help to overcome stalemates, both nationally and internationally, and can encourage ambitious commitments. The Johannesburg Summit, for example, encouraged the United States government to allocate $970 million to fund access to drinking water.

The presence of *diverse stakeholders* at summits also promotes the creation of transnational networks and encourages new partnerships. At the second Rio Summit in 2012, often called 'Rio+20', thousands of parallel sessions were organized, including one meeting for parliamentarians and another for judges.

Finally, summits provide an opportunity for states to *outline priorities* for the international agenda, and to develop and refine shared norms; they can also help to construct a coherent conceptual framework for environmental **governance**. For example, these major summits are partly responsible for the institutionalization of key norms and principles firmly embedded into global environmental governance. These include ideas such as 'sustainable development', the **polluter pays principle**, the **precautionary principle**, **common but differentiated responsibilities**, and the **green economy**. At summits, states have agreed to these principles, adopted plans of action, created new **institutions**, and made financial promises that reflected these key norms and principles.

Yet summit diplomacy has also attracted substantial criticism. Notably, global environmental summits have been criticized for diverting time and resources from other political matters that might be of greater international urgency, such as security threats, famine, or refugees.

Summits have been blamed for merely creating the illusion that action is being taken while they have been weak in delivering on concrete commitments. The norms and principles adopted are often very broad, providing leeway for governments to interpret them in different ways or to use them as a justification for inaction. For instance, differing interpretations of the principle of 'common but differentiated responsibilities' has made it very difficult to reach agreement on developing countries' responsibility for reducing **greenhouse gas** emissions.

Another criticism is that summits can be subject to the whims of either the most obstructive participants or the most powerful ones. For instance, business actors had no defined role at Rio, while they were seen as partners during the Johannesburg Summit, and ended up acting as drivers at Rio+20. While business influence can be positive for environmental governance, business dominance also means that other categories of **non-state actors** have been neglected during recent summits.

A recent concern is the environmental and carbon footprints of summits themselves, which fly out thousands of participants from all over the world. The 2015 Paris climate change summit, which was small in comparison to the summits in Rio and Johannesburg, produced around 300,000 tons of carbon dioxide.

Partly in response to these criticisms, states seem to be investigating smaller venues. These venues can be more restricted in terms of the number of players involved, such as bilateral (US–China for example), minilateral (such as the G20), or regional summits. These venues can also be more specific with regard to the environmental issues they cover, such as those focused specifically on climate change (2015 Paris Summit) or biodiversity (2016 Cancun Summit), among other transboundary environmental issues.

Sources: Andresen 2007; Bakaki and Bernauer 2017; Ferns and Amaeshi 2017; Jinnah 2017; Lövbrand et al. 2017; Meyer et al. 1997; Seyfang and Jordan 2002.

From the first stages of preparation for the Stockholm conference, the issue of economic development emerged as a central focus of negotiations, with developing countries arguing for its inclusion on the negotiating agenda (Najam 2005). Many of these countries had only just escaped the yoke of colonialism, and felt it essential to protect their recently acquired sovereignty, including their sovereign control over their natural resources. Developing countries were also facing severe problems with poverty, and understandably prioritized economic development over environmental protection.

Some developing countries distrusted the environmental concerns expressed by Western governments, fearing they were a covert strategy to maintain economic advantage, or to divert attention away from problems of structural inequality. They found it suspicious that these new environmental concerns were arising at precisely the time when the G77 coalition was being formed, with the purpose of demanding a 'New International Economic Order' at the United Nations General Assembly to redress structural inequalities between developed and developing countries. The distrust among developing countries was such that the organizers of the Stockholm Conference feared some of them might boycott the event (Najam 2005).

In an effort to bring developing countries on board, the conference's Secretary General, Maurice Strong (see Box 6.3), held a preparatory seminar in 1971 on the environment and development. This seminar brought together approximately 30 experts and political decision makers in Founex, Switzerland. Its outcome, the 'Founex Report', concluded that environmental protection and development are not contradictory, but complementary. It argued that lack of development is a cause of environmental damage, and that promoting economic development could help to solve some of the environmental problems faced by developing countries. The Founex Report also argued that developed countries should help developing countries to develop and protect the environment. Assisting developing countries was presented not only as a moral obligation, but also as a rational policy in the best interest of developed countries, as they can only benefit from having stable and reliable partners. The report therefore reassured developing countries that they too had interests in environmental protection, and underscored the role developed countries should play in supporting their engagement. It provided the first normative basis for a rapprochement between the systemic and the structural views presented in Section 6.1.

Box 6.3 Maurice Strong: a bridge-maker between businesses, civil society groups, and governments

Maurice Strong is one of the most influential figures in the history of international environmental politics, having led several important United Nations organizations and summits. He was born in 1929 in Manitoba, Canada, into a poor family. He soon had to make his own living, leaving school at 14 to work in the Canadian Merchant Marine, and subsequently at a trading post in an Inuit village in the Arctic. When he learned of the creation of the United Nations, he knew that he wanted to become involved. In 1947, aged 18, he took a temporary, junior position at the United Nations headquarters. On his own account, he realized once at the United Nations that he would never be promoted to a decision-making post as he had neither a university degree nor political connections. He therefore left the organization, with the intention of returning after building his credentials.

Strong went into the oil industry, where he rapidly advanced, formed his own gas company, and made his fortune. After a few years, he became president of Power Corporation, a multinational corporation that invested in the energy sector. At the same time, he travelled around the world, particularly in West Africa, India, and China. He became involved in the voluntary sector, particularly with the Young Men's Christian Association (YMCA). Because of this international and philanthropic experience, the Canadian prime minister appointed Strong the first head of the new Canadian International Development Agency in 1966.

In 1970, the United Nations Secretary-General, U Thant, appointed Strong to organize and lead the United Nations Conference on the Human Environment, which was held in Stockholm in 1972. Strong's leadership was lauded by many for his ability to take on board the needs and expectations of developing countries, notably by reconciling development needs and environmental protection. As he himself explained: 'After Stockholm, never more could the environment issue be considered only in the narrow context of the pollution problems of the rich, but as deeply relevant to the development needs and aspirations of developing countries, underscoring the imperatives for new dimensions of co-operation and equity in north–south relationships' (Strong 2001). In the wake of this diplomatic success, he was elected Executive Director of the newly created United Nations Environment Programme.

From the mid-1970s to the 2000s, Strong continuously alternated work in the private sector (including as the head of corporations such as Petro-Canada and Toyota) with work in non-profit organizations (including the World Resources Institute, the International Institute for Sustainable Development, and the Stockholm Environment Institute) and **intergovernmental organizations** (including serving the United Nations as Secretary General of the 1992 Rio Summit and becoming a senior advisor to the president of the World Bank in 1995). Because of these diverse experiences, Strong was known as a bridge-maker: a theme throughout his varied career was to promote dialogue across the governmental, for-profit, and not-for-profit sectors. In his owns words, 'lines of communication and decision-making must be given much greater horizontal and trans-sectoral dimensions than are provided for in existing structures' (Strong 1973: 703).

Progressively, though, doubts emerged regarding his genuine capacity to embody the needs of developing countries while following mainstream institutions such as the World Bank, and to embody environmental protection while working hand in hand with multinational corporations. In 2005, his reputation was damaged by suspicions of corruption. Some suspected that he received money from private partners in the United Nations Oil-for-Food programme in Iraq, although no evidence was found to charge him. His departure from the United Nations the same year and his move to China are, according to him, rather due to his feeling that the United Nations had come to an impasse. In any case, the controversy put an end to his career at the United Nations. Maurice Strong died in his home country, Canada, in 2015 at the age of 86.

Sources: Blutstein 2016; Strong 1972, 1973, 1991, 1992, 2000, 2001.

The outcomes of the Stockholm Summit

In part because Maurice Strong managed to attract many developing countries to attend, the Stockholm Conference was one of the largest international conferences ever organized. Delegations from 114 countries took part, at a time when the United Nations only had 131 members, and the environment had not yet become a central issue in international relations. Even the People's Republic of China, which had only just joined the United Nations, participated in the conference.

However, the Soviet Union and other countries in the communist bloc decided not to take part initially. These countries were not opposed in principle to a conference on the environment, but were protesting because the German Democratic Republic (East Germany) was not invited. At that time, the majority of United Nations members did not recognize the existence of two separate German states; only the Federal Republic of Germany (West Germany) was recognized. Maurice Strong did convince the Soviet Union to take part in the preparatory process for the conference, and ensured that the declaration adopted at the conference accounted for the Soviet point of view so that a retrospective agreement was possible (Najam 2005: 319).

The conference's final outcome, the Stockholm Declaration, outlines 26 general environmental principles that reflect systemic as well as structural views. The first principles listed in the Stockholm Declaration echo the systemic view in underscoring the earth's limited resources: Principle 2 addresses the preservation of natural resources 'for the benefit of present and future generations'; Principle 3 underscores that 'the capacity of the earth to produce vital renewable resources must be maintained and, wherever practicable, restored or improved'; Principle 4 advocates for humanity's responsibility to protect 'wildlife and its habitat, which are now gravely imperilled'; Principle 5 emphasizes that non-renewable resources 'of the earth must be employed in such a way as to guard against the danger of their future exhaustion'; and Principle 6 calls for a cessation of the discharge of pollution in 'such quantities or concentrations as to exceed the capacity of the environment to render them harmless'. These examples make clear that the systemic view of the relationship between environment and development is well represented in the Stockholm Declaration.

The Stockholm Declaration's Principles also reflect the structural view in their recognition of inequities between developed and developing countries. For example, Principle 8 states that 'economic and social development is essential for ensuring a favourable living and working environment'; Principle 9 calls for 'accelerated development through the transfer of substantial quantities of financial and technological assistance'; Principle 10 advocates 'adequate earnings for primary commodities and raw materials'; Principle 11 holds that states should offer compensation to address the 'economic consequences resulting from the application of environmental measures'; Principle 12 argues for 'additional international technical and financial assistance' for developing countries; and Principle 15 demands the abandonment of 'projects which are designed for colonialist and racist domination'. All these principles echo requests made by developing countries, and reflect a structural view of the relationship between environment and development.

The liberal view is notably absent from the Stockholm Declaration. Some principles of the declaration even seem to be hostile to liberal laissez-faire economics, such as Principle 13, which defends 'an integrated and coordinated approach to their development planning',

Principle 14, which states that 'rational planning constitutes an essential tool', and Principle 17, which considers that governments must be responsible for 'planning, managing or controlling the environmental resources of States'. Clearly, the Stockholm Declaration implies that environmental protection requires central planning rather than free markets.

Overall, the Stockholm Conference emphasized the priority of environmental concerns, but also recognized the importance of economic development. Although developing countries were initially mistrustful of environmental initiatives, the Stockholm Conference demonstrated that a compromise was possible. The final Declaration does have some inconsistencies, but it has the merit of having brought together developed and developing countries, focusing on a common concern for environmental protection.

Many institutions were created in the wake of the Stockholm Conference and echo this compromise between the systemic and structural views (Meyer et al. 1997). The most important is the United Nations Environment Programme, which was established in 1972. In contrast to the numerous intergovernmental organizations that are based in developed countries, the headquarters of the United Nations Environment Programme is in Nairobi, Kenya. This was a contentious decision, resulting from a hard-fought victory led by Kenya with the support of the G77 to overrule developed country interests in siting it in either New York or Geneva. This victory symbolized the necessity to address developing countries' needs and interests when designing global environmental policies. As we explain in Section 6.3, this balance between systemic and structural views was difficult to maintain because of broader global policies in the 1980s, until the concept of sustainable development restored some coherence to the international debate.

6.3 The Brundtland Report, 1987: the birth of sustainable development

The World Commission on Environment and Development

In the 1980s, the international context changed dramatically from the prevailing atmosphere of the early 1970s. Firstly, the debt crisis considerably weakened the position of developing countries. In the 1970s, many of these countries borrowed heavily from commercial banks in developed countries to finance their industrialization strategies. However, when interest rates increased sharply in the 1980s, their foreign debt exceeded their earning power. As a result, several developing countries, particularly in Latin America, experienced economic recessions and faced increasingly uncompromising creditors in developed countries. This situation put these developing countries in a vulnerable position to have their voice heard in world politics.

From the 1980s onwards, neo-liberal ideas began to dominate debates on economic policy. As the Soviet model waned, United States President Ronald Reagan and British Prime Minister Margaret Thatcher advocated greater market liberalization and increased deregulation, both nationally and internationally. Neo-liberalism was also looked on favourably at the International Monetary Fund and in several other countries, both developed and developing.

New environmental concerns were also emerging following a series of disasters and scientific discoveries. Throughout the 1970s, reports showed that 'acid rain' was affecting not only lakes and forests, but also historic monuments and human health. The Three Mile Island accident of 1979 and the Chernobyl disaster of 1986 alerted the world to the environmental risks of nuclear energy. And in 1984 the explosion at a pesticide factory in Bhopal, India, killed thousands of people and caused irreversible environmental harm. In 1985, a 'hole' was discovered in the **ozone layer**, which allowed more ultraviolet radiation from the sun to reach ground level, increasing the risk of skin cancer. These events were sharp reminders that environmental protection does not just mean protecting natural resources from exploitation; it also means protecting humanity from pollution.

Against this background, in 1983 the United Nations established the World Commission on Environment and Development to develop a global agenda for addressing environmental concerns. The Commission brought together 23 international experts, and was led by Gro Harlem Brundtland, the former Norwegian prime minister (see Box 6.4). Members of the Brundtland Commission held public hearings throughout the world, to listen to a variety of views on the relationship between the environment and development. Their report, entitled *Our Common Future*, is often referred to as the Brundtland Report.

Box 6.4 Gro Harlem Brundtland: the lead architect of sustainable development

Gro Harlem Brundtland was Norway's youngest and first female prime minister. Born in Oslo in 1939, she was a young physician when she became Norway's Minister of Environment in 1974. As Minister of Environment, she won important victories, such as the protection of Europe's largest continuous mountain plain, the Hardangervidda, in the face of powerful opposition from financial interests who wanted to use the area to develop hydroelectric power.

Brundtland became Norway's prime minister at the age of 41 in 1981. During her three terms in office, she became known for her work to enhance the status of women and as an advocate for gender equality. Under her leadership, the number of female students outnumbered men, maternity leave was extended, paternity leave introduced, and 'caring work' gained pension rights. During her second term, she appointed eight women to her 18-member cabinet, a world record.

Brundtland is most well known in global environmental politics for her international work as Chair of the United Nations World Commission on Environment and Development, which was broadly tasked with analysing the impact of environmental degradation and natural resource depletion on economic and social development. After being shortlisted alongside former United States President Jimmy Carter and former British Prime Minister Edward Heath in 1983, United Nations Secretary-General, Javier Pérez de Cuéllar, asked Brundtland to chair this new commission. Brundtland was initially sceptical about taking on the role. However, United Nations Environment Programme Director, Mustafa Tolba, and many others urged her to accept, underscoring that she was the only environment minister in the world to have become prime minister.

The Commission's final report, *Our Common Future*, also known as the Brundtland Report, was released in 1987, in the lead up to the United Nations Conference on Environment and Development (the 'Rio Summit') in 1992. *Our Common Future* laid out a vision for economic growth that is compatible with environmental protection, and is perhaps most well known for its definition of 'sustainable development'. The concept has proven to have much staying power, as reflected in its centrality to the 2015 **Sustainable Development Goals** (SDGs), which became the global blueprint for development planning nearly three decades after the Brundtland Report was released (see Box 6.7). Several members of the Brundtland Commission credit the report's success to Brundtland's skills in moderating discussions, encouraging debate, and compromise.

(continued...)

Building on this impressive legacy, Gro Harlem Brundtland went on to serve the public in various other important ways. Notably, she served as Director of the World Health Organization from 1998 to 2003. In this role, she counts among her successes: making drugs more accessible to people in poor countries, bringing polio closer to eradication, and successfully negotiating a global agreement on tobacco control. She was subsequently appointed by United Nations Secretary-General Ban Ki-Moon as a United Nations Special Envoy for Climate Change (2007–2010), assisting the Secretary-General in consulting with governments and other **stakeholders** about how to facilitate climate change governance in the United Nations system. She was also a founding member of the Elders, a group of independent global leaders, such as Nelson Mandela, Mary Robinson, Desmond Tutu, and others, who work on issues of peace and human rights.

Sources: Borowy 2013; Brundtland 2002; Conca and Dabelko 2015; Robinson 2004; Skard 2015.

The concept of sustainable development

The Brundtland Report famously proposed refocusing the international debate on the concept of sustainable development. The Brundtland Commission drew this concept from the International Union for Conservation of Nature, which had used it since the early 1980s. The Brundtland Report popularized the term, and articulated a definition that remains widely used today:

> *Sustainable development is development that meets the needs of the present without compromising the ability of future generations to meet their own needs. It contains within it two key concepts: the concept of 'needs', in particular the essential needs of the world's poor, to which overriding priority should be given; and the idea of limitations imposed by the state of technology and social organization on the environment's ability to meet present and future needs.*
> (World Commission on Environment and Development 1987: 54)

Defined in this way, sustainable development embodies three goals: economic development, social justice, and environmental protection. The Brundtland Report presents these goals as interdependent, and even inseparable within an 'integrated' approach to economic, social, and environmental policy. They are frequently referred as the three 'pillars' of sustainable development.

The Brundtland Report moved beyond the Stockholm Declaration in drawing on not only systemic and structural views, but also the liberal view. From the systemic view, it took the idea that natural resources are limited. It also uses the structural argument that economic growth in developing countries can enhance rather than harm environmental protection. Finally, it adopted the liberal idea that economic growth can combat poverty and pollution.

The report uses these three views in a nuanced way. As opposed to the classic systemic view, it indicates that the limits on the use of natural resources can be extended using technological development. Unlike archetypal economic liberalism, it considers that some form of state interventionism is required. And in contrast to the structural view, it argues that developing countries must adjust their development pathways to avoid the environmental mistakes made by developed countries since the Industrial Revolution of the 1850s.

The inherent ambiguity of sustainable development as a concept is frequently criticized by academics and activists (Conca 2004; McManus 1996; Zaccai 2012). In particular, many regret that the Brundtland Report did not distinguish more clearly between development and economic growth. These two terms are used interchangeably in the report, which does create some ambiguity. For example, the report identifies growth as a source of environmental destruction; but it also prescribes increased growth as a way of acquiring the tools for reducing this same destruction. Thus, it is unclear whether the report is fundamentally pro-growth or anti-growth. This ambiguity could have been addressed by distinguishing growth from development: arguably, development can be achieved through a better distribution of resources rather than through increases in production levels. Thus, some would have preferred the Brundtland Report to define sustainable development in a way that clearly prioritizes environmental protection and social development over economic growth.

Nevertheless, it is precisely this ambiguity that has given sustainable development its symbolic and diplomatic power (Hopwood et al. 2005). Whereas the Stockholm Declaration only juxtaposes different principles, without addressing their relationships, the concept of sustainable development offers a conceptual focus that brings together various different priorities. In addition, the underlying optimism of this concept, which says it is possible to achieve economic, social, and environmental goals simultaneously, encourages action across sectors. The concept of sustainable development therefore acts as a catalyst, bringing together developed countries, developing countries, and various stakeholders. The 1992 United Nations Conference on the Environment and Development in Rio was a perfect demonstration of this.

6.4 Rio, 1992: the rise of the liberal view

The Earth Summit

In 1992, 20 years after the Stockholm Conference, the United Nations held a second international summit on the environment. Maurice Strong, the Secretary General of the Stockholm Conference and a member of the Brundtland Commission, was then appointed to run the summit as its Secretary General as well.

The theme of the summit was somewhat different from that of its predecessor in Stockholm. Rather than 'Human Environment', the theme was 'Environment and Development', which echoed the official title of the Brundtland Commission. As a symbolic recognition of this fusing of environment and development, it was decided that this summit would be held in a developing country, and accordingly Rio de Janeiro, Brazil was selected.

Developing countries adopted a different strategy at Rio from that 20 years earlier in Stockholm (Hurrell and Sengupta 2012). Rather than taking a defensive and distrustful position towards environmental challenges, developing countries saw the Rio Summit as an opportunity to promote their own interests. In particular, they wanted to draw the international community's attention to the environmental problems that are specific to developing countries. While developed countries were preoccupied by acid rain, forest protection, and the depletion of the ozone layer, developing countries sought to refocus international debates on issues such as desertification and the trade in hazardous waste (Najam 2005).

The Rio Summit was also an opportunity for developing countries to demand more **technology transfer** and additional development assistance. From their point of view, developed countries had a duty to take on the additional costs arising from environmental policies, because they had the resources and they bore most of the historical responsibility for environmental deterioration. From the 1980s, developing countries started to negotiate debt-for-nature swaps with lenders in high-income countries (see Box 6.5). This provided an illustration of the fact that developing countries could make economic gains in exchange for environmental protection. Also in the 1980s, at the negotiations leading up to the Montreal Protocol on ozone layer depletion, developing countries had argued for the creation of a fund to compensate them for the end of the trade in ozone-depleting substances.

Box 6.5   Debt-for-nature swaps—a win-win solution for conservation and development?

Debt-for-nature swaps are financial transactions in which a portion of a developing nation's foreign debt is waived in exchange for local investments in environmental conservation measures. It is a voluntary transaction whereby a debt holder in a developing country negotiates a deal with the lender, typically in a developed country. Central to this deal are provisions in which the foreign debt is alleviated in exchange for a commitment to either invest in conservation and natural resource management projects, or facilitate policy changes and regulations that encourage sustainable development. Thus, debt-for-nature swaps were developed as a potential win-win solution, both alleviating crushing foreign debt and simultaneously addressing the rapid loss of natural resources and environmental degradation that many developing countries face. Financial capital is exchanged for the protection of the world's natural capital.

Some argue that debt-for-nature swaps can become a major source of international nature conservation funding in developing nations. The United States Agency for International Development and its Bilateral Debt-for-Nature Initiatives have been leading nature swaps activities around the world. Successful examples have been recorded in Indonesia, Costa Rica, Guatemala, and the Republic of Seychelles. In 2006 The Nature Conservancy, an American **non-governmental organization** (NGO) working on biodiversity conservation, facilitated one of the largest debt-for-nature swaps in history, protecting a large area of tropical forest in Guatemala. In the Seychelles in 2015, this conservation mechanism allowed for the creation of the second largest marine protected area in the West Indian Ocean. This approach was seen as a viable development strategy, allowing the government to invest in its own local coastal economy, rather than transferring funds overseas to cover its debt.

However, debt-for-nature swaps have also been heavily criticized. Some argue, for example, that they are only effective when there is strong government leadership, effective **enforcement** strategies, good financial management capacity, and strong public support and **compliance**. It is also argued that there should not be conditionalities on debt relief, and that countries should be allowed to invest as they see fit rather than in ways defined by developed countries. Critics also highlight numerous shortcomings and weaknesses in debt-for-nature swaps as effective conservation tools. Since these agreements are voluntary in nature, compliance mechanisms are often weak and ineffective. Debt-for-nature swaps can raise important social equity issues, as the needs and preferences of impacted land users, including indigenous peoples, are often ignored when designing protected areas and preserves. Moreover, in some cases, debt-for-nature swaps fail to address the underlying causes of natural resources mismanagement. In countries like Brazil and Bolivia, debt-for-nature swaps have been unsuccessful, either due to the lending government failing to deliver the negotiated funds and conservation actions, or due to government opposition claiming that these approaches are infringing on the countries' sovereign rights over its natural resources.

Sources: Eitman 2001; Greener 1991; Lubchenco et al. 2016; Neal 1998; Sheikh 2007; United Nations Development Programme 2016.

India and China even made their **ratification** of the Montreal Protocol conditional on the creation of such a fund (Williams 1993: 21). Faced with the insistence of developing countries, and because it was essential to bring them on board to ensure the protection of the ozone layer, developed countries agreed to the creation of the Multilateral Fund. This diplomatic success provided political momentum for developing countries to reinforce their diplomatic goals three years later at the Rio Summit.

The international context also seemed particularly favourable to a new alliance between developed and developing countries. The end of the Cold War meant that the traditional opposition between the communist and the capitalist blocs could be called into question. Multilateralism appeared to have a promising future.

In this climate of optimism, the Rio Summit attracted many official participants: 108 country leaders, 187 delegations, approximately 10,000 government delegates, over 1,400 accredited non-governmental organizations, and nearly 9,000 journalists. It was the biggest international meeting in history. The diversity of participants was just as impressive (Clark et al. 1999). Mayors, indigenous leaders, farmers, representatives of student bodies, directors of multinational companies, and trade union delegates all attended the Rio Summit. Some representatives from civil society took part in the preparatory meetings, in which they were able to present documents to government delegates and speak at formal sessions. In breaking all records for participation, the Rio Summit seemed to herald an era of international governance that would involve local, regional, and transnational stakeholders. Reflecting this integrative and inclusive approach, the 1992 Rio Conference on Environment and Development is also known as the 'Earth Summit'.

The outcome documents of the Rio Summit

The 1992 Rio Conference was highly productive. There were eight main outcomes: (1) States issued a political declaration that clarified the general principles of international environmental law, based on the principles adopted 20 years earlier at Stockholm. (2) They ratified an ambitious action plan for the twenty-first century, known as **Agenda 21**, aiming to identify problems, define goals, and specify action on themes as diverse as chemical substances, access to drinking water, and transportation. (3) The United Nations Framework Convention on Climate Change was concluded, in which industrialized countries committed to reducing their greenhouse gas emissions relative to 1990 levels. (4) Delegates adopted the Convention on Biological Diversity, which concerned conservation of ecosystems, species, and **genetic resources**. (5) An agreement was reached in Rio that negotiations would begin towards a Convention to Combat Desertification, which was signed two years later in 1994. (6) A political declaration on forests was adopted, which set out general principles for forest management. (7) Agreement was reached on reforming the new Global Environment Facility, which was created during the preparation stages of the Summit, to make it an independent organization that would no longer be dependent on the World Bank. (8) A proposal was put forward to create an entirely new institution, the Commission for Sustainable Development, to ensure that Agenda 21 was carried out.

All of the outcomes from the Rio Summit bear the hallmark of sustainable development. The Convention on Biological Diversity, for example, had three main goals: an environmental goal (the conservation of biological diversity), an economic goal (the sustainable use of biological diversity), and a social goal (the fair and equitable sharing of the benefits arising out of biological diversity). Notably, delegates at Rio preferred to create a new institution, the Commission for Sustainable Development, to ensure that Agenda 21 was carried out rather than entrusting the United Nations Environment Programme with this task. This was because the United Nations Environment Programme specialized on the environment, while Agenda 21, and by extension the organization responsible for monitoring its **implementation**, also needed to pay great attention to the economic and social goals of sustainable development.

In some respects, the systemic view on the relationship between environmental protection and economic development was enhanced at the Rio Summit, when compared with the Stockholm Summit. For example, the Rio Declaration included one of the first mentions of the precautionary principle 'to prevent environmental degradation' (Principle 15) (see Box 1.2). It also asked governments to carry out environmental impact studies when planning activities 'that are likely to have a significant adverse impact on the environment' (Principle 17).

Yet, other systemic ideas saw setbacks. For example, concerns about population growth received less attention at the Rio Summit than they had at the Stockholm Summit. Referring to the contested connection between population and environmental degradation, the Stockholm Declaration called on states to 'apply [. . .] demographic policies' (Principle 16). The Rio Declaration softened this language, simply requiring states to 'promote appropriate demographic policies' (Principle 8). Likewise, the proposal by developed countries for a treaty to be adopted at Rio for the halting of deforestation in tropical regions met with strong opposition from developing countries, who wanted to preserve their sovereign rights to use their natural resources. As a result, the deforestation document secured in Rio was merely a declaration of intent rather than a legally binding treaty.

The structural view on the relationship between environment and development is also represented in the Rio outcomes. Nearly all the documents adopted at Rio invoke the sovereign right of developing countries to harness their own natural resources using their own policies. The Convention on Biological Diversity, for example, places genetic resources under the sovereign control of states—until then they were considered to be an element of the common heritage of humankind. The Rio Declaration goes even further. Although it does not create an explicit right to a healthy environment, it clearly asserts that human beings have a right to a 'productive' life (Principle 1) and a 'right to development' (Principle 3).

The most significant advancement of the structural view in the Rio outcomes was the assertion of the principle of common but differentiated responsibilities (Okereke 2008; Stone 2004). This principle essentially states that, although all states must participate in efforts to protect the environment, developed countries must take greater responsibility for this. The Rio Declaration gives two justifications for this principle. First, it explains that developed countries cause more environmental harm, and second, that developed countries have greater financial and technical resources to address these problems (Principle 7). Developing countries might have wished that the Rio Declaration had made explicit mention of two additional justifications: the ecological debt that developed countries have incurred through their historical emissions, and the right that developing countries have to receive assistance in line with their specific needs. These justifications were not explicitly mentioned in the Rio Declaration, but the assertion of the principle of common but differentiated responsibilities, and thus the structural view, is embedded right at the heart of the Declaration.

In concrete terms, the principle of common but differentiated responsibilities is put into practice in international environmental treaties via differentiated commitments, adjusted according to level of development. The United Nations Framework Convention on Climate Change, for example, contains different obligations for developed countries, economies in transition, and developing countries. Developed countries not only have stricter goals for greenhouse gas reduction, but they must also help developing countries to limit their emissions.

Some outcome documents of the Rio Summit do not reflect the structural view on environment and development to the extent hoped for by some developing countries. For example, none of the Rio outcomes gave a precise timetable for developed countries to increase public **development aid**. Furthermore, and contrary to the principle of additionality in international aid contained in the Stockholm Declaration (Principle 12), the Convention to Combat Desertification contains no financial mechanisms to provide additional aid beyond that already provided to developing countries.

For its part, the liberal view on environment and development made substantial inroads at the Rio Summit (Doyle 1998). The Rio Declaration affirms that states must promote a system that 'would lead to economic growth' (Principle 12). Such economic growth is judged to be not only compatible with, but even necessary to 'better address[ing] the problems of environmental degradation' (Principle 12). According to the Rio Declaration, the best way of achieving this growth is to put in place an 'open international economic system' (Principle 12). It is therefore necessary not to 'distort . . . international trade and investment' (Principle 16). More specifically, it is necessary to ensure that environmental policies do not constitute 'a means of arbitrary or unjustifiable discrimination or a disguised restriction on international trade' (Principle 12). Overall, the Rio Declaration asserts that liberalization is a lever for sustainable development and that environmental policies, which by their very nature are restrictive of economic activity, could potentially be an obstacle to this sustainable development.

These expressions of the liberal view in the Rio Declaration, some of which are taken verbatim from trade agreements, were repeated in the other outcomes from the Rio Summit. The United Nations Framework Convention on Climate Change, for example, called on states to 'cooperate to promote supportive and open international economic system that would lead to sustainable economic growth [. . .] thus enabling them better to address the problems of climate change' (Annex 1, Article 3(5)). The Convention to Combat Desertification asserts that states should adopt 'commercial practices that promote growth' (Article 8(3)(a)(ii)). The Statement of Forest Principles states that 'open and free international trade in forest products should be facilitated' (Article 13(a)). These examples illustrate that the liberal view on environment and development was deeply embedded in the Rio Summit outcome documents, although it was nearly absent 20 years earlier at the Stockholm Summit. Nevertheless, overall, the Rio Summit achieved a certain balance between systemic, structural, and liberal views, assisted by the concept of sustainable development.

6.5 Johannesburg, 2002: dilution of the systemic view

The context of the Johannesburg Summit

Ten years after the Rio Summit, the concept of sustainable development had common currency in economic and political circles. It was used by a wide swathe of actors, including journalists, entrepreneurs, and public officials. Even in trade agreements, such as the 1992 North American Free Trade Agreement and the 1994 Marrakesh Agreement establishing the World Trade Organization, there are explicit mentions of sustainable development. It is therefore not surprising that sustainable development was chosen as the theme of the Johannesburg Summit, which was planned for autumn 2002 to mark the tenth anniversary of the Rio Summit.

In the years leading up to the Johannesburg Summit, the international context had been growing increasingly favourable to development aid. Initially, in the early 1990s, official development assistance had substantially reduced. With the end of the Cold War, developing countries were no longer able to play the two rival blocs against each other, and they faced new levels of competition with countries in Eastern Europe, who had joined calls for aid from the West.

But this trend rapidly reversed through a series of summits and commitments in the 2000s (see Box 6.6). In September 2000, world leaders gathered in New York for another United Nations meeting, the Millennium Summit, which made a commitment to create an 'environment [. . .] which is conducive to development and to the elimination of poverty' (Millennium Declaration, paragraph 3). To ensure that this commitment was met, the following year governments adopted the Millennium Development Goals, a series of specific goals, with clear targets such as halving the proportion of the world's population living in extreme poverty by 2015. To contribute to the achievement of these goals, African leaders entered into the New Partnership for Africa's Development in July 2001, with support from leaders of the G8 economic powers. A few months later, in November 2001, a **Conference of the Parties** to the United Nations Framework Convention on Climate Change created a special fund to help developing countries finance projects aimed at adapting to climate change. In the same month, the World Trade Organization Ministerial Conference was taking place in Doha, Qatar, which launched a new round of trade negotiations that were meant to prioritize development in low-income countries. In March 2002, at the International Conference on Financing for Development in Monterrey, Mexico, developed countries made a commitment to significantly increase development aid and to help the most heavily indebted countries. Thus, in the years preceding the Johannesburg Summit, world leaders made a number of ambitious commitments echoing the priorities identified by developing countries.

In this context, the commitments adopted at the 2000 Millennium Summit, the 2001 Doha Conference, and the 2002 Monterrey Conference provided a minimal baseline for the 2002 Johannesburg Summit. It was understood that delegates would not renegotiate to reduce the commitments that they had just made. Yet, from the preparation stages of the Johannesburg Summit, it became obvious that some of the commitments in the political declaration and implementation plan that were to be adopted there would only repeat commitments made at previous summits.

Box 6.6 The politics of environmental aid

Since 1945, wealthier countries have allocated nearly $5 trillion to aid the development of poorer nations. This bilateral aid, often referred to as overseas development assistance (ODA), is given directly by one country to another. In contrast, multilateral aid is given by a donor country to a multilateral organization, such as the World Bank, which then distributes the money to developing countries. Although development aid has traditionally focused on eradicating poverty, as early as the 1990s aid institutions and bilateral donors came to recognize that traditional development challenges are linked in significant ways with environmental issues. For example, in 2010 Norway dedicated up to $1 billion to help Indonesia reduce its greenhouse gas emissions from deforestation.

Since the first United Nations Conference on the Human Environment in Stockholm in 1972, developing states have argued that expectations that poorer nations should pursue economic development in ways that are less damaging to the environment *demand* a resource transfer from richer to poorer states. This is because the costs of pursuing these environmental goals are likely to be substantial. As a result, many global environmental conventions include provisions around the financial commitments needed to address this tension. For example, a multilateral fund was created under the Montreal Protocol on Substances that Deplete the Ozone Layer to meet the incremental costs for developing countries of implementing the Protocol. Similarly, the Global Environment Facility was established in 1992 to manage the multilateral aid process and assist developing countries in implementing the Rio Conventions. Aid institutions have therefore become a key component of global environmental governance.

Environmental aid has also been mainstreamed into development aid. The classic example of this is the World Bank, which in the 1990s included environmental provisions in approximately 23 per cent of its structural adjustment lending portfolio. These provisions, so-called 'environmental conditionalities', required recipient countries to make changes to their domestic environmental policies as a condition of receiving the funding. Environmental conditionalities on lending have been heavily criticized for, among other things, failing to generate long-term institutional reform in recipient countries and requiring institutional reforms that are not a good fit with recipient countries' capacities and interests.

Another contentious question surrounding environmental aid has to do with how to differentiate new commitments of environmental aid from pre-existing development assistance. In particular, requirements to include environmental aid in multilateral environmental agreements have led to concerns that this aid would displace more traditional forms of development assistance. As a result, several environmental treaties now require that environmental aid be 'new and additional'. The big question has been how to identify a baseline for this so called 'additionality', because governments have yet to clearly define what this means in practice.

Another important debate in this area surrounds the impacts of bilateral versus multilateral aid in recipient countries. Some researchers argue that multilateral channels tend to give more agency to recipient countries than bilateral arrangements. Others add that multilateral aid is likely to be more effective, since it may minimize both fragmentation of finance streams and overlap between donors. Further, some channels of bilateral environmental aid more strongly prioritize 'green' aid over 'brown' aid than do multilateral channels. Whereas brown aid generates local benefits (e.g. water sanitation, solid waste treatment, erosion control), green aid generates benefits well beyond the recipient country (e.g. greenhouse gas reductions, ozone preservation). As such, green aid tends to more closely reflect the preferences of the donor country, while brown aid tends to more closely reflect the recipient country's preferences. This raises important questions about equity, with donors' interests outweighing recipients' needs, as well as efficiency, with little coordination among donors working through multiple parallel bilateral environmental aid channels.

Despite a trend towards 'bilateralization' of environmental aid, some issues, such as climate change, still also maintain a strongly multilateral character. Under the Paris Agreement, governments committed to raise $100 billion per year in climate finance for mitigation and **adaptation** by 2020 and established a new multilateral institution, the Green Climate Fund, through which to channel many of those funds. In comparison to bilateral channels, the Green Climate Fund speaks to recipient concerns related to control over finance decisions, with a board that is equally made up of representatives from developed and developing countries. Yet the experience so far of the Green Climate Fund raises another suite of issues related to multilateral environmental funding: donor governments do not always deliver on their financial promises.

Sources: Arndt and Tarp 2017; Gutner 2005; Hicks et al. 2008; Lewis 2003; Marcoux et al. 2013; Park 2016; Roberts et al. 2009; Stadelmann et al. 2011.

The outcomes of the Johannesburg Summit

Instead of seeking only to draw up new commitments from governments, the organizers of the Johannesburg Summit actively encouraged 'type II partnerships' (Bäckstrand 2006). Type II partnerships are those not just between states, but between partners of various kinds, including businesses, intergovernmental organizations, NGOs, and governments (see Chapter 4). More than 200 type II partnerships were agreed in Johannesburg, involving investment of over US$23 million.

Several of these type II partnerships had goals relating to social and economic development in developing countries, and these partly reflected the structural view of the relationship between economic development and environmental protection (Andonova and Levy 2003). For example, several type II partnerships aimed to improve training for officials, to develop education systems, and to promote exports. The majority of these were funded and led by developed countries, intergovernmental organizations, and international NGOs, but their targeted beneficiaries were mainly the populations of developing countries.

Likewise, the political declaration adopted by the delegates paid particular attention to international development and to assistance for underprivileged populations (Najam and Cleveland 2003). It denounces the 'indignity and indecency' of poverty (paragraph 3), calls for a 'caring' global society (paragraph 2), refers to the need to provide 'social development' as well as economic development (paragraph 5), states that inequality poses 'a major threat to global prosperity, security and stability' (paragraph 12), observes that 'the benefits and costs of globalization are unevenly distributed' (paragraph 14), and is concerned that 'the poor of the world may lose confidence in their representatives and the democratic systems' (paragraph 15).

The implementation plan adopted in Johannesburg similarly reflects the structural view. The first chapter of the plan is even devoted to eliminating poverty. In subsequent chapters, particular attention is paid to issues of public health, access to drinking water, food security, and the particular problems faced by African countries and small island nations. It can be concluded from this that the Johannesburg Summit was focused on the social aspect of sustainable development, inspired by ideas from the structural view.

Having said that, the liberal view had not retreated since the Rio Summit. The Johannesburg Declaration stresses that integration of markets, mobility of capital, and increases in investment flows 'have opened new challenges and opportunities for the pursuit of sustainable development' (paragraph 14). The implementation plan states that: 'market distortions' should be eliminated (paragraph 20); the environment should be protected using 'market-oriented approaches' (paragraph 38); 'open, [. . .] multilateral trading and financial systems' should be promoted (paragraph 47); 'public/private initiatives' should be encouraged (paragraph 50); 'an attractive and conducive environment for investment' should be created (paragraph 62); 'market access for goods' should be improved (paragraph 67); 'the benefits for developing countries, as well as countries with economies in transition, from trade liberalization' should be enhanced (paragraph 96); and 'trade agreements' should be established (paragraph 99). Some observers have seen, in these liberal commitments and in the proliferation of type II partnerships, a lack of commitment from states and an implicit admission that private actors, including multinational corporations, should now be considered one of the main drivers of sustainable development (Bäckstrand 2006; Holmes 2012).

The only view from our typology that has lost ground over time at these various summits is the systemic view (see Figure 6.6). Some systemic concerns, such as concern over population

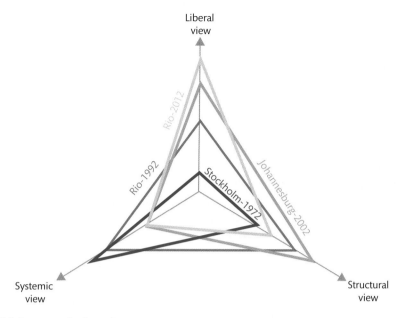

Figure 6.6 Four summits, three views

growth, have been heavily criticized for their disproportionate emphasis on developing country responsibility. The idea that states should regulate birth rates, which was commonly evoked in the 1970s, was rejected once and for all in Johannesburg. Where environmental protection is evoked in the Johannesburg Declaration and implementation plan, it is often mentioned together with structural goals, or with a reminder of the importance of using liberal approaches to environmental problem-solving.

The relative marginalization of the systemic view was not limited to the instruments adopted by governments. Only a minority of the type II partnerships announced at Johannesburg focused on environmental goals. The majority of these partnerships were more concerned with social and economic development issues, and only indirectly contributed to environmental protection (Andonova and Levy 2003). Even in the demonstrations on the streets of Johannesburg, the activists' slogans and demands were more reminiscent of the structural view than the systemic view. It became clear at the Johannesburg Summit that sustainable development was no longer primarily or even necessarily concerned with the systemic view. Some even consider that the Johannesburg Summit marked the 'death of Rio environmentalism' (Park et al. 2008: 1).

6.6 Rio+20, 2012: towards a new equilibrium?

A context of growing antagonism

Twenty years after the Rio Summit, United Nations members attempted to make further diplomatic progress by organizing a new summit on sustainable development in Rio de Janeiro in 2012, the so-called Rio+20 Summit. However, the international context was much less favourable in 2012 than it had been at previous major summits. The effects of the global economic crisis, which began in 2008, were still being felt in many developed countries. The United States was suffering from abnormally high unemployment, and Europe was experiencing a sovereign debt crisis. At a time when many governments were laboriously attempting to reduce public expenditure, it was politically and economically difficult to invest more in environmental protection and foreign aid. The most ambitious domestic environmental measures adopted at that time primarily aimed at creating jobs in sectors such as renewable energy and sustainable transport.

In the 2000s, some developing countries also began to be seen by developed countries as competitors or even rivals. India, China, and Brazil, among others, were recognized as 'emerging countries', or indeed 'emerged' countries, which now had all the economic, technological, and diplomatic capacity they needed to defend their own interests without outside help. The rise of these countries heralded a multipolar world in which emerging powers were seen as stiff competition for established ones.

These concerns are reflected in Figure 6.7; it shows the evolution of total aid for development during the 20-year period between 1995 and 2015, as well as the share of this development assistance devoted to environmental protection. While aid increased between 2005 and 2010, following a series of commitments made in the early 2000s, the level of aid plateaued after 2010, both in absolute total amount per year, and in the share devoted to environmental protection.

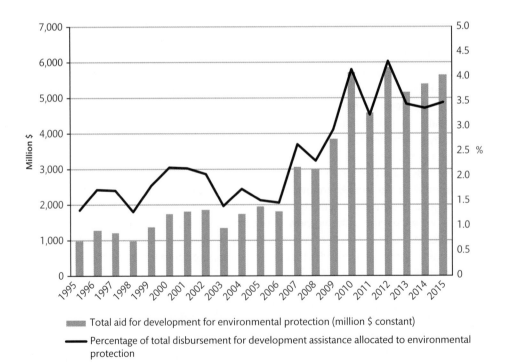

■■■ Total aid for development for environmental protection (million $ constant)

━━ Percentage of total disbursement for development assistance allocated to environmental protection

Figure 6.7 Public development aid for environmental protection (1995–2015)

Source data from: OECD

The governments of several developed countries were particularly reluctant to curb their emissions of greenhouse gases because of concerns that this would hamper their economy due to competition from emerging countries. The United States was especially critical of the fact that emerging countries seemed to do little to reduce their own emissions, even though some of them had become significant emitters of greenhouse gases. On similar grounds, Canada withdrew from the Kyoto Protocol in 2011, having previously ratified it. Meanwhile, many European leaders began advocating a border tax on imports from countries that have not reduced their greenhouse gas emissions, including emerging countries, even though these emerging countries are not subject to specific reduction targets under the Kyoto Protocol. Thus the principle of **common but differentiated responsibilities**, one of the normative legacies of the Rio Summit, was being challenged and reinterpreted in Europe and in North America (Ladly 2012; Walsh et al. 2011).

In this context of increasing antagonism, multilateral environmental diplomacy achieved fewer concrete outcomes in the decade following the Johannesburg Summit than in the decade preceding it. Few new multilateral environmental agreements were concluded during this period, with the notable exception of the 2010 Nagoya Protocol on genetic resources. Although scientific reports from the International Panel on Climate Change and other widely diffused studies, such as the Stern Report on the economics of climate change, warned decision makers of the imminent adverse effects of climate change, climate negotiations progressed very slowly. Notably, the 2009 Copenhagen Conference of the Parties of the United Nations Framework Convention on Climate Change failed to reach an agreement on reducing carbon emissions, primarily due to entrenched disagreement between developed and developing countries.

After the disappointing result of the Copenhagen Conference, most observers had low expectations for the decisions to be adopted in Rio in 2012 (Ivanova 2013). It was clear that Rio+20 would not repeat the success of the first Rio Summit 20 years earlier. And anticipating modest outcomes, several world leaders, in particular the German Chancellor Angela Merkel, American President Barack Obama, and British Prime Minister David Cameron, preferred not to be present. In total, 88 country leaders took part in the summit, compared with 108 at the first Rio Summit.

The Future We Want

The outcome of the Rio+20 Summit was rescued at the last minute by the Brazilian government (Bernstein 2013). In view of the persistent disagreement at the preparatory meetings, Brazil drew up a draft agreement and submitted it to the other countries a few days before the summit began. To bring these countries on board, Brazil removed the most ambitious and controversial ideas from the draft, reducing it to a lowest common denominator constellation of statements and objectives. This text, which was entitled *The Future We Want*, rapidly drew agreement from the other delegations and became the main outcome of the summit.

The Future We Want is approximately 60 pages long, and is both a political declaration that asserts certain principles, and an action plan containing measures to be adopted. Several paragraphs simply repeat the commitments entered into at previous summits: protecting the environment, combating poverty, and liberalizing economies. In fact, the first section of *The Future We Want* is entitled 'Reaffirming Rio principles and past action plans'. Other sections are more innovative.

Among the main innovations in the Rio+20 Summit document is the concept of the 'green economy'. A whole chapter of *The Future We Want* is devoted to this concept, though it is not clearly defined. The green economy is said to be 'one of the important tools available for achieving sustainable development' (paragraph 56). It goes on to say that this is a flexible instrument and should not be a 'rigid set of rules' (paragraph 56).

Some governments that are firm adherents to the structural view, in particular Venezuela, Cuba, and Bolivia, feared that the concept of 'green economy' could be interpreted by liberal thinkers as synonymous with 'green growth'. Green economies would then be understood as liberalized market economies, still oriented towards increased production, but slightly adjusted so that market forces can contribute to environmental protection (Ferguson 2015; McAfee 2016). However, these governments were unsuccessful in their opposition to the concept of green economy being introduced into the final summit document (Chasek 2012; Jacobs 2013).

A second major innovation in *The Future We Want* is the reform of the institutional framework for international sustainable development. Specifically, the decision was taken to replace the Commission for Sustainable Development, which had been created in Rio in 1992, with an 'intergovernmental high level political forum' (paragraph 84). Like the Commission for Sustainable Development before it, this forum is responsible for monitoring sustainable development activities, but it also brings together 'high-level decision makers' to give it greater visibility and decision-making power. *The Future We Want* also called on the United Nations General Assembly to strengthen the United Nations Environment Programme (paragraph 88). It was suggested that universal membership of its governing council should be allowed, its funding increased, its environmental coordination mandate within the United Nations system enhanced, and its regional presence strengthened to assist countries on request.

Another innovation in *The Future We Want* is its emphasis on collection and dissemination of information to encourage behaviour that is supportive of the environment. The United Nations Statistical Commission was asked to formulate 'broader measures of progress to complement GDP' (paragraph 38). This measure should act as an indirect encouragement for states to achieve sustainable development, rather than mere increases in production.

Similarly, *The Future We Want* suggested creating a working group to develop proposals for Sustainable Development Goals, to be submitted to the United Nations General Assembly (paragraph 248). This idea was proposed by Colombia and Guatemala and was inspired by the Millennium Development Goals (see Box 6.7), which acted to guide activities and serve as benchmarks for evaluating the progress of international development between 2000 and 2015.

The Future We Want also encouraged private sector stakeholders to disclose more information about their sustainability practices. Publicly listed companies were encouraged 'to consider integrating sustainability information into their reporting cycle' (paragraph 47). An internet-based registry was also created, to compile the hundreds of commitments voluntarily entered into by all stakeholders at the Rio+20 Summit (paragraph 283).

This insistence on disclosing information and voluntary commitments in *The Future We Want* is partly a reflection of the liberal view. It is interesting to note that although *The Future We Want* contains 5,000 fewer words than the implementation plan from the Johannesburg Summit, it includes three times as many references to the need for 'economic growth'. Conversely, ambitious proposals that were inspired by the structural view were rejected at Rio+20.

Box 6.7 Sustainable Development Goals: defining the global development agenda

At the beginning of the new millennium, 189 world leaders agreed to a new framework to fight poverty worldwide. This framework, which came to be known as the Millennium Development Goals, to be achieved by 2015, outlined eight goals including ensuring environmental sustainability. These goals defined the global development agenda for the first 15 years of the new millennium. They claim important successes, including lifting more than a billion people out of extreme poverty, but also leave much more work to be done in their wake, in terms of both process improvements such as improved participation in decision-making, and substantive progress towards meeting each of the eight goals.

Governments began discussing possibilities for a successor framework to the Millennium Development Goals during the preparatory meetings for the Rio+20 Summit, which would convene in Brazil in June 2012. Colombia and Guatemala first proposed a model for what became the Sustainable Development Goals in 2011, and the idea was eventually incorporated into the Rio+20 outcome document, *The Future We Want*. From the beginning, the Sustainable Development Goals were envisioned as succeeding the Millennium Development Goals, but also improving on them. Notably, the Sustainable Development Goals aimed to make sustainability the centrepiece of development planning and to involve both developing and developed states in meeting development targets.

The process leading to the identification of the Sustainable Development Goals was particularly inclusive. *The Future We Want* called for the creation of an open-ended working group comprising 30 representatives drawn from each of the five United Nations regional groups to negotiate the new Sustainable Development Goals. In an innovative approach to multilateral negotiations, the governments agreed to share the working group's 30 designated seats among 70 countries. For example, Nauru, Palau, and Papua New Guinea shared one seat, as did Zambia and Zimbabwe, as well as China, Kazakhstan, and Indonesia. This process was highly unusual, if not unprecedented, and resulted in greater participation and innovative collaborations between countries that might not otherwise have worked so closely together.

Importantly, *The Future We Want* also called for the inclusion of broad stakeholders in the drafting of the Sustainable Development Goals, including representatives from scientific communities and civil society. The United Nations Development Group, which coordinates development activities across 32 United Nations funds, launched a multipronged outreach programme to solicit such input on the process. This effort included an online poll over several years to collect information on post-2015 development priorities, to which more than 7 million people responded globally.

This inclusive negotiating process was hailed for its strong leadership, and ultimately resulted in the adoption of 17 goals and 169 targets in September 2015, to be achieved by 2030. The Sustainable Development Goals include targets aimed at ensuring access to sustainable energy, reducing inequality within and among countries, ensuring sustainable consumption and production patterns, and taking urgent action to combat climate change.

However, the participatory process for identifying the Sustainable Development Goals also raised some concerns for democratic legitimacy. For example, through a demographic analysis of respondents, Gellers has demonstrated how electronic modes of soliciting input over-represented certain people and under-represented others.

Although the Sustainable Development Goals have been largely positively received for their focus on, for instance, marginalized communities and climate change, they have also raised a host of additional questions and concerns. For example, some have questioned how trade-offs can be assessed in meeting the 17 different goals. Of course, the overarching objective is to meet all 17 goals as quickly as possible. However, in a world of finite human and financial resources, decisions must be made about how to prioritize some goals over others in terms of resource allocation and timing. Whether it is even possible to determine the comparative welfare benefits of some goals over others is open to question. Others have

(continued...)

criticized the Sustainable Development Goals for failing to question the underlying logic of economic growth, for not addressing issues related to **environmental justice** sufficiently, and approaching sustainable development as a series of separate issues rather than adopting an integrated approach.

Some also argue that the main value of the Sustainable Development Goals was in the process of negotiating them, because it forced a global discussion about aspirations and norms—they are not merely metrics to measure the achievement of goals, but an end in themselves. Others take a more forward-looking view, arguing that the success of the Sustainable Development Goals will rest on our ability to measure progress, qualitatively and quantitatively, as well as countries' abilities to translate these overarching global goals into many different scales and contexts. These questions present rich fodder for additional research in the coming years.

Sources: Barbier and Burgess 2017; Biermann et al 2017; Chasek and Wagner 2016; Gellers 2016; Gupta and Vegelin 2016; Kamau et al. 2018; Stevens and Kanie 2016.

For example, a proposal on introducing a tax on financial transactions, which was supported by NGOs and trade union confederations, was not adopted. Similarly, systemic proposals on the rights of Mother Earth, as proposed by the Bolivian President Evo Morales, and a 'universal declaration of the rights of nature', as submitted by the Ecuadorian President Rafael Correa, were also excluded from *The Future We Want*. Although liberalism appears to predominate at Rio+20, there are still elements taken from the systemic and structural views; it is the proportions—rather than the ingredients—that have changed over time.

6.7 Conclusion

The dominant views reflected in the outcome documents of environmental summits underwent a transformation between 1972 and 2012. The Stockholm Summit on the 'human environment' focused on environmental protection and was the summit at which systemic concerns were incorporated most fully. The Rio Summit opened the way to a balance between environment and development, while leaving some space for liberal ideas. In Johannesburg the focus was on development, striking a compromise between liberal and structural views. At Rio+20 the liberal view was predominant, while proposals reflecting the structural and systemic views were marginalized.

The free market has thus become a principle that is inextricably linked with international environmental politics. The Stockholm Declaration of 1972 presented industrialization as a challenge to environmental protection. In contrast, the Johannesburg and Rio+20 declarations saw growth achieved by free trade as the central solution to environmental and international development problems.

This liberalism, combined with elements taken from structural and systemic views, is what Steven Bernstein (2001) calls 'the compromise of **liberal environmentalism**'. This type of liberalism recognizes the need to take into consideration the capacities of developing countries and the limited nature of natural resources, but nonetheless places the emphasis on market forces as a way of achieving sustainable development. Carbon credit trading, the **'polluter pays' principle**, payment for environmental services, and bioprospecting contracts were all developed in the 1990s, and are part of this ideological framework.

This compromise of liberal environmentalism has become so omnipresent that it is now difficult to uphold environmental protection outside this paradigm (Dryzek 2005; Jacques and Lobo 2018; Petersen 2007; Victor and Coben 2005). The majority of key international environmental NGOs and most green political parties now subscribe to liberal environmentalism. Few of them would dare to assert that economic and demographic growth must be reversed in order to achieve environmental protection—this idea is now perceived as a criticism that is only put forward by marginal groups. The dominant discourse, even in many environmental NGOs, is that a 'green economy' can provide both economic development and environmental protection.

It is reasonable to think that it is precisely because environmental concerns have become incorporated into structuralism, and later liberalism, that they have reached the highest political circles. Nevertheless, some regret this dilution of environmental concerns. They question whether this represents the 'death of environmentalism', and call for 'post-environmentalist' approaches, which are less popular but more faithful to systemic principles (Blühdorn and Welsh 2007; Nordhaus and Shellenberger 2007).

One of the main obstacles to a change in the dominant paradigm is the fact that there are many different international institutions involved in environmental governance. As Chapter 7 shows, these institutions are not ideologically neutral. They embody a set of ideas and they contribute to their stabilization.

Critical thinking questions

1. How does the concept of 'sustainable development' fit into the paradigm of 'liberal environmentalism'?
2. How did the early experiences of Vandana Shiva, Maurice Strong, and Gro Harlem Brundtland shape their views on the relationship between environment and development?
3. How did the international political context influence the institutionalization of the structural view between 1972 and 2002?
4. Explain the principle of common but differentiated responsibilities. Do the justifications for this principle appear as convincing today as they did in 1992 in the context of climate change politics?
5. How did each major summit improve on previous summits in terms of the involvement of civil society?
6. Identify two areas of common ground between the reports *Our Common Future* (1987) and *The Future We Want* (2012).

 Test your knowledge and understanding further by trying this chapter's Multiple Choice Questions www.oup.com/he/morin1e

Key references

Bernstein, Steven. 2001. *The Compromise of Liberal Environmentalism*. New York: Columbia University Press.
This classic book discusses the gradual convergence of environmental and economic liberal norms. It identifies the causes of this convergence as well as its implications for policymaking.

Najam, Adil. 2005. 'Developing Countries and Global Environmental Governance: From Contestation to Participation to Engagement'. *International Environmental Agreements* 5 (3): 303–321.

Adil Najam has authored several publications on developing countries' perspective on global environmental politics. In this article, he traces the evolution of developing countries' position from the 1972 Stockholm Summit to the 2002 Johannesburg Summit.

Shiva, Vandana. 1997. *Biopiracy: The Plunder of Nature and Knowledge*. Boston, MA: South End Press.

This book provides a good example of the structuralist view discussed in this chapter. Vandana Shiva argues that the biotechnology industry exercised a new form of colonialism by appropriating developing countries' genetic resources and traditional knowledge, without offering adequate compensation.

Steffen, Will, Johan Rockström, and Robert Costanza. 2011. 'How Defining Planetary Boundaries can Transform our Approach to Growth'. *The Solutions Journal* 2 (3): 59–65.

These authors contributed to the systemic view discussed in this chapter. In this short article, they explain the concept of 'planetary boundaries', referring to the specific limits that humanity must keep within to maintain a global environment that is conductive to human well-being.

 For additional material and resources, please visit the online resources at: www.oup.com/he/morin1e

Chapter references

Andonova, Liliana B., and Marc A. Levy. 2003. 'Franchising Global Governance: Making Sense of the Johannesburg Type II Partnerships'. In *Yearbook of International Cooperation on Environment and Development 2003–2004*, edited by Olav Schram Stokke and Øystein B. Thommessen, 19–31. London: Earthscan.

Andresen, Steinar. 2007. 'The Effectiveness of UN Environmental Institutions'. *International Environmental Agreements: Politics, Law and Economics* 7 (4): 317–336.

Arndt, Channing ,and Finn Tarp. 2017. 'Aid, Environment and Climate Change'. *Review of Development Economics* 21 (2): 285–303.

Bäckstrand, Karin. 2006. 'Democratizing Global Environmental Governance? Stakeholder Democracy after the World Summit on Sustainable Development'. *European Journal of International Relations* 12 (4): 467–498.

Bakaki, Zorzeta, and Thomas Bernauer. 2017. 'Do Global Climate Summits Influence Public Awareness and Policy Preferences Concerning Climate Change?' *Environmental Politics* 26 (1): 1–26.

Barbier, Edward B., and Joanne C. Burgess. 2017. 'The Sustainable Development Goals and The Systems Approach to Sustainability'. *Economics: The Open-Access, Open-Assessment E-Journal* 11 (28): 1–23.

Bernstein, Steven F. 2001. *The Compromise of Liberal Environmentalism*. New York: Columbia University Press.

Bernstein, Steven F. 2013. 'Rio+20: Sustainable Development in a Time of Multilateral Decline'. *Global Environmental Politics* 13 (4): 12–21.

Biermann, Frank, Norichika Kanie, and Rakhyun Kim. 2017. 'Global Governance by Goal-Setting: The Novel Approach of The UN Sustainable Development Goals'. *Current Opinion in Environmental Sustainability* 26–27: 26–31.

Blühdorn, Ingolfur, and Ian Welsh. 2007. 'Eco-Politics Beyond the Paradigm of Sustainability: A Conceptual Framework and Research Agenda'. *Environmental Politics* 16 (2): 185–205.

Blutstein, Harry. 2016. 'Assault on the Summit'. In *The Ascent of Globalisation*, 192–208. Manchester: Manchester University Press.

Borowy, Iris. 2013. *Defining Sustainable Development for Our Common Future: A History of the World Commission on Environment and Development (Brundtland Commission)*. New York: Taylor & Francis.

Brundtland, Gro Harlem. 2002. *Madam Prime Minister: A Life in Power and Politics*. New York: Farrar, Straus and Giroux.

Chasek, Pamela S. 2012. 'Incorporating Regional Priorities into Global Conference'. *Review of European Community and International Environmental Law* 21 (1): 4–11.

Chasek, Pamela S., and Lynn M. Wagner. 2016. 'Breaking the Mold: A New Type of Multilateral Sustainable Development Negotiation'. *International Environmental Agreements: Politics, Law and Economics* 16 (3): 397–413.

Clapp, Jennifer, and Peter Dauvergne. 2011. *Paths to a Green World: The Political Economy of the Global Environment*. Cambridge, MA: MIT Press.

Clark, Ann Marie, Elisabeth J. Friedman, and Kathryn Hochstetler. 1999. 'The Sovereign Limits of Global Civil Society: A Comparison of NGO Participation in UN World Conferences on the Environment, Human Rights, and Women'. *World Politics* 51 (1): 1–35.

Conca, Ken. 2004. 'Environmental Governance after Johannesburg: From Stalled Legalization to Environmental Human Rights'. *Journal of International Law and International Relations* 1 (1–2): 121–138.

Conca, Ken, and Geoffrey Dabelko. 2015. *Green Planet Blues: Critical Views on Global Environmental Politics*. 5th ed. Boulder. CO: Westview Press.

Doyle, Timothy. 1998. 'Sustainable Development and Agenda 21: The Secular Bible of Global Free Markets and Pluralist Democracy'. *Third World Quarterly* 19 (4): 771–786.

Dryzek, John. 2005. *The Politics of the Earth: Environmental Discourses*. Oxford: Oxford University Press.

Eitman, D. J. 2001. 'Maintaining Sovereignty and the Tropical Rainforests: The Promise of Debt-for-Nature Swaps'. *Environs: Environmental Law and Policy Journal* 24 (2): 29–47.

Ferguson, Peter. 2015. 'The Green Economy Agenda: Business as Usual or Transformative Discourse'. *Environmental Politics* 24 (1): 17–37.

Ferns, George, and Kenneth Amaeshi. 2017. 'Struggles at the Summits. Discourse Coalitions, Field Boundaries, and the Shifting Role of Business in Sustainable Development'. *Business and Society* 58 (8): 1533–1571.

Gellers, Joshua C. 2016. 'Crowdsourcing Global Governance: Sustainable Development Goals, Civil Society, and the Pursuit of Democratic Legitimacy'. *International Environmental Agreements: Politics, Law and Economics* 16 (3): 415–432.

Greener, L. P. 1991. 'Debt-for-Nature Swaps in Latin American Countries: The Enforcement Dilemma'. *Connecticut Journal of International Law* 7 (1): 123–180.

Gupta, Joyeeta, and Courtney Vegelin. 2016. 'Sustainable Development Goals and Inclusive Development'. *International Environmental Agreements: Politics, Law and Economics* 16 (3): 433–448.

Gutner, Tamar. 2005. 'Explaining Gaps between Mandate and Performance: Agency Theory and World Bank Environmental Reform'. *Global Environmental Politics* 5 (2): 10–37.

Hicks, Robert L., Bradley C. Parks, J. Timmons Roberts, and Michael J. Tierney. 2008. *Greening Aid: Understanding the Environmental Impact of Development Assistance*. Oxford: Oxford University Press.

Holmes, George. 2012. 'Biodiversity for Billionaires: Capitalism, Conservation and the Role of Philanthropy in Saving/Selling Nature'. *Development and Change* 43 (1): 185–203.

Hopwood, Bill, Mary Mellor, and Geoff O'Brien. 2005. 'Sustainable Development: Mapping Different Approaches'. *Sustainable Development* 13 (1): 38–52.

Hurrell, Andrew, and Sandeep Sengupta. 2012. 'Emerging Powers, North–South Relations and Global Climate Politics'. *International Affairs* 88 (3): 463–484.

Ivanova, Maria. 2013. 'The Contested Legacy of Rio+ 20'. *Global Environmental Politics* 13 (4): 1–11.

Jacobs, Michael. 2013. 'Green Growth'. In *Handbook of Global Climate and Environmental Policy*, edited by Robert Falkner, 197–214. Oxford: Wiley Blackwell.

Jacques, Peter J., and Rafaella Lobo. 2018. 'The Shifting Context of Sustainability: Growth and the World Ocean Regime'. *Global Environmental Politics* 18 (4): 85–106.

Jinnah, Sikina. 2017. 'Makers, Takers, Shakers, Shapers: Emerging Economies and Normative Engagement in Climate Governance'. *Global Governance* 23 (2): 285–306.

Kamau, Macharia, Pamela Chasek, and David O'Connor. 2018. *Transforming Multilateral Diplomacy: The Inside Story of the Sustainable Development Goals*. Abingdon: Routledge.

Ladly, Sarah Davidson. 2012. 'Border Carbon Adjustments, WTO-Law and the Principle of Common but Differentiated Responsibilities'. *International Environmental Agreements* 12 (1): 63–84.

Lewis, Tammy L. 2003. 'Environmental Aid: Driven by Recipient Need or Donor Interests?' *Social Science Quarterly* 84 (1): 144–161.

Lövbrand, Eva, Mattias Hjerpe, and Björn-Ola Linnér. 2017. 'Making Climate Governance Global: How UN Climate Summitry Comes to Matter in a Complex Climate Regime'. *Environmental Politics* 26 (4): 580–599.

Lubchenco, J., E. B. Cerny-Chipman, J. N. Reimer, and S. A. Levin. 2016. 'The Right Incentives Enable Ocean Sustainability Successes and Provide Hope for the Future'. *Proceedings of the National Academy of Sciences* 113 (51): 14507–14514.

Marcoux, Christopher, Bradley C. Parks, Christian M. Peratsakis, J. Timmons Roberts, and Michael J. Tierney. 2013. 'Environmental and Climate Finance in a New World: How Past Environmental Aid Allocation Impacts Future Climate Aid'. WIDER Working Paper, No. 2013/128. Helsinki: UN University World Institute for Development Economics Research.

McAfee, Kathleen. 2016. 'Green Economy and Carbon Markets for Conservation and Development: A Critical View'. *International Environmental Agreements: Politics, Law and Economics* 16 (3): 333–353.

McManus, P. 1996. 'Contested Terrains: Politics, Stories and Discourses of Sustainability'. *Environmental Politics* 5 (1): 48–73.

Meadows, Donella H., Dennis L. Meadows, Jørgen Randers, and William W. Behrens III. 1972. *The Limits to Growth: A Report for the Club of Rome's Project on the Predicament of Mankind*. New York: Universe Books.

Meyer, John W., David John Frank, Ann Hironaka, Evan Schofer, and Nancy Brandon Tuma. 1997. 'The Structuring of a World Environmental Regime, 1870–1990'. *International Organization* 51 (4): 623–651.

Najam, Adil. 2005. 'Developing Countries and Global Environmental Governance: From Contestation to Participation to Engagement'. *International Environmental Agreements* 5 (3): 303–321.

Najam, Adil, and Cutler J. Cleveland. 2003. 'Energy and Sustainable Development at Global Environmental Summits: An Evolving Agenda'. *Environment, Development and Sustainability* 5 (1–2): 117–138.

Neal, S. M. 1998. 'Bringing Developing Nations on Board the Climate Change Protocol: Using Debt-for-Nature Swaps to Implement the Clean Development Mechanism'. *Georgetown International Environmental Law Review* 11 (1): 163–178.

Nordhaus, Ted, and Michael Shellenberger. 2007. *Break Through: From the Death of Environmentalism to the Politics of Possibility*. New York: Houghton Mifflin Harcourt.

Okereke, Chukwumerije. 2008. 'Equity Norms in Global Environmental Governance'. *Global Environmental Politics* 8 (3): 25–50.

Park, Jacob, Ken Conca, and Matthias Finger (eds). 2008. *The Crisis of Global Environmental Governance: Towards a New Political Economy of Sustainability*. Abingdon and New York: Routledge.

Park, Jeongwon B. 2016. 'Toward the Green Comfort Zone: Synergy in Environmental Official Development Assistance'. *Global Environmental Politics* 16 (4): 1–11.

Petersen, Lars Kjerulf. 2007. 'Changing Public Discourse on the Environment: Danish Media Coverage of the Rio and Johannesburg UN Summits'. *Environmental Politics* 16 (2): 206–230.

Roberts, J. Timmons, Bradley C. Parks, Michael J. Tierney, and Robert L. Hicks. 2009. 'Has Foreign Aid Been Greened?' *Environment: Science and Policy for Sustainable Development* 51 (1): 8–21.

Robinson, John. 2004. 'Squaring the Circle? Some Thoughts on the Idea of Sustainable Development'. *Ecological Economics* 48 (4): 369–384.

Rockström, Johan, Will Steffen, Kevin Noone, Åsa Persson, F. Stuart III Chapin, Eric Lambin et al. 2009. 'Planetary Boundaries: Exploring the Safe Operating Space for Humanity'. *Ecology and Society* 14 (2): article 32. Available at: http://www.ecologyandsociety.org/vol14/iss2/art32/, accessed October 2019.

Seyfang, Gill, and Andrew Jordan. 2002. 'The Johannesburg Summit and Sustainable Development: How Effective Are Environmental Conferences?'. In *Yearbook of International Co-operation on Environment and Development*, edited by Olav Schram Stokke and Øystein B. Thommessen, 19–39. London: Earthscan.

Sheikh, Pervase A. 2007. 'Debt-for-Nature Initiatives and the Tropical Forest Conservation Act (TFCA): Status and Implementation'. Congressional Research Service Report for Congress. Order Code RL31286.

Shiva, Vandana. 1989. *Staying Alive: Women, Ecology and Development*. London: Zed Books.

Shiva, Vandana. 1991. *The Violence of the Green Revolution: Third World Agriculture, Ecology, and Politics*. London: Zed Books.

Shiva, Vandana. 1997. *Biopiracy: The Plunder of Nature and Knowledge*. Boston, MA: South End Press.

Shiva, Vandana. 2004. 'The Future of Food: Countering Globalisation and Recolonization of Indian Agriculture'. *Futures* 36 (6–7): 715–732.

Shiva, Vandana. 2005. *Earth Democracy: Justice Sustainability and Peace*. London: Zed Books.

Shiva, Vandana. 2014. *The Vandana Shiva Reader*. Lexington: The University Press of Kentucky.

Skard, Torild. 2015. *Women of power: Half a century of female presidents and prime ministers worldwide.* Bristol: Policy Press.

Stadelmann, Martin, J. Timmons Roberts, and Axel Michaelowa. 2011. 'New and Additional to What? Assessing Options for Baselines to Assess Climate Finance Pledges'. *Climate and Development* 3 (3): 175–192.

Steffen, Will, Katherine Richardson, Johan Rockström, Sarah E. Cornell, Ingo Fetzer, Elena M. Bennett et al. 2015. 'Planetary Boundaries: Guiding Human Development on a Changing Planet'. *Science* 347 (6223): 1259855-1–1259855-10.

Steffen, Will, Johan Rockström, and Robert Costanza. 2011. 'How Defining Planetary Boundaries Can Transform Our Approach to Growth'. *The Solutions Journal* 2 (3): 59–65.

Stevens, Casey, and Norichika Kanie. 2016. 'The Transformative Potential of the Sustainable Development Goals (SDGs)'. *International Environmental Agreements: Politics, Law and Economics* 16 (3): 393–396.

Stone, Christopher D. 2004. 'Common and Differentiated Responsibilities in International Law'. *The American Journal of International Law* 98 (2): 276–301.

Strong, Maurice, F. 1972. 'The United Nations and the Environment'. *International Organization* 26 (2): 169–172.

Strong, Maurice, F. 1973. 'One Year after Stockholm: An Ecological Approach to Management'. *Foreign Affairs* 51 (4): 690–707.

Strong, Maurice, F. 1991. 'ECO '92: Critical Challenges and Global Solutions'. *Journal of International Affairs* 44 (2): 287–300.

Strong, Maurice, F. 1992. 'Energy, Environment and Development'. *Energy Policy* 20 (6): 490–494.

Strong, Maurice, F. 2000. *Where on Earth are we Going?* Canada: Vintage Canada.

Strong, Maurice, F. 2001. Keynote speech for the Symposium on Global Environmental Governance in the 21st Century, 27 November 2001, Ritsumeikan University, Kyoto, Japan.

United Nations Development Programme. 2016. *Debt for Nature Swaps: Financing Solutions for Sustainable Development.* New York: UNDP.

Victor, David G., and Lesley A. Coben. 2005. 'A Herd Mentality in the Design of International Environmental Agreements?' *Global Environmental Politics* 5 (1): 24–57.

Walsh, Sean, Huifang Tian, John Whalley, and Manmohan Agarwal. 2011. 'China and India's Participation in Global Climate Negotiations'. *International Environmental Agreements* 11 (3): 261–273.

Williams, Marc. 1993. 'International Trade and the Environment: Issues, Views and Challenges'. *Environmental Politics* 2 (4): 80–97.

Williams, Marc. 2005. 'The Third World and Global Environmental Negotiations: Interests, Institutions and Ideas'. *Global Environmental Politics* 5 (3): 48–69.

World Commission on Environment and Development. 1987. *Our Common Future.* Oxford: Oxford University Press.

Zaccai, Edwin. 2012. 'Over Two Decades in Pursuit of Sustainable Development: Influence, Transformation, Limits'. *Environmental Development* 1 (1): 79–90.

Part 4

Institutions and policies

7 International institutions

As several environmental problems have transnational implications, governments have been eager to establish international institutions to address these problems collectively. In the aftermath of the landmark 1972 Stockholm Summit on the Human Environment, states created several international institutions specifically dedicated to environmental protection. Over time, and in keeping with broader trends in global politics, these institutions have begun to interact with institutions that specialize on other topics. This chapter tracks international environmental institutions' development and impacts over time.

 Learning objectives

After reading this chapter, readers will be able to:

● Identify and historically situate the main international organizations and international regimes dealing with environmental protection;

● Explain the types of autonomy enjoyed by intergovernmental organizations devoted to environmental protection;

● Categorize the types of interactions that occur between different international institutions in global environmental governance; and

● Discuss the main reform proposals to reorganize global environmental governance architecture, as well as their advantages and drawbacks.

Introduction

What is the benefit of investing time and resources in solving transboundary environmental problems if other countries do not adopt similar measures? This question highlights the tension between collective and individual interests, a tension that characterizes most, if not all, global environmental issues (see Chapter 5). One important way to address this tension is to set up international **institutions** to facilitate cooperation between states.

Robert Keohane defines institutions as 'persistent and connected sets of rules (formal and informal) that prescribe behavioural roles, constrain activity, and shape expectations' (Keohane 1989: 3). Keohane further identifies three more specific categories of international institutions: international **regimes**, **intergovernmental organizations**, and **social norms**. Whereas social norms are addressed in Chapter 2, this chapter focuses on intergovernmental organizations and international regimes.

International regimes are sets of 'principles, norms, rules, and decision-making procedures around which actor expectations converge in a given issue-area' (Krasner 1982: 185).

One key aspect of this definition is the notion of issue areas: each regime evolves around one specific topic, or issue area. We speak of the **biodiversity** regime, or the desertification regime, for example.

Intergovernmental organizations are often thought to have three characteristics, which differentiate them from other types of international institutions. Centrally, these characteristics also help explain why, unlike other types of institutions, intergovernmental organizations are often able to become independent actors in their own right (Biermann and Siebenhüner 2009; Jinnah 2010, 2014). Firstly, intergovernmental organizations are brick and mortar institutions. They are 'material entities possessing physical location (or seats), offices, personnel, equipment, and budgets' (Young 1989a: 33), meaning that they have permanent bureaucracies and bodies (secretariats, chief executives, etc.), with budgets and physical headquarters. Secondly, intergovernmental organizations are created by international law, often backed by a corresponding charter, that gives them international recognition and international legal personality. This means that although intergovernmental organizations have a certain autonomy in the fulfilment of their functions and competencies, they can also be held responsible for any illegal actions they might engage in. Thirdly, intergovernmental organizations are created by states, which differentiates them from **non-governmental organizations**, business organizations, and administrative organizations like the International Standardization Organization.

Although these terms are often used interchangeably, there is important analytical utility in separating out international regimes and intergovernmental organizations as distinct concepts. For example, historically, an individual regime was largely thought to be made up of one intergovernmental organization along with its related treaties and **protocols**. However, with the proliferation of international institutions and the broadening scope of intergovernmental organizations, it is now widely understood that several intergovernmental organizations can be part of the same regime. For example, as shown in Figure 7.2 in Section 7.3, both the United Nations Food and Agriculture Organization and the International Tropical Timber Organization are part of the international regime on forests. In fact, an intergovernmental organization can also be part of several overlapping international regimes. For example, the United Nations Educational, Scientific and Cultural Organization (UNESCO), which primarily addresses scientific knowledge management, is also part of the international biodiversity regime through its World Heritage Convention, which seeks to conserve outstanding biodiverse sites across the globe.

There is a rich body of literature focusing on international institutions (i.e. international regimes and intergovernmental organizations), analysing their activities and their effects. The remainder of this chapter explores this literature, identifying key themes and debates. We analyse how institutional institutions have addressed environmental concerns (Section 7.1). We then discuss how international environmental institutions exhibit differing levels of autonomy (Section 7.2), before going on to look at the interactions between international institutions, in particular the dynamics of synergy and conflict between them (Section 7.3). Finally, we discuss the literature on actual or planned reforms to the institutional architecture for global environmental **governance** (Section 7.4).

7.1 The birth of environmental concerns in international institutions

Two explanations for the proliferation of international environmental institutions

Numerous international institutions deal with environmental protection. Table 7.1 displays some of the main intergovernmental organizations involved in global environmental governance. Each of these organizations oversees one or more environmental treaties, often with the support of a secretariat that may be financially provided by, but largely independent of, the parent organization (see Box 7.3). For example, the United Nations Environment Programme oversees several convention secretariats, including those for the Convention on

Table 7.1 A few intergovernmental organizations and the treaties associated with them

International organizations	Environmental agreements
International Union for Conservation of Nature	Ramsar Convention on Wetlands (1971)
United Nations Environment Programme	CITES Convention on Trade in Endangered Species (1972)
	Barcelona Convention on the Mediterranean (1976)
	Convention on Migratory Species (1979)
	Vienna Convention for the Protection of the Ozone Layer (1985)
	Basel Convention on Hazardous Waste (1989)
	Convention on Biological Diversity (1992)
	Rotterdam Convention on Chemicals (1998)
	Stockholm Convention on Persistent Organic Pollutants (2001)
	Minamata Convention on Mercury (2013)
Food and Agriculture Organization of the United Nations	International Treaty on Plant Genetic Resources (2001)
International Maritime Organization	London Convention on Marine Pollution (1954)
	MARPOL Convention (1973)
United Nations Educational, Scientific and Cultural Organization	World Heritage Convention (1971)
International Tropical Timber Organization	International Agreement on Tropical Timber (1986)
United Nations Economic Commission for Europe	Convention on Transboundary Air Pollution (1979)
	Espoo Convention on Environmental Impact Assessment (1991)
	Aarhus Convention on Access to Information and Justice on Environmental Matters (1998)
General Assembly of the United Nations	United Nations Framework Convention on Climate Change (1992)
Commission for the Conservation of Antarctic Marine Living Resources	Convention on the Conservation of Antarctic Resources (1980)
International Atomic Energy Agency	Convention on Nuclear Accidents (1986)
African Union	Bamako Convention on Hazardous Wastes (1991)

Source: The authors, based on the original treaty text.

Biological Diversity and the Vienna Convention for the Protection of the Ozone Layer. One notable exception is the Ramsar Convention on Wetlands, which is not attached to an inter-governmental organization, but instead is managed by the International Union for Conservation of Nature, a hybrid organization with state and non-state members.

The number of international environmental institutions has grown rapidly over time. As of 2019, states have concluded more than 3,000 **international environmental agreements** since the beginning of the twentieth century (Mitchell 2019). This proliferation largely results from two processes: *the establishment of new institutions*, and *the expanding scope of existing ones* (see Table 7.2; Kim 2013). On the former, global environmental summits have been one of the key moments for the creation of such organizations (see Chapter 6). For example, the United Nations Environment Programme was created in 1972, following the Stockholm Summit, and the United Nations Convention on Climate Change was agreed at the 1992 Rio Earth Summit.

The decision to *create a new intergovernmental organization* is sometimes born from dis-satisfaction among states regarding existing organizations' ability to address environmental issues (Oh and Matsuoka 2017). For example, after the failure of the League of Nations to regu-late whaling from 1920 to 1946, governments created the independent International Whaling Commission in 1946 (Meyer et al. 1997). Then, due to their dissatisfaction with the moratorium on whaling adopted by the International Whaling Commission in 1982, Iceland and Norway created a new organization, the North Atlantic Marine Mammal Commission in 1992.

The second mode through which international environmental institutions proliferate is by *expanding the scope of existing international institutions*. Several international institutions that did not originally focus on the environment have gradually come to operate in this field. For example, in the 1980s the Organisation for Economic Co-operation and Development, the United Nations Food and Agriculture Organization, the World Health Organization, and the United Nations Industrial Development Organization began to study closely the benefits and risks posed by **genetically modified organisms**.

It is common for intergovernmental organizations to favour extending their existing man-dates, rather than creating a new organization. When one organization has a certain level of expertise in a particular field, it tends to cultivate and support this expertise to guarantee its

Table 7.2 The emergence of environmental issues in the organizational landscape

	Within the United Nations	Outside the United Nations
Creation of a new institution	Examples: • United Nations Environment Programme • Global Environment Fund • High-Level Political Forum on Sustainable Development	Examples: • European Environment Agency • International Whaling Commission • OSPAR Convention for the Protection of the Marine Environment of the North-East Atlantic
Extension of an existing institution's mandate	Examples: • United Nations Educational, Scientific and Cultural Organization • United Nations Industrial Development Organization • Food and Agriculture Organization of the United Nations	Examples: • Organisation for Economic Co-operation and Development • International Energy Agency • Association of Southeast Asian Nations

own development, and sometimes even its continued relevance and financial survival in a world of scarce resources. Existing expertise can also attract new experts to an organization and facilitate the negotiation of new agreements to cover new and emerging related issues.

Often, this organizational expansion starts with simple political declarations, which are subsequently supplemented by more detailed **framework conventions**, and later by more specific protocols and amendments. In this way, for many organizations a dynamic of positive feedback favours mandate expansion to cover new and emerging issues, while still also maintaining the original issue focus of the organization. For example, this dynamic helps explain why the International Maritime Organization, which already dealt with marine pollution, took charge of the 1973 International Convention for the Prevention of Pollution from Ships.

As a result of these expansion processes, a wide range of international institutions deal with environmental issues. Some of these institutions are hosted within the United Nations system, while others have been created outside that system. There are several explanations why certain new international environmental organizations are created independently of the United Nations (Andresen 2001). One main explanation involves the scale of action. Regional problems, such as the pollution of a specific ecosystem, are often dealt with by regional organizations, outside the United Nations (Balsiger and Prys 2016). This is the case, for example, with the Convention for the Protection of the Marine Environment of the North-East Atlantic (known as the OSPAR Convention). In contrast, problems with global impact, such as **ozone layer** depletion, are often addressed through the United Nations system, such as through the United Nations Environment Programme. Confusingly, some regional issues are also addressed by multilateral organizations, such as the 1975 Mediterranean Action Plan, established under the United Nations Environment Programme to address common challenges of marine environmental degradation.

The greening of international institutions

What motivates existing intergovernmental organizations to embrace new environmental missions, and what are the consequences of this expansion? A debate about why and how these intergovernmental organizations have handled environmental concerns emerged in the 1990s (Park 2007). The debate focused on whether they would truly embrace environmental concerns ('greening process') or if they would simply embrace environmental concerns strategically as an opportunity to raise their profile on the international political agenda ('greenwashing dynamic'). Many analysts agree that the greening of institutions that do not specialize in the environment is 'positive, but insufficient' for addressing environmental issues in international politics (Andresen 2001: 19).

To differentiate the 'greening' from the **'greenwashing'** of international institutions, it is useful to distinguish internal from external factors—without ruling out the possibility of interactions between the two (Luken 2009: 161). Factors internal to the organization are linked to its organizational culture and the standards followed by its staff; they are more likely to bring about new concerns at the heart of the organization. In contrast, external factors are related to the need to find new resources or activities to revitalize the institution or to respond to criticism from civil society. Forced conversion from an external source is more likely to lead to strategic and superficial changes.

Yet, in some cases, external factors can also lead to the 'greening' of international institutions. One classic example that is widely documented in the literature is the greening of the World Bank (see Box 7.1). This process began in the 1980s in response to environmental NGOs highlighting the bank's allocation of loans to development projects that had disastrous environmental consequences. This NGO activity both acted as a catalyst for the bank to adopt an environmental strategy, and motivated states to create a new financial institution specifically dedicated to environmental projects: the Global Environment Facility (see Box 7.2).

Box 7.1 The politics of funding environmental projects: the World Bank

The World Bank is an international financial institution that provides loans to countries for capital programmes, including industrial agriculture and large infrastructure projects (e.g. roads, dams, and energy investments). It was created in 1944 following World War II, as one of the three Bretton Woods institutions, whose aim was to rebuild the post-war economy and promote international economic cooperation. Its twin goals are to reduce poverty and increase economic prosperity, which are closely tied to the bank's purposes of promoting private foreign investment and international trade. Developed countries, primarily the US, dominate decision-making at the World Bank, which weights decision-making power according to the amount of money a country contributes to the bank.

World Bank projects have been criticized by environmental groups for producing negative environmental consequences. Environmental campaigns in the 1980s pointed to the World Bank's contribution to forest destruction, for instance, by financing logging, road-building through forested areas, pesticide-intensive agricultural projects, and mega-dams that flooded large riparian areas and forced migration. At that time, the World Bank only considered environmental issues when they posed problems for the success of its projects; environmental degradation resulting from its projects was considered unavoidable. One of these projects was the construction of the Polonoroeste road through the Amazon, which began in 1981. Although this project helped to connect the various regions of Brazil, it also had a catastrophic impact on biodiversity and on the living conditions of local populations. The World Bank thus drew criticism from NGOs and governments alike, but also from the US Congress, which threatened to suspend its contributions to the bank unless it would begin to engage in these issues.

Although at first the World Bank was resistant to charges of environmental malfeasance associated with its projects, it started to implement some limited environmental initiatives in the 1970s, such as the establishment of a new environmental unit and an environmental advisor. By the late 1980s and early 1990s, the World Bank had created a new environmental department, increased environment-related staff, required **environmental impact assessments** on all of its projects, and increased lending for environmentally beneficial projects. Despite these changes, many continued to criticize the environmental degradation caused by large-scale World Bank-supported projects and the bank's inadequate **implementation** of its new environmental policies.

Several large-scale assessments of the bank's work followed in the 1990s. These studies showed that the greening of the bank was still only superficial, and was simply a response to external pressures from important donors and NGOs. The World Bank merely adopted environmental standards that were close to its traditional policies, like including an impact assessment for current projects, rather than changing its policies significantly. Yet, a few specialists have noted some important changes in the bank, such as creating an 'Environmentally and Socially Sustainable Development Network' as part of its internal structure in 1996, and adopting its own environmental strategy in 2001. It is also important to recognize that the bank has made more significant efforts on environmental issues than it has on other cross-sectional issues such as gender equality.

Sources: Lindenthal and Koch 2013; Park 2005; Reed 1997; Siebenhüner 2008; Zawahri and Weinthal 2014.

So far, other international financial institutions have not engaged in any meaningful discussion on a potential greening strategy. The New Development Bank (created in 2014) and the Asian Infrastructure and Investment Bank (created in 2016), which were created in response to dissatisfaction among emerging countries about their limited decision-making share at the World Bank, have communicated conflicting messages. On one hand, they finance projects with no conditionality criteria, which means that funded projects do not need to respect the World Bank's environmental or social standards. On the other hand, their agenda explicitly includes **sustainable development**, for instance in financing 'infrastructure and sustainable development projects' in emerging economies and **developing countries** (Hochstetler 2014). However, the way this sustainable development dimension will be implemented remains uncertain.

The United Nations Industrial Development Organization is another intergovernmental organization whose greening has raised similar debates. It initially had no activities related to environmental matters, working to support the industrial development of developing countries. In the 1980s it went through a crisis of confidence on the part of its member states, alongside a financial crisis, and this pushed it to invest in emerging fields such as the environment. In particular, it offered its services for the management of the multilateral fund of the Vienna Convention for the Protection of the Ozone Layer, and created an action group specifically to tackle environmental issues. In 1992, it succeeded in becoming an agency responsible for hosting the Vienna Convention, and the action group invested efforts in environmental projects, such as the protection of a large ecosystem in the Gulf of Guinea. These early environmental projects were a success for the Industrial Development Organization, whose funding was renewed by member states in response to these projects. Indeed, its portfolio changed radically over time. In 1992, 98 per cent of the projects it funded involved industrial development, while only 2 per cent were environmental. But by 2004, only 43 per cent of its projects were industrial, and environmental projects had jumped to 57 per cent (Luken 2009: 159). However, much like the World Bank, some of this greening appears only superficial. Though the number of environmental projects funded by the United Nations Industrial Development Organization has increased, their quality remains contested. The organization has focused on obtaining increased funding from the multilateral fund of the Vienna Convention and the Global Environment Facility, rather than ensuring that its projects are consistent with specific environmental objectives.

7.2 The autonomy of international institutions

Three perspectives on autonomy

Autonomy is one of the key variables used by scholars to analyse the actions of international institutions. Simply put, autonomy is the ability of international institutions to act independently of the preferences of their member states. States can delegate to intergovernmental organizations the authority to execute various governance tasks, including adopting regulations, monitoring **compliance**, enforcing rules, adjudicating disputes, and implementing projects (Nielson and Tierney 2003). Institutional autonomy varies between organizations. However, Jessica Green and Jeff Colgan (2013) argue that institutions operating in global environmental governance enjoy a particularly high degree of autonomy in comparison to those in other fields, for three main reasons: the field relies on technical expertise that institutions can often provide; it is characterized by a high level of complex interdependence, meaning that coordination by international institutions is very helpful; and it is commonly considered as unthreatening to states' core interests, so states are prepared to cede autonomy to these international institutions.

Three theoretical perspectives are central to understanding institutional autonomy (Hall and Taylor 1996). The first is the contractual *rational choice* perspective (see also Chapter 3). According to this perspective, states rationally establish contracts among them to maximize their individual interests. They will only create and become members of an institution if it serves their interests. This means that their choice will be rational ('rational choice') in terms of maximizing interests. The autonomy of intergovernmental organizations therefore depends directly on the interests of the states that create them. For example, when governments are confronted with a high level of uncertainty or when their preferences are less well formulated, as in new or highly technical issues, they are rationally more inclined to delegate a higher level of autonomy to intergovernmental organizations so that they may deal with this uncertainty (Jinnah 2014; Koremenos et al. 2001). The difficulty lies in creating the initiatives and guarantees that are needed to persuade reluctant governments to set up relatively autonomous international institutions (Thompson 2010; Urpelainen 2012). States might fear that a highly autonomous organization will drift away from its original mandate or will be captured by specific national interests.

The second perspective on institutional autonomy is the *historical institutionalist* framework. Much like rational choice scholars, scholars using this perspective recognize the importance of governments in the creation of international institutions. However, they believe that institutions, once created, alter the preferences of their member states: they create a climate of trust, encourage the sharing of information, reduce transaction costs, and ultimately favour cooperation. Instead of static contracts, international institutions are seen as dynamic forums supporting constant self-reinforcement. Although international institutions are created by governments to set their long-term cooperative relationships, the institutions themselves create the conditions in which governments are able to increase their cooperation even more. Thus, for historical institutionalists, institutions gradually gain autonomy (Young et al. 2008). As such, institutional autonomy can also vary over time as new issues emerge, state preferences develop, and conditions of trust evolve in an international institution (Jinnah 2014).

The third theoretical perspective is *sociological institutionalism*. An extreme interpretation of this perspective is that intergovernmental organizations are not just static contracts, or even dynamic forums, but rather autonomous actors that are relatively independent of their creators. The sociological institutionalist perspective challenges more mainstream understandings in international relations about the role of secretariats—the administrative arms of international organizations and often international treaties (see Figure 7.1). Secretariats are bureaucracies consisting of full-time professionals, organized in a hierarchical structure and operating under defined sets of rules. They typically lack formal decision-making authority and are often understood in international relations theory as agents of their state principals. This is in part why international relations scholarship has historically considered secretariats as neutral administrative actors, functionaries of member states, which merely carry out the delegated tasks prescribed to them, such as organizing meetings and distributing documents. However, in a sociological institutionalist perspective, scholars have also demonstrated that secretariats can exhibit high levels of autonomy under certain conditions, such as when they are addressing new or highly technical issues and/or when they serve a function that no other actors can fulfil (Jinnah 2014).

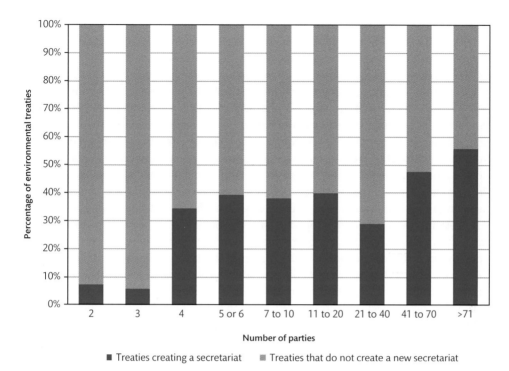

Figure 7.1 Relationship between the number of parties to an environmental treaty and the creation of a secretariat

Source data from: https://iea.uoregon.edu/

Organizations have their own bureaucratic culture, strategic interests, and normative preferences. As actors, they use their expertise and political legitimacy in an attempt to influence international debates. They can influence the processes and outcomes of international governance and even shape the preferences of member states (Jinnah 2014). The relative autonomy of these institutions is not, therefore, imparted by governments, nor is it gradually acquired through interactions with them, but rather it is established from within, when they are created. Due to this high level of autonomy, it is not uncommon, according to sociological institutionalists, for a discrepancy to form over time between the dominant ideas within an institution and those that circulate in its social environment, made up of its member states, other institutions, and **non-state actors** (Bauer 2006).

Assessing autonomy: The case of UNEP

An analysis of the United Nations Environment Programme's autonomy illustrates how these three theoretical perspectives operate in practice. If we examine this institution from a rational choice point of view, it becomes apparent that its member states have deliberately deprived it of autonomy (Ivanova 2007, 2012). When it was created in 1972, some developed countries feared the United Nations Environment Programme would be too strong a supporter of strict environmental regulations. Others feared that developing countries would take advantage of the organization, if the opportunity arose, to promote their own demands for a new global economic order (see Chapter 6). The collective decision was therefore made to maintain the United Nations Environment Programme as a programme, not a full organization, meaning that it cannot sign treaties, adopt regulations, or organize large environmental summits (Ivanova 2007: 339).

From a rational choice perspective, the autonomy of the United Nations Environment Programme is also hindered by a lack of material resources. Compared with other international institutions, its budget and the number of employees are relatively limited. The Programme does not have its own independent funding source—it receives less than 1 per cent of funding from the United Nations regular budget, the rest being covered mostly by voluntary contributions from the member states. Moreover, the fact that the United Nations Environment Programme was established in Nairobi, Kenya, is a significant organizational constraint. The decision to base it in a developing country was a hard-fought battle led by Kenya and the G77, despite concerns from developed countries about efficiency. Indeed, the location has caused technical and logistical problems due to reduced infrastructure and telecommunications resources, and distance from the usual international seats of power, such as New York or Geneva (Ivanova 2010: 48). When it comes to adding sustainable development issues to the agenda and allocating more financial resources to environmental protection, governments have several times preferred to create new institutions, such as the Global Environment Facility (Box 7.2), rather than adapting the United Nations Environment Programme.

Box 7.2 The Global Environment Facility: a key financial mechanism

The 1987 **Brundtland Commission** recommended the creation of a new funding organization explicitly to address problems arising at the intersection of the environment and development. Consequently, the Global Environment Facility was set up as a pilot project in 1991, with the United Nations Development Programme, the United Nations Environment Programme, and the World Bank identified as the three initial partners implementing the Facility's projects. In 1994, in response to criticism from developing countries and NGOs, the Facility was restructured, and became fully operational as an independent international organization headquartered in Washington.

Since 1994, the Global Environment Facility has served as the primary financial mechanism for several international environmental treaties, including the Convention on Biological Diversity and the United Nations Framework Convention on Climate Change. The Facility manages funding to support government projects and programmes in the areas of biodiversity, international waters, land degradation, chemicals and waste, and climate change mitigation. For example, it supports projects related to sustainable **conservation** and management of protected areas, and has a fund for climate **adaptation** projects in developing countries. Between 1991 and 2016, the Facility invested around $14.5 billion, and leveraged $75.4 billion in additional resources for 3,946 projects in 167 countries.

The governance of the Global Environment Facility is based on a compromise between the wishes of developed and developing countries. In short, the developing countries, along with NGOs and United Nations agencies, wanted the governance of the new mechanism to reflect the values of the United Nations system: transparency, accountability, democracy, and universality. On the other hand, the developed countries and the World Bank favoured a structure similar to the World Bank, which emphasizes efficiency, management, executive abilities, and decision-making based on which country contributes the most money. The end result is a hybrid between the two systems. The Facility's Governing Council decides which projects to finance, and consists of 32 members appointed by constituencies of member countries. Of these Council members, 14 are from developed countries, 16 from developing countries, and 2 from economies transitioning from a centrally planned to a market economy.

While the decision-making structure appears more egalitarian, and both developing and developed countries are actively involved, the balance of power in the Council is still weighted in favour of developed countries. This is primarily due to procedures for replenishing the fund, which allows major donors to make prerequisites for the funding in the form of 'policy recommendations'. After the Facility decides to provide a grant, one of the three implementing agencies is responsible for negotiating and implementing the project. Research shows that poorer countries contribute more to a project when the implementing agency is the World Bank than when a United Nations organization is given this task, suggesting that a state's economic strength affects their ability to bargain with more non-egalitarian international organizations.

Considering the need for financial backing to help solve environmental problems, and the need to address trade issues alongside environmental issues, the Global Environment Facility is an important player in global environmental politics. Understanding which interests dominate decision-making procedures seems to be key for understanding institutional outcomes and their implications for global environmental governance.

Sources: Bayer et al. 2015; Boisson de Chazournes 2005; Sovacool et al. 2017; Streck 2001.

Historical institutionalism, however, helps to temper this rational choice perspective on the United Nations Environment Programme's autonomy. The Programme has gradually shifted from a passive role managing pre-identified problems to a more active role defining new issues (Siebenhüner 2008). It has contributed in particular to formalizing and negotiating numerous multilateral agreements regarding the environment, including the Convention on the Conservation of Migratory Species of Wild Animals, the Montreal Protocol on Substances that Deplete the Ozone Layer, and the Convention on Biological Diversity. It has also participated in the implementation of multilateral agreements through training in developing countries. Finally, it has set up support measures, such as its ozone action programme and information platforms, to facilitate the sharing of knowledge.

In the historical institutionalist perspective, through these efforts the United Nations Environment Programme has been able to gradually gain the trust of states and eliminate any initial resistance, in developed countries as well as developing ones. In 1999, for example, the United Nations General Assembly created a Global Ministerial Environment Forum to bring together environment ministers on a regular basis. Although this forum never formally governed the United Nations Environment Programme, it still had a strong influence on it as it was deliberately organized at the same time and in the same location as the Board of Directors of the Programme. The Global Ministerial Environment Forum thus helped to increase the visibility and political legitimacy of the United Nations Environment Programme on both national and international levels. Moreover, at the Rio+20 Summit in 2012 governments agreed to grant the Programme more autonomy. Its budget was increased and stabilized, its council was reformed to allow all member states of the United Nations a seat, and its physical presence in various regions of the world was reinforced. To mark this change, the United Nations Environment Programme's Board of Directors was renamed the 'United Nations Environment Assembly', and its first meeting was held in Nairobi in June 2014.

Finally, from a sociological institutionalist perspective, insisting on the importance of international civil servants, the United Nations Environment Programme has long enjoyed important elements of autonomy. In line with sociological institutionalism, the very first leaders of the United Nations Environment Programme's secretariat, Maurice Strong (see Box 6.3) and Mostafa Tolba, endowed a spirit of autonomy on the organization from the very beginning. Importantly, they worked to strengthen the organization's expertise and to develop its relations with important partners, beyond the member states.

An important element of the United Nations Environment Programme's autonomy is its technical expertise, which enables it to formulate authoritative opinions regarding the state of the environment across the world. For example, the Programme has access to several control networks and satellites, allowing it to monitor deforestation and gather maritime data. This information can then be shared via an environment alert service and through reports on the state of the planet, such as the series of publications entitled 'The Global Environment Outlook'. The United Nations Environment Programme's technical knowledge allows it to provide important guidance to states and others on global environmental challenges.

United Nations Environment Programme leaders also strategically overcome its financial and institutional limitations by establishing partnerships. It often works with other United Nations specialized agencies and private partners. For instance, it has been working hand in hand with corporations to develop the 1997 Global Reporting Initiative, which creates standards for assessing the social, economic, and environmental performance of businesses. The United Nations Environment Programme has also supported the development of environmental laws and institutions in Africa through the Partnership for the Development of Environmental Laws and Institutions in Africa programme (1994–2006), in collaboration with the United Nations Development Programme, the World Bank, the International Union for the Conservation of Nature, and donor countries (Tarasofsky and Hoare 2004: 10). The United Nations Environment Programme is thus recognized as one of the international institutions that is most able to organize a network of public, private, and mixed institutions around the subject of sustainable development (Abbott and Snidal 2010).

Box 7.3 Convention secretariats as political players

Secretariats' activities can influence politics via several different mechanisms. A secretariat might provide critical background information to help states make decisions, train state actors on institutional rules, lobby a state actor to introduce a new idea into a negotiating process, and/or write draft decisions in dispute-settlement procedures. In these ways, secretariats can actually shape power relations between states by designing rules and institutions, restructuring capacities and relationships among states, and shaping norms and ideas. For example, in the early 1990s the Convention on Biological Diversity secretariat originally developed, through an information document prepared for its members states, the suite of practices that define how the Convention cooperates with other international biodiversity institutions, for instance through joint work programmes on issues of common concern.

Some scholars have argued that the fragmented landscape of international politics, characterized by a plethora of overlapping international treaties and regimes, provides opportunities for secretariats to exert influence. Secretariats can use their networks, capacities, and expertise to coordinate across multiple overlapping regimes—something that states are often unable to do on a large scale. This enables secretariats to influence who is involved in governance and what is being governed, making certain outcomes more or less likely. For example, the secretariat of the United Nations Framework Convention on Climate Change played a heavy role in engaging subnational and private actors through the Momentum for Change initiative, which is intended to highlight forms of climate action occurring on different scales.

Recent scholarship has further argued that secretariats are most likely to influence politics when they fulfil roles that few other actors can perform, and when states lack strong preferences on an issue. A secretariat's ability to influence governance also depends on how much autonomy it has, or the extent to which it can act without direct instruction from its member states. Some scholars have demonstrated, for example, how the secretariat of the United Nations Framework Convention on Climate Change is heavily constrained by rules imposed by member states, whereas the secretariat of the Convention on Biological Diversity has considerable autonomy, and could thus play a larger role in shaping negotiations. Additional factors that come into play in shaping secretariats' influence include the mandate of the secretariat, organizational factors such as size and budget, and both the secretariat's and member states' perceptions of the secretariat's role. Recent research has shown that an increase in available resources can provide secretariats with more autonomy, even if they were initially highly constrained. In addition, delegation theory suggests that states can influence secretariats by adjusting their budgets and thus the scope of their work.

It is also important to note that not all secretariats seem to have a great deal of influence. For example, research shows that the Division for Sustainable Development, which served the now defunct Commission on Sustainable Development, had little influence on procedures and outcomes in the Commission, although it did have some influence in promoting the participation of **major groups** and developing countries.

Importantly, recent research has also demonstrated how secretariats themselves obscure their influence, to avoid perceptions of partiality or bias. Whereas secretariat influence could be seen as supporting particular state interests, scholars have argued that secretariats typically see themselves as 'guardians' of the treaties and institutions they serve, rather than as political actors per se. Some scholars have highlighted that in serving as guardians of their institutions they also serve as guardians of the established world order, where powerful states most often define what those institutions contain and stand for. Interestingly, research shows that some powerful states, such as the United States, sought to maximize the autonomy of the United Nations Environment Programme secretariat in anticipation that they would be able to exert influence over it. This approach was in contrast to that of developing countries, which sought to ensure intergovernmental control.

Sources: Bauer and Ege 2017; Biermann and Siebenhüner 2009; Jinnah 2014; Jörgens et al. 2017; Kolleck et al. 2017; Manulak 2017; Michaelowa and Michaelowa 2017; Widerberg and van Laerhoven 2014.

The development of such entrepreneurship by civil servants working in the United Nations Environment Programme has created a certain amount of turmoil and tension. In reaction to what has sometimes been perceived as overstepping their limits, several convention secretariats supported by the United Nations Environment Programme have gradually become more autonomous and their officers have asked for independence from the Programme (see Box 7.3).

7.3 Interactions between international institutions

From institutional interactions to regime complexes

Since the 2000s, growing attention has been paid to interactions between international institutions. This new focus can be explained by the rapid increase in the number of international institutions, which has created significant institutional density and led to normative and functional overlap between institutions (Biermann et al. 2009; Oberthür and Stokke 2011; Raustiala and Victor 2004).

As the number of international institutions has proliferated and their scope expanded, the concept of individual institutions and/or regimes has become inadequate for understanding international political dynamics. Inspired by Oran Young's early work on interactions, or interplay, between international institutions (see Box 7.4), the concept of regime complexes has emerged to help capture this new complexity. The term was first coined by Kal Raustiala and David Victor (2004), to describe the global governance institutions for **genetic resources**. Raustiala and Victor observed that the management of genetic resources was not unfolding within a single regime, but was crossing different international regimes, such as the biodiversity conservation regime as well as regimes outside the environmental field, such as those addressing intellectual property rights. They also noticed strategic behaviour by states with regard to these different international regimes. Certain states were practising 'forum shopping', by choosing to voice their concerns in institutions whose rules and norms closely corresponded to their interests.

Box 7.4 A foundational thinker on global environmental institutions: the work of Oran Young

Much of our understanding of international environmental institutions builds on the foundational theoretical, empirical, and methodological contributions of Professor Oran Young. Young's scholarship over the course of 50 years has theoretically uncovered why international environmental institutions form, how they are designed, and the conditions under which they are effective in reaching their goals. His scholarship explores how environmental regimes play key roles in helping societies solve a wide range of problems emerging from human activity (such as urban development) that affect the environment, and conversely environmental impacts (such as drought) on human societies.

Oran Young is one of the most prolifically published and cited authors on these issues. His early work was strongly theoretical, writing primarily on international relations and institutional processes (such as mediation, bargaining, and international interdependence) in the realm of security and international crises. During the 1970s, Young's writing shifted slightly to theorize more extensively about international regimes and international cooperation, and to focus empirically more on environmental affairs and Arctic issues. His 1977 book entitled *Resource Management at the International Level: The Case of the North Pacific* became a foundational work in global environmental governance due to its contribution to the development of international regimes as a unit of analysis. His scholarship on the Arctic has further brought to light emerging security, economic, and environmental issues in the region.

Importantly, Young's research on international regimes suggests that clear and carefully designed rules and decision-making procedures can foster international cooperation among actors (including states), which can help to avoid overuse of natural resources and pollution sinks. This work was particularly important, in that it challenged assumptions that were dominant at the time in the field of international relations about the barriers to international cooperation in the absence of centralized authority.

Young's research has also explored why and when international institutions form, finding that they can form spontaneously, be negotiated, or be imposed by dominant states. The functions of international institutions vary, ranging from simply regulating decision-making, pooling resources, or promoting and generating (international) norms. Young distinguishes between the 'effectiveness' of environmental and resource regimes (solving or mitigating the problems for which they were created), versus 'effects' that include the broader and indirect impacts an institution may have beyond the specific environmental problem it targets (see Chapter 8). For instance, an international institution on arms control can influence world peace, but also environmental quality, international trade, and political stability. Young's work has further catalysed a lot of research surrounding the interplay between international regimes. For example, he highlights the interaction between climate change and ozone regimes with respect to both their shared funding mechanism, and their diverging treatment of some chemicals, such as chlorofluorocarbons, which are both ozone-depleting substances and potent **greenhouse gases**.

In addition to studying international institutions, Young has also contributed to building them. He helped establish a variety of international committees on science and environmental change. For example, Young was the founding chair of the Committee on the Human Dimensions of Global Change of the National Academy of Science in the United States; launched the Working Group on Arctic International Relations; served as a vice president of the International Arctic Science Committee; carried out projects for the Standing Committee of Parliamentarians of the Arctic Region; and chaired the steering committee of the Arctic Governance Project. His enrolment in these committees also demonstrated his will to inform policy through science.

Sources: Mitchell 2013; Young 1977, 1979, 1982, 1989b, 1999a, 1999b, 2002, 2013, 2016.

The regime complex concept quickly took off in global governance scholarship and has been widely cited and used to study a broad range of issue areas. As it became more widely used, the definition became more specific. For example, Amandine Orsini, Jean-Frédéric Morin, and Oran Young have defined a regime complex as a 'network of three or more international regimes that relate to a common subject matter; exhibit overlapping membership; and generate substantive, normative, or operative interactions recognized as potentially problematic whether or not they are managed effectively' (Orsini et al. 2013: 29). Figure 7.2 represents two regime complexes in global environmental politics, one centred on biodiversity and the other on climate change. It shows how several international regimes interact in global climate change governance. For example, the regime on forests interacts with the climate regime because forests are potential **carbon sinks**, and the ozone layer regime interacts with climate because some substitutes for ozone-depleting substances also have a huge impact on global warming.

Importantly, the fact that an environmental problem is governed by a regime complex does not mean that this problem is itself necessarily complicated. It means, however, that this problem is governed by a structure of institutions, which holds properties beyond the sum of the different institutions that make it up. For instance, ideas from one of the institutions that make up the regime complex might quickly and more easily diffuse to the other institutions within the regime complex. For example, the negative environmental externalities of biofuel production, initially recognized in the European Union Directive on Renewable Energy, were subsequently taken into account by the United Nations Framework Convention on Climate Change and the World Bank, due to the cross-participation of non-state actors to these three processes (Orsini and Godet 2018).

The concept of regime complex is related to, but distinct from, other conceptualizations surrounding the density of international institutions in international politics. Notably, other scholars use the concept of *fragmentation* to describe the multitude of overlapping institutions operating in international environmental law (Biermann et al. 2009; Zelli and van Asselt 2013). *Fragmentation* is more normative than a regime complex, as it traditionally points to the need for increased synergy among various institutional elements.

The concept of regime complex has been criticized on a number of grounds. One critique is that the concept focused too strongly on intergovernmental organizations, neglecting other types of institutions, including informal organizations, civil society institutions, and private actors. Increasingly however, authors have studied the emergence and influence of private actors within regime complexes as well (Green and Auld 2017; Orsini 2013). On climate change for instance, a wide set of institutions govern climate change, including intergovernmental

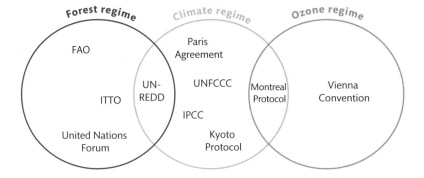

FAO: Food and Agriculture Organization
IPBES: Intergovernmental Science-Policy Platform on Biodiversity and Ecosystem Services
IPCC: Intergovernmental Panel on Climate Change
ITTO: International Tropical Timber Organization
UNFCC: United Nations Framework Convention on Climate Change
UN-REDD: United Nations Collaborative Programme on Reducing Emissions from Deforestation and Forest Degradation in Developing Countries

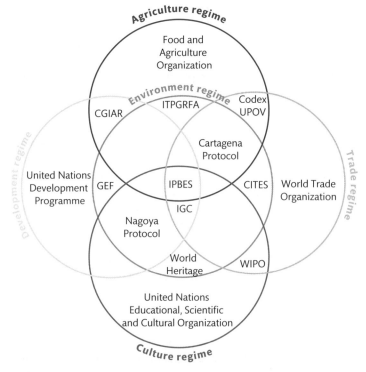

CGIAR: Consultative Group on International Agricultural Research
CITES: Convention on International Trade in Endangered Species
Codex: Codex Alimentarius Commission
FAO: Food and Agriculture Organization
GEF: Global Environment Facility
IGC: Intergovernmental Committee
IPBES: Intergovernmental Science-Policy Platform on Biodiversity and Ecosystem Services
ITPGRFA: International Treaty on Plant Genetic Resources for Food and Agriculture
UPOV: Union for the Protection of New Varieties of Plants
WIPO: World Intellectual Property Organization

Figure 7.2 Environmental regime complexes centred on biodiversity and climate change

agreements, development banks, international scientific panels, transnational private regulations, agencies specialized on energy, free trade agreements, and international networks of cities (Abbott 2012; Keohane and Victor 2011).

The concept of regime complex also involves a risk of tautological reasoning as the structure (the regime complex) both influences its units (its individual institutions) and is also made up of these same units. Scholars have called for the reintroduction of clear sequencing in the study of the different evolutionary steps of regime complexes to clarify the links between the units and the structure (Morin and Orsini 2014). Empirically, some have argued that we need further detailed case studies to refine our analytical tools and better support the generalizability of current research results (Alter and Raustiala 2018). Regardless of these criticisms, the term continues to gain relevance. Scholars work, among others, on potential policy solutions to effectively manage regime complexes, including as related to who should be held responsible for decision-making in a regime complex system.

Characterizing interactions between international institutions

There are at least four types of interactions between international institutions. First, institutional interactions can be of a *cognitive nature*, reflecting the fact that several institutions produce information on interconnected empirical issues. For example, the Convention on International Trade in Endangered Species and the World Customs Organization have cognitive interactions: the former has produced numerous reports expressing its point of view on customs inspections for endangered species, which were then considered by the latter in its work on border control.

Second, the interactions between international institutions can be *commitment-based* when states must comply with closely related, or sometimes even conflicting, obligations set out in different institutions to which they belong. For example, Indonesia's commitments under its bilateral trade agreements related to the export of palm oil interact with its commitments within the Association of Southeast Asian Nations on the restriction of transboundary air pollution. Burning, which is highly polluting, is the main technique used to clear land for setting up new palm plantations. This means that Indonesia's commitments under these different institutions are contradictory.

Third, institutional interactions can be *behavioural* in nature when they relate to how member states comply with their commitments under overlapping institutions. For example, Brazil is engaged in biodiversity conservation under the Convention on Biological Diversity, but it also has several marine protected areas projects through the World Bank. Both commitments are quite synergetic in theory but their implementation could be problematic, especially if the World Bank environmental criteria are less stringent than those of the Convention on Biological Diversity.

Fourth, interactions can be related to *impacts* when decisions under one regime impact outcomes under another regime. For example, since cod eats herring, a European agreement on cod fishing quotas will have a negative impact on the herring protection agreements made with Norway, as more cod means less herring (Oberthür and Gehring 2011: 37–42).

All four types of interaction can result in conflicts or synergies between institutions. The interaction between the ozone and climate regimes described earlier, for example, is one of conflictual interaction. In contrast, the interactions between the World Customs Union and the Convention on International Trade in Endangered Species discussed above are synergistic.

Table 7.3 Modes of interaction between regimes

		Norms	
		Compatible	Divergent
Rules	Compatible	**Type I** Largely synergistic *(The Convention on Biological Diversity and the Ramsar Convention)*	**Type II** To some extent synergistic *(The International Tropical Timber Agreement and the Convention on Biological Diversity)*
	Divergent	**Type III** Reciprocally harmful *(The Montreal and Kyoto Protocols)*	**Type IV** High conflict potential *(The Cartagena Protocol and the Agreement on Sanitary and Phytosanitary Measures)*

Source: authors, categorization inspired by Rosendal 2001.

Further, these interactions can emerge across regime norms or regime rules. Norms are understood as general standards underpinning the institutions and rules are specific prescriptions for behaviour (Rosendal 2001). Table 7.3 shows the different types of interactions between regimes, with examples involving environmental institutions.

Type I interactions are those in which both the norms and rules of the institutions involved are synergistic or compatible—for example, interactions between the Convention on Biological Diversity and the Ramsar Convention on Wetlands, which share the core norm of conservation and use protected areas as instruments.

Type II interactions are those in which the institutions' norms differ but their rules are compatible. The interaction between the International Tropical Timber Organization and the Convention on Biological Diversity is one example. The core norm of the International Tropical Timber Organization is to increase trade in tropical wood, which is in opposition to biodiversity conservation, the key norm of the Convention on Biological Diversity. However, in establishing quotas on wood trade as a rule to achieve their objective, the International Tropical Timber Organization does not conflict with the Convention on Biological Diversity.

In Type III interactions, the institutions involved share common norms, but their rules conflict or are incompatible. For example, the Montreal Protocol on Substances that Deplete the Ozone Layer and the United Nations Framework Convention on Climate Change have compatible norms of environmental protection, but diverge with respect to at least one of their rules. The Montreal Protocol encourages the use of hydrofluorocarbons in place of chemicals that damage the ozone layer. At the same time, these chemical compounds are a potent greenhouse gas targeted under the Kyoto Protocol. As such, both agreements share environmental protection norms, but they have incompatible rules and are therefore mutually detrimental. This is why in 2016 the parties to the Montreal Protocol negotiated the Kigali Amendment aimed at phasing down hydrofluorocarbons and replacing them with climate-friendly substances, which entered into force on 1 January 2019.

Lastly, Type IV interactions are the most problematic and involve incompatible norms and incompatible rules. There are no instances where these interactions exist between international institutions specializing in environmental issues. However, they can occur between institutions of different policy fields, such as between environmental and trade institutions.

This is the case, for example, for the Cartagena Protocol on Biosafety and the World Trade Organization's Agreement on Sanitary and Phytosanitary Measures (see Box 1.2). The former restricts trade of genetically modified organisms and includes provisions based on the **precautionary principle**. The latter favours trade in agricultural products and is based on risk assessment procedures. Their approaches to scientific evidence related to risks over genetically modified organisms is so drastically different that some interpretations of the Cartagena Protocol can lead to domestic measures that are incompatible with the obligation of the World Trade Organization's agreement (Oberthür and Gehring 2006).

Conceptualizing interactions through time

There are four phases in the regime complex life cycle, which illuminate the importance and nature of interactions between multiple institutions as they change over time. When regimes working on a common theme are isolated and maintain no effective relationship, the regime complex is *fragmented*. At a later stage—*competition*—the regimes compete to take up a key position in the complex. At the third stage institutions *specialize* in specific roles or subthemes within the complex. And at the fourth stage—*integration*—the complex becomes unified. A stable equilibrium can be maintained at each of these stages, but it is also possible for a regime complex to go through these various stages sequentially (Morin and Orsini 2014).

The regime complex on genetic resources, for example, has evolved through all of these four stages. This complex was fragmented until the 1980s: the international trade, agriculture, and intellectual property regimes—reflected in the General Agreement on Tariffs and Trade, the Food and Agriculture Organization, and the World Intellectual Property Organization respectively—were largely disconnected. From the early 1990s, with the adoption of the Convention on Biological Diversity and the Agreement on the Trade-Related Aspects of Intellectual Property Rights under the World Trade Organization, the complex entered into a stage of competition. For instance, while the Food and Agriculture Organization promoted farmers' rights to freely use genetic resources, the Agreement on the Trade-Related Aspects of Intellectual Property Rights promoted the rights of corporate innovators to require farmers who use patented technologies to pay for those products. Also, some institutions, such as the Convention on Biological Diversity, promoted the protection of **traditional knowledge** often held by indigenous and local communities, whereas others, such as the World Intellectual Property Organization, promoted the protection of restrictive intellectual property rights to knowledge. This highly conflictive normative atmosphere between international institutions operating in the regime complex led these institutions to become highly specialized. For example, the Food and Agriculture Organization took charge of genetic resources ex-situ, stored in gene banks or botanic gardens, whereas the Convention on Biological Diversity focused on the use of resources in-situ. The complex has since become progressively more integrated. For example, parties to the Convention on Biological Diversity gradually accepted the fact that intellectual property issues are largely resolved at the World Trade Organization or the World Intellectual Property Organization. Today, the structure of the regime complex for genetic resources is more or less organized around four unified poles: environment, intellectual property, agriculture, and trade. As a result, genetic resources can be exchanged and traded under precise rules for access and use.

International institutions do not necessarily strive for greater compatibility, as compatibility can also mean redundancy. Researchers and practitioners alike are now, therefore, questioning the possibility of reforming global environmental governance to reduce institutional conflicts and redundancy, to increase synergy and efficiency, or at least to better orchestrate cooperation between international institutions.

7.4 Designing global environmental governance

Creating a World Environment Organization?

Due to the limits of current environmental institutions such as the United Nations Environment Programme, and because of the redundant and fragmented proliferation of institutions more generally, there are recurrent debates surrounding the reform of global environmental governance. Some have argued that a discussion is needed on how to apply the sustainable development principles of 'reducing', 'reusing', and 'recycling' to the realm of international institutions (Papa 2015). Debates arise periodically at the United Nations General Assembly, the United Nations Economic and Social Council, and the United Nations Environment Programme. They also regularly appear on the agenda of major environmental summits such as the Rio+20 summit in 2012.

In these debates, several have proposed creating a World Environment Organization that would strengthen global environmental governance by upgrading the United Nations Environment Programme from a programme to a more autonomous and broader agency. This reform would also help reduce institutional fragmentation by designating one core institution to deal with environmental issues. Three primary models have been put forward for such an organization: a *cooperation model*, a *centralization model*, and a more *hierarchical model* (Biermann 2011). The *cooperation model* would involve creating a new forum that would expand the range of actors involved, to include NGOs and firms as well as the existing international institutions. Such a forum would encourage coordination and a better representation of different constituencies. In contrast, the *centralization model* would mean abolishing all the existing international environmental institutions, including the United Nations Environment Programme and all the secretariats of environmental treaties, to create one unique organization that would bring all fields of activity under the same umbrella. Finally, the *hierarchical model* would involve creating a core council, based on the United Nations **Security Council**, in which a limited number of key states would take part and make important decisions concerning the environment and the division of labour among the different international institutions.

It is often argued that a World Environment Organization would offer a number of benefits. First, it would offer increased political visibility by centralizing all environmental decisions, and increase organizational legitimacy by clarifying decision-making. It would also ensure greater consistency between environmental institutions as common discussions would be easier. It would remedy the current geographic dispersion of environmental institutions between Nairobi, Bonn, Geneva, New York, Montreal, and Washington, and condensing global environmental politics into a single forum would be more efficient. By creating an equivalent environmental organization, it would also help to offset the influence of the World Trade Organization and other powerful organizations. The collection of funds for environmental purposes is likely to be easier, and finally, it could potentially improve adherence to multilateral environmental agreements, especially if membership of the World Environment Organization would automatically entail signing up to some key multilateral treaties.

Despite these potential benefits and strong support from several governments—such as France and Germany, who reiterated their willingness to create a new organization at the 2012

Rio Earth Summit—the idea of creating a World Environment Organization has not gained much political traction and it is unlikely to happen any time soon. This can be partly explained by several disadvantages from the viewpoints of different actors. For existing international institutions, the creation of a World Environment Organization might lead to a loss of power, a threat that makes those who benefit from the existing power structure in the international system very reluctant. Different administrative cultures, and diverging understandings in individual governments of what global environmental politics should be, have stalled discussions and held back governments from developing a united vision of what a World Environment Organization would look like in practice (Vijge 2013). There is also a concern that states not wishing to participate in the newly created World Environment Organization would be excluded from global debates about the environment. A further concern is that creating an organization specifically dedicated to the environment would breach the principles of transversality and integration, which claim that environmental protection should be taken into account in all fields of international politics (transversality) and integrated into these fields (integration). The creation of a new intergovernmental organization might lead to cumbersome decision-making and bureaucratic processes, and although one specialized organization would be more visible, it would also be more vulnerable to pressures from interest groups. Some also argue that the current system, although fragmented, is flexible and is better suited to the specific needs and complexity of global environmental politics (Andresen 2001; Kellow 2012; Keohane and Victor 2011). Peter Haas (2004: 7) summarizes this point of view well:

> The best institutional structure for dealing with complex and uncertain policy environments is loose, decentralized, dense networks of institutions and actors that are able to quickly relay information, and provide sufficient redundancies in the performance of functions so that the elimination or inactivity by one institution does not jeopardize the entire network.

Overall, the idea of enhancing multilateralism, and more precisely environmental multilateralism, is also sometimes strongly criticized by certain political actors, most of all by right-wing populist political leaders, parties, and movements (Fraune and Knodt 2018). These actors favour unilateralism as, among other reasons, they lack trust in intergovernmental organizations.

Reforming global environmental governance at the margins

Rather than setting up a World Environment Organization, a series of more modest changes to the global governance architecture have been adopted. For example, 20 years after its creation, it became evident that the Commission on Sustainable Development was not meeting expectations and was not generating political momentum. Certain countries participated in it only sporadically and non-state actors gradually lost interest in this institution (Chasek 2000). Delegations that attended were often limited to representatives from environment ministries, meaning that the Commission failed to convince governments of the transversality of environmental issues. The Commission on Sustainable Development became simply a 'talk shop' (Kaasa 2007: 107; see also Andresen 2007). Therefore, in 2012 states decided to abolish it and replace it with the High-Level Political Forum on Sustainable Development. The mandate of this forum is similar to that of the Commission on Sustainable Development, but since it regularly attracts heads of state, it is better positioned to influence the political mobilization of its various actors. As such, it has embraced a stronger political role, being the main United Nations platform on sustainable development and playing a central role in the follow-up and review of the **Sustainable Development Goals** (see Box 6.7) at the global level. Since 2014, the United Nations Environment Programme has also had its own General Assembly, that addresses critical environmental challenges.

Today, in many respects, it seems less necessary to significantly reform the United Nations Environment Programme. Initially, the idea of creating a World Environment Organization was primarily motivated by a desire to offset the World Trade Organization. There was a particular fear that the Dispute Settlement Body of the World Trade Organization would place excessive pressure on international environmental regimes and that it would establish a de facto legal hierarchy favouring trade regulations at the expense of environmental ones. But, 25 years after the World Trade Organization was created, it appears that this Dispute Settlement Body is not such an immediate threat to environmental regimes as was initially feared (see Chapter 10).

Furthermore, it seems that the potentially conflictive relationships between international institutions do not necessarily need to be adjudicated by legal mechanisms or resolved through the creation of new multilateral organizations. More flexible and informal mechanisms might also help to avoid frontal collisions and favour synergy between international regimes (Johnson and Urpelainen 2012; Raustiala and Victor 2004). 'Orchestration' has been suggested as one such flexible solution: 'intergovernmental organisations engage in orchestration when they enlist intermediary actors on a voluntary basis, by providing them with ideational and material support, to address target actors in pursuit of intergovernmental governance goals' (Abbott et al. 2015; see also Betsill et al. 2015). For instance, the United Nations Environment Programme's Finance Initiative, created in 1992, is a partnership between the United Nations Environment Programme and the global financial sector, to promote sustainable finance. The nexus approach (Boas et al. 2016), whereby all sectors are integrated for better synergy, is a similar, more recent, perspective. The idea of the nexus approach is to create more integrated and cross-sectoral strategies, as do the Sustainable Development Goals. The nexus approach and corresponding cross-sectoral management would also be useful to manage what have become 'multipurpose' goods, such as agricultural goods which are used for an increasing number of purposes, including food but also energy or medical uses (Bastos Lima 2018).

Responding to these calls for flexible solutions, several interorganizational partnerships have been set up on an ad hoc basis to catalyse dialogue between international institutions. Secretariats are often key players in establishing and managing these partnerships (Jinnah 2014). For example, the Collaborative Partnership on Forests was established in 2001 between 14 organizations that manage programmes related to international forests policies, including the United Nations Food and Agriculture Organization, the United Nations Forum on Forests, the United Nations Environment Programme, the World Bank, the Global Environment Facility, the International Union for Conservation of Nature, and the secretariat of the United Nations Framework Convention on Climate Change. For biodiversity issues, a liaison group, made up of representatives from the five secretariats of the Convention on Biological Diversity, the Convention on the Trade of Endangered Species, the Convention on Migratory Species, the Ramsar Convention on Wetlands, and the World Heritage Convention, was set up in 2004 to enhance synergies between the actions of different treaties.

Similarly, frequent summits between heads of state help to smooth out potentially conflictive interactions between regimes. The G7 summits and the G20 summits, for example, are an opportunity to address several subjects at once, to focus on the most pressing issues, and to reach difficult compromises without the constraint of a rigid institutional structure (Kim and Chung 2012). This practice, which is becoming more and more frequent, could potentially evolve into a sort of 'inclusive minilateralism' diplomacy, which would serve as a middle ground between sclerotic multilateralism, where decisions are difficult to take due to diverging state interests, and restricted membership 'club governance', which lacks legitimacy (Eckersley 2012). Such 'inclusive minilateralism' could be used as a springboard for international discussions, and progressively include more members for a global reach (Gampfer 2016).

Moreover, regional governance allows certain laborious aspects of multilateral negotiations to be overcome (Balsiger and VanDeveer 2012; see Box 7.5), even if not all environmental problems can be addressed at this scale. Regionalism simplifies the process by reducing the number of actors and bringing together those who share common cultural references and who face similar problems, enabling connections to be more easily made between environmental issues and other subjects such as transport, immigration, and trade. Regional organizations could play the role of coordinating agencies between state and non-state actors and could adjust territoriality to better deal with ecoregions, as is the case in the European Alps for example (Balsiger 2012).

Box 7.5 The European Union as a green international actor?

The European Union is perceived to be more than just another intergovernmental organization, due to its high level of supranationality. The concept of supranationality means that the European institutions often take decisions for the Union's member states. In global environmental politics, the supranational exceptionalism of the European Union has often been coupled with the vision of Europe as a green leader.

The 2007 Treaty on the Functioning of the European Union states that the Union will work for the sustainable development of Europe and, in its external dimension, promote 'measures at international level to deal with regional or worldwide environmental problems, and in particular combating climate change'. The European Union has developed two innovative ways of implementing these general goals.

First, it adopted the so-called 'environmental policy integration' provision according to which 'environmental protection requirements must be integrated into the definition and implementation of the Union's policies and activities, in particular with a view to promoting sustainable development'. Environmental policy integration is part of the Union's cohesion policy, and has two dimensions: horizontal and vertical. Horizontal policy integration means that all sectors have to include environmental objectives. For example, the Common Agricultural Policy also has the aim to avoid environmentally harmful farming activities. Vertical policy integration means that all environmental efforts have to contribute to other policy objectives. For instance, the European Union Energy Strategy 2050 is also meant to dynamize the European job market by creating a business case for new environmentally friendly technology corporations.

Second, the Treaty on the Functioning of the European Union developed a procedure through which the Union can participate as a **party** to the building of international environmental treaties. Ultimately, the European Council remains the institution that authorizes the signing of any agreement, but this procedure means that both the European Union and its member states can be parties to international environmental agreements and can negotiate these agreements together. The European Union is currently a full member (in addition to its member states) of about 30 international environmental agreements including the Minamata Convention on Mercury, the Convention on International Trade in Endangered Species, and the Paris Agreement.

(continued...)

The European Union's environmental policy has increased in quantity, in scope, and in impact over the last five decades. Its policies have, moreover, become increasingly complex, affecting almost all sectors of society and all levels of political activity. Thus, the European external environmental agenda is not unilaterally controlled by one unique authority but is distributed among an important set of actors.

The leadership role of the European Union is well illustrated by international climate change politics. The European Union has been a strong supporter of the United Nations Framework Climate Change Convention and its related Kyoto Protocol and Paris Agreement. The Union has also played a proactive role in convincing other institutions to engage with climate change. For instance, at the International Civil Aviation Organization, the European Union is advocating for aviation sector involvement in international climate efforts. The Union has also established its own emissions trading system, which has contributed to other important players, such as China, following suit. In December 2019, the European Commission presented an ambitious roadmap, the *European Green Deal*, to make Europe the first climate-neutral continent by 2050.

Although many have highlighted the European Union's environmental leadership, others argue that this leadership is now waning. In particular, the European Union has adopted a defensive stance on two important issues of climate governance: climate finance and adaptation. Moreover, the success of the Paris Agreement will depend on the willingness of governments to progressively strengthen their climate commitments. It is not clear that the Union itself will meet its climate targets. In May 2018, ten families brought a claim to the General Court of the European Court of Justice in the 'People's climate case', in which citizens sued several European member states for lack of climate action. Nevertheless, the very fact that the European institutions give rights to European citizens to contest environmental politics is, for others, a strong sign of green leadership.

Sources: Adelle et al. 2018; Biedenkopf et al. 2017; Delreux 2011, 2014; Delreux and Happaerts 2016; Falkner 2007; Lindenthal 2014; Oberthür and Groen 2018; Zito 2005.

In summary, though the problem of managing international institutions remains, it appears more and more evident that this problem should not necessarily—or even ideally—be resolved by profoundly changing global environmental governance.

7.5 Conclusion

This chapter shows that an increasing number of international institutions embrace environmental objectives, that environmental institutions benefit from a varying degree of autonomy, but that proliferation also means that global environmental governance might suffer from a lack of coordination. Until now, states have been more likely to adapt current institutions than to significantly modify their entire governance structure.

Although environmental institutions are numerous and demonstrate a high level of dynamism, shortfalls still remain. More than conflicts between institutions, important lacunas are the lack of international institutions on certain issue areas. Currently, no multilateral treaty directly deals with the problems of drinking water, greenhouse gas emissions from cruise ships, coral bleaching, or Arctic haze (see Box 7.6). Even when treaties are adopted, states tend to favour minimal agreements, which are sometimes incomplete or contain ambiguities. The obligations provided in multilateral environmental agreements are therefore often difficult to interpret. It is also essential to assess the effectiveness of international institutions. Chapter 8 discusses this issue and introduces the range of **policy instruments** that intergovernmental organizations, states, and non-state actors mobilize to tackle environmental issues.

Box 7.6 Regulating greenhouse gas emissions in international aviation and maritime transport

International aviation and maritime transport account for a significant share of global greenhouse gas emissions. Each of these two sectors accounts for more than 2 per cent of global emissions. Moreover, the share of international aviation and shipping emissions is expected to grow.

These emissions pose a challenge for international regulation efforts because they are released into international airspace and waters. The responsibility for emissions is also difficult to parse between countries of origin, destination, and/or incorporation. It is therefore difficult to assign the corresponding responsibly to a single jurisdiction. This explains why these sectors were excluded from the scope of the United Nations Framework Convention on Climate Change and the Paris Agreement. Instead, the task of developing regulations for international aviation and shipping were left to two United Nations specialized agencies in the governance of these sectors: the International Civil Aviation Organization and the International Maritime Organization.

The International Civil Aviation Organization has focused on technological solutions to increase fuel efficiency, the development of alternative fuels such as biofuels for air transport, improvements in air traffic management, and also on market-based policies for incentivizing emission reductions. After years of deliberation, in 2016 the International Civil Aviation Organization adopted a Carbon Offsetting and Reduction Scheme for International Aviation, which aims to stabilize greenhouse gas emissions at 2020 levels. It requires airlines to monitor their emissions from international flights and to offset their growth in emissions by purchasing emission-reduction credits. The scheme has been criticized by many because it will be voluntary until 2027, only covers emissions from international travel and only those over 2020 levels, and is an offsetting scheme, which may not lead to actual reductions in emissions because emissions can simply be displaced to another industry or location. Some argue that more policies are needed to restrict demand, such as a moratorium on airport expansion in wealthy countries.

A similar process has evolved for maritime emissions in the International Maritime Organization. Although there have been some developments in the past decade, progress has been insufficient to substantially reduce emissions from this sector. In 2011, the Organization adopted mandatory energy efficiency measures for new ships built after 2025, and in 2016 its parties agreed to a data collection system for the fuel consumption of large ships. In 2018 the Organization adopted an 'initial strategy' to reduce total greenhouse gas emissions by at least 50 per cent by 2020, compared to 2008, while pursuing efforts to phase them out entirely in the longer term. Many NGOs have noted that while the strategy is long overdue, the lack of concrete mandatory measures is inconsistent with the urgent need to drastically reduce emissions. Recently, the widespread deployment of relevant technologies, such as alternative fuels and renewable energy, as well as efficiency improvements, improvements in ship design, and operational measures, have all demonstrated potential to provide substantial emission reductions. This suggests there is no single route to decarbonization, and underscores the need for multiple approaches pursued in parallel to address these issues.

Sources: Balcombe et al. 2019; Bows-Larkin 2015; Keen et al. 2013; Macintosh and Wallace 2009; Miola et al. 2011.

Critical thinking questions

1. How might the relative autonomy of an intergovernmental organization affect its interactions with other intergovernmental organizations? Provide specific examples.
2. Explain, from the rational choice, historical institutionalist, and sociological institutionalist perspectives, the failure to significantly reform environmental governance.
3. Compare how the United Nations Environment Programme and the World Bank have addressed environmental issues over the last 30 years.

4. What are the four types of interactions between international institutions? Provide some examples of conflictive and synergistic interactions between international institutions.

5. How might a World Environment Organization alleviate or accentuate tensions between environmental and non-environmental regimes?

 Test your knowledge and understanding further by trying this chapter's Multiple Choice Questions www.oup.com/he/morin1e

Key references

Biermann, Frank, and Bernd Siebenhüner (eds). 2009. *Managers of Global Change: The Influence of International Environmental Bureaucracies*. Cambridge, MA: MIT Press.

This edited volume demonstrates how international civil servants matter for global environmental politics. Using nine detailed case studies, it identifies the parameters allowing international bureaucrats to have more or less autonomy with regard to the member states across several international institutions.

Jinnah, Sikina. 2014. *Post-Treaty Politics: Secretariat Influence in Global Environmental Governance*. Cambridge, MA: MIT Press.

This book builds on the previous one in identifying the conditions under which secretariats are most likely to exert influence and power in international affairs. Specifically, it argues that secretariats are most likely to exert influence when state preferences are weak and when secretariat functions are not easily replaced by other actors. It examines secretariat influence through the lens of how secretariats help to manage institutional interaction between regimes.

Meyer, John W., David John Frank, Ann Hironaka, Evan Schofer, and Nancy Brandon Tuma. 1997. 'The Structuring of a World Environmental Regime, 1870–1990'. *International Organization* 51 (4): 623–651.

This article traces the historical formation of environmental governance over the twentieth century. It focuses in particular on the proliferation of institutions, including environmental NGOs, treaties, intergovernmental organizations, and national ministries.

Oberthür, Sebastian., and Olav Schram Stokke (eds). 2011. *Managing Institutional Complexity: Regime Interplay and Global Environmental Change*. Cambridge, MA: MIT Press.

This edited volume proposes a detailed categorization of institutional interactions and applies this to numerous cases in the global environmental field, including Arctic governance, genetic resources, fisheries, and climate and energy.

 For additional material and resources, please visit the online resources at: www.oup.com/he/morin1e

Chapter references

Abbott, Kenneth W. 2012. 'The Transnational Regime Complex for Climate Change'. *Environment and Planning C: Government and Policy* 30 (4): 571–590.

Abbott, Kenneth W., Philipp Genschel, Duncan Snidal, and Bernhard Zangl (eds). 2015. *International Organizations as Orchestrators*. Cambridge: Cambridge University Press.

Abbott, Kenneth W., and Duncan Snidal. 2010. 'International Regulation Without International Government: Improving IO Performance Through Orchestration'. *Review of International Organizations* 5 (3): 315–344.

Adelle, Camilla, Katja Biedenkopf, and Diarmuid Torney. 2018. *European Union External Environmental Policy: Rules, Regulation and*

Governance Beyond Borders. Basingstoke: Palgrave Macmillan.

Alter, Karen J., and Kal Raustiala. 2018. 'The Rise of International Regime Complexity'. *Annual Review of Law and Social Science* 14: 329–349.

Andresen, Steinar. 2001. 'Global Environmental Governance: UN Fragmentation and Co-ordination'. In *Yearbook of International Cooperation on Environment and Development 2001–2002*, edited by Olav Schram Stokke and Øystein B. Thommessen, 19–25. London: Earthscan.

Andresen, Steinar. 2007. 'The Effectiveness of UN Environmental Institutions'. *International Environmental Agreements: Politics, Law and Economics* 7 (4): 317–336.

Balcombe, Paul, James Brierley, Chester Lewis, Line Skatvedt, Jamie Speirs, Adam Hawkes, and Iain Staffell. 2019. 'How to Decarbonise International Shipping: Options for Fuels, Technologies and Policies'. *Energy Conversion and Management* 182 (February): 72–88.

Balsiger, Jörg. 2012. 'New Environmental Regionalism and Sustainable Development in the European Alps'. *Global Environmental Politics* 12 (3): 58–78.

Balsiger, Jörg, and Miriam Prys. 2016. 'Regional Agreements in International Environmental Politics'. *International Environment Agreements* 16 (2): 239–260.

Balsiger, Jörg, and Stacy D. VanDeveer. 2012. 'Navigating Regional Environmental Governance'. *Global Environmental Politics* 12 (3): 1–17.

Bastos Lima, Mairon G. 2018. 'Toward Multipurpose Agriculture: Food, Fuels, Flex Crops, and Prospects for a Bioeconomy'. *Global Environmental Politics* 18 (2): 143–150.

Bauer, Michael W., and Jorn Ege. 2017. 'A Matter of Will and Action: The Bureaucratic Autonomy of International Public Administrations'. In *International Bureaucracy: Challenges and Lessons for Public Administration Research*, edited by Michael W. Bauer, Christoph Knill, and Steffen Eckhard, 13–42. London: Palgrave Macmillan.

Bauer, Steffen. 2006. 'Does Bureaucracy Really Matter? The Authority of Intergovernmental Treaty Secretariats in Global Environmental Politics'. *Global Environmental Politics* 6 (1): 23–49.

Bayer, Patrick, Christopher Marcoux, and Johannes Urpelainen. 2015. 'When International Organizations Bargain: Evidence from the Global Environment Facility'. *Journal of Conflict Resolution* 59 (6): 1074–1100.

Betsill, Michele, Navroz K. Dubash, Matthew Paterson, Harro van Asselt, Antto Vihma, and Harald Winkler. 2015. 'Building Productive Links between the UNFCCC and the Broader Global Climate Governance Landscape'. *Global Environmental Politics* 15 (2): 1–10.

Biedenkopf, Katja, Patrick Müller, Peter Slominski, and Jørgen Wettestad. 2017. 'A Global Turn to Greenhouse Gas Emissions Trading? Experiments, Actors, and Diffusion'. *Global Environmental Politics* 17 (3): 1–11.

Biermann, Frank. 2011. 'Reforming Global Environmental Governance: The Case for a United Nations Environment Organisation (UNEO)'. Stakeholder Forum's Programme on Sustainable Development Governance towards the UN Conference on Sustainable Development in 2012.

Biermann, Frank, Philipp Pattberg, Harro van Asselt, and Fariborz Zelli. 2009. 'The Fragmentation of Global Governance Architectures: A Framework for Analysis'. *Global Environmental Politics* 9 (4): 14–40.

Biermann, Frank, and Bernd Siebenhüner. 2009. *Managers of Global Change: The Influence of International Environmental Bureaucracies*. Cambridge, MA: MIT Press.

Boas, Ingrid, Frank Biermann, and Norichika Kanie. 2016. 'Cross-Sectoral Strategies in Global Sustainability Governance: Towards a Nexus Approach'. *International Environmental Agreements: Politics, Law and Economics* 16 (3): 449–464.

Boisson de Chazournes, Laurence. 2005. 'The Global Environment Facility (GEF): A Unique and Crucial Institution'. *RECIEL* 14 (3): 193–201.

Bows-Larkin, Alice. 2015. 'All Adrift: Aviation, Shipping, and Climate Change Policy'. *Climate Policy* 15 (6): 681–702.

Chasek, Pamela S. 2000. 'The UN Commission on Sustainable Development: The First Five Years'. In *The Global Environment in the Twenty-first Century: Prospects for International Cooperation*, edited by Pamela S. Chasek, 378–398. New York: United Nations University.

Delreux, Tom. 2011. *The EU as International Environmental Negotiator*. Surrey: Ashgate.

Delreux, Tom. 2014. 'EU Actorness, Cohesiveness and Effectiveness in Environmental Affairs'. *Journal of European Public Policy* 21 (7): 1017–1032.

Delreux, Tom, and Sander Happaerts. 2016. *Environmental Policy and Politics in the European Union*. The European Union Series. London: Palgrave Macmillan.

Eckersley, Robyn. 2012. 'Moving Forward in the Climate Negotiations: Multilateralism or Minilateralism?' *Global Environmental Politics* 12 (2): 24–42.

Falkner, Robert. 2007. 'The Political Economy of "Normative Power" Europe: EU Environmental Leadership in International Biotechnology Regulation'. *Journal of European Public Policy* 14 (4): 507–526.

Fraune, Cornelia, and Michèle Knodt. 2018. 'Sustainable Energy Transformations in an Age of Populism, Post-Truth Politics, and Local Resistance'. *Energy Research & Social Science* 43: 1–7.

Gampfer, Robert. 2016. 'Minilateralism or the UNFCCC? The Political Feasibility of Climate Clubs'. *Global Environmental Politics* 16 (3): 62–88.

Green, Jessica F., and Graham Auld. 2017. 'Unbundling the Regime Complex: The Effects of Private Authority'. *Transnational Environmental Law* 6 (2): 259–284.

Green, Jessica F., and Jeff Colgan. 2013. 'Protecting Sovereignty, Protecting the Planet: State Delegation to International Organizations and Private Actors in Environmental Politics'. *Governance* 26 (3): 473–497.

Haas, Peter M. 2004. 'Addressing the Global Governance Deficit'. *Global Environmental Politics* 4 (4): 1–15.

Hall, Peter A., and Rosemary C. R. Taylor. 1996. 'Political Science and the Three New Institutionalisms'. *Political Studies* 44 (5): 936–957.

Hochstetler, Kathryn. 2014. 'Infrastructure and Sustainable Development Goals in the BRICS-Led New Development Bank'. CIGI Policy Brief 46. Ontario: CIGI.

Ivanova, Maria. 2007. 'Designing the United Nations Environment Programme: A Story of Compromise and Confrontation'. *International Environmental Agreements* 7 (4): 337–361.

Ivanova, Maria. 2010. 'UNEP in Global Environmental Governance: Design, Leadership, Location'. *Global Environmental Politics* 10 (1): 30–59.

Ivanova, Maria. 2012. 'Institutional Design and UNEP Reform: Historical Insights on Form, Function and Financing.' *International Affairs* 88 (3): 565–584.

Jinnah, Sikina. 2010. 'Overlap Management in the World Trade Organization: Secretariat Influence on Trade–Environment Politics'. *Global Environmental Politics* 10 (2): 54–79.

Jinnah, Sikina. 2014. *Post-Treaty Politics: Secretariat Influence in Global Environmental Governance.* Cambridge, MA: MIT Press.

Johnson, Tana, and Johannes Urpelainen. 2012. 'A Strategic Theory of Regime Integration and Separation'. *International Organization* 66 (4): 645–677.

Jörgens, Helge, Nina Kolleck, Barbara Saerbeck, and Mareike Well. 2017. 'Orchestrating (Bio)diversity: The Secretariat of the Convention of Biological Diversity as an Attention-Seeking Bureaucracy'. In *International Bureaucracy: Public Sector Organizations*, edited by M. Bauer, C. Knill, and S. Eckhard, 73–95. London: Palgrave Macmillan.

Kaasa, Stine Madland. 2007. 'The UN Commission on Sustainable Development: Which Mechanisms Explain its Accomplishments?' *Global Environmental Politics* 7 (3): 107–129.

Keen, Michael, Ian Parry, and Jon Strand. 2013. 'Planes, Ships and Taxes: Charging for International Aviation and Maritime Emissions'. *Economic Policy* 28 (76): 701–749.

Kellow, Aynsley. 2012. 'Multi-Level and Multi-Arena Governance: The Limits of Integration and the Possibilities of Forum Shopping'. *International Environmental Agreements* 12 (4): 327–342.

Keohane, Robert O. 1989. *International Institutions and State Power.* Boulder, CO: Westview Press.

Keohane, Robert O., and David G. Victor. 2011. 'The Regime Complex for Climate Change'. *Perspectives on Politics* 9 (1): 7–23.

Kim, Joy Aeree, and Suh-Yong Chung. 2012. 'The Role of the G20 in Governing the Climate Change Regime'. *International Environmental Agreements* 12 (4): 361–374.

Kim, Rakhyun E. 2013. 'The Emergent Network Structure of the Multilateral Environmental Agreement System'. *Global Environmental Change* 23 (5): 980–991.

Kolleck, Nina, Mareike Well, Severin Sperzel, and Helge Jörgens. 2017. 'The Power of Social Networks: How the UNFCCC Secretariat Creates Momentum for Climate Education'. *Global Environmental Politics* 17 (4): 106–126.

Koremenos, Barbara, Charles Lipson, and Duncan Snidal. 2001. 'The Rational Design of International Institutions'. *International Organization* 55 (4): 761–799.

Krasner, Stephen D. 1982. 'Structural Causes and Regime Consequences: Regimes as Intervening Variables'. *International Organization* 36 (2): 185–205.

Lindenthal, Alexandra. 2014. 'Aviation and Climate Protection: EU Leadership within the International Civil Aviation Organization'. *Environmental Politics* 23 (6): 1064–1081.

Lindenthal, Alexandra, and Martin Koch. 2013. 'The Bretton Woods Institutions and the Environment: Organizational Learning within the World Bank and the International Monetary Fund (IMF)'. *Administrative Sciences* 3 (4): 166–201.

Luken, Ralph A. 2009. 'Greening an International Organization: UNIDO's Strategic Responses'. *Review of International Organizations* 4 (2): 159–184.

Macintosh, Andrew, and Lailey Wallace. 2009. 'International Aviation Emissions to 2025: Can Emissions Be Stabilised without Restricting Demand?' *Energy Policy* 37 (1): 264–73.

Manulak, Michael W. 2017. 'Leading by Design: Informal Influence and International Secretariats'. *Review of International Organizations* 12 (4): 497–522.

Meyer, John W., David John Frank, Ann Hironaka, Evan Schofer, and Nancy Brandon Tuma. 1997. 'The Structuring of a World Environmental Regime, 1870–1990'. *International Organization* 51 (4): 623–651.

Michaelowa, Katharina, Michaelowa, Axel. 2017. 'The Growing Influence of the UNFCCC Secretariat on the Clean Development Mechanism'. *International Environmental Agreements* 17 (2): 247–269.

Miola, A., M. Marra, and B. Ciuffo. 2011. 'Designing a Climate Change Policy for the International Maritime Transport Sector: Market-Based Measures and Technological Options for Global and Regional Policy Actions'. *Energy Policy* 39 (9): 5490–5498.

Mitchell, Ronald B. 2013. 'Oran Young and International Institutions'. *International Environmental Agreements* 13 (1): 1–14.

Mitchell, Ronald B. 2019. *International Environmental Agreements Database Project, 2002–2019*. Available at: https://iea.uoregon.edu/, accessed October 2019.

Morin, Jean-Frédéric, and Amandine Orsini. 2014. 'Policy Coherency and Regime Complexes: The Case of Genetic Resources'. *Review of International Studies* 40 (2): 303–324.

Nielson, Daniel L., and Michael J. Tierney. 2003. 'Delegation to International Organizations: Agency Theory and World Bank Environmental Reform'. *International Organization* 57 (2): 241–276.

Oberthür, Sebastian, and Thomas Gehring. 2006. 'Institutional Interaction in Global Environmental Governance: The Case of the Cartagena Protocol and the World Trade Organization'. *Global Environmental Politics* 6 (2): 1–31.

Oberthür, Sebastian, and Thomas Gehring. 2011. 'Institutional Interaction. Ten Years of Scholarly Development'. In *Managing Institutional Complexity: Regime Interplay and Global Environmental Change*, edited by Sebastian Oberthür and Olav Schram Stokke, 25–58. Cambridge, MA: MIT Press.

Oberthür, Sebastian, and Lisanne Groen. 2018. 'Explaining Goal Achievement in International Negotiations: The EU and the Paris Agreement on Climate Change'. *Journal of European Public Policy* 25 (5): 708–727.

Oberthür, Sebastian, and Olav Schram Stokke (eds). 2011. *Managing Institutional Complexity: Regime Interplay and Global Environmental Change*. Cambridge, MA: MIT Press.

Oh, Chaewoon, and Shunji Matsuoka. 2017. 'The Genesis and End of Institutional Fragmentation in Global Governance on Climate Change from a Constructivist Perspective'. *International Environmental Agreements* 17 (2): 143–159.

Orsini, Amandine. 2013. 'Navigating the Regime Complexes for Forestry and Genetic Resources'. *Global Environmental Politics* 13 (3): 34–55.

Orsini, Amandine, and Claire Godet. 2018. 'Food Security and Biofuels Regulations: The Emulsifying Effect of International Regime Complexes'. *Journal of Contemporary European Research* 14 (1): 4–22.

Orsini, Amandine, Jean-Frédéric Morin, and Oran R. Young. 2013. 'Regime Complexes: A Buzz, A Boom or a Boost for Global Governance?' *Global Governance* 19 (3): 27–39.

Papa, Mihaela. 2015. 'Sustainable Global Governance? Reduce, Reuse, and Recycle Institutions'. *Global Environmental Politics* 15 (4): 1–20.

Park, Susan. 2005. 'How Transnational Environmental Advocacy Networks Socialize International Financial Institutions: A Case Study of the International Finance Corporation'. *Global Environmental Politics* 5 (4): 95–119.

Park, Susan. 2007. 'The World Bank Group: Championing Sustainable Development Norms?' *Global Governance* 13 (4): 535–556.

Raustiala, Kal, and David G. Victor. 2004. 'The Regime Complex for Plant Genetic Resources'. *International Organization* 58 (2): 277–309.

Reed, David. 1997. 'The Environmental Legacy of Bretton Woods: The World Bank'. In *Global Governance: Drawing Insights from the Environmental Experience*, edited by O. R. Young, 227–246. Cambridge, MA: MIT Press.

Rosendal, G. Kristin. 2001. 'Impacts of Overlapping International Regimes: The Case of Biodiversity'. *Global Governance* 7 (1): 95–117.

Siebenhüner, Bernd. 2008. 'Learning in International Organizations in Global Environmental Governance'. *Global Environmental Politics* 8 (4): 92–116.

Sovacool, Benjamin K., May Tan-Mullins, David Ockwell, and Peter Newell. 2017. 'Political Economy, Poverty, and Polycentrism in the Global Environment Facility's Least Developed Countries Fund (LDCF) for Climate Change Adaptation'. *Third World Quarterly* 38 (6): 1249–1271.

Streck, Charlotte. 2001. 'Global Environment Facility— A Role Model of International Governance?' *Global Environmental Politics* 1 (2): 71–94.

Tarasofsky, Richard G., and Alison L. Hoare. 2004. *Implications of a UNEO for the Global Architecture of the International Environmental Governance System*. Paris: IDDRI, with the support of France's Ministry of Ecology and Sustainable Development.

Thompson, Alexander. 2010. 'Rational Design in Motion: Uncertainty and Flexibility in the Global Climate Regime'. *European Journal of International Relations* 16 (2): 269–296.

Urpelainen, Johannes. 2012. 'Geoengineering and Global Warming: A Strategic Perspective'. *International Environmental Agreements* 12 (4): 375–389.

Vijge, Marjanneke J. 2013. 'The Promise of New Institutionalism: Explaining the Absence of a World or United Nations Environment Organisation'. *International Environmental Agreements* 13 (2): 153–176.

Widerberg, Oscar, and Frank van Laerhoven. 2014. 'Measuring the Autonomous Influence of an International Bureaucracy: The Division for Sustainable Development'. *International Environmental Agreements* 14 (4): 303–327.

Young, Oran R. 1977. *Resource Management at the International Level: The Case of the North Pacific.* New York: Pinter and Nichols.

Young, Oran R. 1979. *Compliance and Public Authorities: A Theory with International Applications.* Baltimore: Johns Hopkins University Press.

Young, Oran R. 1982. *Resource Regimes: Natural Resources and Social Institutions.* Berkeley: University of California Press.

Young, Oran R. 1989a. *International Cooperation: Building Regimes for Natural Resources and the Environment.* Ithaca, NY: Cornell University Press.

Young, Oran R. 1989b. 'The Politics of International Regime Formation: Managing Natural Resources and the Environment'. *International Organization* 43 (3): 349–375.

Young, Oran R. 1999a. *The Effectiveness of International Environmental Regimes: Causal Connections and Behavioral Mechanisms.* Cambridge, MA: MIT Press.

Young, Oran R. 1999b. *Governance in World Affairs.* Ithaca, NY: Cornell University Press.

Young, Oran R. 2002. *The Institutional Dimensions of Environmental Change: Fit, Interplay, and Scale.* Cambridge, MA: MIT Press.

Young, Oran R. 2013. *Governance in World Affairs.* Ithaca, NY: Cornell University Press.

Young, Oran R. 2016. 'The Co-Production of Knowledge about International Governance: Living on the Science/Policy Interface'. In *New Earth Politics: Essays from the Anthropocene*, edited by Simon Nicholson and Sikina Jinnah, 75–96. Cambridge, MA: MIT Press.

Young, Oran R., Leslie A. King, and Heike Schroeder. 2008. *Institutions and Environmental Change: Principal Findings, Applications, and Research Frontiers.* Cambridge. MA: MIT Press.

Zawahri, Neda, and Erika Weinthal. 2014. 'The World Bank and Negotiating the Red Sea and Dead Sea Water Conveyance Project'. *Global Environmental Politics* 14 (4): 55–74.

Zelli, Fariborz, and Harro van Asselt. 2013. 'The Institutional Fragmentation of Global Environmental Governance: Causes, Consequences, and Responses'. *Global Environmental Politics* 13 (3): 1–13.

Zito, Anthony. R. 2005. 'The European Union as an Environmental Leader in a Global Environment'. *Globalizations* 2 (3): 363–375.

8 Policy instruments and effectiveness

This chapter introduces several debates surrounding the effectiveness of global environmental governance. These debates are closely linked to the choice of policy instruments states make within international regimes. The chapter explains the modalities, diffusion, and political effects of these policy instruments. Although the concept of policy instruments may appear technical and neutral, we show how instruments can actually shape, modify, and even undermine global environmental politics.

 Learning objectives

After reading this chapter, readers will be able to:

- Assess the effectiveness of international environmental policy instruments, using a variety of different approaches;
- Describe the modalities of different instruments used for environmental protection;
- Explain how and why instruments diffuse between states; and
- Discuss the political effects of policy instruments and in particular their potential to change power dynamics.

Introduction

Global environmental politics is teeming with a wide variety of public **policy instruments** available to public authorities and private operators to fulfil their commitments under international **regimes**. These include regulations, administrative standards, scientific indicators, financial targets, and accounting practices, among others. Whereas international **institutions** frame the general norms, principles, and rules for tackling environmental problems, instruments provide the toolbox of policy mechanisms that actors in global environmental politics use to implement those norms, principles, and rules. In some cases, the choice of instruments is made at the international level and applied in exactly the same way by a group of states. In other cases, the choice of policy instruments is left to the discretion of states, who can then choose among different alternatives to fulfil their international commitments. Even so, because states interact and exchange information and practices, similarities and trends appear in the way they select their policy instruments.

Instruments are not politically neutral. They have long been neglected by analysts of global environmental politics, who have considered them to be technical and therefore apolitical. However, instruments have been increasingly contested because their implicit underlying assumptions often rest on strong political and/or normative ideas. Some instruments, for example, rest on the assumption that **market mechanisms** are the most effective means to reduce environmental degradation or that strong legally based **enforcement** mechanisms are necessary to ensure **compliance**. These assumptions are often hidden behind a veil of technicality: instruments are the necessary additives for political action, and are all the more powerful because they go practically unnoticed.

This chapter presents the current debates in global environmental politics regarding the effectiveness of policy instruments. It examines how global environmental politics is implemented through instruments, and illuminates how such instruments are in fact strongly political, with broad impacts. A state's choice of policy instrument affects not only the effectiveness of international institutions, but also the global distribution of power.

The chapter is organized into four parts. We first discuss several ways of measuring regime effectiveness in global environmental politics (Section 8.1). As we will go on to explain, the study of policy instruments stems in large part from this debate, as environmental regimes rest on a wide diversity of policy instruments. We then present different categories of instruments used in global environmental politics and explain their modalities (Section 8.2), before considering the diffusion of such instruments across national borders (Section 8.3). Finally, we reflect on the political effects of international and national instruments, which influence their ability to solve environmental problems (Section 8.4).

8.1 The effectiveness of global environmental politics

The three steps for measuring policy effectiveness

The question of effectiveness is central in global environmental politics for scholars and policymakers alike: how well do our international institutions mitigate environmental degradation? Are the effects of our initiatives the ones we expected? In order to answer these questions, scholars have defined several ways to measure **policy effectiveness**.

Some scholars have measured policy effectiveness in three steps: *output*, *outcome*, and *impact* (Andresen 2007; Böhmelt and Vollenweider 2013; Conliffe 2011). First, applied to international environmental politics, *output* in this context refers to the concrete results of international discussions, such as international treaties, declarations, regulations, programmes, and recommendations. For instance, the Paris Agreement is an output of the negotiations of the **Conference of the Parties** to the United Nations Framework Convention on Climate Change. *Outcome* relates to the actual behavioural changes induced by outputs. The stronger the outcomes generated by a particular output, the more effective that output is considered to be. Following the same example, one of the outcomes of the Paris Agreement is that in 2019 more than 180 states were in the process of implementing their bottom-up mitigation plans, known as their nationally determined contributions. *Impact* measures the environmental progress made as a result of these outcomes. In other words, impact is a measurement of the extent to which outcomes helped reach the defined objective of the policy being examined. For example, the impact of nationally determined contributions on climate change is a function of the extent to which they result in emission reductions, and thus help states stay within the 2°C warming target set out in the Paris Agreement.

Measuring effectiveness by assessing environmental impact is an attractive proposition for those who care about the state of the environment. However, impacts are particularly difficult to assess, for at least three reasons. First, scientific data on the state of the environment is often fragmented or incomplete, especially in **developing countries** due to a lack of capacity. And for some environmental issues, environmental changes are difficult to measure because they can only be observed over long periods of time.

Second, impacts must be measured against precise benchmarks. This is difficult because the objectives that act as reference points for evaluating impact are often formulated in a very vague manner. In the negotiation process, ambiguity is often favoured to facilitate political compromise, at the expense of precision. For example, the Paris Agreement mentions both a +1.5°C and a +2°C target as maximum levels of global warming. Some environmental agreements can also have modest objectives. Compliance with these treaties is easy, but does little for the environment (Downs 2000; Downs et al. 1996). In some cases, several competing interpretations of the objectives are also possible. Going back to the climate change example, establishing that countries have reduced their CO_2 emissions is not enough to assess the *impact* of the Paris Agreement on mitigating climate change. In order to evaluate impact, one needs to know whether states have reduced their emissions sufficiently to achieve this objective. Complicating matters, there are several ways to assess 'sufficiency' in this context. Some believe, as mentioned earlier, that the baseline should be the official objective of the regime, shared by all parties—the 2°C limit. Others claim that the benchmark should be defined outside the Paris Agreement, for instance by the scientific community, such as through the **Intergovernmental Panel on Climate Change**, because the objectives of the Paris Agreement might be too modest.

Third, the establishment of a causal relationship between policy outputs and behavioural outcomes, as well as between outcome and impact, is challenging. Despite sophisticated techniques, such as the quantification of a no-treaty counterfactual situation and the determination of a collective optimum, the causal chain linking the adoption of a treaty to a reduction in pollutant emissions remains long, indirect, and uncertain. Because of the complexity of social, political, economic, and natural systems, multiple intervening, mediating, moderating, and confounding variables can be at play and can lead to an over- or underestimation of a treaty's impact. When significant progress is observed, it cannot always be attributed to the adoption of a particular international decision (Aakvik and Tjotta 2011; Ringquist and Kostadinova 2005; Vollenweider 2013). For example, it might be that a reduction in CO_2 emissions observed at the global level is caused by non-state climate action, such as market forces that drive up the cost of fossil fuels, rather than by the targeted behavioural changes of the parties to the Paris Agreement. Because impact is so difficult to evaluate, analysts often focus instead on outcomes or outputs as measures of the overall effectiveness of environmental policies.

Figure 8.1 shows the correlation between the number of environmental agreements ratified by a state and its corresponding environmental performance (as measured by the Environmental Performance Index, which merges 24 indicators based on output measures, such as the number of protected marine areas created by states, as well as impact measures, such as the emission of air pollutants). Looking at Figure 8.1, it seems that the more treaties a country has ratified, the stronger its environmental performance. However, the reasons for this correlation are unclear and it should not be taken as a causal relation (Brandi et al. 2019). For example, it could be the case that countries adopt treaties because they are already displaying good performance in particular areas (Desombre 2000). Or perhaps a third factor, such as the degree of democracy, drives both treaty **ratification** and environmental performance.

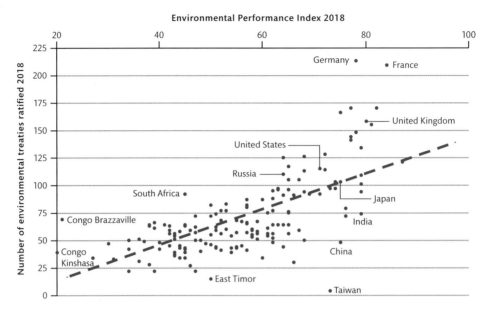

Figure 8.1 Number of treaties ratified and environmental performance

Source data from: https://iea.uoregon.edu/; epi.yale.edu

 Take your learning further by viewing the interactive version of this figure
www.oup.com/he/morin1e

Several hypotheses may explain why a country's environmental performance is not clearly linked to the number of treaties it has ratified (Wilson 2008). It could be that certain environmental agreements have collateral effects, modifying the behaviour of countries that are not party to those agreements. As such, a country's environmental performance could improve even if it did not sign a treaty on that issue. For example, the European Union's adoption of the Cartagena Protocol on Biosafety, dealing with the global trade in **genetically modified organisms**, has had effects in other developed economies because of the size of the EU market. Alternatively, it could be that changes in behaviour surrounding one environmental issue have an impact on other environmental issues besides the one initially targeted. Environmental performance on one issue might decrease because of spillover effects. For instance, the 1987 Montreal Protocol on the **ozone layer** is considered as one of the most effective **international environmental agreements** as it helped mitigate the depletion of the ozone layer. However, some of the chemical substitutes that states are permitted to use under the Protocol have important climate warming impacts. Can the Montreal Protocol be truly effective if in solving one environmental problem it simultaneously makes another one worse? It could also be that there is no significant causal link between countries signing treaties and their adoption of related national policies, because the adoption of such policies might have preceded and even catalysed the decision to sign the new treaty.

Measuring effectiveness: the case of international regimes

In addition to looking at outputs, outcomes, and impacts, analysts have proposed various other analytical frameworks that can be applied to case studies to help understand the effectiveness of policy, and in particular of international environmental regimes. For example, in 1993 Peter Haas, Robert Keohane, and Marc Levy put forward three metrics for evaluating environmental regimes' effectiveness, applied to a study of seven environmental issues. Referring to the 'three Cs', they argued that the effectiveness of environmental regimes is a function of three outputs and/or outcomes: increasing *concern*, enhancing the *contractual* environment, and increasing national *capacity*. In other words, a highly effective regime, in their view, would raise actors' awareness about an environmental issue (i.e. increase concern), help actors to agree on reciprocal commitments (i.e. enhance the contractual environment), and give actors the means to achieve those commitments (i.e. enhance capacity) (Haas et al. 1993).

Oran Young (1999) suggests an additional framework for measuring effectiveness, which identifies six pathways through which regimes could influence actors and processes, and thus impact effectiveness. Specifically, Young argues that regime effectiveness increases when the regime increases the utility function of the proposed solutions to tackle environmental problems, enhances cooperation between states, bestows authority on the environmental problems at hand, facilitates learning, defines roles, and realigns interests. Young's framework has been applied to multiple qualitative case studies. For example, Young's edited volume (1999) found the Convention on Long-Range Transboundary Air Pollution to be one of the strongest learning facilitators, making states aware of the importance of the transboundary pollution issue, whereas fisheries management regimes in the Barents Sea have been less effective on this metric, due to scientific uncertainty.

Case studies are particularly useful for theory building. But they might not be representative, and their scope of generalization is uncertain. So, alongside detailed case studies, other studies have attempted to measure effectiveness in ways that allow us to compare across regimes more easily. This has led scholars to quantify effectiveness, by aggregating the scores of different effectiveness indicators. For example, Carsten Helm and Detlef Sprinz (2000) provide an in-depth analysis of the transboundary air pollution regime in Europe and conclude that its effectiveness is low, being 39 per cent and 31 per cent effective for sulphur and nitrous control respectively.

One problem in using these studies to understand effectiveness is that they use different formulas to quantitatively assess effectiveness, so we cannot compare findings across studies. In an attempt to make effectiveness assessment methods more consistent, and building on former studies, two major projects began in the 2000s: the Oslo-Seattle Project (Miles et al. 2001) and the International Regimes Database Project (Breitmeier et al. 2006). These are both 'quali-quantitative' projects, meaning they are based on qualitative indicators but look at a large number of cases.

The Oslo-Seattle Project (Helm and Sprinz 2000; Hovi et al. 2003a) provides one of the most formalized and explicit effectiveness measures in global environmental politics. One innovative element of this measure is to include a counterfactual evaluation that considers the effects that could have been expected if a regime had not been adopted (Underdal 1997). This counterfactual evaluation is based either on interviews with the regime's practitioners and specialists, or on data regarding the environmental situation before the regime was set up. A second innovative aspect of the Oslo-Seattle Project is that it evaluated effectiveness in comparison to a collective optimum, meaning the optimal impact that could be reached through the regime. Including both indicators—effectiveness of regime and collective optimum—allows scholars to assign an effectiveness measure between 0 and 1, where 0 is not effective and 1 is very effective. This is presented as a fraction:

$$\text{Total effectiveness} = \frac{\text{(effectiveness of the adopted regime} - \text{effectiveness without the regime)}}{\text{(effectiveness of the collective optimum} - \text{effectiveness without the regime)}}$$

This calculation has given rise to several debates and reactions (Hovi et al. 2003b; Young 2003). Ronald Mitchell (2006) and Oran Young (2003) have emphasized the importance of comparing environmental problems that have similar structures, and not painting vastly different regimes with the same brush. Other critiques argue that using qualitative indicators to reach a final numerical score is inaccurate as it oversimplifies reality and gives the wrong impression that the indicator is robust. Despite these criticisms, the Oslo-Seattle Project measure of effectiveness is still used today and is regularly improved (Grundig 2012).

The second project aiming to create a standardized system for effectiveness measurement is the International Regimes Database Project. Unlike the Oslo-Seattle Project, the International Regimes Database Project does not analyse effectiveness as an average score across an entire regime, but instead breaks down effectiveness measurement according to the different legal components of a regime (i.e. its various conventions and protocols). Moreover, the database has a broader scope: whereas the Oslo-Seattle Project considers 44 cases (Miles et al. 2001), the International Regimes Database includes 92 regime elements (Breitmeier et al. 2006). The database also offers a coding system for numerous **explanatory variables** of regime effectiveness, such as a treaty's funding mechanism, the presence (or not) of an associated expert group, or the asymmetry of power relations between the treaty's member states. These variables are analysed one by one using a comparative quali-quantitative method. After the regime's numerical scores are analysed, each evaluation is supplemented with a detailed qualitative analysis. The International Regimes Database Project thus addresses some of the criticisms of the Oslo-Seattle Project by giving a more detailed assessment of the different components of each regime and by adding a qualitative explanation for each of its results. However, it is still regarded by some as an incomplete measure that could at best be used as a first step in broadly evaluating regime effectiveness, before going into more accurate, detailed qualitative research efforts.

Whatever method is used, there remains a divide between those who think that environmental agreements are generally effective and those who think that environmental performance would be the same without them (Vollenweider 2013: 345). Regardless of these divisions, these studies raise interesting questions about why regimes display differing degrees of effectiveness. Among other factors, such as problem structure, scientific (un)certainty, and state capacities, effectiveness also depends on the specific policy instruments used by states to implement their international commitments (Sprinz 2000). Since the 2000s, a growing number of analysts have attempted to categorize these instruments and analyse their differential impacts on effectiveness. In the remainder of the chapter we turn to these instruments and their political effects.

8.2 Types of policy instruments

States adopt domestic public policy instruments to comply with their international commitments. In that sense, instruments can play a crucial role in the effectiveness of global environmental politics. There are two broad types of policy instruments that are of particular relevance for global environmental **governance**: instruments that are meant to implement international commitments; and instruments that are meant to verify that states actually achieve their objectives. Both types of instrument are important to study for measuring the outcome dimension of effectiveness.

The modalities of implementation instruments

Implementation instruments can be classified according to their modality of execution (Delreux and Happaerts 2016; Jordan et al. 2012). In other words, they can be distinguished by examining how they achieve their policy objective. Four modalities can be distinguished: *regulation*, *incentives*, *persuasion*, and *service*.

The first modality, *regulation*, is an approach based on legal obligations. Initially associated with centralized 'command and control' mechanisms, such as caps on emissions from smokestacks, this modality evolved towards 'smart regulation' at the end of the 1990s (Gunningham and Sinclair 2017). In contrast to 'command and control' mechanisms, smart regulations are based on a more flexible approach of co-regulation or self-regulation. Regulatory instruments include prohibitions, moratoriums, restrictions, labelling, and mandatory **environmental impact assessments**. For example, the 1991 Protocol on Environmental Protection to the Antarctic Treaty requires states to conduct environmental impact studies for all projects carried out in Antarctica, to ensure that their impact is only minor and temporary (Article 8).

The second modality groups together instruments that provide positive or negative *incentives*. These instruments encourage or discourage actors to change their behaviour, without requiring a specific behavioural change. The main incentive instruments include pollution markets, taxes and tariffs, conditional funding, voluntary labels and certifications, and compensation mechanisms. Figure 8.2 illustrates that environmental taxes are used worldwide, and can account for up to 4 per cent of gross domestic product and around 10 per cent of tax revenues in certain countries. The rationale behind environmental taxes is to increase the price of environmentally harmful goods and activities, and thereby discourage their consumption and production. However, taxes do not prohibit specific behaviours, and actors can still choose to pay for the environmental externalities of their goods and activities if they wish. Box 8.1 discusses the effectiveness of carbon taxes.

A third group of instruments uses *persuasion* to change actors' behaviour. This involves co-operation and information strategies that aim to convince a target group to change its behaviour. Although persuasion instruments may appear weak at first glance because they involve

Box 8.1 Market-based instruments for addressing climate change

Greenhouse gas emissions must be reduced to address climate change. One way to achieve these reductions is via 'command and control' instruments, where governments mandate regulated entities to make behavioural changes, such as requiring emission reductions from a power plant. In recent decades, market-based instruments have increasingly been used alongside traditional command and control instruments. Market-based instruments are economic instruments that use elements of markets to internalize environmental externalities. In the case of greenhouse gas emissions, market-based instruments aim to incentivize firms or individuals to reduce their greenhouse gas emissions by putting a 'price' on greenhouse gases, thereby requiring polluting entities to account for the costs of their emissions. These instruments include emissions/carbon trading and carbon taxes.

Although not as prolifically used as emissions trading systems (see Chapter 10), carbon taxes are more straightforward, efficient, and increasingly important. A tax, collected and managed by a public authority, could be levied on greenhouse gas emissions. Polluters would be taxed commensurate with their pollution levels. Key questions involved in the design of carbon taxes include who is taxed, how much they are taxed, how this tax rate changes over time, and how the tax revenue would be used. Revenue from the tax could be used, for example, to stimulate innovations in low carbon technology or fund projects to help particularly vulnerable communities adapt to the effects of climate change.

As of May 2018, there are 26 carbon taxes implemented or scheduled globally, primarily at the national level. The Canadian provinces of British Columbia and Alberta have carbon taxes in place on the provincial level. The earliest national carbon taxes were implemented in the early 1990s by Finland, Poland, Norway, Sweden, and Denmark, though the vast majority of carbon taxes have been implemented within the decade up to 2018. Due to the many different elements involved in designing a carbon tax, most differ significantly, making it hard to make comparisons across tax schemes.

The effectiveness of carbon taxes is hotly debated. On one hand, carbon taxes are preferred by some because they place responsibility for greenhouse gas emissions on polluters; the infrastructure for taxation is mostly already in place; the taxes could raise badly needed funds for **adaptation** and other uses; and the concept is relatively simple compared to other market instruments, such as emissions trading systems. Notably, carbon trading and carbon taxes are not mutually exclusive; a carbon tax and an emissions trading system could both be implemented in the same jurisdiction. A few jurisdictions are doing this already, notably some countries in the European Union, such as France and Portugal, and in the Nordic countries.

On the other hand, due to the globalized nature of the world economy, and particularly the importance of international trade and competition, some scholars have raised concerns about unilaterally implementing carbon taxes. Specifically, there is concern that implementing a costly carbon tax in one jurisdiction could lead to 'carbon leakage', whereby a reduction in emissions in that jurisdiction is offset by a rise in emissions in another. Research shows that emissions flow from jurisdictions that lack carbon pricing to jurisdictions that do have a carbon tax through the import of emission-intensive goods, and that this transfer of emissions is increasing.

To address these concerns, and help to 'level the playing field', some argue that border tax adjustments—an added price based on the carbon content of goods—should be applied to imported goods. According to proponents, doing this would ensure a domestic price on carbon, and either create an incentive for foreign producers to lower the carbon intensity of their goods, or penalize nations that do not take climate action. However, others argue that due to a number of difficulties surrounding the implementation of border tax adjustments, such as trade rules against discrimination, they are unable to effectively put a price on a substantial amount of emissions from imported goods.

Sources: Andrew et al. 2010; Avi-Yonah and Uhlmann 2009; Bachram 2004; Bernstein et al. 2010; Fankhauser et al. 2010; Layfield 2013; Metcalf and Weisbach 2009; Neuhoff 2011; Sakai and Barrett 2016.

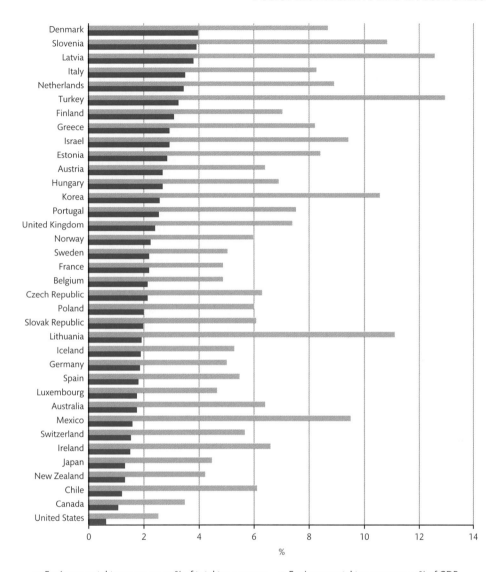

Figure 8.2 Environmentally related tax revenue (2018)

Source data from: OECD 2018

Includes tax on energy products, motor vehicles, pollutant emissions and resource extraction.

no coercive element, the power of ideas should not be underestimated. Certain reports, such as *Our Common Future* by the **Brundtland Commission**, and certain political documents such as **Agenda 21**, adopted at the 1992 **Rio Summit**, have helped to bring about paradigm shifts, by presenting ideas that define what is desirable and possible in global environmental governance writ large (see Chapter 6).

The fourth modality is *service*, meaning the direct provision of goods, services, or funding to induce behavioural change. The International Convention for the Prevention of Pollution from Ships (also known as the MARPOL Convention), for example, provides training for state parties in acquiring and using special installations for oil tankers, to avoid pollution from oil and other harmful products during routine operations and to prevent accidental spillages of such substances. Other service-oriented instruments provide funding intended to help developing countries to fulfil their international obligations under environmental treaties. This is the case for the Ramsar Convention's Fund for Wetland Conservation (created in 1990), the Montreal Protocol's Multilateral Fund (created in 1991), and the United Nations Framework Convention on Climate Change's Green Climate Fund (created in 2010).

Table 8.1 illustrates these different modalities of implementation instruments. This table, however, is only a simplified categorization. The reality is more complex, as several instruments combine several of the modalities. The Kyoto Protocol, for example, included both a regulatory dimension, with specific objectives for reducing greenhouse gas emissions, and an incentive dimension, with an emissions trading system. Also, impact assessments combine regulation—it is mandatory to conduct the assessment—and persuasion—the scientific evidence is supposed to be persuasive and to guide policy decisions, even when decision makers are not legally required to adopt adapted policies.

Table 8.1 Implementation instruments

Regulation	**Prohibitions**
	• To unload cleaning water from oil vats within 50 miles of the coast, OILPOL Convention (1954)
	• To hunt seals south of the 60th degree, Convention for the Protection of Antarctic Seals (1972)
	Moratoria
	• On commercial whaling, International Whaling Commission (1984)
	• On the ivory trade, CITES Convention (1989)
	Limitations
	• Trade of protected species, CITES Convention (1975)
	• On fisheries, International Commission for the Conservation of Atlantic Tunas (1969)
	Labelling
	• Genetically modified organisms intended for introduction into the environment, Cartagena Protocol (2000)
	• Dangerous chemicals, European Regulation 1272/2008 (2008)
	Prior informed consent
	• For the import of hazardous waste, Basel Convention (1989)
	• For the import of genetically modified organisms intended for introduction into the environment, Cartagena Protocol (2000)
	Impact studies
	• For any project in the region, Madrid Protocol of the Antarctic Treaty (1991)
	• For any transboundary project, Espoo Convention (1991)

Incentives	**Taxes and fees**
	• For the production of electricity from renewable energies, European Directive 2001/77/EC (2001)
	• European Regulatory Plan on Energy (1992)
	Credit markets
	• Greenhouse gas emissions, European Emissions Trading System (2005)
	• Clean Development Mechanism, Kyoto Protocol (1997)
	Conditional financing
	• World Bank Projects (1990)
	• Projects of the Global Environment Facility (1991)
	Compensation
	• To prevent deforestation, United Nations Collaborative Program for Reducing Emissions from Deforestation and Forest Degradation in Developing Countries (2008)
	• To avoid exploitation of oil, Yasuni Fund for the protection of a natural reserve in Ecuador (attempt, 2007)
	Labels and certifications
	• For ecological products, European Ecolabel 'Flower' (1992)
	• For wood, Forest Stewardship Council (1993) *
Persuasion	**Reports and documents**
	• The Limits to Growth, by the Club of Rome (1972) *
	• Our Common Future, by the Brundtland Commission (1987)
	Interface organizations between science and politics
	• Intergovernmental Panel on Climate Change (1988)
	• Intergovernmental Science-Policy Platform on Biodiversity and Ecosystem Services (2012)
	Statements and principles
	• Rio Declaration on the Environment and Development (1992)
	• Equator Principles on the management of social and environmental risks by financial institutions (2010) *
	Objectives and action plans
	• Agenda 21 (1992)
	• Sustainable Development Goals (2015)
	Guidelines
	• Bonn Guidelines on Access to Genetic Resources (2002)
	• Revised Guidelines of the Organisation for Economic Co-operation and Development for multinational enterprises (2011)
	Models
	• Champions of the Earth Award of the United Nations Environment Program (2004)
	• African Model Legislation on Genetic Resources (2000)
Service	**Capacity building**
	• Technology transfer on clean energy, Asia-Pacific Partnership on Clean Development and Climate (2005)
	• Provision of suitable equipment to minimize marine pollution by carriers, MARPOL Convention (1973/1978)
	Funding
	• Wetland Conservation Fund, Ramsar Convention (1990)
	• Multilateral Fund for the implementation of the Montreal Protocol (1991)
	• UNFCCC Green Climate Fund (2010)

* Initiatives of non-state actors

The modalities of verification instruments

Verification instruments are also key to ensuring that states' environmental commitments are respected. Two types of verification instruments can be distinguished: *compliance instruments* and *enforcement instruments*. Compliance is the degree of consistency between the norms, principles, and rules set out in international regimes and the corresponding behaviour. *Compliance instruments* aim at verifying the actions that states are undertaking. *Enforcement instruments* are the adjustments and measures carried out to correct for non-compliance. Table 8.2 details the main compliance and enforcement instruments used in global environmental governance. Because verification instruments are meant to control compliance and enforcement, they mostly rely on the regulatory modality, such as reporting for compliance or sanctions for enforcement. But a few verification instruments use persuasion, such as compliance rankings or naming and shaming, to catalyse enforcement.

The most widely used instruments for verifying compliance are reporting mechanisms. The vast majority of multilateral environmental agreements require their parties to periodically submit reports on the domestic implementation of their obligations. One objective of reporting is to support states in keeping track of their national actions; another is to make those actions more transparent and therefore enforceable. For example, the Paris Agreement's pledge and review mechanism relies on reporting. Under the pledge and review mechanism, parties are required to pledge emission-reduction targets, and produce biennial reports on the implementation status of those targets, with a view to reviewing and ratcheting them up during each subsequent compliance period (Keohane and Oppenheimer 2016).

Although a seemingly simple compliance mechanism, reporting requirements are not always followed. Some countries fail to meet their reporting obligations, or submit reports that lack detail or are inconsistent in their evaluation criteria. In attempts to encourage compliance, the secretariats of several international environmental agreements, such as the secretariat of the Convention on International Trade in Endangered Species of Wild Fauna and Flora, compile their parties' reports into a 'report on reports', so that all reports are visible for anyone to access and analyse. At the same time, many countries, particularly developing countries, have long argued that the reporting requirements across the many environmental conventions they are party to are onerous, especially because these reporting requirements and formats are not streamlined. These countries cite a lack of domestic capacity to produce different reports for the many different but closely related treaties to which they are party.

Reporting is mostly performed on a self-reporting basis. However, some environmental agreements encourage states to publicly identify other states that they suspect are out of compliance. The 1989 Convention on the Control of Transboundary Movements of Hazardous Wastes and their Disposal, for instance, states that: 'Any **Party** which has reason to believe that another Party is acting or has acted in breach of its obligations under this Convention may inform the Secretariat thereof' (Article 19).

While states have accepted some verification measures undertaken by their peers, they are more reluctant to delegate verification instruments to international institutions. There are a few exceptions, where states have delegated control tasks to supranational authorities, including reporting that is carried out by external reviewers. For example, the International Whaling Commission was revised in 1977 to authorize, with the consent of the targeted states, bilateral exchanges of observers, who visit boats and sites on land to evaluate implementation. The observers then report any infractions to the Commission. Similarly, in 1991 the Organisation for

Table 8.2 Verification instruments

Compliance instrument	Enforcement instrument
Surveillance system	**Public denunciations**
• Cooperative Program for Monitoring and Evaluation of the Long-range Transmission of Air Pollutants in Europe (1984)	• 'Fossil of the Day' Award to the delegation that contributed the most to blocking climate negotiations (since 1999) *
• Satellite surveillance, Antarctic Treaty (1959)	• 'Captain Hook' Awards to the greatest plunderer
Filing of complaints by citizens	of genetic resources (since 2002) *
• For environmental responsibility, European Court of Justice (2010)	**Calls for a boycott**
• For failure to enforce its legislation, North American Commission for Environmental Cooperation (1994)	• Boycott of products using tropical timber, Greenpeace (1990) *
Rankings and indices	• Boycott of cosmetic products tested on animals, NatureWatch (2000) *
• Environmental Performance Index, Yale University (2000)	**Suspension of benefits**
• Living Planet Report by WWF (1998)	• Decommissioning of World Heritage Sites of
Reports and investigations	the United Nations Educational, Scientific and
• Investigation procedure of the Montreal Protocol on the Ozone Layer (1992)	Cultural Organization (1972)
• Expert report to review the implementation of environmental provisions, Free Trade Agreement between the European Union and Korea (2011)	• Suspension of aid, Multilateral Fund of the Montreal Protocol (1987)
• Paris Agreement's pledge and review mechanism	**Postponements of commitments**
• CITES reports on reports	• Postponement of emission-reduction targets from one commitment phase to another, Kyoto Protocol (2005)
• Bilateral exchanges of observers, who visit boats and on-land sites, International Whaling Commission (1997)	**Liability and redress**
Disclosure of information and self-assessment	• International Convention on Civil Liability for Oil Pollution Damage (1969)
• Produced by organizations that decide to become members of the Global Reporting Initiative (1997) *	• Paris (1960) and Brussels (1963) Conventions of the Organisation for Economic Co-operation and Development for nuclear accidents
• Biosafety Clearing-House, Cartagena Protocol (2000)	**Sanctions and penalties**
Audit and evaluation by third parties	• Suspension of trade in all CITES-listed species for Guinea (2013)
• To verify the compliance with ISO 14001 standards *	• Monetary penalties for non-compliance with
• Peer review provided for by the Organisation for Economic Co-operation and Development (1991)	environmental standards to encourage trade, Free Trade Agreement between the United States and Australia (2004)
Arbitration and courts	
• International Commission for the Protection of the Rhine against Pollution (1950)	
• International Tribunal for the Law of the Sea (1982)	
• European Court of Justice	

*Initiatives of non-state actors

Economic Co-operation and Development set up a system for reviewing the environmental performance of its member states. This process is based on the 'peer review' technique, with the peers being other member states. More recently, the 2015 Paris Agreement on climate change adopted the so-called 'Measurement, Reporting and Verification' procedure, which includes a technical expert review to assess the parties' nationally determined contributions.

The Co-operative Programme for Monitoring and Evaluation of the Long-range Transmission of Air Pollutants in Europe is an exception to states' general reluctance to delegate verification to international instruments. Set up by the 1984 **Protocol** to the 1979 Geneva Convention on Transboundary Air Pollution, this programme functions as a network of monitoring stations located in several state parties, that evaluates air pollution. It collects information on air pollution across Europe and sends it to the Geneva Convention's executive body in an annual report.

Another mechanism for verifying compliance is the enquiry procedure. Most enquiry procedures are launched by parties to an international agreement, and operate by asking states suspected of not complying fully to conduct an enquiry or to authorize experts to conduct an enquiry to evaluate any deficiencies in compliance. This is the case, for example, with the Convention on International Trade in Endangered Species of Wild Fauna and Flora. Under the Convention, any party concerned about trade in endangered species by another party can bring the matter to that party or to the Convention secretariat. Occasionally, it is made possible for international secretariats to independently launch an enquiry procedure. For example, the Montreal Protocol's secretariat has exceptional prerogative to conduct enquiries into its parties' compliance level. The secretariat can trigger a 'non-compliance' procedure on the basis of information sent (or not sent) by states as part of the Protocol's reporting system. It can also initiate an enquiry procedure using non-compliance information collected from sources other than its parties, including **non-state actors** such as **non-governmental organizations**.

If parties to an environmental agreement are found to be out of compliance, enforcement instruments can be used. However, enforcement instruments are rare in global environmental politics because states prefer to maintain their **sovereignty**, and therefore their control over their own policies. Moreover, when they do exist, enforcement instruments mostly consist of discussions with the non-compliant state about how to bring the state into compliance. Some environmental agreements conduct such discussions in ad hoc arbitration mechanisms. In very rare cases, enquiry procedures lead to sanctions, when non-compliant behaviours are identified or confirmed. For instance, the compliance body of the Convention on International Trade in Endangered Species of Wild Fauna and Flora can decide to suspend all trade in related species by non-compliant states. These procedures are generally quite vague and rarely used, however. States can also bring charges of non-compliance to the Permanent Court of Arbitration, the International Tribunal of the Law of the Sea, the International Court of Justice, or the European Court of Justice. Of these, only the European Court of Justice enables unilateral action, meaning that under all of the other dispute settlement venues, both the plaintiff and the defendant have to agree on bringing a case together (Matisoff 2010). It is also possible for states to apply non-compliance sanctions outside an environmental agreement, such as through trade sanctions. However, states have very rarely used such unilateral measures (Urpelainen 2010; see also Chapter 10).

Because of the sovereignty-related concerns, sanctioning systems can be counterproductive in global environmental governance: actors are reluctant to join treaties that use too strong verification instruments. For example, under the International Convention on Civil Liability for Oil Pollution Damage (1969), its 1992 Protocol, and its 2000 Amendments, in case of a marine oil spill, compensation may be paid by the transporters and oil company to anyone who suffers from oil pollution. However, the agreements also set out significant limits to this compensation due to the risk that transporters might refuse to participate in the mechanism, meaning that no party would adopt the agreement (Hay 2010).

In other cases, sanctions can be counterproductive because they would worsen environmental degradation. For example, a sanction foreseen in the United Nations Educational,

Scientific and Cultural Organization World Heritage Convention is to declassify World Heritage Sites if the state does not comply with the Convention management practices. The problem is that declassification does not help to improve the environment, since the site is then left totally unprotected.

For these reasons, environmental agreements often favour an approach to non-compliance that is based on **capacity building**, such as providing additional resources to countries that are unable to meet their commitments. A capacity-building approach is also more in line with recognizing the different national contexts for compliance (Weiss and Jacobson 1998). For example, the 2013 Minamata Convention on Mercury has a specific international programme for capacity-building as a mechanism to support compliance. The Convention also provides that this mechanism 'shall be facilitative in nature and shall pay particular attention to the respective national capabilities and circumstances of Parties' (Article 15(1)).

We can further refine the typology of implementation and verification instruments by looking at some additional characteristics, such as schemes developed by states versus non-state actors. In contrast to the state-led instruments discussed above, an example of a non-state enforcement instrument is the 'Fossil of the Day' award, a daily prize given by the Climate Action Network to countries judged to have been the most obstructionist in the United Nations climate change negotiations. The award, initiated in 1999 by the German NGO Forum, has gained visibility over the years, and acts as an enforcement instrument based on persuasion, according to the naming and shaming logic. A refinement could also be made by distinguishing voluntary schemes and obligatory ones. For example, the Western Hemisphere Shorebird Reserve Network, a network of 66 protected areas in six countries, relies on a voluntary approach, where the site owners voluntarily register their sites as protected areas. In contrast, the Natura 2000 protected areas, in the same sector, are based on a European directive in which member states are required to register a certain percentage of their natural areas as protected areas.

A rich body of scholarship questions the effectiveness of instruments of all modalities. Are regulation-based instruments more effective than incentive-based instruments? Can verification instruments be effective even if they are not based on sanctions? Are instruments set up by non-state actors only effective if states support them? These questions have sparked lively debates. Some claim that voluntary instruments can be surprisingly effective. The Helsinki Convention on the Protection of the Marine Environment of the Baltic Sea and the Convention on Long-range Transboundary Air Pollution provide support for this argument. They compel states to limit their harmful emissions without imposing that limitation on them. Rather, they rely on information exchange, consultation, or research in order to secure state compliance, and have been successful at doing so. However, voluntary commitments are more likely to be respected if they are expressed at a high political level, are easy to verify, and are collectively monitored (Skjærseth 2010; Tallberg 2002). Moreover, the effectiveness of voluntary instruments can be explained by the fact that they allow states to commit to a level, and on a timeline, that they are realistically capable of achieving. But compliance with these voluntary instruments doesn't necessarily correlate with effectiveness, because states following minimal levels of commitment will still be considered compliant, even if this yields little to no positive environmental impact (Harrison 1998).

Therefore, there is uncertainty about the relative effectiveness of specific instruments. So it is surprising to see that certain types of instruments quickly diffuse and become widely used while others remain marginal. As Section 8.3 discusses, the diffusion of a particular type of instrument can be explained by many factors besides its proven effectiveness.

8.3 The diffusion of instruments

How instruments diffuse

International agreements could dictate the precise types of instruments that their parties should use to implement their international obligations. Often, however, international agreements leave these decisions to the discretion of the parties. This is done to allow states to decide for themselves which types of instruments would be most effective in implementing their international obligations, given their specific domestic contexts (e.g. politics, laws, capacities, etc.). Given the diversity of domestic contexts, we would expect this to lead to a diverse set of policy instruments, but in practice policy instruments are often consistent from one state to the other. We also see similarities across international instruments in this regard. How does this happen?

When the instruments adopted by different political authorities (domestic or international) are similar, they are referred to as isomorphic. Isomorphism is relatively common and is usually not the result of simultaneous independent decisions taken by different authorities. In most cases, a policy innovation appears in a particular context and then diffuses to other contexts, creating similarities. The diffusion dynamics of several different instruments are illustrated in Table 8.3.

Diffusion can occur along two dimensions: horizontal or vertical. *Horizontal diffusion* means that an instrument is adopted by various other actors at the same political level. For example, climate change action plans have spread to cities all over the world, as cities learn from one another through transnational networks (Hakelberg 2014; see also Box 4.6). *Vertical diffusion* happens across two or more political levels. Diffusion can happen from a lower to a higher level; this is known as the 'internationalization' of domestic regulations (Desombre 2000). As shown in Table 8.3, vehicle pollution standards spread from an American state level to the federal level; national environmental policy plans spread from the national to the European level; and emissions objectives spread from the national to the international level. Diffusion can also occur from a higher to a lower political level. As Table 8.3 shows, national environmental policy plans diffused from the international level to the national level as a condition of World Bank loans and for environmental performance assessment by the Organisation for Economic Co-operation and Development.

Diffusion can occur between international institutions that address the same environmental issue (i.e. within a regime complex—see Chapter 7). For example, specialized ecolabels in the forestry sector have spread to different geographical areas. Diffusion can also occur across regimes that address different issues: **Prior Informed Consent** procedures, which were initially applied to **dangerous wastes** transfers, are now applied to imports of genetically modified organisms as well.

Finally, diffusion can occur between *public* and *private initiatives*. For example, the specialized ecolabels in forestry, which were first developed through partnerships between non-governmental organizations and timber growers such as the Forest Stewardship Council (see Box 4.7), have since been adopted by some governments such as Canada and the United States, for example through the Sustainable Forestry Initiative label.

Table 8.3 Examples of instrument diffusion

	First occurrence	First wave of diffusion	Second wave of diffusion
Vehicle pollution standards	1960–California law	1965–Federal US law	1968–Japan law on air pollution; 1970–European Directive 70/220/EEC
Access to information	1978–US law; 1983–Article 111 of the constitution of the Netherlands	1990–European Directive 90/313/EEC on free access to environmental information	1992–2000–Legislation in the former communist countries; 1992–Principle 10 of the Rio Declaration; 1998–Aarhus Convention
General ecolabels	1978–German ecolabel 'The Blue Angel'	1992–European ecolabel 'The Flower'	
Prior informed consent	1989–Basel Convention on hazardous waste	1991–Bamako Convention on Hazardous Wastes; 1998–Rotterdam Convention on Hazardous Chemicals; 2000–Cartagena Protocol on genetically modified organisms	2012–European Regulation no. 649/2012 on dangerous chemicals
National environmental policy plans	1989–Netherlands plan; 1992–Chapter 8.7 of Agenda 21	1992–5th European Environmental Action Programme; 1992–World Bank sets national plans as loan condition; 1993–Organisation for Economic Co-operation and Development sets environmental strategy as a criterion for assessing environmental performance	1995–2003–Plans in several European countries; 1997–UN General Assembly resolution calling on states to adopt an environmental strategy by 2002
Targets for emission of atmospheric pollutants	1990–Amendments to the US Clean Air Act	1997–Kyoto Protocol	2005–European Emissions Trading System
Environmental taxes on energy	1991–Swedish regulation; 1992–Danish regulation	1992–European regulatory plan	1992–Netherlands regulations; 1992–2000–The European Union and the Organisation for Economic Co-operation and Development promote these taxes internationally, but without success
Specialized ecolabels	1993–Forest Stewardship Council	1994–Sustainable Forestry Initiative, North America; 1995–Sustainable Forest Management of the Canadian Standards Association, Canada; 1996–Marine Stewardship Council; 1999–Forest Certification Systems Recognition Program (PEFC), Europe	
Moratoria on genetically modified organisms	1998–2004– European moratorium	1998–2013–Mexican moratorium on corn; 1999–2005 Chinese moratorium	

Sources: Busch et al. 2005; Gupta and Falkner 2006; Ovodenko and Keohane 2012.

Types of instruments that have diffused prolifically

The four types of instruments that have diffused most prolifically are those that are voluntary, commodified, based on transparency, and developed by private actors (Busch et al. 2005). *Voluntary* approaches emerged in the 1990s following certain problems created by regulation-based approaches. Imposing uniform standards can be economically ineffective because standards take a long time to develop and revise, and they do not incentivize industries to make any effort beyond what the standards require (Harrison 1998). In contrast, voluntary contributions could push some industries to go beyond their usual practices because, for instance, they may discover a new market case for environmental innovation (see Chapter 4).

Instruments that result in *commodification* of the environment have also diffused prolifically. Peter Newell (2005: 268) defines commodification as 'a trend towards viewing the market as the source of innovation, efficiency and incentives necessary to combat environmental degradation without compromising economic growth'. This tendency originates from industry pressures and a lack of government financial capacity. For example, the 1992 Rio Declaration calls on states to use economic instruments. Agenda 21 also advocated a master plan encouraging the creation of new markets in the anti-pollution and resource management sectors. This diffusion of commodifying instruments has grown increasingly strong since these instruments were adopted in 1992 (Dinar et al. 2011; Fuentes-George 2013; see Box 8.2). For example, emissions trading systems have proliferated across the globe.

Box 8.2 The commodification of nature: payments for ecosystem services

Ecosystem services are the benefits people obtain from ecosystems. Payments for ecosystem services instruments protect ecosystems by paying resource users/managers for conserving ecosystems that provide benefits to humans. There are four categories of ecosystem services: *provisioning services* such as food, fuel, ores, timber, and water; *regulation services* that affect climate, disease, water quality, etc.; *cultural services* that provide recreational, aesthetic, spiritual, and educational benefits; and *support services* such as soil formation, nutrient cycling, and photosynthesis. Forests provide all of these categories of services: food provided by a forest, such as nuts and berries, is a provisioning service; the storage of carbon in trees is a regulation service; recreational opportunities, such as hiking and birdwatching, are cultural services; and finally, cycling of nutrients is a support service.

Payments for ecosystem services are economic instruments designed to stop the destruction, depletion, and degradation of ecosystems. The main idea is as follows: landowners and users tend to be poorly motivated to protect ecosystem services on their land because such services are otherwise unvalued in economic terms. Therefore, land users can only be encouraged to protect ecosystem services if they are given a financial incentive, or payment, to implement more sustainable land use management. These payments come from beneficiaries of the environmental service—either directly, or from governments acting on behalf of the beneficiaries. By connecting ecosystem service providers—those who own and manage land—and the users of the services in a contractual arrangement, a market or quasi-market is created, in which the previously free ecosystem service is valued as a commodity.

The concept is based in neoclassical environmental economics, which considers environmental degradation to be a result of market failure. In this view, markets are unable to internalize the true costs of environmental degradation, or 'externalities'. This means that individuals can 'free ride' by gaining benefits from using **public goods**—goods that are difficult to exclude users from and whose use does not reduce its availability for others—without incurring costs. As such, payments for ecosystem services are part of the broader class of market-based instruments for environmental policy.

Costa Rica has one of the most frequently analysed national payment for ecosystem instruments, called the 'Pagos por Servicios Ambientales'. This scheme was the first formal, countrywide programme to pay providers of ecosystem services, and it is partly credited for helping the country achieve significant reforestation. The instrument targets four ecosystem services: greenhouse gas mitigation; **conservation** of **biodiversity**; regulation of the hydraulic system, including provision of water; and scenic beauty for tourism and leisure. Private landowners are paid for conserving their land, with the funding coming from a tax on fossil fuels. Additional funding has come from international donors such as the Global Environment Facility, the World Bank, Conservation International, and the German aid agency. The instrument has been a source of inspiration for similar programmes in Latin America, and Costa Rica has hosted dozens of official delegations from other countries who want to study the instrument. However, the instrument has also been criticized for distributing uniform payments that do not take into account the costs of conserving land (against the benefits owners would obtain from developing the land), for distributing payments inefficiently, and for providing payments for services that would have been provided anyway.

Payment for ecosystem service instruments remains controversial. There are some who are critical of the commodification and commercialization of nature that such schemes entail, as well as the uncertainties associated with the valuation of ecosystem services. These projects' negative social impacts have been documented, including enclosure, and reinforcement of existing inequalities and conflicts over access to and control of resources. Enclosure, in which individuals or communities lose access to a resource, can happen in a number of different ways. Users that lack formal ownership also face obstacles to participating in the programme and receiving payments. In the case of collective ownership, some members of a community can lose access to a resource. Because ownership can be poorly defined, and in some cases contested (and the concept itself can be understood differently in different cultures), clarifying who owns what and who has rights of access and use is a social and political process that can result in 'losers' who are no longer able to rely on access to a resource for their livelihoods.

Sources: Farrell 2014; Fuentes-George 2013; Hansen et al. 2015; Kinzig et al. 2011; Pagiola et al. 2005; Pascual et al. 2010; Rodríguez de Francisco and Boelens 2015; Sattler and Matzdorf 2013; Schomers and Matzdorf 2013.

There has also been a proliferation in instruments that aim to increase *transparency* in environmental policymaking (Ciplet et al. 2018). Since the 1990s, governments have frequently organized public consultations surrounding environmental decision-making (Langley 2001) although their reasoning for doing so varied. For central and eastern countries, the rationale was to strengthen emerging democratic processes. In China it was about increasing citizens' capacity to evaluate government performance, without making it possible for them to question governmental choices (Florini 2010). Irrespective of the domestic motivations for adopting them, the number and types of public consultation instruments have increased globally, encouraged in part by the 1998 Aarhus Convention on Access to Information, Public Participation in Decision-making and Access to Justice in Environmental Matters (Mason 2010) and the 2018 Regional Agreement on Access to Information, Public Participation and Justice in Environmental Matters in Latin America and the Caribbean.

Transparency-enhancing mechanisms, such as public consultations, have become commonplace in the creation of any new environmental policy. For instance, the 2015 Paris Agreement on climate change relies on an 'enhanced transparency framework', with recurrent public reports on states' progress regarding implementation. This, in turn, builds trust and makes countries comply with their pledges (Gupta and van Asselt 2019). In the private sector, a growing amount of information is also made publicly available following pressure from consumers, investors, and states: most companies annually publish a report on their environmental impact. They also regularly disclose information related to their specific fields of activity. For instance, in the context of **genetic resources**, several companies that use natural resources make public their agreements with local governments for access to those resources (Van Alstine 2014).

Instruments that catalyse *privatization* of governance have also proliferated. This means that non-state actors (see Chapter 4) increasingly participate in the choice and deployment of policy instruments, independently or along with states. In the forest management sector, for example, there has been a transition from a sustainable forest management regime controlled by states to a voluntary certification regime controlled by civil society, such as the Forest Stewardship Council. The diffusion of non-state certification schemes is actively supported by certain **intergovernmental organizations**, such as the World Bank and regional development banks (Chan and Pattberg 2008).

Why instruments diffuse

There are four primary explanations for diffusion, which are not necessarily mutually exclusive: *coercion, competition, learning,* and *socialization* (Dobbin et al. 2007). The first explanation, *coercion,* occurs when the motivation to adopt a new instrument is exogenous, imposed by external actors. This can be done through negative incentives, for instance when adopting a particular type of instrument is a condition for securing a loan or aid, receiving a good environmental evaluation, or avoiding the imposition of trade or security sanctions. For example, the World Bank has participated in the diffusion of national environmental policy plans through its lending programme. In 1988 Madagascar was the first country to benefit from such a plan, following World Bank funding.

The second explanation for diffusion involves *competition,* where instruments are adopted from another political context in order to maintain competitiveness between actors. This is particularly common with respect to foreign investment. For example, if a car manufacturer is required to adopt higher (i.e. more expensive) pollution standards to sell its vehicles in a particular country, it is in the manufacturer's interest to ensure that its competitors are subject to the same pollution standards, even if they do not sell their vehicles in that country. That manufacturer may then lobby other governments to adopt the higher standards so it can maintain competitiveness in these markets. In addition, it can be in the interest of other countries' governments to adopt compatible standards so that their car manufacturers are not obliged to develop different cars for different export markets, which also drives up costs of production (Prakash and Potoski 2006; Saikawa 2013; Vogel 1995). Competition can result in a 'race to the top' as in the car manufacturing example, but it could also lead to a '**race to the bottom**' if the instruments adopted enable, for instance, lower pollution standards (see Chapter 10).

The third explanation for diffusion is *learning.* Learning involves reproducing an instrument in a new political context when it has proven to be effective elsewhere. Adopting lessons from the experience of others is generally a safer strategy than proceeding randomly through trial and error. This is one of the reasons why emissions trading systems, which have proven effective in the American context for sulphur emission reductions, have diffused to climate change regimes for reducing greenhouse gas emissions. States sometimes put forward proposals inspired by either successful national practices or previous international agreements, to save time during international negotiations. Learning can also be strategically supported by states through capacity building projects. For example, because the European Union wanted to connect its own carbon market to those in other regions, it provided expertise and training to Chinese officials to aid in the diffusion of carbon markets to China (Biedenkopf et al. 2017).

The learning explanation is usually based on rationality and efficiency: governments replicate instruments that work. For example, market-based instruments, such as emissions trading or pollution taxes, are often chosen based on a rational economic logic. That is, they allow environmental objectives to be reached at a lower cost (Urpelainen 2010). But instruments also sometimes diffuse through learning for reasons other than costs. Victor and Coben (2005) note, for example, that the majority of international regimes that regulate atmospheric pollution set maximum quantities for emissions of pollutants because states perceive them as efficient and easy to implement. This policy choice is surprising, as incentive-based instruments, such as a tax, can be more effective than a regulatory approach in reducing pollution. Indeed, setting maximum quantities for the emission of pollutants is less likely to be effective because these measures are not immediate—actors have a certain period of time over which they can pollute—and as economic actors cannot foresee the costs of this type of limitation they often practise free-riding. In contrast, taxes have consequences for prices, can be applied immediately, and give a clear indication of the costs. What this means is that states have often bounded rationality and prefer to follow the solutions provided by other states rather than looking for more effective instruments.

Finally, when diffusion is based on normative or causal beliefs such as an instrument's soundness or fairness, rather than on material interests, diffusion occurs through *socialization*. The diffusion of bans on genetically modified organisms and the spread of instruments for access to information have mainly occurred through processes of socialization. This is also the case for several instruments that have been transposed from American law to international environmental law, such as in the case of whale protection. In 1972, the US Congress adopted the Marine Mammal Protection Act. This law prohibits any person living in the United States from killing, hunting, injuring, or tormenting any marine mammal species, even species that are not under threat of extinction. In 1986, the International Whaling Commission took inspiration from this American law and adopted a ban on commercial hunting of all whale species.

The diffusion of instruments can take many different forms, and find diverse explanations based on interests, effectiveness, or values. As such, the choice of instruments is perhaps less rational than it may seem, and the forces behind their diffusion perhaps more profound. Instruments raise questions that are essentially political. We turn to these questions in Section 8.4.

8.4 What are the political effects of instruments?

Much of the management literature on instruments tends to adopt a managerial and prescriptive stance (Vollenweider 2013). In other words, it sees instruments as neutral tools that provide ready-to-use solutions. This is surprising because environmental policy is politically contested, with different perceptions about the economic costs and benefits of environmental policies and how those costs and benefits are or should be distributed among actors.

In global environmental governance, instruments have generally been studied as non-neutral devices, meaning that they have political effects rather beyond their initial objectives. Two broad schools of thought have developed that give different weights to the potential positive impacts of instruments as policy tools and their potential negative effects on environmental protection and broader power distribution.

Ecological modernization and instruments as solutions providers

The first school of thought believes the positive impacts of instruments outweigh their potential counterproductive effects. In other words, from this perspective, instruments' effectiveness in catalysing political action counterbalances the possibly negative impacts of instruments, such as the reduction of actors' room for manoeuvre in a specific policy area. This school argues that instruments prolong, specify, and make possible political action, and as such can even rebalance governance systems.

This school of thought relies on the effectiveness of instruments to solve **sustainable development** issues and is generally based on the **ecological modernization** paradigm (Hajer 1995). According to this paradigm, it is possible to limit negative environmental impacts by using instruments as facilitators for green technology development (see Box 8.3). Two forms of ecological modernization coexist (Szarka 2012). A first, 'techno-optimistic' form presents instruments as obvious solutions to environmental problems, the selection of which can be left to experts and public decision makers. This is the 'zero regret' and 'win-win' discourse that supports developing instruments for environmental protection according to a top-down approach.

Box 8.3 The international politics of green technology innovation and transfer

Technology that is useful in solving environmental problems is often called 'green technology'. While there is no single definition for green technology, one that is commonly used derives from Agenda 21, which defines green technologies as those that protect the environment, emit fewer pollutants, use resources more sustainably, and/or recycle more by-products. Importantly, the term does not apply solely to individual technologies, but also to practices and procedures, goods and services, and equipment. An entire chapter of Agenda 21 is devoted to promoting greater access to and the transfer of technology, and the idea of **technology transfer** is reflected in several important multilateral environmental agreements, including the United Nations Framework Convention on Climate Change and the Convention on Biological Diversity.

The importance of green technology development and transfer is especially pronounced in meeting climate change goals. Addressing climate change demands technological advancement, including for reducing resource inputs and emissions outputs, and to scale up the use of renewable technologies. Technology is also crucial to adaptation, for instance through improved irrigation techniques, levees for protecting coasts from sea level rise, and new varieties of drought-resistant crops. Indeed, technology transfer was identified in the 2007 Bali Action Plan under the United Nations Framework Convention on Climate Change as a priority area for international climate action. Further negotiations under this Convention resulted in the creation of a Technology Mechanism to facilitate the transfer of technology. One way it accomplishes this is by assisting developing countries to create strategies and road maps for adopting various technologies based on their individual needs.

While the need for technology development and transfer in addressing climate change is widely agreed on, there is considerable disagreement over how this should be achieved. The role of intellectual property rights, in particular, is at the centre of one of the most contentious debates in international climate negotiations. A polarized debate has developed between mostly developing countries, who argue that intellectual property rights are a barrier to the transfer of green technology, and most developed countries, who argue that these rights are necessary for incentivizing innovation. The intellectual property system is the most widely used policy for encouraging technological innovation in the private sector. It is designed to allow companies to obtain benefits from investing in the research and development of something that benefits everybody—technological advancement. However, the drawback of intellectual property is that it can inhibit the diffusion, or transfer, of the very technology that intellectual property is designed to stimulate. As such, it can also stifle further innovation. Proposals put forward by developing countries to overcome these barriers, such as compulsory licensing, in which a government allows a domestic company to produce a patented product without the approval of the patent holder, have been strongly opposed by developed countries.

Despite these disagreements over intellectual property, many innovative mechanisms to facilitate access to green technologies are being developed. One example of this is green patent databases, which gather patented innovations in a certain area into a single database, making it easier for those in need of green technologies to connect with investors and inventors. Facilitating these connections is intended to reduce high transaction costs, and make it easier to license and utilize green patents. The World Intellectual Property Organization launched a GREEN initiative in 2013, comprised of two components: a searchable database of green patents, and a platform for connecting those who need technology and those who can provide it. An assessment of this initiative shows that the filing of patents for green technologies related to energy have exponentially increased over the last decade, although this has slowed in recent years. Furthermore, over 60 per cent of green energy patents originate from only four countries: Japan, the United States, Germany, and increasingly China.

Additionally, patent pledges are designed to allow anyone to use a patented technology, simplifying procedures for accessing the technology. For example, the World Business Council for Sustainable Development launched the Eco-Patent Commons in 2008 in collaboration with a number of multinational corporations such as IBM, Nokia, and Sony. The Eco-Patent Commons is made up of patents that are donated, meaning users can utilize the patents for free and patent holders pledge not to enforce their exclusive rights so long as the innovation is used in a product or process that has some environmental benefit. Although recent research has not found evidence that the Eco-Patent Commons increased the diffusion of the donated technologies, it may yet be too early to assess this.

Despite some promising opportunities for tackling the intertwined issues of green technology innovation and diffusion, most analysts agree that these issues, particularly the role of intellectual property rights, are likely to remain controversial in the coming years. A broader question involves how to transfer the 'know how', or knowledge, needed to use and further develop green technologies, beyond just the transfer of hardware or practices.

Sources: Abdel-Latif 2015; Hall and Helmers 2013; Meeûs and Strowel 2012; Raiser et al. 2017.

A second, reflexive form of ecological modernization emphasizes the societal decisions necessary to facilitate the development and diffusion of these instruments. From this perspective, for instruments to work, it is necessary to overcome and counteract the reluctance of the most powerful groups, especially industrial pressure groups. For example, according to supporters of this more reflexive ecological modernization, if electric vehicles are not widely used in the United States, it is because of obstruction from the major American automobile manufacturers; if preferential renewable energy tariffs have been so difficult to maintain in

Europe, this is because they have been criticized by industry groups as violations of free competition. Since technology is an element that the private sector often masters more effectively than public actors (Tjernshaugen 2012), then in order to promote reflexive ecological modernization it is necessary to restore balance by involving all **stakeholders** in the decision-making process.

Governmentality and instruments as inequalities providers

The second school of thought on the political effects of instruments views them in a more critical light. It highlights subtle power struggles around the choice and development of instruments, using in particular the governmentality concept borrowed from Michel Foucault (Methmann 2011: 70). Governmentality (Foucault 1991) states that instruments can gain autonomy and deviate from the initial goals of the policymakers who designed them (see Box 8.4). Instruments can reinforce powerful interests, fail to solve environmental problems, wrongly modify environmental representations, and bring institutional inertia. More than instruments per se, it is the broader social environment in which they operate that exacerbates their potential negative effects. Changing these social structures—such as in the case of a 'green state', which suggests better representing nature's interests in national decision-making processes (Eckersley 2018) or a 'just transition', which takes into account the social costs of environmental transitions (Healy and Barry 2017) for example—could rectify some of these problems (see also Chapter 2).

Instruments often reflect and accentuate power imbalances between actors. For example, although the Nagoya Protocol suggests that states take measures to improve access to justice in case of misappropriation of genetic resources, these devices remain inaccessible to indigenous populations (Orsini et al. 2014). A similar difficulty arises for developing countries wishing to use verification instruments such as interstate dispute settlement mechanisms. This is because proceedings can take decades, during which a very complex political game involving strategic use of media or attempts to bargain can unfold, a game that requires a lot of financial and discursive resources (Dieperink 2011). Likewise, certifications such as those by the International Standardization Organization generate costs that are not always easy for developing countries to take on, which can therefore have the effect of favouring products and practices from developed countries.

In addition to accentuating power imbalances, instruments can have unexpected negative practical effects. For example, technical standards are useful to set objectives but can also reduce companies' motivation to do better. Bans are essential to stop damaging activities but can also create counterproductive collateral effects. One example is the ban on trade in elephant ivory adopted by parties to the Convention on International Trade in Endangered Species of Wild Fauna and Flora in 1989. Although this ban is intended to protect elephants, some have argued that it has increased contraband as ivory has become an even more valuable material now it is no longer available legally (see also Box 8.4).

Instruments can also have negative effects by changing actors' perceptions of environmental problems. American efforts to develop technologies to reduce vehicle emissions, such as carbon monoxide, hydrocarbons, and nitrogen oxide, have been fruitful. However, they have also led to increased vehicle traffic as people have started to think that cars were environmentally sustainable (Szarka 2012: 95). In contrast, certain instruments over-regulate

Box 8.4 Unintended consequences in policymaking

Policies can have unintended consequences. In some cases, they may even exacerbate rather than alleviate the problem they are designed to address. This is a phenomenon that some economists call 'the cobra effect'. The reference is to an anecdote going back to colonial India, in which the British authorities were concerned about the danger posed by cobra snakes, and they therefore encouraged the local population to hunt the cobras. As a motivator, they offered a reward to everyone who brought back a snake corpse. Faced with this new incentive, some Indians began raising cobras for extra income. When the British authorities became aware of this, they repealed the reward system, but as a consequence the cobra breeders, having no reason to continue, released the snakes into the wild. Thus, what was intended as a strategy to eradicate cobras, instead contributed to their dispersal.

The example of the cobras is not an isolated case. The French colonial authorities experienced a similar repercussion in Hanoi, Vietnam. The sewer system they built there to improve public health became a favoured home and breeding ground for rats, which are often vectors of disease. To solve the rat problem, the French authorities at first employed Vietnamese labourers to catch the rats. However, the rat infestation was so enormous that the efforts were unsuccessful. Consequently, to involve more people in the hunt, the authorities offered a reward for each rat tail turned in to the authorities, which prompted some Vietnamese in the suburbs of Hanoi to start breeding rats. Hence, policies implemented to solve problems in the interest of the collective resulted in unintended consequences due to actions motivated by individual economic interests.

There are also contemporary examples of the cobra effect. For example, a ban on harvesting trees from an ecosystem where endangered species live may encourage forest owners to cut down their trees for timber sales prematurely, before an endangered species is found there. Similarly, the traffic policy in some megacities of banning half the cars on alternate days may in fact encourage households to own two cars instead of just one, so that they can change between the two and so drive every day. The ban on the export of certain species of fish and tropical birds may lead to an increase in catches to compensate for the larger number of animals that die during transport because of the containment required for smuggling activities. Additionally, some subsidies, which are based on the amount of emission reductions, may encourage businesses to temporarily increase their emissions so that the effect of the reduction, and thus the amount of the subsidy, is higher.

Finally, one-off sales of ivory are an important example of the cobra effect. In 1997, for example, three African countries, Botswana, Namibia, and Zimbabwe, were permitted under the Convention on International Trade in Endangered Species to auction off 50 tonnes of government-held ivory to Japanese traders. Other countries that have attempted to gain permission to hold a one-off sale, such as Tanzania and Zambia, are major sources and conduits for the illegal ivory trade. These countries argued that their national elephant populations were reaching high levels due to their wildlife management practices, and that they could use the proceeds from such an auction to finance further conservation efforts. However, others argued that the auction would stimulate demand for ivory, and lead to a spike in illegal ivory. Still others argued that ivory sales could jeopardize revenue from tourism, either through tourist boycotts or by triggering further poaching. Although limited data prevents a comprehensive assessment of these arguments, some research shows that a small spike in poaching on the local level followed the one-off sales. Others find no evidence to support the spike in poaching following a one-off sale, although they still caution against any legal ivory trade without constraining demand and ensuring robust monitoring and regulation measures are in place. An alternative approach is to burn stockpiles of ivory, sending the message that profiting from the trade of ivory is unacceptable, and preventing the supply of ivory from stimulating demand or leaking to the black market.

These examples highlight the importance of careful policy design, which considers potential unintended consequences and perverse incentives.

Sources: Bulte et al. 2007; Davis 2008; Lueck and Michael 2003; Stiles 2004; Vann 2003; Wasser et al. 2010.

certain substances for their potential harmful effect on the environment. The 2001 Stockholm Convention on Persistent Organic Pollutants provides a list of chemical products whose use should be prohibited or restricted, with a limited number of exceptions. However, these provisions halt the development of potentially innovative uses from them, which might have actually been environmentally safe. Less stringent instruments, such as taxing their use for example, might have been enough to achieve environmental protection goals, while still maintaining their innovation potential (Urpelainen 2010).

In addition, instruments can inappropriately cause institutional inertia. Because instruments are adapted to institutions that are already in place, they favour continuity and incremental reform rather than radical change. For example, several international financial institutions such as the World Bank, the International Monetary Fund, and regional development banks have pushed for the privatization of water supply services in developing countries. However, the management of water supplied by private companies also came with drawbacks such as an increase in water tariffs, which can restrict access to water for poorer parts of the population. Privatization can also sometimes result in low water quality due to lack of transparency in the way water is managed. While better state control over water prices and quality is needed, it has become very difficult after several decades of private control to bring the state back into water provision in developing countries such as Ivory Coast, Bolivia, or Brazil because the institutional inertia of privatized systems is so great (Tecco 2008: 137).

8.5 Conclusion

The types of instruments that states choose to implement their international commitments can have large impacts on the effectiveness of international regimes. States have invested extensive resources in drafting innovative and varied instruments to implement and verify their commitments in international institutions. These instruments have diffused and some have been used recurrently on diverse environmental issues.

More importantly, the political effects of instruments are real. Instruments can confirm power inequalities, create perverse incentives for more environmental degradation, or block innovation. States should be mindful of these political impacts and, as necessary, adjust their instruments to minimize negative political effects in pursuit of their policy goals. For example, it should be possible for the choice of instruments for each policy problem to evolve over time, even if that means changing or combining instruments to make them more flexible (Boockmann and Thurner 2006; Eyckmans and Finus 2007; Urpelainen 2013). One possible model for such an approach might be the European emissions trading system, which was rolled out in several phases in order to allow adjustments from one phase to the other. These adjustments have now diffused into the Chinese emissions trading system as well (Wettestad 2014).

Increased international discussion is needed on experimentation with instruments and their change. This is partly what a growing literature on experimentalist governance (Zeitling 2015) is doing, but there is a need for more attention to this area of inquiry. In the meantime, states have other major challenges to face in global environmental politics and in particular security issues, that we develop in Chapter 9.

Critical thinking questions

1. What are the modalities of execution reflected in the instruments used to mitigate climate change?
2. Explain some of the mechanisms of diffusion for instruments in global environmental politics.
3. What factors help to explain why instruments diffuse across states?
4. What are the major types of instruments that have diffused prolifically in global environmental politics? Provide some specific examples from an environmental issue area you care about.

 Test your knowledge and understanding further by trying this chapter's Multiple Choice Questions www.oup.com/he/morin1e

Key references

Bang, Guri, Jon Hovi, and Tora Skodvin. 2016. 'The Paris Agreement: Short-Term and Long-Term Effectiveness'. *Politics and Governance* 4 (3): 209–218.
This article discusses different dimensions of the effectiveness of the Paris Agreement, including output ambition, compliance, and long-term structural change. The authors doubt the effectiveness of the agreement in both the short term and the long term.

Busch, Per-Olof, Helge Jörgens, and Kerstin Tews. 2005. 'The Global Diffusion of Regulatory Instruments: The Making of a New International Environmental Regime'. *The Annals of the American Academy of Political and Social Science* 598 (1): 146–167.
This article explains the spontaneous worldwide diffusion of regulatory instruments for environmental protection in the 1990s. The research shows that diffusion does not rest exclusively on material explanations, but most of all on legitimacy justifications and concern about conformity with international norms.

Pagiola, Stefano, Agustin Arcenas, and Gunars Platais. 2005. 'Can Payments for Environmental Services Help Reduce Poverty? An Exploration of the Issues and the Evidence to Date from Latin America'. *World Development* 33 (2): 237–253.
The authors explain that Payments of Environmental Services mechanisms were not initially designed to reduce poverty, but that they could achieve this aim if designed properly. Looking at the local context in Latin America, they identify clear property rights, adaptation to the local context, and participation by poor people as important factors for such synergies to happen.

Brown Weiss, Edith, and Harold Karan Jacobson (eds). 1998. *Engaging Countries: Strengthening Compliance with International Environmental Accords*. Cambridge, MA: MIT Press.
This edited volume discusses what happens once states adopt international environmental agreements, scrutinizing their level of implementation and compliance. It sheds light on states' different implementation and compliance performance and identifies explanatory factors for this diversity of behaviours.

 For additional material and resources, please visit the online resources at: www.oup.com/he/morin1e

Chapter references

Aakvik, Arild, and Sigve Tjotta. 2011. 'Do Collective Actions Clear Common Air? The Effect of International Environmental Protocols on Sulphur Emissions'. *European Journal of Political Economy* 27 (2): 343–351.

Abdel-Latif, Ahmed. 2015. 'Intellectual Property Rights and the Transfer of Climate Change Technologies: Issues, Challenges, and Way Forward'. *Climate Policy* 15 (1): 103–26.

Andresen, Steinar. 2007. 'The Effectiveness of UN Environmental Institutions'. *International Environmental Agreements: Politics, Law and Economics* 7 (4): 317–336.

Andrew, Jane, Mary A. Kaidonis, and Brian Andrew. 2010. 'Carbon Tax: Challenging Neoliberal Solutions to Climate Change'. *Critical Perspectives on Accounting* 21 (7): 611–618.

Avi-Yonah, Reuven S., and David M. Uhlmann. 2009. 'Combating Global Climate Change: Why a Carbon Tax is a Better Response to Global Warming Than Cap and Trade'. *Stanford Environmental Law Journal* 28 (1): 3–50.

Bachram, Heidi. 2004. 'Climate Fraud and Carbon Colonialism: The New Trade in Greenhouse Gases'. *Capitalism Nature Socialism* 15 (4): 5–20.

Bernstein, Steven, Michele Betsill, Matthew Hoffman, and Matthew Paterson. 2010. 'A Tale of Two Copenhagens: Carbon Markets and Climate Governance'. *Millennium: Journal of International Studies* 39 (1): 161–173.

Biedenkopf, Katja, Sarah Van Eynde, and Hayley Walker. 2017. 'Policy Infusion Through Capacity Building and Project Interaction: Greenhouse Gas Emissions Trading in China'. *Global Environmental Politics* 17 (3): 91–114.

Böhmelt, Tobias, and Jürg Vollenweider. 2013. 'Information Flows and Social Capital Through Linkages: The Effectiveness of the CLRTAP Network'. *International Environmental Agreements: Politics, Law and Economics* 15 (2): 105–123.

Boockmann, Bernhard, and Paul W. Thurner. 2006. 'Flexibility Provisions in Multilateral Environmental Treaties'. *International Environmental Agreements* 6 (2): 113–135.

Brandi, Clara, Dominique Blümer, and Jean-Frédéric Morin. 2019. 'When Do International Treaties Matter for Domestic Environmental Legislation?'. *Global Environmental Politics* 19 (4): 14–44.

Breitmeier, Helmut, Oran R. Young, and Michael Zürn. 2006. *Analyzing International Environmental Regimes: From Case Study to Database*. Cambridge, MA: MIT Press.

Bulte, Erwin H., Richard Damania, and G. Cornelis Van Kooten. 2007. 'The Effects of One-Off Ivory Sales on Elephant Mortality'. *The Journal of Wildlife Management* 71 (2): 613–618.

Busch, Per-Olof, Helge Jörgens, and Kerstin Tews. 2005. 'The Global Diffusion of Regulatory Instruments: The Making of a New International Environmental Regime'. *The Annals of the American Academy of Political and Social Science* 598 (1): 146–167.

Chan, Sander, and Philipp Pattberg. 2008. 'Private Rule-Making and the Politics of Accountability: Analyzing Global Forest Governance'. *Global Environmental Politics* 8 (3): 103–121.

Ciplet, David, Kevin M. Adams, Romain Weikmans, and J. Timmons Roberts. 2018. 'The Transformative Capability of Transparency in Global Environmental Governance'. *Global Environmental Politics* 18 (3): 130–150.

Conliffe, Alexandra. 2011. 'Combating Ineffectiveness: Climate Change Bandwagoning and the UN Convention to Combat Desertification'. *Global Environmental Politics* 11 (3): 44–63.

Davis, Lucas W. 2008. 'The Effect of Driving Restrictions on Air Quality in Mexico City'. *Journal of Political Economy* 116 (1): 38–81.

Delreux, Tom, and Sander Happaerts. 2016. 'Environmental Policy Instruments'. In *Environmental Policy and Politics in the European Union*, edited by T. Delreux and S. Happaerts, 141–162. London: Routledge.

Desombre, Elizabeth R. 2000. *Domestic Sources of International Environmental Policy. Industry, Environmentalists, and US Power*. Cambridge, MA: MIT Press.

Dieperink, Carel. 2011. 'International Water Negotiations Under Asymmetry, Lessons from the Rhine Chlorides Dispute Settlement (1931–2004)'. *International Environmental Agreements* 11 (2): 139–157.

Dinar, Ariel, Shaikh Mahfuzur Rahman, Donald F. Larson, and Philippe Ambrosi. 2011. 'Local Actions, Global Impacts: International Cooperation and the CDM'. *Global Environmental Politics* 11 (4): 108–133.

Dobbin, Frank, Beth Simmons, and Geoffrey Garrett. 2007. 'The Global Diffusion of Public Policies: Social Construction, Coercion, Competition, Or Learning?' *Annual Review of Sociology* 33: 449–72.

Downs, George W. 2000. 'Constructing Effective Environmental Regimes'. *Annual Review of Political Science* 3 (1): 25–42.

Downs, George W., David M. Rocke, and Peter N. Barsoom. 1996. 'Is the Good News About Compliance Good News About Cooperation?' *International Organization* 50 (3): 379–406.

Eckersley, Robyn. 2018. 'The Green State in Transition: Reply to Bailey, Barry and Craig'. *New Political Economy*, 1–11 September.

Eyckmans, Johan, and Michael Finus. 2007. 'Measures to Enhance the Success of Global Climate Treaties'. *International Environmental Agreements* 7 (1): 73–97.

Fankhauser, Samuel, Cameron Hepburn, and Jisung Park. 2010. 'Combining Multiple Climate Policy Instruments: How Not To Do It'. *Climate Change Economics* 1 (3): 209–225.

Farrell, Katharine N. 2014. 'Intellectual Mercantilism and Franchise Equity: A Critical Study of the Ecological Political Economy of International Payments for Ecosystem Services'. *Ecological Economics* 102: 137–146.

Florini, Ann. 2010. 'The National Context for Transparency Based Global Environmental Governance'. *Global Environmental Politics* 10 (3): 120–131.

Foucault, Michel. 1991. *The Foucault Effect: Studies in Governmentality*. Chicago: University of Chicago Press.

Fuentes-George, Kemi. 2013. 'Neoliberalism, Environmental Justice, and the Convention on Biological Diversity: How Problematizing the Commodification of Nature Affects Regime Effectiveness'. *Global Environmental Politics* 13 (4): 144–163.

Grundig, Frank. 2012. 'Dealing with the Temporal Domain of Regime Effectiveness: A Further Conceptual Development of the Oslo-Potsdam Solution'. *International Environmental Agreements* 12 (2): 111–127.

Gunningham, Neil, and Darren Sinclair. 2017. 'Smart Regulation'. In *Regulatory Theory: Foundations and Applications*, edited by Peter Drahos, 133–148. Acton, Canberra: Australian National University Press.

Gupta, Aarti, and Robert Falkner. 2006. 'The Influence of the Cartagena Protocol on Biosafety: Comparing Mexico, China and South Africa'. *Global Environmental Politics* 6 (4): 23–55.

Gupta, Aarti, and Harro van Asselt. 2019. 'Transparency in Multilateral Climate Politics: Furthering (or Distracting from) Accountability?' *Regulation and Governance* 13 (1): 18–34.

Haas, Peter M., Robert O. Keohane, and Marc A. Levy (eds). 1993. *Institutions for the Earth—Sources of Effective International Environmental Protection*. Cambridge, MA: MIT Press.

Hajer, Marteen A. 1995. The Politics of Environmental Discourse: Ecological Modernization and the Policy Process. Oxford: Oxford University Press.

Hakelberg, Lukas. 2014. 'Governance by Diffusion: Transnational Municipal Networks and the Spread of Local Climate Strategies in Europe'. *Global Environmental Politics* 14 (1): 107–129.

Hall, Bronwyn H., and Christian Helmers. 2013. 'Innovation and Diffusion of Clean/Green Technology: Can Patent Commons Help?' *Journal of Environmental Economics and Management* 66 (1): 33–51.

Hansen, Melissa, Mine Islar, and Torsten Krause. 2015. 'The Politics of Natural Resource Enclosure in South Africa and Ecuador'. *Conservation and Society* 13 (3): 287–298.

Harrison, Kathryn. 1998. 'Talking with the Donkey: Cooperative Approaches to Environmental Protection'. *Journal of Industrial Ecology* 2 (3): 51–72.

Hay, Julien. 2010. 'How Efficient can International Compensation Regimes be in Pollution Prevention? A Discussion of the Case of Marine Oil Spills'. *International Environmental Agreements* 10 (1): 29–44.

Healy, Noel, and John Barry. 2017. 'Politicizing Energy Justice and Energy System Transitions: Fossil Fuel Divestment and a "Just Transition"'. *Energy Policy* 108: 451–459.

Helm, Carsten, and Detlef Sprinz. 2000. 'Measuring the Effectiveness of International Environmental Regimes'. *The Journal of Conflict Resolution* 44 (5): 630–652.

Hovi, Jon, Detlef F. Sprinz, and Arild Underdal. 2003a. 'The Oslo-Potsdam Solution to Measuring Regime Effectiveness: Critique, Response, and the Road Ahead'. *Global Environmental Politics* 3 (3): 74–96.

Hovi, Jon, Detlef F. Sprinz, and Arild Underdal. 2003b. 'Regime Effectiveness and the Oslo-Potsdam Solution: A Rejoinder to Oran Young'. *Global Environmental Politics* 3 (3): 105–107.

Jordan, Andrew, David Benson, Rüdiger Wurzel, and Anthony Zito. 2012. 'Environmental Policy: Governing by Multiple Policy Instruments?' In *Constructing a Policy-Making State?: Policy Dynamics in the EU*, edited by Jeremy Richardson, 104–124. Oxford: Oxford University Press.

Keohane, Robert O., and Michael Oppenheimer. 2016. 'Paris: Beyond the Climate Dead End through Pledge and Review?' *Politics and Governance* 4 (3): 142–151.

Kinzig, A. P., C. Perrings, F. S. Chapin, S. Polasky, V. K. Smith, D. Tilman, and B. L. Turner. 2011. 'Paying for Ecosystem Services—Promise and Peril'. *Science* 334 (6056): 603–604.

Langley, Paul. 2001. 'Transparency in the Making of Global Environmental Governance'. *Global Society* 15 (1): 73–92.

Layfield, David. 2013. 'Turning Carbon into Gold: The Financialisation of International Climate Policy'. *Environmental Politics* 22 (6): 901–917.

Lueck, Dean, and Jeffrey A. Michael. 2003. 'Preemptive Habitat Destruction under the Endangered Species Act'. *Journal of Law and Economics* 46 (1): 27–60.

Mason, Michael. 2010. 'Information Disclosure and Environmental Rights: The Aarhus Convention'. *Global Environmental Politics* 10 (3): 10–31.

Matisoff, Daniel C. 2010. 'Are International Environmental Agreements Enforceable? Implications for Institutional Design'. *International Environmental Agreements* 10 (3): 165–186.

Meeûs, Jérôme de, and Alain Strowel. 2012. 'Climate Change and the Debate around Green Technology Transfer and Patent Rules: History, Prospect and Unresolved Issues'. *The WIPO Journal* 3 (2): 179–197.

Metcalf, Gilbert E., and David Weisbach. 2009. 'The Design of a Carbon Tax'. *Harvard Environmental Law Review* 33 (2): 499–556.

Methmann, Chris. 2011. 'The Sky is the Limit: Global Warming as Global Governmentality'. *European Journal of International Relations* 19 (1): 69–91.

Miles, Edward L., Arild Underdal, Steinar Andresen, Jörgen Wettestad, John B. Skjærseth, and Elaine M. Carlin (eds). 2001. *Environmental Regime Effectiveness: Confronting Theory with Evidence*. Cambridge, MA: MIT Press.

Mitchell, Ronald. 2006. 'Problem Structure, Institutional Design, and the Relative Effectiveness of International Environmental Agreements'. *Global Environmental Politics* 6 (3): 72–89.

Neuhoff, Karsten. 2011. *Climate Policy after Copenhagen: The Role of Carbon Pricing*. Cambridge: Cambridge University Press.

Newell, Peter. 2005. 'Towards a Political Economy of Global Environmental Governance'. In *Handbook of Global Environmental Politics*, edited by Peter Dauvergne, 187–202. Cheltenham: Edward Elgar Publishing.

Orsini, Amandine, Sebastian Oberthür, and Justyna Pozarovska. 2014. 'Transparency in the Governance of Access to and Benefit Sharing from Genetic Resources'. In *Transparency in Global Environmental Governance: Critical Perspectives*, edited by Aarti Gupta and Michael Mason, 157–180. Cambridge, MA: MIT Press.

Ovodenko, Alexander, and Robert O. Keohane. 2012. 'Institutional Diffusion in International Environmental Affairs'. *International Affairs* 88 (3): 523–541.

Pagiola, Stefano, Agustin Arcenas, and Gunars Platais. 2005. 'Can Payments for Environmental Services Help Reduce Poverty? An Exploration of the Issues and the Evidence to Date from Latin America'. *World Development* 33 (2): 237–253.

Pascual, Unai, Roldan Muradian, Luis C. Rodriguez, and Anantha Duraiappah. 2010. 'Exploring the Links between Equity and Efficiency in Payments for Environmental Services: A Conceptual Approach'. *Ecological Economics* 69 (6): 1237–1244.

Prakash, Aseem, and Matthew Potoski. 2006. 'Racing to the Bottom? Trade, Environmental Governance, and ISO 14001'. *American Journal of Political Science* 50 (2): 350–364.

Raiser, K., H. Naims, and T. Bruhn. 2017. 'Corporatization of the Climate? Innovation, Intellectual Property Rights, and Patents for Climate Change Mitigation'. *Energy Research & Social Science* 27: 1–8.

Ringquist, Evan J., and Tatiana Kostadinova. 2005. 'Assessing the Effectiveness of International Environmental Agreements: The Case of the 1985 Helsinki Protocol'. *American Journal of Political Science* 49 (1): 86–102.

Rodríguez de Francisco, Jean Carlo, and Rutgerd Boelens. 2015. 'Payment for Environmental Services: Mobilising an Epistemic Community to Construct Dominant Policy'. *Environmental Politics* 24 (3): 481–500.

Saikawa, Eri. 2013. 'Policy Diffusion of Emission Standards: Is There a Race to the Top?' *World Politics* 65 (1): 1–33.

Sakai, Marco, and John Barrett. 2016. 'Border Carbon Adjustments: Addressing Emissions Embodied in Trade'. *Energy Policy* 92: 102–110.

Sattler, Claudia, and Bettina Matzdorf. 2013. 'PES in a Nutshell: From Definitions and Origins to PES in Practice—Approaches, Design Process and Innovative Aspects'. *Ecosystem Services* 6 (December): 2–11.

Schomers, Sarah, and Bettina Matzdorf. 2013. 'Payments for Ecosystem Services: A Review and Comparison of Developing and Industrialized Countries'. *Ecosystem Services* 6: 16–30.

Skjærseth, Jon Birger. 2010. 'Exploring the Consequences of Soft Law and Hard Law: Implementing International Nutrient Commitments in Norwegian Agriculture'. *International Environmental Agreements* 10 (1): 1–14.

Sprinz, Detlef F. 2000. 'Research on the Effectiveness of International Environmental Regimes: A Review of the State of the Art'. Paper prepared for the Final Conference of the EU Concerted Action on Regime Effectiveness. Institut D'educación Contínua (IDEC), Barcelona, 9–12 November 2000.

Stiles, Daniel. 2004. 'The Ivory Trade and Elephant Conservation'. *Environmental Conservation* 31 (4): 309–321.

Szarka, Joseph. 2012. 'Climate Challenges, Ecological Modernization, and Technological Forcing: Policy Lessons from a Comparative US–EU Analysis'. *Global Environmental Politics* 12 (2): 87–109.

Tallberg, Jonas. 2002. 'Paths to Compliance: Enforcement, Management, and the European Union'. *International Organization* 56 (3): 609–643.

Tecco, Nadia. 2008. 'Financially Sustainable Investments in Developing Countries Water Sectors: What Conditions Could Promote Private Sector Involvement?' *International Environmental Agreements* 8 (2): 129–142.

Tjernshaugen, Andreas. 2012. 'Technological Power as a Strategic Dilemma: CO_2 Capture and Storage in the International Oil and Gas Industry'. *Global Environmental Politics* 12 (1): 8–29.

Underdal, Arild. 1997. 'Patterns of Effectiveness: Examining Evidence from 13 International Regimes'. Paper presented at the 38th Annual Meeting of the International Studies Association. The Westin Harbour Castle Hotel, Toronto, Canada.

Urpelainen, Johannes. 2010. 'Enforcing International Environmental Cooperation: Technological Standards Can Help'. *The Review of International Organisations* 5 (4): 475–496.

Urpelainen, Johannes. 2013. 'A Model of Dynamic Climate Governance: Dream Big, Win Small'. *International Environmental Agreements* 13 (2): 107–125.

Van Alstine, James. 2014. 'Transparency in Resource Governance: The Pitfalls and Potential of "New Oil" in Sub-Saharan Africa'. *Global Environmental Politics* 14 (1): 20–39.

Vann, Michael G. 2003. 'Of Rats, Rice, and Race: The Great Hanoi Rat Massacre, an Episode in French Colonial History'. *French Colonial History* 4: 191–203.

Victor, David G., and Lesley A. Coben. 2005. 'A Herd Mentality in the Design of International Environmental Agreements?' *Global Environmental Politics* 5 (1): 24–57.

Vogel, David. 1995. *Trading Up: Consumer and Environmental Regulation in a Global Economy.* Cambridge, MA: Harvard University Press.

Vollenweider, Jürg. 2013. 'The Effectiveness of International Environmental Agreements'. *International Environmental Agreements* 13 (3): 343–367.

Wasser, Samuel, Joyce Poole, Phyllis Lee, Keith Lindsay, Andrew Dobson, John Hart, Iain Douglas-Hamilton et al. 2010. 'Elephants, Ivory, and Trade'. *Science* 327 (5971): 1331–1332.

Weiss, Edith Brown, and Harold Karan Jacobson. 1998. *Engaging Countries: Strengthening Compliance with International Environmental Accords.* Cambridge, MA: MIT Press.

Wettestad, Jørgen. 2014. 'Rescuing EU Emissions Trading: Mission Impossible?' *Global Environmental Politics* 14 (2): 64–81.

Wilson, Jeremy. 2008. 'Institutional Interplay and Effectiveness: Assessing Efforts to Conserve Western Hemisphere Shorebirds'. *International Environmental Agreements* 8 (3): 207–226.

Young, Oran R. 1999. *The Effectiveness of International Environmental Regimes: Causal Connections and Behavioral Mechanisms.* Cambridge, MA: MIT Press.

Young, Oran R. 2003. 'Determining Regime Effectiveness: A Commentary on the Oslo-Potsdam Solution'. *Global Environmental Politics* 3 (3): 97–104.

Zeitling, Jonathan (ed.) 2015. *Extending Experimentalist Governance?: The European Union and Transnational Regulation.* Oxford: Oxford University Press.

Part 5

Cross-cutting issues

Natural resources, security, and conflicts

The relationship between the environment and security can be examined in several ways. On one hand, this relationship raises questions about the consequences of environmental degradation for security. Can scarcity of natural resources increase tension in societies and trigger armed conflicts? How can environmental degradation impact human living conditions? On the other hand, the causal relationship between the environment and security can be addressed from the opposite direction, by examining the impacts of armed conflicts on environmental degradation. What are the environmental impacts of armed conflicts? How can international institutions mitigate these environmental impacts? This chapter explores possible answers to these questions.

Learning objectives

After reading this chapter, readers will be able to:

- Explain the concept of 'environmental security' and its different interpretations;

- Understand the relationship between resource scarcity and violent conflicts;

- Explain why the concept of human security challenges the established world order; and

- Analyse how international institutions regulate any environmental degradation caused by military operations.

Introduction

The concept of 'environmental security' is omnipresent, but is nonetheless ambiguous and contested (Ney 1999). What exactly needs to be secured, and what are the security threats? Is environmental security about state security, faced with the loss of natural resources? Or is it about protecting individuals and communities from environmental degradation and reduced access to key environmental resources? Or protecting the biosphere, faced with unsustainable human activity?

A first step in clarifying these questions is to disentangle two related but distinct causal arguments. In the relationship between environment and security, environmental degradation can be analysed either as a cause or as a consequence of security issues. Examining how environmental degradation triggered a military conflict, for example, raises completely different questions to studying the environmental consequences of the same conflict. The two directions of causality are equally interesting, but they need to be analysed separately.

A second step needed to clarify these debates is to adopt clear definitions. Security is the freedom from threat. In the context of international relations, security has traditionally been understood in relation to the survival of the state, and the main threats to state security are armed conflicts. For the purpose of this chapter, *conflicts* are defined as any type of disagreement. They can be either violent (also called armed conflicts) or resolved peacefully through legal or political means. Conflicts can occur either at the domestic level (intrastate or civil conflicts) or at the international level (interstate conflicts). War is the ultimate challenge to state security. Following other authors in international relations, we define a war as an armed conflict that leads to at least 1,000 violent deaths within a 12-month period (Sarkees and Schafer 2000).

Based on these clarifications, this chapter addresses the relationship between security and environmental degradation from four different angles. First, we examine the concept of 'environmental security' and how it is used by scholars and political actors (Section 9.1). Then we discuss whether, and how, environmental degradation leads to armed conflicts (Section 9.2), and go on to look at the effect of environmental degradation on human security (Section 9.3). The last section of this chapter reverses the causal direction and examines the impact of conflicts on the environment (Section 9.4).

9.1 The ambiguous concept of environmental security

Until the 1980s, most security experts favoured a state-centric understanding of security. This understanding focused on protecting the political integrity of the state when faced with military threats, mostly from other states. Later, as the tensions of the Cold War eased, a growing number of security experts came to see this narrow understanding of security as too limited (Buzan and Hansen 2009; Ullman 1983).

Three observations led to the establishment of a connection between security and environmental issues. First, it was recognized that armed violence is not the only form of violence: pollution and poverty could also be understood as violent experiences. Second, national threats are not solely military: an entire range of threats, including sea-level rise and fish stock depletion, could just as readily restrict a government's policy options as a military threat. Third, it is not only the state that must be protected: individuals and their environment should also be protected to allow each person to thrive in harmony with nature.

The concept of environmental security does not have a single meaning. The term was originally coined to refer to the '**securitization**' of the environment. With the end of the Cold War a period began in which many issue areas, which had not previously been directly connected to the concept of security, were 'securitized' (Buzan et al. 1998). Poverty, nationalism, food, drug trafficking, migration, pandemics—and also the environment—were reframed as security concerns. For the first time, atmospheric pollution and hazardous wastes were seen to present threats to human well-being in a similar way that tanks and missiles do.

But, starting in the 2000s, the concept of environmental security was sometimes used with a different meaning. It referred less to securitization of the environment than to the 'environmentalization' of security **institutions** and practices (Allenby 2000). It seemed clear that the protection of the environment required a holistic approach and could not be isolated from other topics of international cooperation, including trade, finance, **development aid**, and security. Thus, people began to question the environmental impact and potential con-tributions to environmental protection of traditional security institutions and practices (US Department of Defense 1995).

Certain political actors have contributed to the securitization of the environment and the environmentalization of security for strategic reasons, whether to draw attention to a concern they consider to be neglected or to divert resources allocated to another issue (Detraz 2011; Hartmann 2010). For environmental activists, mobilizing the language of 'environmental se-curity' helps to frame the protection of the environment as a fundamental political priority, which justifies spending significant public funds. Several **non-governmental organizations** therefore use the concept of security to campaign for renewable energy sources and for bet-ter access to drinking water (Fischhendler and Katz 2012). For military organizations, add-ing environmental protection to their objectives allows for the rebranding of the army as a positive force contributing to the common good. This was notably a discursive strategy used by the North Atlantic Treaty Organization (NATO) after the Cold War in order to justify its renewed relevance and the maintenance of its budgets (Barnett 2001: 82).

Several political leaders have made the same link between environment and security in their political discourse. In 1989 Mikhail Gorbachev, Secretary General of the Communist Party in the Soviet Union, declared that 'The threat from the skies today is not so much nuclear missiles as **ozone layer** depletion and global warming' (cited in Myers 2009: 48). As for Amer-ican President Bill Clinton, he told his Chinese counterpart Jiang Zemin that 'The greatest threat to our security that you present is that all of your people will want to get rich in exactly the same way we got rich' (cited in Friedman 1996). In the same vein, in 2007 a representa-tive from the Polynesian micro-state of Tuvalu, which is highly threatened by rising sea levels, claimed that 'the world had moved from the cold war to the "warming war", in which chimney stacks and exhaust pipes were the weapons' (United Nations **Security Council** 2007).

The linkage between security and environment is now deeply politically ingrained, and a wide range of institutions and practices are dedicated to this connection (Floyd 2010; Hayes and Knox-Hayes 2014). For example, the 2015 United States National Security Strategy, which articulated the global security policy of the United States administration under President Barack Obama, explicitly addresses environmental security. It identifies climate change as one of the 'top strategic risks to our interests' as it contributes to 'increased natural disaster, refugee flows and conflicts over basic resources like food and water' (United States National Security Strategy 2015: 12). The environment is also one of the issues regularly addressed by **intergovernmental organizations** dedicated to security. In 2007, for example, the United Kingdom initiated debates at the United Nations Security Council on the potential conse-quences of climate change for security, including border disputes, food shortages, instabili-ties around migration, and humanitarian crises (Conca et al. 2017: 3).

This connection between the environment and security has become so anchored in our collective understanding of what security includes, that few observers are surprised when the Nobel Peace Prize is awarded to environmentalists. In 2004, for example, the Nobel Peace Prize went to Wangari Muta Maathai, the founder of the Green Belt Movement, a non-governmental organization working on reforestation in Kenya. Three years later, in 2007, the Nobel Peace Prize went to former US Vice President Al Gore and the **Intergovernmental Panel on Climate Change** for their efforts in raising awareness about climate change. Although these recipients do not explicitly contribute to issues of peace and security as traditionally understood, it is now widely appreciated that working towards environmental protection and working towards peace are closely linked.

Nonetheless, the normative assumption that security and environment should be linked together is not unanimously agreed on. Certain activists and scholars believe that using the concept of security risks contaminates environmental policymaking with ill-suited state-centric assumptions (Conca et al. 2017; Detraz 2011; Deudney 1990, 1999; Dyer 2001; Fox and Sneddon 2007). They consider that the state and its military institutions are not well suited to solve environmental problems, and even less so the transnational ethical issues posed by environmental degradation. Environmental protection requires international cooperation, whereas military organizations exist to prepare for international violent conflicts. On this basis, some argue that it would be inappropriate, for example, to use military means to fight against poaching and trafficking of endangered species (Duffy et al. 2019). In contrast, others believe it would be ill-advised to leave the concept of security to those who are primarily interested in military conflicts (Litfin 1999; Trombetta 2008). They consider that environmental protection requires structural changes in all spheres of society, and to ignore the impact of traditional security practices would further perpetuate a non-viable international order.

An equally ambiguous and contested concept is the notion of 'environmental migrants'. The relationship between the environment and migration is just as complex and multifaceted as the relationship between the environment and security. This ambiguity gives rise to multiple competing framings of the issue, some focusing on the environmental impacts of migration and others on the migratory consequences of environmental degradation (see Box 9.1). As Section 9.2 discusses, the problem becomes even more complicated when tripartite relations between the environment, migration, and security are considered together.

Box 9.1 The difficulty in classifying environmental migrants

Can environmental degradation be so detrimental to human living conditions that it triggers the massive displacement of populations? This question generates growing policy and academic interest. In the 1980s, studying environmental migrants was still an exploratory endeavour. Today, the existence and growing importance of the phenomenon is widely recognized.

In 1995, Myers and Kent established predictions concerning the migratory fluxes caused by growing populations, rising sea levels, and natural disasters. These authors began with an assessment of 25 million environmental migrants in 1995 and estimated that this number would double by 2010. Since then, several reports have estimated the potential number of environmental migrants, without reaching a consensus, but giving a clear indication that predictions have been underestimating the phenomenon. Indeed, the International Organization for Migration estimated that in 2008, 20 million people had already been displaced by extreme weather events, a number that does not take into account other categories of environmental migrants who are suffering from long-term environmental degradation. Forecasts vary from 25 million to 1 billion environmental migrants by 2050, with 200 million being the most widely cited estimate.

Studies have distinguished different scenarios that would lead to environmental migration. First, environmental migration can happen on a short-term scale when it is caused by extreme weather events such as droughts, floods, or hurricanes. In that case, it is considered forced migration. Environmental migration can also be the consequence of long-term environmental change, such as sea-level rise or the degradation of living conditions such as food shortages due to lower agricultural productivity. In that case, the boundary between forced and voluntary migration is less easy to draw. To catch this distinction between forced and voluntary migration, some experts have proposed to distinguish 'environmental refugees' from 'environmental migrants'. The problem is that while it usually refers to forced migration, the term 'refugees' also tends to refer to people crossing national borders. It therefore only includes environmental migrations that take place internationally, and excludes internal migration. The International Organization for Migration estimated that rapid-onset disasters such as flooding in 2016 internally displaced around 300,000 people in Ethiopia, 40,000 in Kenya, 70,000 in Somalia, and thousands more in the United Republic of Tanzania and Madagascar. Actually, figures tend to show that displacement within the same country is more common than international displacement. To add another level of difficulty with regard to the definition, the International Organization for Migration usually makes a distinction between temporary and permanent migration. For example, migration due to sea-level rise will be permanent, while environmental migration due to extreme weather is more likely to be only temporary.

In methodological terms, it is difficult to establish causal links between environmental change and migration. While the number of displaced people following a sudden disaster such as an oil spill or a hurricane can be estimated relatively easily, displacement resulting from slower environmental processes such as desertification, loss of **biodiversity**, or changes in temperature are more difficult to assess. Much like the link between environmental change and violence is contested, the link between environmental change and migration is also disputed, particularly since the environmental variable is part of complex causal links. Since environmental, economic, and security conditions are closely linked, it is difficult to empirically distinguish between environmental, economic, and political motivations for migration. However, that environmental change and degradation are aggravating factors is clear.

Despite these conceptual ambiguities and methodological difficulties, certain international instruments recognize that environmental disturbances can lead to the displacement of populations and that states have responsibilities in the face of these movements. For example, the 2009 African Union Convention for the Protection and Assistance of Internally Displaced Persons in Africa states that the signatory states 'shall take measures to protect and assist persons who have been internally displaced due to natural or human made disasters, including climate change' (Article 5(4)).

Nonetheless, at this time, 'environmental refugees' have no specific legal status at the multilateral level. Certain researchers, activists, and political decision makers ardently wish for this shortcoming to be addressed, in the name of human rights and **environmental justice**. One possibility would be to widen the reach of the Geneva Convention of 1951 and the United Nations High Commissioner for Refugees by including environmental refugees. Another option would be to create a new system to recognize, protect, and resettle environmental migrants. However, these two possibilities seem unlikely in the short term, due in part to the numerous debates about defining all the facets of the phenomenon. For instance, framing the issue as a 'refugee' issue is likely to securitize it, that is, to link it to international security issues. This framing could possibly lead to increasing border control. Alternative framings include efforts by the International Organization for Migration that aim to present migration as a necessary mechanism for climate change **adaptation**.

Sources: Biermann and Boas 2010; Gemenne 2011; International Organization for Migration 2018; Myers and Kent 1995; Ransan-Cooper et al. 2015.

9.2 Environmental degradation as a trigger for armed conflict

From Malthus to Homer-Dixon

The hypothesis that environmental degradation can lead to armed conflict has attracted attention for a long time. Since the nineteenth century, Malthusians have denounced the pressures that humans exert on their environment, pressures that can have dramatic social, economic, and political consequences (see Chapter 2). They see population growth and natural resource scarcity as significant threats, which could lead to destructive episodes such as wars, food shortages, and pandemics. From their point of view, the environment should not be protected for its intrinsic value, but because environmental degradation poses severe social risks, and can ultimately result in the premature deaths of thousands of people (Meadows et al. 1972).

Interest in the idea that environmental degradation can cause armed conflict surged in the early 1990s, at a time of particularly deadly civil wars in Africa, including in Rwanda, Sierra Leone, Djibouti, Somalia, Burundi, Congo, and Mali (Bächler 1999; Kaplan 1994). Several researchers therefore focused on these conflicts and explored the role of the natural environment in the disintegration of the state apparatus and the outbreak of violence. According to some of these researchers, the environmental degradation associated with rapid population growth can lead to natural resource scarcity and ultimately to the collapse of society, and even to genocide (Diamond 2005; see also Box 9.2).

Box 9.2 Avoiding ecological collapse: what can we learn from Easter Island?

Easter Island is a fascinating place due to its isolation in the middle of the Pacific Ocean, the mysterious origins of its population, and its iconic Moai statues. Perhaps most intriguing to scholars of environmental decline is the fate met by its society a few centuries ago, when a period of rapid population growth triggered intensive resource use and severe ecological decline. This in turn led to chaos, deadly conflicts, and ultimately societal collapse. By the time the Europeans arrived in 1722, the insular population had fallen from 15,000 to 2,000 souls. The people of Easter Island had drained their forest resources to use trees as transport systems for hundreds of gigantic stone statues that they erected and aligned all around the island. This led to the breakdown of their economy, famine, war, and even cannibalism. Some people therefore examine Easter Island as an exemplary case of ecological decline. Some use it as a cautionary tale for modern societies, particularly those where the state is unable to implement institutional reforms on the management of natural resources.

The puzzle here is why Easter Islanders faced ecological decline and societal collapse, while other island populations, such as the Solomon and Nauru islands, survived similar environmental crises. The Easter Island case offers an opportunity to identify the factors that enhance or impede a society's ability to adapt to an environmental crisis. Two factors seem to be particularly important. First, the success of the Solomon and Nauru islands may be explained by the presence of more robust political institutions, which allowed them to channel the discontent of their populations. Although Easter Islanders had access to the necessary technology and know-how, they failed in large part due to the absence of institutional reforms to control their pressure on natural resources. Second, the Solomon and Nauru islands participated in regional **regimes** for cooperation and commerce, which were lacking in the Easter Island case. Studies of the ecological decline in Easter Island point to its extreme isolation, in addition to the rigidity of its institutions, as a determining factor in the failure of its civilization to handle the crisis.

Applied to the international level, if the world can be thought of as an island facing a major environmental crisis, the case of Easter Island is an argument for strong institutions and cooperation initiatives. However, although the case is very demonstrative in illustrating the dramatic consequences of an unmanaged environmental crisis, its lessons are still very vague and cannot be easily implemented without further detail on *how* to build such institutions and collaborations. These are even more needed as Easter Island is now facing a new and even more challenging environmental crisis: the issue of sea-level rise, which will need to be solved globally.

Sources: Boersema 2015; Diamond 2005; Erickson and Gowdy 2000; Matthew and Gaulin 2001; McAnany and Yoffee 2010; Reuveny and Decker 2000; Roman et al. 2017.

Environmental degradation can also lead to conflicts in rich and politically stable countries, although these conflicts are generally less violent. For example, the depletion of fish stocks in the North Atlantic has led to tensions between countries wishing to secure access to fish (Mitchell 1976). Iceland and the United Kingdom conducted a series of confrontations over fishing right in 1976, termed the 'Cod Wars', and Canada and Spain were involved in a similar dispute in 1995, known as the 'Turbot War' (see Box 5.1). Although they were not traditional military conflicts, these episodes produced naval pursuits, forced inspections of foreign boats, and led to diplomatic incidents of rare intensity between members of the North Atlantic Treaty Organization (NATO).

A significant theoretical contribution related to the link between increased resource scarcity and armed conflict comes from the work of political scientist Thomas Homer-Dixon (1991, 1994, 1999). By studying various cases including Rwanda, the Gaza strip, South Africa, Chiapas, and Pakistan, Homer-Dixon developed a theoretical model in which ecological imbalances play a catalysing role in the development of conflicts, without being necessarily their immediate or sole cause.

More specifically, the Homer-Dixon model starts with pressures on natural resources (see Figure 9.1). Homer-Dixon identifies three types of pressures: the *degradation of resources*, *growing demand for resources* due to population or economic growth, and change in terms of *access to resources* due to inequalities within social groups. According to Homer-Dixon, these three types of shortage can lead to economic decline and the weakening of the social fabric. Two social processes can then come about. In some cases, a particular social or ethnic group can attempt to procure the resources they are lacking, to the detriment of the rest of the population. In other cases, the shortage will force part of the population to migrate, often to ecologically fragile regions, causing further environmental harm. These two scenarios can lead to tensions between rival groups, battles to control resources, and pressure on the state, causing its collapse and pushing the society towards violent conflict.

The Homer-Dixon model is neither simplistic nor determinist. In other words, it does not state that environmental shortages directly and necessarily lead to violent conflict. Homer-Dixon willingly recognizes that factors such as the prior existence of political polarization, a low level of democratization, and the fragility of institutions increase the risk of environmental conflict.

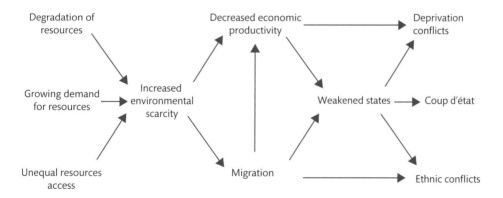

Figure 9.1 The Homer-Dixon model
Source: adapted from Homer-Dixon 1994

He also recognizes that some societies manage to adapt to the increased scarcity of natural re-sources, and to avoid violence despite unfavourable conditions. However, he supports the idea that societies that do not adapt to the depletion of natural resources risk becoming economi-cally, socially, and politically weakened, and this weakness increases the likelihood of violence.

Critiques of the Homer-Dixon model

Despite its nuances and caveats, the Homer-Dixon model remains controversial. Some studies corroborate this theoretical model as a whole or in part (Hauge and Ellingsen 1998; Raleigh 2011; Reuveny 2007; Tir and Diehl 1998). However, most scholars of the Homer-Dixon model strongly criticize it from several angles. Here we look at six of the most common critiques, as they provide an opportunity to deepen our understanding of the relationship between security and the environment.

A first critique is a methodological one. Homer-Dixon's work is decried for being biased, starting with the selection of cases. Since Homer-Dixon chose to focus on some countries rather than others according to the presence of intergroup violence, it is not surprising that he finds a link between resource scarcity and the outbreak of violence. He would perhaps have reached different conclusions if he had selected cases characterized by a lack of resources, but not necessarily by the presence of violence (Levy 1995). Likewise, his conclusions would undoubtedly have been different if he had focused on violence among individuals and in households rather than that between different social groups (Deligiannis 2012).

A second critique questions the role of environmental degradation in the triggering of intrastate violence (Bergholt and Lujala 2012; Floyd and Matthew 2013; Gleditsch 1998; Kahl 2006; Peluso and Watts 2001; Salehyan 2008; Theisen 2008). Shortages of natural resources are part of an economic, political, and historical context, and they are not always associated with environmental degradation. Ethnic and political rivalries, poverty, inequality, the quality of institutions, trade structure, culture, and relative isolation all have an impact on the way an environmental crisis is managed and on the displacement of populations. It therefore becomes difficult to establish even an indirect causal relationship between an environmental problem and a civil war.

Third, the role of migration in spreading violent conflict—a fundamental element of the Homer-Dixon model—is contested. Environmental migration can contribute to conflicts either directly or indirectly (Warnecke et al. 2010). In the direct scenario, environmental stress creates mass migration, which generates tensions in the host regions. In the indirect scenario, environ-mental stress first creates a local conflict, which leads to migration of refugees, and through them the diffusion of this conflict to new places. Critics point out that the first scenario is rare, as migrations directly caused by environmental degradation tend to be incremental movements similar to economic migrations rather than sudden mass migrations. Several authors have also highlighted the positive effects of such incremental migration on host societies, refuting the theory of underlying conflict (Barnett 2003; Hartmann 2010). As for indirect spreading of con-flict, there is no clear causal link between the arrival of refugees and the propagation of conflict, even during mass displacements caused by a war (Martin 2005; Warnecke et al. 2010).

A fourth critique of the Homer-Dixon model concerns its scope of generalization. The model seems to be relevant for certain specific cases, mainly in countries that have only seen slow eco-nomic growth, are politically isolated, and are not governed by stable democratic institutions.

But this relevance becomes more and more limited as economies develop, international co-operation becomes more dense, and democratic institutions become more firmly established (Matthew et al. 2003). A growing number of societies now have the capacity to adapt to resource scarcity by finding technical or political solutions. For example, scarcity of water resources has led to the development of techniques that help to reduce demand for water, such as micro-irrigation, in turn reducing the likelihood of local conflicts that aim to secure access to water. Further, certain societies that are well integrated into the global economic system, such as Japan and Singapore, have demonstrated a strong capacity for diversifying their economy through technological development despite having very few natural resources (Le Billon 2001).

A fifth critique of Homer-Dixon's model questions its implicit assumptions on a more normative level. According to this critique, the Homer-Dixon model conveys a world view according to which sources of instability come from **developing countries** that are unable to adapt to changing contexts on their own. This implicitly suggests that solutions are to be found through extending the Western model of liberal democracy, which is seen as both stable and flexible (Barnett 2000). In doing this, the Homer-Dixon model turns attention away from the responsibility of global structural inequality in worsening environmental degradation and so triggering violent conflicts in developing countries (De Châtel 2014; Slettebak 2012). Worse still, several authors have expressed their concern about the performative effects of the Homer-Dixon model which, through repetition, may become a self-fulfilling prophecy (Gleditsch 2012; Haas 2002). In other words, if political leaders are exposed to the idea that there is a causal relationship between the growing scarcity of natural resources and the outbreak of violence, they are more likely to prepare themselves to face this violence and, through their defensive actions, risk creating precisely the conditions that allow violence to break out.

Finally, certain empirical studies indicate that environmental degradation and natural resource depletion lead to greater cooperative behaviour and mutual assistance (Conca and Dabelko 2002; Myers 1986). For example, in the 1970s, in the middle of the Cold War, atmospheric pollution in Europe gave the Eastern and Western blocs a rare opportunity to cooperate. Similarly, several countries that were previously at war set up 'peace parks'—protected cross-border zones symbolizing and sealing their willingness to cooperate (Ali 2007). During natural disasters, it is not rare for rival countries to offer assistance to one another, which can help to build trust in the long term (Kelman 2011; Renner and Chafe 2007). The most notorious example of environmental shortages bringing about cooperation rather than conflict is that of fresh water. Although several communities only have limited access to fresh water, surprisingly few armed conflicts are waged over access to drinking water, and hundreds of cooperation agreements have been signed on this issue (see Box 9.3 and Figure 9.2). In turn, environmental cooperation can induce a more positive view of other countries, increase perceptions of interdependence, develop channels of communication, align expectations, and help to bring about societal changes. Together, these outcomes of environmental cooperation reduce the risk of future conflicts.

The paradox of plenty

Instead of studying the relationship between environmental shortages and violent conflicts as the Homer-Dixon model does, another interesting line of research explores the relationship between abundance of resources and violent conflict. This relationship is known as the

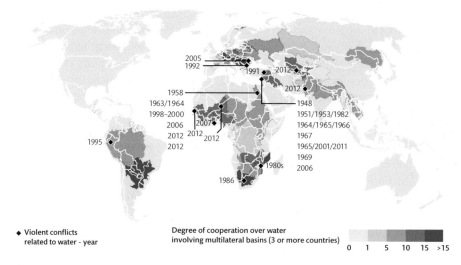

Figure 9.2 Cooperation and conflicts over water

Source data from: www.transboundarywaters.orst.edu; http://worldwater.org; www.fao.org

Box 9.3 The myth of water wars

The hypothesis of a water war, in the Middle East or elsewhere, is frequently mentioned in political and media discourse. At first glance, since clean water is a vital resource and is unequally distributed, it can seem logical that wars would occur in order to procure this liquid gold, particularly in arid regions. Nonetheless, no modern interstate war has been recorded that aimed primarily at gaining access to clean water. On some accounts, the last international water war was waged between the Sumerian city-states of Umma and Lagashde, almost 4,500 years ago! For water, as with several other issues in international environmental politics, causal links that at first seem logical or intuitive can be difficult to confirm.

Of course, several states that share a waterway or water basin are currently involved in armed conflict. This is the case for India and Pakistan in their conflict over the Kashmir region. The statistical probability of a war between two states sharing a waterway is higher than that between two adjacent states that do not share one. However, these wars are practically never carried out *primarily* for access to water.

Nor does the absence of a fully fledged war mean that there are not interstate disagreements regarding access to water. Tensions surrounding this issue are common, and often initiated by a dam project or massive pollution in a country upstream. However, these disagreements remain latent or are resolved politically or legally rather than through military means. When episodes of violence break out, they are either too limited to be classified as wars, or the issue of water is only marginal compared with other causes of the conflict.

These empirical observations suggest that the use of violence for access to water is neither rational from a strategic point of view, nor efficient from a hydrographic point of view, and nor is it economically viable. In the majority of cases, it is more efficient for a state suffering from lack of water resources to import water-intensive goods, such as agricultural products, than it is to instigate a war to ensure access to water to enable it to produce these goods itself.

There is, however, evidence showing that water is a trigger for international cooperation. Historically, bordering states have had strong incentives to cooperate in situations of tension. There are indeed hundreds of bilateral or regional interstate agreements that govern shared water resources. For example, India and Pakistan negotiated the Indus Waters Treaty in 1960 in spite of their political disagreements over Kashmir—a treaty which, moreover, has survived two Indo-Pakistani wars, and which has been amended several times. Based on this historical context, research on freshwater **governance** has focused more on the conditions that favour cooperation than on those that favour conflict. Among the variables that increase the statistical probability that an agreement on water will be signed, scholarship suggests the level of democratization of bordering countries, their economic interdependence, and the presence of a hegemonic power capable of imposing a regional order. Nonetheless, the past is not a guarantee of the future. The possibility of a water war cannot be completely ruled out, particularly in a context of significant desertification and increasing climate change.

Sources: Alam 2002; Bernauer et al. 2012; Bernauer and Böhmelt 2014; Dinar 2008; Fischhendler 2015; Gleick 2014; Petersen-Perlman et al. 2017; Tir and Ackerman 2009; Wolf 1997, 2007; Zeitoun and Warner 2006.

'paradox of plenty' or the 'resource curse'. Under this perspective, a high concentration of natural resources in a particular region can cause violent conflicts to break out (Colgan 2010, 2013; Collier 2007; De Soysa 2002, 2013). An abundance of natural resources inspires greed and can be exploited by private interests, with the risk of accentuating economic inequalities, undermining democracy, and turning already weak states into failed states (Collier and Hoeffler 2005; Reno 2000; Sachs and Warner 2001). Several examples support this 'resource curse' argument, particularly on the role of diamonds in the civil wars affecting Sierra Leone, Angola, and Liberia, or the role of oil in Chad, Sudan, and the Caucasus.

Yet the causal relationship between the abundance of natural resources and conflicts should not be exaggerated. As Figure 9.3 illustrates, this relationship is relatively weak. It shows on one axis natural resource rents (including rent from extraction of oil, natural gas, coal, minerals, and forests) as a percentage of gross domestic product for 84 countries for which the data is available. The other axis presents the number of battle-related deaths from 1990 to 2016 for these countries. Countries that experienced deadly conflicts are not necessarily those where natural resources are the primary type of exports. This is true for Afghanistan and Sri Lanka, for example. Likewise, several resource-intensive countries like Norway and Australia have not been torn apart by violent conflicts. The risk for resource abundance to degenerate into violent conflict is primarily found in countries with low income per capita and weak political institutions.

Climate change and conflict

A new generation of studies revisit the causal relationship between environmental degradation and violent conflict by focusing on the impact of climate change. According to certain historians, changes to the climate have increased the incidence rate of wars in the last millennium, particularly in Europe and Asia (Tol and Wagner 2010; Zhang et al. 2006, 2011). Retracing the connection between climate disturbances in the eighteenth and nineteenth centuries and the French revolutions of 1789 and 1848, one study finds that the whims of nature were partly responsible for the shortages that fed public discontent (Le Roy Ladurie 2006). Likewise, climate change might be one of the indirect causes of the Syrian civil war. Syria experienced an exceptionally severe drought from 2007 to 2010, which impoverished farming communities and led to massive internal migrations, creating favourable conditions for social tensions (De Châtel 2014; Gleick 2014; Kelley et al. 2015).

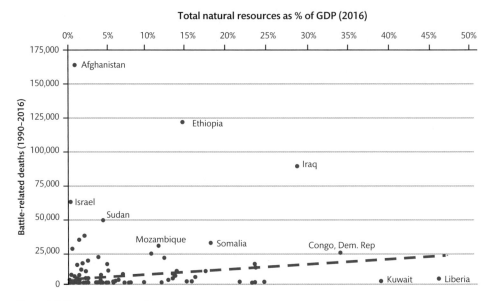

Figure 9.3 The resource curse?

Source data from: World Bank; Uppsala Conflict Data Program

 Take your learning further by viewing the interactive version of this figure
www.oup.com/he/morin1e

According to some statistical estimates, each time the climate heats up by a value equivalent to one standard deviation from the mean temperature, the frequency of interpersonal violence increases by 4 per cent, and intergroup conflicts increase by 14 per cent (Hsiang et al. 2013). Other quantitative studies indicate that significant variations in rainfall, whether during particularly arid or rainy years, correlate to several types of violent conflicts including protests, riots, general strikes, and rebellions (Hendrix and Salehyan 2014; Hendrix and Glaser 2007; Hsiang et al. 2011; Nel and Righarts 2008). With the acceleration in climate change and natural disasters foreseen for the coming decades, these studies leave us with a bleak vision of the future. Some even predict a 54 per cent rise in armed conflicts in the next few decades (Burke et al. 2009).

These pessimistic scenarios should be interpreted cautiously. The results of the statistical studies mentioned are fragile and ambivalent. In fact, several of the studies do not manage to establish a strong correlation between variations in climate and conflict (Buhaug 2010; Linke et al. 2017; Nardulli et al. 2015; Salehyan 2014). Measurement problems, theoretical ambiguity, and contested empirical tests prevent any bold and definitive conclusion. Climate seems to play at most a marginal role in triggering hostility compared with the fragility of political, social, and economic institutions. Certain studies even indicate that variations in climate and natural disasters lead to greater cooperation between social groups in order to face this adversity together (Adano et al. 2012; Slettebak 2012; Theisen et al. 2011; Theisen 2012). Other studies find that the threat comes mostly from the massive investments made in reducing **greenhouse gas** emissions, since these can cause economic downturn in developing countries and this slowing can create the conditions that can lead to armed conflicts (Gartzke 2012).

The question of the relationship between environmental degradation and conflict remains complex and controversial.

9.3 Human and environmental security

The concept of human security

Environmental degradation not only threatens state security, as discussed in Section 9.2, but also human security. Human security expands the notion of what needs securing from the state to its people (McDonald 2013). Although there is no agreed definition of the concept of human security, most analysts agree that, at a minimum, it consists of protecting the physical integrity and dignity of human beings so that they can meet their fundamental needs, such as subsistence and protection. For analysts of human security, the emphasis is not on the risk that environmental degradation may lead to conflict, but rather the role of environmental degradation in preventing individuals from thriving (Barnett et al. 2010; Hobson et al. 2014). While a foreign invasion or a *coup d'état* threaten the security of a state and primarily concern state security, a health epidemic or poverty threaten the well-being of humans and directly concern human security.

Several human security scholars criticize the national security paradigm (Detraz 2011; McDonald 2013). They believe that states can be a source of threat for their own populations. For example, in supporting automobile use through manufacturing and fossil fuel subsidies, states threaten human security by supporting policies that lead to increased emissions, and the host of associated public health and environmental problems that arise from that trend (Paterson 2000). In a similar way, several states have signed treaties on sharing water resources to facilitate their infrastructure projects, such as hydroelectric dams, even though such projects can disturb local populations and ecosystems in the long term (Fox and Sneddon 2007). For human security analysts, the state is not necessarily a shield guaranteeing individual security to its citizens, but can also be a source of threat to that security.

Approaching environmental protection through a human security lens can thus prove to be subversive. Sources of human insecurity no longer seem to be external to humans and their social and political structures, but integral to them. For example, the damage caused by natural disasters cannot be attributed to forces of nature alone. Some environmental degradation caused by humans, whether soil erosion or greenhouse gas emissions, contributes to the increased frequency and severity of so-called 'natural' disasters (Steffen et al. 2007). Extreme weather events, in particular, are far more frequent than they were 50 years ago (see Figure 9.4). Certain experts call the current geological period the **Anthropocene**, since the human impact on the earth system is so profound that it is the primary cause of much of the current disruption to the system (see Box 0.1). Furthermore, humans have contributed to their own susceptibility to environmental change by building cities in vulnerable areas, such as flood plains, and by making themselves dependent on international trade and fossil fuels (Leichenko and O'Brien 2008).

Some of the regions that are most exposed to natural disasters are also the least well equipped to face them, because they do not have the economic, social, and political resources that would allow them to adapt to these impacts. In order to better prepare for these changes, some human security scholars call for significant changes in, for example, consumption levels, production methods, transport systems, and urban planning. Some argue that these changes

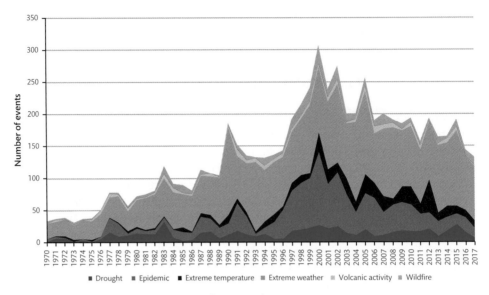

Figure 9.4 Number of natural disaster events (1970–2017)

Source data from: http://www.emdat.be/

will only be possible if we can radically overturn modes of governance at all levels of society, from local to international (Dalby 2009).

Human security in global environmental governance

The concept of human security remains relatively marginalized in the practice of international relations. Some states such as Canada, Ireland, Japan, Norway, and Switzerland, as well as intergovernmental institutions such as the United Nations Development Programme, have integrated a human security lens into their standard discourse. The 2014 assessment report from the Intergovernmental Panel on Climate Change even had an entire chapter devoted to human security.

However, the structures and institutions in place continue to favour state security rather than human security (Eckersley 2007; Özerdem 2010). It is not difficult to imagine a government favouring its national **sovereignty** over human security when faced with environmental threat. Think, for example, of a government whose territory might be threatened by rising sea levels. Now suppose that this government comes to possess a risky geoengineering technology, such as stratospheric aerosol injection, that could potentially disrupt the global climate in unintended ways (see Box 1.6). The government might very well decide to unilaterally deploy this geoengineering technology, putting human beings at risk all over the globe in a desperate attempt to protect its own territory (Rabitz 2016). An alternative to this unilateral act of geoengineering, more in line with the human security paradigm and a cosmopolitan ethic, would be to relocate the population elsewhere. This alternative, however, might put the political survival of the government at risk, something that few political leaders are willing to consider.

Although human security protections remain under-institutionalized in international law, the more specific question of human rights provides some promise to address parallel concerns (Nicholson and Chong 2011). In 1972, the Declaration of the United Nations Conference on the Human Environment explicitly associated human rights with environmental protection: 'Man has the fundamental right to freedom, equality and adequate conditions of life, in an environment of a quality that permits a life of dignity and well-being, and he bears a solemn responsibility to protect and improve the environment for present and future generations' (principle 1).

Since this declaration was adopted in 1972, a few international treaties have formally integrated environmental and human rights concerns. This was notably the case for the 1981 African Charter of Human and Peoples' Rights, which states that 'all peoples shall have the right to a general satisfactory environment favourable to their development' (Article 24). The 1988 Additional Protocol to the American Convention on Human Rights in the area of economic, social, and cultural rights further recognizes a 'right to live in a healthy environment' (Article 11), and the Indigenous and Tribal Peoples Convention of 1989 demands that states take measures 'for safeguarding the persons, institutions, property, labour, cultures and environment of the peoples concerned' (Article 4). Several national legal instruments, including various national constitutions, echo these treaties and also recognize the right to a healthy environment.

Until now, however, plaintiffs and tribunals have been hesitant in making use of the right to a healthy environment, where it is recognized, to force states and private parties to modify their polluting practices. This hesitancy comes in part from the fear of possible tensions between different human rights. For example, how can economic rights and the right to give birth be balanced with the right to a healthy environment when, in places, economic growth and population growth put excessive pressure on the environment? What balance should be established between the right to food and the need to reduce the expansion of arable land in order to maintain a necessary rich biodiversity? Laws are not always well equipped to mediate these ethical issues. One exception was the 2011 verdict from an Ecuadorian tribunal that found the oil company Texaco (now Chevron) responsible for polluting the Amazon rainforest with oilfield waste, jeopardizing the quality of life for several indigenous communities, and imposed a fine on the company of almost US$10 billion. Although cases like this may alleviate some of the hesitation about exercising the right to a healthy environment, in this case the enforcement of the Ecuadorian court decision was successfully contested in US tribunals.

This chapter has so far addressed the impact of environmental changes on security in terms of armed conflict and in terms of human security. However, an biocentric understanding (see Chapter 2) of the object of security can also be the environment itself, if one considers that the environment should be protected from states and human activities. In fact, one source of threat to the security of the environment is military conflict. Through this lens, environmental degradation appears not only as a cause, but also as an effect of violence. Section 9.4 looks at this second causal relationship by examining the effects of armed conflict on the environment.

9.4 Environmental impact of security policies

War and environmental security

Several wars have resulted in major environmental degradation. Arthur H. Westing, one of the first researchers to study the environmental impacts of war, explains that the forces of nature often interact with military forces in the collective imagination: 'The ancient Greeks envied Zeus his ability to hurl thunderbolts. Moses was said to have been able to control the Red Sea in such a way as to drown the Egyptian forces that were pursuing the Israelites' (Westing 2013: 84). Therefore, it is not surprising if modern generals also wish to mobilize the powerful forces of nature for their military enterprises.

Environmental warfare refers to the intentional manipulation of the environment as a strategic tool to hostile ends (see Box 9.4). The primary example is the use of the scorched-earth strategy, which derived its name from the practice of destroying grain fields in order to starve the enemy, which has been used for millennia. Today, this policy refers to the destruction of any type of resource or infrastructure that may benefit the enemy. For instance, during World War II, the Chinese army destroyed the Huayuankow embankment in the Yellow River in order to prevent Japanese troops advancing. Several thousand Japanese soldiers drowned, along with 750,000 Chinese civilians; the floods also destroyed the homes of millions of Chinese people, as well as millions of hectares of arable land (Schwabach 2000: 134). Another striking example of intentional damage is the use of the herbicide **Agent Orange** by the American army during the Vietnam War. The widespread use of this herbicide was intended to expose the enemy by defoliating forests and to starve the population by depriving it of harvests (Zierler 2011). More recently, during the Gulf War in 1991, Saddam Hussein's troops deliberately spilled a massive amount of petrol in order to prevent the American land forces from disembarking. This spill caused considerable damage to marine ecosystems, gravely affected fishing, and compromised a desalination plant essential to the production of drinking water in the region (Caggiano 1993).

In certain cases, armed conflicts can also lead to accidental environmental damage. For example, during the Kosovo War in 1999, the North Atlantic Treaty Organization's forces bombed a petrochemical factory in Pančevo, apparently in order to cut off the Serbian troops' access to fuel. This bombing released toxic chemical substances into the air and water, creating one of the greatest environmental disasters in terms of volume and toxicity in recent history (Schwabach 2000).

The biggest threat of environmental warfare is that of the 'nuclear winter'. The Brundtland Report of 1987 (see Chapter 6) evokes a catastrophic scenario: 'Among the dangers facing the environment, the possibility of nuclear war, or military conflict of a lesser scale involving weapons of mass destruction, is undoubtedly the gravest' (World Commission on Environment and Development 1987: 286). The explosions, fires, and radioactive fallout caused by global nuclear conflict would not only lead to immediate destruction of human and natural systems, but would also have lasting effects on the earth's climate (Gleditsch 1998; Sagan and Turco 1993). A nuclear war could result in what some refer to as **ecocide**, understood as the destruction of an entire ecosystem (Drumbl 1998).

Regulating the environmental impact of conflicts

Several international treaties address the risk of nuclear bombs leading to serious environmental destruction (Schmitt 2000; Westing 1985). One of the first was the 1963 Partial Test Ban Treaty, which prohibits nuclear weapons tests in the atmosphere, in outer space, and underwater. The logic underlying this restriction was that any nuclear explosion in these shared ecosystems would be likely to cause radioactivity outside the territorial limit of the state that conducts the test. Since 1996, the Comprehensive Nuclear-Test-Ban Treaty has prohibited

Box 9.4 The threat of environmental terrorism

Some world leaders link environmental issues to terrorism. The United States government condemned the 'environmental terrorism' of Iraq, which had set fire to oil wells in Kuwait in 1991. In 2011, the French President Nicolas Sarkozy denounced the 'environmental terrorism' of those who opposed nuclear energy by feeding the population's fears about the security of nuclear plants in France. In Canada, in 2012, the Conservative government included certain forms of environmentalism in its antiterrorist strategy, considering them as threats in need of surveillance. Although the term 'environmental terrorism' has a strong resonance with political leaders and the media, it is generally ill-defined if it is defined at all. The concept sometimes includes behaviours whose motivations and effects are radically different from one another. Very often, it is confused with ecological terrorism, which actually has very different motivations. As such, while considering the implications of environmental or ecological terrorism, it is important to establish what such terms mean.

At least two conditions must be present in order to speak of 'environmental terrorism'. First, environmental terrorism is a behaviour or action that *infringes* national or international law. To participate legally in public debates by highlighting the environmental impacts of certain political decisions, such as a state's decision not to reduce greenhouse gas emissions, is not enough to be classed as environmental terrorism, even though these impacts can seem terrifying. Second, environmental terrorism must *target* the environment as a symbol in order to inspire fear in the wider population. Environmental damage is not simply collateral damage: it is targeted for its symbolic value. When local fishermen massacred dozens of protected turtles in 1996 as a protest against the fishing quotas in the Galapagos Islands, this was indeed an act of environmental terrorism. In the case of the oil wells set alight by Saddam Hussein during the Gulf War, however, experts were divided on the intention behind Hussein's actions. Although some argued this was environmental terrorism, others believed that Hussein was aiming to destroy wealth and not the environment.

The frequency of acts of environmental terrorism has so far been limited, even if their potential effects could be colossal. For example, it might be considered environmental terrorism if a rogue state unilaterally deployed some form of geoengineering technology, such as stratospheric aerosol injection, as a means to alter the climate system and gain benefits over its enemies. This scenario is implausible in the near term, given the nascent state of technological development, but it could emerge in future, should these technologies ever be developed for use at large scale.

In contrast, 'ecological terrorism' is performed in the name of the environment, most of the time by individuals or radical groups when they destroy resources and infrastructure while campaigning for the protection of the environment. In contrast to environmental terrorism, ecological terrorism aims to support ecological priorities. By drawing media attention, it raises public awareness about environmental destruction. Groups like Earth First!, the Earth Liberation Front, and the Animal Liberation Front are movements driven by **biocentrism** and profound environmentalism. They are suspected of using techniques such as setting fire to polluting vehicles, sabotaging pipelines, cyberattack, and tree spiking. Several governments also consider the organization Sea Shepherd, which tracks and obstructs whaling vessels, as an ecological terrorist organization.

However, there are also grey areas, and what constitutes ecological terrorism is not always clear-cut. Individuals and organizations accused of ecological terrorism reject the term entirely. They consider themselves to be acting as liberators, using violence exclusively for self-defence, since they aim to protect the biosphere, including humans, from the violence caused by the pollution and destruction of the environment. Both in environment and in the traditional security domain, what some consider terrorism, others consider liberation.

Sources: Al-Damkhi and Al-Fares 2010; Chalecki 2002; Leader and Probst 2003; Posluszna 2015; Rabitz 2016; Schwartz 1998; Watson and Wyatt 2014.

its signatories from carrying out any nuclear weapon test explosion, as even underground explosions were found to generate transnational radioactive emissions. The 2017 Treaty on the Prohibition of Nuclear Weapons even prohibits assistance and encouragement in the development, testing, production, stockpiling, stationing, transfer, use, and threat of use of nuclear weapons (Article 1). It also instructs each state **party** to take 'appropriate measures towards the environmental remediation of areas' contaminated by nuclear testing (Article 6). In parallel, a series of regional agreements have established nuclear-weapon-free zones, including in the South Pacific Region, in Central Asia, in South Asia, and in Africa. **Compliance** with these treaties is deemed to be high in general, although some countries have yet to ratify them. France, for example, never ratified the Partial Test Ban Treaty and was still conducting nuclear weapons tests in the atmosphere over the South Pacific in the 1970s.

Other treaties deal with the risks created by chemical weapons. After the experience of using mustard gas during World War I, the 1925 Geneva Protocol was adopted to prohibit the use of toxic and bacteriological weapons. This ban was reinforced in 1972 with the adoption of the Biological Weapons Convention and in 1993 with the Chemical Weapons Convention, which prohibit not only the use but also the manufacture and storage of these weapons. These conventions do not directly aim to protect the environment, but they do so indirectly since the use of chemical and biological weapons can have grave consequences for the environment.

In 1976, in response to the use of Agent Orange during the Vietnam War, the United Nations adopted the Convention on the Prohibition of Military or Any Other Hostile Use of Environmental Modification Techniques. The first article of this Convention prohibits the use of environmental modification techniques if they have 'widespread, long-lasting or severe effects as the means of destruction, damage or injury to any other state Party'. As examples of environmental modification, the Convention mentions earthquakes, tsunamis, changes to a region's ecological balance, and modifications to atmospheric, climatic, or oceanic conditions. Though these possibilities largely seemed like science fiction when the Convention was being negotiated, developments in geoengineering have created new risks (see Box 1.6). Nonetheless, the scope of this Convention is limited, and does not cover all environmental modification techniques. Those carried out for peaceful purposes or affecting a non-signatory state are excluded from it, as is the environmental destruction that may result from the use of conventional weapons.

Other treaties aim to reduce environmental risks created by military conflicts more directly. The 1977 Additional Protocol I of the Geneva Convention limits the environmental damage permitted during an international armed conflict, prohibiting 'attacks on the natural environment by way of reprisals', and specifies that 'care shall be taken in warfare to protect the natural environment against widespread, long-term and severe damage' (Article 55). The 2002 Rome Statute of the International Criminal Court goes one step further by considering 'intentionally launching an attack in the knowledge that such attack will cause incidental [. . .] widespread, long-term and severe damage to the natural environment which would be clearly excessive in relation to the concrete and direct overall military advantage anticipated' to be a war crime (Article 8).

Although these international measures aim to limit the environmental impact of armed conflicts, armed forces' activities contribute to environmental degradation even in times of peace: air, water, and soil pollution, as well as the use of natural resources by armed forces, are environmental stress factors (Jorgenson et al. 2010). For example, the United States Department of Defense is the largest consumer of energy in the United States. For this reason, armed forces around the world are changing their practices and attempting to reduce their environmental footprint. The Pentagon is now subject to the National Environmental Policy Act and must conduct **environmental impact assessments** of its activities. Likewise, the North Atlantic Treaty Organization has begun to integrate environmental assessment into its management practices, especially regarding its management of dangerous materials, wastewater treatment, and energy use (Boiral and Verna 2004).

Yet, from a biocentric perspective, the measures intended to reduce the **ecological footprint** of military forces appear insufficient. They remain relatively marginal measures that barely call into question the international order founded on state power. If one of the main threats to human security and to the biosphere arises out of military activities, reducing energy consumption seems at best insufficient, and at worst a smokescreen giving a false impression of ecological responsibility. For example, in the 2000s, while the United States Department of Defense publicly expressed its concern for environmental security, it burned its solid waste in Iraq and Afghanistan in open air pits, producing hazardous emissions harmful for both US soldiers and local civilians (Bonds 2016). It was also found that the United States has left radioactive wastes and other toxic materials in its clandestine military bases around the world (Colgan 2018). This dissonance between the discourse and practices reveals how persistent the traditional interstate security paradigm is, and how ambiguous the concept of environmental security remains. Is it a question of preventing the environment from disturbing interstate stability, or preventing state action from causing lasting damage to the ecological balance?

9.5 Conclusion

The relationships between natural resources, security, and conflicts are complex and intertwined. Conceptually, broadening the notion of security allows environmental protection to be problematized in terms of environmental or human security, even though grey areas remain such as the notions of 'environmental migrants' or 'environmental terrorism'. New theoretical models have been created in order to establish a link between environmental degradation and armed conflict, but they still do not stand up to all empirical testing. At the institutional level, while several measures have been adopted to limit the impact of armed conflict on the environment, their effectiveness is openly questioned. However, empirically, it is clear that many armed conflicts have major environmental consequences, whether the environment is deliberately targeted or whether it is the victim of collateral damage.

Critical thinking questions

1. How do concepts of 'environmental security' and 'human security' compare, and what analytical purchase do they offer beyond what national security can offer?
2. How does research into 'environmental migrants' help to confirm, deny, or complete the Homer-Dixon model?

3. When do natural resources favour interstate cooperation rather than conflict?
4. How might the use of environmental modification techniques for military purposes be considered as terrorism?

 Test your knowledge and understanding further by trying this chapter's Multiple Choice Questions www.oup.com/he/morin1e

Key references

Barnett, Jon, Richard A. Matthew, and Karen L. O'Brien. 2010. 'Global Environmental Change and Human Security: An Introduction'. In *Global Environmental Change and Human Security*, edited by Richard A. Matthew, Jon Barnett, Bryan McDonald, and Karen L. O'Brien, 3–32. Cambridge, MA: MIT Press.

This chapter reviews the literature on global environmental change and human security, and discusses how the concept of human security can renew research on environmental change.

Dalby, Simon. 2009. *Security and Environmental Change*. Cambridge: Polity Press.

This book offers a critical political economy perspective on environmental security. It discusses how the world economic system destabilizes our environment and makes populations more vulnerable.

Homer-Dixon, Thomas. 1994. 'Environmental Scarcities and Violent Conflict: Evidence from Cases'. *International Security* 19 (1): 5–40.

This article presents a theoretical model linking environmental scarcity to violent internal conflict. It also presents empirical findings from several case studies in developing countries.

Floyd, Rita. 2010. *Security and the Environment: Securitisation Theory and US Environmental Security Policy*. New York: Cambridge University Press.

Informed by the Copenhagen School of securitization theory, this book studies the discourse of the United States government on environmental security. Based on interviews with key players, it focuses on the administration of Presidents Clinton and Bush.

 For additional material and resources, please visit the online resources at: www.oup.com/he/morin1e

Chapter references

Adano, Wario R., Ton Dietz, Karen Witsenburg, and Fred Zaal. 2012. 'Climate Change, Violent Conflict and Local Institutions in Kenya's Drylands'. *Journal of Peace Research* 49 (1): 65–80.

Alam, Undala Z. 2002. 'Questioning the Water Wars Rationale: A Case Study of the Indus Waters Treaty'. *The Geographical Journal* 168 (4): 341–353.

Al-Damkhi, Ali M., and Rana A. Al-Fares. 2010. 'Terrorist Threats to the Environment in Iraq and Beyond'. *Global Environmental Politics* 10 (1): 1–6.

Ali, Saleem H. 2007. *Peace Parks: Conservation and Conflict Resolution*. Cambridge, MA: MIT Press.

Allenby, Braden R. 2000. 'Environmental Security: Concept and Implementation'. *International Political Science Review* 21 (1): 5–21.

Bächler, Günther. 1999. *Violence through Environmental Discrimination: Causes, Rwanda Arena, and Conflict Model*. London: Kluwer Academic Publishing.

Barnett, Jon. 2000. 'Destabilizing the Environment–Conflict Thesis'. *Review of International Studies* 26 (2): 271–288.

Barnett, Jon. 2001. *The Meaning of Environmental Security: Ecological Politics and Policy in the New Security Era*. London: Zed Books.

Barnett, Jon. 2003. 'Security and Climate Change'. *Global Environmental Change* 13 (1): 7–17.

Barnett, Jon, Richard A. Matthew and Karen L. O'Brien. 2010. 'Global Environmental Change and Human Security: An Introduction'. In *Global Environmental Change and Human Security*, edited by Richard A. Matthew, Jon Barnett, Bryan Mcdonald, and Karen L. O'Brien, 3–32. Cambridge: MIT Press.

Bergholt, Drago, and Päivi Lujala. 2012. 'Climate-Related Natural Disasters, Economic Growth, and Armed Civil Conflict'. *Journal of Peace Research* 49 (1): 147–162.

Bernauer, Thomas, and Tobias Böhmelt. 2014. 'Basins at Risk: Predicting International River Basin Conflict and Cooperation'. *Global Environmental Politics* 14 (4): 116–138.

Bernauer, Thomas, Tobias Böhmelt, Halvard Buhaug, Nils P. Gleditsch, Theresa Tribaldos, Eivind B. Weibust, and Gerdis Wischnath. 2012. 'Water-Related Intrastate Conflict and Cooperation (WARICC): A New Event Dataset'. *International Interactions* 38 (4): 529–545.

Biermann, Franck, and Ingrid Boas. 2010. 'Preparing for a Warmer World: Towards a Global Governance System to Protect Climate Refugees'. *Global Environmental Politics* 10 (1): 60–88.

Boersema, Jan J. 2015. *The Survival of Easter Island: Dwindling Resources and Cultural Resilience.* Cambridge: Cambridge University Press.

Boiral, Olivier, and Gérard Verna. 2004. 'La protection de l'environnement au service de la paix (Note)'. *Études internationales* 35 (2): 261–286.

Bonds, Eric. 2016. 'Legitimating the Environmental Injustices of War: Toxic Exposures and Media Silence in Iraq and Afghanistan'. *Environmental Politics* 25 (6): 395–413.

Buhaug, Halvard. 2010. 'Climate not to Blame for African Civil Wars'. *Proceedings of the National Academy of Sciences* 107 (38): 16477–16482.

Burke, Marshall B., Edward Miguel, Shanker Satyanath, John A. Dykema, and David B. Lobell. 2009. 'Warming Increases the Risk of Civil War in Africa'. *Proceedings of the National Academy of Sciences* 106 (49): 20670–20674.

Buzan, Barry, and Lene Hansen. 2009. *The Evolution of International Security Studies.* New York: Cambridge University Press.

Buzan, Barry, Ole Wæver, and Jaap De Wilde. 1998. *Security: A New Framework for Analysis.* Boulder, CO: Lynne Rienner Publishers.

Caggiano, Mark J. T. 1993. 'The Legitimacy of Environmental Destructions in Modern Warfare: Customary Substance over Conventional Form'. *Boston College Environmental Affairs Law Review* 20 (3): 479–506.

Chalecki, Elizabeth L. 2002. 'A New Vigilance: Identifying and Reducing the Risks of Environmental Terrorism'. *Global Environmental Politics* 2 (1): 46–64.

Colgan, Jeff D. 2010. 'Oil and Revolutionary Governments: Fuel for International Conflict'. *International Organization* 64 (4): 661–694.

Colgan, Jeff D. 2013. 'Fueling the Fire: Pathways from Oil to War'. *International Security* 38 (2): 147–180.

Colgan, Jeff D. 2018. 'Climate Change and the Politics of Military Bases'. *Global Environmental Politics* 18 (1): 33–51.

Collier, Paul. 2007. *The Bottom Billion: Why the Poorest Countries are Failing and What Can Be Done About It.* Oxford: Oxford University Press.

Collier, Paul, and Anke Hoeffler. 2005 'Resource Rents, Governance, and Conflict'. *Journal of Conflict Resolution* 49 (4): 625–633.

Conca, Ken, and Geoffrey Dabelko (eds). 2002. *Environmental Peacemaking.* Washington, DC: Woodrow Wilson Centre Press and Johns Hopkins University Press.

Conca, Ken, Joe Thwaites, and Goueun Lee. 2017. 'Climate Change and the UN Security Council: Bully Pulpit or Bull in a China Shop'. *Global Environmental Politics* 17 (2): 1–20.

Dalby, Simon. 2009. *Security and Environmental Change.* Cambridge: Polity Press.

De Châtel, Francesca. 2014. 'The Role of Drought and Climate Change in the Syrian Uprising: Untangling the Triggers of the Revolution'. *Middle Eastern Studies* 50 (4): 521–535.

De Soysa, Indra. 2002. 'Ecoviolence: Shrinking Pie or Honey Pot?' *Global Environmental Politics* 2 (4): 1–36.

De Soysa, Indra. 2013. 'The Resource Course'. In *Environmental Security: Approaches and Issues,* edited by Rita Floyd and Richard A. Matthew, 36–63. London: Routledge.

Deligiannis, Tom. 2012. 'The Evolution of Environment-Conflict Research: Toward a Livelihood Framework'. *Global Environmental Politics* 12 (1): 78–100.

Detraz, Nicole. 2011. 'Threats or Vulnerabilities? Assessing the Link between Climate Change and Security'. *Global Environmental Politics* 11 (3): 104–120.

Deudney, Daniel. 1990. 'The Case against Linking Environmental Degradation and National Security'. *Millennium* 19 (3): 461–476.

Deudney, Daniel. 1999. 'Environmental Security: A Critique'. In *Contested Grounds: Security and Conflict in the New Environmental Politics,* edited by Daniel H. Deudney and Richard A. Matthew, 187–219. Albany, NY: SUNY Press.

Diamond, Jared. 2005. *Collapse: How Societies Choose To Fail or Succeed.* London: Penguin Books.

Dinar, Shlomi. 2008. *International Water Treaties: Negotiation and Cooperation along Transboundary Rivers*. London: Routledge.

Drumbl, Mark A. 1998. 'Waging War Against the World: The Need to Move from War Crimes to Environmental Crimes'. *Fordham International Law Journal* 22 (1): 122–153.

Duffy, Rosaleen, Francis Masse, Emile Smidt, Esther Marijnen, Bram Büscher, Judith Verweijen et al. 2019. 'Why we Must Question the Militarisation of Conservation'. *Biological Conservation* 232: 66–73.

Dyer, Hugh. 2001. 'Environmental Security and International Relations: The Case for Enclosure'. *Review of International Studies* 27 (3): 441–450.

Eckersley, Robyn. 2007. 'Ecological Intervention: Prospects and Limits'. *Ethics and International Affairs* 21 (3): 293–316.

Erickson, Jon D., and John M. Gowdy. 2000. 'Resource Use, Institutions, and Sustainability: A Tale of Two Pacific Island Cultures'. *Land Economics* 76 (3): 345–354.

Fischhendler, Itay. 2015. 'The Securitization of Water Discourse: Theoretical Foundations, Research Gaps and Objectives of the Special Issue'. *International Environmental Agreements: Politics, Law and Economics* 15 (3): 245–255.

Fischhendler, Itay, and David Katz. 2012. 'The Use of "Security" Jargon in Sustainable Development Discourse: Evidence from UN Commission on Sustainable Development'. *International Environmental Agreements* 12 (1): 1–22.

Floyd, Rita. 2010. *Security and the Environment: Securitisation Theory and US Environmental Security Policy*. New York: Cambridge University Press.

Floyd, Rita, and Richard A. Matthew. 2013. *Environmental Security: Approaches and Issues*. London: Routledge.

Fox, Coleen A., and Chris Sneddon. 2007. 'Transboundary River Basin Agreements in the Mekong and Zambezi Basins: Enhancing Environmental Security or Securitizing the Environment?' *International Environmental Agreements* 7 (3): 237–261.

Friedman, Thomas. 1996. 'Foreign Affairs; Gardening with Beijing'. *New York Times*, 17 April. Available at: www.nytimes.com/1996/04/17/opinion/foreign-affairs-gardening-with-beijing.html, accessed October 2019.

Gartzke, Erik. 2012. 'Could Climate Change Precipitate Peace?' *Journal of Peace Research* 49 (1): 177–192.

Gemenne, François. 2011. 'How They Became the Human Face of Climate Change: Research and Policy Interactions in the Birth of the "Environmental Migration" Concept'. In *Migration and Climate Change*, edited by Etienne Piguet, Antoine Pécoud, and Paul de Guchteneire, 225–259. New York: Cambridge University Press.

Gleditsch, Nils Petter. 1998. 'Armed Conflict and the Environment: A Critique of the Literature'. *Journal of Peace Research* 35 (3): 381–400.

Gleditsch, Nils Petter. 2012. 'Whither the Weather? Climate Change and Conflict'. *Journal of Peace Research* 49 (1): 3–9.

Gleick, Peter H. 2014. 'Water, Drought, Climate Change, and Conflict in Syria'. *Weather, Climate, and Society* 6 (3): 331–340.

Haas, Peter M. 2002. 'Constructing Environmental Conflicts from Resource Scarcity'. *Global Environmental Politics* 2 (1): 1–11.

Hartmann, Betsy. 2010. 'Rethinking Climate Refugees and Climate Conflict: Rhetoric, Reality and the Politics of Policy Discourse'. *Journal of International Development* 22 (2): 233–246.

Hauge, Wenche, and Tanja Ellingsen. 1998. 'Beyond Environmental Scarcity: Causal Pathways to Conflict'. *Journal of Peace Research* 35 (3): 299–317.

Hayes, Jarrod, and Janelle Knox-Hayes. 2014. 'Security in Climate Change Discourse: Analyzing the Divergence between US and EU Approaches to Policy'. *Global Environmental Politics* 14 (2): 82–101.

Hendrix, Cullen S., and Sarah M. Glaser. 2007. 'Trends and Triggers: Climate, Climate Change and Civil Conflict in Sub-Saharan Africa'. *Political Geography* 26 (6): 695–715.

Hendrix, Cullen S., and Idean Salehyan. 2012. 'Climate Change, Rainfall, and Social Conflict in Africa'. *Journal of Peace Research* 49 (1): 35–50.

Hobson, Christopher, Paul Bacon, and Robin Cameron. 2014. *Human Security and Natural Disasters*. New York: Routledge.

Homer-Dixon, Thomas. 1991. 'On the Threshold: Environmental Changes as Causes of Acute Conflicts'. *International Security* 16 (2): 76–116.

Homer-Dixon, Thomas. 1994. 'Environmental Scarcities and Violent Conflict: Evidence from Cases'. *International Security* 19 (1): 5–40.

Homer-Dixon, Thomas. 1999. *Environment, Scarcity, and Violence*. Princeton, NJ: Princeton University Press.

Hsiang, Solomon M., Marshall Burke, and Edward Miguel. 2013. 'Quantifying the Influence of Climate on Human Conflict'. *Science* 341 (6151): 1212–1228.

Hsiang, Solomon M., Kyle C. Meng, and Mark A. Cane. 2011. 'Civil Conflicts are Associated with the Global Climate'. *Nature* 476 (7361): 438–441.

International Organization for Migration. 2018. *World Migration Report 2018*. Geneva: IOM.

Jorgenson, Andrew K., Brett Clark, and Jeffrey Kentor. 2010. 'Militarization and the Environment: A Panel Study of Carbon Dioxide Emissions and the

Ecological Footprints of Nations, 1970–2000'. *Global Environmental Politics* 10 (1): 7–29.

Kahl, Colin H. 2006. *States, Scarcity, and Civil Strife in the Developing World*. Princeton, NJ: Princeton University Press.

Kaplan, Robert D. 1994. *The Coming Anarchy: Shattering the Dreams of the Post Cold War*. New York: Random House.

Kelley, C. P., S. Mohtadi, M. A. Cane, R. Seager, and Y. Kushnir. 2015. 'Climate Change in the Fertile Crescent and Implications of the Recent Syrian Drought'. *Proceedings of the National Academy of Sciences* 112 (11): 3241–3246.

Kelman, Ilan. 2011. *Disaster Diplomacy: How Disasters Affect Peace and Conflict*. Abingdon: Routledge.

Le Billon, Philippe. 2001. 'The Political Ecology of War: Natural Resources and Armed Conflicts'. *Political Geography* 20 (5): 561–584.

Le Roy Ladurie, Emmanuel. 2006. *Histoire humaine et comparée du climat: Tome 2, disettes et révolutions (1740–1860)*. Paris: Fayard.

Leader, Stefan H., and Peter Probst. 2003. 'The Earth Liberation Front and Environmental Terrorism'. *Terrorism and Political Violence* 15 (4): 37–58.

Leichenko, Robin, and Karen O'Brien. 2008. *Environmental Change and Globalization: Double Exposures*. Oxford: Oxford University Press.

Levy, Marc. 1995. 'Is the Environment a National Security Issue?' *International Security* 20 (1): 35–62.

Linke, Andrew M., Frank D. W. Witmer, John O'Loughlin, J. Terrence Mccabe, and Jaroslav Tir. 2018. 'Drought, Local Institutional Contexts, and Support for Violence in Kenya'. *Journal of Conflict Resolution* 62 (7): 1544–1578.

Litfin, Karen T. 1999. 'Constructing Environmental Security and Ecological Interdependence'. *Global Governance* 5 (3): 359–377.

Martin, Adrian. 2005. 'Environmental Conflicts between Refugee and Host Communities'. *Journal of Peace Research* 42 (3): 329–346.

Matthew, Richard A., and Ted Gaulin. 2001. 'Conflict or Cooperation? The Social and Political Impacts of Resource Scarcity on Small Island States'. *Global Environmental Politics* 1(2): 48–70.

Matthew, Richard A., Ted Gaulin, and Bryan McDonald. 2003. 'The Elusive Quest: Linking Environmental Change and Conflict'. *Canadian Journal of Political Science* 36 (4): 857–878.

McAnany, Patricia A., and Norman Yoffee (eds). 2010. *Questioning Collapse: Human Resilience, Ecological Vulnerability, and the Aftermath of Empire*. Cambridge: Cambridge University Press.

McDonald, M. 2013. 'Discourses of Climate Security'. *Political Geography* 33 (1): 42–51.

Meadows, Donella H., Dennis L. Meadows, Jørgen Randers, and William W. Behrens III. 1972. *The Limits to Growth: A Report for the Club of Rome's Project on the Predicament of Mankind*. New York: Universe Books.

Mitchell, Bruce. 1976. 'Politics, Fish, and International Resource Management: The British–Icelandic Cod War'. *Geographical Review* 66 (2): 127–138.

Myers, Norman, 1986. 'The Environmental Dimension to Security Issues'. *Environmentalist* 6(4): 251–257.

Myers, Norman. 2009. 'Environmental Security Concerns: Sources'. In *Energy and Environmental Challenges to Security*, edited by Stephen Stec and Baraj Besnic, 41–53. Dordrecht : Springer (in cooperation with NATO Public Diplomacy Division).

Myers, Norman, and Jennifer Kent. 1995. *Environmental Exodus: An Emergent Crisis in the Global Arena*. Washington, DC: Climate Institute.

Nardulli, Peter F., Buddy Peyton, and Joseph Bajjalieh. 2015. 'Climate Change and Civil Unrest: The Impact of Rapid-Onset Disasters'. *Journal of Conflict Resolution* 59 (2): 310–335.

Nel, Philip, and Marjolein Righarts. 2008. 'Natural Disasters and the Risk of Violent Civil Conflict'. *International Studies Quarterly* 52 (1): 159–185.

Ney, Steven. 1999. 'Environmental Security: A Critical Overview'. *Innovation* 12 (1): 7–30.

Nicholson, Simon, and Daniel Chong. 2011. 'Jumping on the Human Rights Bandwagon: How Rights-Based Linkages Can Refocus Climate Politics'. *Global Environmental Politics* 11 (3): 121–136.

Özerdem, Alpaslan. 2010. 'The "Responsibility to Protect" in Natural Disasters: Another Excuse for Interventionism? Nargis Cyclone, Myanmar'. *Conflict, Security & Development* 10 (5): 693–713.

Paterson, Matthew. 2000. *Understanding Global Environmental Politics: Domination, Accumulation, Resistance*. London: Palgrave Macmillan.

Peluso, Nancy L., and Micheal Watts. 2001. *Violent Environments*. Ithaca, NY: Cornell University Press.

Petersen-Perlman, Jacob D., Jennifer C. Veilleux, and Aaron T. Wolf. 2017. 'International Water Conflict and Cooperation: Challenges and Opportunities'. *Water International* 42 (2): 105–120.

Posluszna, Elzbieta. 2015. *Environmental and Animal Rights: Extremism, Terrorism, and National Security*. Oxford: Butterworth-Heinemann.

Rabitz, Florian. 2016. 'Going Rogue? Scenarios for Unilateral Geoengineering'. *Futures* 84: 98–107.

Raleigh, Clionadh. 2011. 'The Search for Safety: The Effects of Conflict, Poverty and Ecological Influences on Migration in the Developing World'. *Global Environmental Change* 21 (1): S82–S93.

Ransan-Cooper, Hedda, Carol Farbotko, Karen E. McNamara, Fanny Thornton, and Emilie Chevalier. 2015. 'Being(s) Framed: The Means and Ends of Framing Environmental Migrants'. *Global Environmental Change* 35 (November): 106–115.

Renner, Michael, and Zoë Chafe. 2007. *Beyond Disasters: Creating Opportunities for Peace*. Washington DC: Worldwatch Institute.

Reno, William. 2000. 'Shadow States and the Political Economy of Civil Wars'. In *Greed and Grievance: Economic Agendas in Civil Wars*, edited by Mats Berdal and David M. Malone, 43–68. Boulder, CO: Lynne Rienner Publishers.

Reuveny, Rafael. 2007. 'Climate Change-Induced Migration and Violent Conflict'. *Political Geography* 26 (6): 656–673.

Reuveny, Rafael, and Christopher S. Decker. 2000. 'Easter Island: Historical Anecdote or Warning for the Future?' *Ecological Economics* 35 (2): 271–287.

Roman, S., S. Bullock, and M. Brede. 2017. 'Coupled Societies are More Robust Against Collapse: A Hypothetical Look at Easter Island'. *Ecological Economics* 132 (February): 264–278.

Sachs, Jeffrey D., and Andrew Warner. 2001. 'Natural Resources and Economic Development: The Curse of Natural Resources'. *European Economic Review* 45 (4–6): 827–838.

Sagan, Carl, and Richard P. Turco. 1993. 'Nuclear Winter in the Post-Cold War Era'. *Journal of Peace Research* 30 (4): 369–373.

Salehyan, Idean. 2008. 'From Climate Change to Conflict? No Consensus Yet'. *Journal of Peace Research* 45 (3): 315–326.

Salehyan, Idean. 2014. 'Climate Change and Conflict: Making Sense of Disparate Findings'. *Political Geography* 43 (November): 1–5.

Sarkees, Meredith Reid, and Phil Schafer. 2000. 'The Correlates of War Data on War: An Update to 1997'. *Conflict Management and Peace Science* 18 (1): 123–144.

Schmitt, Michael N. 2000. 'War and the Environment: Fault Lines in the Prescriptive Landscapes'. In *The Environmental Consequences of War*, edited by Jay E. Austin and Carl E. Bruch, 87–136. Cambridge: Cambridge University Press.

Schwabach, Aaron. 2000. 'Environmental Damage Resulting from the NATO Military Action against Yugoslavia'. *Columbia Journal of Environmental Law* 25 (1): 117–140.

Schwartz, Daniel M. 1998. 'Environmental Terrorism: Analyzing the Concept'. *Journal of Peace Research* 35 (4): 483–496.

Slettebak, Rune T. 2012. 'Don't Blame the Weather! Climate-Related Natural Disasters and Civil Conflict'. *Journal of Peace Research* 49 (1): 163–176.

Steffen, Will, Paul J. Crutzen, and John R. McNeill. 2007. 'The Anthropocene: Are Humans Now Overwhelming the Great Forces of Nature?' *Ambio* 36 (8): 614–621.

Theisen, Ole Magnus. 2008. 'Blood and Soil? Resource Scarcity and Internal Armed Conflict Revisited'. *Journal of Peace Research* 45 (6): 801–818.

Theisen, Ole Magnus. 2012. 'Climate Clashes? Weather Variability, Land Pressure, and Organized Violence in Kenya, 1989–2004'. *Journal of Peace Research* 49 (1): 81–96.

Theisen, Ole Magnus, Helge Holtermann, and Halvard Buhaug. 2011. 'Climate Wars? Assessing the Claim that Drought Breeds Conflict'. *International Security* 36 (3): 79–106.

Tir, Jaroslav, and John Ackerman. 2009. 'Politics of Formalized River Cooperation'. *Journal of Peace Research* 46 (5): 623–640.

Tir, Jaroslav, and Paul F. Diehl. 1998. 'Demographic Pressure and Interstate Conflict: Linking Population Growth and Density to Militarized Disputes and Wars, 1930–89'. *Journal of Peace Research* 35 (3): 319–339.

Tol, Richard S. J., and Sebastian Wagner. 2010. 'Climate Change and Violent Conflict in Europe over the Last Millennium'. *Climatic Change* 99 (1): 65–79.

Trombetta, Maria Julia. 2008. 'Environmental Security and Climate Change: Analysing the Discourse'. *Cambridge Review of International Affairs* 21 (4): 585–602.

Ullman, Richard H. 1983. 'Redefining Security'. *International Security* 8 (1): 129–153.

United Nations Security Council. 2007. 'Security Council Holds First-Ever Debate On Impact Of Climate Change On Peace, Security, Hearing Over 50 Speakers'. 5663rd Meeting (CS/9000). Security Council press release, 11 April. Available at: https://www.un.org/press/en/2007/sc9000.doc.htm, accessed October 2019.

United States National Security Strategy. 2015. Available at: http://nssarchive.us/wp-content/uploads/2015/02/2015.pdf, accessed October 2019.

US Department of Defense. 1995. *Report of the Defense Science Board Task Force on Environmental Security*. Washington, DC: USDOD.

Warnecke, Andrea, Dennis Tänzler, and Ruth Vollmer. 2010. *Climate Change, Migration and Conflict: Receiving Communities Under Pressure?* Washington, DC: The German Marshall Fund of the United States.

Watson, Hayley and Tanya Wyatt. 2014. 'Politics, Power and the Media: The Visibility of Environmental and Eco Terrorism'. In *Invisible Crimes and Social Harms*, edited by P. Davies, P. Francis, and T. Wyatt, 44–60. London: Palgrave Macmillan.

Westing, Arthur H. 1985. 'Environmental Warfare'. *Environmental Law* 15 (4): 645–666.

Westing, Arthur H. 2013. *Arthur H. Westing: Pioneer in the Environmental Impact of War*. Heidelberg: Springer.

Wolf, Aaron T. 1997. 'International Water Conflict Resolution: Lessons from Comparative Analysis'. *Water Resources Development* 13 (3): 333–365.

Wolf, Aaron T. 2007. 'Shared Waters: Conflict and Cooperation'. *Annual Review of Environment and Resources* 32: 241–269.

World Commission on Environment and Development. 1987. *Our Common Future*. Oxford: Oxford University Press.

Zeitoun, Mark, and Jeroen Warner. 2006. 'Hydro-Hegemony—A Framework of Analysis of Transboundary Water Conflicts'. *Water Policy* 8 (5): 435–460.

Zhang, David D., C. Y. Jim, George C.-S. Lin, Yuan-Qing He, James J. Wang, and Harry F. Lee. 2006. 'Climatic Change, Wars and Dynastic Cycles in China over the Last Millennium'. *Climatic Change* 76 (3): 459–477.

Zhang, David D., Harry F. Lee, Cong Wang, Baosheng Li, Qing Pei, Jane Zhang, and Yulun An. 2011. 'The Causality Analysis of Climate Change and Large-Scale Human Crisis'. *Proceedings of the National Academy of Sciences* 108 (42): 17296–17301.

Zierler, David. 2011. *The Invention of Ecocide: Agent Orange, Vietnam, and the Scientists Who Changed the Way We Think about the Environment*. Athens: University of Georgia Press.

Trade and the environment

This chapter explores the complex and multifaceted relationship between international trade and environmental protection. The global trade regime's normative principles, legal rules, and real-world consequences often contradict environmental governance. For example, there is tension between trade and environmental governance with respect to the commercialization of endangered species, export of hazardous wastes, emissions involved in transporting goods, and patentability of living organisms. However, there are also synergies, which enable trade liberalization and environmental protection to reinforce one another. For example, trade forces were key drivers in the reduction of ozone-depleting substances and the affordability of pollution abatement technologies. This chapter explores these conflicts and synergies by first discussing the literature that examines the positive and negative impacts that trade has on the environment. It goes on to look at the trade dimensions of various environmental regimes, and then environmental dimensions of the trade regime, within both the World Trade Organization and preferential trade agreements.

 Learning objectives

After reading this chapter, readers will be able to:

- describe the various ways in which trade and environmental issues intersect with one another, and the potential synergies and conflicts that can arise from these interactions;

- deploy theoretical arguments to discuss how and why trade can both cause environmental problems and serve as a solution to them;

- explain how trade agreements use environmental provisions to achieve their objectives, and conversely how multilateral environmental agreements use trade provisions to achieve their own objectives; and

- discuss the effectiveness of the global trade regime in addressing environmental issues.

Introduction

The relationship between international trade and environmental protection is complex. On one hand, international trade can accelerate environmental degradation, for example through increased transportation emissions (see Box 7.6). On the other hand, international trade can alleviate environmental problems by facilitating the dispersal of environmentally friendly products, such as pollution control technologies. In addition, many multilateral environmental treaties include trade measures as a means to secure environmental objectives. The 2001 Stockholm Convention on **Persistent Organic Pollutants**, for example, restricts the trade (i.e. import and export) of certain toxic chemicals. In parallel, an increasing number of trade agreements contain environmental provisions. For example, the 2018 Comprehensive and Progressive Agreement for Trans-Pacific Partnership contains provisions that address environmental issues, including **biodiversity** loss and illegal fishing, by notably requiring parties to implement the Convention on International Trade in Endangered Species (CITES) and eliminating over time the use of fishing subsidies that contribute to overfishing.

This chapter explores the multifaceted relationship between international trade and the environment. Section 10.1 explores various theoretical perspectives on whether trade is good or bad for environmental protection. We then turn to the empirical connections by discussing, first, how states have used multilateral environmental agreements to deploy trade measures as a means of environmental protection (Section 10.2), and then how the global trade **regime** has engaged with environmental issues, including by incorporating environmental provisions into international trade agreements (Section 10.3).

10.1 Is trade good or bad for the environment?

The complex relationship between international trade and environmental protection

International trade can be a driver of environmental degradation. As market demand increasingly drives goods such as textiles and agricultural products across borders, the environmental costs of production, transport, use, and disposal can increase. Consider, for example, the carbon emissions involved in transporting mangos from Mexico to Australia, cars from Japan to Europe, and plastic recycling waste from the United States to China (see Box 10.1). In addition to transport-related impacts, international market demand can increase environmental degradation associated with the production of goods. Scholars have shown, for example, that international trade is an emerging driver of deforestation in the Brazilian Amazon, due to increasing market demand for beef and soya beans in places like China and Russia (Karstensen et al. 2013). Trade can also facilitate 'pollution displacement', whereby polluting processes or entities are transferred from one country or jurisdiction to another, or more indirectly, where a reduction in pollution in one jurisdiction leads to an increase in another.

International trade can also bring environmentally friendly products, such as renewable energy technologies, to new markets. These 'green' products can displace less environmentally friendly options in the marketplace, potentially decreasing environmental degradation. Similarly, international trade can be managed to give preference to certain environmental products. There are ongoing discussions, for example, in the World Trade Organization about decreasing tariffs (fees charged on imports at the border) on environmental goods. Environmental goods include such products as catalytic converters, waste water treatment technologies, and hazardous waste treatment equipment (Steenblik 2005). States could also use the global trade regime to further environmental protection efforts by phasing out market distortions, such as subsidies, on environmentally harmful products like fossil fuels. However, both options are highly contentious and countries do not all share enthusiasm for them (see below).

Box 10.1 Recycling waste trade between China and the US

Trade in waste products intended for recycling received closer attention in February 2013 when China, the world's largest importer of wastes for recycling, announced its operation 'Green Fence'. Green Fence was a policy campaign launched by the Chinese government which aimed to address a domestic environmental crisis resulting from mismanaged waste by reducing imports of illegal plastic waste—defined by Chinese law as 'certain banned materials'—such as medical waste and drums used for chemical storage. As the country with the largest recycling imports of scrap metals, plastic, and paper—receiving almost half of the world's plastic waste (a cumulative 45 per cent) since 1992—the impact of China's new waste trade policy has been felt in countries all over the world.

In 2017, the Chinese government announced a new complementary initiative, the National Sword initiative, which completely banned the import of 24 types of materials, including plastics and other types of solid waste, and further tightened the limits for allowed contaminated materials. As part of China's **implementation** efforts, the country notified the World Trade Organization that they intended to issue import bans. With this new policy China went a step further than Green Fence, by both restricting imports and signalling plans for a full ban on plastic waste, unsorted scrap paper, discarded textiles, and more. The Chinese government also introduced strong **enforcement** mechanisms to suppress smuggling activities, and ensure plastic recycling and disposal facilities operated with adequate pollution control measures. In November 2017, the Chinese government went on to declare a 0.5 per cent allowable contamination limit for most of the recycled waste materials not included in the ban, which is considered an unattainably low level among industry experts. Most recently, in March 2018, China announced its Blue Sky implementation initiative, which is intended to enforce the import restrictions issued under National Sword through coordinated customs inspections, shipment slowdowns, investigations into falsified import documents, and arrests of smugglers. This was followed in April 2018 by an announcement expanding the ban on imported materials, including extending it to post-industrial plastics. China declared in July 2018 that it intends to ban the import of all recyclable materials by 2020.

The long-term effects of China's import ban remain speculative. It is certain, however, that China's import ban has given some developed countries an acute waste management challenge due to their lack of investment in domestic recycling infrastructure. One concern, though, is that instead of investing in new recycling facilities or waste reduction initiatives, high waste producing countries will either find alternative ways to dispose of their waste, which could lead to more plastic ending up in landfill or the oceans, or find loopholes to get around the restrictions and bans. The latter concern is stressed by He et al. (2018), who note that plastic waste may continue to find its way into China via transit hubs such as Hong Kong and the Philippines, where it will be given preliminary processing and then re-exported to China. They suggest that the issue of recycling waste should also be addressed in bilateral and multilateral trade agreements between China and its neighbouring countries, and that exporting countries should take greater responsibility for the quality of the recycling waste they send abroad. They note, for instance, that the United States has no domestic system in place for monitoring the nature and quality of the plastic waste it exports, and it is not a party to the 1989 Basel Convention, which regulates international trade in hazardous waste.

Sources: Brooks et al. 2018; He et al. 2018; O'Neill 2018.

Theoretical perspectives on the trade–environment relationship

Theoretical arguments surrounding the relationship between trade and environment have been put forth by scholars from several disciplines, including political science, economics, political economy, and sociology. The most classic arguments are rooted in diverging inter-pretations of economic theories of competitive advantage. As early as the beginning of the nineteenth century, economist David Ricardo argued that because countries face different costs of production (for the same good), all countries benefit when goods are produced and exported from places where production costs are least expensive relative to other goods (Ricardo 1817). Extending this argument, other economists have argued that international trade drives lower prices and thus results in overall benefits to welfare, even if some countries experience more benefits than others. Connecting these arguments to environmental issues, many economists have suggested that welfare benefits, in turn, result in higher levels of environmental protection.

In contrast, other economists argue that the environmental costs of international trade outweigh the limited benefits. They note that Ricardo's theory of comparative advantage operates on the assumption that capital cannot cross borders, yet in today's world of financial liberalization, capital can do just that. These economists argue that if countries with differing environmental standards trade freely, industries face incentives to relocate to countries where they are not required to internalize (i.e. take into account the environmental costs of their production by, for example, controlling pollution). Some economists argue that this ultimately sacrifices environmental standards to international competition, as industry will relocate to countries with lower environmental standards (Daly 1993).

A classic exchange between economists Jagdish Bhagwati and Herman Daly illustrates these principles. Bhagwati argues that environmentalists should support international trade and economic growth because: (i) growth creates the tax base and revenue necessary for protecting the environment; (ii) countries with higher incomes tend to have greater public support for environmental protection; (iii) 'green' technology could become available elsewhere more easily under a system of free trade; and (iv) trade restrictions may ultimately increase environmental degradation. In addition, protectionism may maintain inefficient firms that could overconsume resources. Ultimately, Bhagwati argues that free trade will result in rising income levels and consumption patterns across the world, and eventually in greater environmental protection (Bhagwati 1993).

In contrast, Daly is wary that the environmental costs of such a system may increase faster than the benefits from production (Daly 1993). He argues that free trade isn't actually profitable or efficient, because transporting goods is so energy-intensive, and because roughly the same amount of similar goods are often imported and exported simultaneously. Furthermore, increased competition resulting from international trade lowers standards for efficiency, distributive equity, and ecological sustainability, because firms compete against each other under differing levels of regulation (Daly 1993). Overall, Daly argues in favour of sustainable levels of resource use as a way to address environmental problems, a prospect that is threatened by rising consumption patterns across the world (Daly 1993). As is apparent, these economists disagree over many elements, including what the environmental effects of free trade *actually are*.

More critical explanations of the relationship between trade and environment delve deeply into the nature of capitalism itself to take into account the broader impacts of trade on power inequalities and social development. These critiques maintain that there is a fundamentally antagonistic relationship between capitalism, which has structural characteristics based on expansion and accumulation, and the environment, which has finite limits and constraints (Foster et al. 2011). One such example, the concept of **metabolic rift**, a term coined in 1999 by influential environmental sociologist John Bellamy Foster, refers to a changing relationship between humans and the rest of nature under a capitalist mode of production, in which humans are increasingly alienated from the rest of nature, resulting in unsustainable use and demands for energy (Foster et al. 2011). Moreover, this explanation maintains that the origins and further growth of capitalism require imperialism and ecological exploitation, whereby developed (i.e. imperialist) countries gain control of and funnel developing countries' resources—land, raw materials, and labour—into the process of capital accumulation which enriches the elites in developed countries (Clark and Foster 2009).

In the context of international trade, the metabolic rift is further deepened and globalized because developed countries draw on natural resources from abroad after their own domestic resources have been depleted. Some authors refer to a 'planetary rift' instead of a 'metabolic rift' to indicate such trends (Foster 2012). Consider nineteenth-century Britain and the United States. Both countries' soil had been diminished of nutrients after years of industrial agriculture, where food and fibre crops were transferred to cities, rather than returned to the soil (Clark and Foster 2009). To compensate for its own internal environmental degradation, Britain increasingly sought control over guano, a natural fertilizer, from Peru. However, this led to an international metabolic rift, as nutrients were transported from South America to England and other industrializing nations, leaving Peru without these essential nutrients. Thus, as allowed by international trade, there are now global dimensions to unsustainable resource use.

A related concept from environmental sociology and political economy, known as *the treadmill of production framework*, is used to explain how capital-intensive economic growth results in increasing levels of social inequality and environmental degradation (Buttel 2004). According to the treadmill of production framework, as more capital accumulated in the United States and elsewhere following World War II, it was invested in new forms of production and technology with the aim of increasing returns on investment (Gould et al. 2004). However, these new technologies and practices required greater chemical and energy inputs than earlier techniques, which relied heavily on labour (Gould et al. 2004). This has implications for resource demand and waste production, as well as social welfare. With each new round of investment, employment decreases, environmental degradation increases, and profits increase. The investment and production cycle begins again, with laid off workers supporting further investment in new technologies and production methods on the assumption that such investment will lead to new employment opportunities (Gould et al. 2004). As a result of the last few decades of financial liberalization and increased globalization of the economy, investment and production, and by extension environmental degradation, has shifted abroad, resulting in improvements of some environmental indicators in several developed countries, but ultimately leading to increasing environmental degradation in **developing countries** (Gould et al. 2004). Thus, the treadmill of production now operates on a global scale, facilitated by international trade and foreign investment.

Trade as a driver of environmental degradation

In parallel to theoretical debates on the nature and potential explanations of trade and environment relations, there is also a rich academic literature that tries to *empirically* assess the impacts of international trade on the environment. Part of this literature sees trade as a driver of environmental degradation. For example, the main driver of increased air pollution emissions in the United States shipping sector is international trade (Gallagher 2005), and there is also a positive correlation between increased international trade volumes and the number of alien invasive species (Paini et al. 2016; Westphal et al. 2008). In addition, these invasive pathways are tied to the transportation of goods across borders. Zebra mussels, for example, a highly invasive species native to the Caspian Sea, made their way to North America in the ballast water of commercial ships in the late 1980s (Roberts 1990). Zebra mussels have since transformed freshwater ecosystems in North America by outcompeting native species (Strayer et al. 1999; Strayer 2009). Invasive species have also impacted the agricultural sector in sub-Saharan Africa, by causing crop losses and threatening food security, with the United States and China representing the greatest sources of invasive species (Paini et al. 2016).

Several empirical studies qualify theoretical expectations. For instance, although many theoretical models predict that liberalized international trade in the agricultural sector will lead to either a reduction in environmental degradation or only marginal effects (OECD 2005), some of the empirical literature shows that negative impacts can occur. As the metabolic rift concept discussed earlier illustrates, the international trade in intensive (high-yielding) agricultural crops results in a global redistribution of nutrients, such as carbon, nitrogen, and phosphorous. This both occurs through the physical transfer of nutrients in traded agricultural commodities, as well as through trade in nutrients required for intensive agricultural production. This changing distribution of chemical nutrients has widespread impacts on the environment, including negative impacts on air and water quality (Schipanski and Bennett 2012). International agricultural trade can also result in the displacement of small-scale farmers, who may not be able to compete with commercially grown imported (or exported) crops. Another result can be the expansion of agriculture into previously undeveloped spaces of high environmental value. For example, in the case of small-scale corn farmers in Mexico, to compensate for reduced income resulting from increasing corn imports from the United States, many farmers expanded their agricultural activity into nearby forests and jungles, resulting in deforestation and biodiversity loss (Soto 2012).

One often overlooked impact that trade can have on the environment is represented by measures of *embodied carbon* (Chen and Chen 2011; Kanemoto et al. 2014; Tang et al. 2013; Zhang et al. 2014). As carbon dioxide emissions are typically accounted for where goods are produced, we have a distorted view of any given country's actual contribution to climate change. This is because this contribution is also a function of the amount of carbon dioxide embodied in the goods we consume. As such, countries with low emissions but relatively high rates of consumption may be net carbon dioxide importers (e.g. Switzerland and the United States), whereas others that rely on export economies may be net carbon dioxide exporters (e.g. China) (Davis and Caldeira 2010; see Figure 10.1). Some have argued that countries should address the issue of consumption-based carbon emissions through carbon tariffs: border taxes that account for the carbon embodied in imported products (Böhringer et al. 2018; Gros and Egenhofer 2011). The idea behind a carbon tariff is that it places a price on carbon and so encourages the production of goods in a less carbon-intensive manner. There are a multitude of design questions associated with such a scheme, including how to compensate developing countries for welfare losses, for example by channelling tax revenue back to those countries (Lininger 2015).

Similar discussions have arisen in relation to water embodied in exports, often agricultural products. This is sometimes referred to as *virtual water*, or the amount of water used in the production process of a commodity (Hoekstra and Hung 2005). For example, the amount

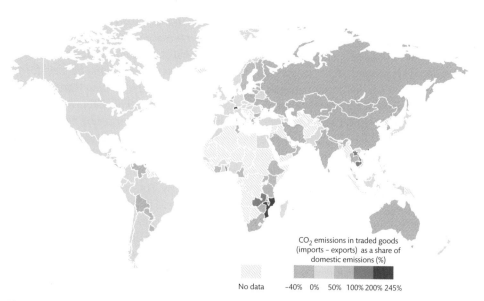

CO₂ emissions in traded goods
(imports – exports) as a share of
domestic emissions (%)

No data   –40% 0%   50% 100% 200% 245%

Figure 10.1 CO$_2$ emissions in traded goods as a share of domestic emissions

Source data from: Peters, G.P., et al. (2011). Growth in emission transfers via international trade from 1990 to 2008. *PNAS*, 108 (21): 8903–8908. https://doi.org/10.1073/pnas.1006388108.

of water needed to grow a kilogram of grain more than doubles when the grain is grown in an arid environment rather than under favourable climate conditions (Hoekstra and Hung 2005). In this sense, some countries can be said to provide virtual water to water-scarce countries by way of exporting water-intensive crops (and vice versa) (Biro 2012).

Trade as a solution to environmental problems

Other empirical studies concentrate on international trade as a solution to environmental degradation. For example, trade between developing countries and either the United States or the European Union is correlated with increased environmental performance in the developing countries (Prakash and Potoski 2017). Developing countries' export dependence on the European Union has been found to be correlated with their reductions in carbon dioxide emissions following the Kyoto Protocol (Prakash and Potoski 2017). However, this doesn't occur when developing countries trade with each other or with other developed countries (Gamso 2017). This is attributed to the United States and European Union's willingness and ability to pressure their trade partners to strengthen domestic environmental protection (when it serves their interests), as well as the large consumer demand in the European Union and the United States for 'green' products, incentivizing other exporters to create green products (Gamso 2017).

An increasing consumer demand for 'green' products and services is embodied in the discourse and practice of 'green consumerism' (see also Chapter 4). Green consumerism, as reflected in consumer, government, and corporate discourse, refers to 'the production, promotion, and preferential consumption of goods and services on the basis of their pro-environment claims' (Akenji 2014: 13), although notably the concept is contested, both in terms of what counts as 'green' and the responsibilities of consumers in improving business practices (Autio et al. 2009). Green consumerism assumes that as consumers' awareness of the ecological impacts of their consumption increases, they will make specific choices when participating in markets that place pressure on retailers, manufacturers, and service providers to make major improvements in how they produce, transport, and provide goods and services (Akenji 2014).

Prominent examples of green products include electric cars and energy-efficient appliances. Notable examples of approaches to green consumerism include **eco-labelling** code and standards initiatives, public awareness campaigns, certificates for green production and processes, procurement of green goods by public **institutions**, and public and private recycling programmes (Akenji et al. 2011). Fashion is an emergent example of an industry impacted by green consumerism. Eco-fashion is a rising trend characterized by the production of clothing with a long lifetime that is produced with little environmental impact, although the clothing supply chain is so complicated that it is difficult to do this holistically (Niinimäki 2010). The Sustainable Apparel Coalition, formed in 2011, is an international industry-led consortium that seeks to promote sustainable production and raise awareness of the ecological impacts of clothing (Dauvergne and Lister 2012).

Some note that many large corporations increasingly integrate environmental goals into their business strategies, and are making progress in achieving these goals—although they are still far off, and these approaches are nevertheless fundamentally limited (Dauvergne and Lister 2012). Many are critical of green consumerism because it places the responsibility for bringing the economic system in line with ecological imperatives on consumers (rather than corporations or policymakers), while consumer preference is unable to provide the structural and systematic changes required to do this, and because it can distract from the urgent structural changes that are needed (Akenji 2014; Seyfang 2005), including transforming much more fundamentally how high-consumption individuals and societies live, travel, produce, and consume. Additionally, many 'green' products still have environmental impacts, such as electric vehicles, which involve large emissions of CO_2 when produced. Scholars argue that corporations engage in green consumerist practices to secure or maintain their position in the market (Akenji 2014), or to enhance their **governance** power, in terms of their ability to set the agenda, make rules, and oversee implementation (Dauvergne and Lister 2012). For the consumer, engaging in green consumerism just provides a 'warm glow' (Autio et al. 2009), although it can be a first step towards generating broader public awareness of environmental issues and how individual behaviour contributes to these issues (Seyfang 2005).

Another example of trade as a potential solution to environmental problems is the solar photovoltaic industry, which involves many international supply chains, and as a result is characterized by a high degree of international trade, especially as China has recently become a major manufacturer of solar modules (Meckling and Hughes 2017). As firms in these supply chains have accumulated experience in deploying solar technology, and as cumulative capacity has grown and economies of scales are achieved, the cost of solar photovoltaic has dropped significantly in recent decades, more than 100-fold since 1976 (see Figure 10.2; Lafond et al. 2018). Therefore, international trade has helped to make solar economically feasible as a renewable source of energy. Indeed, one of the main benefits of international trade is increased production, or, in general, economic growth. However, even the generation of solar energy has environmental impacts, for example because solar arrays require material inputs and most likely large amounts of land.

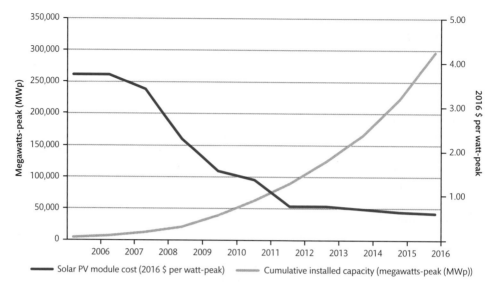

Figure 10.2 Solar prices vs cumulative capacity worldwide 2006–2016

Source data from: Lafond, F., et al. (2017). How well do experience curves predict technological progress? A method for making distributional forecasts. *Technological Forecasting and Social Change*, 128: 104–117. https://doi.org/10.1016/j.techfore.2017.11.001.

 Take your learning further by viewing the interactive version of this figure
www.oup.com/he/morin1e

Pollution havens versus pollution halos

There are also many grey areas and open debates concerning whether trade exerts an upward or downward pressure on the environment, mixing theoretical reasoning and empirical evidence. One classic debate surrounds the 'pollution haven' hypothesis, which argues that pollution-intensive industries will migrate to countries where environmental policies and standards are weakest. These havens are typically thought to be developing countries, because firms will choose to produce where the regulatory regime does not require them to internalize their costs of production (Daly 1993). This dynamic in turn, the argument goes, can cause a **race to the bottom**, where countries compete to lower their environmental standards in order to attract industry (see Chapter 8). Empirical studies have not borne out this claim, however, with firms' decisions on location rarely depending on environmental regulations (Carruthers and Lamoreaux 2016; Wei and Smarzynska 1999). Some argue that this is because the costs of **compliance** with environmental regulations in developed countries are not actually that high, and therefore other factors affect location decisions more, particularly the cost of labour (Batabyal 1995).

Others suggest that because developed countries increasingly seek to import environmentally intensive goods for domestic consumption from developing countries, 'the race to the bottom' hypothesis is a fallacy (Muradian and Martinez-Alier 2001). In other words, rather than generating a global 'race to the bottom', competitive pressures instead create environmental improvements and enhanced environmental standards in developed countries, and ecological degradation in developing countries, which experience a 'stuck at the bottom' effect, where these countries are unable to move beyond specialization in the exploitation of natural resources (Muradian and Martinez-Alier 2001). Further, the evidence is mixed among those studies that do find a connection between regulatory competition and decision-making surrounding firms' geographic location. Some of these studies find that firms with weak **corporate social responsibility** metrics, for example, are indeed more likely to relocate to countries with weak environmental regulations (Dam and Scholtens 2008). Others demonstrate that some firms actually move to countries with stronger environmental standards because they are looking for transparency and stability (Kirkpatrick and Shimamoto 2008). Similarly, some argue that firms prefer to operate in countries with stronger environmental standards in order to justify investments in new technology, because there is little risk that the standards will suddenly be raised (Leonard 2006).

Scholars have also demonstrated variation in how countries respond to trade pressures on the basis of the pollution type. For example, Cao and Prakash (2010, 2012) have shown that states respond to trade pressure in the area of air pollution differently than for water pollution. They suggest that this is because, in an export economy, there are generally fewer industries that contribute to air pollution compared to those that contribute to water pollution, meaning that the sectors that contribute to air pollution are 'likely to be less sensitive to pressures from trade competitors' than industries that contribute to water pollution (Cao and Prakash 2010: 492). Whether or not the 'pollution haven' hypothesis is empirically correct, the fear that firms will migrate to countries with lower levels of environmental protection is real. This fear is evident in many trade agreements, including the 2018 Comprehensive and Progressive Agreement for Trans-Pacific Partnership, which sets out that parties must not seek to gain trade or investment advantage by weakening their environmental laws or by failing to enforce them.

Still others have argued that when firms from developed countries relocate to developing countries, they bring better environmental practices, or so-called 'pollution halos', with them. As with pollution havens, however, the evidence is somewhat mixed. For example, the opposite effect has been demonstrated in a study uncovering how American firms brought cars without catalytic converters to China (Gallagher 2006). Other studies have shown that increased trade and investment has led to increased stringency in environmental regulations in China (Zeng and Eastin 2007). Many debates have focused not on *whether* pollution halos exist, but rather on the conditions under which they do exist. For example, 'pollution halos' exist in some regions, such as the Middle East and North Africa (Asghari 2013). Others have found evidence of pollution halos in specific sectors, such as energy, where firms may have access to greener technology (Zarsky 1999).

In a related argument, David Vogel (2009) demonstrates that countries with large markets can dictate higher environmental standards because the costs of leaving such markets are too high for firms compared to the other costs of doing business. This can actually result in an upward harmonization of environmental standards as firms meet the requirements of the most stringent markets, rather than produce different products for different markets. Because Vogel demonstrated this phenomenon through his examination of the diffusion of motor vehicle emission standards from California to other American states and even other countries, it is now famously known as the 'California effect' (see also Chapter 4). A similar argument has been made regarding an upward harmonization of environmental standards towards European Union standards, as firms find it more efficient to produce goods for a single market standard. This phenomenon has been termed the 'Brussels effect' (Bradford 2012).

There is no easy answer to the question: Is trade good or bad for the environment? Those that have offered 'black and white' answers have been motivated by theoretically determined models of potential outcomes, rather than clear data and empirical evidence of effects. That said, there are prolific empirical linkages between the governance of international trade and the governance of global environmental politics. Section 10.2 explores some of these empirical linkages by looking at how states have incorporated trade mechanisms in various environmental regimes.

10.2 Trade dimensions of environmental regimes

There are several clear examples of environmental problems with trade connections: for example, international trade in endangered wildlife species, such as elephants, sharks, and bluefin tuna, hunted for their commercial value on the international market. In 2018, bluefin tuna fetched more than $11,000 per kilogram at Tokyo's Toyosu market (Elassar 2018). Due to the many close ties between international trade and environmental degradation, several multilateral environmental agreements engage trade in one of two ways. In these agreements, states either address environmental issues that are clearly trade-related, typically using trade measures to secure objectives, or they use trade measures as a means of addressing environmental problems even when the problems themselves may not be directly related to international trade. This section unpacks both situations. It develops two examples of the former, wildlife trade and trade in hazardous waste, under the Convention on International Trade in Endangered Species and the Basel Convention on Hazardous Wastes and their Disposal respectively. It also briefly discusses trade provisions under the Cartagena Protocol on Biosafety. It then explains two examples of the latter: emissions trading under the Kyoto Protocol on climate change, and trade bans on ozone-depleting substances under the Montreal Protocol on Substances that Deplete the Ozone Layer. Although we focus on these four multilateral environmental agreements here, many others, including the Rotterdam Convention on **prior informed consent** and the Minamata Convention on Mercury, also use trade-related measures.

Trade-related environmental issues: wildlife and hazardous waste

There are thousands of species that are threatened or may become so due to international trade in their parts and derivatives. Elephants are one of the most well-known examples. Driven largely by markets in parts of Asia, elephant ivory is largely valued for its aesthetic and ornamental purposes, but it was also historically used for products such as billiard balls, needles, chopsticks, and piano keys. Ivory trafficking is estimated to bring in about $4 billion per year (Weintraub 2018), and at its peak in 2014 the wholesale price of elephant ivory was $2,100 per kilogram. This was in part driven by the fact that until 2017 China allowed *domestic* trade in ivory. Since the domestic ban on ivory trade was announced in China, the price of ivory has dropped to $730 per kilogram in 2017 (a 65 per cent decrease), and there has been an 80 per cent decline in seizures of ivory entering China (Xiang and Wei 2017). Another high-profile example of a species that has become threatened due to international trade is sharks, with the total declared value of trade in shark products approaching $1 billion per year (Dent and Clarke 2015). Some shark species, such as hammerhead, basking, and great white sharks, are hunted for their fins, which are traded for human consumption (i.e. shark fin soup) and for traditional medicinal purposes, and can fetch more than $20,000 for a single fin depending on the species. A 2013 study estimated that 100 million sharks are killed each year as part of this trade, with most populations for which data is available showing an unsustainable decline in numbers (Worm et al. 2013).

To address the problem of species being endangered by trade, an international treaty was negotiated, called the Convention on International Trade in Endangered Species (known as CITES). This Convention is one of the oldest multilateral environmental agreements, entering into force in 1975, and now enjoys near-universal participation among states (183 parties) as of 2019. Its overarching objective is to 'ensure that international trade in specimens of wild animals and plants does not threaten their survival' (CITES n.d.). It seeks to achieve this objective by restricting international trade in certain species of plants and animals through a system of detailed lists and associated permits.

Although CITES has had some success in protecting some commercial species, such as seahorses and Nile crocodiles (Martin 2016), it has historically struggled to adequately protect species that have high commercial value (Jinnah 2014). A classic example of this is the bluefin tuna, which is highly threatened and has been proposed for listing within CITES several times over the years, but has never secured enough votes for protection, despite strong scientific evidence supporting its high level of threat due to international trade (Madigan et al. 2017; Vincent et al. 2014). This is probably because bluefin tuna are one of the most expensive fresh seafood species in the world (Collette et al. 2011), leading some countries to place short-term economic interests in catching the fish ahead of longer-term **conservation** interests in protecting them to ensure the survival of the species (Jinnah 2014). CITES has similarly struggled to protect species such as elephants, whose population declines are driven by illegal trafficking and domestic markets (Wittemyer 2016).

Moreover, some argue that trade bans can actually result in an increase in trade of vulnerable species because they lead to a rise in the commercial value of a banned species, which can in turn drive black markets (Rivalan et al. 2007). Although CITES has taken steps in recent years to address problems of wildlife trafficking, its efforts have been insufficient to inhibit the rapid growth of transnational environmental crime, which includes wildlife trafficking. As such, although the trade controls set up by CITES are an important piece of global strategy to combat damaging wildlife trade, it must be complemented by non-trade measures as well, such as domestic conservation efforts. Further, because CITES only addresses legal trade in wildlife, additional measures, such as criminal penalties, must also be developed to aggressively address illicit trade.

The risks associated with the transboundary movement of hazardous waste is another issue that has been addressed through the use of trade restrictions. The deliberate transboundary shipment of waste—from brick dust to laptops to plastics to nuclear waste—has been a persistent challenge for global environmental governance. Countries transport wastes across borders for various different reasons. It may be that the closest, cheapest, or most specialized treatment or disposal facility for a particular type of waste is in another country. Alternatively, what is seen as waste in some countries can be considered raw materials in others (Wyler and Sheikh 2013). Waste streams between developed and developing countries have grown increasingly larger over time. There are deep concerns about developed countries dumping wastes cheaply in poorer countries, as well as increased waste trade among poorer countries (Lepawsky 2018).

Scholarship on the trade in hazardous waste has revealed that most trade has been legal, and carried out among wealthy countries—and yet it still posed significant risks to importing

countries, in particular to human health and the environment, as a result of the nature of hazardous waste and the expense of managing wastes safely, which falls on private actors (O'Neill
2000). Early scholarly analyses and governance interventions regarding the cross-border flow
of waste tended to treat wastes as risky externalities of production, and to focus on rich developed countries dumping their hazardous waste in developing countries (O'Neill 2019). Much
of this attention was spurred by a series of 'toxic ships', which transported hazardous wastes
from developed countries to developing countries (see Box 10.2).

Box 10.2   The Bamako Convention: addressing hazardous waste dumping in developing countries through a regional agreement

In 1988, thousands of barrels of highly toxic hazardous waste were dumped in the village of Koko,
Nigeria. An Italian businessman convinced a Nigerian farmer to store these barrels on his land for
approximately $100 per month. The barrels, disguised as building materials, were improperly sealed,
leading to serious health effects for the residents of Koko. This incident and similar ones throughout the
African continent brought widespread international attention to the issue of dumping large quantities
of hazardous materials in less developed countries, particularly in Africa. The United Nations Economic
Commission for Africa, which was established by the Economic and Social Council of the United Nations
to promote the economic and social development of Africa, referred to the practice as 'toxic terrorism',
and the president of Kenya, Daniel arap Moi, in 1988 called it 'garbage imperialism'.

In response, the Organization of African Unity (which preceded the African Union) and the Economic
Commission for Africa, with the assistance of the United Nations Environment Programme produced
the Ban of the Import into Africa and the Control of Transboundary Movement and Management
of Hazardous Wastes within Africa, more commonly called the Bamako Convention, in 1991. The
Convention entered into force in 1998 and as of January 2019, 28 African countries have ratified it.

The Convention aims to protect the health of African populations and the environment by banning
the import of any hazardous or radioactive waste into African nations. It is an important example of a
regional environmental governance instrument that uses restrictions on trade to secure environmental
objectives. The Bamako Convention also includes measures designed to minimize and control the
transboundary movement of hazardous waste within the African continent. For example, it requires
shipment-specific notices, supports a precautionary approach, and prohibits the dumping of hazardous
wastes into the sea and in domestic water systems. The Convention treats illegal traffic as a criminal and
extraditable offence, contains compulsory enforcement measures, and requires member countries to
enact domestic penalties for people involved in the illegal transfer of hazardous waste. During the first
Conference of the Parties in Bamako, Mali in 2013, African ministers of environment declared that 'the
import of hazardous waste into Africa is a crime against humanity'.

Although the Bamako Convention is an important step towards addressing the issue of hazardous
waste dumping in Africa, numerous challenges remain apparent. Notably, many of the commitments
parties made at the first Conference of the Parties have not been fulfilled, including delivering on
finance. Furthermore, many countries have not communicated or reported necessary information, nor
implemented domestic obligations. These challenges are in part a result of a myriad of complex issues
facing African countries, including high levels of poverty, massive development needs, poor governance,
and limited technical capabilities. Therefore, while the Bamako Convention afforded African countries
greater autonomy to develop a hazardous waste governance system that is more amenable to African
interests, there may be a trade-off, in that the parties to the Bamako Convention generally lack the
capacity to implement it. Many developed countries continue to dump hazardous waste in Africa.

Sources: Jones 1993; Kaminsky 1992; Saleh and Abene 2016.

The issue of the dumping of waste from rich to poor countries and at sea, and concern about the ability of developing economies to adequately manage waste, also fostered an international response to these issues with the development of a new treaty, the 1989 Basel Convention on the Control of Transboundary Movements of Hazardous Wastes and their Disposal. The Convention entered into force in May 1992, and has 186 country members as of 2019. It aims to enable environmentally sound management of hazardous wastes by minimizing generation of wastes, reducing transboundary movement, and disposing of wastes close to the point of generation. It encourages cooperation between parties in the form of technical assistance and information sharing, and runs a network of training and capacity-building centres throughout the world.

The Convention has also two main provisions related to trade. First, it prohibits trade in hazardous wastes with non-parties to the Convention, a provision which was intended to encourage membership. However, it also has the potential unintended consequence of diverting trade from countries that may be able to more safely manage and dispose of such wastes, such as the United States, which as one of the world's largest waste exporters has not joined the treaty.

Second, the Convention rests on a prior informed consent system in which importing countries must be notified and provide written consent before any hazardous wastes can be shipped to these countries. Although the rationale behind this type of notification and consent system is to ensure transparency and minimize abuses such as the 'toxic ship' episodes in the 1980s, these procedures could be seen as non-tariff barriers to trade—they could then possibly be in conflict with World Trade Organization rules, which prohibit most restrictions on international trade (see also Section 10.3).

Despite these provisions, many felt that the Convention did not go far enough. The Basel Convention Ban Amendment, which would have prevented the movement of hazardous waste from developed to developing countries altogether, never got enough support to enter into force. African nations and others were concerned that the Basel Convention only attempts to regulate, rather than ban, this practice by requiring that exporters notify and gain the consent of importing countries. These African countries argued that they did not have the institutional and technological means to effectively implement the notification and consent system, and therefore a ban on imports was necessary. They also argued that the Basel Convention's definition of hazardous wastes is too narrow (notably it exempts radioactive waste), and that the lack of compulsory enforcement measures would limit its effectiveness. Moreover, some developing countries remain concerned about illegal trade, economically motivated dumping, 'sham' recycling (unsafe dumping under the pretext of recycling), and 'dirty' recycling (recycling from hazardous wastes that is harmful to the environment or people involved) (Krueger 2001). Developing countries and **non-governmental organizations** (such as the Basel Action Network and Greenpeace) argued for a new amendment, called the 'Ban Amendment', to end waste trading except between a subset of wealthy countries, and as applied to wastes shipped for final disposal and for recycling (Krueger 2001). Although the Ban Amendment was adopted in 1995, it has yet to secure enough **party ratifications** to enter into force. The Ban is opposed by those who prefer the existing notification and consent system, which includes many developed countries, some developing countries that have waste recycling industries, and the international recycling industry (Krueger 2001).

The nature of the hazardous waste management problem has shifted over time, including in terms of the materials at issue, and therefore the actors involved and the regulatory politics. The growth of trade in electronic waste (e-waste), which refers to all electrical and electronic equipment that has been discarded without intention for reuse, has resulted in a growth in exports of these wastes from developed to developing countries. This is an important problem because electronic wastes can contain hundreds of toxic substances that contaminate ecosystems and human bodies, particularly for the labourers who rummage through e-waste to gather parts for recycling (Iles 2004). Moreover, developing countries generally do not have the infrastructure for appropriate waste management (Osibanjo and Nnorom 2007). Despite bans on exports of e-waste from the European Union to developing countries, illegal trade persists and has even attracted the attention of Interpol.

Another important emerging issue is the accumulation of plastic waste in the oceans (see Box 5.4), which comes from domestic, industrial, and fishing activities, but primarily from land-based sources via runoff (Auta et al. 2017; Li et al. 2016). Some argue that international trade in plastic waste should be encouraged as a solution to plastic pollution, because plastic can be exported to countries that can more cheaply recycle the waste, thereby encouraging recycling. However, developed countries, which have better waste management infrastructure, are the primary exporters of plastic waste, and the plastic overwhelmingly goes to developing countries, primarily in East Asia and the Pacific, which are still in the process of implementing effective waste management infrastructure (Brooks et al. 2018). International trade in waste plastic further increases the risk that the plastic will be mismanaged, and end up in the ocean. It is also important to note that only 9 per cent of the total plastic waste generated had been recycled as of 2015, and because most plastic can only be recycled once or twice, '[r]ecycling delays, rather than avoids, final disposal' (Geyer et al. 2017: 2).

Finally, a persistent issue surrounding the global trade in waste is storing and disposing of nuclear waste. There remains some interest in regional, international, and multinational disposal options, in part because some countries with nuclear power programmes are still looking to export their nuclear waste, despite action in other countries to manage such waste responsibly. This raises concerns related to national **sovereignty**, governance, funding, and security (Di Nucci and Isidoro Losada 2015). The complexity and importance of these issues point towards a growing need for improvements in the governance of global waste management.

The 2000 Cartagena Protocol on Biosafety also contains trade measures that could potentially be seen to conflict with trade rules. The Protocol regulates the international trade in **genetically modified organisms**, for example by requiring exporters of certain genetically modified organisms to receive the 'advance informed agreement' of an importing country prior to import. The Cartagena Protocol requires that importing countries base their decisions to restrict the imports of genetically modified organisms on a scientifically based risk assessment (Newell and Mackenzie 2000). This is consistent with the World Trade Organization's 1994 Agreement on the Application of Sanitary and Phytosanitary Measures, which requires that import restrictions on genetically modified organisms for sanitary or phytosanitary reasons must be based on sufficient evidence and a risk assessment that conforms to certain standards (Oberthür and Gehring 2006). The Cartagena Protocol has more expansive provisions than the 1994 Agreement, particularly in allowing for precautionary action, in allowing the exporter to carry out the risk assessment, and by also requiring an assessment of socio-economic considerations. However, in an effort to avoid conflicting regulations, these differing provisions are not necessarily inconsistent with the 1994 WTO Agreement, although this is subject to interpretation (Oberthür and Gehring 2006).

Because of potential conflicts with trade law, some scholars hypothesize that there may actually be a 'chilling effect' on countries' willingness either to negotiate strong multilateral environmental agreements that use trade provisions to secure environmental objectives, or to implement the provisions of those that already exist (Conca 2000; Eckersley 2004). Yet no dispute was ever raised at the World Trade Organization against such domestic laws implementing a multilateral environmental agreement. This could be related, at least in part, to environmental exemptions in trade law that allow countries to reconcile environmental policies and trade.

Using trade measures to address environmental issues: climate change and ozone depletion

Whereas the Basel Convention and CITES explicitly address trade-related environmental problems, other multilateral environmental agreements use market-based instruments to address environmental issues which are only tangentially related to international trade. This is in part because market-based instruments can help to achieve environmental objectives at lower cost and because powerful states have pushed for their inclusion in some cases.

States have incorporated trade measures into the 1987 Montreal Protocol on Substances that Deplete the Ozone Layer. The Montreal Protocol seeks to address stratospheric **ozone layer** depletion by reducing and eventually eliminating the production and use of chlorofluorocarbons and other ozone-depleting substances, which were widely used as aerosol propellants, refrigerants, and in industrial processes. In order to do this, it uses measures to restrict trade in these substances, products containing them, and the technologies used for producing them. In particular, parties to the Protocol were required to ban the import of ozone-depleting substances from non-parties, and exports of these substances were also subsequently banned (Brack 2018).

The motivation behind these trade measures was to promote the broadest possible participation and compliance with the Montreal Protocol, and the Protocol has been quite successful in achieving those objectives. However, the trade restrictions put developing countries in a difficult position, because they lacked the financial means and technological capabilities to create substitutes for chlorofluorocarbons, unlike developed countries. Therefore, developing countries pushed for technical and financial assistance that would provide them with affordable access to chemical substitutes, as well as the basis for their own chemical manufacturing industries (Litfin 1994). Importantly, the Multilateral Fund was created in 1991 to help developing countries meet their commitments under the Protocol.

The Kyoto Protocol on climate change uses emissions trading to reduce **greenhouse gas** emissions. Emissions trading systems, sometimes called 'cap and trade' systems, are the most common form of market-based mechanism for reducing greenhouse gas emissions (World Bank and Ecofys 2018). They entail a government or other regulatory authority setting a 'cap'—an upper limit on emissions—and then selling or giving a corresponding number of 'allowances' or 'permits' to emitters (MacKenzie 2009). In the case of carbon trading, these allowances are units of carbon dioxide-equivalent emissions (calculated on the basis of how much each pollutant contributes to global warming in comparison to carbon dioxide)

(MacKenzie 2009). Allowances can be traded in markets, where entities for which emission reductions would be costly can instead buy additional allowances from other entities that can reduce emissions relatively cheaply (MacKenzie 2009). Thus, the key selling point of carbon trading is that emissions can be reduced where it is cheapest to do so, and businesses have the flexibility to either reduce emissions or buy additional allowances (Newell and Paterson 2010). Over time, the regulatory authority lowers the cap, making the allowances more scarce and increasing the incentive to invest in low carbon technologies and practices.

Under the Kyoto Protocol's first commitment period (2008–2012), all developed country parties agreed to emission-reduction targets (some countries took on additional targets during the second commitment period, 2013–2020). These targets required them to reduce emissions by a percentage below 1990 levels. The targets were then expressed as allowed emissions for each country, and were divided into 'assigned amount units'. After meeting their targets, countries that had units to spare could then sell them in an emissions trading system. For example, if Japan could reduce its emissions below its Kyoto target by increasing nuclear power, it could quantify those additional reductions, and offer them for sale on the international carbon market. Then other states for whom buying Japan's surplus assigned amount units is cheaper than reducing emissions domestically, could do so and use those assigned amount units towards meeting their own emission-reduction commitments under the Protocol.

In addition to the carbon market between developed country parties, the Kyoto Protocol also established an innovative system to allow for emissions trading between developed and developing countries. This new system was called the Clean Development Mechanism. Under the Clean Development Mechanism, developed countries could invest in emission-reduction projects in developing countries, which did not have binding emission-reduction targets under the Kyoto Protocol, in order to generate emission-reduction credits. The developing countries would then sell those carbon credits, known as 'certified emission reductions', to developed country investors. For example, the China Guanmenyan Hydropower Project, located along the Lishui River in Hunan Province, was expected at the time of its registration in 2008 to reduce annual greenhouse gas emissions by over 90,000 tons of carbon dioxide equivalent by displacing some of the power coming from power plants that use fossil fuels; these emission reductions could then be sold to a developed country investor to meet its emission-reduction commitments (Clean Development Mechanism 2006).

The Clean Development Mechanism was envisioned as an engine for **sustainable development**, while simultaneously giving developed countries increased flexibility to meet their commitments at the least expense. However, many studies have criticized its actual delivery on the former aim (Olsen 2007; Sutter and Parreño 2007). Central to these critiques has been the observation that projects have been poorly distributed across the world, with very few in places like sub-Saharan Africa. Rather, 75 per cent of all Clean Development Mechanism projects were hosted in India, Brazil, China, and Mexico (Olsen 2007). Scholars have also criticized the 'additionality' of Clean Development Mechanism projects (Paulsson 2009). In other words, they question the extent to which projects result in emission reductions that wouldn't have been realized otherwise, a core requirement of generating certified emission reductions under the Kyoto Protocol.

The future of emissions trading under the 2015 Paris Agreement remains unclear. The Paris Agreement does not explicitly refer to emissions trading or **market mechanisms** at all.

Rather, Article 6 encourages 'voluntary cooperation' between parties in meeting their new voluntary, bottom-up emission-reduction targets (their 'nationally determined contributions'). It further provides that this might include the use of 'internally transferred mitigation outcomes'. Although their details are yet to be determined, these instruments are likely to involve some sort of market mechanism for sharing mitigation responsibility among countries. Thus far, much of the discussion among Paris Agreement parties has revolved around designing an accounting structure for such a mechanism and creating safeguards to ensure environmental integrity. The parties have also discussed ways to distribute proceeds, such as for example collecting these proceeds into a fund to assist developing countries in adapting to climate change.

Carbon markets are also a dominant feature of global climate governance beyond the Paris Agreement (Bernstein et al. 2010; Newell and Paterson 2010). The European Union emissions trading system, launched in 2005, remains the world's largest, although it will probably be surpassed by China's domestic emissions trading system once it is operational. In the Americas, Mexico began piloting an emissions trading system in 2018, Columbia and Chile are considering doing the same, California has extended its own emissions trading system to 2030, and British Columbia and Washington state have also launched systems of their own. Importantly, linkages between emissions trading systems are being made, which allow for allowances to be traded from one system to another. For example, California's emissions trading system is linked with the Quebec system. Moreover, some businesses have also implemented internal and sector-wide emissions trading systems (Kolk and Pinkse 2004).

10.3 Environmental dimensions of the global trade regime

The global trade regime addresses environmental issues in a variety of ways. Centrally, the World Trade Organization's environment-related negotiations and jurisprudence have strongly shaped the way we understand the relationship between trade and environmental governance. In addition, many **preferential trade agreements** (i.e. those between two or more countries) have also been active sites of environmental governance, incorporating increasingly far-reaching environmental provisions, including investment provisions, that expand on the environmental provisions that originated with the World Trade Organization (Jinnah and Morin 2020).

We therefore begin this section with a discussion of environmental governance in the World Trade Organization, before turning to an exploration of how this has extended into preferential trade agreements in recent years, and how investment provisions have also engaged with environmental governance. We then briefly reflect on the influence of environmental governance on the global trade regime.

Environmental governance at the World Trade Organization

Before unpacking the World Trade Organization's treatment of environmental issues, it is important to understand the basic principles of how the organization operates. The 1994 agreement establishing the World Trade Organization provides an overarching framework under which sit more than 30 agreements, annexes, and lists of commitments, which cover trade in goods and services as well as intellectual property. If one World Trade Organization member believes that another member is in violation of its obligations under the organization's agreements, that member can request the formation of a dispute settlement panel to hear the dispute, and can also appeal panel decisions to an Appellate Body. Unlike dispute resolution under multilateral environmental agreements, the World Trade Organization's dispute settlement system allows for compensation measures to bring about compliance with its rules. This can be quite effective even though its decisions do not carry binding precedent on future decisions.

The core principle of the World Trade Organization is **non-discrimination**, which is embodied by two obligations: *most favoured nation* and *national treatment*. Under the *most favoured nation* principle, all members must be treated the same way with respect to domestic rules and practices surrounding international trade. Members cannot grant special favour to one member compared to another. Provisions under certain multilateral environmental agreements, such as the Basel Convention which prohibits trade in hazardous waste products between parties and non-parties, could be seen as in violation of the most favoured nation principle. Under *national treatment*, members must treat domestic and imported 'like products' (i.e. products that are the same or very similar) equally with respect to domestic laws and policies, such as taxes. The term 'like product' has been important to several World Trade Organization disputes relating to the environment. Some dispute settlement panels have explored whether two products that are functionally the same but have different environmental impacts—for example in the energy inputs of production—are indeed 'like products' and should therefore be treated identically. World Trade Organization jurisprudence includes whether 'dolphin-safe' tuna is a like product with tuna caught using non-dolphin-safe methods, or if a brick that contains asbestos is the same as one that does not.

The centrepiece of World Trade Organization jurisprudence on environmental issues for many years was an environmental exception contained in the General Agreement on Tariffs and Trade. Article XX of that agreement allows members to implement environmental laws and policies that would otherwise conflict with their obligations, as long as certain conditions are met. Specifically, Article XX provides protection for domestic environmental policies that are '*necessary* to protect human, animal or plant life or health', or that are '*relat[ed] to* the conservation of a natural resource' [emphasis added]. Although seemingly straightforward, interpretation of these provisions has largely hinged on the italicized words, *necessary* and *related to*. In addition, interpretation of these provisions has also hinged on the 'chapeau', or opening clause, of Article XX, which requires that these domestic environmental policies must also be implemented in a way that 'does not constitute arbitrary or unjustified discrimination' or 'a disguised restriction on international trade'. Article XX disputes have covered a wide swathe of issues, ranging from biodiversity to public health to requirements for reformulated gasoline (see Table 10.1).

Narrow interpretations of these clauses in early World Trade Organization panel decisions found that several domestic environmental laws did not qualify for Article XX exceptions, and were therefore in violation of World Trade Organization rules. These early rulings, such as the famous Shrimp/Turtle case, were heavily criticized by environmental activists (see Box 10.3). Although some of these early decisions 'threatened to render environmental exceptions unusable' (Charnovitz 2007: 695), more recently Appellate Body decisions have reversed controversial panel decisions, ruling that domestic environmental laws do in fact meet some or all of the conditions of Article XX, including in the Shrimp/ Turtle cases (see Box 10.3).

Table 10.1 Disputes involving Article XX(b) and (g) of the General Agreement on Tariffs and Trade (1980–2018)

Year complaint filed	Title of dispute	Issue	Key findings
1980	United States–Prohibition of Imports of Tuna and Tuna Products from Canada	United States introduced a ban on tuna and tuna products imports from Canada in retaliation for the arrests of United States tuna fishermen	United States withdrew the import ban, which was subsequently found to be inconsistent with Article XI (Elimination of Quantitative Restrictions), and was not justified under Article XX(g).
1987	Canada–Measures Affecting Exports of Unprocessed Herring and Salmon	Canadian regulations prohibited export of certain unprocessed herring and salmon. United States filed complaint.	Canadian export prohibitions were found to be inconsistent with Article XI, and were not justified under Article XX(g).
1990	Thailand–Restrictions on the Importation of and Internal Taxes on Cigarettes	Thailand prohibited cigarette imports but allowed domestic cigarette sales. United States filed complaint.	Thailand's import prohibitions were found to be inconsistent with Article XI, and not 'necessary' within the meaning of Article XX(b).
1991	United States–Restrictions on Imports of Tuna	United States banned tuna imports originating from Mexico for failing to meet dolphin protection standards set by United States.	United States import ban was found to be not applicable under Article III (National Treatment) and inconsistent with Article XI. It could not be justified under Article XX(b) or (g). Panel report was not adopted.
1992	United States–Restrictions on Imports of Tuna II	United States ban on tuna imports from Mexico covered intermediary nations. European Economic Community filed complaint.	United States import ban on intermediary and primary nations was found to be not covered under Article III, inconsistent with Article XI, and could not be justified under Article XX(b) or (g).
1993	United States–Taxes on Automobiles	European Union issued a complaint about three United States measures on automobiles: a luxury tax, gas guzzler tax, and the Corporate Average Fuel Economy (CAFE) regulation, which sets different rules for calculating the average fuel economy of imported and domestic vehicles.	The panel found that the luxury and gas guzzler taxes were consistent with Article III, but the CAFE regulation was inconsistent with Article III. Panel found that the CAFE regulation could not be justified under Article XX(g) or (d).
1995	United States–Gasoline	The United States Clean Air Act sets out different rules for regulating domestic and imported gasoline. Brazil and Venezuela filed complaints.	Panel found that the different rules were in violation of Article III, and did not fall under Article XX(g). Appellate Body found that the rules fell within the scope of Article XX(g), but constituted discrimination under Article XX chapeau.
1997	United States–Shrimp	United States banned the import of shrimp and shrimp products from countries that did not use a certain type of net designed to protect sea turtles. Complaints filed by India, Malaysia, Pakistan, and Thailand.	Panel and Appellate Body found the ban was in violation of Article XI, and although covered by Article XX(g) was considered discriminatory under Article XX chapeau.

Year complaint filed	Title of dispute	Issue	Key findings
1998	European Communities–Asbestos	France banned asbestos and asbestos-containing products to protect human health. Canada filed complaint.	Panel found that the ban was inconsistent with Article III, but granted an exception for the ban under Article XX(b). Appellate Body ruled that Canada did not prove ban was in violation of Article III; also upheld justification for ban as exemption under Article XX(b).
2000	United States–Shrimp (Article 21.5–Malaysia)	United States revised guidelines for implementing ban on shrimp products. Malaysia filed complaint that ban was still discriminatory.	Appellate Body and Panel both found that the revised guidelines were justified under Article XX(g), and met the conditions of the chapeau of Article XX.
2005	Brazil–Retreaded Tyres	Brazil banned the import of retreaded tyres. European Union filed complaint.	Panel found Brazil's ban on retreaded tyres was inconsistent with Articles XI and III. Panel and Appellate Body both found that while the ban was justified under Article XX(b), it was not justified (albeit for different reasons) under Article XX chapeau.
2009	China–Raw Materials	China imposed export duties, quotas, and other requirements on various raw materials. Complaints filed by European Community, Mexico, and United States.	Panel and Appellate Body found that China's export restraints were inconsistent with several commitments under its Accession Protocol and that the restraints could not be justified under Article XX(b) or (g).
2011	EC–Seal Products	European Union regulations placed prohibitions on the import and sale of seal products. Complaints filed by Canada and Norway.	Panel and Appellate Body found that seal product prohibitions were inconsistent with Article I (Most-Favoured-Nation Treatment) and Article III, that these prohibitions could be considered under Article XX(a) (necessary to protect public morals), but the European Union had not demonstrated that the prohibitions met requirements of Article XX chapeau. Panel also found the bans could not be justified under Article XX(b) (Appellate Body made no decision on this).
2012	China–Rare Earths	China placed export duties, quotas, and other limitations on various forms of rare earths (elements that have magnetic and conductive properties, commonly used in electronics) as well as tungsten and molybdenum. United States, European Union, and Japan filed complaints.	China's export duties were found by the Panel and Appellate Body to be inconsistent with its Accession Protocol, and could not be justified under Article XX. Panel also found that the export quotas were inconsistent with Article XI, and could not be justified under Article XX(g). Appellate Body upheld Panel's application of Article XX(g).

Source: compiled by the authors with data provided by the World Trade Organization.

Box 10.3 The World Trade Organization Shrimp/Turtle dispute

Perhaps the most (in)famous environmental dispute under the World Trade Organization is the 1998 Shrimp/Turtle dispute which pitted India, Malaysia, Thailand, and Pakistan against the United States. The dispute was prompted by concerns in the United States that methods used to catch shrimp—shrimp trawling nets—resulted in the unintended drowning of marine turtles who got caught in those nets as by-catch. Prompted in part by domestic pressures from civil society organizations such as the Earth Island Institute to address this issue, the United States instituted a ban on the import of shrimp and shrimp products under its Endangered Species Act if those products were not caught using methods that protect marine turtles through 'turtle excluder devices'.

India, Malaysia, Thailand, and Pakistan challenged the American law, arguing that it violated World Trade Organization rules. Because shrimp harvested using turtle excluder devices and shrimp harvested using trawling nets and other devices are essentially the same product (i.e. 'like products'), banning one and not the other violated non-discrimination obligations. Additionally, they argued that this violated the most favoured nation clause because it allowed the import of a *like product* from one member state, but not others. The United States defended its law as an environmental exemption under Article XX of the General Agreement on Tariffs and Trade. Specifically, it argued that the law was 'related to the conservation of a natural resource' under Article XX(g) and was 'necessary for the protection of human, animal, and plant life and health' under Article XX(b).

However, the Panel rejected the exemption under Article XX because the law constituted 'unjustifiable discrimination' under Article XX. The United States appealed the case, but the Appellate Body also found that the law constituted 'arbitrary and unjustifiable discrimination'. Importantly, the law was too rigid in requiring countries to adopt essentially the same policies, rather than allowing flexibility to meet the same goal (i.e. sea turtle conservation) by other comparable means. The Appellate Body also ruled that the United States treated countries differently, for example in its efforts to negotiate solutions to the problem, and in the domestic certification process through which countries' compliance with the law was evaluated.

Although the World Trade Organization ruling has faced much criticism for what many see as its striking down of a domestic environmental law, the Appellate Body decision underscored, for the first time, the legitimacy of the Article XX exemptions. Importantly, it stated: 'we have *not* decided that sovereign states should not act together bilaterally, plurilaterally or multilaterally, either within the World Trade Organization or in other international forums, to protect endangered species or to otherwise protect the environment. Clearly, they should and do.' The take home lesson from this decision was that environmental protection is important and should be granted certain protections, but that World Trade Organization members must be very cautious when applying such measures to ensure that they do not constitute disguised restrictions on international trade.

In focusing on a charismatic species, such as sea turtles, the case brought much non-governmental organization and public attention to issues at the intersection of trade and the environment. This was evidenced, for example, by the environmental activists in sea turtle costumes who took part in the massive protests, which eventually shut down the World Trade Organization's ministerial conference in Seattle in 1999 just after the ruling was made. This so-called 'battle in Seattle' was a turning point for trade–environment politics, which was in part fuelled by the ruling in this case, which many environmental activists viewed as 'anti-environment'.

Sources: DeSombre and Barkin 2002; Kulovesi 2011; Neumayer 2004.

Recently, the World Trade Organization's dispute settlement body has begun to hear a series of environment-related cases that relate to the permissibility of subsidies for renewable energy. These cases are critical because they could impact the ability of states to support decarbonization efforts. For example, in 2010 Japan and the European Union challenged a Canadian feed-in tariff. A feed-in tariff seeks to encourage investment in renewables by guaranteeing a set price for renewable energy that is generated and sold into the grid. The Canadian feed-in tariff in question guaranteed minimum electricity prices for solar and wind sources only if a baseline domestic content requirement was met (Verkuijl et al. 2017). The domestic content requirement could be seen as a violation of Canada's national treatment obligation under the World Trade Organization, and indeed the organization's dispute settlement body ruled against Canada for that reason.

Renewable energy cases are also very interesting to study because although fossil fuel subsidies are prolific (see Figure 10.3), outnumbering those for renewables by a ratio of 4:1, to date only subsidies for renewables have been challenged at the World Trade Organization (Asmelash 2015; Van de Graaf and van Asselt 2017). Scholars have posed several explanations for why renewables subsidies have been challenged in the World Trade Organization while fossil fuel subsidies have not. These explanations include that: challenges to renewables subsidies enjoy a higher likelihood of success because the discriminatory nature of feed-in tariffs is not contested; renewable energy equipment companies have pushed their governments to challenge subsidies for their competitors in other countries; and countries are less likely to challenge long-standing subsidies than newer ones (Asmelash 2015; Meyer 2017; Wold et al. 2012).

Besides its dispute settlement function, the World Trade Organization is also a forum for negotiations in its Committee for Trade and Environment in Special Session. World Trade Organization member states are discussing several environmental issues, including those related to clarifying the relationship between World Trade Organization rules and trade

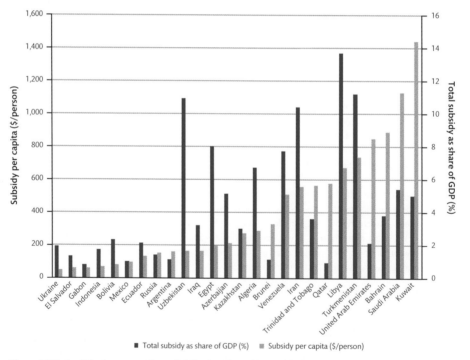

Figure 10.3 Fossil fuel consumption subsidies in selected countries, 2017

Source data from: World Bank, and based on IEA data from IEA (2017). *Fossil-fuel subsidies by country*, www.iea.org/statistics. All rights reserved; as modified by Oxford University Press.

measures taken under multilateral environmental agreements, such as those discussed above. World Trade Organization members are also discussing how to decrease fish subsidies, which are a major driver of overfishing globally, and how to reduce tariffs on environmental goods and services. They have made some progress on both of these tracks. Negotiations on a plurilat-eral Environmental Goods and Services Agreement began in 2014, to develop a system of tariff reductions on products like renewable energy technologies and products used in processes such as waste treatment systems. However, as of January 2019 negotiators have been unable to reach agreement. This may be, in part, because key World Trade Organization members, including the United States, China, and the European Union, have been involved in tense dip-lomatic discussions surrounding environmental goods, such as solar panels and biofuels, which has chilled their interest in pursuing agreement in the World Trade Organization on these issues.

Environmental governance through preferential trade agreements

The provisions contained in the World Trade Organization's core agreements have been influen-tial in shaping how states have treated environmental issues in subsequent **preferential trade agreements** (Jinnah and Morin 2020). There are currently more than 600 preferential trade agreements in force, 86 per cent of which include environmental provisions (Morin et al. 2018). These agreements are thus also emerging as important sites of global environmental politics.

Many of the environmental provisions in preferential trade agreements are weak, merely restating the goal of sustainable development or mirroring the environmental exceptions found in Article XX of the General Agreement on Tariffs and Trade discussed earlier. How-ever, in recent years many preferential trade agreements have reached well beyond the environmental provisions in Article XX (see Figure 10.4). Some of the environmental provi-sions found in trade agreements require that trading partners: implement multilateral envi-ronmental agreements; cooperate on environmental issues; strengthen or enforce existing

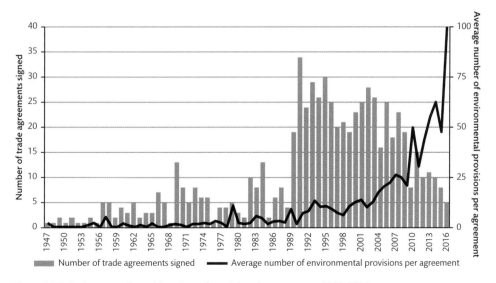

Figure 10.4 Environmental provisions in preferential trade agreements 1947–2016

Source data from: Morin, J.F., A. Dür and L. Lechner (2018), Mapping the trade and environment nexus: Insights from a new dataset. *Global Environmental Politics*, vol. 18(1): 122-139. MIT Press. https://doi.org/10.1162/GLEP_a_00447

environmental laws; protect endangered species; regulate fishing activities; or address climate change by adopting and implementing specified multilateral environmental agreements (Jinnah and Morin 2020; Morin and Jinnah 2018). For example, the 2018 Comprehensive and Progressive Trans-Pacific Partnership, negotiated among 11 countries, contains broader environmental provisions than previously seen in any trade agreement (Cimino-Isaacs and Schott 2016). Among others, it contains new measures for transparency surrounding fish subsidies, which contribute to overfishing and illegal, unreported, and unregulated fishing. Although the agreement doesn't mention climate change explicitly, it does call for a 'transition to a low emission economy' and encourages parties to cooperate on such things as low emission technologies and renewable energy development.

The United States follows a *legalistic approach*, which requires that trading partners adhere to a high level of environmental protection, reflected in strong environmental regulations, and requiring effective enforcement of these laws (Morin and Rochette 2017). Moreover, the United States keeps to an *adversarial* approach with respect to dispute settlement and enforcement of environmental provisions in its preferential trade agreements (Morin and Rochette 2017). Although early agreements followed a more cooperative model, since 2008 all environmental provisions under American preferential trade agreements have enjoyed the full range of remedies available under the agreements' dispute settlement procedures (Jinnah and Morin 2020). This means that sanctions could, in principle, be used to enforce environmental provisions, including those related to implementation of multilateral environmental agreements (Jinnah 2011). Additionally, while the European Union's sectoral approach addresses specific environmental issues, the United States' approach has tended towards enforcement of broad environmental standards (Jinnah and Morgera 2013).

In line with its leadership on many other environmental issues, the European Union has also been active in including environmental provisions in its preferential trade agreements (Morin and Rochette 2017; Poletti and Sicurelli 2016). The European approach is more *cooperative* than the United States approach in some ways, as for example dispute settlement occurs through consultation or arbitration, and the enforcement of environmental provisions is not subject to sanctions (Jinnah and Morgera 2013). Usually their preferential trade agreements include few mechanisms for monitoring compliance with environmental provisions, standards, or agreements. Instead, the European Union tends to integrate, along with environmental provisions, norms that encourage dialogue, the exchange of information, cooperation on transboundary issues, and technical or financial assistance for enhancing the capacity of trade partners to engage in environmental protection. Additionally, the European Union generally uses a *sectoral approach*, where specific environmental issues that affect trading partners are addressed, rather than a general one (Morin and Rochette 2017). For example, its 2002 agreement with Lebanon addresses desertification, while the 2014 agreement with Moldova addresses fisheries and climate action.

Some Latin American countries have also been leaders in developing certain types of environmental provisions in their trade agreements. For example, Peru and Colombia have pushed for the inclusion of biodiversity provisions in their agreements. These are designed to implement access and **benefit sharing** provisions which govern how **genetic resources** can be used, and how the benefits from that use are shared between users and providers (Morin and Gauquelin 2016). These provisions encourage compliance with obligations that are contained in the Convention on Biological Diversity and the Nagoya Protocol. The 2013 Columbia–Costa Rica preferential trade agreement also includes a provision stating that states should ensure that access to traditional indigenous knowledge is subject to prior and informed consent.

Global environmental governance and investment law

Finally, investment law is also an important site of environmental governance in the global trade regime. There are now more than 3,000 bilateral investment treaties and free trade agreements that contain investment chapters (Tienhaara 2018). Many of these agreements protect foreign investors against regulations (including environmental ones) that are tantamount to expropriation. In other words, if an environmental regulation is seen as impacting a foreign firm's expected investment, for example by prohibiting the commercialization of its product, the host state can be liable for damages to the foreign firm under the trade agreement. Many of these agreements, including the North American Free Trade Agreement, establish an international dispute settlement mechanism through which private investors can directly claim damages from states (see Table 10.2). The number of such cases has increased significantly in the 2000s, not only against developing countries, but also against developed countries. These claims can be significant, with some investors claiming more than $100 million in damages.

One potential negative implication of these investor–state dispute settlement provisions is that the prospect of a dispute could have a **chilling effect** on the development of new environmental regulations or on the enforcement of existing ones (Tienhaara 2006; see Box 10.4). That is, states might be hesitant to enact new environmental rules for fear that they could be sued by foreign investors if those rules impacted investment returns. It is unclear if the chilling effect is occurring empirically. However, irrespective of this, environment-related disputes have been hugely controversial. Some civil society groups argue, for example, that these disputes undermine the democratic process by allowing private actors to restrict the regulatory sovereignty of countries to adopt environmental regulations (Ranald 2015).

In response to controversial disputes, most recent agreements include new safeguards and provisions for investor–state dispute settlement related to environmental policymaking (Gagné and Morin 2006; Miles 2016). For example, Canada's model provisions for bilateral investment treaties are particularly clear on this issue, saying that: 'non-discriminatory measures of a Party that are designed and applied to protect legitimate public welfare objectives, such as health, safety and the environment, do not constitute indirect expropriation'.

Some recent trade agreements are also now circumscribing the reach of investor–state dispute settlement. For instance, whereas the 1994 North American Free Trade Agreement was heavily criticized by environmentalists for its strong investor–state dispute settlement provisions (Gaines 2007), investor–state dispute settlement has been eliminated between the United States and Canada under the 2018 renegotiated version of this agreement (the United States-Mexico-Canada Agreement). However, a more limited investor–state dispute settlement mechanism will be available for investors from the United States in some sectors in Mexico, notably the energy sector, after these investors have exhausted all domestic remedies. Therefore, most of the disputes presented in Table 10.2 would not be possible under this renegotiated agreement.

Are trade agreements effective in addressing environmental issues?

Evidence surrounding the effectiveness of environmental provisions in trade agreements is mixed. Recent studies have found that trade agreements with detailed environmental provisions are associated with reduced emission levels of carbon dioxide and suspended particulate matter, compared to agreements without such provisions (Baghdadi et al. 2013;

Table 10.2 Canada's environmental disputes under the NAFTA Investment Chapter (1993–2018)

Year complaint filed	Complaining investor	Issue	Status
1997	Ethyl Corporation	Canada adopted a ban on the gasoline additive MMT.	Out-of-court settlement of US$13 million.
1998	S. D. Myers Inc. (from United States)	Canada prohibited the export of some dangerous waste to the United States.	Tribunal awarded CAN$6.9 million to S. D. Myers.
2001	Chemtura (from United States)	Canadian ban of Lindane, an agricultural pesticide.	Tribunal dismissed the claim.
2006	V. G. Gallo (from United States)	Ontario government banned the dumping of municipal waste in Adams Mine Lake.	Tribunal dismissed the claim.
2008	Clayton and Bilcon (from United States)	Governments of Canada and Nova Scotia did not approve the construction of a marine terminal in an environmentally sensitive region, following an environmental impact assessment.	Canada found liable for breach. Investors claimed US$101 million. Award decision pending.
2008	Dow Agro Science (from United States)	Quebec government banned the use of certain chemical pesticides.	The parties reached a settlement. Dow withdrew its claim and the provincial government acknowledged that the pesticide does not pose an unacceptable risk to human health or the environment.
2008	William Jay Greiner and Malbaie River Outfitters (from United States)	Quebec government reduced the number of salmon fishing licences and restricted access to certain salmon fishing areas.	The claimant withdrew the claim.
2011	St-Mary's VCNA (from United States)	Provincial government prevented a site from being converted from agricultural to extractive industrial use due to concerns related to groundwater.	The parties reached a settlement.
2012	Windstream Energy (from United States)	Ontario decided to defer freshwater offshore wind development to conduct impact assessment and develop environmental regulations.	Tribunal awarded CAN$28.1 million to Windstream.
2012	Lone Pine Resources (from United States)	Quebec government revoked all permits for oil and gas exploration and exploitation under the St Lawrence River, following an environmental impact study.	Pending. Investor claims US$118.9 million.
2014	J. M. Longyear (from United States)	The investor did not receive the provincial tax incentive for sustainable forestry management.	The claimant withdrew the claim.

Source: compiled by the authors with data provided by the Canadian government.

Box 10.4 Vattenfall vs Germany dispute

In 2009, the Swedish energy company Vattenfall brought a landmark case against Germany in the World Bank's International Centre for Settlement of Investment Disputes. The dispute concerned a coal-fired power plant that Vattenfall was constructing near the German city of Hamburg. At the heart of Vattenfall's claim was the city of Hamburg's regulatory permissions process, which imposed environmental restrictions on the power plant project that were designed to minimize pollution into the Elbe River. Vattenfall argued that requirements placed on the project after construction began made the project economically infeasible, which amounted to indirect expropriation and required compensation of 1.4 billion euros (approximately US$1.6 billion). Therefore, Vattenfall claimed that the Hamburg regulatory authorities had violated its right to fair and equitable treatment and the right to not be subject to indirect expropriation under the Energy Charter Treaty, a multilateral treaty that protects energy investments, including in Germany. This dispute was the first investor–state arbitration procedure against Germany.

The power plant had from the start sparked opposition from local environmentalists and political groups, who were concerned about its local environmental impacts, and also with the climate impacts of the coal-fired plant due to greenhouse gas emissions. Nevertheless, the City of Hamburg began to issue permits for the plant from 2007, the terms of which were dependent on the final permit. The City of Hamburg argued that the additional environmental restrictions it imposed in this final permit were necessary to implement the European Union's Water Framework Directive, which sets standards for water quality that member states must adhere to. It is also important to note that part way through the regulatory process, a more environmentally friendly local authority was elected. It was at this point that the local authority mandated more stringent environmental protections. Thus, Vattenfall argued that the local German authorities acted inconsistently throughout the process. According to Vattenfall, the additional restrictions were unforeseen and unexpected, and because the restrictions threatened the economic vitality of the project, the local authorities had effectively expropriated the project. Vattenfall claimed that Germany, which is the responsible party under the Energy Charter Treaty, should be required to compensate Vattenfall 1.4 billion euros for the cost of the project.

Germany ultimately reached an agreement with Vattenfall, which suspended the arbitration proceedings. Germany agreed to replace the more stringent permits with the original permits, and also to release Vattenfall from obligations to construct and operate additional infrastructure. Some see this outcome as Germany agreeing to water down environmental protection, for fear of having to pay a private company for lost profits resulting from the costs of implementing environmental regulations. Others argue that regardless of how the arbitration would ultimately end, the time and resources Germany was required to put into the case were enough to deter the new regulations.

This raises a number of issues. First, the case raises concerns for some that public pressure for more stringent environmental regulation may be unable to override regulatory decisions, throwing the efficacy of the democratic process into question. The case also suggests that investment treaties may restrict the ability of states to implement regional or internationally agreed environmental laws and regulations. The dispute is notable because it effectively reversed public regulatory measures designed to protect the environment, as Germany had to agree to less stringent environmental requirements on the construction of the power plant to avoid paying compensation. Some are concerned that the Vattenfall case has had a chilling effect on public environmental regulatory efforts in Europe. The case further fuelled public opposition in Germany to the proposed Transatlantic Trade and Investment Partnership between the United States and the European Union, which also included a mechanism that allows investors to bring international claims against governments.

Vattenfall brought a second case against Germany in 2012, challenging Germany's decision to phase out nuclear power plants by 2022—Vattenfall is a major owner in two nuclear plants. Germany made this decision following the 2011 disaster at Japan's Fukushima nuclear power plant, but anti-nuclear sentiment has a long history in German politics, resulting from long-standing concerns over where nuclear waste would be stored and also shock from the 1986 Chernobyl nuclear catastrophe in the Soviet Union. Vattenfall is seeking 4.7 billion euros (roughly US$5.37 billion) in compensation. The case is ongoing; most recently in 2018, Germany's attempt to have the case thrown out was rejected.

Sources: Bernasconi-Osterwalder and Hoffman 2012; International Centre for Settlement of Investment Disputes 2011; Jacur 2015; Jahn and Korolczuk 2012.

Martínez-Zarzoso 2018; Zhou et al. 2017). It remains unclear, however, which specific provisions have this positive impact and how it relates to the way they are actually implemented. Case studies suggest that the more mandatory and enforceable environmental commitments are, the more likely governments are to take actions to protect the environment (Matisoff 2010; Jinnah and Lindsay 2016). Others argue that benefits, such as reduced tariffs for countries that commit to specific environmental actions, can also act as an incentive for environmental action (Nordhaus 2015; see Box 10.5).

Nevertheless, there is evidence suggesting that softer provisions, such as support for **capacity building**, can lead to increased environmental cooperation, which can in turn lead to improved domestic environmental protection (Yoo and Kim 2016; Bastiaens and Postnikov 2017). There is also evidence to suggest there are still many untapped potential ways to address environmental issues, especially climate change, through trade agreements (Morin and Jinnah 2018; Box 10.6).

While environmental provisions are not as common in preferential trade agreements between developing countries, these countries are gradually including more environmental provisions over time (Berger et al. 2017). Some include more environmental provisions than others. For example, Mexico has included environmental provisions in its preferential trade agreements with other developing countries that are similar to those in the North American Free Trade Agreement—and in some cases, these provisions are more substantial.

Box 10.5 Climate clubs: using trade barriers to support climate mitigation

Doubtful about the capacity of multilateral treaties to lead to substantial reductions in greenhouse gas emissions, some scholars advocate alternative approaches to international climate governance. One of these approaches, called the 'climate club' model, involves 'minilateralism'—that is, cooperation among a small number of key countries, often those that are more ambitious in tackling climate change or those that are major greenhouse gas emitters.

There are different models of climate clubs. One of the most ambitious and widely discussed models was developed by Yale economist William Nordhaus, who won the Nobel prize in 2018 for his work on carbon pricing. According to his model, countries join the club by agreeing to both set a defined carbon price and impose tariffs on goods imported from non-members. Facing these increased tariffs, non-members have an incentive to join the club and accept carbon pricing.

Proponents of climate club models argue that because a club consists of a smaller number of like-minded countries, countries are more likely to cooperate with one another and more likely to commit to ambitious climate action within a club format. Proponents also recognize that a safe climate system is very difficult to provide, because actors have an incentive to free-ride—to benefit from the actions taken by others to provide the public good (in this case a safe climate), but without taking costly actions themselves to contribute to it. A climate club might address this free-riding problem by providing benefits to members of the club, such as reduced barriers to trade. Moreover, by imposing costs such as tariffs on non-members, climate clubs incentivize countries to join and remain in the club.

Despite proponents' optimism that climate club models could lead to ambitious and effective climate action, climate clubs are criticized in both theory and practice for a number of reasons. Some have argued that climate clubs, and minilateralism in general, lack legitimacy from the perspective of other states, due to the small number of actors involved. Similarly, some have said that current forms of minilateralism are elitist and procedurally unjust because they might exclude the most vulnerable countries. These authors also argue that minilateralism increases the capacity of powerful states to shape the normative and institutional architecture of global climate governance.

Sources: Eckersley 2012; Hovi et al. 2016; Nordhaus 2015; Odell 2018; Sprinz et al. 2018; Stua 2017; Weischer et al. 2012.

Box 10.6 Addressing climate change through trade agreements

What contribution do trade agreements make to addressing climate change? In a recent study, Jean-Frédéric Morin and Sikina Jinnah asked this precise question. They used the Trade and Environment Database (TREND) to analyse the climate change provisions contained in 688 preferential trade agreements. They examined climate provisions along four dimensions: scope and diversity (*innovation*), legal strength (*legalization*), relative presence in the overall preferential trade agreement population (*replication*), and the type of countries that have endorsed them (*distribution*). They argued that for preferential trade agreements to significantly contribute to climate governance, they must include comprehensive provisions, be highly enforceable, be quantitatively numerous across several agreements, and cover countries that qualitatively matter the most for climate governance.

They found that innovation in preferential trade agreements is high, with some agreements containing more specific and enforceable climate-related provisions than those in the Kyoto Protocol and the Paris Agreement. For example, 138 provisions in agreements outline provisions related to renewable energy and energy efficiency, aiming at reducing carbon dioxide emissions. These include provisions that promote the use of renewable technologies, and encourage cooperation between countries on these topics. Despite this high degree of innovation, however, Morin and Jinnah also found that these provisions are weakly 'legalized', fail to replicate broadly in the global trade system, and in some cases were not adopted by the largest greenhouse gas emitters. Therefore, they argue that the contribution of these agreements to addressing climate change remains limited.

There are many possible reasons for this limited contribution, including a hesitancy from some states to create commitments to greenhouse gas reductions, and possibly the perceived distance between climate provisions and core trade objectives. One solution might be to address issues at the heart of this intersection, such as carbon taxes, fossil fuel subsidies, emissions trading, and lower tariffs on energy efficient technologies.

Although many countries are increasingly interested in such a solution, concerns about competition could reduce the effectiveness of these policies. However, if trading partners include provisions on border adjustments for carbon prices in their trade agreements, this could drive up the price on carbon-intensive goods. Trading partners could also agree in their trade agreements to phase out subsidies for fossil fuels, providing certainty that countries will not lose their ability to compete internationally by unilaterally removing subsidies. Finally, countries can use trade agreements to lower tariffs on technologies that could help countries lower their carbon emissions, and so enhance access to these technologies.

These climate- and trade-related provisions hold great potential to enhance the contribution of preferential trade agreements to climate governance. Importantly, the inclusion of climate-related trade provisions is considered more feasible in the short term than enacting legal changes in the World Trade Organization that would ensure countries can enact stringent climate policies without violating their obligations. Some argue that preferential trade agreements that span multiple regions and include many countries could diffuse climate protection rules more widely, which would also ensure that competitive pressures do not dilute climate-related regulations.

Sources: Brack et al. 2013; Das et al. 2018; Droege et al. 2016; Jinnah and Morin 2020; Morin et al. 2018; Morin and Jinnah 2018.

On the other hand, India has argued that environmental issues should be governed in other venues, and it has resisted the inclusion of environmental provisions in its preferential trade agreements, and the shift towards governing trade and environment issues more broadly (ICTSD 2010). Nevertheless, recent empirical global trends and patterns of legal diffusion suggest that environmental provisions are likely to be included in preferential trade agreements in the future.

10.4 **Conclusion**

Despite powerful theoretical arguments surrounding this debate, the conditions under which trade liberalization leads to increased or decreased environmental impact is still in need of additional empirical analysis. Nonetheless, there are many on-the-ground intersections between these two areas of international politics. Several multilateral environmental agreements, such as the Montreal and Kyoto Protocols, use trade measures to secure their objectives. At the same time, trade agreements are increasingly being used to push forward environmental policies, with concrete impacts on, for example, environmental treaty performance and the global distribution of environmental norms and policies. There are also additional issues, such as **traditional knowledge**, that are increasingly being addressed through the global trade regime and have impacts on the environment. As these points of intersection become increasingly common, it will be important to continue to evaluate these connections empirically to ensure mutual supportiveness between global trade and environmental regimes.

Critical thinking questions

1. How do theoretical models differ with respect to the relationship between economic growth and the environment?
2. How might trade have positive effects on the environment? Or negative effects?
3. What are pollution halos and pollution havens, and why might they occur?
4. Provide examples of two multilateral environmental agreements that contain trade provisions and describe how each agreement does so.
5. What obligations do World Trade Organization members have with respect to non-discrimination? What are the implications of these obligations for environmental protection?
6. How might the scope and enforcement of any future climate change provisions differ if they were implemented in United States trade agreements versus those of the European Union?

 Test your knowledge and understanding further by trying this chapter's Multiple Choice Questions www.oup.com/he/morin1e

Key references

Clapp, Jennifer. 2001. *Toxic Exports: The Transfer of Hazardous Wastes from Rich to Poor Countries.* Ithaca, NY: Cornell University Press.

This book examines the causes of hazardous waste and technology transfer from rich to poor countries, as well as the political responses to it. Clapp explains that waste transfer is driven by forces of economic globalization in a world characterized by inequality. The political responses, including bans on toxic waste export and technology transfer, are flawed because, as Clapp argues, when one form of toxic export is stopped, it is replaced by another form of toxic waste.

Gallagher, Kevin P. 2009. 'Economic Globalization and the Environment'. *Annual Review of Environment and Resources* 34 (1): 279–304.
  This article reviews the scholarly literature on economic globalization and the environment. It highlights the importance of: the direct effects of globalization on the environment; the impacts of 'South–South' integration; and improvements in methodologies and instruments for estimating the impacts of trade and environment policies.

Jinnah, Sikina, and Jean-Frédéric Morin. 2020. *Greening through Trade: How American Trade Policy is Linked to Environmental Protection Abroad.* Cambridge, MA: MIT Press.
  This book investigates how the United States shapes environmental politics through its trade agreements. It explores key questions such as why the United States includes environmental provisions in its trade agreements, whether trade agreements can enhance the effectiveness of multilateral environmental agreements, how the United States diffuses environmental norms and policies to its trade partners, and whether environmental provisions first included in the United States' trade agreements are incorporated into the trade agreements of other countries.

O'Neill, Kate. 2000. *Waste Trading among Rich Nations: Building a New Theory of Environmental Regulation.* Cambridge, MA: MIT Press.
  This book examines why some countries are net importers of waste while others are net exporters. O'Neill provides a theoretical framework for comparing differences in environmental regulations across countries and applies this empirically to waste trading among the UK, Germany, France, Australia, and Japan. Key elements of the theoretical framework include institutional structure (centralized or decentralized), policy access (open or closed to the public), and regulatory style (rigid or flexible).

 For additional material and resources, please visit the online resources at: **www.oup.com/he/morin1e**

Chapter references

Akenji, Lewis. 2014. 'Consumer Scapegoatism and Limits to Green Consumerism'. *Journal of Cleaner Production*, Special Volume: Sustainable Production, Consumption and Livelihoods: Global and Regional Research Perspectives 63 (January): 13–23.

Akenji, Lewis, Yasuhiko Hotta, Magnus Bengtsson, and Shiko Hayashi. 2011. 'EPR Policies for Electronics in Developing Asia: An Adapted Phase-in Approach'. *Waste Management & Research* 29 (9): 919–930.

Asghari, Maryam. 2013. 'Does FDI Promote MENA Region's Environment Quality? Pollution Halo or Pollution Haven Hypothesis'. *International Journal of Scientific Research in Environmental Sciences* 1 (6): 92–100.

Asmelash, Henok Birhanu. 2015. 'Energy Subsidies and WTO Dispute Settlement: Why Only Renewable Energy Subsidies Are Challenged'. *Journal of International Economic Law* 18 (2): 261–285.

Auta, Helen. S., Chijioke U. Emenike, and Shahul H. Fauziah. 2017. 'Distribution and Importance of Microplastics in the Marine Environment: A Review of the Sources, Fate, Effects, and Potential Solutions'. *Environment International* 102 (May): 165–176.

Autio, Minna, Eva Heiskanen, and Visa Heinonen. 2009. 'Narratives of "Green" Consumers—the Antihero, the Environmental Hero and the Anarchist'. *Journal of Consumer Behaviour* 8 (1): 40–53.

Baghdadi, Leila, Inmaculada Martínez-Zarzoso, and Habib Zitouna. 2013. 'Are RTA Agreements with Environmental Provisions Reducing Emissions?' *Journal of International Economics* 90 (2): 378–390.

Bastiaens, Ida, and Evgeny Postnikov. 2017. 'Greening Up: The Effects of Environmental Standards in EU and US Trade Agreements'. *Environmental Politics* 26 (5): 847–869.

Batabyal, Amitrajeet A. 1995. 'Development, Trade, and the Environment: Which Way Now?' *Ecological Economics* 13 (2): 83–88.

Berger, A., C. Brandi, D. Bruhn, and M. Chi. 2017. 'Towards "Greening" Trade? Tracking Environmental Provisions in the Preferential Trade Agreements of Emerging Markets'. Discussion Paper/Deutsches Institut Für Entwicklungspolitik 2017, 2. Bonn: Deutsches Institut für Entwicklungspolitik GmbH.

Bernasconi-Osterwalder, Nathalie, and Rhea Tamara Hoffman. 2012. 'The German Nuclear-Phase-Out Put to the Test in International Investment Arbitration? Background to the new dispute Vattenfall v. Germany (II)'. International Institute for Sustainable Development briefing note. Available at: https://www.libre-echange.info/IMG/pdf/german_nuclear_phase_out.pdf, accessed 12 January 2019.

Bernstein, Steven, Michele Betsill, Matthew Hoffmann, and Matthew Paterson. 2010. 'A Tale of Two Copenhagens: Carbon Markets and Climate Governance'. *Millennium* 39 (1): 161–173.

Bhagwati, Jagdish. 1993. 'The Case for Free Trade'. *Scientific American* 269 (5): 42–49.

Biro, Andrew. 2012. 'Water Wars by Other Means: Virtual Water and Global Economic Restructuring'. *Global Environmental Politics* 12 (4): 86–103.

Böhringer, Christoph, Jared C. Carbone, and Thomas F. Rutherford. 2018. 'Embodied Carbon Tariffs'. *The Scandinavian Journal of Economics* 120 (1): 183–210.

Brack, Duncan. 2018. *International Trade and the Montreal Protocol*. 2nd. ed. London and New York: Routledge.

Brack, Duncan, Michael Grubb, and Craig Windram. 2013. *International Trade and Climate Change Policies*. London: The Royal Institute of International Affairs and Earthscan.

Bradford, Anu. 2012. 'The Brussels Effect'. *Northwestern University Law Review* 107 (1): 1–68.

Brooks, Amy L., Shunli Wang, and Jenna R. Jambeck. 2018. 'The Chinese Import Ban and its Impact on Global Plastic Waste Trade'. *Science Advances* 4 (6): eaat0131.

Buttel, Frederick H. 2004. 'The Treadmill of Production: An Appreciation, Assessment, and Agenda for Research'. *Organization & Environment* 17 (3): 323–336.

Cao, Xun, and Aseem Prakash. 2010. 'Trade Competition and Domestic Pollution: A Panel Study, 1980–2003'. *International Organization* 64 (3): 481–503.

Cao, Xun, and Aseem Prakash. 2012. 'Trade Competition and Environmental Regulations: Domestic Political Constraints and Issue Visibility'. *The Journal of Politics* 72 (1): 62–82.

Carruthers, Bruce G., and Naomi R. Lamoreaux. 2016. 'Regulatory Races: The Effects of Jurisdictional Competition on Regulatory Standards'. *Journal of Economic Literature* 54 (1): 52–97.

Charnovitz, Steve. 2007. 'The WTO's Environmental Progress'. *Journal of International Economic Law* 10 (3): 685–706.

Chen, Z. M., and G. Q. Chen. 2011. 'Embodied Carbon Dioxide Emission at Supra-National Scale: A Coalition Analysis for G7, BRIC, and the Rest of the World'. *Energy Policy* 39 (5): 2899–2909.

Cimino-Isaacs, Cathleen, and Jeffrey J. Schott. 2016. *Trans-Pacific Partnership: An Assessment*. Washington, DC: Peterson Institute for International Economics.

CITES. n.d. Website. Available at: https://www.cites.org/eng/disc/what.php, accessed October 2019.

Clark, Brett, and John B. Foster. 2009. 'Ecological Imperialism and the Global Metabolic Rift: Unequal Exchange and the Guano/Nitrates Trade'. *International Journal of Comparative Sociology* 50 (3-4): 311–334.

Clean Development Mechanism. 2006. 'Project Design Document Form Version 03.1. for China Guanmenyan Hydropower Project'. UNFCCC. Available at: https://www.netinform.net/KE/files/pdf/GSP_Guanmenyan_33MW_Hydro_PDD_20070110.pdf, accessed 21 January 2019.

Collette, B. B., K. E. Carpenter, B. A. Polidoro, M. J. Juan-Jordá, A. Boustany, D. J. Die, C. Elfes et al. 2011. 'High Value and Long Life—Double Jeopardy for Tunas and Billfishes'. *Science* 333 (6040): 291–292.

Conca, Ken. 2000. 'The WTO and the Undermining of Global Environmental Governance'. *Review of International Political Economy* 7 (3): 484–494.

Daly, Herman E. 1993. 'The Perils of Free Trade'. *Scientific American* 269 (5): 50–57.

Dam, Lammertjan, and Bert Scholtens. 2008. 'Environmental Regulation and MNEs Location: Does CSR Matter?' *Ecological Economics* 67 (1): 55–65.

Das, Kasturi, Harro van Asselt, Susanne Droege, and Michael Mehling. 2018. *Making the International Trade System Work for Climate Change: Assessing the Options*. n.d.: Climate Strategies.

Dauvergne, Peter, and Jane Lister. 2012. 'Big Brand Sustainability: Governance Prospects and Environmental Limits'. *Global Environmental Change* 22 (1): 36–45.

Davis, Steven J., and Ken Caldeira. 2010. 'Consumption-Based Accounting of CO_2 Emissions'. *Proceedings of the National Academy of Sciences* 107 (12): 5687–5692.

Dent, Felix, and Shelley Clarke. 2015. 'State of the Global Market for Shark Products'. FAO Fisheries and Aquaculture Technical Paper No. 590. Rome: Food and Agriculture Organization. Available at: http://www.fao.org/3/a-i4795e.pdf, accessed October 2019.

DeSombre, Elizabeth R., and J. Samuel Barkin. 2002. 'Turtles and Trade: The WTO's Acceptance of Environmental Trade Restrictions'. *Global Environmental Politics* 2 (1): 12–18.

Di Nucci, Maria Rosaria, and Ana María Isidoro Losada. 2015. 'An Open Door for Spent Fuel and Radioactive Waste Export?' In *Nuclear Waste Governance: An International Comparison*, edited by Achim Brunnengräber, Maria Rosaria Di Nucci, Ana Maria Isidoro Losada, Lutz Mez, and Miranda A. Schreurs, 79–97. Energiepolitik Und Klimaschutz [Energy Policy and Climate Protection]. Wiesbaden: Springer Fachmedien Wiesbaden.

Droege, Susanne, Harro van Asselt, Kasturi Das, and Michael Mehling. 2016. *The Trade System and Climate Action: Ways Forward under the Paris Agreement*. n.d.: Climate Strategies.

Eckersley, Robyn. 2004. 'The Big Chill: The WTO and Multilateral Environmental Agreements'. *Global Environmental Politics* 4 (2): 24–50.

Eckersley, Robyn. 2012. 'Moving Forward in the Climate Negotiations: Multilateralism or Minilateralism?' *Global Environmental Politics* 12 (2): 24–42.

Elassar, Alaa. 2018. 'Massive Tuna Net $3.1Million at Japan Auction'. CNN website. Available at: https://www.cnn.com/2019/01/05/asia/giant-tuna-sets-record-at-japan-auction/index.html, accessed October 2019.

Foster, John B. 2012. 'The Planetary Rift and the New Human Exemptionalism: A Political-Economic Critique of Ecological Modernization Theory'. *Organization & Environment* 25 (3): 211–237.

Foster, John B., Richard York, and Brett Clark. 2011. *The Ecological Rift: Capitalism's War on the Earth*. New York: Monthly Review Press.

Gagné, Gilbert, and Jean-Frédéric Morin. 2006. 'The Evolving American Policy on Investment Protection: Evidence from Recent FTAs and the 2004 Model BIT'. *Journal of International Economic Law* 9 (2): 357–382.

Gaines, Sanford E. 2007. 'Environmental Policy Implications of Investor–State Arbitration under NAFTA Chapter 11'. *International Environmental Agreements: Politics, Law and Economics* 7 (2): 171–201.

Gallagher, Kelly Sims 2006. *China Shifts Gears: Automakers, Oil, Pollution, and Development*. Cambridge, MA: MIT Press.

Gallagher, Kevin P. 2005. 'International Trade and Air Pollution: Estimating the Economic Costs of Air Emissions from Waterborne Commerce Vessels in the United States'. *Journal of Environmental Management* 77 (2): 99–103.

Gamso, Jonas. 2017. 'Trade Partnerships and Environmental Performance in Developing Countries'. *The Journal of Environment & Development* 26 (4): 375–399.

Geyer, Roland, Jenna R. Jambeck, and Kara Lavender Law. 2017. 'Production, Use, and Fate of All Plastics Ever Made'. *Science Advances* 3 (7): e1700782.

Gould, Kenneth A., David N. Pellow, and Allan Schnaiberg. 2004. 'Interrogating the Treadmill of Production: Everything You Wanted to Know about the Treadmill but Were Afraid to Ask'. *Organization & Environment* 17 (3): 296–316.

Gros, Daniel, and Christian Egenhofer. 2011. 'The Case for Taxing Carbon at the Border'. *Climate Policy* 11 (5): 1262–1268.

He, Kehan, Quanyin Tan, Lixia Zheng, and Jinhui Li. 2018. 'Adapting to New Policy Environment—Past Pattern and Future Trend in US–Sino Waste Plastic Trade Flow'. *International Journal of Sustainable Development & World Ecology* 25 (8): 703–712.

Hoekstra, Arjen, and P. Q. Hung. 2005. 'Globalisation of Water Resources: International Virtual Water Flows in Relation to Crop Trade'. *Global Environmental Change* 15 (1): 45–56.

Hovi, Jon, Detlef F. Sprinz, Håkon Sælen, and Arild Underdal. 2016. 'Climate Change Mitigation: A Role for Climate Clubs?' *Palgrave Communications* 2 (1): article 16020.

ICTSD. 2010. 'Indian Official Says Trade and Environment Should Not Mix'. International Centre for Trade and Sustainable Development website. Available at: https://www.ictsd.org/bridges-news/bridges/news/indian-official-says-trade-and-environment-should-not-mix, accessed 4 October 2018.

Iles, Alastair. 2004. 'Mapping Environmental Justice in Technology Flows: Computer Waste Impacts in Asia'. *Global Environmental Politics* 4 (4): 76–107.

International Centre for the Settlement of Investment Disputes. 2011. 'Award of the Arbitral Tribunal'. ICSID Case No. ARB/09/6, 11 March 2011, Washington, DC. Available at: https://www.italaw.com/sites/default/files/case-documents/ita0890.pdf, accessed 12 January 2019.

Jacur, Francesca Romanin. 2015. 'The *Vattenfall v. Germany* Disputes: Finding a Balance Between Energy Investments and Public Concerns'. In *Bridging the Gap between International Investment Law and the Environment*, edited by Yulia Levashova, Tineke E. Lambooy, and Ige Dekker, 339–356. Legal

Perspectives on Global Challenges Series. The Hague: Eleven Legal Publishing.

Jahn, Detlef, and Sebastian Korolczuk. 2012. 'German Exceptionalism: The End of Nuclear Energy in Germany!' *Environmental Politics* 21 (1): 159–164.

Jinnah, Sikina. 2011. 'Strategic Linkages: The Evolving Role of Trade Agreements in Global Environmental Governance'. *The Journal of Environment & Development* 20 (2): 191–215.

Jinnah, Sikina. 2014. *Post-Treaty Politics: Secretariat Influence in Global Environmental Governance*. Cambridge, MA: MIT Press.

Jinnah, Sikina, and Abby Lindsay. 2016. 'Diffusion Through Issue Linkage: Environmental Norms in US Trade Agreements'. *Global Environmental Politics* 16 (3): 41–61.

Jinnah, Sikina, and Elisa Morgera. 2013. 'Environmental Provisions in American and EU Free Trade Agreements: A Preliminary Comparison and Research Agenda'. *Review of European, Comparative & International Environmental Law* 22 (3): 324–339.

Jinnah, Sikina, and Jean-Frédéric Morin. Forthcoming 2020. *Greening through Trade: How American Trade Policy is Linked to Environmental Protection Abroad*. Cambridge, MA: MIT Press.

Jones, Wordsworth Filo. 1993. 'The Evolution of the Bamako Convention: An African Perspective'. *Colorado Journal of International Environmental Law and Policy* 4 (2): 324–342.

Kaminsky, Howard S. 1992. 'Assessment of the Bamako Convention on the Ban of Import into Africa and the Control of Transboundary Movement and Management of Hazardous Wastes within Africa'. *Georgetown International Environmental Law Review* 5 (1): 77–90.

Kanemoto, Keiichiro, Daniel Moran, Manfred Lenzen, and Arne Geschke. 2014. 'International Trade Undermines National Emission Reduction Targets: New Evidence from Air Pollution'. *Global Environmental Change* 24 (1): 52–59.

Karstensen, Jonas, Glen P. Peters, and Robbie M. Andrew. 2013. 'Attribution of CO_2 Emissions from Brazilian Deforestation to Consumers between 1990 and 2010'. *Environmental Research Letters* 8 (2): 024005.

Kirkpatrick, Colin, and Kenichi Shimamoto. 2008. 'The Effect of Environmental Regulation on the Locational Choice of Japanese Foreign Direct Investment'. *Applied Economics* 40 (11): 1399–1409.

Kolk, Ans, and Jonatan Pinkse. 2004. 'Market Strategies for Climate Change'. *European Management Journal* 22 (3): 304–314.

Krueger, Jonathan. 2001. 'The Basel Convention and the International Trade in Hazardous Wastes'. In *Yearbook of International Co-Operation on Environment and Development 2001–02*, edited by Olav Schram Stokke and Øystein B. Thommessen, 43–51. London: Earthscan.

Kulovesi, Kati. 2011. *The WTO Dispute Settlement System: Challenges of the Environment, Legitimacy and Fragmentation*. Alphen aan den Rijn, Netherlands: Kluwer Law International B.V.

Lafond, François, Aimee Gotway Bailey, Jan David Bakker, Dylan Rebois, Rubina Zadourian, Patrick McSharry, and J. Doyne Farmer. 2018. 'How Well Do Experience Curves Predict Technological Progress? A Method for Making Distributional Forecasts'. *Technological Forecasting and Social Change* 128: 104–117.

Leonard, H. Jeffrey. 2006. *Pollution and the Struggle for the World Product: Multinational Corporations, Environment, and International Comparative Advantage*. Cambridge: Cambridge University Press.

Lepawsky, Josh. 2018. *Reassembling Rubbish: Worlding Electronic Waste*. Cambridge, MA: MIT Press.

Li, Waichin C., H. F. Tse, and Lincoln Fok. 2016. 'Plastic Waste in the Marine Environment: A Review of Sources, Occurrence and Effects'. *Science of The Total Environment* 566–567 (October): 333–349.

Lininger, Christian. 2015. 'Design Options for Consumption-Based Policy Approaches: A Literature Review'. In *Consumption-Based Approaches in International Climate Policy*, edited by Christian Lininger, 205–226. Springer Climate. Cham, Switzerland: Springer International Publishing.

Litfin, Karen. 1994. *Ozone Discourses: Science and Politics in Global Environmental Cooperation*. New York: Columbia University Press.

MacKenzie, Donald. 2009. 'Making Things the Same: Gases, Emission Rights and the Politics of Carbon Markets'. *Accounting, Organizations and Society* 34 (3–4): 440–455.

Madigan, Daniel. J., Andre Boustany, and Bruce. B. Collette. 2017. 'East not Least for Pacific Bluefin Tuna'. *Science* 357 (6349): 356–357.

Martin, Rowan. 2016. *CITES II or The Second Convention on International Trade in Endangered Species of Wild Fauna and Flora*. SSRN Scholarly Paper No. ID 2861388. Available at: https://papers.ssrn.com/abstract=2861388, accessed 20 September 2019.

Martínez-Zarzoso, I. (2018). 'Assessing the Effectiveness of Environmental Provisions in Regional Trade Agreements: An Empirical Analysis'. ECD Trade and Environment Working Papers, No. 2018/02.

Paris: OECD Publishing. Available at: https://doi.org/10.1787/5ffc615c-en, accessed 30 September 2019.

Matisoff, Daniel C. 2010. 'Are International Environmental Agreements Enforceable? Implications for Institutional Design'. *International Environmental Agreements: Politics, Law and Economics* 10 (3): 165–186.

Meckling, Jonas, and Llewelyn Hughes. 2017. 'Globalizing Solar: Global Supply Chains and Trade Preferences'. *International Studies Quarterly* 61 (2): 225–235.

Meyer, Timothy. 2017. 'Explaining Energy Disputes at the World Trade Organization'. *International Environmental Agreements: Politics, Law and Economics* 17 (3): 391–410.

Miles, Kate. 2016. 'Investor–State Dispute Settlement: Conflict, Convergence, and Future Directions'. In *European Yearbook of International Economic Law*, edited by M. Bungenberg, C. Herrmann, M. Krajewski, and J. P. Terhechte, 7: 273–308. Cham, Switzerland: Springer International Publishing.

Morin, Jean-Frédéric, Andreas Dür, and Lisa Lechner. 2018. 'Mapping the Trade and Environment Nexus: Insights from a New Data Set'. *Global Environmental Politics* 18 (1): 122–139.

Morin, Jean-Frédéric, and Mathilde Gauquelin. 2016. 'Trade Agreements as Vectors for the Nagoya Protocol's Implementation'. CIGI Paper No. 115, November. Waterloo, Ontario: Centre for International Governance Innovation. Available at: https://www.cigionline.org/publications/trade-agreements-vectors-nagoya-protocols-implementation, accessed October 2019.

Morin, Jean-Frédéric, and Myriam Rochette. 2017. 'Transatlantic Convergence of Preferential Trade Agreements Environmental Clauses'. *Business and Politics* 19 (4): 621–658.

Morin, Jean-Frédéric, and Sikina Jinnah. 2018. 'The Untapped Potential of Preferential Trade Agreements for Climate Governance'. *Environmental Politics* 27 (3): 541–565.

Muradian, Roldan, and Joan Martinez-Alier. 2001. 'Trade and the Environment: From a 'Southern' Perspective'. *Ecological Economics* 36 (2): 281–297.

Neumayer, Eric. 2004. 'The WTO and the Environment: Its Past Record Is Better than Critics Believe, but the Future Outlook is Bleak'. *Global Environmental Politics* 4 (3): 1–8.

Newell, Peter, and Ruth Mackenzie. 2000. 'The 2000 Cartagena Protocol on Biosafety: Legal and Political Dimensions'. *Global Environmental Change* 10 (4): 313–317.

Newell, Peter, and Matthew Paterson. 2010. *Climate Capitalism: Global Warming and the Transformation of the Global Economy*. Cambridge: Cambridge University Press.

Niinimäki, Kirsi. 2010. 'Eco-Clothing, Consumer Identity and Ideology'. *Sustainable Development* 18 (3): 150–162.

Nordhaus, William. 2015. 'Climate Clubs: Overcoming Free-Riding in International Climate Policy'. *American Economic Review* 105 (4): 1339–1370.

Oberthür, Sebastian, and Thomas Gehring. 2006. 'Institutional Interaction in Global Environmental Governance: The Case of the Cartagena Protocol and the World Trade Organization'. *Global Environmental Politics* 6 (2): 1–31.

Odell, J. S. 2018. *Our Alarming Crisis Demands Border Adjustments Now*. Geneva: ICTSD.

OECD. 2005. *Agriculture, Trade and the Environment: The Arable Crop Sector*. Paris: OECD Publishing. Available at: https://doi.org/10.1787/19901194, accessed October 2019.

Olsen, Karen Holm. 2007. 'The Clean Development Mechanism's Contribution to Sustainable Development: A Review of the Literature'. *Climatic Change* 84 (1): 59–73.

O'Neill, Kate. 2000. *Waste Trading among Rich Nations: Building a New Theory of Environmental Regulation*. Cambridge, MA: MIT Press.

O'Neill, Kate. 2018. 'The New Global Political Economy of Waste'. In *A Research Agenda for Global Environmental Politics*, edited by Peter Dauvergne and Justin Alger, 87–136. Cheltenham: Edward Elgar Publishing.

O'Neill, Kate. 2019. *Waste*. Cambridge: Polity Press.

Osibanjo, Oladele, and I. C. Nnorom. 2007. 'The Challenge of Electronic Waste (e-Waste) Management in Developing Countries'. *Waste Management & Research* 25 (6): 489–501.

Paini, Dean R., Andy W. Sheppard, David C. Cook, Paul J. De Barro, Susan P. Worner, and Matthew B. Thomas. 2016. 'Global Threat to Agriculture from Invasive Species'. *Proceedings of the National Academy of Sciences* 113 (27): 7575–7579.

Paulsson, Emma. 2009. 'A Review of the CDM Literature: From Fine-Tuning to Critical Scrutiny?' *International Environmental Agreements: Politics, Law and Economics* 9 (1): 63–80.

Peters, Glen P., Jan C. Minx, Christopher L. Weber, and Ottmar Edenhofer. 2011. 'Growth in emission transfers via international trade from 1990 to 2008'. *Proceedings of the National Academy of Sciences* 108 (21): 8903–8908.

Poletti, Arlo, and Daniela Sicurelli. 2016. 'The European Union, Preferential Trade Agreements, and the International Regulation of Sustainable Biofuels'. *JCMS: Journal of Common Market Studies* 54 (2): 249–266.

Prakash, Aseem, and Matthew Potoski. 2017. 'The EU Effect: Does Trade with the EU Reduce CO_2 Emissions in the Developing World?' *Environmental Politics* 26 (1): 27–48.

Ranald, Patricia. 2015. 'The Trans-Pacific Partnership Agreement: Reaching Behind the Border, Challenging Democracy'. *The Economic and Labour Relations Review* 26 (2): 241–260.

Ricardo, David. 1817. *Principles of Political Economy and Taxation*. London: Murray.

Rivalan, Philippe, Virginie Delmas, Elena Angulo, Leigh S. Bull, Richard J. Hall, Franck Courchamp, Alison M. Rosser, and Nigel Leader-Williams. 2007. 'Can Bans Stimulate Wildlife Trade?' *Nature* 447 (7144): 529–530.

Roberts, Leslie. 1990. 'Zebra Mussel Invasion Threatens US Waters: Damage Estimates Soar into the Billions for the Zebra Mussel, Just One of Many Invaders Entering US Waters via Ballast Water'. *Science* 249 (4975): 1370–1372.

Saleh, Ponsah, and Nanyen Mannok Abene. 2016. 'Africa and the Problem of Transboundary Movement of Hazardous Waste: An Assessment of Bamako Convention of 1991'. *Journal of Law, Policy and Globalization* 48: 47–53.

Schipanski, Meagan E., and Elena M. Bennett. 2012. 'The Influence of Agricultural Trade and Livestock Production on the Global Phosphorus Cycle'. *Ecosystems* 15 (2): 256–268.

Seyfang, Gill. 2005. 'Shopping for Sustainability: Can Sustainable Consumption Promote Ecological Citizenship?' *Environmental Politics* 14 (2): 290–306.

Soto, Gloria. 2012. 'Environmental Impact of Agricultural Trade Liberalization under NAFTA'. *Politics & Policy* 40 (3): 471–491.

Sprinz, Detlef F., Håkon Sælen, Arild Underdal, and Jon Hovi. 2018. 'The Effectiveness of Climate Clubs under Donald Trump'. *Climate Policy* 18 (7): 828–838.

Steenblik, Ronald. 2005. 'Environmental Goods: A Comparison of the APEC and OECD Lists'. OECD Trade and Environment Working Paper No. 2005-4. Paris: OECD Publishing.

Strayer, David L. 2009. 'Twenty Years of Zebra Mussels: Lessons from the Mollusk That Made Headlines'. *Frontiers in Ecology and the Environment* 7 (3): 135–141.

Strayer, David L., Nina F. Caraco, Jonathan J. Cole, Stuart Findlay, and Michael L. Pace. 1999. 'Transformation of Freshwater Ecosystems by Bivalves: A Case Study of Zebra Mussels in the Hudson River'. *BioScience* 49 (1): 19–27.

Stua, Michele. 2017. 'Climate Clubs and Their Relevance Within the Paris Agreement'. In *From the Paris Agreement to a Low-Carbon Bretton Woods: Rationale for the Establishment of a Mitigation Alliance*, edited by Michele Stua, 31–47. Cham, Switzerland: Springer International Publishing.

Sutter, Christoph, and Juan Carlos Parreño. 2007. 'Does the Current Clean Development Mechanism (CDM) Deliver its Sustainable Development Claim? An Analysis of Officially Registered CDM Projects'. *Climatic Change* 84 (1): 75–90.

Tang, Xu, Simon Snowden, and Mikael Höök. 2013. 'Analysis of Energy Embodied in the International Trade of UK'. *Energy Policy* 57 (June): 418–428.

Tienhaara, Kyla. 2006. 'What You Don't Know Can Hurt You: Investor–State Disputes and the Protection of the Environment in Developing Countries'. *Global Environmental Politics* 6 (4): 73–100.

Tienhaara, Kyla. 2018. 'Regulatory Chill in a Warming World: The Threat to Climate Policy Posed by Investor–State Dispute Settlement'. *Transnational Environmental Law* 7 (2): 229–250.

Van de Graaf, Thijs, and Harro van Asselt. 2017. 'Introduction to the Special Issue: Energy Subsidies at the Intersection of Climate, Energy, and Trade Governance'. *International Environmental Agreements: Politics, Law and Economics* 17 (3): 313–326.

Verkuijl, Cleo, Harro van Asselt, Tom Moerenhout, Liesbeth Casier, and Peter Wooders. 2017. *Tackling Fossil Fuel Subsidies through International Trade Agreements*. London: Climate Strategies.

Vincent, Amanda C. J., Yvonne J. Sadovy de Mitcheson, Sarah L. Fowler, and Susan Lieberman. 2014. 'The Role of CITES in the Conservation of Marine Fishes Subject to International Trade'. *Fish and Fisheries* 15 (4): 563–569.

Vogel, David. 2009. *Trading Up: Consumer and Environmental Regulation in a Global Economy*. Cambridge, MA: Harvard University Press.

Wei, Shang-Jin, and Smarzynska, Beata. 1999. 'Pollution Havens and Foreign Direct Investment: Dirty Secret or Popular Myth?' Policy Research Working Papers. Washington, DC: World Bank.

Weintraub, Karen. 2018. 'Elephant Tusk DNA Helps Track Ivory Poachers'. *New York Times*, Science section, 25 September. Available at: https://www.nytimes.com/2018/09/19/science/ivory-poaching-genetics.html, accessed October 2019.

Weischer, Lutz, Jennifer Morgan, and Milap Patel. 2012. 'Climate Clubs: Can Small Groups of Countries Make a Big Difference in Addressing Climate Change?'

Review of European Community & International Environmental Law 21 (3): 177–192.

Westphal, Michael I., Michael Browne, Kathy MacKinnon, and Ian Noble. 2008. 'The Link between International Trade and the Global Distribution of Invasive Alien Species'. *Biological Invasions* 10 (4): 391–398.

Wittemyer, George. 2016. 'Illegal Wildlife Trade: Look to the Elephants'. *Science* 353 (6307): 1507.

Wold, Chris, Grant Wilson, and Sara Foroshani. 2012. 'Leveraging Climate Change Benefits through the World Trade Organization: Are Fossil Fuel Subsidies Actionable?' *Georgetown Journal of International Law* 43 (3): 635–694.

World Bank and Ecofys. 2018. *State and Trends of Carbon Pricing 2018*. Washington, DC: World Bank. Available at: https://openknowledge.worldbank.org/handle/10986/29687, accessed October 2019. License: CC BY 3.0 IGO.

Worm, Boris, Brendal Davis, Lisa Kettemer, Christine A. Ward-Paige, Demian Chapman, Michael R. Heithaus, Steven T. Kessel, and Samuel H. Gruber. 2013. 'Global Catches, Exploitation Rates, and Rebuilding Options for Sharks'. *Marine Policy* 40 (July): 194–204.

Wyler, Liana Sun, and Pervaze A Sheikh. 2013. *International Illegal Trade in Wildlife: Threats and US Policy*. Congressional Research Service 26.

Xiang, Luan, and Liu Wei. 2017. 'China Takes Historic Step to Ban Ivory Sales'. *Xinhua* website, 30 December. Available at: http://www.xinhuanet.com/english/2017-12/30/c_136861722.htm, accessed October 2019.

Yoo, In Tae, and Inkyoung Kim. 2016. 'Free Trade Agreements for the Environment? Regional Economic Integration and Environmental Cooperation in East Asia'. *International Environmental Agreements: Politics, Law and Economics* 16 (5): 721–738.

Zarsky, Lyuba. 1999. 'Havens, Halos, and Spaghetti: Untangling the Evidence about Foreign Direct Investment and the Environment'. In *Foreign Direct Investment and the Environment*, 43–73. Paris: OECD Publishing.

Zeng, Ka, and Josh Eastin. 2007. 'International Economic Integration and Environmental Protection: The Case of China'. *International Studies Quarterly* 51 (4): 971–995.

Zhang, Zengkai, Ju'e Guo, and Geoffrey J. D. Hewings. 2014. 'The Effects of Direct Trade within China on Regional and National CO_2 Emissions'. *Energy Economics* 46 (November): 161–175.

Zhou, Li, Xi Tian, and Zhengyi Zhou. 2017. 'The Effects of Environmental Provisions in RTAs on PM2.5 Air Pollution'. *Applied Economics* 49 (27): 2630–2641.

Databases and useful websites

Climate Action Tracker, https://climateactiontracker.org/

The Climate Action Tracker was developed by three independent research centres. It quantifies climate change commitments, and assesses whether countries are on track to meet them. It also aggregates country action at the global level, determining likely temperature increase by the end of the century.

Climate Watch, https://www.climatewatchdata.org/

This website offers data and visualizations of states' actions related to climate change, including greenhouse gas emissions, as well as commitments to reduce them. In addition, it provides several analytical tools that map out trends, both present and future, related to climate change.

CDP Disclosure Insight Action, https://data.cdp.net/

This website, developed by the non-governmental organization CDP (formerly Carbon Disclosure Project), offers data about environmental commitments and actions taken by local actors, such as cities, regions, and companies, on a wide variety of environmental issues ranging from water or renewable energy to climate hazards.

Environmental Data Explorer, http://geodata.grid.unep.ch

The Environmental Data Explorer is used by the United Nations Environment Programme and its partners in the preparation of their reports on environmental issues. This database features over 500 variables at the national, regional, and global levels, and includes statistics and geospatial databases, on topics such as freshwater, forests, harmful emissions, climate change, and natural disasters.

Environmental Justice Atlas, https://ejatlas.org/

Created by academic researchers at the Universitat Autonoma de Barcelona, this website maps and documents social conflicts around environmental issues. These conflicts include social mobilizations against an economic activity or a policy proposal. Conflicts are related to nuclear energy, mining, waste management, land, water management, and natural reserves, among other environmental issues.

Environmental Performance Index, https://epi.envirocenter.yale.edu/

This website allows us to comparatively evaluate how different countries perform on environmental issues. It presents an environmental performance index for 180 countries, based on 24 performance indicators such as air pollution and lead exposure, to provide an overview of states' progress in achieving established environmental policy goals. It also offers visualization tools and summary reports. The index has been developed by Yale University and Columbia University in collaboration with the World Economic Forum.

Environmental Studies Section of the International Studies Association, http://environmental-studies.org

This website features the activities of the International Studies Association's Environmental Studies Section, including publications, newsletters, and conferences related to international environmental politics.

Environmental Sustainability Index, http://sedac.ciesin.columbia.edu/es/esi/

The Environmental Sustainability Index, developed under the umbrella of the National Aeronautics and Space Administration (NASA) since 2000, presents a tool to measure the general evolution of the earth's environmental sustainability over time. The website offers reports and other environmental data, as well as several complementary sources. It also offers a large gallery of maps created using the website's data on various environmental issues.

Environmental Treaties and Resource Indicators, http://sedac.ciesin.columbia.edu/data/collection/entri

This website is a searchable database, developed under the umbrella of the National Aeronautics and Space Administration (NASA), of more than 600 environmental treaties, offering information including their status and their member countries. It also provides the full texts of the agreements as well as country profiles, and allows for word searches in both treaty texts and Conference of Party decisions.

European Environmental Agency, https://www.eea.europa.eu/data-and-maps

The European Environmental Agency is an agency of the European Union, whose task is to provide information on the environment. Its website offers various data, maps, and graphs comparing the consumption of natural resources and emissions of pollutants in the European countries.

FAOSTAT, http://faostat3.fao.org

FAOSTAT is a website on food and agriculture statistics, maintained by the United Nations Food and Agriculture Organization. An important part of this website also relates to environmental data, such as freshwater use, demographic data, forest land, and greenhouse gas emissions. The website also features reports on numerous topics, including food security.

Global Climate Action, http://climateaction.unfccc.int

Launched by the United Nations Conference on Climate Change, France and Peru in 2014, the Global Climate Action website offers data on transnational environmental initiatives aimed at addressing climate change.

International Institute for Sustainable Development Reporting Services, http://www.iisd.ca

This website, developed by a non-governmental organization, offers daily summary reports as well as analyses of major international negotiations on the environment and development through its free online publication, the *Earth Negotiations Bulletin*. It also contains archives going back to 1992.

Informea, https://www.informea.org/

This website, which is maintained by the United Nations, gathers information on multilateral environmental agreements by region, country, and theme (including biodiversity, chemicals and waste, climate change and atmosphere, and marine and freshwater). It also provides a list of cases and complaints made under these agreements and a list of relevant publications.

International Environmental Agreements Database, http://iea.uoregon.edu

This database was created by Ronald Mitchell at the University of Oregon, and lists thousands of multilateral regional and bilateral agreements on the environment. Most of them are available in full text.

International Regimes Database, https://iea.uoregon.edu/ird

This tool was developed by a team of German and American researchers. They coded various characteristics of 23 international environmental regimes—for instance, the political context in which they were negotiated, their attributes, their consequences, and their dynamics. Regimes include those that address Antarctica, desertification, and wetlands.

Measuring-progress.eu, https://measuring-progress.eu/

This interactive tool, developed as part of a European Union-funded research project, aggregates indicators from other sources to measure progress towards the green economy. Its database features indicators divided into five main topics: environmental sustainability, social justice, quality of life, economic sustainability and resilience, and effective governance, as well as annotations on the interpretation of the indicators.

Organisation for Economic Co-operation and Development Data on the Environment, https://data.oecd.org/environment.htm

This database, maintained by the Organisation for Economic Co-operation and Development, includes a full section on environmental issues. It features data on various environmental issues, such as air and climate, forests, waste, and water, as well as publications providing analyses of this data.

Our World in Data, https://ourworldindata.org

This website, which was developed by the University of Oxford, aims to offer visual representations of the world based on data in various areas, including the environment. More specifically, it provides visualizations and accompanying analyses for several environmental issues, such as CO_2 emissions, natural disasters, and air pollution.

Trade and Environment Database Analytics, http://www.TRENDanalytics.info

The TREND dataset was developed by Jean-Frédéric Morin. It offers an exhaustive and detailed codification of environmental provisions in over 680 trade agreements adopted since 1947. The provisions coded include both issue-specific provisions (on forests, fisheries, etc.) and institutional provisions. The website, created by the German Development Institute, features visualization tools and links to publications based on the data collected.

Transboundary Freshwater Dispute Database, www.transboundarywaters.orst.edu

This database, developed by the Oregon State University, lists over 400 international agreements on freshwater, from the nineteenth century to the present day, as well as over 6,000 events (both cooperative and conflictual) on this theme. It also features a database of transboundary watersheds, along with a number of publications.

World Bank Open Data, http://data.worldbank.org/

World Bank Open Data is an online resource developed by the World Bank group. It includes data on a large number of topics, including many related to international environmental policy, such as climate change (rising sea levels, energy emissions), rural development (agricultural production, fertilizer use), and natural resources (protection of marine resources, forests, biodiversity).

World Resources Institute, www.wri.org/resources

The World Resources Institute is an international research organization that offers data and maps on six main themes related to the environment and development: climate, energy, food, forests, water, and cities. The data covers over 50 countries. The website also features many publications, graphics, and other useful information.

Glossary

*Glossary terms in the text are indicated by **blue bold** font.*

Adaptation attempts on the part of individuals and societies to respond to environmental change or impacts. The term is most often used in the context of climate change, and is often contrasted to mitigation (see 'Climate mitigation').

Agenda 21 action plan adopted at the Earth Summit in 1992. It identifies global environmental and development issues and defines related objectives and means of action. See also 'Rio Summit'.

Agent Orange herbicide used as a strategic weapon by the United States during the Vietnam War to defoliate forests and ruin harvests, giving rise to important environmental damage and health issues.

Alliance of Small Island States coalition of 44 small island and low-lying coastal countries that share development challenges and concerns about the environment, especially regarding their vulnerability to the adverse effects of climate change.

Anthropocene epoch during which human activities have had a profound impact on the earth's ecosystems and geology, including through climate change.

Benefit sharing principle according to which the benefits arising from the use of natural resources should be shared equitably with the country and/or indigenous or local communities from which the resources originate.

Biocentrism world view according to which living things have intrinsic value, regardless of the use humans can make of them.

Biodiversity variability among living organisms from all sources, including terrestrial, marine, and other aquatic ecosystems, and the ecological systems of which they are part. Includes diversity within and between species and ecosystems.

Biosecurity risks associated with agriculture and food production, including the risks posed by genetically modified organisms.

Boundary organization organization that aims to bridge the gap between scientific research and its practical applications by connecting knowledge producers and users.

Brundtland Commission (also known as World Commission on Environment and Development) body established by the United Nations General Assembly in 1983 and chaired by Gro Harlem Brundtland. It was dissolved after adopting the Brundtland Report, *Our Common Future*, in 1987.

Cap and trade market-based instrument through which a political authority sets a global cap for pollution emissions and distributes emission credits among unitary actors, who can then trade these credits among them.

Capacity building assistance provided to a state or non-state actor to strengthen its institutions and its own ability to take effective action in a given field, including environmental protection.

Carbon sink natural or artificial reservoir that absorbs carbon, thus lowering the concentration of greenhouse gases in the atmosphere. Carbon sinks include some forests and the oceans.

Carrying capacity maximal pressure from human activity that an ecosystem or the earth as a whole can support while retaining the capacity to sustain itself.

Chilling effect the hypothesis that threats of sanctions or other strong enforcement mechanisms, often present in international trade law, make states reluctant to adopt environmental measures that have adverse effects on trade or foreign investment.

Climate mitigation efforts to reduce greenhouse gas emissions, for instance by switching from fossil fuels to renewable energy sources.

Club of Rome group of entrepreneurs, decision makers, and scientists created in 1968 out of apprehension for the future of humanity. Its first report, published in 1972 and entitled *The Limits to Growth*, raised concerns about the impact of economic growth on the environment.

Common but differentiated responsibilities and respective capabilities principle that all states share the general responsibility to promote sustainable development and protect the environment, but that those responsibilities vary between states—for example, based on their contribution to a particular problem. It further underscores that states should contribute to environmental problem-solving according to their respective capabilities.

Common goods goods that are non-excludable but rivalrous, meaning that all can access them but that they exist in a finite quantity. Common goods are thus subject to the tragedy of the commons, where unregulated access leads to their depletion. See also 'Public goods' and 'Rivalrous goods'.

Compliance compatibility between the actions taken by an actor and the rules that bind it.

Conference of the Parties the prime governing body of an international convention, where states meet on a periodic basis to take decisions related to the implementation of the convention.

Conservation an approach to natural resource management that allows for nature to be used for human well-being in a sustainable way, even if that use does not preserve the environment in a pristine state. See also 'Preservation'.

Contact group informal group created during international negotiations, bringing together a restricted number of parties in order to reach a consensus more easily. Working groups are the formal equivalent of contact groups.

Corporate social responsibility voluntary measures taken by businesses to minimize the social and environmental costs of their activities.

Customary international law a source of international law (along with treaties, principles, and judicial decisions) that is derived from the practice of states. Customary international law may not necessarily be formalized in a legal text, but it is nonetheless deemed binding if it reflects the general practice of states and states consider such practices to be obligatory.

Dangerous waste (also called hazardous or toxic waste) substances or objects that are intended to be disposed of and present risks to human health or the environment. Management and disposal of dangerous waste are governed by the Basel Convention.

Deep ecology a biocentric perspective according to which environmental protection justifies measures that will have adverse consequences for human societies. See also 'Biocentrism'.

Developing countries countries that have a relatively low level of economic development, and also often have a relatively low level of human development. Given the absence of widely accepted objective criteria to identify developing countries, they are often self-designated, as opposed to least-developed countries. See also 'Least-developed countries'.

Development aid financial assistance provided by (inter)governmental or non-governmental organizations to developing countries to support their long-term development.

Ecocide total destruction or loss of an ecosystem. Meant to establish a parallel between genocides as crimes against humanity and ecocides as crimes against nature.

Eco-label voluntary certification scheme allowing a product to be specially labelled as respecting a given set of environmental production standards.

Ecological footprint a measure aiming to quantify the impact of human activity on the environment. It is often used by neo-Malthusians to denounce the disproportionate use of resources by humans compared to the environment's capacity to sustain itself. See also 'Malthusianism'.

Ecological modernization theory based on the idea that economic progress does not necessarily create additional environmental costs.

Ecosystem services benefits derived from the natural functioning of ecosystems, for instance waste decomposition or pollination, as a type of common good.

Effectiveness see 'Policy effectiveness'.

Emissions trading see 'Cap and trade'.

Enforcement range of measures available to ensure that legal rules or commitments are properly implemented.

Entropy process through which available energy becomes unrecoverable after it has been used, leading some experts to raise concerns about potential energy shortages caused by human activity.

Environmental impact assessment evaluation procedure aiming to determine the likely impact of a proposed activity on the environment.

Environmental justice either the belief that environmental benefits and burdens should be divided equally, or a theory of justice that tackles ethical questions arising from environmental degradation.

Environmental Kuznets curve parabolic curve establishing a relationship between economic development and environmental quality. It suggests that a country's growing per capita income will be associated with environmental degradation up to a turning point, after which any additional increase in income will lead to environmental improvement instead.

Epistemic community network of people with shared expertise, such as scientific or traditional knowledge, who work together to influence governmental policy outcomes.

Explanatory variable object or situation whose value does not depend on another variable.

Externality positive or negative consequence of an economic activity experienced by a third party that is not involved in its production or consumption.

Framework convention initial legal agreement creating broad obligations for states, setting the stage for the negotiation of additional protocols defining more specific commitments.

Genetic resources genetic material of plant, animal, microbial, or other origin that contains functions of heredity and/or biochemical components whose use has actual or potential value.

Genetically modified organism any living organism that possesses a novel combination of genetic material obtained through the use of modern biotechnology.

Global Compact voluntary agreement launched in 2000 between businesses and several United Nations agencies to promote corporate social responsibility through ten principles, including environmental responsibility. See also 'Corporate social responsibility'.

Governance refers to the use of institutions, social structures, or instruments to manage collective issues, including environmental protection.

Green economy economy that favours a better quality of life and contributes to sustainable development and poverty eradication by being low carbon, resource efficient, and socially inclusive. One of the main themes of the 2012 Rio+20 Conference.

Greenhouse gas gaseous constituent of the atmosphere, either natural or anthropogenic, that absorbs and re-emits infrared radiation, warming the planet's surface through the greenhouse effect.

Greenwashing action of embracing environmental concerns strategically as an opportunity to raise ones' political or commercial profile.

Heritage of humankind global commons or elements whose value is seen as transcending national sovereignty, meaning that they should not be appropriated and that all nations should be able to enjoy them.

Implementation process of putting legal commitments into effect, for instance through the adoption of national laws or the creation of domestic programmes.

Institution set of rules that mediate social interactions by prescribing behavioural roles, constraining activity, and shaping expectations. Institutions include organizations, regimes, and social norms.

Instrument see 'Policy instrument'.

Intergovernmental organization formal structure governed by legal rules and created by states to facilitate international cooperation and manage collective problems.

Intergovernmental Panel on Climate Change international boundary organization created in 1988 by the World Meteorological Organization and the United Nations Environment Programme, that is charged with providing summaries and assessments of climate change science and related issues, which policymakers can use to formulate policy decisions. See also 'Boundary organization'.

Intergovernmental Science-Policy Platform on Biodiversity and Ecosystem Services international boundary organization created in 2012. The Platform conducts assessments of biodiversity, and provides policy support, capacity building, and knowledge. See also 'Boundary organization'.

Intermediate variable variable that interferes with a causal relation between two phenomena.

International environmental agreement an international treaty through which states cooperate on environmental issues of common concern.

International regime see 'Regime'.

Least-developed countries low-income countries confronting severe structural impediments to sustainable development, as identified by the United Nations Social and Economic Council's Committee for Development Policy based on their income, human assets, and economic vulnerability.

Liberal environmentalism world view according to which market forces, insofar as they account for inequalities among countries and the limited availability of natural resources, can be used to achieve sustainable development.

Major groups categorization of non-state actors into nine groups, adopted by states during the United Nations Conference on Environment and Development held in Rio in 1992.

Malthusianism school of thought that sees the earth as a finite system with limited natural resources. It posits that a balance must be maintained between the consumption and regeneration of resources so as not to exceed the earth's carrying capacity. See also 'Carrying capacity'.

Market mechanism a type of policy instrument that aims to reduce pollution by placing a price on a regulated substance and so making it more expensive to pollute. Often used in the context of carbon dioxide emissions, for example through carbon taxes or emissions trading markets.

Metabolic rift a Marxist term used to describe the growing separation in the relationship between humans and the rest of nature under a capitalist mode of production, resulting in unsustainable uses of energy and outputs of waste.

Non-discrimination a central tenet of international trade law wherein all parties to a trade agreement must enjoy equal benefits.

Non-governmental organization organization that is independent of government and brings together individuals or other non-governmental organizations to manage common interests or achieve a common goal.

Non-state actors actors that are independent of government. Although no set definition exists, they can include non-governmental organizations, unions, corporations, and individuals. See also 'Non-governmental organization'.

Observer status that grants non-member states, intergovernmental organizations, or non-state actors the right to take part in the activities of a convention or an organization, but without the right to vote.

Ozone layer layer of stratospheric ozone that protects the earth from the sun's ultraviolet radiation. Its depletion due to the use of the chlorofluorocarbons poses important risks for human health and the environment.

Party state or intergovernmental organization that has completed the necessary procedures to become legally bound by an international agreement, often including both a signature and a ratification step.

Payment for ecosystem services (sometimes known as payment for environmental services) payments offered to voluntary providers of environmental services, such as reforestation, watershed services, and biodiversity conservation, as an incentive to encourage environmental protection.

Persistent organic pollutants pollutants that possess toxic properties, resist degradation, bioaccumulate, and are transported, through air, water, or migratory species, across international boundaries and deposited far from their place of release, where they accumulate in terrestrial and aquatic ecosystems.

Policy effectiveness actual contribution of an environmental policy to the improvement of the environment or other related objectives.

Policy instrument tool that actors in global environmental politics use to implement norms, principles, and rules.

Polluter pays principle principle of international law according to which a polluter should be held accountable for its emissions by paying to repair the damage caused by those emissions to human health or the environment.

Precautionary principle principle of international law according to which the lack of scientific certainty regarding the environmental impacts of an activity should not impede the adoption of measures to prevent potential risks.

Preferential trade agreement a trade agreement between two or more countries, which provides for preferential treatment (e.g. reduced tariffs) with respect to trade in goods and/or services.

Preservation the idea that humans should intervene as little as possible in the natural environment so as to maintain such environments in as close to their natural and/or pristine state as possible. See also 'Conservation'.

Prevention principle principle that once the environmental impacts of an activity are scientifically proven, states have a duty to take all available actions to minimize these impacts.

Prior informed consent consent given by a government or other actor, for instance an indigenous or local community, before an activity is carried out that is potentially harmful to humans or the environment, such as the import of hazardous waste or toxic substances.

Prisoner's dilemma standard situation in game theory that shows that two rational actors might not cooperate even if this would be an optimum solution.

Protocol legal instrument adopted under the auspices of an existing treaty (often a framework convention) to define more specific obligations with regard to a given issue. See also 'Framework convention'.

Public goods goods that are non-excludable, meaning that it is impossible to keep others from enjoying the good, and non-rivalous, meaning that someone's enjoyment of the good does not limit the possibility for others to also enjoy it. See also 'Common goods' and 'Rivalrous goods'.

Race to the bottom the idea that corporations will move their investments and operations to places where environmental laws and policies are weakest in order to reduce their costs of production. The idea is contested.

Ratification legal step completed by a state or other actor to signify that it accepts being bound by a legal instrument. Usually follows a first step of signature, where states or other actors accept the text in its final version, and signal an intent to follow the spirit of the treaty, but are not yet legally bound by it.

Regime set of principles, norms, rules, and procedures governing the behaviour of actors in a given issue area of international cooperation.

Rio Summit (also called the Earth Summit) 1992 meeting of the United Nations Conference on Environment and Development, during which the Rio Declaration and Agenda 21 were adopted. See also 'Agenda 21'.

Rivalrous goods goods that cannot be consumed jointly by different actors. The consumption of one unit of a rivalrous good reduces the amount of that good available for other actors. See also 'Common goods' and 'Public goods'.

Securitization the process of transforming certain topics, including climate or the environment, into international security issues, opening up the possibility of resorting to emergency responses to deal with such issues.

Security Council organ created by the United Nations Charter comprising five permanent members with veto power and ten rotating members. It is responsible for the maintenance of international peace and security on behalf of all United Nations member states.

Social norm line of conduct defining socially appropriate behaviour for a specific entity.

Sovereignty in international law, describes the status of a state that has a permanent population, a territory, a government, and absolute authority in its relations with other states. All states are characterized by sovereign equality.

Stakeholder individual or collective actor that has an active interest in a topic or policy.

Sustainable development principle according to which development should meet the needs of the present without compromising the ability of future generations to meet their own needs, in light of three interdependent pillars: economic development, social justice, and the environment. First gained widespread recognition in the Brundtland Report in 1987. See also 'Brundtland Commission'.

Sustainable Development Goals 17 goals and related targets adopted by a United Nations General Assembly resolution to promote sustainable development for the period 2015 to 2030.

Technology transfer transfer of more advanced technologies by governments, intergovernmental organizations, research institutes, non-governmental organizations, or businesses to entities that do not possess them, often to help them meet their obligations under an international agreement.

Traditional knowledge knowledge, know-how, and practices that are passed on from generation to generation within a community. It includes traditional medicines and traditional artworks.

Tragedy of the commons phenomenon where a non-excludable but rivalrous common good, if its use is left unregulated, will be depleted due to the aggregation of individual rational decisions to use the good. See also 'Public goods', 'Rivalrous goods', and 'Common goods'.

Vulnerability susceptibility to experiencing the negative impacts of a phenomenon, for instance a natural disaster, often due to geographical characteristics or insufficient capacity to adapt to a changing environment.

Working group see 'Contact group'.

Index

Tables, figures, glossary terms and boxes are indicated by an italic *t*, *f*, *g*, and *b* following the page number.

A

Aarhus Convention on Access to Information, Public Participation in Decision-Making and Access to Justice in Environmental Matters 12–13*f*, 22, 128, 231*t*, 277
abatement costs 96–101, 98*t*, 99*f*
Abbott, Kenneth 250
Aboriginal peoples *see* indigenous communities
access to genetic resources and benefit sharing 24, 66, 102, 119, 182, 183*b*, 359*g*
acid rain 31*b*, 33*b*, 35, 204
see also transboundary air pollution
adaptation 359*g*
see also climate change mitigation and adaptation
additionality 211, 212*b*
adjusted net savings 196, 196*f*
administrative units 104–7, 105*b*
advice strategy of non-state actors 141–2, 141*t*, 144*b*
advocacy groups 9, 63, 128
see also non-governmental organizations (NGOs)
Advocates Coalition for Development and Environment 132
Afghanistan 115*f*, 303, 311
Africa
armed conflicts 298, 303
desertification negotiations 22, 116*b*, 117*b*, 137
development aid 212
development of environmental laws and institutions 239
elephants 70–1
environmental migration 296*b*
hazardous waste dumping 20, 330*b*, 331
invasive species 323
non-state actors 137
resource curse 303
African Charter of Human and Peoples' Rights 307
African Group 113, 115*f*, 120
African Union 231*t*, 296*b*
African Wildlife Foundation 137
Agarwal, Anil 83

Agenda 21 12–13*f*, 147*b*, 209, 210, 267, 276, 281*b*, 359*g*
Agent Orange 308, 310, 359*g*
Agreement Governing the Activities of States on the Moon and Other Celestial Bodies 174
Agreement on Application of Sanitary and Phytosanitary Measures 31*b*, 246, 247, 332
agricultural biodiversity 197*b*
agriculture
climate-smart 134
International Treaty on Plant Genetic Resources for Food and Agriculture 12–13*f*, 62, 180, 231*t*
trade and environmental degradation 323
see also Food and Agriculture Organization; genetically modified organisms (GMOs)
aid
development 207–9, 212, 212*b*, 216, 216*f*, 360*g*
neo-Malthusianism and 72
air pollution *see* transboundary air pollution
Albania 115*f*
Algeria 115*f*, 340*f*
alien species 38–9, 323
All-China Environment Federation 129
Alliance of Small Island States (AOSIS) 82, 115*f*, 116*b*, 119, 359*g*
Al Sabban, Mohamed 120
Amazon rainforest 105*b*, 175, 184, 234*b*, 307, 319
American Convention on Human Rights 307
America's Pledge 149*b*
Angola 115*f*, 303
Animal Liberation Front 309*b*
animal rights 66
Antarctic Treaty regime 32, 69
common heritage of humankind principle 171–2, 172*f*, 175
Convention on the Conservation of Antarctic Marine Living Resources 12–13*f*, 19, 69, 171, 231*t*

Madrid Protocol on Environmental Protection 12–13*f*, 171, 265
Anthropocene 1, 2*b*, 305, 359*g*
anthropocentrism 61–3, 65–6, 131
Antigua and Barbuda 115*f*
AOSIS *see* Alliance of Small Island States (AOSIS)
arbitration mechanisms 272
Arctic communities 38, 130*b*
Arctic Council 38, 130*b*, 185
Argentina 113, 115*f*, 340*f*
armed conflict
climate change and 303–5
environmental degradation as cause of 297–305, 299*f*, 302*b*, 302*f*
environmental impacts of 307–11
environmental warfare 307–8
Homer-Dixon model 299–301, 299*f*
myth of water wars 301, 302*b*, 302*f*
paradox of plenty 301–3, 304*f*
resource curse 301–3, 304*f*
Asian Infrastructure and Investment Bank 235
assessments *see* environmental impact assessments
Association of Southeast Asian Nations 245
atmospheric pollution *see* transboundary air pollution
Australia 82, 113, 114, 115*f*, 267*f*, 303
Austria 115*f*, 267*f*
autocracies, state preferences of 100–1, 101*f*
aviation industry 251*b*, 253*b*
awareness, public 4, 8*b*, 9, 33*b*, 73, 126, 263, 325
Azerbaijan 340*f*

B

Bahamas 115*f*
Bahrain 115*f*, 340*f*
Bali Action Plan 281*b*
Baltic Sea 32–4, 273

Bamako Convention on the Ban of the Import into Africa and the Control of Transboundary Movement and Management of Hazardous Wastes within Africa 12–13f, 20, 231t, 330b
Bangladesh 115f
Ban Ki-Moon 205b
Barbados 115f
Basel Convention on the Control of Transboundary Movements of Hazardous Wastes and their Disposal 12–13f, 20, 47, 138, 185, 231t, 271, 320b, 331, 336
BASIC 115f
Belarus 115f
Belgium 115f, 267f
Belize 115f
Benedict, Richard 36b
beneficiary pays principle 81
benefit sharing 24, 66, 102, 119, 182, 183b, 359g
Benin 115f
Bernstein, Steven 220
Bhagwati, Jagdish 321
Bhopal disaster, India 147b, 205
Bhutan 115f
biocentrism 61–2, 63–6, 131, 307, 309b, 311, 359g
biodiversity 6t
    agricultural 197b
    anthropocentrism and 62
    declines in 126–7
    epistemic communities 35
    indigenous communities and 38
    institutional interactions 245, 246, 247, 250
    megadiverse countries 118–19, 181f
    negotiation leadership 118–19
    non-governmental organizations and 126–7, 132, 137–8, 139
    regime complex 243f
    sovereignty rights over 180–2, 181f, 183b, 210
    see also Convention on Biological Diversity
biofuels 44b, 244
biological weapons 310
biopiracy 139, 180
bioprospecting 139, 220
bioregionalism 63
biosafety/biosecurity 105b, 359g
    business involvement 102, 142, 144b
    Cartagena Protocol on Biosafety 12–13f, 23, 30, 31b, 31f, 105b, 113, 120, 142, 144b, 246, 262, 332

interstate coalitions 113
    negotiation leadership 120
    numbers of scientific publications 31f
    precautionary principle 30, 31b, 45
biotechnology industry 35, 102, 134, 136, 142, 144b, 180, 181f, 182, 183b
Birdlife International 131, 138
birth control policies 72–3, 75
Blair, Tony 152
bluefin tuna 328, 329
Bolivarian Alliance for the Peoples of Our America (ALBA) 80, 114, 115f
Bolivia 80, 113, 115f, 208b, 218, 220, 340f
Bonn Convention on the Conservation of Migratory Species of Wild Animals 12–13f, 69, 231t, 238–9, 250
boomerang effect 130b
Bosnia and Herzegovina 115f
Botswana 71, 115f, 283b
bottom-up approach 108b, 117b
boundary organizations 45–8, 359g
Brazil 116b, 216
    Amazon rainforest 105b, 175, 184, 234b, 319
    Clean Development Mechanism projects 334
    debt-for-nature swaps 208b
    greenhouse gas emissions 83f
    institutional interactions 271–2
    interstate coalitions 114
    trade disputes 337t
    see also Rio+20 Summit on Sustainable Development; Rio Summit on the Environment and Development
Brezhnev, Leonid 42b
Brundtland Commission and Report 60, 85–6, 193, 204–7, 205b, 238b, 267, 308, 359g
Brundtland, Gro Harlem 205b
Brunei 115f, 340f
Brussels effect 327
Bulgaria 115f
bureaucracy see administrative units; secretariats
Burkina Faso 115f
Burundi 115f, 298
Business Charter for Sustainable Development 147b
businesses 129, 132–6, 200b, 280
    biosafety negotiations and 102, 142, 144b

biotechnology industry 35, 102, 134, 136, 142, 144b, 180, 181f, 182, 183b
    climate change negotiations and 134, 135b, 149b
    corporate social responsibility 146, 147b, 360g
    discursive resources 138
    Eco-Patent Commons 281b
    Global Compact 147b, 361g
    Global Reporting Initiative 147b, 239
    green consumerism 324–5
    influence during policy phases 139–40
    intellectual property rights 41f, 134, 138, 180, 181f, 183b, 197b, 247, 281b
    ISO 14001 standard 102–4, 103f
    material resources 137
    neo-Gramscian perspective 133–4
    pluralist perspective 134–6
    political regime type and 101–4, 103f
    solar photovoltaic industry 325, 326f
    strategies of influence 141, 142, 143, 144b
    transnational initiatives 149b, 151b

C

California effect 136, 327
Cambodia 115f
Cameroon 115f
Canada 115f
    climate change negotiations and 104, 217
    emissions trading systems 335
    environmental taxes 266b, 267f
    environmental terrorism 309b
    feed-in tariff 339–40
    fisheries 166b, 176, 299
    Great Lakes 185
    greenhouse gas emissions 82, 83f
    human security concept 306
    interstate coalitions 113, 114
    investor–state disputes 343, 344t
    military presence in Arctic 184
    plastic pollution 140b
    polar bears 58
    trade disputes 337t, 339–40
    Trail Smelter dispute 176, 177b
Cao, Xun 327
capacity building 268t, 273, 279, 346, 359g

cap and trade 359g
   see also emissions trading
      systems
Cape Verde 115f
carbon capture and storage 44b
carbon credit trading see carbon
      markets
carbon dioxide emissions see
      greenhouse gas emissions
carbon dioxide removal
      technologies 44b
carbon markets 105b, 135b, 149b,
      168–9, 220, 266b, 268, 268t,
      276, 279, 333–5
Carbon Offsetting and Reduction
      Scheme for International
      Aviation 253b
carbon pricing 346b
   see also carbon markets
carbon sinks 113, 114, 359g
carbon tariffs 323, 346b
carbon taxes 105b, 266b
   see also environmental taxes
carrying capacity 72, 73, 75–6,
      194–5, 359g
Carson, Rachel 9, 10
Cartagena Protocol on
      Biosafety 12–13f, 23, 30, 31b,
      31f, 105b, 113, 120, 142, 144b,
      246, 262, 332
Carter, Jimmy 73, 205b
Casa, Fernando 110–11
causal beliefs 55
   conservationism versus
      preservationism 66–71, 67b
   neo-Malthusianism versus
      cornucopian theory 71–9, 74f,
      75f, 78f
Central African Republic 115f
Centre for International
      Environmental Law 141
certification schemes 151b, 274,
      275t, 278, 325
Chad 115f, 303
chairs, negotiation 110–13
chemicals, hazardous
   Agent Orange 308, 359g
   chemical disasters 64b, 147b,
      205, 308
   prior informed consent 12–13f, 23
   Rotterdam Convention
      12–13f, 23, 231t
   Stockholm Convention 12–13f,
      23, 231t, 284, 318–19
chemical weapons 310
Chernobyl nuclear disaster
      205, 345b
chicken game 109
Chile 113, 115f, 267f, 335
chilling effect 333, 343, 345b, 359g

China 115f, 116b, 216, 219b
   Clean Development Mechanism
      projects 334
   climate change negotiations and
      99, 108
   emissions trading system
      279, 284, 335
   environmental warfare 308
   greenhouse gas emissions
      82, 83f, 99
   ivory trade 71, 328
   Montreal Protocol and
      208–9
   patents 281b
   recycling waste trade 320b
   solar photovoltaic industry 325
   trade disputes 337t
   trade openness 100
Chipko movement 64b, 197b
chlorofluorocarbons (CFCs) 5t, 10f,
      36b, 98, 133, 335
CITES see Convention on Interna-
      tional Trade in Endangered
      Species of Wild Fauna and
      Flora (CITES)
city networks, transnational
      146–9, 148f, 149b
civil society organizations see
      non-governmental organiza-
      tions (NGOs)
Clapp, Jennifer 178b
Clean Development Mechanism
      22, 110, 113, 114, 334
ClientEarth 143
Climate Accountability Institute
      133
Climate Action Network 132, 273
climate change 2, 5t
   1.5°C threshold 46b
   2°C threshold 42
   Arctic communities and 38
   conflict and 303–5
   cultural cognition hypothesis
      33b
   environmental security 295
   numbers of scientific
      publications 31f
   sea level rise 82, 116b, 295, 296b
climate change mitigation and
      adaptation 359g
   carbon tariffs 323, 346b
   carbon taxes 105b, 266b
   city networks 146–9, 149b
   climate clubs 346b
   emissions trading systems 105b,
      135b, 149b, 168–9, 220, 266b,
      268, 268t, 276, 279, 333–5
   geoengineering 43, 44b, 67, 306,
      309b
   intergenerational equity 80–2

   intragenerational equity
      82–5, 83f
   measuring policy effectiveness
      260, 261
   nationally determined
      contributions 60, 108b, 260
   technology transfer 281b
   trade agreements and
      346b, 347b
   see also climate change negotia-
      tions; climate change regime
climate change negotiations 46b
   bottom-up approach 108b
   business involvement
      134, 135b, 140
   contact and working groups 110
   developing countries and
      41–2, 82–5, 83f, 217
   ecological vulnerability and 99
   emerging countries and 217
   epistemic communities 35
   indigenous representation 130b
   interstate coalitions
      113–14, 115f, 116b
   national delegations 106, 111f
   need for political input 43
   negotiation chairs 110, 112
   negotiation leadership
      118, 119, 251b
   NGO involvement 130, 130b,
      131, 132, 137, 138, 139, 142
   numbers of non-state observers
      127, 127f
   obstructionist behaviour
      120, 273
   polycentric governance 153
   prisoner's dilemma logic
      and 108
   state political regime and 100,
      104
   Stern Review 81–2, 217
   Talaona Dialogue 153
   transnational initiatives
      145, 146–9, 146f, 149b
   Vatican and 60b
   voluntary approach 108b
climate change regime
   Clean Development Mechanism
      22, 110, 113, 114, 334
   common but differentiated
      responsibility 84, 211, 217
   Green Climate Fund 212b, 268
   implementation instru-
      ments 266b, 268
   institutional interactions 246
   instrument diffusion 279
   Intergovernmental Panel on
      Climate Change (IPCC) 40f,
      42, 45, 46b, 135b, 217, 295,
      306, 361g

climate change regime (*Continued*)
  regime complex 243*f*, 244–5
  trade and 333–5
  see also Kyoto Protocol; Paris
    Agreement on climate change;
    United Nations Framework
    Convention on Climate
    Change
climate clubs 346*b*
climate engineering *see*
  geoengineering
climate justice *see* environmental
  justice
climate models 32, 42
climate-smart agriculture 134
climate system, knowledge of 39
Climate Tracker 139
Clinton, Bill 295
club goods 165*t*
club governance 251
Club of Rome 8*b*, 28, 73, 359*g*
Coalition of Rainforest
  Nations 113, 115*f*
coalitions, interstate 113–14, 115*f*,
  116*b*, 118–19
Coben, Lesley 279
cobra effect 283*b*
codes of conduct 66, 147*b*
Cod Wars 299
Cold War 39, 42*b*, 69, 72, 174, 209,
  212, 294, 295, 301
Colgan, Jeff 235–6
Collaborative Partnership on
  Forests 250
collective action problems
  marine pollution 178*b*
  see also common heritage of
    humankind; sovereignty over
    natural resources; tragedy of
    the commons
Colombia 113, 115*f*, 184, 218,
  219*b*, 335, 342
command and control mechanisms
  265, 266*b*
Commission for Sustainable
  Development 114, 209, 210,
  218, 240*b*, 249
Commission for the Conservation
  of Antarctic Marine Living
  Resources 231*t*
commodifying instruments
  276, 276*b*
  see also market mechanisms
common but differentiated responsibility 9, 84, 200*b*, 210–11,
  217, 359*g*
common goods 164–5, 165*t*, 359*g*
  market mechanisms and
    168–9, 169*t*

polycentric governance 170
private property rights and 166*b*,
  168–9
regulations and 166–7,
  166*b*, 169*t*
subsidies and 167–8, 169*t*
taxation and 168, 169*t*
  see also common heritage of hu-
    mankind; public goods; sover-
    eignty over natural resources;
    tragedy of the commons
common heritage of human-
  kind 164, 170–5, 210, 361*g*
  Antarctica 171–2, 172*f*, 175
  international seabed
    174–5, 175*f*
  outer space
    172–4, 173*b*
common pool resource problems
  173*b*
  see also tragedy of the commons
Communal Areas Management
  Programme for Indigenous
  Resources, Zimbabwe 130*b*
communitarianism 59–60
Comoros 115*f*
comparative advantage theory
  320–1
compensation mechanisms
  268*t*, 272
compliance 360*g*
compliance instruments
  268, 270–2, 270*t*
Comprehensive and Progressive
  Agreement for Trans-Pacific
  Partnership 319, 327, 342
Comprehensive Nuclear Test Ban
  Treaty 12–13*f*, 308–10
computer modelling
  air pollution models 42*b*
  climate models 32, 42
  uncertainty of 28–9
conditional financing 212*b*, 235,
  268*t*, 274
Conferences of the Parties 360*g*
  to Convention on International
    Trade in Endangered
    Species 58
  to United Nations Framework
    Convention on Climate
    Change 42, 46*b*, 108*b*, 114,
    120, 127, 142, 212, 217
conflict *see* armed conflict
conservation
  Antarctic marine living resources
    12–13*f*, 19, 69, 171, 231*t*
  anthropocentrism and 62
  conspicuous 58*b*
  International Union for

Conservation of Nature 70,
  102, 103*f*, 139, 206, 231*t*, 232,
  239, 250
marine protected areas
  166*b*, 208*b*, 245
migratory species 12–13*f*, 69,
  231*t*, 238–9, 250
protected areas 175, 273
Ramsar Convention on Wetlands
  of International Importance
  12–13*f*, 62, 69, 231*t*, 232, 246,
  250, 268
  see also whaling; wildlife trade
    and trafficking
Conservation International
  138, 276*b*
conservationism 66–8, 67*b*, 70–1,
  131, 360*g*
  see also preservationism
conspicuous conservation 58*b*
constructivism 11, 95
contact groups 110, 360*g*
Convention Concerning the Protection of the World Cultural and
  Natural Heritage *see* World
  Heritage Convention
Convention for the Conservation of
  Antarctic Seals 69
Convention for the Preservation of
  Wild Animals, Birds and Fish in
  Africa 62
Convention for the Protection of
  Birds Useful to Agriculture 62
Convention for the Protection
  of the Marine Environment
  of the North-East Atlantic
  (OSPAR Convention) 233
Convention on Access to Informa-
  tion, Public Participation in
  Decision-Making and Access to
  Justice in Environmental Mat-
  ters 12–13*f*, 22, 128, 231*t*, 277
Convention on Biological Diversity
  12–13*f*, 21, 32, 38, 65, 142,
  144*b*, 209–10, 231*t*, 239
  Cartagena Protocol on Biosafety
    12–13*f*, 23, 30, 31*b*, 31*f*, 105*b*,
    113, 120, 142, 144*b*, 246, 262,
    332
  conservationism 70
  institutional interactions 245,
    246, 247, 250
  interstate coalitions 119
  Nagoya Protocol 12–13*f*, 24, 66,
    110–11, 130*b*, 139, 182, 183*b*,
    217, 282
  non-state actor involvement
    102, 127*f*, 136, 139
  secretariat 240*b*

sovereignty over natural resources 180, 182, 183*b*, 210
technology transfer 281*b*
traditional knowledge 38, 130*b*, 183*b*, 247
Convention on Environmental Impact Assessment in a Transboundary Context 12–13*f*, 21, 231*t*
Convention on International Liability for Damage Caused by Space Objects 173
Convention on International Trade in Endangered Species of Wild Fauna and Flora (CITES) 12–13*f*, 18, 48, 106, 231*t*, 329
    business involvement 102
    compliance instruments 271, 272
    elephants and ivory trade 70–1, 282, 283*b*, 328
    institutional interactions 245, 246, 250
    polar bears 58
    preservationism 69
Convention on Long-range Transboundary Air Pollution 12–13*f*, 19, 31*f*, 42*b*, 166, 231*t*, 263, 271–2, 273
Convention on Nature Protection and Wild Life Preservation in the Western Hemisphere 62, 69
Convention on Nuclear Accidents 12–13*f*, 231*t*
Convention on Nuclear Safety 12–13*f*
Convention on the Conservation of Antarctic Marine Living Resources (CCAMLR) 12–13*f*, 19, 69, 171, 231*t*
Convention on the Conservation of Migratory Species of Wild Animals 12–13*f*, 69, 231*t*, 238–9, 250
Convention on the Control of Transboundary Movements of Hazardous Wastes and their Disposal 12–13*f*, 20, 47, 138, 185, 231*t*, 271, 320*b*
Convention on the Law of the Sea 12–13*f*, 107, 110, 112, 166*b*, 174–5, 176–8
Convention on the Prohibition of Military or Any Other Hostile Use of Environmental Modification Techniques 12–13*f*, 66, 310
Convention on the Protection and Use of Transboundary Watercourses and International Lakes 12–13*f*

Convention on the Transboundary Effects of Industrial Accidents 12–13*f*
Convention to Combat Desertification 12–13*f*, 22, 30, 109, 116*b*, 117*b*, 137, 138, 209, 211
Co-operative Programme for Monitoring and Evaluation of the Long-range Transmission of Air Pollutants in Europe 271–2
Copenhagen Conference 42, 119, 127, 217
cornucopian theories 75–9, 78*f*
corporate social responsibility 146, 147*b*, 360*g*
corporations *see* businesses
Correa, Rafael 220
cost accounting, historical 80–2
Costa Rica 113, 115*f*, 208*b*, 276*b*, 342
costs of abatement 96–101, 98*t*, 99*f*
Côte d'Ivoire 115*f*
counterfactual evaluation 263–4
counter-summits 142–3
credit markets *see* emissions trading systems
critical theories 11, 95
Croatia 115*f*
CropLife International 144*b*
Crutzen, Paul 2*b*
Cuba 80, 115*f*, 218
cultural cognition hypothesis 33*b*
cultural ecofeminism 64*b*
cultural ecosystem services 276*b*
customary law 360*g*
Cyprus 115*f*
Czech Republic 115*f*, 267*f*

D

Daly, Herman 321
dangerous waste 360*g*
    see also hazardous wastes
d'Eaubonne, Francoise 64*b*
debt crises 204, 216
debt-for-nature swaps 208, 208*b*
Declaration on the Responsibilities of the Present Generations Towards Future Generations 171
deep ecology 63, 360*g*
deep seabed 174–5, 175*f*
deforestation *see* forests and deforestation
Delbeke, Jos 105*b*
democracies, state preferences of 100–4, 101*f*, 103*f*
Democratic Republic of the Congo 115*f*
democratization 105

demographic growth 71–3, 74, 75, 76, 76*b*, 210, 297–8, 298*b*, 299
Denmark 39, 115*f*, 266*b*, 267*f*
dependent variables 360*g*
Depledge, Joanna 46*b*, 120
desertification 7*t*
    African countries and 22, 116*b*, 117*b*, 137
    interstate coalitions 116*b*
    lack of international cooperation on 30, 34
    Land Degradation Neutrality Fund 117*b*
    negotiation leadership 117*b*
    United Nations Convention to Combat Desertification 12–13*f*, 22, 30, 109, 116*b*, 117*b*, 137, 138, 209, 211
developing countries 360*g*
    climate change negotiations 41–2, 82–5, 83*f*
    common but differentiated responsibility 9, 84, 200*b*, 210–11, 217, 359*g*
    common heritage of humankind principle and 174, 175
    conservationism 70–1
    debt crisis 204
    debt-for-nature swaps 208, 208*b*
    development aid 207–9, 212, 212*b*, 216, 216*f*
    emerging countries 116*b*, 216, 217, 235
    environmental agreements 199, 199*f*
    environmental aid 207–9, 212, 212*b*, 216, 216*f*
    environmental Kuznets curve and 77–8, 78*f*
    expertise from 46*b*
    Forest Stewardship Council and 151*b*
    Global Environment Facility and 238*b*
    greenhouse gas emissions 41, 82–5, 83*f*
    Group of 77 (G77) 113, 115*f*, 116*b*, 120, 201, 204, 237
    hazardous waste dumping 20, 329–32, 330*b*
    inequalities in scientific research and 39–42, 40*f*, 41*f*
    intragenerational equity 82–5, 83*f*
    leadership in negotiations 117*b*
    least-developed countries 115*f*, 361*g*

developing countries (*Continued*)
  Montreal Protocol and 208–9, 212*b*, 335
  neo-Malthusianism and 71–3, 74
  non-state actors 137
  pollution haven hypothesis and 326–7
  population growth 71–3, 74
  preferential trade agreements 346–7
  Rio Summit and 207–8, 209, 210–11
  sovereignty over natural resources 180–2, 183*b*, 201, 210
  Stockholm Conference and 201, 203, 204
  structural inequalities 196–8, 197*b*, 197*f*
  technology transfer 207–8
  trade and environment 324, 326–7, 346–7
  verification instruments and 282
development *see* economic development and environment; sustainable development
development aid 207–9, 212, 212*b*, 216, 216*f*, 360*g*
differentiated responsibility *see* common but differentiated responsibility
diffusion
  policy 274–9, 275*t*, 362*g*
  technology 207–8, 281*b*, 363*g*
disasters
  chemical 64*b*, 147*b*, 205, 308
  natural 296*b*, 301, 304, 305, 306*f*
  nuclear 12–13*f*, 136, 204–5, 231*t*, 345*b*
discursive resources of non-state actors 138–9
dispute settlement mechanisms
  investor-state 343
  verification instruments as 282
  World Trade Organization 250, 335–40, 337*t*, 339*b*, 340*f*
Djibouti 115*f*, 298
Doha Conference 212
Dolšak, Nives 67*b*
domestic politics 96–107, 98*t*, 99*f*
Dominica 110, 115*f*
Dominican Republic 115*f*
drinking water
  see freshwater
Dryzek, John 55
dumping *see* hazardous wastes
DuPont 133

E

early warning systems 360*g*
Earth
  carrying capacity 72, 73, 75–6, 194–5, 359*g*
  Gaia hypothesis 8*b*, 63–5
  images from space 8*b*
Earth First! 63, 128, 309*b*
Earth Liberation Front 309*b*
Earthlife Africa 131
Earth Negotiations Bulletin 107
Earth Summit *see* Rio Summit on the Environment and Development
Easter Island 298*b*
ecocentrism 360*g*
  see also biocentrism
ecocide 65–6, 308, 360*g*
eco-fashion 325
ecofeminism 63, 64*b*, 197*b*
eco-labels 151*b*, 274, 275*t*, 278, 325, 360*g*
ecological economics 79
ecological footprint 73, 74*f*, 194–5, 195*f*, 311, 360*g*
ecological modernization 76, 280, 360*g*
ecological terrorism 309*b*
ecological vulnerability 96–101, 98*t*, 99*f*
Economic and Social Council to the United Nations 248, 330*b*
Economic Commission for Africa 330*b*
Economic Commission for Europe 42*b*, 231*t*
economic development and environment 192–8
  Brundtland Commission and Report 60, 85–6, 193, 204–7, 205*b*, 238*b*, 267, 308, 359*g*
  debt-for-nature swaps 208, 208*b*
  green economy 139, 200*b*, 218, 361*g*
  Johannesburg Summit 12–13*f*, 60, 145, 147*b*, 193, 200*b*, 211–12, 214–15, 215*f*
  liberal environmentalism 220–1, 361*g*
  liberal view 194*f*, 195–6, 196*f*, 198, 203, 206, 211, 214, 215*f*, 218, 220, 221
  Rio+20 Summit 12–13*f*, 66, 79, 128, 142–3, 193, 200*b*, 215–20, 215*f*
  structural view 194*f*, 196–8, 197*b*, 197*f*, 201, 203–4, 206, 210–11, 214, 215*f*, 218, 220, 221

systemic view 194–5, 194*f*, 195*f*, 198, 201, 203–4, 206, 210, 214–15, 215*f*, 220, 221
  see also Rio Summit on the Environment and Development; Stockholm Conference on the Human Environment
economic growth 195–6, 196*f*, 218
  in Brundtland Report 205*b*, 206, 207
  The Limits to Growth 8*b*, 28, 73
  neo-Malthusianism versus cornucopian theory 71–9, 74*f*, 75*f*, 78*f*
  in Rio Declaration 211
Eco-Patent Commons 281*b*
ecosystem services 360*g*
  cultural services 276*b*
  payments for 220, 276*b*, 362*g*
  provisioning services 276*b*
  regulation services 276*b*
  support services 276*b*
ecosystem vitality index 197–8, 197*f*
Ecuador 66, 80, 115*f*, 220, 307, 340*f*
effectiveness *see* policy effectiveness
Egypt 115*f*, 340*f*
Ehrlich, Paul 9, 10, 72–3, 76*b*
Elders 205*b*
electoral systems 104
electronic waste 332
elephants 70–1, 282, 283*b*, 328
El Salvador 115*f*, 340*f*
embodied carbon 323
emerging countries 116*b*, 216, 217, 235
emissions trading systems 105*b*, 135*b*, 149*b*, 168–9, 220, 266*b*, 268, 268*t*, 276, 279, 333–5
endangered species *see* Convention on International Trade in Endangered Species of Wild Fauna and Flora (CITES); wildlife trade and trafficking
energy
  biofuels 44*b*, 244
  fossil fuel subsidies 340, 340*f*
  nuclear 43, 136, 345*b*
  see also renewable energy
enforcement 360*g*
enforcement instruments 268, 270–1, 270*t*, 272–3
enquiry procedure 272
entrepreneurial leadership 119–20
entropy 79, 360*g*

environmental agreements *see* international environmental agreements
environmental aid 207–9, 212, 212*b*, 216, 216*f*
environmental conditionalities on lending 212*b*, 235, 268*t*, 274
Environmental Defense Fund 132
environmental externalities 79, 133, 147*b*, 168, 244, 265, 266*b*, 276*b*, 361*g*
environmental goods 100, 319, 324–5, 341
environmental impact assessments 12–13*f*, 21, 37, 47, 260–2, 265, 268*t*, 311, 360*g*
Environmental Integrity Group 114, 115*f*
environmental justice 360*g*
  Aarhus Convention 12–13*f*, 22, 128, 231*t*, 277
  discursive resources and 138–9
  ecocide 65–6, 308, 360*g*
  ecofeminism 63, 64*b*, 197*b*
  Escazú Agreement 12–13*f*, 128, 277
  intergenerational equity 80–2
  intragenerational equity 82–5, 83*f*, 175
  see also common heritage of humankind
environmental Kuznets curve 77–9, 78*f*, 361*g*
environmental migrants 296, 296*b*, 300
environmental modification techniques 12–13*f*, 66, 310
environmental security 293–311
  ambiguous concept of 294–6
  climate change and conflict 303–5
  ecological terrorism 309*b*
  environmental degradation as cause of armed conflict 297–305, 299*f*, 302*b*, 302*f*
  environmental impacts of armed conflict 307–11
  environmental migration 296, 296*b*, 300
  environmental terrorism 309*b*
  environmental warfare 307–8
  Homer-Dixon model 299–301, 299*f*
  human rights and 306–7
  human security and 305–7
  myth of water wars 301, 302*b*, 302*f*
  paradox of plenty 301–3, 304*f*
  resource curse 301–3, 304*f*
  societal collapse 298, 298*b*

environmental taxes 105*b*, 168, 169*t*, 265, 266*b*, 267*f*, 268*t*, 275*t*, 279
environmental terrorism 309*b*
environmental warfare 307–8
epistemic communities 11, 34–7, 36*b*, 361*g*
Equatorial Guinea 115*f*
Equator Principles 147*b*
equity
  intergenerational 80–2
  intragenerational 82–5, 83*f*, 175
  see also environmental justice
Eritrea 115*f*
Escazú Agreement on Access to Information, Public Participation and Justice in Environmental Matters in Latin America and the Caribbean 12–13*f*, 128, 277
Espoo Convention on Environmental Impact Assessment in a Transboundary Context 12–13*f*, 21, 231*t*
Estonia 115*f*, 267*f*
ethics 43–5
  anthropocentrism versus biocentrism 61–6
  birth control policies 72–3, 75
  conservationism versus preservationism 66–71, 67*b*
  ecocide 65–6, 308, 360*g*
  geoengineering 43, 44*b*, 67, 306, 309*b*
  intergenerational equity 80–2
  intragenerational equity 82–5, 83*f*, 175
  neo-Malthusianism and 72–3, 75
  speciesism 66
  whaling 35, 59, 67*b*
  see also common heritage of humankind; environmental justice; rights
Ethiopia 70, 115*f*, 120, 142, 296*b*
European Commission 105*b*, 119
European Court of Justice 251*b*, 272
European Network for Ecological Reflection and Action 130*b*
European Roundtable of Industrialists 129
European Union 115*f*, 251*b*
  autonomy of 185
  climate change negotiations 42, 118, 119, 251*b*

desertification negotiations 117*b*
Directive on Renewable Energy 244
emissions trading system 105*b*, 251*b*, 279, 284, 335
environmental policy integration 251*b*
fisheries 166*b*
genetically modified organisms (GMOs) 31*b*, 262
Natura 2000 protected areas 273
negotiation leadership 118, 119, 251*b*
preferential trade agreements 342
trade and environment 324, 327
trade disputes 337*t*, 339–40
exclusive economic zones 166*b*, 175*f*, 176–8
experts 37–8
  see also epistemic communities
externalities 79, 133, 147*b*, 168, 244, 265, 266*b*, 276*b*, 361*g*
Extractive Industries Transparency Initiative 152
extreme weather events 296*b*, 305, 306*f*

F

Farman, Joseph 36*b*
fashion industry 325
feed-in tariffs 339–40
feminism *see* ecofeminism
Fiji 115*f*
financial mechanisms and funding 268*t*
  conditional financing 212*b*, 235, 268*t*, 274
  Environmental Defense Fund 132
  Global Environment Facility 152, 209, 212*b*, 234, 235, 237, 238*b*, 250, 276*b*
  Green Climate Fund 212*b*, 268
  Land Degradation Neutrality Fund 117*b*
  Multilateral Fund 209, 212*b*, 268, 335
  Prototype Carbon Fund 145
  United Nations Fund for International Partnerships 152
  Wetland Conservation Fund 268
  World Heritage Fund 171
Finland 32–4, 104, 115*f*, 266*b*, 267*f*

fisheries and overfishing 6t, 166b
    anthropocentrism and 62
    certification scheme 151b
    conflict and 166b, 176, 299
    exclusive economic zones 166b,
        175f, 176–8
    global trends 10f
    institutional interactions 245
    subsidies 341, 342
    tragedy of the commons 166b
    treaties 12–13f, 62
    Turbot War 166b, 176, 299
Florianópolis Declaration 67b
Food and Agriculture Organiza-
        tion 114, 142, 166b, 230, 231t,
        232, 247, 250
food security 214, 323
footprint see ecological footprint
forests and deforestation 7t
    Amazon rainforest 105b, 175,
        184, 234b, 307, 319
    certification schemes 151b, 274,
        275t, 278
    Collaborative Partnership on
        Forests 250
    ecosystem services 276b
    global trends 10f
    indigenous communities
        and 130b
    institutional interactions
        246, 250
    instrument diffusion 274, 275t
    International Tropical Timber
        Agreements 12–13f, 231t
    interstate coalitions
        113, 114, 116b
    lack of international cooperation
        on 30, 34, 151, 210
    non-state actors and 143
    at Rio Summit 209, 210
    transnational initiatives
        151, 151b
    World Bank and 234b
Forest Stewardship Council 151b,
        274, 275t, 278
forum shopping 241
fossil fuels
    oil industry 74, 75f, 134, 138
    oil spills 18, 98–9, 134, 267–8,
        272, 308
    subsidies 340, 340f
    see also Organization of the
        Petroleum Exporting Countries
        (OPEC)
'Fossil of the Day' award 273
Foster, John Bellamy 321–2
Foucault, Michel 280
Founex Report 201
fragmentation, institutional 244

framework conventions 361g
    see also United Nations Frame-
        work Convention on Climate
        Change
France 115f
    environmental taxes 267f
    environmental terrorism 309b
    exclusive economic zone 178
    genetically modified organisms
        (GMOs) 45
    greenhouse gas emissions 83f
    ministry of the environment 105
    nuclear weapons 310
    ozone negotiations and 98
    plastic pollution 140b
    revolutions 303
    trade disputes 337t
Francis (Pope) 60b
free riding 56, 279, 346b
freshwater
    cooperation and conflicts
        over 301, 302b, 302f
    extraction trends 10f
    pollution 5t, 327, 345b
    privatization of supply ser-
        vices 284
Friends of the Earth 9, 129, 131,
        141, 147b
Fukushima nuclear disaster 345b
funding see financial mechanisms
        and funding
fur industry 102
Future We Want, The 12–13f, 79,
        128, 217–20

G
G7 140b, 178b, 250
G20 250
G77 113, 115f, 116b, 120, 201,
        204, 237
Gabon 115f, 340f
Gaia hypothesis 8b, 63–5
Gambia 115f
game theory 107–8, 109
General Agreement on Tariffs and
        Trade 247, 336, 337t, 339b,
        341
genetically modified organisms
        (GMOs) 361g
    business involvement 144b
    Cartagena Protocol on Bio-
        safety 12–13f, 23, 30, 31b, 31f,
        105b, 113, 120, 142, 144b, 246,
        262, 332
    institutional interactions 246
    instrument diffusion
        274, 275t, 279
    interstate coalitions 113

labelling 136
    need for political input 43, 45
    precautionary principle
        30, 31b, 45
    prior informed consent
        268t, 274
    structural inequalities and 197b
    trade in 332–3
genetic resources 361g
    access and benefit sharing 24,
        66, 102, 119, 182, 183b, 359g
    anthropocentrism and 62
    epistemic communities 35
    indigenous communities and 38,
        130b, 183b, 247, 282
    information disclosure 277
    institutional interactions 247
    International Treaty on Plant Ge-
        netic Resources for Food and
        Agriculture 12–13f, 62,
        180, 231t
    Nagoya Protocol 12–13f, 24, 66,
        110–11, 130b, 139, 182, 183b,
        217, 282
    'negotiation burden' problem
        142
    negotiation leadership 118–19
    non-governmental organizations
        and 130b, 132
    prior informed consent 21, 24,
        183b, 342
    regime complex 241
    sovereignty rights over 180–2,
        181f, 183b, 210
    traditional knowledge 38, 130b,
        183b, 247, 342
    see also Convention on
        Biological Diversity
Geneva Conventions 310
geoengineering 43, 44b, 67, 306,
        309b
Georgescu-Roegen, Nicholas 79
Georgia 114, 115f
geostationary orbit 165
Germany 76, 83f, 104, 115f, 140b,
        203, 267f, 281b, 345b
Gibbs, Lois 64b
Global 2000 report 73
Global Climate Coalition 135b, 140
Global Compact 147b, 361g
Global Environment Facility 152,
        209, 212b, 234, 235, 237, 238b,
        250, 276b
Global Industry Coalition 144b
Global Ministerial Environment
        Forum 239
Global Pact for the Environment 60
Global Reporting Initiative
        147b, 239

global warming 5t, 108b
  1.5°C threshold 46b
  2°C threshold 42
  see also climate change
Global Witness 130
GMOs see genetically modified
  organisms (GMOs)
golden rice 144b
Gorbachev, Mikhail 295
Gore, Al 46b, 295
governance 361g
  polycentric 14, 152–3, 170
  privatization of 277
  reform of global environmental
    247–52
  regional 251
  transnational 145–56, 146f, 148f,
    149b, 151b
governmentality 280–4
Great Pacific Garbage Patch 178b
Greece 115f, 267f
Green Belt Movement
  64b, 130b, 295
Green Climate Fund 212b, 268
green consumerism 324–5
green economy 139, 200b,
  218, 361g
greenhouse gas emissions
  5t, 361g
  aviation industry 251b, 253b
  businesses and 135b
  carbon dioxide removal tech-
    nologies 44b
  carbon taxes 105b, 266b
  cultural cognition hypothesis
    33b
  developing countries 41, 82–5,
    83f, 217
  embodied carbon 323
  emissions trading systems 105b,
    135b, 149b, 168–9, 220, 266b,
    268, 268t, 276, 279, 333–5
  global trends 10f
  hydrochlorofluorocarbons 246
  intergenerational equity 80–2
  intragenerational equity
    82–5, 83f
  measuring policy effective-
    ness 260, 261
  nationally determined contribu-
    tions 60, 108b, 260
  shipping 253b, 322–3
  trade and 323, 324f
  transnational governance 145
  see also climate change
Greenhouse Gas Protocol 145
Green, Jessica 235–6
green parties 104
green patent databases 281b

Greenpeace 9, 67b, 126, 129–30,
  131, 132, 136, 137, 138, 139,
  140, 141, 147b
green technology 280, 281b
greenwashing 233, 361g
Grenada 115f
Grossman, Gene 77
Group of 7 (G7) 140b, 178b, 250
Group of 20 (G20) 250
Group of 77 (G77) 113, 115f, 116b,
  120, 201, 204, 237
growth see economic growth;
  population growth
guano 322
Guatemala 115f, 208b, 218, 219b
Guinea 115f
Guinea-Bissau 115f
Gulf War 308, 309b
Guyana 115f, 184

H
Haas, Ernst 38
Haas, Peter 11, 34, 36b,
  249, 263
Haiti 115f
Hardin, Garrett 10, 72–3, 164
Hayek, Friedrich von 29
hazardous chemicals
  Agent Orange 308, 359g
  chemical disasters 64b, 147b,
    205, 308
  prior informed consent
    12–13f, 23
  Rotterdam Convention
    12–13f, 23, 231t
  Stockholm Convention 12–13f,
    23, 231t, 284, 318–19
hazardous wastes 329–32,
  330b, 360g
  Bamako Convention 12–13f, 20,
    231t, 330b
  Basel Convention 12–13f, 20,
    47, 138, 185, 231t, 271, 320b,
    331, 336
  businesses and 138
  electronic waste 332
  Love Canal disaster, US 64b
  nuclear waste 43, 311,
    332, 345b
  plastic pollution 10f, 139, 140b,
    178b, 332
  plastic recycling waste 320b
  prior informed consent 20, 268t,
    274, 331
heads of state summits 250–1
Heath, Edward 205b
hegemony 133–4
Helm, Carsten 263

Helsinki Convention on the Protection of the Marine Environment of the Baltic Sea 273
Helsinki Protocol on the Reduction of
  Sulphur Emissions 12–13f, 31f
heritage of humankind see common heritage of humankind
High-Level Political Forum on Sustainable Development 249
historical cost accounting 80–2
historical institutionalism
  236, 238–9
Hodges, Timothy 110–11
Homer-Dixon model
  299–301, 299f
Homer-Dixon, Thomas
  299–300
Honduras 115f
Hubbert, Marion King 74, 75f
human intervention, causal effect
  of 66–71
human rights 130, 306–7
Human Rights Watch 130
human security 305–7
Hungary 115f, 267f
Hussein, Saddam 308, 309b
hybrid cars 58b
hydrochlorofluorocarbons
  133, 246

I
Iceland 67b, 115f, 166b, 232,
  267f, 299
ideological debates 54–86
  anthropocentrism versus
    biocentrism 61–6
  conservationism versus preserva-
    tionism 66–71, 67b
  intragenerational equity versus
    intergenerational equity
    80–5, 83f
  neo-Malthusianism versus
    cornucopian theory 71–9, 74f,
    75f, 78f
  universalism versus communi-
    tarianism 56–61, 57f
impact assessments see environmental impact assessments
implementation 361g
implementation instruments
  265–8, 268t, 273
incentive instruments 265, 266b,
  268t, 279
  see also environmental taxes;
    market mechanisms
inclusive minilateralism
  diplomacy 251
independent variables 361g

India 116*b*, 216
  Bhopal disaster 147*b*, 205
  Chipko movement 64*b*, 197*b*
  Clean Development Mechanism
    projects 334
  cobra effect 283*b*
  cooperation over water 302*b*
  genetically modified organisms
    (GMOs) 197*b*
  greenhouse gas emissions 82,
    83*f*
  Montreal Protocol and 208–9
  preferential trade agree-
    ments 347
  trade disputes 337*t*, 339*b*
  trade openness 100
Indigenous and Tribal Peoples
    Convention 130*b*, 307
indigenous communities 282
  Amazon rainforest 184, 307
  counter-summits 142–3
  genetic resources and 38, 130*b*,
    183*b*, 247, 282
  human rights 307
  Inuit 58, 185
  polar bear hunting 58
  representation in international
    politics 128, 130*b*
  traditional knowledge 38, 130*b*,
    138, 183*b*, 247, 342, 363*g*
  whaling 59, 67*b*
Indigenous Peoples' International
    Centre for Policy Research and
    Education 130*b*
individual transferable quota
    systems 166*b*
Indonesia 102, 115*f*, 208*b*, 212*b*,
    219*b*, 245, 340*f*
Industrial Biotechnology Associa-
    tion 136
industry *see* businesses
Indus Waters Treaty 302*b*
inequalities
  intergenerational equity 80–2
  intragenerational equity 82–5,
    83*f*, 175
  policy instruments as inequalities
    providers 280–4
  in scientific research 39–42,
    40*f*, 41*f*
  structural 196–8, 197*b*, 197*f*
  see also environmental justice
informal pressure strategies of
    non-state actors 141*t*, 142
information, access to
  Aarhus Convention 12–13*f*, 22,
    128, 231*t*, 277
  Escazú Agreement
    12–13*f*, 128, 277

instrument diffusion 275*t*, 279
  see also knowledge
innovation 75–9
institutional fragmentation 244
institutional interactions 241–7,
    243*f*, 244*t*, 250
institutionalism
  historical 236, 238–9
  liberal 11, 95
  sociological 236–7, 239–40
institutions 361*g*
  see also international institutions
instrument diffusion 274–9, 275*t*,
    362*g*
instruments *see* policy instruments
intellectual leadership 119, 120
intellectual property rights 41*f*,
    134, 138, 180, 181*f*, 183*b*,
    197*b*, 247, 281*b*
intended nationally determined
    contributions 108*b*
intergenerational equity 80–2
  see also common heritage of
    humankind
intergovernmental organisations
  nexus approach 250
  orchestration 250
intergovernmental organiza-
    tions 229, 230, 361*g*
  autonomy of 235–40
  greening of 233–5, 234*b*
  historical institutionalist
    perspective 236, 238–9
  proliferation of 231–3,
    231*t*, 232*t*
  rational choice perspective
    236, 237
  reform of global environmental
    governance 247–52
  sociological institutionalist
    perspective 236–7, 239–40
Intergovernmental Panel on
    Climate Change (IPCC) 40*f*,
    42, 45, 46*b*, 135*b*, 217, 295,
    306, 361*g*
Intergovernmental Science-Policy
    Platform on Biodiversity and
    Ecosystem Services 47, 361*g*
intermediate variables 361*g*
internally displaced persons 296*b*
International Atomic Energy
    Agency 231*t*
International Chamber of Com-
    merce 129, 135*b*, 147*b*
International Civil Aviation
    Organization 251*b*, 253*b*
International Climate Change
    Partnership 135*b*, 149*b*
International Conference on

Financing for Development,
    Monterrey 212
International Convention for the
    Prevention of Pollution from
    Ships (MARPOL) 18, 98–9,
    178*b*, 231*t*, 233, 267–8
International Convention for the
    Regulation of Whaling
    18, 67*b*
International Convention on Civil
    Liability for Oil Pollution Dam-
    age 272
International Convention on the
    Removal of Wrecks 12–13*f*
International Council for Local En-
    vironmental Initiatives 148–9
International Court of Justice
    185, 272
International Criminal Court
    65, 66, 310
International Emissions Trading
    Association 135*b*
international environmental agree-
    ments 12–13*f*, 18–24, 231*t*,
    232, 361*g*
  distribution by development
    level 199, 199*f*
  measuring effectiveness
    of 260–5, 262*f*
  numbers ratified 97*f*
  ratification and democracy
    101, 101*f*
  ratification and environmental
    performance 261–2, 262*f*
  ratification and wealth 99, 99*f*
  see also summit diplomacy
International Indigenous
    Peoples Forum on Climate
    Change 130*b*
International Institute for Environ-
    ment and Development 143
International Institute for Sustain-
    able Development 107, 132
international institutions 229–53
  autonomy of 235–40, 238*b*, 240*b*
  greening of 233–5, 234*b*
  historical institutionalist
    perspective 236, 238–9
  interactions between 241–7,
    243*f*, 244*t*, 250
  nexus approach 250
  orchestration 250
  proliferation of 231–3, 231*t*, 232*t*
  rational choice perspective
    236, 237
  reform of global environmental
    governance 247–52
  regime complexes 11, 241–5,
    243*f*, 246–7

sociological institutionalist perspective 236-7, 239-40
International Labour Organization 130b
International Maritime Organization 178b, 231t, 233, 253b
International Monetary Fund 204, 284
international negotiations 107-20
  bottom-up approach 108b, 117b
  contact and working groups 110, 360g
  game theory and 107-8, 109
  interstate coalitions 113-14, 115f, 116b, 118-19
  leadership 117-20, 117b, 251b
  national delegations 104-7, 105b, 110, 111f
  negotiation chairs 110-13
  voluntary approach 108b, 117b
  see also climate change negotiations; ozone negotiations; summit diplomacy
International Organization for Migration 296b
international regimes 229-30, 241b, 363g
  measuring effectiveness of 263-4
  norms and rules 244t, 246
  regime complexes 11, 241-5, 243f, 246-7
International Regimes Database Project 263, 264
international relations theories 11, 14
international seabed 174-5, 175f
International Seabed Authority 174
International Standardization Organization 282
International Treaty on Plant Genetic Resources for Food and Agriculture 12-13f, 62, 180, 231t
International Tribunal of the Law of the Sea 272
International Tropical Timber Agreements 12-13f, 231t
International Tropical Timber Organization 114, 139, 143, 230, 231t, 246
International Union for Conservation of Nature (IUCN) 70, 102, 103f, 139, 206, 231t, 232, 239, 250
International Whaling Commission 59, 67b, 100, 140, 232, 271, 279

interstate coalitions 113-14, 115f, 116b, 118-19
intragenerational equity 82-5, 83f, 175
Inuit communities 58, 185
invasive species 38-9, 323
investment law 343, 344t, 345b
IPCC see Intergovernmental Panel on Climate Change (IPCC)
Iran 115f, 340f
Iraq 115f, 308, 309b, 311, 340f
Ireland 115f, 267f
ISO 14001 standard 102-4, 103f
Israel 115f, 267f
Italy 115f, 140b, 267f
IUCN see International Union for Conservation of Nature (IUCN)
ivory trade 71, 282, 283b, 328

J
Jamaica 115f
Japan 115f
  environmental taxes 267f
  human security concept 306
  interstate coalitions 113, 114
  ivory trade 71
  ministry of the environment 105
  North Pacific Fur Seal Convention 62
  patents 281b
  trade disputes 337t, 339-40
  whaling 67b, 100
Jiang Zemin 295
Johannesburg Summit on Sustainable Development 12-13f, 60, 145, 147b, 193, 200b, 211-12, 214-15, 215f
Jordan 115f
JUSCANZ 114
justice see environmental justice

K
Kazakhstan 115f, 219b, 340f
Keck, Margaret 130b
Kent, Jennifer 296b
Kenya 64b, 115f, 130b, 204, 237, 295, 296b
Keohane, Robert 229, 263
Kessler syndrome 173b
Kiribati 115f
knowledge
  knowledge-based politics 37-8
  political foundations of 38-42, 40f, 41f
  traditional 38, 130b, 138, 183b, 247, 342, 363g

types of scientific 34
see also information, access to; science and politics
Koester, Veit 113
Koh, Tommy 112
Korea 114, 115f, 267f
Kosovo War 308
Krueger, Alan 77
Kuwait 115f, 309b, 340f
Kuznets curve, environmental 77-9, 78f, 361g
Kuznets, Simon 77
Kyoto Protocol 12-13f, 22, 31f, 32
  Clean Development Mechanism 22, 110, 113, 114, 334
  common but differentiated responsibility 84
  contact and working groups 110
  ecological vulnerability and 99
  emerging countries and 217
  emissions trading systems 333-4
  implementation instruments 268
  institutional interactions 246
  legally binding commitments 108b
  negotiation chairs 112
  negotiation leadership 118, 119
  non-state actor involvement 135b, 138, 140, 142
  obstructionist behaviour 120
  prisoner's dilemma logic and 108
  state political regime and 104

L
labelling 136, 151b, 268t, 274, 275t, 278, 325, 360g
Land Degradation Neutrality Fund 117b
Lang, Winfried 112
Laos 115f
Latin America
  debt crisis 204
  Escazú Agreement 12-13f, 128, 277
  interstate coalitions 113, 114
  preferential trade agreements 342
Latin American Initiatives Group (GRILA) 113, 114
Latvia 115f, 267f
Law of the Sea see United Nations Convention on the Law of the Sea
League of Nations 232

least-developed countries 115f, 361g
Lebanon 115f, 342
Lesotho 115f
Levy, Marc 263
liberal ecofeminism 64b
liberal environmentalism 220-1, 361g
liberal institutionalism 11, 95
liberalism 55
Liberia 115f, 303
Libya 115f, 340f
Liechtenstein 114, 115f
Limits to Growth, The 8b, 28, 73
Litfin, Karen T. 66
Lithuania 115f, 267f
litigation 142, 143
Living Planet Report 126-7
Lomborg, Bjørn 39, 82
London Convention Relative to the Preservation of Fauna and Flora in their Natural State 62
Long Range Transport Project 42b
Love Canal disaster, US 64b
Lovelock, James 8b, 63
Luxembourg 115f, 267f

M
Maathai, Wangari 64b, 130b, 295
Madagascar 115f, 296b
Madrid Protocol on Environmental Protection to the Antarctic Treaty 12-13f, 171, 265
major groups 128, 129, 131, 361g
Malawi 115f
Malaysia 115f, 120, 142, 337t, 339b
Maldives 100, 115f
Mali 115f, 298
Malta 115f
Malthusianism 297-8, 362g
    see also neo-Malthusianism
Malthus, Thomas 71-2
Man and the Biosphere Programme 8b, 9
Mandela, Nelson 205b
Marine Mammal Protection Act, US 120, 279
marine pollution 18, 98-9, 134, 178b, 231t, 233, 267-8, 272
marine protected areas 166b, 208b, 245
marine resources 178b
    Convention on the Conservation of Antarctic Marine Living Resources (CCAMLR) 12-13f, 19, 69, 171, 231t
    exclusive economic zones 166b, 175f, 176-8

sovereignty rights over 176-8, 178b
    see also fisheries and overfishing
Marine Stewardship Council 151b, 275t
maritime transport see shipping
market mechanisms 70, 149b, 214, 265, 266b, 268t, 362g
    emissions trading systems 105b, 135b, 149b, 168-9, 220, 266b, 268, 268t, 276, 279, 333-5
    environmental taxes 105b, 168, 169t, 265, 266b, 267f, 268t, 275t, 279
    genetic resources 182
    instrument diffusion 276, 279
    payments for ecosystem services 220, 276b, 362g
    tragedy of the commons and 168-9, 169t
MARPOL Convention 18, 98-9, 178b, 231t, 233, 267-8
Marrakesh Agreement 211
Marshall Islands 115f
material resources of non-state actors 137
Mauritania 115f
Mauritius 115f
Meadows, Dennis 28, 73
Meadows, Donella 28, 73
Mediterranean Sea 12-13f, 32, 35, 138, 231t, 233
megadiverse countries 118-19, 181f
Merchant, Carolyn 64b
mercury pollution 12-13f, 24, 178b, 231t, 273
Merkel, Angela 217
metabolic rift 321-2, 323, 362g
Mexico 114, 115f, 267f, 334, 335, 337t, 340f, 346
Miami Group 113
Micronesia 115f
microplastics 140b, 178b
migration, environmental 296, 296b, 300
migratory species 12-13f, 69, 231t, 238-9, 250
Millennium Development Goals 212, 218, 219b
Millennium Summit 212
Miller, Andrew R. 67b
Minamata Convention on Mercury 12-13f, 24, 178b, 231t, 273
minilateralism 251, 346b
ministries of the environment 104-7, 105b
Mitchell, Ronald 264

mitigation see climate change mitigation and adaptation
models see computer modelling
Moldova 115f, 342
Momentum for Change initiative 240b
Monaco 114, 115f
Mongolia 115f
Monsanto 144b
Monterrey Conference 212
Montreal Protocol on Substances that Deplete the Ozone Layer 12-13f, 20, 31f, 36b, 98, 110, 112, 185, 208-9, 212b, 239, 246, 262, 268, 272, 333
Morales, Evo 220
Morocco 115f
most favoured nation principle 336
Mozambique 115f
Muir, John 67
Multilateral Fund 209, 212b, 268, 335
Myanmar 115f
Myers, Norman 296b

N
Nagoya Protocol on Access to Genetic Resources and the Fair and Equitable Sharing of Benefits Arising from their Utilization 12-13f, 24, 66, 110-11, 130b, 139, 182, 183b, 217, 282
Najam, Adil 117b
Namibia 71, 115f, 283b
naming and shaming 136, 142, 271, 273
nanotechnology 29b
Narain, Sunita 83
National Aeronautics and Space Administration (NASA) 8b
national delegations 104-7, 105b, 110, 111f
national environmental policy plans 274, 275t
nationally determined contributions 60, 108b, 260-5
national parks 62, 69, 131
national treatment principle 336
NATO see North Atlantic Treaty Organization (NATO)
Natura 2000 protected areas 273
natural disasters 296b, 301, 304, 305, 306f
natural resources
    armed conflict and 297-305, 299f, 302b, 302f
    Homer-Dixon model 299-301, 299f

market mechanisms and
168-9, 169t
metabolic rift 322
myth of water wars 301,
302b, 302f
paradox of plenty 301-3, 304f
polycentric governance 170
private property rights and
166b, 168-9
regulations and 166-7,
166b, 169t
resource curse 301-3, 304f
subsidies and 167-8, 169t
taxation and 168, 169t
see also common heritage of
humankind; fisheries and
overfishing; freshwater;
genetic resources; marine
resources; sovereignty over
natural resources; tragedy of
the commons
Nature Conservancy 137, 208b
nature's rights proposal 65-6, 220
Nauru 115f, 219b, 298b
Nechisar National Park,
Ethiopia 70
neem 183b
negotiating coalitions 113-14,
115f, 116b, 118-19
'negotiation burden' problem 142
negotiation chairs 110-13
negotiation leadership 117-20,
117b, 251b
negotiations see climate change
negotiations; international negotiations; ozone negotiations;
summit diplomacy
neo-liberalism 204
neo-Malthusianism 71-5, 74f, 75f
Nepal 115f
Netherlands 115f, 267f
New Development Bank 235
Newell, Peter 276
New International Economic
Order 201
New Zealand 66, 114, 115f, 166b,
267f
nexus approach 250
Nicaragua 115f
Niger 115f
Nigeria 115f, 134, 330b
Nobel Peace Prize 46, 130, 295-6
non-discrimination principle 362g
non-governmental organizations
(NGOs) 9, 126-7, 128, 129-32,
362g
businesses and 136, 147b
conservationism 70, 131
counter-summits 142-3

defining 129-30
discursive resources 138-9
environmental security concept
and 295
indigenous representation 130b
influence during policy
phases 139-40
liberal environmentalism 139
litigation 142, 143
material resources 137
observer status 127, 127f, 141-2,
362g
organizational resources 137-8
plastic pollution and 140b
preservationism 67, 67b, 131
strategies of influence 141,
142-3
transnational initiatives 151b
whaling moratorium and
35, 67b
non-regression 362g
non-state actors 126-9, 200b, 362g
advice strategy 141-2, 141t,
144b
corporate social responsibility
146, 147b, 360g
counter-summits 142-3
discursive resources 138-9
indigenous organizations
128, 130b
influence during policy
phases 139-40
informal pressure strate-
gies 141t, 142
litigation 142, 143
major groups 128, 129, 131,
361g
material resources 137
'negotiation burden' problem 142
numbers of 127, 127f
observer status 127, 127f, 141-2,
362g
organizational resources 137-8
policy instruments 273, 278
political regime type and 101-4,
103f
polycentric governance 152-3
promotion strategy 141t, 143,
144b
public pressure strategies 141t,
142-3
strategies of influence 141-3,
141t, 144b
transnational governance
145-56, 146f, 148f, 149b, 151b
see also businesses; non-
governmental organizations
(NGOs)
Nordhaus, William 346b

norms see regime norms and rules;
social norms
North American Free Trade
Agreement 211, 343, 344t
North Atlantic Marine Mammal
Commission 232
North Atlantic Treaty Organization
(NATO) 295, 299, 308, 311
North Pacific Fur Seal
Convention 62
Northwest Atlantic Fisheries
Organization 166b
Norway
environmental aid 212b
environmental taxes 266b,
267f
fisheries 245
human security concept 306
interstate coalitions 113, 114
natural resources 303
trade disputes 337t
whaling 67b, 232
nuclear accidents 12-13f, 136,
204-5, 231t, 345b
nuclear energy 43, 136, 345b
nuclear waste 43, 311, 332, 345b
nuclear weapons 12-13f, 174, 185,
308-10
nuclear winter 308

O
Obama, Barack 217, 295
observer status 127, 127f,
141-2, 362g
Ocean Plastics Charter 140b, 178b
oceans
acidification 44b
Convention on the Law of the
Sea 12-13f, 107, 110, 112,
166b, 174-5, 176-8
exclusive economic zones 166b,
175f, 176-8
geoengineering 44b, 67
international seabed
174-5, 175f
marine protected areas 166b,
208b, 245
plastic pollution 140b,
178b, 332
sea level rise 82, 116b, 295, 296b
see also fisheries and overfishing;
shipping
OECD see Organisation for
Economic Co-operation and
Development (OECD)
oil industry 74, 75f, 134, 138
oil spills 18, 98-9, 134, 267-8,
272, 308

Oman 115*f*
OPEC *see* Organization of the Petroleum Exporting Countries (OPEC)
orbital space debris 173*b*
orbit, geostationary 165
orchestration 250
Organisation for Economic Co-operation and Development (OECD) 42*b*, 147*b*, 232, 271, 274
organizational resources of non-state actors 137–8
Organization of African Unity 330*b*
Organization of the Petroleum Exporting Countries (OPEC) 115*f*, 116*b*, 120
Oslo Protocol on Further Reduction of Sulphur Emissions 31*f*
Oslo-Seattle Project 263–4
OSPAR Convention 233
Ostrom, Elinor 152, 169–70
Our Common Future see Brundtland Commission and Report
outer space 8*b*, 12–13*f*, 172–4
geostationary orbit 165
orbital space debris 173*b*
overfishing *see* fisheries and overfishing
Oxfam International 130
ozone layer 362*g*
ozone layer depletion 5*t*, 36*b*, 205
chlorofluorocarbons (CFCs) 5*t*, 10*f*, 36*b*, 98, 133, 335
global trends 10*f*
numbers of scientific publications 31*f*
ozone negotiations
developing countries and 208–9
epistemic communities 35, 36*b*
negotiation chairs 110, 112
non-state actor involvement 133
ozone regime
enquiry procedure 272
institutional interactions 246
Montreal Protocol on Substances that Deplete the Ozone Layer 12–13*f*, 20, 31*f*, 36*b*, 98, 110, 112, 185, 208–9, 212*b*, 239, 246, 262, 268, 272, 333
Multilateral Fund 209, 212*b*, 268, 335
trade and 185, 333, 335
Vienna Convention for the Protection of the Ozone Layer 12–13*f*, 19, 31*f*, 32, 36*b*, 110, 133, 231*t*, 235

P

Pakistan 115*f*, 302*b*, 337*t*, 339*b*
palm oil production 102, 245
Panama 115*f*
Pan European Forest Certification Council 151*b*
Papua New Guinea 115*f*, 219*b*
paradox of plenty 301–3, 304*f*
Paraguay 115*f*
Paris Agreement on climate change 12–13*f*, 24, 42, 46*b*
carbon footprint of 200*b*
common but differentiated responsibility 84
contact and working groups 110
ecological vulnerability and 99
emissions trading systems 334
Green Climate Fund 212*b*, 268
intragenerational versus inter-generational equity 82
measuring effectiveness 260, 261
nationally determined contributions 60, 108*b*, 260
non-state actor involvement 139, 143
polycentric governance 153
prisoner's dilemma logic and 108
reporting mechanism 271
transparency framework 277
United States withdrawal from 108, 148, 149*b*
Vatican and 60*b*
voluntary approach 108*b*
Partial Nuclear Test Ban Treaty 30–2, 308, 310
participation *see* public participation
parties 362*g*
see also Conferences of the Parties
Partnership for the Development of Environmental Laws and Institutions in Africa 239
patent pledges 281*b*
patents 41*f*, 180, 181*f*, 183*b*, 197*b*, 281*b*
payments for ecosystem services 220, 276*b*, 362*g*
peace parks 301
peer review technique 271
Pérez de Cuéllar, Javier 205*b*
Permanent Court of Arbitration 272
persistent organic pollutants 23, 362*g*
Stockholm Convention 12–13*f*, 23, 231*t*, 284, 318–19

persuasion instruments 265–7, 268*t*, 271, 273
Peru 115*f*, 322, 342
pesticides
Bhopal disaster, India 147*b*, 205
Rotterdam Convention 12–13*f*, 23, 231*t*
Stockholm Convention 12–13*f*, 23, 231*t*, 284, 318–19
Philippines 115*f*
Pinchot, Gifford 67
plastic pollution 10*f*, 139, 140*b*, 178*b*, 332
plastic recycling waste 320*b*
Poland 115*f*, 266*b*, 267*f*
polar bears 58
policy diffusion 274–9, 275*t*, 362*g*
policy effectiveness 260–5, 262*f*, 362*g*
policy instruments 259–84, 362*g*
arbitration mechanisms 272
behavioural outcomes of 260–2
capacity building 268*t*, 273, 279, 346, 359*g*
commodifying instruments 276, 276*b*
compliance instruments 268, 270–2, 270*t*
diffusion of 274–9, 275*t*, 362*g*
ecological modernization and 280
enforcement instruments 268, 270–1, 270*t*, 272–3
enquiry procedure 272
governmentality and 280–4
impacts of 260–2
implementation instruments 265–8, 268*t*, 273
incentive instruments 265, 266*b*, 268*t*, 279
as inequalities providers 280–4
measuring effectiveness of 260–5, 262*f*
non-state actors and 273, 278
persuasion instruments 265–7, 268*t*, 271, 273
political effects of 279–84, 281*b*, 283*b*
public consultation instruments 277
regulatory instruments 265, 266*b*, 268*t*, 271, 279
reporting mechanisms 268*t*, 271–2
sanctions 100, 272, 342
service-oriented instruments 267–8, 268*t*
as solutions providers 280, 281*b*

transparency-enhancing mechanisms 277–8
unintended consequences 280–4, 283*b*
verification instruments 268–73, 270*t*, 282
voluntary approaches 108*b*, 117*b*, 273, 276, 278
political regime, state preferences and 100–4, 101*f*, 103*f*
polluter pays principle 80–1, 168, 200*b*, 220, 362*g*
pollution
    displacement of 319
    freshwater 5*t*, 327, 345*b*
    marine 18, 98–9, 134, 178*b*, 231*t*, 233, 267–8, 272
    mercury 12–13*f*, 24, 178*b*, 231*t*, 273
    plastic 10*f*, 139, 140*b*, 178*b*, 332
    pollution havens and pollution halos 326–7
    see also transboundary air pollution
polycentric governance 14, 152–3, 170
population growth 71–3, 74, 75, 76, 76*b*, 210, 297–8, 298*b*, 299
Portugal 115*f*, 267*f*
post-environmentalism 221
power to destroy 119
Prakash, Aseem 327
precautionary principle 30, 31*b*, 45, 147*b*, 200*b*, 210, 362*g*
preferential trade agreements 362*g*
    environmental provisions in 341–2, 341*f*, 343, 346–7, 346*b*, 347*b*
preservationism 66–71, 67*b*, 131, 362*g*
    see also conservationism
preventive action principle 31*b*, 177*b*, 185, 362*g*
prior informed consent 362*g*
    genetically modified organisms 268*t*, 274
    genetic resources 21, 24, 183*b*, 342
    hazardous chemicals 12–13*f*, 23
    hazardous wastes 20, 268*t*, 274, 331
    instrument diffusion 274, 275*t*
prisoner's dilemma 108, 362*g*
privatization
    of governance 277
    of water supply services 284
promotion strategy of non-state actors 141*t*, 143, 144*b*
property rights

tragedy of the commons and 166*b*, 168–9
    see also intellectual property rights
proportional representation 104
protected areas 175, 273
    marine 166*b*, 208*b*, 245
protocols 362*g*
    see also framework conventions
Prototype Carbon Fund 145
provisioning ecosystem services 276*b*
public awareness 4, 8*b*, 9, 33*b*, 73, 126, 263, 325
public consultation instruments 277
public goods 165*t*, 276*b*, 363*g*
    see also common goods
public participation
    Aarhus Convention 12–13*f*, 22, 128, 231*t*, 277
    Escazú Agreement 12–13*f*, 128, 277
public pressure strategies of non-state actors 141*t*, 142–3
Public Research and Regulation Initiative 144*b*

Q

Qatar 115*f*, 340*f*

R

race to the bottom 278, 326, 363*g*
race to the top 278
radical ecofeminism 64*b*
radioactive waste 43, 311, 332, 345*b*
Ramsar Convention on Wetlands of International Importance 12–13*f*, 62, 69, 231*t*, 232, 246, 250, 268
ratification 363*g*
    democracy and 101, 101*f*
    environmental performance and 261–2, 262*f*
    wealth and 99, 99*f*
rational choice theory 96–100, 120–1, 236, 237
rationality 279
Raustiala, Kal 11, 241
Reagan, Ronald 36*b*, 73, 204
realism 11, 95
recycling waste trade 320*b*
Reducing Emissions from Deforestation and Forest Degradation Mechanism 113, 130*b*
refugees, environmental 296*b*, 300

regime complexes 11, 241–5, 243*f*, 246–7
regime norms and rules 244*t*, 246
regimes 363*g*
    see also international regimes
Regional Acidification Information System 42*b*
regional development banks 278, 284
regional governance 251
regulation ecosystem services 276*b*
regulatory instruments 265, 266*b*, 268*t*, 271, 279
    tragedy of the commons and 166–7, 166*b*, 169*t*
renewable energy
    environmental Kuznets curve and 77, 78–9, 78*f*
    feed-in tariffs 339–40
    solar photovoltaic industry 325, 326*f*
    subsidies 339–40
reporting mechanisms 268*t*, 271–2
Republic of the Congo 115*f*
Research Foundation for Science, Technology and Ecology 197*b*
resource curse 301–3, 304*f*
resources *see* genetic resources; marine resources; natural resources
Responsible Care code of conduct 147*b*
Ricardo, David 321
rights
    animal rights 66
    human rights 130, 306–7
    intellectual property rights 41*f*, 134, 138, 180, 181*f*, 183*b*, 197*b*, 247, 281*b*
    nature's rights proposal 65–6, 220
    property rights and tragedy of the commons 166*b*, 168–9
    right to a healthy environment 307
Rio+20 Summit on Sustainable Development 12–13*f*, 66, 79, 128, 142–3, 193, 200*b*, 215–20, 215*f*
Rio Summit on the Environment and Development 9, 60, 105, 193, 200*b*, 207–11, 215*f*, 363*g*
    Agenda 21 12–13*f*, 147*b*, 209, 210, 267, 276, 281*b*, 359*g*
    desertification negotiations 116*b*, 117*b*, 209, 211
    interstate coalitions 116*b*
    non-state actors 128, 132–3, 139, 147*b*

Rio Summit on the Environment and Development (*Continued*)
  outcomes 209–11
    Rio Declaration 12–13*f*, 31*b*, 65, 185, 209, 210–11, 276
rivalrous goods 165, 165*t*, 363*g*
Robinson, Mary 205*b*
Romania 115*f*
Rome Statute of the International Criminal Court 65, 66, 310
Rotterdam Convention on the Prior Informed Consent Procedure for Certain Hazardous Chemicals and Pesticides in International Trade 12–13*f*, 23, 231*t*
Royal Society for the Protection of Birds 67
Rural Advancement Foundation 139
Russia 62, 83*f*, 118, 340*f*
  see also Soviet Union
Rwanda 115*f*, 298

S
St. Kitts and Nevis 115*f*
St. Lucia 115*f*
St. Vincent and the Grenadines 115*f*
sanctions 100, 272, 342
São Tomé and Príncipe 115*f*
Sarkozy, Nicolas 309*b*
satellites 165
Saudi Arabia 115*f*, 120, 340*f*
Schmidheiny, Stephen 132–3
science and politics 27–48
  boundary organizations 45–8, 359*g*
  communications between 43–5
  co-production of 37–43
  cultural cognition hypothesis 33*b*
  epistemic communities 11, 34–7, 36*b*, 361*g*
  ethical questions 43–5
  geoengineering 43, 44*b*, 67, 306, 309*b*
  inequalities in scientific research 39–42, 40*f*, 41*f*
  knowledge-based politics 37–8
  nanotechnology 29*b*
  political foundations of knowledge 38–42, 40*f*, 41*f*
  precautionary principle 30, 31*b*, 45, 147*b*, 200*b*, 210, 362*g*
  scientific uncertainty 28–34, 31*f*

of transboundary air pollution 42*b*
sclerotic multilateralism 251
seabed, international 174–5, 175*f*
sea level rise 82, 116*b*, 295, 296*b*
seas *see* oceans
Sea Shepherd Conservation Society 67*b*, 132, 309*b*
sea turtles 138, 336, 337*t*, 339*b*
secretariats 236–7, 240*b*, 250
securitization 294–5, 363*g*
security *see* environmental security
Security Council 295, 363*g*
Senegal 83*f*, 115*f*
service-oriented instruments 267–8, 268*t*
Sexton, Alison 58*b*
Sexton, Steven 58*b*
Seychelles 115*f*, 208*b*
shaming *see* naming and shaming
sharks 328–9
shipping
  greenhouse gas emissions 253*b*, 322–3
  prevention of pollution from 18, 98–9, 178*b*, 231*t*, 233, 267–8
Shiva, Vandana 180, 183*b*, 197*b*
Shrimp/Turtle dispute 336, 337*t*, 339*b*
Shue, Henry 81
Sierra Club 67, 131
Sierra Leone 115*f*, 298, 303
Sikkink, Kathryn 130*b*
Simon, Julian 75–6, 76*b*
Singapore 115*f*
Slovakia 115*f*, 267*f*
Slovenia 115*f*, 267*f*
smart regulations 265
social ecofeminism 64*b*
socialist ecofeminism 64*b*
social norms 55, 170, 229, 363*g*
  intragenerational equity versus intergenerational equity 80–5, 83*f*
societal collapse 298, 298*b*
sociological institutionalism 236–7, 239–40
solar geoengineering 43, 44*b*, 67, 306, 309*b*
solar photovoltaic industry 325, 326*f*
Solomon Islands 115*f*, 298*b*
Somalia 115*f*, 296*b*, 298
South Africa 83*f*
  see also Johannesburg Summit on Sustainable Development
South Korea 114, 115*f*, 267*f*
South Sudan 115*f*
sovereignty 363*g*

sovereignty over natural resources 12–13*f*, 163–4, 170, 176–87, 201, 210
  environmental cooperation and 184–7, 186*t*
  genetic resources 180–2, 181*f*, 183*b*, 210
  marine resources 176–8, 178*b*
  trade-offs 186–7, 186*t*
  Trail Smelter dispute 176, 177*b*
Soviet Union 42*b*, 203
  see also Russia
space debris, orbital 173*b*
space exploration 8*b*
  see also outer space
Spain 115*f*, 166*b*, 176, 267*f*, 299
speciesism 66
Sprinz, Detlef 98, 98*t*, 263
Sprout, Harold 10
Sprout, Margaret 10
Sri Lanka 115*f*, 303
stakeholders 363*g*
state behaviour types 98, 98*t*
state preferences 95–121
  abatement costs and 96–101, 98*t*, 99*f*
  challenges of reconciling 107–9, 108*b*
  contact and working groups and 110
  domestic sources of 96–107, 98*t*, 99*f*
  ecological vulnerability and 96–101, 98*t*, 99*f*
  international sources of 107–20
  interstate coalitions and 113–14, 115*f*, 116*b*, 118–19
  negotiation chairs and 110–13
  negotiation leadership and 117–20, 117*b*
  political regime and 100–4, 101*f*, 103*f*
  representation of 104–7, 105*b*, 110, 111*f*
Stern, Nicholas 81–2
Stern Review 81–2, 217
Stockholm Conference on the Human Environment 9, 10, 42*b*, 67*b*, 105, 193, 199–204, 200*b*, 202*b*, 215*f*
  Stockholm Declaration 12–13*f*, 60, 65, 185, 203–4, 210, 307
Stockholm Convention on Persistent Organic Pollutants 12–13*f*, 23, 231*t*, 284, 318–19
Stoermer, Eugene F. 2*b*
strategies of influence of non-state actors 141–3, 141*t*, 144*b*

stratospheric aerosol injection 44b, 306, 309b
Strong, Maurice 132-3, 201, 202b, 203, 207, 239
structural inequalities 196-8, 197b, 197f
structural leadership 118-19, 120
subsidies
  fish 341, 342
  fossil fuel 340, 340f
  renewable energy 339-40
  tragedy of the commons and 167-8, 169t
Sudan 115f, 303
summit diplomacy 200b
  heads of state summits 250-1
  Johannesburg Summit 12-13f, 60, 145, 147b, 193, 200b, 211-12, 214-15, 215f
  Rio+20 Summit 12-13f, 66, 79, 128, 142-3, 193, 200b, 215-20, 215f
  see also Rio Summit on the Environment and Development; Stockholm Conference on the Human Environment
support ecosystem services 276b
supranationality 251b
Suriname 115f
sustainability, strong 79
Sustainable Apparel Coalition 325
sustainable development 363g
  Brundtland Commission and Report 60, 85-6, 193, 204-7, 205b, 359g
  Clean Development Mechanism and 334
  Commission for Sustainable Development 114, 209, 210, 218, 240b, 249
  concept of 70, 86, 200b, 206-7
  conservationism and 70
  corporate social responsibility and 147b
  genetically modified organisms and 144b
  interstate coalitions 114
  Johannesburg Summit 12-13f, 60, 145, 147b, 193, 200b, 211-12, 214-15, 215f
  non-state actors and 128, 130, 132-3, 147b
  Rio+20 Summit 12-13f, 66, 79, 128, 142-3, 193, 200b, 215-20, 215f
  Rio Summit and 209-11
  transnational initiatives 145
Sustainable Development Goals (SDGs) 12-13f, 205b, 218, 219b, 249, 363g

Sustainable Forestry Initiative 151b, 274
Swaziland 115f
Sweden 32-4, 104, 115f, 136, 266b, 267f
  see also Stockholm Conference on the Human Environment
Switzerland 105b, 114, 115f, 267f, 306
Syria 115f, 303

T

Tajikstan 115f
Talaona Dialogue 153
Tanzania 115f, 283b, 296b
taxation, environmental 105b, 168, 169t, 265, 266b, 267f, 268t, 275t, 279
technology
  green 280, 281b
  innovation 75-9
  nanotechnology 29b
  technology transfer 207-8, 281b, 363g
  see also biotechnology industry
temperature, global 5t, 108b
  1.5°C threshold 46b
  2°C threshold 42
  'termination shock' problem 44b
terrorism
  ecological 309b
  environmental 309b
Thailand 115f, 337t, 339b
Thatcher, Margaret 204
thermoeconomics see ecological economics
Third World Network 130, 130b
Three Mile Island accident 204-5
Togo 115f
Tolba, Mustafa 112, 205b, 239
Tonga 115f
trade agreements 141, 211, 319, 327
  environmental provisions in 341-2, 341f, 343, 346-7, 346b, 347b
  investment law 343, 344t, 345b
trade and environment 101-2, 318-48
  climate change regime and 333-4
  embodied carbon 323
  environmental goods 100, 319, 324-5, 341
  environmental governance at World Trade Organization 335-41, 337t, 339b, 340f

environmental provisions in preferential trade agreements 341-2, 341f, 343, 346-7, 346b, 347b
  genetically modified organisms 332-3
  green consumerism 324-5
  investment law 343, 344t, 345b
  metabolic rift 321-2, 323
  ozone regime and 185, 333, 335
  plastic recycling waste 320b
  pollution displacement 319
  pollution havens and pollution halos 326-7
  Shrimp/Turtle dispute 336, 337t, 339b
  theoretical perspectives 320-2
  trade as driver of environmental degradation 322-4, 324f
  trade as solution to environmental problems 324-5, 326f
  trade disputes 250, 335-40, 337t, 339b, 340f
  trade openness and abatement costs 99-100
  trade-related environmental issues 328-33, 330b
  treadmill of production framework 322
  see also Convention on International Trade in Endangered Species of Wild Fauna and Flora (CITES); transboundary movement of hazardous wastes; wildlife trade and trafficking
Trade and Environment Database (TREND) 347b
trade sanctions 100, 272, 342
traditional knowledge 38, 130b, 138, 183b, 247, 342, 363g
tragedy of the commons 164-70, 187-8, 363g
  critics of 169-70
  potential solutions to 165-9, 166b, 169t
  see also common heritage of humankind; sovereignty over natural resources
Trail Smelter dispute 176, 177b
transboundary air pollution 42b
  Convention on Long-range Transboundary Air Pollution 12-13f, 19, 31f, 42b, 166, 231t, 263, 271-2, 273

transboundary air pollution
(*Continued*)
Co-operative Programme for
Monitoring and Evaluation
of the Long-range Trans-
mission of Air Pollutants in
Europe 271–2
institutional interactions 245
numbers of scientific publications 31*f*
palm oil production and
102, 245
trade and 327
Trail Smelter dispute 176, 177*b*
see also acid rain
transboundary movement of
hazardous wastes 329–32,
330*b*
Bamako Convention 12–13*f*, 20,
231*t*, 330*b*
Basel Convention 12–13*f*, 20,
47, 138, 185, 231*t*, 271, 320*b*,
331, 336
nuclear waste 332
plastic recycling waste 320*b*
transnational city networks 146–9,
148*f*, 149*b*
transnational governance 145–56,
146*f*, 148*f*, 149*b*, 151*b*
transparency-enhancing
mechanisms 277–8
treadmill of production framework 322
treaty negotiations *see* climate
change negotiations; international negotiations; ozone negotiations; summit diplomacy
Treaty on the Functioning of the
European Union 251*b*
Treaty on the Prohibition of Nuclear
Weapons 12–13*f*, 310
Trinidad and Tobago 115*f*, 340*f*
Trump, Donald 148
Tunisia 115*f*
Turbot War 166*b*, 176, 299
Turkey 267*f*
Turkmenistan 115*f*, 340*f*
Turkson, Peter 60*b*
turtle conservation 138, 336,
337*t*, 339*b*
Tutu, Desmond 205*b*
Tuvalu 98, 115*f*, 295
type II partnerships 145, 214, 215

U
Uganda 115*f*
Ukraine 115*f*, 340*f*
Umbrella Group 113–14, 115*f*

uncertainty, scientific 28–34, 31*f*
UNESCO 9, 62, 171, 230, 231*t*,
272–3
United Arab Emirates 115*f*, 340*f*
United Kingdom 62, 115*f*, 140*b*,
204, 267*f*, 295, 299, 322
United Nations 233
Global Compact 147*b*, 361*g*
Millennium Development
Goals 212, 218, 219*b*
Reducing Emissions from Defor-
estation and Forest Degrada-
tion Mechanism 113, 130*b*
Sustainable Development Goals
(SDGs) 12–13*f*, 205*b*, 218,
219*b*, 249, 363*g*
United Nations Conference on
Sustainable Development *see*
Rio+20 Summit on Sustainable
Development
United Nations Conference on the
Environment and Develop-
ment, Rio de Janeiro 9, 60,
105, 193, 200*b*, 207–11, 215*f*,
363*g*
Agenda 21 12–13*f*, 147*b*, 209,
210, 267, 276, 281*b*, 359*g*
desertification negotia-
tions 116*b*, 117*b*, 209, 211
interstate coalitions 116*b*
non-state actors 128, 132–3,
139, 147*b*
outcomes 209–11
Rio Declaration 12–13*f*, 31*b*, 65,
185, 209, 210–11, 276
United Nations Conference on
the Human Environment,
Stockholm 9, 10, 42*b*, 67*b*,
105, 193, 199–204, 200*b*,
202*b*, 215*f*
Stockholm Declaration 12–13*f*,
60, 65, 185, 203–4, 210, 307
United Nations Conference on Trade
and Development 116*b*
United Nations Convention on the
Law of the Sea 12–13*f*, 107,
110, 112, 166*b*, 174–5, 176–8
United Nations Convention to
Combat Desertification
12–13*f*, 22, 30, 109, 116*b*,
117*b*, 137, 138, 209, 211
United Nations Development Pro-
gramme 219*b*, 238*b*, 239, 306
United Nations Economic and
Social Council 248, 330*b*
United Nations Economic Commis-
sion for Africa 330*b*
United Nations Economic Commis-
sion for Europe 42*b*, 231*t*

United Nations Educational, Scien-
tific and Cultural Organization
(UNESCO) 9, 62, 171, 230,
231*t*, 272–3
United Nations Environmental
Programme 117*b*
United Nations Environment
Programme 9, 36*b*, 46*b*, 105,
112, 127, 129, 202*b*, 204, 210,
218, 231–2, 231*t*, 233, 237–40,
238*b*, 248, 249–50, 330*b*
United Nations Food and
Agriculture Organization 114,
142, 166*b*, 230, 231*t*, 232,
247, 250
United Nations Forum on Forests 114, 250
United Nations Framework
Convention on Climate
Change 12–13*f*, 21, 31*b*, 31*f*,
43, 84, 106, 110, 209, 211, 217,
231*t*, 232, 244
Bali Action Plan 281*b*
Copenhagen Conference 42,
119, 127, 217
Green Climate Fund 212*b*, 268
institutional interactions 246
Momentum for Change initiative 240*b*
non-state actor involve-
ment 127, 127*f*, 131, 139, 141
obstructionist behaviour 120
secretariat 240*b*, 250
technology transfer 281*b*
see also Kyoto Protocol; Paris
Agreement on climate change
United Nations Fund for International Partnerships 152
United Nations General Assembly 12–13*f*, 60, 65, 176, 200,
201, 218, 231*t*, 239, 248
United Nations High Commissioner
for Refugees 296*b*
United Nations Industrial Development Organization 232, 235
United Nations Seabed Committee 112
United Nations Security Council 295, 363*g*
United Nations Statistical Commission 218
United States 115*f*
acid rain 33*b*
businesses 102, 135*b*, 136, 140
California effect 136, 327
climate change negotiations 120
climate change negotiations
and 99, 104, 108, 135*b*, 140,
148, 149*b*

debt-for-nature swaps 208b
desertification negotiations 117b
emissions trading systems 335
environmental impact assessments 311
environmental security 295
environmental taxes 267f
environmental warfare 308
genetically modified organisms (GMOs) 45, 144b
Great Lakes 185
greenhouse gas emissions 82, 83f
Gulf War 308
interstate coalitions 113, 114
invasive species 323
Love Canal disaster 64b
Marine Mammal Protection Act 120, 279
marine pollution 98–9
military's impacts on environment 311
national parks 69
National Security Strategy 295
negotiation leadership 120
neo-liberalism 204
neo-Malthusianism 73
North Pacific Fur Seal Convention 62
oil production 75f
ozone negotiations 36b, 133
patents 281b
plastic pollution and 140b
political foundations of knowledge 39
preferential trade agreements 342
rate of ratifying environmental agreements 104
recycling waste trade 320b
representation at negotiations 106
Shrimp/Turtle dispute 336, 337t, 339b
space exploration 8b
trade and environment 324, 327
trade disputes 337t, 339b
Trail Smelter dispute 176, 177b
Vietnam War 308
whaling moratorium and 67b, 100
United States Agency for International Development 208b
United States Supreme Court 134
universalism 56–61, 57f
Uruguay 113, 115f
Uzbekistan 115f, 340f

V
Vaahtoranta, Tapani 98, 98t
Vatican 60b
Vattenfall 345b
vehicle emission standards 274, 275t, 327
Venezuela 80, 115f, 184, 218, 337t, 340f
verification instruments 268–73, 270t, 282
Victor, David 11, 241, 279
Vienna Convention for the Protection of the Ozone Layer 12–13f, 19, 31f, 32, 36b, 110, 133, 231t, 235
Vietnam 115f, 283b
Vietnam War 308
virtual water 323–4
Vogel, David 327
voluntary approaches 108b, 117b, 147b, 273, 276, 278
Voluntary Human Extinction Movement 63
vulnerability 363g
see also ecological vulnerability

W
war see armed conflict
Warsaw International Mechanism for Loss and Damage 82
Washington Convention see Convention on International Trade in Endangered Species of Wild Fauna and Flora (CITES)
water
cooperation and conflicts over 301, 302b, 302f
embodied in exports 323–4
extraction trends 10f
privatization of supply services 284
see also oceans
water pollution 5t, 327, 345b
see also marine pollution
Watson, Paul 132
Western Hemisphere Shorebird Reserve Network 273
Westing, Arthur H. 307–8
Wetland Conservation Fund 268
wetlands see Ramsar Convention on Wetlands of International Importance
whaling 12–13f, 18, 35, 59, 67b, 100, 232, 271, 279
Whanganui River, New Zealand 66

wildlife
elephants 70–1, 282, 283b, 328
invasive species 38–9, 323
polar bears 58
sea turtles 336, 337t, 339b
see also whaling
Wildlife Conservation Society 131, 137
wildlife trade and trafficking 6t, 328–9
bluefin tuna 328, 329
elephants and ivory trade 70–1, 282, 283b, 328
institutional interactions 245, 246, 250
sharks 328–9
see also Convention on International Trade in Endangered Species of Wild Fauna and Flora (CITES)
working groups see contact groups
World Bank 145, 212b, 234, 234b, 238b, 239, 244, 245, 250, 274, 276b, 278, 284
World Business Council for Sustainable Development 132–3, 145, 147b, 281b
World Charter for Nature 65
World Commission on Environment and Development 60, 85–6, 193, 204–7, 205b, 359g
World Conservation Union 138
World Customs Organization 245, 246
World Environment Organization 247–9
World Health Organization 205b, 232
World Heritage Convention 62, 171, 230, 231t, 250
World Heritage Fund 171
World Heritage Sites 171, 273
World Industry Council for the Environment 133
World Intellectual Property Organization 142, 183b, 247, 281b
World Meteorological Organization 46b
World Resources Institute 132, 143, 145
World Summit on Sustainable Development, Johannesburg 12–13f, 60, 145, 147b, 193, 200b, 211–12, 214–15, 215f

World Trade Organization 100,
118, 142, 211, 212, 248, 250,
319, 331
    Agreement on Application of
    Sanitary and Phytosanitary
    Measures 31b, 246, 247, 332
    Committee for Trade and Environ-
    ment in Special Session 340–1
    dispute settlement 250, 335–40,
    337t, 339b, 340f
    environmental governance
    at 335–41, 337t, 339b, 340f
    General Agreement on Tariffs
    and Trade 247, 336, 337t,
    339b, 341

    most favoured nation
    principle 336
    national treatment principle 336
    Shrimp/Turtle dispute
    336, 337t, 339b
World Values Survey 56, 57f
world views 55
    anthropocentrism versus
    biocentrism 61–6
    universalism versus
    communitarianism
    56–61, 57f
Worldwatch Institute 132
World Wildlife Fund (WWF) 126–7,
129, 132, 137, 141, 151b

Y

Yemen 115f
Young, Oran 230, 241, 241b, 242,
263, 264

Z

Zambia 115f, 219b, 283b
zebra mussels 323
Zehr, Stephen 33b
Zero Population Growth 76b
Zimbabwe 71, 115f, 130b, 219b,
283b